The Critical Margolis

SUNY series in American Philosophy and Cultural Thought
―――――――
Randall E. Auxier and John R. Shook, editors

The Critical Margolis

Joseph Margolis

Edited and with a Preface by
Russell Pryba

Published by State University of New York Press, Albany

© 2021 State University of New York

All rights reserved

Printed in the United States of America

No part of this book may be used or reproduced in any manner whatsoever without written permission. No part of this book may be stored in a retrieval system or transmitted in any form or by any means including electronic, electrostatic, magnetic tape, mechanical, photocopying, recording, or otherwise without the prior permission in writing of the publisher.

For information, contact State University of New York Press, Albany, NY
www.sunypress.edu

Library of Congress Cataloging-in-Publication Data

Names: Margolis, Joseph, 1924– author. | Pryba, Russell, editor.
Title: The critical Margolis / Joseph Margolis, Russell Pryba.
Description: Albany : State University of New York Press, [2021] | Series: SUNY series in American philosophy and cultural thought | Includes bibliographical references and index.
Identifiers: LCCN 2020036146 | ISBN 9781438483078 (hardcover : alk. paper) | ISBN 9781438483085 (pbk. : alk. paper) | ISBN 9781438483092 (ebook)
Subjects: LCSH: Philosophy, American—20th century.
Classification: LCC B945.M361 P79 2021 | DDC 191—dc23
LC record available at https://lccn.loc.gov/2020036146

10 9 8 7 6 5 4 3 2 1

Circumstances have obliged me to view my survival this first hundred years in terms of preparing for the publication of the book before you now. The miracle is that the labor has drawn me closer to the creaturely lives of everyone I now encounter: family, friends, children, students, colleagues, medical caregivers, working people, people of every color, strangers, even rascals. I cannot thank any sizable part of that multitude in person. I name three persons only to signify my gratitude for whatever time I've shared with them and any of the others: Michael Ramirez, MD, Eva, and Jenny, without whom not, and trust no one will think himself or herself forgotten.

Contents

Acknowledgments	ix
Editor's Preface to *The Critical Margolis* Russell Pryba	xi
Primary Works by Joseph Margolis	xix
Preamble: Pragmatism's Solidarity	1

PART ONE

1	Relativism and Cultural Relativity	23
2	Objectivism and Relativism	47
3	Science as a Human Undertaking	65
4	Reclaiming Naturalism	97

PART TWO

5	Change and History	147
6	Mind and Culture	191
7	Selves and Other Texts	231

PART THREE

8	The Definition of the Human	263
9	What, After All, Is a Work of Art?	289
10	The Eclipse and Recovery of Analytic Aesthetics	321

PART FOUR

11	Life without Principles	351
12	The Nature of Normativity	387
13	A Reasonable Morality for Partisans and Ideologues	451
Notes		477
Index		551

Acknowledgments

Chapters with light revisions are reprinted with permission from these original publications.

1. "Relativism and Cultural Relativity." Chapter 2 of *What, After All, Is a Work of Art?* Pennsylvania State University Press, 1999.

2. "Objectivism and Relativism." Chapter 3 of *Pragmatism without Foundations: Reconciling Realism and Relativism*. Basil Blackwell, 1986.

3. "Science as a Human Undertaking." Chapter 8 of *Science without Unity: Reconciling the Human and Natural Sciences*. Basil Blackwell, 1987.

4. "Reclaiming Naturalism." Chapter 2 of *Pragmatism's Advantage: American and European Philosophy at the End of the Twentieth Century*. Stanford University Press, 2010.

5. "Change and History." Chapter 9 of *Historied Thought, Constructed World: A Conceptual Primer for the Turn of the Millennium*. University of California Press, 1995.

6. "Mind and Culture." Chapter 10 of *Historied Thought, Constructed World: A Conceptual Primer for the Turn of the Millennium*. University of California Press, 1995.

7. "Selves and Other Texts." Chapter 6 of *Selves and Other Texts: The Case for Cultural Realism*. Pennsylvania State University Press, 2001.

8. "The Definition of the Human." Prologue to *The Arts and the Definition of the Human: Towards a Philosophical Anthropology*. Stanford University Press, 2009.

9. "What, After All, Is a Work of Art?" Chapter 3 of *What, After All, Is a Work of Art?* Pennsylvania State University Press, 1999.

10. "The Eclipse and Recovery of Analytic Aesthetics." Chapter 1 of *Selves and Other Texts: The Case for Cultural Realism*. Pennsylvania State University Press, 2001.

11. "Life without Principles." Chapter 5 of *Life without Principles: Reconciling Theory and Practice*. Basil Blackwell, 1996.

12. "The Nature of Normativity." Chapter 4 of *Toward a Metaphysics of Culture*. Routledge, 2016.

13. "A Reasonable Morality for Partisans and Ideologues." Chapter 1 of *Moral Philosophy after 9/11*. Pennsylvania State University Press, 2004.

Editor's Preface to *The Critical Margolis*

Russell Pryba

The Critical Margolis assembles important philosophical writings, selected from Joseph Margolis's vast body of publications, produced over recent decades. His new preamble was completed by the time of his ninety-sixth birthday, even as he continues to compose more books. This collection is critical in three different senses. Primarily, it assembles essays that are essential for understanding Margolis's diverse array of theoretical commitments in the various subfields of philosophy to which he has contributed. Readers will acquire a familiarity with Margolis's positions in core areas of philosophy and the relative terrain he occupies amongst his philosophical peers, especially Hilary Putnam and Richard Rorty, in the mid-twentieth to early twenty-first centuries. This book is intended to represent the critical, or essential, statements of Margolis's heterodox philosophical commitments.

A title such as "The Essential Margolis" would fail to capture the second way in which this title can be understood. Although Margolis is no Kantian, *critical* is also meant here in the sense of critique. Margolis consistently attempts to comprehend the conditions of the possibilities of human thought, language, art, culture, history, and philosophy through thematizing the process of enculturation that ontically transforms the native biological powers of *Homo sapiens* into those of the hybridized, historicized human self.

In the course of articulating his theories of enculturation and self-formation, Margolis has been thoroughly critical in a third manner: by formulating his pragmatism as a viable alternative to analytic and continental traditions and a serious rival to the views of his philosophical contemporaries. In the course of presenting pragmatism as a philosophical option able to incorporate the best lines of thought from other traditions without resorting to any doctrinal adherence to the totality of another program, Margolis directly addresses and criticizes most of the prominent philosophers of the second half of the twentieth century, from Quine, Danto, and Putnam to Derrida, Rorty, Brandom, and a host of similarly significant thinkers.

Joseph Margolis's philosophical career began during a period when pragmatism was being eclipsed, so his own recovery of the most promising parts of pragmatism (presented in many chapters of this volume) is surely an impressive, if not somewhat astounding, accomplishment. Context is everything. Margolis, although certainly not unique in this regard, was perfectly situated to be educated by the last generation of academics directly connected to the classic pragmatism of Charles Peirce, William James, and especially John Dewey. He was also in place to observe how that line of thought was rendered almost irrelevant by the increasingly scientific turn of analytic philosophy and then situated at the frontlines of pragmatism's reclamation as the middle way between the overarching reductionism of analytic philosophers and the transcendental extravagances of continental philosophers. Before Putnam, before Rorty, there was Margolis.

Joseph Margolis was born in 1924 in Newark, New Jersey. After serving in World War II, he entered Columbia University for graduate studies in philosophy and was awarded the PhD in 1953 with a dissertation entitled "The Art of Freedom: An Essay in Ethical Theory."[1] At the time, the philosophy department at Columbia was still heavily informed by the pragmatism of John Dewey, even if the broader scene in mid-century Anglo-American philosophy had long since ceased viewing the humanistic philosophy of Dewey as a live option compared to the supposedly more robust imports of positivism and logical empiricism.[2] One suspects that Margolis's graduate education during the 1950s would have had the feeling of being immersed in a waning historical movement that no longer possessed the internal vitality and energy of its first sixty years—an irony, no doubt, for a philosophical movement like pragmatism that assesses the meaning and value of an idea by its practical consequences in actual experience. Margolis was always determined to make pragmatism relevant, wherever it is most needed.

Even in his earliest publications in aesthetics and ethics in the late 1950s, Margolis takes direct critical aim at the reigning dogmas and figures ascendant at that time. (Take Margolis's engagement with Monroe Beardsley as one example.)[3] Margolis is fond of calling his own philosophical views "heterodox," and if there is a philosophical position dismissed by dominant philosophical camps, one is likely to see it taken under consideration by Margolis. Of course, it is not *because* a view is unfashionable that one can often find it defended in Margolis's writings. Rather, it is because the fashions and trends of philosophy, itself a historicized endeavor of encultured human selves, can only be adequately understood from within that perspective. Furthermore, since so much of what have passed as the orthodoxies of philosophy in the twentieth century is deeply inconsistent with the perspective of philosophy as a human endeavor, Margolis's deep commitment to his philosophical anthropology naturally leads him to endorse philosophical options that are ruled out by more reductionist or transcendental thinkers and tendencies.

While this volume offers many of the most important writings exemplifying and explaining Margolis's primary philosophical viewpoints, it is neither comprehensive nor focused on his philosophical development. For example, his early work in value theory, especially in analytic aesthetics, is eschewed here in favor of later essays such as "The Eclipse and Recovery of Analytic Aesthetics." That selectivity allows this volume to situate the progress of his thought relative to broader trajectories and trends that could not yet have been evident when Margolis was first contributing to their formulations.[4] As another example of situated thinking, while Margolis is a more-than-able historian of philosophy (whether discussing his contemporaries or examining figures of the Western philosophical canon), his discussions of the history of philosophy, such as his favoring of Hegel over Kant, are always delivered to serve arguments for philosophical alternatives that he himself favors.[5] The best example of this feature of Margolis's writing is his contribution to the history and development of pragmatism. In Margolis's preamble to this volume, he again casts himself as a modest historian of pragmatism and its prospects, including its unexpected revival at the hands of Rorty and Putman at the end of the last century.[6]

As important as Margolis's accounts are as a chronicle of the history of pragmatism, they are best understood as his own positive contribution to the development of philosophical pragmatism as the best way forward through the morasses of late analytic and continental philosophy toward a holistic account of the human person and the cognitive powers that personhood engenders. If philosophy is "unabashedly eclectic now," as Margolis puts it in his preamble to this volume, it is in no small part due to the sustained and compelling advocacy of a range of philosophical positions previously thought by Margolis himself to be unrecoverable by the broader profession, the arguments for which are often couched as *reductiones* of the more well-worn theories of his prominent contemporaries in his historical writings.

Margolis's contributions to the rediscovery of what he identifies as "pragmatism's advantage" have served to inspire so many others who find in his work a philosophical way forward that might capture the irreducible richness of the human world (especially the marvels of language, art, and culture) without sacrificing an equally strong commitment to the rigors of scientific methodology and progress—the latter bounded, of course, by the understanding that science is, as Margolis calls it, a "human undertaking."

As the reader new to Margolis will readily discover, he is always highly critical, in this sense of *critique*, of the perceived argumentative missteps of many of the most prominent contemporary and historical figures in philosophy. When reading Margolis, one cannot fail to recognize the audacious scope of his critiques of the trajectory of Western philosophy. He seems to be able to hold the entirety of the Western philosophical tradition—historical, analytic, and continental—in his intellectual grasp, and, at times, all in the span of a single paragraph! The range of thinkers Margolis engages with in these papers is immense. It is difficult to fathom the sheer accomplishment of merely understanding the philosophical complexities of all the philosophers about whom Margolis writes—let alone treats as a foil against which to articulate his own unique philosophical perspective. All of this makes Margolis's writing philosophically dense and stylistically complex, and, over the course of a long and fruitful career, he has often taken up similar themes in different stages of his philosophical development and in different contexts.

The selections in this volume assist the reader with finding and understanding definitive statements of Margolis's numerous philosophical views. His views are complexly intertwined, and he often uses figures in the history of philosophy as signposts for whole swaths of philosophical argumentation that may at times remain merely implicit in his narratives. Therefore, the chapters in this volume are chosen to illustrate the internal coherence of Margolis's thought, so that one chapter can be used as an aid in the interpretation of the others. Some may find this feature of his work frustrating and a significant impediment to engaging fully with his ideas. As such, the intent of the present volume is to collect in one place the most important and complete statements of Margolis's philosophical views, drawn together from a variety of his books over the course of many decades, in order to give the reader a sense of both the breadth and daring originality of his philosophical vision. In turn, subsequent engagements with Margolis's expansive corpus (which it is hoped this volume will inspire) can be grounded in an understanding of the unifying themes and philosophical core that might be difficult to discern by a single reading of any of his individual works.

It is not a simple task to summarize the complexity of Margolis's thought. Thus, although all too facile, resorting to an enumeration of the various "isms" that might aptly describe some aspect of Margolis's philosophical commitments can prove helpful. As he himself has regularly noted, the heterodox positions he defends do not yield to simple characterizations or unifications. Nevertheless, peppered throughout his philosophical output one can identify arguments and positions that can be fairly characterized as relativist, historicist, antiessentialist, antifoundationalist, humanist, pragmatist, antireductionist, naturalist, and emergentist, among others. Margolis is arguably the most notable defender of relativism since Protagoras, first as a logic of interpretation in the aesthetic domain, and subsequently expanding outward to other domains of inquiry.[7]

It is interesting to consider that, both developmentally and philosophically, Margolis's thought germinates in the domains of philosophical aesthetics and the philosophy of art. This fact, the reversal in Margolis's philosophical inquiry of the traditional subjugation of art to science, perhaps goes some distance in explaining the attraction to philosophical options, most notably relativism, that would not seem nearly as viable (or even coherent) to a philosopher with a different orientation to questions of the relevance of the arts to philosophy more generally. It is thus suitable that this volume begins with two chapters on relativism and that the chapters in part 3 address the implications of Margolis's defense of this view for the ontology of art and the inadequacy of the aesthetic theories of Monroe Beardsley, Nelson Goodman, and Arthur Danto.

The importance of relativism and historicism in Margolis's thought, and ultimately his commitment to the philosophical promise of pragmatism, can be further explained through understanding the linchpin of Margolis's philosophical vision: his theory of the human person as a "natural artifact." The articulation of this view can be found in numerous chapters in this volume. I particularly note here "The Definition of the Human," "Reclaiming Naturalism," and "Life without Principles," although one could reasonably list every chapter in this collection under this theme, as they all either explicitly or implicitly address or rely on this philosophical insight. Its importance and implications permeate the totality of Margolis's thought. In "Life without Principles"—in a footnote, no less—Margolis effectively demotes Hume from the rank of moral theorist that the likes of Aristotle and Kant occupy because Hume nowhere provides a satisfactory account of the self. This is the same complaint that Margolis makes in another domain (aesthetics) against Arthur Danto. This clarifies the importance of philosophical anthropology (the philosophy of the self) to Margolis's entire philosophical endeavor; it is what most frequently grounds his critiques of other thinkers whom he finds inadequate. Since the self for Margolis is a hybrid artifact, the result of the process of enculturation that is historicized and relativized to the societies in which the process is enacted, any claim to invariant structures of the self that ground morality, perception, knowledge, or the like (such as Hume's account of the "passions") is excluded in Margolis's account of the human person. Thus, Margolis's emergentist ontology of personhood requires his relativism (which is also articulated in this chapter and many others in this volume), uniting these two master themes in his philosophy.

For Margolis, it is the processes of language acquisition and enculturation—what, borrowing from Hegel, Margolis calls primary and secondary *Bildung*—that transforms a member of the biological species *Homo sapiens* into a biological-cultural-metaphysical hybrid, which emerges from and is embodied by its biological bases but which cannot be reduced to or, ultimately, explained by those (now transformed) biological powers. This fundamental metaphysical transformation enables and empowers human persons to create, perceive, interpret, and enjoy works of art; to engage in politics and be capable of morality; and to construct philosophical theories about ourselves and our connection to the natural world, along with all of our other human powers and activities. Furthermore, the entire range of human abilities cannot be adequately explained solely in terms of biological or physical features of the natural world without reference to our hybridization as culturally emergent human selves. Seen as such, the theory of the cultural emergence of human selves grounds (without any claims being made to invariant foundations) Margolis's critiques of prominent philosophical positions in more local debates. Illustrations are plentiful: consider his searching criticism of Jaegwon Kim's reductive physicalism in the philosophy of mind, his refutation of Arthur Danto's theory of the transfiguration of "mere real things" into artworks and its accompanying theory of perception, his better alternative to Hilary Putnam's internal realism, and his naturalizing replacements for unnecessary transcendentalizing from Kant. These are just some of the many disputes that the attentive reader will encounter in the chapters assembled here.

The chapters of this collection are organized thematically. Part 1 addresses Margolis's defense of relativism, his pragmatic naturalism, and the rejection of the unity-of-science model through the endorsement of Intentionality (a Margolisian term of art distinct from its usage in Husserl) as the means of reconciling the human and natural sciences. Part 2 presents Margolis's enormously complex historicism and how it informs his philosophy of mind and epistemology—again, through the articulation and defense of his core ideas of the Intentionality of the cultural world and the irreducibility of human selves to the mere physical or biological. The last chapter in this section, "Selves and Other Texts," in addressing questions of meaning, reference, and denotation connects the historicism applied to questions of mind, knowledge, and perception in the previous chapters of the section to the questions in the philosophy of art taken up in part 3. To see how Margolis's definition of a work of art as a physically embodied, culturally emergent entity in "What, After All, Is a Work of Art?" is structurally analogous to his conception of the human person as a natural artifact is to see how deeply the puzzles of the cultural world inform Margolis's master insight about what it is to be human. Part 4 takes up the questions of morality, normativity, and prescriptivity from within the broader framework of Margolis's philosophical commitments articulated in the previous sections.

Although an attempt was made to thematically organize the essays reprinted here in a way that is informative and suggestive of the connections between the chapters contained in each section, the reader can reasonably start with any chapter that sparks a particular interest and find within it the totality of Margolis's philosophy expressed through the lens of a particular question or problem. Therein lies the genius, and the puzzle, of the philosophy of Joseph Margolis.

From relativism in the logic of interpretation to pluralism in metaphysics, the doctrines of radical historicism and flux, and his original philosophical anthropology and theory of culture, it may seem that throughout his career Margolis has often been on the wrong side of philosophical fashions. Yet now, with this volume as a guide, one hopes that the rest of philosophy is finally ready to catch up with his inspiring vision. With that guiding hope in mind, rather than attempting a grand narrative of the philosophical themes and their relationships that are constitutive and definitive of the Margolisian corpus, this introduction and the collection that follows leave it to the reader to interpret those themes for themselves.

Given Margolis's relativistic logic of the interpretation of texts (and the other utterances of the human self, including the self itself), there could be no other philosophically adequate possibility. For those readers who are already familiar with some or perhaps most of Margolis's published writings, there will be inevitable disagreements about the selections included herein; perhaps one's favorite piece is not among the *Critical* writings. However, in keeping with the spirit with which Margolis himself philosophizes, this collection is directed toward the future. Thus, it is my hope that this volume succeeds in introducing a new generation of inquirers to the powerful and suggestive philosophical achievement of Joseph Margolis.

Primary Works by Joseph Margolis

The Language of Art and Art Criticism: Analytic Questions in Aesthetics (1965)
Psychotherapy and Morality: A Study of Two Concepts (1966)
Values and Conduct (1971)
Knowledge and Existence: An Introduction to Philosophical Problems (1973)
Negativities: The Limits of Life (1975)
Persons and Minds: The Prospects of Nonreductive Materialism (1978)
Art and Philosophy: Conceptual Issues in Aesthetics (1980)
Culture and Cultural Entities: Toward a New Unity of Science (1984)
Philosophy of Psychology (1984)
Pragmatism without Foundations: Reconciling Realism and Relativism (1986)
Psychology: Designing the Discipline, with Peter T. Manicas, Rom Harré, and Paul F. Secord (1986)
Science without Unity: Reconciling the Human and Natural Sciences (1987)
Texts without Referents: Reconciling Science and Narrative (1989)
The Truth about Relativism (1991)
The Flux of History and the Flux of Science (1993)
Historied Thought, Constructed World: A Conceptual Primer for the Turn of the Millennium (1995)
Interpretation Radical but not Unruly: The New Puzzle of the Arts and History (1995)
Life without Principles: Reconciling Theory and Practice (1996)
What, After All, Is a Work of Art? Lectures in the Philosophy of Art (1999)
The Quarrel between Invariance and Flux: A Guide for Philosophers and Other Players, with Jacques N. Catudal (2001)
Selves and Other Texts: The Case for Cultural Realism (2001)
Reinventing Pragmatism: American Philosophy at the End of the Twentieth Century (2002)

The Unraveling of Scientism: American Philosophy at the End of the Twentieth Century (2003)
Moral Philosophy after 9/11 (2004)
History, Historicity and Science (2006)
Introduction to Philosophical Problems (2006)
The Arts and the Definition of the Human: Toward a Philosophical Anthropology (2009)
Culture and Cultural Entities: Toward a New Unity of Science (2009)
On Aesthetics: An Unforgiving Introduction (2009)
Pragmatism's Advantage: American and European Philosophy at the End of the Twentieth Century (2010)
The Cultural Space of the Arts and the Infelicities of Reductionism (2010)
Pragmatism Ascendent: A Yard of Narrative, A Touch of Prophecy (2012)
Toward a Metaphysics of Culture (2016)
Three Paradoxes of Personhood: The Venetian Lectures (2017)

Preamble

Pragmatism's Solidarity

When the editor of this collection first broached publication plans and listed the essays to include, I didn't quite appreciate how well he spied the unmarked unity of what might have been taken to be a haphazard lot of randomly produced pieces. In fact, let me confess, I didn't rightly recall having actually written all the pieces mentioned, although their themes and treatment were and remain undeniably mine.

I began my graduate studies in the late 1940s, somewhat before John Dewey's death and shortly after my service in the Second World War, with a curriculum that strongly favored pragmatism and naturalism, though, as I soon discovered, I had begun at a time when pragmatism might easily have expired as an active movement. I recall turning to the journals, essentially on my own, to gain a working command of the most debated issues favored by the different parties of what was then disjunctively separated as analytic and continental philosophy and saw at once the good sense of avoiding mere tribal loyalties. I became fairly wide-ranging in my reading and professional taste—dialectically and comparatively, so to say—well before it became the academic fashion (as it has), and I've remained so to this day.

But then, curiously, I found that I had also recovered something of a firmer grip on pragmatism's extraordinary appeal, spontaneously arrayed against the boldest proposals of the remaining movements of Western philosophy, despite pragmatism's continuing decline. Positivism, I might add, very possibly the most forceful and daring of the movements of the early twentieth century, had already suddenly collapsed—unnervingly, in fact, defeated by its own most passionate premises. It began to dissolve as a movement well before the rise of Nazism, the conjoint effect of which was to scatter its best-known talents to the winds and into distinctly alien, even if not unfriendly, spaces. I saw at once how fragile philosophy could be, even in the work of its most admired figures. Think for a moment of the career and reception of figures like Heidegger and Husserl—and Carnap and Quine—if the juxtaposition seems plausible at all. (It would have seemed bizarre to many, less than fifty years ago, to bring them together in a single breath.) Philosophy, you must agree, is more fickle than any new enthusiast could possibly suppose. (I confess I find myself musing, even now, how sorry I am that I have no more than the barest understanding of Asian thought.)

Pragmatism began as a minor flurry following the end of the American Civil War, with the publication (in the 1870s) of some strikingly original, very simply written papers by a youngish Charles Peirce that feature what Peirce came to call the "pragmatic maxim," which, I daresay, is still, deservedly, the compelling (but modestly formulated) nerve of its continuing conviction, 150 years later. It ceased to be a parochial vision, however, during its completely unanticipated second surge, which may be dated approximately from the 1960s and '70s to the end of the last century, sparked, surprisingly, without any memorable manifesto or new discovery of any kind—beyond philosophy's newfound openness—by way of a somewhat negligible, rather weary quarrel (in good part centered on trading charges of having yielded to one or another form of relativism—imagine!) between two otherwise lively, much-admired younger philosophers. I'm speaking, of course, of Richard Rorty and Hilary Putnam—both now gone—each dubiously self-identified as a pragmatist, each well informed regarding the entire span of Western philosophy, involving the best work of the European positivists and logical empiricists; the particular contributions of figures as diverse as C. I. Lewis, Josiah Royce, Frege, Russell, Carnap, Cassirer, Quine, Sellars, and Wittgenstein; the various conceptual experiments of Kant and Hegel and their successors (the Frankfurt School, for instance); and, even more adventurously, the work of figures like Heidegger and the phenomenologists and hermeneuts.

Western philosophy is unabashedly eclectic now. No philosophical movement is likely to survive for long that insists on the sort of doctrinal purity or single-mindedness of any of the principal cohorts active at the end of the twentieth century. There is, it appears, no royal road to follow any longer, no preeminent exemplars of that stripe. Count that an unintended, subterraneanly pragmatistic concession, a sobering sense of the unlikelihood of arriving at any singular consensus regarding the best philosophical prospects and impulses of our time—there were no Olympian figures at the end of the twentieth century.

Nevertheless, I venture to say the main philosophical quarrel of the new century features (that's to say, cannot escape) the question of the compatibility or incompatibility of what has become of pragmatism and rationalism. I take this to be (as well) an essential part of my own program, though I continue to practice in a distinctly freewheeling way. We are forever in search of new sources of conceptual confidence. In any case, I read the pragmatic maxim as committed to the primacy of flux over fixity (ontologically) and a theory of knowledge and understanding that insists on the strongest possible disjunction between the so-called empirical and the purely formal (mathematical and logical) sciences; the denial of any would-be necessary synthetic or unconditionally universal truths ranging over the whole of nature; the affirmation of the inherently informal, contingently plausible, instrumentally limited, improvisational, diverse, never completely grounded or uniquely systematized cognitive practices—addressed to the natural or experienced world and the impossibility of a noncircular demonstration of the validity of any would-be method of determining the content of an objective body of knowledge of the world and of the true meaning of the propositions of factual discourse.

Modern rationalism has produced at least two distinct, ultimately linked, immensely influential, and wide-ranging doctrines that pragmatism treats, straightforwardly, as utterly arbitrary and/or unconditionally false. I agree entirely with the pragmatist verdict. I don't deny that recent advocates have experimented with deliberately weakened versions of the original uncompromising claims; but it is precisely the original doctrines that must be addressed and either defeated or stalemated, if pragmatism is to vindicate its second surge compellingly. In their strictest forms, pragmatism and rationalism cannot be reconciled. The attempted compromises are not philosophically uninteresting; nevertheless, they can do no more than displace the original agon. The judgment is obvious enough if one formulates the question in either the Kantian or Fregean idiom.

The Kantian strategy features the supposedly self-evident standing of synthetic a priori (necessary) truths—which is in fact the thrust of what is standardly called transcendentalism, usually cast in the architectonic form favored by either Kant or Husserl or in some modification of either's model—or else weakened in various logical or conceptual ways (so as to count as a variant of pragmatism) by such figures as Vaihinger, Cassirer,

Habermas, or Pihlström. The Fregean strategy (which acknowledges a somewhat elusive, hardly explicitly articulated bond with Kant) affirms the regulative primacy of a strict mathematical modeling (or platform) of the formal (allegedly necessary) rigor of a true science (more or less in the spirit of Frege's *Begriffsschrift* or of any reasonable analogue)—notably without much success (as far as I can see)—either in relatively formal terms, as in Russell, Carnap, Suppes, or Macbeth, or more laxly by figures associated with the so-called Pittsburgh School (Sellars, Brandom, and O'Shea, particularly).

I find the executive premise of each of these two branches of rationalism decidedly unconvincing: both, I should say—extending the use of a notion of C. I. Lewis's in a way Lewis would probably not approve, meaning by that construing (by sheer fiat) certain analytic truths as synthetically necessary—are what amounts to no more than a purely "stipulative" gain (Lewis's term). Sellars's own efforts are quite perfunctory (in his early essays) and transparently self-defeating (in, say, the important but very risky essay "Philosophy and the Scientific Image of Man"); Brandom's posit of the primacy of "inferentialism" (following Sellars) is completely subverted by his own pointed admission of the massive "nonmonotonicity" of pragmatic inference and the reliance on extremely preliminary analogies along with the very different algorithmic speculations of artificial-intelligence reasoning and the like. O'Shea is simply respectful of, but also deeply puzzled by, possible answers to the question of what Sellars might actually have achieved. We require a logic; I don't deny that. But an ineluctable formal methodology of science, as well? I've never seen a convincing rationale spanning the empirical and mathematical sciences—certainly not in the most irenic efforts of the unity-of-science persuasion (in Hempel, for example).

The main lines of this part of the pragmatist undertaking have been thoroughly examined by now: they remain open to improvement, of course, but the argument is in large rightly regarded as a settled part of the legacy of classic pragmatism. Certainly, Peirce, toward the end of his life, possibly in acknowledging the force of some of Josiah Royce's late arguments, possibly even in reading some of Dewey's simpler claims, begins (with a fresh sense of conceptual economy) to replace his well-known, still-Kantian-tinged infinitist fallibilism (and idealism) with a distinctly leaner, empirically riskier, more opportunistic, and more instrumentally realist methodological policy that openly favors any technically informed but seemingly unconfirmable guesswork on the part of hands-on scientists. Peirce explicitly names this the "logic of abduction"—that is, the guesswork of informed ignorance, in light of the practical impossibility of rendering so many of our best hypotheses completely and suitably explicit (in testable form), in advance of confirmatory observation and experiment. I see a decided convergence here with the robustly pragmatist theories of science advanced (most effectively) by figures like Ian Hacking and Nancy Cartwright as well as by Otto Neurath and John Dewey. Peirce himself did not survive long enough to complete a full first pass at the intended simplification. But he does say, explicitly, that abduction is the key to the meaning of the pragmatic maxim—I view that as a sizable revision.

The intended change strongly supports the primacy of flux over fixity and the abandonment of all Kant-like extravagances. But it also begins to exploit the daring, genuinely novel idea that knowledge—scientific knowledge, preeminently—must encompass the informed ignorance (my phrasing), the import of the unconfirmable abductions of notably gifted experimental minds, whose most-admired conceptual guesses go deeper than the truth of any merely isolated propositions. (I think here, particularly, of Faraday.) I have no doubt that this is the gist of Peirce's last thoughts about abduction. Nevertheless, Peirce's actual texts lacked time enough to have cured properly. To read Peirce now—in this way—is to replace the usual wooden (analytic) conception of truth and knowledge with a more flexible notion of the intellectual flourishing of an entire form of life. I daresay this goes Wittgenstein a step better, in disclosing a more complex kinship between pragmatism and its conceptual cousins. Here, I should say, pragmatism is less a rival of rationalism then a newly discerned constituent of any and every viable theory of disciplined knowledge—which, of course, is hardly capable of validating its own labors.

That's to say Peirce finally grasps the full simplicity of (1) the effective impossibility of correctly or confirmably filling all the tolerated lacunae of presumed empirical knowledge and (2) the legitimacy of counting as still-inchoate parts of a reasonably settled body of empirical knowledge conjectured regularities ventured as promising abductions, in accord with (1). Circularity and ignorance are plausibly acknowledged to be both benign and ineliminable. Effectively, Peirce begins to abandon infinite-regress arguments (which he speaks of in terms of "Hope" rather than of belief). Here, as I suggest, he's speaking of the instrumentalist success of a form of life. In this sense, there's a touch of fiction in Peirce's realism—already implicated in the pragmatic maxim (and, I should add, in Kant). The real world cannot fail to include our sense of how the world appears to us. Apparently, on pragmatist grounds, realism need not be unconditionally or systematically completely determinate.

As I say, Peirce did not live long enough to formulate an adequate version of his intended revision, though he made a compelling start. In any event, we may advance the thesis in his name. He makes a virtue of the endlessness of the entire cognitive venture, though he abandons, in the bargain, his earlier asymptotic treatment of fallibilism. Fallibilism was, in fact, an infelicitous doctrine, both conceptually and operatively. But there can be no doubt that Peirce came to regard his theory of abduction as an essential improvement of the pragmatist conception of science and knowledge.

Peirce was surely advancing a doctrine of considerable daring, in which science or knowledge (rightly conceived) need never completely eliminate either ignorance or actual error! This stunning innovation is puzzling at first but far more flexible and instructive than his own infinitist fallibilism or the analysts' conception of knowledge as justified true belief, or anything of the sort. The new maneuver fits very well with the essential incompatibility of pragmatism and rationalism and the simplification of empirical realism—and may indeed justify a significant change in prevailing attempts to formulate a useful theory of knowledge. Abduction tends to favor reflecting on gaps in empirical inquiry and in the systematicity of science itself, whereas fallibilism remains theoretically abstract and centered on what to regard as an adequate account of the truth conditions of isolated propositions.

There is, however, no Archimedean point in Peirce's abductive theory: we are always in the middle of the journey, our cognitive bearings never more than seemingly secured at the "receding shore." (See Nicholas of Cusa's well-known speculation regarding "learned ignorance.") Peirce's two doctrines are substantially opposed—distantly linked to the confrontation between pragmatism and rationalism but not actually thus engaged. There can be no uniquely fixed referential mapping of the whole of reality, from any merely human vantage, and our cognitive achievement cannot fail to be defined in societally managed terms—say, by identifying what "there is" (in the world) that might serve our particular form of life. We secure our bearings only in a fluxive way: informally, symbiotically—which is to say, in acknowledging the inseparability of ontological and epistemological questions within First Philosophy.

I daresay the notion of the infinitude of inquiry is the wrong sort of guess, on pragmatism's behalf, although inquiry is, admittedly, endless. Fallibilism was in fact a paradoxical proposal for pragmatists who favor any sort of "instrumentalist" constraint (Dewey's term), which has (can have) no confidence in the long-term direction of realist inquiry, however mathematized.

Peirce fretted about this particular fiction, although he always addressed it (scrupulously) in terms of Hope rather than of belief, so that, as he began to grasp the very different, more suitable virtue of the abductive thesis, he drew on fallibilism with less and less confidence. (The textual evidence is admittedly meager, but the argument is all but unavoidable.) Inquiry always remains open to local, ad hoc doubt and disconfirmation—which owes more to the surprises of history than to the subtleties of infinitesimals.

The abductive argument, then, addresses the question of socially shared competences, whereas fallibilism does not venture beyond the lonely (possibly fictitious) mathematics of empirical truth. (There's not much of a contest there.) Rationalism could never be satisfied with the first option, and pragmatism could never learn when to trust the second.

I find a welcome and surprising analogy, here, to my own proposal regarding the artifactuality of the self: the self, I say, cannot be determinately located in bodily or biological terms, although it exists (if conceded at all) in a bodily way. It has no settled locus of its own; it is marked only functionally—in terms of its relationship to (that's to say, its possessing) the mental and behavioral states and processes that it's entitled to avow. The self is the imputed site or agent of such avowals: it's assigned to its own content, or its content is ascribed to it—as with Strawson's familiar objection to the "no-ownership" thesis of mental life. All this is fitted to the needs and interests and modes of awareness that we learn to assign to the self itself. There cannot be any humanly discernible, uniquely fixed, all-inclusive, necessary system of the world—say, of Kant's or Husserl's or Carnap's or Spinoza's sort (except by "stipulation"—C. I. Lewis's term—as with Spinoza). Any instrumentally successful cognitive schema, however fraught with contingency and ignorance, is all we actually need or can rightly claim (according to pragmatism's outlook). But then, if we can produce one such viable and cognizable conception, we cannot deny that we can invent another.

Furthermore, I see no reason a mongrel theory of the self need be rejected, if (1) it can be shown to facilitate one or another useful application to the world, (2) it is distinctly convenient in doing that (according to our lights), and (3) we ourselves are willing to treat its evident infelicities as tolerable trade-offs for its admitted convenience. It may in fact be the only way to proceed, viewed from the vantage of the sort of variant pragmatism I've been sketching: it confirms the ubiquity of abduction itself. Of course, we cannot avoid the mongrel liberties of mundane language if (as is patently true) the right theory on every important philosophically contested distinction (the theory of mind, for instance) cannot be expected to have been successfully embedded in any mundane language.

In fact, I'm fully prepared to say that all this is already true of Descartes's "cogito" and Kant's "Ich denke"—and Spinoza's "natura." Any viable human language can support a large run of such theories, and doubtless does. A *Lebensform* may (and must) be viable in ways that need not be acceptable among individual propositions that prove to be confirmably false but were thought to be reliably true. The reason for such tolerance has to do with the complex facility of the socially entrenched executive role of the mundane language of one's own *Bildung* (qua self) or of one or another suitable surrogate. For, even here, there is no exclusively necessary or unconditionally adequate language. What is normally required is no more than a fair measure of what I call an "equilibration" between the general fitness of our mundane language (for our usual needs) and whatever more specialized instruments we may wish to access (for further cognizable gains). But, surely, it cannot be supposed that all the theories thus embedded in our particular variant of a given primary language are demonstrably preferable to the possible contribution of any other theory that might actually favor (for cause) a different idiom.

I should perhaps explain that, by a *mongrel expression*, I mean any expression, in ordinary or technical use, that would be wrongly charged as literally or linguistically faulty, defective, or misleading—on some pertinent present occasion (conceptually, logically, grammatically, doctrinally, in terms of literal meaning or acknowledged theory, or in some sense akin)—when the very use of the expression has been accorded (as by a supposed consensus or tolerable ad hoc intention) the power to block or erase or bypass (without penalty and without any need to explain the liberty) the apparent error itself. Mongrel expressions usually facilitate, in this way, the assured fluency of a continuing discourse or conversation already in play: the avoidance of awkward circumlocutions, unwanted quarrels and distractions, or unresolved vulnerabilities of style and substance that are unlikely (and are known to be unlikely) to advance the purpose of a given discourse.

For example, in philosophical as well as ordinary usage, the idiom of mind/body dualism—the seeming nerve of Descartes's theory of mind—is often expressly used to block the need to defend that theory (at least here and now) or perhaps any particular theory of mind, admitting the hazards of any such attempt. Descartes himself gives various perfunctory accounts of his dualism, even plays with it seriously and philosophically. However, he also lets it be known—as in responding to the persistent question put to him by the Princess Elisabeth—that he does indeed have a theory of what an integral human being is, which he promises to provide but never does. Even the opponents of dualism find the idiom mongrelly convenient and well-nigh unavoidable. No one misunderstands, and no one has a compellingly adequate theory of mind to end the dodge. In much the same spirit, I think we may regard the first-cause argument as a mongrel gesture, not unlike Stephen Hawking's joke—it is a joke, isn't it?—that ex nihilo is the best possible theory of Creation.

A very different example of a mongrel practice appears in American English, which permits one to use singular and plural pronominal expressions as uniformly singular in sense, in certain commonplace grammatical settings—as in using the pronoun *they* to convey what may be said of some loosely marked someone (or "someone or other"), even where particular or named individuals have already been mentioned in an otherwise suitably articulated antecedent clause. Its purpose, of course, is largely verbal. Vincent Descombes mentions an intriguing puzzle case requiring a very different resolution that arises in translating Edmund Burke into suitable French: in Burke's political text, the term *people* takes a singular form; English normally allows both the singular (the collective, so to say) and the plural (the aggregative) reading of *the people*, whereas *le peuple* is normally read (Descombes claims) as plural in French (*le peuple sont . . .*), which would produce an inaccurate (as opposed to an ungrammatical) translation! (I cannot vouch for Descombes's reading.) Strenuous philosophical distinctions tend to require adventurous mongrel liberties: we don't really understand the mind very well; therefore, we tolerate extravagant expressions ("he searched his mind," for instance, or ". . . his memory"), which everyone may read as they wish, since it releases us from any need to provide a theory of memory to justify the idiom. I understand that some Asian languages (such as Chinese) tend to avoid featuring the detailed mental life of individual selves; they favor instead a behavioral or objectual vocabulary, which would seem to require mongrel provisions if we are to escape cross-cultural misunderstanding. When successful socially, the mongrel option often appears as idiomatic.

I suggest it is part of pragmatism's improvement, after its second surge, that we acknowledge that every mundane language (which is, or evolves from, the language of our original *Bildung*) must afford as many mongrel liberties as may be needed. Surely, Descartes's dualism is more a mongrel convenience than a merely false theory—or so we may plausibly affirm. Theorists as different as Rudolf Carnap and Paul Churchland may, therefore, have made much the same mistake as Wilfrid Sellars and Daniel Dennett in supposing that since a mongrel advantage would have been a mere mistake if it had been meant to be taken as straightforwardly true, it must, even now, be a corrigible mistake—and thus correctly displaced now. But that's an option Peirce has shown us how and why to block. (Our theories of mind are known to be distinctly primitive and inexact.) Abduction itself is linked to the obvious truth that many of the mongrel conveniences embedded at some level of discourse in mundane language are unlikely to be easily replaced by sounder theories (of any known stripe) that we either already possess or know how to construct.

Just think a little more carefully about providing an adequate theory of truth or knowledge or meaning or, say, the determinate and systematic structure of the self, for starters. These issues cannot avoid producing *petitios*. The fact is we lack any reliable such theories; the fluency of a natural language does not presuppose that such theories can always (or even often) be satisfactorily drawn, on demand, from their own conceptual resources. Language is surely a repository of sorts of our evolving categories and theories, but, though our sciences prosper, our higher-order theories of what the sciences are thought to achieve develop much more unreliably. The analysis of our most fundamental categories (those just mentioned, say) tends to generate endlessly many insoluble *petitios*. And yet, we hardly ever simply fail. Our mongrel strategies tend to be helpful in avoiding mere stalemate and *petitio*. We seem to understand the sense in which we succeed in our inquiries—but not, perhaps, in the (higher-order) sense in which we could actually state, without paradox, precisely what we (now) know "there is" or what and how we know what there is.

We have perhaps succeeded in much the same sense in which, in *Philosophical Investigations*, Wittgenstein "succeeds" in explaining what is entailed in the notion of following a rule. After exhausting all the explicit questions he's been forced to consider when another speaker claims to be following the same rule (though by unanticipated, even baffling alternative means), Wittgenstein is forced to confess, in following the rule, "I obey the rule *blindly*" (§219). That's to say: the knowledge and understanding exercised may be tacit in some sense akin to the import of Polanyi's well-known use of the expression "tacit knowledge," which seems (to me) to be close enough to Peirce's use of "abductive" guesses to suggest a kind of convergence. Nevertheless, all of these maneuvers leave unresolved a second-order paradox at the level of explication that confirms the mystery of cognitive success (viewed as practice) and of failure at the level of explicating the precise nature of such success. It's the mystery of knowledge that presents itself as ignorance that we cannot capture. It may be enough for pragmatism, since pragmatism is already committed to the *petitio* of explicating knowing fact and understanding meaning. But rationalism would find itself defeated by any such concession. It could never allow it.

I come now to the last of my proposed innovations meant to strengthen classic pragmatism beyond its second surge: an innovation especially effective against the pretensions of the strong forms of rationalism and transcendentalism. I have in mind a neglected premise that cannot be rightly fathomed without acknowledging the artifactuality of the self: namely, the posit of historicity, read as an existential feature of the artifactual self itself—a hybrid transformation of the primate *Homo sapiens* yielded (as I argue) in the very process of mastering a first (one's own) home language. Somehow, such mastery is a perfectly ordinary feat achieved within a perfectly ordinary form of *Bildung* that is itself the "final" phase in the normal evolution of the human being. Darwin, I claim, utterly fails to grasp the unique complexity of this last extraordinary phase of the novel form of evolution that separates the human career from the rest of animal evolution's further, future possibilities.

I should add at once that I regard the whole of epistemology as benignly circular—argumentatively: no foundationally grounded cognitive capture of reality can ever be compellingly demonstrated. Nevertheless, it remains entirely reasonable to suppose that the actual practices of mundane inquiry are rightly counted—however revisably—as a genuine system of objective knowledge. Our sciences, as Peirce came to realize, are very clever forms of ignorance. I suggest, therefore, that we think of pragmatism as committed, evolutionarily, at the very least, to the reliability of our culturally inherited forms of inquiry—more in terms of *Bildung* and socially favored options than of supposedly validative transcendental invariances or of biochemical processes alone.

I'm prepared to concede that the mundane validation of the macroscopic achievements of our strongest sciences are often cast, provisionally, as mongrel liberties (often involving microtheoretical abbreviations), selected from among alternatively serviceable such options, whereas the achievements themselves are often much too impressive to be denied actualist standing—say, in accord with the pragmatic maxim. (Think here of the invention of the electric light bulb and the atomic bomb.) Our formulations tend to combine cognitional generalities with specifically evidentiary factors, linking ingredients drawn (sometimes incommensurably) from different levels of reference and description, though said to be (for theoretical reasons) addressed to the same events and phenomena. Clearly, such liberties are bound to change with changing literacy. We cannot easily do without these liberties, and we cannot be expert enough, in chance conversation, to avoid them.

The very idea of recovering the true foundations of would-be knowledge cannot be more than a deceptive *petitio*. Cognitive practices are largely inherited, though they remain revisable, within the span of evolving possibilities that belong to our shared history. Mundane knowledge, then, is existential and existentially validated in just this indirect sense: in being benignly bound to our contingent *Bildung*. We cannot track objective truth directly; we can do no more than name what we take to be our most reliable practices read as provisional exemplars of what is confirmably actual. The actuality of the artifactual self extends to the actuality of our cognitive convictions. Hence, it's instructive to take note of the peculiar vagueness and abstractness of Kant's "Ich denke" (in the first *Critique*) and of Husserl's canny tale of the transcendental ego's eidetic powers. Such characterizations appear to be no more than obiter dicta—and so they are: they lack explicit linkage to any form of successful *Bildung*. But that's to suggest that the validation of our cognitive powers is best managed individually, by attending to existential habits of mind that may be drawn from the salient practices of the mundane world itself. One way or another, pragmatism reverses transcendentalism's priorities. It favors contingent truths collected in ways that are existentially linked to our original *Bildung* and to societal endorsement. Rationalism and transcendentalism can do very little more than retreat to claims of self-evidence. But there is no reliable run of necessary synthetic truths to draw on, and the instances Kant and Husserl actually favor are distinctly quarrelsome.

In effect, the circularity of epistemology and philosophical semantics confirms that the grounding of such disciplines (if they may be said to be grounded at all) cannot avoid the mundane assurances of our original *Bildung* (qua selves). I admit it's not enough for apodictic validation, but it does expose the fact that such propositions as those of Descartes's "cogito," Husserl's pure phenomenology, and Kant's various synthetic a priori truths and principles cannot claim any enabling *Bildung* and cannot demonstrate convincingly the self-evident certainty of their a priori claims—or, for that matter, the need to confirm, or the confirmability of, any such claims. I think here of Kant's postulated rational obligation confronting mankind to promote (in a sincere and optimistic spirit) the progressive fulfilment of its ultimate moral/political goal, perpetual peace, and the would-be rational necessity to ensure the completeness of its table of categories required for the entire range of truth-bearing inquiries. Here, pragmatism ventures no further than it believes mankind can responsibly explore or demonstrate.

I may, in fact, be nearly alone in championing the self's artifactuality. The self is neither a fiction, of course, nor a perceptual object; it's an aptly enlanguaged transform of the functional unity of *Homo sapiens*' primate life. It's an elusive (ontological or quasi-ontological) form of being that begins among languageless infants, as Wittgenstein seems to suggest, as a grammatically anticipatory empty category that, through continual reflexive iteration, yields (as normal infants mature, governed by an enlanguaging *Bildung*) a novel awareness (not a perception) of their (that is, of every infant creature's) functioning as the unitary site of its perceptions, experience, thoughts, memory, inferences, intentions, commitments, and the like. Its elusiveness is the upshot of its lacking any fixed or determinate material location. It manifests itself only functionally, as the incarnate, spontaneous site or agency of inner mental life and purposive behavior. It's accessible only relationally: that is, as the site of the objects it can avow it is aware of or can control. (I remind you that we're speaking here of the symbiosis of First Philosophy.)

I treat the entire feat as existential, meaning, by that, to mark the original grounding and worldly orientation of the mundane self's identity. It's a stunning fact that there is no doctrine or conjecture regarding an original *Bildung* (from primate to self) in Aristotle or in the transcendentalisms of Kant and Husserl. It's an understandable lapse, of course, but it does signal the ultimate incompleteness of nearly all of Western philosophy. The continuity of the animal and the human must be assured, factually, if anything like Darwin's account of evolution is reasonably accurate (as far as it goes)—for Darwinism confirms the viability of an endless variety of forms of life that depend on the use of cognitive resources of a decidedly contingent, if not lowly, sort.

Kant's and Husserl's versions of the transcendental ego hang in the air: to have had any fruitful application to the mundane world, they would have had to borrow from, or share, the contingent experience of the mundane self itself. But that would be to admit the conceptual dependence of the apodictic on the contingencies of what passes for mundane knowledge. But, then, to speak of the a priori conditions of sensory perception (as with Kant) is already to admit the conceptual dependence (the pertinent applicability) of synthetic a priori truths in legitimating the empirical truth of worldly claims. Husserl does not explain the cognitive or ontological relationship between the mundane self and the transcendental self: the two sorts of self seem to be disjoint (in Husserl's text), but is that possible? (How would the transcendental ego know that it was addressing worldly contingencies correctly?) Kant assigns the functional unity of the sensory and the rational in terms of the coordinated functioning of separate faculties within perceptual episodes, but he cannot demonstrate that his would-be collection of the categories of the understanding (*Verstand*) are ever both necessary and complete for the entire run of empirical judgments—or that his collection actually harbors selected necessary synthetic truths needed to ground the confirmability of contingent empirical claims.

History and historicity, please note, would be meaningless in a world confined to necessary truths. But they are hardly meaningless in our world. Indeed, they qualify, existentially, as I say, the very nature of the mundane self, and thus they qualify the primacy of worldly cognition over would-be transcendental capabilities in some contexts, at least. But then, surely, the mundane and the transcendental must be sufficiently distinct (as well as paired) if mundane evidence were actually to be able to defeat a would-be transcendental claim—for instance, if the supposedly exceptionless universality of a would-be law of nature could be shown to be subject to an unsuspected, contingently historied revision or exception, on the strength (say) of newly discovered mundane facts. Of course, the historied claim would also be subject to further revision, but that would strengthen the game in the same direction. I press the point because Husserl appears to override, unconditionally, the contingencies of historicity by appealing to the so-called "a priori of history," which he treats as ahistorical (timeless)—which either it cannot be or, if it can, it cannot then effectively defeat historicized claims as such. I find a deep paradox here that Husserl cannot rightly resolve, except by arbitrary fiat. The mundane and the transcendental (in Husserl) seem to have separate lives, but they must inhabit the same world somewhere, if *The Crisis of the European Sciences and Transcendental Phenomenology* is to make sense. (The argument is uncertain.)

In the *Crisis* volume, historicity appears to be tolerated, for the most part, in a sense reasonably close to its ordinary meaning: it's the point of its inclusion in Husserl's review of the history of early modern physics. However, in an appendix to the *Crisis* volume, the "a priori of history"—which proves to be ahistorical—ultimately overrides historicized claims as being no more than illusory or ephemeral. But the history of physics could not have progressed in the way it has if it had not relied on the benign skepticism of historicity. I take Husserl's unyielding disjunction between the mundane and the transcendental to be too extreme to account for the actual achievements of modern physics. Better to give up transcendentalism than to discount the existential aspects of mundane science.

To be entirely candid, I cannot see how progress in physics, beyond Galileo, could possibly advance without continually consulting the mundane history of physics, regardless of the would-be regulative function of the a priori of history. Surely, even that function of the "a priori" cannot fail to yield to historied discovery, as Ernst Cassirer demonstrates in the third volume of his *Philosophy of Symbolic Forms* collection. If we reject (with Kant) the constitutive function of the a priori vis-à-vis the transcendental analysis of physical objects, we cannot fail to treat Kant's regulative function in a historicized way.

We will have merely shifted the burden of historical discovery to the "transcendental" level of inquiry. We would then, effectively, have erased the essential difference between the mundane and the transcendental.

I daresay the argument in favor of historicity—cast in what may be called mundane terms, the terms of one's own home language (however modified through life)—is well-nigh impregnable: effective enough to stalemate or defeat, say, Husserl's notably courageous (but ultimately retrograde, possibly even self-contradictory) transcendental countermeasure, drawn from the *Crisis* volume but bested (as I believe) in a single stroke, and hence, then, applicable as well against Kant's Critical transcendentalism, for cognate but somewhat different reasons.

I've already argued that the transformation of the human primate—qua self—is ontologically equivalent to the original invention and distributed mastery of language among the infant primates of the species. But if it is, then it would not be unreasonable to claim that *Homo sapiens* has, quite literally, changed its nature—in developing into the discursively apt history it becomes. The evolutionary cycle, culminating in the formation of the (artifactual) self, cannot be satisfactorily described or explained in terms restricted to merely self-regulating biological processes. The formation and maturation of the self require the entwined functioning of biological processes and the contingently invented powers of a societally managed *Bildung*.

Thereafter, the essential mark of the human lies with its enlanguaged technologies, which change and evolve in profoundly varied ways despite the near constancy of its formative biology. The self (societies of selves) transforms the entire world in an enlanguaged way. That's to say, the specifically human world—in a way not unlike that in which a canvas daubed with paint may be spontaneously transformed into an interpretable painting—begins to exhibit discernibly incarnate meanings, significance, and semiotic and significative features that embody and reflect the entire play of human histories: the endless narratives of the new creatures and objects of the specifically human world. (I shall in a moment collect these emergent forms as uniquely Intentional.)

In fact, I cannot see any plausible way to theorize about the cognitional relationship between the mundane self and the would-be transcendental ego (whether with Husserl or with Kant) without reference to the contribution of the mediating transformation—into a self or person—of the primate *Homo sapiens*. Husserl's transcendental phenomenology cannot fail to depend on the prior cognitive resources of mundane language, because it already shares the prior discursive resources of mundane language. In that ineluctable sense, history and historicity are, plainly, existential (enabling) factors but not, of course, cognitive faculties in their own right. Husserl's treatment of eidetic discernment (after the *epoché*) seems to make that a facultative innovation, possibly not strictly dependent on the acquisition of language. There's a gap in every form of rationalist or transcendental philosophy that marks the failure to demonstrate the cognitive privilege every such philosophy requires. Historicity serves, then, as our mundane reminder of the presence of all such lacunae. Transcendentally necessary truths must rest on some subset of the prior contingent truths of mundane language to have any earthly relevance at all. (Husserl tends to prioritize thinking over speech.) How is that possible in Husserl's world?

No doubt all this is suspiciously simple, not likely to be believed in any first pass at an adequate brief. The argument itself depends on a deep but elementary correction in philosophical reasoning. The correction strikes me as distinctly Darwinian, in a good sense: that's to say, it requires a judgment or decision as to the cognitional primacy of the existential or the a priori over the other. Alternatively put: it's a question of whether human cognition is initially grounded in contingent animal ways, thereafter sustained by further contingencies due to the invention and mastery of language, or whether, somehow, regardless of the Darwinian concession, the human self or person, uniquely endowed for its intended gain, discovers (within its newfound powers) a commanding self-evident, autonomous source of necessary synthetic truths, the right use of which assuredly outflanks the provisional truths standardly affirmed in the language of its original *Bildung*. (You cannot fail to see the uncertainties of Husserl's account.)

We may read the contest as an agon between a mundane and a transcendental conception of science, language, and practical knowledge.

But what it finally comes to is a choice between the merely ephemeral appearance of historicality and the existential persistence of historicity in every form of history. If the issue never escapes stalemate, then philosophy cannot be more than an ideology, but if the evidence leads convincingly to a decisive finding, then, disjunctively, either pragmatism defeats rationalism hands down or rationalism denies pragmatism any ultimately trustworthy role—cognitionally—especially with regard to history.

My own verdict holds that the two programs are incompatible, that pragmatism is at least factually plausible, and that rationalism and transcendentalism cannot demonstrate that they are ever more than obiter dicta applied to the natural world. I see no other option in the offing: any compromise between mundane contingency and a priori apodicticity must count as a retreat from (say) a Fregean or Kantian insistence on the mathematical rigor needed in resolving foundational questions about secure knowledge (whether in the formal sciences or with regard to nature at large). But, of course, it's entirely possible that there are worthier forms of philosophical inquiry (and cognitive assurance) that are neither principally pragmatist nor principally rationalist. (I doubt there are, but I'm prepared to rest my case.)

I have already taken the liberty of casting the matter in terms I have yet to explain fully. I see no harm in that, though I must return to add some further support for the verdict mentioned. I'm more than inclined to believe that any Fregean enthusiasm in favor of the mathematized rigor of physics is just a mistake and that any Kantian synthetic a priori is no more than a temporarily aggrandized philosophical fashion (protected much too long), now little more than a *façon de parler*.

You have only to recall that Kant is markedly uneasy about the difficulty of demonstrating the necessary completeness of his table of fundamental categories. The fact is, the question makes no sense at all, when not relativized to our contingently changing interests, to the actual development of our best sciences, to changes in our conception of systematicity, and, of course, to the upshot of the play of historicity itself. Reichenbach, for example, notes that causality appears to be best confined and applied to our macroscopic world (effectively, the mundane world), not misapplied (as he signals) to quantum events, and, more recently, philosophers of physics—Steven French and John Worrall, for instance—are strongly tempted by the seeming viability of radical ontological economies aptly introduced at one level of hierarchized generalization but perhaps not, perspicuously, at another. My own conjecture holds that we very much rely on the historical and historied aptness and flexibility of what I've begun to call our mundane language: an evolving language suitably linked to the contingencies of our original *Bildung* (in becoming selves) and to the historical vision of the human world within which we ourselves appear to fit best. We speculate transcendentally from the existential vantage of mundane language. But, then, transcendentalism cannot possibly win. There can be no known philosophical solace here that lies entirely beyond existential solidarity.

The linchpin of my argument—a conjecture, I admit—may be put this way: whatever the inadequacies of the Darwinian account, evolution confirms that the primate *Homo sapiens* must have acquired survival skills of a competitively advanced sort by more than merely innate capabilities; the mature human primate must have been capable of learning from experience, in spite of lacking language. I take this line of reasoning to signify that we cannot fail to acknowledge perceptual and experiential concepts as distinct from linguistic concepts or, for that matter, to acknowledge a not-insignificant overlap between perceptual and linguistic concepts that may have facilitated the fluency with which languageless infants are known to master their home language, the language of their initial *Bildung*. Nevertheless, Western philosophers are often quite reluctant to admit the fact, reluctant to draw the explicit inference that concepts need not be exclusively linguistic or discursive. (See, for instance, John McDowell's claims in his Woodbridge Lectures.)

Since this is also the enabling condition, according to my argument, of the very formation of the artifactual self, I suggest that this first language (however modified or, conceivably, replaced) plays a special role in the normal functioning of any apt or well-formed person. In that sense, since the language one acquires accounts for the formation or construction of one's own self and for the dawning of history and historicity, it's bound to gain a distinctive existential status peculiar to itself, as the contingent platform or precondition for the entire subsequent span of what may be learned within the space of a single career. That makes it entirely plausible that even putatively rationalist and transcendental proposals (say, favoring necessary synthetic truths, apodicticity, and the like) cannot easily overcome such deeply entrenched contingent discoveries as those regarding the benign skepticism of historicity. At the very least, the transcendentalists may find themselves obliged to mount a suitable argument in behalf of their own convictions, since mundane language may indeed prove to be an ineliminable part of the enabling conditions for rationalist and transcendental proposals themselves—even if such proposals are mistakenly advanced or mistakenly construed. I don't find any compelling rejoinders in the arguments of, say, Husserl, Kant, Frege, Descartes, or Spinoza—or in the lesser (rationalist or quasi-rationalist) claims of figures like Carnap, Hempel, Sellars, McDowell, or Brandom. Transcendentalism suddenly seems extremely weak.

If the foregoing argument succeeds, pragmatism will have defeated rationalism and transcendentalism from an unexpected vantage—and moved on to an entirely fresh premise regarding the artifactuality of the human self. To be sure, there will be many additional conceptual innovations to consider, effectively linked to a systematic account of the whole of human life, under the novel constraint of the artifactuality thesis. I, for one, find myself attracted particularly to the bearing of the innovations sketched, with special regard to the theory of human agency and the interpretation of human culture—and, from there, to the study of the moral/political world that agency and interpretation begin to define. But I shall stop here, abruptly, since whatever further time may be allotted me at this late moment must make room for unfamiliar rejoinders that may well oblige me to reconsider my own convictions more carefully. Shared ignorance defines the public membership of a seemingly private inquiry.

Let me confess, finally, that I've failed to formulate the unifying thread of the foregoing collection of pragmatist topics drawn from the original sources of the "critical" selection of the chapters that follow. These chapters are meant to sample a considerable number of the revisionary themes I've pursued over the years in reinterpreting (in a loyal way) the main lines of classic pragmatism. But the larger innovation that makes itself felt incipiently in the pages that follow (and in the original publications) eclipses ordinary or parochial pragmatism and goes on to metaphilosophical proposals.

Primarily, I'm persuaded that the history of philosophy has changed so profoundly that the revisions and extensions here proposed begin to yield a metaphilosophical application to the most promising contemporary philosophies—pragmatist or not. The principal premise of the latter sort is, indeed, marked by the pendulum swing (over the whole of the history of philosophy) favoring flux over fixity; the open-ended incompletability of philosophy over any supposedly accessibly completed philosophical plenum; the insuperably historied nature of human life and societal existence; and the primacy of empirical contingency regarding thought and reason, knowledge, practical life, action, and commitment over any or all presumptions of rational or transcendental apodicticity of any kind addressed to our understanding of the natural world.

I add a second metaphilosophical premise: namely, the epistemological primacy of the human cultural world over the natural world, with regard especially to the role of language in the formation of selves or persons and questions regarding truth and meaning, knowledge and science, thought and reason, action, commitment, production, and inner mental experience. These two premises (and their implications) count, then, as a completely fresh construal of First Philosophy (preserving the insuperability of the paradoxes of ontology and epistemology). I treat cognition as a form of learned ignorance, full of persistent gaps but instrumentally sufficient (and suitably revisable) for all our uses and interests, and I endorse (and explain) the use of mongrel liberties (deliberate but palpable fictions that everyone supports) posing as philosophical solutions (which they cannot be) in the face of the most formidable puzzles of First Philosophy (such as the true nature of selves or persons, the nature of mind and the resolution of mind/body dualism, the analysis of meaning and the predication of truth, and the rejection of rationalist and transcendental apodicticity and strict universality or necessary synthetic truths). All of these themes (and more) are featured in the pragmatist chapters that follow.

It's my intention—if mortal time permits—to present the general lines of a metaphilosophical reading of these same premises, offered to any reasonable philosophy committed to the flux of the real world and the existential primacy of history in human affairs. I take the proposal to adumbrate the largest plausible revision of the entire undertaking of philosophy since Parmenides' initial (and fateful) pronouncement. In that sense, it's the profound informality of philosophy that I wish to promote. It concedes the primacy of mundane language and macroscopic objects addressed to our perceptual powers, which yields continually to piecemeal improvement achieved in good part within the dependent precision of its specialized inquiries, without being effectively displaced by any such adjustments. The primacy of encultured human life over the would-be disclosures of, say, a mathematized physics or mathematics itself simply confirms the plain fact that the fully enlanguaged human agent (self or person) is the operative agent of both the human and physical sciences. I take the failure of any convincing *reductio* or elimination of the self—failure up to the present, at least—to be tantamount to the defeat of any would-be transcendental or rationalist necessity regarding the natural world. And I take that to justify our confidence in the provisional resolution of philosophically persistent puzzles—along instrumentalist lines.

Joseph Margolis
Philadelphia, Penn.
May 2020

PART ONE

One

Relativism and Cultural Relativity

It is a truism at once baffling and reassuring that there are apt bilinguals for every known natural language. It is the corollary, of course, of an equally baffling and equally reassuring truism—namely, that a newborn child can have learned any language as their first language if they can have learned the language they eventually acquire. And yet, at the point of mature competence, everyone is aware of the deep uncertainty of understanding the speech and behavior of others belonging to the same culture as well as to another culture. In fact, we may as well admit that we are not always sure whether we understand ourselves at certain critical moments or, indeed, sure about what we may have done or said or made at some moment in our past. Plato broadly suggests in the *Ion* that the gods make captive the minds of poets in order to express through them their own thoughts. But the gods are notoriously difficult to understand. Furthermore, we are hardly confident about what it is we do when we understand ourselves, one another, those of our own culture, and those of another culture. No one, I think, has satisfactorily answered these questions.

When we ponder these familiar puzzles, we begin to suspect that often—possibly always—what we call *understanding* and *knowledge* may not be capable of being as crisp, as univocal, or as confirmable as we should like. If, to take a compelling example, I stand before a number of Paul Klee's enigmatic drawings, I am aware that part of their great charm rests in the fact that I can place them with assurance in an art tradition with which I am well acquainted, though I am unable to state their meaning and what their purposive structure is with a precision and assurance matching their obvious mastery. I fall back to weaker claims, and I take Klee's works to convey not a dearth of evidence I might otherwise have collected but a sign I am at the limit of what evidence could possibly be added that could bring my interpretive conjectures to any single, final, exclusive truth about their meaning.

I am impressed with the uncertainty (that is, the certainty) that what Klee produced might not be able to support any uniquely valid description, interpretation, or explanation of its meaning and that what holds for Klee's drawings holds everywhere, or for the most part, or often enough that we must make conceptual room for such occasions. Others may not believe as I do, may not be struck in the same way I am. It is for that reason I confess that I am a relativist, though I am aware that others are not.

Of course, in mentioning Klee's works, I am not insisting so much on the possibility of alternative interpretations of any particular piece as on the initially problematic nature of first confronting a Klee. Anyone familiar with the usual Klee prints and paintings knows how difficult it is to determine what to regard as the right way to read them. No telltale clues reassure us, confirming that we're simply right, after all. We are obliged to construct (within our sense of the tradition of receiving art) what we judge to be a fair way of entering the (Intentional) "world" of any particular Klee. (I am convinced that the same is true as well in getting our bearings on, say, a more legible Vermeer.) But the deeper point is that *how* we enter Klee's "world" is a function of how we ourselves have been formed and altered by the ongoing history of painting we suppose we are able to master, well after the original Klees were produced.

In the West, the history of relativism is a conceptual disaster: not, as one might imagine, because of the futile efforts in its defense but rather because of the remarkable constancy of philosophy's adverse judgment that relativism cannot possibly be made coherent. It is an extraordinary fact that, from ancient times to the beginning of the twenty-first century, there have been no more than one or two principal objections against the coherence of relativism—already formulated by Plato and Aristotle—which have been thought so decisive that we still invoke the ancient arguments almost without modification.

As far as I know, there is no other doctrine of comparable importance—skepticism (which is altogether different) springs to mind—that shows the same degree of philosophical inertia. The ancients thought of the matter primarily in logical or formal terms (even if ontologically or epistemologically), and, in the modern world, the ancient puzzles have been additionally complicated by the general admission of historical and cultural diversity (the consequence, I should say, of philosophy's reflections on the meaning of the French Revolution). You see the difference at once when comparing Plato's *Theaetetus* and Aristotle's *Metaphysics* 4 (both addressed to Protagoras) to the more diffuse accounts of Thomas Kuhn's *Structure of Scientific Revolutions* and Michel Foucault's "Nietzsche, Genealogy, History."[1] Of course, the modern exemplars are hardly canonical in the same sense the ancient texts are thought to be. But the plain fact is the ancient arguments are remarkably easy to defeat (though they have hardly been strengthened over the centuries) and the modern discussions are not so much arguments one way or another as unavoidable confirmations of the kind of cultural site at which the threat of relativism must be met. Any proper defense of relativism must address both themes.

I am convinced that the ancient and modern ways of rejecting relativism depend on the same unearned convictions—namely, that whatever is truly real possesses some unchangeable structure, that whatever changes occur in the real world may be explained only in terms of what is changeless, and that whatever we come to know of reality involves a grasp (however approximate) of that underlying structure.

The opponents of relativism are aware that its deepest defense relies on it *not* being demonstrable that this executive conviction can ever be shown to be necessary or inviolable in reality or in thought—that is, to avoid paradox or self-contradiction. Aristotle is entirely explicit on the matter. In fact, what I have just offered is a summary of his argument in *Metaphysics* 4, and Plato's sketch of Protagoras's thesis on the meaning of truth shows how opposing the canonical view of fixity (in at least one way, certainly not in every eligible way) instantly produces a self-defeating paradox.

Protagoras seems to have been aware of the underlying confrontation between necessary invariance and flux; very possibly, he meant his famous doctrine, "Man is the measure," to accord with the rejection of Parmenides' dictum, which (we may suppose) Plato and Aristotle wished to reconcile with the reality (or the appearance of reality) of the changing everyday world. But I must also warn you that part of the argument that is needed cannot altogether escape certain formal considerations. (I intend to press these to advantage.)

You see how complicated the underlying quarrel is. I have no wish to pursue it here, though its relevance can never be rightly ignored. In the modern world, the ancient doctrine of invariance is most compellingly championed in the familiar dictum that nature is governed by universal, changeless, and exceptionless laws and that the work of the sciences is directed toward their discovery or approximation.[2] The fact is, now, even that notion is no longer thought unassailable: the laws of nature, we suppose, may (without contradiction) be artifacts or idealizations of some sort from the informal and imperfect regularities of the observed world.[3] Furthermore, the world of human culture—of language, languaged thought, history, technology, art, and, most provocatively, whatever we suppose are the competence of science and the conditions of the world's intelligibility—is clearly contingently formed, impressively variable in structure, eminently alterable by human intervention, problematically intelligible under conditions that change with changing history, and endlessly novel and creative.

In that sense, the prospects of defending relativism are paradigmatically focused in the puzzles of interpreting the art world—for, it may be argued, if relativism can be defended in the world of the arts, then, assuming that modal invariance cannot be secured philosophically and that it cannot be unreasonable to regard our conceptual resources as common coin for theorizing about nature and culture alike, what is gained in one corner of inquiry may be pressed into service in another. Seen that way, you realize that the contest regarding the defense of relativism harbors rather grand pretensions—for instance, about essentialism and the fixed conditions of intelligibility. I set these aside here, but only as an economy. The fact remains that the classic defeat of relativism is given in ontological or logical terms brought into accord with an acceptable ontology.

Now, the defense of relativism joins two lines of reasoning: one is more or less confined to formal, uninterpreted, or logical considerations bearing on the treatment of truth or what we should take our truth-values to be, as far as admissible inferences go; the other addresses what, regarding one or another local sector of reality and knowledge, favors or disfavors the relativistic preferences arrived at in the first. The division is obviously artificial, since the intended benefits of the first are offered in the service of the second, and the possibilities the second suggests must be shown not to produce difficulties for the first.

For convenience, I tag inquiries of the first sort *alethic* and inquiries of the second sort *ontic* and *epistemic*; also, I urge that they be viewed as no more than distinct aspects of a single indivisible inquiry. You see, therefore, that a responsible relativism must provide an alternative logic on which its larger rationale depends, but it cannot pursue the large claim if it does not exceed the alethic issue. By the same token, attacks on relativism that are purely formal but are thought to bear on epistemic or ontic issues (once the coherence or nonparadoxicality of relativism is admitted) are, to put it mildly, philosophically irresponsible.

The alethic question is entitled to a certain priority, however, because if it may be shown that relativism's logic cannot but be self-defeating, there would be little point to going on to the ontic and epistemic questions artworks and other cultural artifacts oblige us to consider (that is, in defense of relativism). But, of course, if you take seriously the inseparability of the two sorts of question, you see at once that its priority is no more than a convenience, for what the appropriate logic should be, in servicing, say, the interpretation of the arts, will be a function of what we take the objective features of the arts to be. Alethic, ontic, and epistemic questions are inseparable from one another relative to truth claims because they are inseparable within objective inquiries. To deny this would be no more than to favor another version of the invariantist thesis: for instance, to claim that, regarding reality, only some form of bivalence (taking *true* and *false* as disjunctive and exhaustive truth-values) could possibly serve coherently and adequately. That is exactly Aristotle's claim in the *Metaphysics*.

No evidence shows that one cannot depart, coherently, from an all-encompassing bivalence, and there is no reason to object to the compatibility of employing both a bivalent and a relativistic logic—wherever wanted—provided only that such policies be properly segregated, on grounds of relevance, so as to avoid avoidable difficulties. It is also excessive to insist that no such division of labor may be conducted in as informal a way as we please, for all that is needed is that we fit the picture of our practice to what is reasonably close to the actual practice.

It is *not* a necessary part of the relativist's brief, for instance, that in accommodating diverse interpretations of Velázquez's *Las Meninas*, which, on the evidence, cannot be reconciled with a bivalent logic,[4] we should be obliged to forego the advantage that there are indeed uncontested descriptive claims about *Las Meninas* that rightly fit a bivalent model and even provide, as such, the initial grounds on which relativistically disputed interpretations of the painting effectively vie for objective standing.

That comes as a surprise, though it is hardly problematic. In fact, it suggests the general irrelevance of that larger well-known canard holding that relativism can only be "true" relativistically—that if relativism holds anywhere, it must hold everywhere, which is plainly arbitrary and absurd. What the canard insists on is simply that no relativism can be coherently formulated. As it turns out, that implicates a version of the usual sense of

Socrates' devastating defeat of Protagoras in Plato's *Theaetetus*. But, as I say, such an interpretation is neither inescapable nor plausible, given Protagoras's great reputation in the ancient world and the options available to us still. (Protagoras cannot have been as stupid as the counterargument requires.)

I have introduced three important caveats in approaching the alethic question. I find them reasonable and compelling. More than that, they are not noticeably skewed in relativism's favor. Before going on and in order to avoid misunderstanding, I restate them here: (1) alethic, ontic, and epistemic questions are inseparable in analyzing would-be truth claims; (2) the proper "logic" of any set of truth claims is a function of what we take to be the domain of inquiry and the conditions of knowledge; and (3) no formal reason precludes us from mingling the logics of different sorts of truth claims, provided only they are rightly segregated on grounds of relevance.

These are very slim constraints, but they touch on much more fundamental questions than I am willing to pursue here. I allow them to surface for strategic reasons, but they are too global for the local issues that metonymically arise in interpreting the arts. I give fair warning, however, that if what I have been saying is reasonably correct, there will be no defensible disjunction between inquiries into nature and inquiries into culture (though they are plainly not the same); in that case, if relativism seems apt in cultural matters, then it cannot (I say) be altogether inapt among the natural sciences. That, however, is not my concern here.

Item (2) is the operative thesis of the tally just given. I read it in the spirit of Aristotle's *Rhetoric* (in the spirit of holding that the valid forms of argument are embedded in social practices), but (2) is not in accord with Aristotle's actual policy, because, of course, Aristotle is committed to ontic invariance and the necessity of bivalence, and there is no compelling argument in favor of either. The most recent formulas directed against relativism in interpreting artworks claim either (a) that relativism (which eschews bivalence) cannot do more, or anything other, than what can be done with a bivalent logic or (b) that if one insists on departing from bivalence, one inevitably produces results no one would sensibly favor. I reject both claims. I should add, however, that the interpretive theories of Monroe Beardsley and E. D. Hirsch (which adhere to bivalence) are indeed philosophically responsible, albeit uncompelling.[5]

In any case, I draw your attention to the measure of philosophical freedom I've secured by proceeding as I have, for the opponents of relativism usually ignore the inseparability of alethic and both ontic and epistemic matters. They claim we must adhere in an invariant way to bivalence wherever truth claims are at stake, but they neglect to explain why our local "logic" should not be tailored to what we believe a given sector of reality can rightly support in the way of truth claims, and they cannot satisfactorily explain why a restriction in the scope of bivalence should be thought to produce an insuperable paradox. For instance, they surely cannot show that a three-valued logic is inherently self-defeating or that a would-be bivalent logic cannot accommodate truth-value gaps.[6] Here, of course, I am approaching the logical needs of an interpretive practice addressed to the Intentional complexities of artworks. I therefore invite your patience.

I can now provide an answer to the alethic question. The following are the essential elements of a relativistic logic—where, by a *logic*, I mean nothing more than a policy regarding the formal conditions for the choice and assignment of truth-values affecting admissible inferences in the space in which they are applied, without (yet) specifying the evidentiary grounds on which they are empirically assigned: (1) the concept and practice of a bivalent logic are assumed to be in general play in all our inquiries, but the bivalent values themselves (true/false) are restricted in scope or denied application among selected truth claims admitted to the domain in question; (2) within relativism's scope, the values *true* and *false* are treated asymmetrically: *false* is retained, but *true* is denied application, and a many-valued set of truth-values (not a three-valued set—one that merely adds *indeterminate* to the usual bivalent pair) replaces *true*, so that *not false* is no longer equivalent, as in standard bivalent logic, to *true* but is equivalent instead to values drawn from the replacing many-valued values; (3) within the scope of (1)–(2), truth claims that on a bivalent account would be formally contradictory or incompatible may be logically compatible when assigned one or another of the replacing values; these may be termed "incongruent" values, meaning that what they permit would be incompatible on a bivalent logic but is (now) formally consistent within the alethic scope intended and, also, that further constraints of inconsistency and contradiction may be admitted (on substantive grounds) involving opposing the value *false* and one or another of the replacing values; (4) bivalent and relativistic logics remain compatible and may be jointly used, provided only the scope and relevance constraints binding different sets of truth-values and their applications are segregated—in as ad hoc a way as we please; (5) the resultant logic may, when rightly joined to ontic and epistemic considerations, be as realist in import as the applications of any standard bivalent logic; and (6) the values invoked remain entirely formal—lack all epistemic and ontic import—until the domain in which they are applied is pertinently interpreted.

To offer a small clue about items (1)–(6), I should say that I can easily believe what Roland Barthes called "readerly" and "writerly" reading—in effect, a bivalent and a relativistic reading of Balzac's *Sarrasine*—may be jointly supported (without contradiction).[7] I also believe descriptive considerations are bound to form the common evidentiary ground for both practices, so that they may still be assigned the value *true* (in the bivalent sense) but may then be used to justify confirming that a relativistic reading is as "objective" in its own sphere as bivalent claims are in the bivalent sphere.

Plainly, the rationale for so speaking will depend on how we characterize the interpretable properties of a literary piece like *Sarrasine*. How could the supposed normative but purely formal invariance of bivalence possibly decide the right way to proceed in accommodating would-be interpretations of *Sarrasine*? It seems an awkward question for the enemies of relativism. Furthermore, we may invoke bivalent values wherever we speak of consistency of usage—that is, when using terms in the same way in different contexts—but that shows the benign sense in which we may reconcile bivalence and many-valued values. Alternatively, of course, consistency and noncontradiction arise in many-valued contexts just as they do in bivalent ones.

A few explanatory remarks may be helpful here. First, I treat cultural entities in a realist way—in other words, no more than that they are real and that their properties may be fairly said to be discerned. In this minimal sense, *realism* is neutral as between bivalence and a relativistic logic (though, of course, many would not be willing to admit as much). Second, on my view, a relativism regarding interpretation is not precluded from treating certain descriptive (even certain interpretive) attributions bivalently; that is just what I had in mind in admitting an informal and relatively ad hoc mix of bivalent and relativistic values in interpreting familiar artworks (for instance, in speaking of Hamlet's procrastination). But admitting this much goes no distance toward admitting *any* antecedently fixed general range of application of bivalent values in interpretive contexts, and what we should understand as the right relationship between description and interpretation depends on our theory of what an artwork is. It certainly cannot be decided by appeal to how things may go (analogously) in speaking, say, of physical objects. This is often overlooked.[8] Third, in defending relativism, it is irrelevant that interpreters often believe their own accounts preclude other "incongruent" interpretations if a disciplined practice (as among professional critics and scholars)—that is, a collective practice, as opposed to an individual idiosyncrasy—finds it worth conceding that such interpretations may be jointly valid. And, fourth, the entire issue is worth very little if the alethic questions are disjoined from a reasonably ramified account of the ontology of art and the epistemology of interpretation. It is extraordinary how many discussants disregard these very modest constraints.

The marvel is that it is so terribly easy to accommodate (in a formal way) the practice of contemporary literary and art criticism as at once objective *and* relativistic. The objections of the ancients and of contemporary antirelativists like Monroe Beardsley and E. D. Hirsch have no force at all, or if they do, it rests on ontic and epistemic grounds suited to one or another domain of inquiry—*not* for the formal reasons usually advanced—which is precisely what I wish to champion.[9]

Many who have been sympathetic to the relativist's view of criticism but who both despair of ever recovering the required alethic policy and are simply unwilling to oppose bivalence must themselves now come to terms with the obvious coherence of the relativist's alethic policy. This is especially true of those who have been tempted to drop the notion that interpretive judgments take truth-values at all (for instance, an otherwise excellent study by Torsten Pettersson of interpretive options in poetry).[10] They, too, are now obliged to explain their stance in terms that have nothing to do with avoiding formal difficulties. That is a considerable gain.

I should perhaps add that I am entirely willing to label my many-valued values in any way that suits the occasion at hand (*apt, reasonable, plausible*, or the like). All I insist on is that, thus far at least, they are merely alethic—that is, not yet interpreted epistemically or ontically. It is, of course, entirely possible that such values as *apt* or *plausible* should also be construed in evidentiary ways. However, if you allow them here in the alethic sense, they are not yet epistemically informed. I should say that something similar obtains in a many-valued logic that admits *probable* or *probably true*, although they are characteristically linked to a bivalent logic and likely to be intended in nonrelativistic ways. There may be many such loosely similar distinctions to consider. (Relativist values, however, are not probabilistic values of any kind.)

We have reached a stalemate, then, on the alethic issue. Whatever advantages accrue to bivalence or relativism depend entirely on our picture of the world in which they apply. Even that is a stunning gain—for if you review the history of relativism, you will not fail to see that it has never been conceded that a relativism close to Protagoras's conception could possibly escape one or another lethal paradox. That now turns out to have been a mistake.

I trust you approve my initial constraints on the airing of relativism's prospects. I have, in the foregoing, confined my analysis to the alethic in order to demonstrate, within the usual terms the canonical opponents of relativism insist on, that relativism remains as coherent as bivalence—and need not even refuse to be linked to the use of bivalence. In arguing thus, I may have prompted objections of two related sorts that I should like to offset. Many will say that if you treat relativism in the alethic way, you have yourself fallen in with relativism's opponents; you must believe that a relativistic logic is, on objectivist grounds, the right logic to prefer everywhere. By *objectivism*, I mean no more than that there is an independent order of reality—including artworks and other cultural entities—and that we are fortunately endowed with the cognitive capacity to discern its determinate structure as it exists independently.[11]

No. What I have offered in the foregoing is an attempt to vindicate relativism within the terms of reference the opponents of relativism insist on: my limited claim here is that they fail under that constraint. But I also want to insist, first of all, that the entire alethic policy I am advocating is *not* detachable from the encompassing ontic and epistemic considerations relative to which a relativistic logic (or a bivalent logic, for that matter) works at all and, second, that here the invariances and modal necessities of the objectivist orientation are to be rejected.

You will notice that I have avoided introducing flux or historicity or incommensurability in speaking of the mere alethic structure of relativism. That was meant to preclude certain irrelevant objections. Nevertheless, once, on independent grounds, you acknowledge historicity, the range of application for a relativistic logic is bound to be much larger than might otherwise be supposed. Relativism is hardly interesting when presented as a mere abstract possibility. It gains standing only by being put to use in one important sector of inquiry or another. Here, of course, I am attempting to show its advantage in the criticism of the arts, but I set no antecedent limitations on its use. On the contrary, you see that vindicating relativism in the formal sense is only a small part of recovering the puzzle that the modernist/postmodernist dispute obscures.

I

Matters change abruptly once we turn from formal to substantive considerations, for relativism has its best inning in judgments about cultural phenomena. Even if admitting that were tantamount to admitting a restriction on relativism's range of application, nothing would be lost: as I have said, relativism need not be an all-or-nothing affair. The opponents of relativism forever point to inquiries that (as they believe) could not possibly recommend a relativistic logic. Perhaps. But if relativism may be defended piecemeal, for different sectors of inquiry, this objection would be irrelevant. There are also, I may say, arguments to the effect that physical nature is itself a distinction drawn from within the scope of culturally qualified phenomena. I cannot do full justice to these deeper speculations—they would be out of place—but they might easily affect our sense of the conceptual link between nature and culture and the fortunes of Protagorean relativism. In particular, if realism with regard to physical nature must take a constructivist form, as I believe it must, then the prospects of relativism will be greatly enhanced, even with respect to the physical sciences. I shall leave the matter thus—quite unresolved.

It is hard to convey how far we've come. To grasp the full force of what has already been said, you must realize that what is still needed to clinch the argument in relativism's favor is simply to show a proper fit between some sector or sectors of inquiry and the accommodating logic. That's all. Wherever we want to admit incongruent truth claims, we need only fall back to a relativistic logic. The question remains whether there are any such sectors of inquiry—whether it would be no more than stonewalling to deny they exist. Of course they do! I shall come to the argument in a moment. But, more to the point, you must realize that what remains to be supplied is not so much a further formal defense of relativism as an ontic and epistemic characterization of the phenomena of certain exemplary inquiries and of what it is possible to claim and confirm about them. These, it may be hoped, can be shown to fit especially well the peculiar resources of a relativistic logic. What this shows is the misplaced zeal with which relativism is usually condemned and the profound mistake of conflating relativism with skepticism—or worse. For to justify relativism is to qualify the logical variety of admissibly objective truth claims and to explain why relativism should be favored in certain domains at least. That runs absolutely contrary to skepticism's objective—as well as anarchism's and nihilism's, for that matter.

One extremely tame concession is too easily confused with the relativist's claim. We need to be clear about this possibility in order to dismiss it as a false pretender. The irony is that, when certain further distinctions are put in play, the tame concession in question—often dubbed cultural relativity—suddenly takes on a meaning that *does* indeed bear in an important way on relativism's (ontic and epistemic) fortunes. Nevertheless, by itself, it is a truth no one would ever dream of disputing or rightly suppose was equivalent to the relativist's thesis—for, of course, if it were the true nerve of the issue, we would all be both instant relativists and relieved to say so.

By *cultural relativity*, then, I mean no more than the pedestrian fact that different societies have different histories, languages, customs, values, theories, and the like. I do *not* mean, in that sense, that what is true is also different among different peoples or that knowledge differs among different peoples because knowledge must be relativized to what is already relativized in the way of truth. Such a position would be a conceptual blunder as well as a complete non sequitur. What, substantively, is claimed to be true will doubtless differ from one cultural orientation to another, but truth and knowledge, as such, cannot be construed, on pain of contradiction. as culturally variable—for that would mean what is (rightly) true might also be (rightly) false. This is the reason for distinguishing between truth and truth claims.

Simply put, the theme of cultural relativity is a matter of first-order fact, whereas the relativist's thesis is a matter of second-order legitimation. That languages and customs differ is no more than a tiresome first-order fact, but that a relativistic logic should fit certain inquiries better than a bivalent logic, *without yet implicating any variability in truth or knowledge as such*, is a question open to serious second-order philosophical dispute. I see no quarrel here. By themselves, the bare facts regarding cultural relativity have no philosophical importance at all. They acquire importance only when they are pressed in the direction of the blundering thesis I have just flagged or of whatever accords with relativism proper. This matter is almost universally overlooked.

What is potentially interesting about cultural relativity is that the differences noted between cultures may also obtain within them—that intersocietal differences are no different in any principled way from intrasocietal differences; therefore, it is just as philosophically difficult to fix objective truth and knowledge within any one society or culture as it is to do so between very different societies or cultures. That, I should say, was the absolutely splendid thesis of W. V. Quine's enormously influential book *Word and Object*, though that connection is never pointedly addressed in *Word and Object* (in the sense relevant to relativism) or anywhere else in Quine's publications.[12] Of course, it is also the central thesis of Kuhn's *Structure of Scientific Revolutions* and Foucault's "Nietzsche, Genealogy, History," which, by and large, are inchoate relativisms addressed to the possible philosophical importance of cultural relativity and historical change. For what Kuhn and Foucault were willing to concede—which Quine was not—was that what we count as truth and knowledge (that is, the legitimated concepts, not the bare, first-order facts accumulated by different societies) are *artifacts of history* in the very same way first-order facts are. Yet that is no longer mere cultural relativity but relativity housing relativism, the conjunction of alethic and ontic/epistemic issues.

We don't actually know what Kuhn's and Foucault's theories of relativism were. They were never explicit enough. Kuhn was content to deny that we could ever directly discern any principle of neutrality regarding objective truth (objectivism), and Foucault had no patience with the question. The usual philosophical error spun from the facts of cultural relativity is, in effect, the same error Socrates attributes to Protagoras in the well-known exchange with Protagoras's student, in the *Theaetetus*. "True," for Protagoras, Socrates affirms, means "true-for-*x*." Truth is an inherently relational notion, relativized to whatever contingently, merely appears—or is believed—true by this person or that, or by the same person at different times. This has become the standard reading of Protagoras's doctrine over twenty-five hundred years.[13] Of course, if that is what relativism comes to, then certainly relativism is absurd—because it is self-defeating in an insuperable way.

One could never, for instance, say what anyone took to be true by their own or anyone else's lights; every effort to do so would be caught in the relationalism of the original definition of *true*. I trust it is clear that I have, by what has already been offered in the way of analyzing relativism's logic, completely obviated the need to fall back to this preposterous reading of either cultural relativity or Protagoras's doctrine. We must go further. I do acknowledge that a bewildering number of commentators suppose either that cultural relativity *is* what relativism comes to or that, in virtue of cultural relativity, adopting relativism is tantamount to admitting Socrates' formula.[14] But that is surely a non sequitur. I am unconditionally opposed to such readings.

All this is by way of clearing the air. The primary point about cultural relativity is not mere first-order variety but rather that, within such variety, we must single out the possible import of its being the case that expressive, representational, stylistic, rhetorical, symbolic, semiotic, linguistic, traditional, institutional, and otherwise significant features of artworks and other cultural phenomena fall within the scope of the culturally variable. If such properties are subject to cultural relativity, then it must dawn on us that we may not be able to defend the objectivity of truth claims about them in the usual bivalent way. We may have to fall back to the relativist's option. Such is the full connection between the two questions I originally distinguished.

I call all such properties (the expressive and the representational, for instance) "Intentional" properties, which means they designate meanings assignable to certain structures or meaningful structures as a result of the various forms of culturally informed activity (speech, deeds, manufacture, artistic creation), such that suitably informed persons may claim to discern these properties and interpret them objectively. *Intentionality* is a term of art here, which I designate by capitalizing the initial *I*. I use the term predicatively, to mark a family of sui generis properties confined to the cultural world—that is, to designate the collective, intrinsically interpretable features of societal life. I do *not* equate the term to the essentially solipsistic, ahistorical, and acultural forms of intentionality featured in the theories of Brentano and Husserl, yet I apply *Intentionality* in a way that still provides for something like the use they intended, but only under enculturing conditions (the conditions of acquiring, in infancy, a natural language and a grasp of the practices of one's surrounding society).[15]

That is a large story of its own, which I cannot properly relate here.[16] I merely co-opt the benefit of admitting its relevance. The most strategic theorem it offers—not the most important for our question—rests with the fact (congenial to cultural relativity) that Intentional properties are quite real. For convenience, I recommend the following postulate: the Intentional is equal to the cultural. For what is normally contested (remember Danto) in admitting the world of human culture is whether it is real at all—as real (say) as physical nature—and, qua real, marked by the sui generis properties I've just collected (the Intentional). That, of course, lays a proper ground for the objectivity of interpretive truth claims that is conveniently indifferent to the alethic quarrel between bivalent and relativistic logics.

There's much more to the story than that. I'm being more than cautious in drawing your attention to the unfinished tale on which the completion of the argument favoring relativism depends. It's not needed in any narrow sense here, but it would help to reassure you that, both prephilosophically and philosophically, questioning the reality of the cultural world would produce an instant and insuperable paradox. On my own argument, it would involve questioning our own existence. As I see matters, we ourselves ("selves") are also artifacts of cultural life formed by transforming the members of *Homo sapiens* into linguistically and culturally apt subjects, marked (by that process) for discerning the Intentional features of whatever, as selves, we make and do. To put the point in its most provocative form, one could assert that no principled ground exists on which to disjoin the realist reading of human selves and the realist reading of the artifacts of their world; both are culturally constituted in similar ways, and both are subject to similar interpretive interests. I would not press the point, except for the fact that the most fashionable analytic theories in the West (particularly in the philosophy of mind) completely discount the reality of the cultural (and the intentional in general) or make it entirely derivative, logically, from whatever may be specified in purely biological or computational terms.[17]

Even that might not be troubling, since these theorists often have little interest in the philosophical problems of the cultural world. But what should we say when leading theorists of the arts—Arthur Danto, most notably—commit themselves to the *denial* of the reality of the cultural (or the Intentional)?[18] I must alert you to the fact that even a bivalent account of the objectivity of literary and art criticism would utterly founder on anything like Danto's thesis; so that admitting the reality—a fortiori, the discernibility—of the Intentional structure of artworks and human careers lays a needed ontic and epistemic ground for the would-be objectivity of critical interpretations and histories, *whether construed bivalently or relativistically, objectivistically or constructivistically*. Allow the gain, if you will, however provisionally: it does not quite reach to what is decisive for or against relativism, but it makes the debate worth the bother.

Let me summarize what I have already established in this chapter, with an eye to securing a further goal. Thus far, we have (1) distinguished a relativistic logic from a bivalent logic and shown its formal coherence; (2) discovered that the defense of relativism, as in a relativistic theory of interpretation or history, is largely occupied with demonstrating, ontically and epistemically, a certain suitable fit between manageable inquiries in one or another sector of the world and the resources and advantages of a relativistic logic; (3) acknowledged that no insurmountable paradox results from using a bivalent and a relativistic logic together, even in a lax and ad hoc way; and (4) determined that relativism and cultural relativity are entirely different doctrines, since the first is a second-order thesis and the second is a first-order thesis. We want, of course, to know how relativism and cultural relativity may be fruitfully linked so that an obviously robust practice—such as the ongoing work of a professional cohort of historians or art critics, or lawyers or moralists, for that matter—could be sustained or would strike us as worthwhile (not prone to any serious loss of investigative rigor) and would actually be less arbitrary and more rewarding than champions of the bivalent canon suppose.

The general answer is plain enough: on the one hand, the defenders of the bivalent canon cannot make their own case everywhere and, indeed, inevitably betray their awareness that they cannot; on the other hand, we already have the supportive of the pluralized practices of interpretive critics and historians. The essential clue is this: the switch from bivalence to relativistic values is not a change in rigor at all but a change in what we understand to be the nature of the *objects* on which the relevant rigor is to be practiced. In claiming that the Intentional structure of artworks definitely favors relativism over bivalence, I take the general failure on the part of most critics of relativism to analyze Intentionality to be knockdown evidence of their failure to address the full question of relativism itself. For Intentional attributes are not determinate—though, under interpretive conditions, they are determinable—when compared with what is usually taken to be the determinate nature of physical or non-Intentional attributes. It's this issue that needs to be pursued—along with, of course, its bearing on the question of objectivity.

I can well imagine that Barthes's intuitive discipline in reading *Sarrasine* may set a higher mark for acceptable relativistic interpretations than conventional bivalent readings of established texts. Harold Bloom's ingenious reading of Nathanael West's *Miss Lonelyhearts*, for instance, is, despite Bloom's own antirelativistic proclivities, a fine example of a relativistic exercise akin to Barthes's.[19]

It may also be that a potential social benefit results from calling *all* pretensions of objectivity into question at the present time. I am willing to concede the possibility, but it is not my principal concern here. Nevertheless, I'll add in all frankness that to reject objectivity because one rejects objectivism is excessive—and more than misleading—because we obviously need *some* normative sense of the rigor of inquiry and the attribution of truth-values. Whatever is best in that sense is what we must recover as objectivity. (There's a danger here of being misunderstood.) But strict postmodernism is conceptual anarchy: whatever first-order recovery may be defended implicates some form of second-order legitimation.[20]

For present purposes, I bridge the difference between the two issues by admitting straight out that what counts as objectivity is—ineluctably—a reasoned artifact of how we choose to discipline our truth claims in any sector of inquiry. The assumption is that there is simply no way to *discover* the true norms of objectivity in any domain at all. Acceptable norms will have to be constructed as one or another disputed second-order proposal fitted to what we claim are our best first-order interests in this domain or that. What's important is that such a construction is not tantamount to relativism—in the straightforward sense that even our adherence to a bivalent logic (in physics, say) may have to take a constructivist turn. Constructivism is not, as such, equivalent to relativism.

Kuhn may well be right to say that it is "hopeless" to pretend to discover the changeless marks of objectivity.[21] Some claim to see in this a return to Socrates' interpretation of Protagoras. But that would be a mistake, a complete non sequitur, for, as already remarked, *true* is laid down in the *Theaetetus* as meaning "true-for-*x*" and is thereafter rigorously applied (when possible), whereas here it is not a question of the meaning or criteria of *true* at all but of how, socially, the practices of what we call objective inquiry are first formed. There is no ulterior judgment to the effect that what is posited as a defensible practice in this regard is tantamount to, or entails, the finding that that (also) is true-for-*x* (where *x* is now the society that supports the practice).

II

I freely admit there's a puzzle here, one very close to what I wish to secure—that is, a fifth theorem in the tally I have just collected. But it cannot be captured by the relationalist formula drawn from the *Theaetetus* or from any simple Kuhnian or Foucauldian analogue applied to history. That would merely repeat the disaster of the standard history of relativism, formed, without protest, from ancient times to the present. We are in uncertain waters here, not because of deeper doubts about relativism but because of the primitive state of all our inquiries into cultural life. The entire rationale for shifting from bivalence to relativism depends on how clear we really are about the *nature* of an artwork or a self.

You see this instantly if you recall the bivalent arguments of Beardsley and Hirsch. Why do they insist on the inviolability of bivalence in literary and art criticism? Beardsley claims no fundamental difference exists between the describability of a stone and the describability of a poem, except that poems have "meanings" for properties and stones do not. Surely, that's preposterous. Beardsley himself admits he cannot tell when a meaning is in a poem or merely imputed to it.[22] He certainly cannot offer us anything like a rule or criterion in support of his bivalent claim. For his part, Hirsch denies that poems are objects of any kind. They are, he suggests, what may be imaginatively reconstructed by discerning, among the ordered words of a text, evidence of the original intent of the one who first assembled them.

And how is that done? Hirsch claims that every possible poetic utterance—effectively, the intentional ordering of words—quite naturally instantiates one or another fixed genre of utterance formed within the ethos of the would-be poet's voice. Still, human history itself, Hirsch admits, makes it impossible to fix any of these supposedly essential genres; the entire enterprise is an improvisational fantasy ("probabilized," Hirsch says) that cannot do more than pretend to discover the invariant forms of meaning.[23]

It's the elusive nature of artworks that forces us to give up a strict bivalence. (If art is Intentionally structured and if Intentionality is determinable—interpretively—but not independently determinate, in the way physical objects are said to be, then bivalence must be threatened.) Also, of course, on Hirsch's own account, authors need not know what it is they themselves "intend"; their conformity with objective genres decides the issue. Yet Hirsch's solution cannot escape the indeterminacies of the hermeneutic circle.

This brings me to the missing theorem we need: (5) the very nature of cultural entities and phenomena—artworks, histories, sentences, actions, societies, persons—is such that, for obvious ontic and epistemic reasons, they cannot support any objective description or interpretation confined exclusively along bivalent lines. The decisive point is that no one can even say what the logic of criticism should be, unless they can also say what the nature of a poem or a painting is, relative to discursive and interpretive truth claims.

For his part, Arthur Danto never tells us what an artwork or a history *is*, except to say no actual artworks exist. Presumably, this is because their intentional features—representationality and expressivity—are rhetorically assigned "mere real things," in virtue of which they become rhetorically accessible. They cannot be more, since, it seems, the intentional features in question are never more than rhetorically ascribed, so they cannot be objectively discerned. Possibly, no histories exist either. Or, if they do, then artworks do not, and Danto will have succumbed to an incoherent claim (a vicious regress). Even though artworks are plainly uttered by human artists as the Intentionally structured expressions they are, Intentional properties will (have to) be real in the case of persons but be deemed unreal in artworks. Apparently, for Danto, artworks are what we imagine, fictively, when, by rhetoric or "transfiguration," we construe "mere real things" (physical objects or utensils, chiefly) as belonging to an ethos or an "artworld."[24] But what's the basis for any would-be objective claims about the meaning of a painting *within* that world? Danto never says. Beardsley and Hirsch are more adventurous but hardly more successful, for they are prepared to risk their own peculiar theories of what an artwork is. Plainly, we cannot hope to fob off any theory of interpretation—good, bad, or indifferent—if we have no theory of the Intentional structure of artworks or human careers.

I have just stated the reason for favoring relativism. Relativism is not inherently a subversive doctrine, a way of destroying the fabric of decent society. It is, rather, the upshot of a quite sober reckoning of the false pretensions of a canon that might well wreck us with its own misguided zeal. Imagine that the champions of some political status quo insisted they had found the true norms of invariant human nature and therefore were obliged to treat moral, legal, political, and religious questions in accord with a strict bivalence informed by those ulterior truths; that would be the analogue of Beardsley's and Hirsch's doctrines. They can't possibly work: the Intentionality of the human world is far too complex, far too equivocal, far too mongrelized, far too transient, and far too easily altered by our own efforts to determine its meaning. Here, you begin to see the advantage of conceding no more than the Intentionality of artworks and the formal resources of relativism.

Please explain yourself, you're bound to say. Don't just rail against the honest labor of more conventional theorists. Tell us how you would reconcile relativism and objectivity—in criticism, for example. Tell us that, or go away! Fair enough. I accept the complaint, but my answer stares you in the face. A proper elucidation would doubtless be interminable, but the essential clue is clear enough: Intentional properties—expressive, semiotic, representational, and all the other significative properties I've gathered under the umbrella term *Intentional*—cannot be determined criterially, algorithmically, evidentially, except in ways that are already subaltern to the consensual (not criterial) tolerance of the apt agents of the collective practices of a particular society. That is the reason all analogies drawn from physical nature won't do, for cultural phenomena exhibit and physical phenomena lack Intentional properties. Hence, what we mean by description and interpretation is not quite the same in the two domains (though they are not disjoint, either).

In our own time, the thesis may be drawn, in different ways, from Wittgenstein's notions of a *Lebensform* and a "language game,"[25] and from Kuhn and Foucault as well. Historically, I am convinced it captures the leanest way to read Hegel's notions of *sittlich* as well as *Geist*.[26] It appears as a recognizable stream of thought running from Hegel through Marx, Nietzsche, Dilthey, Heidegger, Horkheimer, and Gadamer, down to Foucault. If you grasp the point, you see at once it is not possible to segregate the theory of interpreting artworks from a general theory of cultural reality. Professional work will have its local policy, to be sure, but its logic and its sense of a viable practice will be governed by our general conception of the sui generis features of the culture we share—any culture, as we now understand matters.

The important point to bear in mind is that a proper analysis of Intentionality is in no way hostage to relativism. It's the other way around: Intentional properties, which distinguish the world of human culture—a fortiori, literary and art criticism and, on a plausible argument, even explanatory theories in the physical sciences—will ultimately signal what our alethic, ontic, and epistemic policies should be.

The entire contest can be decided by reviewing two corollaries of my characterization of Intentionality—applied, if adopted, to the special concerns of professional critics, historians, or the like. First of all, predication in general cannot be epistemically managed on criterial or algorithmic grounds unless, per impossibile, Platonism is proved viable. I claim that general predicates, and Intentional predicates in particular, cannot be extended to new instances, except informally, in terms of what, consensually, may be tolerated as effective or incremental extensions from acknowledged exemplars. Any difficulties incurred—for example, in the sciences, with respect to would-be laws, prediction, explanation, or technological control—can be readily resolved along alternative lines that will proceed informally as well.[27]

But the hopelessness of all theories of universals—realist, nominalist, conceptualist—remains confirmed quite independently of all that. If so, then bivalence will *always* be subject to a policy of accommodating predicative similarities that cannot themselves be strictly applied (algorithmically, for instance) in bivalent terms. This concession is generally ignored by the opponents of relativism, even though the tolerance that must be admitted is not inherently relativistic in its own right. Bivalence itself must be applied in a constructivist way to predicables. Even a bivalent treatment of predicative truth must acknowledge that informality.

If you add to this (the first corollary) the obvious adjustment—that the particular exemplars on which extended predicative tolerance depends will always be subject to replacement, on the strength of changing convictions of what to look for in the way of observable similarities—then *whatever* we judge to be objective in the predicative way will elude the impossible strictures any bivalent policy informed by one or another form of invariance. What I say here is that objectivity must be a constructed artifact of our consensual practice—whether construed bivalently or relativistically. Furthermore, what holds for predication holds for reference and denotation and for all linguistic powers that bear on servicing truth claims. I challenge the opponents of relativism to explain how, if Platonism cannot be convincingly invoked, the objective practice of making and confirming truth claims can possibly be restricted in the bivalent way. I think there cannot be a satisfactory answer.

The second corollary concerns Intentional predicates and the nature of artworks in particular. Imagine someone asks you for the meaning of Anselm Kiefer's use of Nazi symbolism in his enormously intriguing paintings—which may be judged (by opposed lines of reasoning) to be celebrating or exorcising the world's unresolved memory of that terrible past. How should we decide such a dispute? I suggest you take stock of the following notions. First, any predicative attribution will favor the *sittlich*—in the minimal (perhaps pirated) sense I have already sketched but not previously named. (I now borrow the term in the slimmest possible way from Hegel.) The "is" of predicative similarity lacks, in the last instance, crisp, distinctive criteria or strict algorithms of application, because to presume otherwise would be to favor something resembling a form of Platonism or strict interpretive readings. Thus, if the scope of a general predicate—any predicate—is extended in real-world terms, it escapes utter arbitrariness only by appealing to the *sittlich*, the actual laxer practices of a society of apt speakers. Questions of the fit between such extensions and the theoretical and practical interests of those speakers affect only the choice among various lines of extension amid an indefinite run of such possibilities. Such a choice never assuredly affords more powerful epistemic resources. Hence, the fortunes of bivalence cannot fail to be subordinated to deeper epistemic and ontic considerations.

By parity of reasoning, our aptitude for discerning relevant similarities in a run of would-be cases—any cases—signifies our mastery of the same *sittlich* practices within the bounds of which such similarities obtain or are reasonably extended. In the art world, Intentional properties bring into play meanings and other significative structures (Kiefer's images, for instance). So, I mention as a second consideration, Intentional properties complicate the initial question of perceptual similarity (in any generous sense of *similarity*) by drawing in (within the bounds of the first) specifically interpretive attributions of semiotic similarities. Is Prokofiev's *Classical*

Symphony Mozartean, for instance? Is *Miss Lonelyhearts* a fair analogue of Milton's *Paradise Regained*?

To admit these questions is to admit the unlikelihood of adhering to a strict bivalence, yet without refusing the advantage of a laxer use of bivalence under consensual conditions. If you bear in mind that ordinary discourse is the usual exemplar of our treatment of truth claims—both in the sense that any would-be greater precision of reference and predication is tethered to the possibilities of conversational precision and in the sense that, at the conversational level, consensual solidarity (again, *not* in any excessively disjunctive way) cannot fail to be in play—you must grasp as well that the precision of critical discourse (like the precision of science) cannot usually exceed the precision with which we understand ourselves and one another. In this sense, relativism is a reminder of our epistemic frailties. How could it be otherwise?

I have deliberately kept the argument to the slimmest possible assumptions—that is, to the internal coherence of a relativistic logic and to the contingent standing of arguments that favor an exclusive appeal to bivalence.

Beyond that, if you merely add the indefensibility of objectivism, the indemonstrability of modal necessities *de re* and *de cogitatione*, and the conceptual difference between cultural relativity and relativism itself, there would seem to be no conceivable way in which to disqualify invoking relativism in interpretive contexts (or elsewhere), if an analysis of the domains in question would otherwise justify doing so.

Now, in cultural matters, some form of constructivism seems inevitable, and if in pursuing the import of the analysis of predication, reference, and discursive contexts we find we cannot segregate our discourse about the natural world and the world of human culture, then some sort of constructivism will be implicated once again. As I have said, however, constructivism is *not* tantamount to relativism.

Neither is cultural relativity, nor the relativity of truth-value assignments on evidentiary grounds formed in accord with the first-order patterns of cultural relativity. All that is often overlooked—or misconstrued. Certainly, to concede that saying assigning "true" to a given statement is relative to a society's evidentiary practice is not equivalent to agreeing that *true* means "true-for-x" in anything like the relational sense Socrates cleverly imposes on Theaetetus. Beyond that, if human thought is, as I suggest, historicized as well, and if objectivity must (as in the predicative case) be artifactually constructed in accord with our consensual practices, then

(I suggest) it is well-nigh impossible that relativism will not have a very strong inning in interpretive and other cultural contexts (and elsewhere). Nevertheless, I insist I have built the argument up from the least contestable considerations.

But what of artworks? What of their ontic structure—relative to our quarrel? The answer must be judged in a double way (alethically and also in epistemic/ontic terms). First, artworks (like persons, actions, and sentences) are not fully determinate but are, rather characteristically, interpretively determinable in Intentional ways because Intentional properties are themselves not fully determinate. (Only if meanings were properties and at least as determinate as the properties of physical objects would Intentionality be determinate at all. But Intentionality, remember, is a fluxive artifact of history, inherently subject to interpretation and reinterpretation under the historicized conditions of human life.) Second, in spite of the preceding statement, and in spite of having such a nature, artworks are reasonably *determinate in number*, individuatable, and reidentifiable. This goes against the entire tradition of philosophy. In particular, it goes against Aristotle's *Metaphysics* 4 and the standard attack on Protagoras. You begin to glimpse, therefore, the subversive possibilities of the rather bland line of speculation I am offering here.

In fact, I am now able to bring the entire argument to a trim close in a way that is hospitable to both the usual bivalent practice and the radical possibilities relativists would be unwilling to disallow. All that would be needed would be to abandon the standard convictions that bivalence cannot be coherently breached and that reality must possess determinate, unchanging structures. On the foregoing argument, those conceptual dinosaurs cannot be restored to their towering eminence. All that needs to be added is a third consideration—namely, that the boundary conditions for interpretive discourse, as far as both referential fixity and what should be relevantly construed as the salient features (the nature) of a particular work are concerned, are themselves decided in accord with the same *sittlich* practices noted above or by endorsing one or another critical revision of them.

Beyond that, practice goes on as before. I see in this an explanation of the ironic possibilities of Barthes's having favored *scriptible* ("writerly") interpretations without disallowing *lisible* ("readerly") interpretations—that is, roughly, what I am sorting as relativistic and bivalent criticism. Each proceeds by imposing its own restrictions and liberties. Each may be consensually endorsed, and the two practices may be reconciled. This signifies that many further questions will have to be resolved to make a reasonably tight case. Nevertheless, the best-known challenges to relativism fall within the terms I've sketched.

Here, criticism recovers the resources collected in the name of cultural relativity. Here, surely, criticism follows the inventive glory of the arts themselves. I find the Western emblem of the world's diversity displayed, however problematically, in Picasso's *Les demoiselles d'Avignon*, for within that interrupted painting one sees the impossibility of avoiding the spontaneous urge to bend the Intentional forms of one society to the art and criticism of another. The acknowledged importance of *Les demoiselles* signifies both that one cannot fully grasp the significance of the painting in terms of historical resources confined in any way to what is internal to the Western tradition *ante* and that one cannot rightly grasp its Intentional structure by reference to any well-formed hermeneutically defined genre within the standard practices of painting. Admit the practice and give in to the irresistible temptation, within the bounds of the theory I propose, and you will find that you have already become a friend of relativism.

I venture a final thought on the distinction between relativism and cultural relativity. The distinction is quite simple. I mean by "cultural relativity" nothing more than a version of cultural pluralism, in which the puzzles of relativism need not (but may) arise. The standard example, in poetry, appears in one of Wordsworth's Lucy poems, which is said to support (with equal plausibility) opposed readings of the poet's thoughts on the occasion of losing his beloved and/or the import of his reflections on the dismal lesson of the prevailing physical sciences. This draws our attention to two topics that must be addressed: one, the endless openendedness of interpretation (an issue akin to historicity); the other, the materiality of thought (an issue that addresses the nature of the human and the causal efficacy of agental [mental] episodes). But I cannot pursue these matters here.

Two

Objectivism and Relativism

I

Whoever would defend relativism must, on pain of self-confessed stupidity, construe it in a way that is not self-contradictory or self-refuting, and yet it is notorious that its opponents regularly and comfortably identify it in a blatantly stupid form.[1] We cannot help suspecting the objector's practice, because, quite obviously, the intended lesson needs to be repeated much too frequently to be taken entirely at face value, and because there is no straightforward reason for supposing that the defenders of relativism are that stupid. On the other hand, there is the perfectly reasonable concern—against would-be relativists—that they should not be permitted to tailor the notion at will solely to escape the damning charge: they must afford an account that suitably bears on a fair portion of those issues that seem to have led to the original complaint. A fair way of passing between these two dangers suggests itself: let us stipulate independent conditions or constraints that a responsive and interesting form of relativism is likely to satisfy, of both the consistency and pertinence sorts, without rushing to declare *what* the relativist thesis is or must be. That ought to satisfy all within the field of combat—except, of course, those whose own pleasant game is thereby exposed. The point of the exercise would be to restore a clear sense of the viability of relativism—against the backdrop of its obviously accelerating appeal in the contemporary world but in sympathy with the conviction that, if it is viable, it will surely affect in a profound way our understanding of human rationality and the puzzle of legitimating the alternative forms of inquiry that the human race seems forever bound to encourage. It should be possible in this way to draw objections to relativism that are not simply occupied with the allegedly inevitable self-refutation.

What shall we need? Well, we shall want to set formal conditions on the truth-values (or truth-like values) the relativist's judgments, propositions, claims, or suitable analogues can take, in virtue of which conditions sufficiently close to or like the usually imputed self-refutation obtain, but without the obvious penalty. We shall want to show in some way what grounds may be offered for holding that, in *some* sector of inquiry at least (precisely because of the nature of the domain, but not necessarily in all sectors of inquiry), it is as reasonable to restrict such judgments in the accommodating way as to refuse to do so and that doing so really does address our deeper concerns about the alleged scope of the relativist thesis. It may prove to be that certain global versions of relativism (for instance, forms of Protagorean relativism)[2] may not be coherent in the sense required. If so, then surely reasonable relativists would abandon such versions and retreat to a more restricted, modular, or modest version and try to make the case out that even that sort of relativism is stronger than its opponents would be willing to grant. There might have to be a compromise on both sides, and both sides may be sobered by the discovery.

The minimal formal condition required seems straightforward: simply take sets of the offending judgments—supposed to be contradictory or self-refuting—and restrict the truth-values or truth-like values they can be assigned so that, in accord with the new values but not with the old, and without otherwise altering the content of what is claimed, the judgments in question are no longer contradictory or self-refuting. They might now be said to be incongruent, precisely because on a bivalent (or bipolar) model of truth and falsity they would be incompatible but now are not. That this is not yet sufficient for any interesting form of relativism is clear enough if we remind ourselves that merely *probabilized* judgments go some distance in meeting the condition—for example, that it is probable that Nixon knew about Watergate in advance and that it is probable that Nixon did not know about Watergate in advance. Usually, probabilized judgments are supposed to be assignable the bipolar (bivalent) truth-values *true* and *false* and so would normally be taken to generate (contrary to what we want) contradictions when assigned such values. But the direction in which the formal constraints would need to be spelled out is reasonably clear and reasonably manageable. All we need do is restrict the admissible values—values such as *plausible* and *implausible*, disallowing bivalent truth and falsity—so that the offending contradictions and self-refutations are precluded (without, of course, needing to disallow contradiction or self-refutation in other ways). We should be home free. Of course, the defense may be thought uninteresting. But it certainly clears the air. For instance, it disables at a stroke such claims as the following: "implicitly or explicitly, the relativist claims that his or her position is true, yet the relativist also insists that since truth is relative, what is taken as true may also be false. Consequently, relativism itself may be true *and* false. One cannot consistently state the case for relativism without undermining it."³ It is true that the relativistic countermove is a purely formal one, so it can hardly be thought sufficiently persuasive against more substantive suspicions. By parity of reasoning, however, so, too, are formal complaints of the sort just cited (the charge of Protagoreanism). One suspects, therefore, that objections of an altogether different sort lurk in the neighborhood and that constraints of another sort will thus be needed.

Seen this way, relativism is best taken as something more than—but at least as including—a thesis (and the accompanying rationale for it) regarding the assignment of suitably weakened truth-values (or truth-like values) to certain sets of judgments. Narrowly construed, its rationale supplies a theory about the properties or nature of some part of the world, or of some part of the conditions of inquiry with respect to that part of the world, or both, supporting such assignments. Could we, then, in the interest of an honest canvass, add constraints that, joined with suitably amplified versions of the merely formal (alethic) conditions mentioned, would place at greater risk (hence, might mark the greater promise of) the somewhat spare relativism already sketched? Why not?

What might be added? The following conditions seem particularly promising:

1. Relativism should not be construed as, or as reducible to, any form of skepticism, nihilism, irrationalism, anarchism, or the like, although it may be that a well-defended relativism would lend comfort to doctrines of these sorts.

2. Relativism should be construed as precluding, within its scope, any form of foundationalism, essentialism, logocentrism, or similar doctrine—without being thought restricted merely to their denial.

3. Relativism should be construed as compatible with but not as entailing historicism, although strong forms of historicism should be construed as entailing relativism.

4. Relativism should be construed as more comprehensive if its rationale is made to depend on the distinctive features of a given domain of inquiry than if it merely imposes external cognitive limitations on all who inquire in that domain.

5. Relativism should not be construed in terms of judgments merely relativized (or "relationalized") to alternative conceptual schemes or cognizing agents, or in terms of the putative incommensurability of such schemes, or in terms of being cognitively confined within the boundaries of particular such schemes to the exclusion of others, and a theory should not be construed as relativistic merely because it provides for making and appraising judgments that entail an appeal to the categories of particular conceptual schemes—or to schemes subject to the conditions just disfavored.

6. Relativism should not be construed as precluding comparative or normative judgments of the usual sort and range (for instance, of better or worse, or of more or less adequate) conceded within theories that subscribe to bipolar (bivalent) truth-values.

7. Relativism should not, when restricted to particular domains of inquiry, be construed as incompatible in principle with cognitive claims, outside its own scope, that favor bivalent truth-values.

8. Relativism should not be construed as, or as reducible to, pluralism and should be construed as entailing but not as entailed by pluralism.

9. Relativism should be construed as neutral regarding, and as not committed to either affirming or denying (or requiring or precluding), the cognitive adequacy of any otherwise coherent or self-consistent conceptual scheme.

10. Relativism should not be construed as affirming or entailing (or denying, for that matter) the facts of cultural diversity or cultural relativity, whatever they may be, synchronically across cultures or diachronically within particular cultures.

11. Relativism should not be required to resolve claims or disputes by way of supplying evidence or cognitive resources greater or more fruitful than what is normally admitted within any given science or inquiry. In particular, it should not be required to be stated in a global or inclusive rather than a restricted form or in a form more inclusive in scope than any nonrelativistic theory it may contend with; it should be construed as a theory fitted in a conceptually competitive way to the practices of particular forms of inquiry.

These obviously informal conditions make a very reassuring set. Doubtless there are other such conditions that would be worth considering in exploring a reasonably ramified version of relativism. But it is hard to suppose that these fail to touch on the points at issue in very nearly all—one is tempted to say, all—of the best-known quarrels about relativism in the recent literature. If so, then any theory that could satisfactorily meet these and similar conditions would be a full-fledged form of relativism, quite apart from whether it were specifically linked (as well it might be) to larger issues regarding the practices of science and rational inquiry.

II

Here we may take advantage of a recent account, one of the latest to air the issues raised by our eleven conditions, that offers a decidedly sanguine view about avoiding what it calls the twin disorders of objectivism and relativism. It promises a convenient economy, because it denies relativism the option of satisfying all or nearly all the conditions mentioned and because it surveys the views of most of the principal opponents of the "disorders" in question. There are actually very few sustained statements of this sort to be had. If we could offset the countermoves it collects from a sprawling literature, then we might conveniently focus in a brief span the actual prospects of a genuinely disciplined relativism. In fact, if the attack fairly represents a dominant (or the dominant) line of objection to relativism, the best line of defense may well lie (1) in undermining the alleged conceptual dependence of relativism on objectivism and (2) in providing a sense in which relativism effectively addresses an ineliminable problem raised *both* by the dependence alleged and by the opposed strategy. We may anticipate that the upshot of a successful effort of such a sort would be to bring a merely formally coherent relativism (together with its supporting rationale) into accord with our eleven substantive conditions.

Consider the following specimen view. In his recent book *Beyond Objectivism and Relativism*, Richard Bernstein offers the following terminological distinctions: "By 'objectivism,' I mean the basic conviction that there is or must be some permanent, ahistorical matrix or framework to which we can ultimately appeal in determining the nature of rationality, knowledge, truth, reality, goodness, or rightness. . . . The objectivist maintains that unless we can ground philosophy, knowledge, or language in a suitably rigorous manner we cannot avoid radical skepticism."[4] The relativist not only denies the positive claims of the objectivist but goes further. In its strongest form, relativism is the basic conviction that when we turn to the examination of those concepts that philosophers have taken to be the most fundamental—whether it is the concept of rationality, truth, reality, right, the good, or norms—we are forced to recognize that in the final analysis all such concepts must be understood as relative to a specific conceptual scheme, theoretical framework, paradigm, form of life, society, or culture: "For the relativist, there is no substantive overarching framework or single metalanguage by which we can rationally adjudicate or univocally evaluate competing claims of alternative paradigms."[5]

Some clarifying observations are in order. First, Bernstein means to include as objectivists, for understandable reasons, not only the rationalists and empiricists, and all foundationalists and essentialists, but also Kant and Husserl, although Husserl considered the term *objectivist* inapplicable to the special apodictic certainty appropriate to his own favored form of "transcendental subjectivity."[6] In any case, *objectivism* is a convenient catchall. Second, it is true that relativism is incompatible with an inclusive objectivism. But it hardly follows that "relativism . . . is not only the dialectical antithesis of objectivism; it is itself parasitic upon objectivism."[7] That this is neither true nor required nor even particularly central to relativism is worth emphasizing, since relativism is (trivially) incompatible with accounts of knowledge and science opposed to objectivism-*and*-relativism (Bernstein's target) that insist nevertheless that cognitive claims are capable of a measure of objectivity.

(Here, at some risk, we may include as specimen views of the *non*relativist, *non*objectivist sort those of the following, at least: Popper, Kuhn, Lakatos, Hesse, Gadamer, Habermas, Ricœur, Davidson, Putnam; Charles Taylor, MacIntyre, and Winch.) Thus, if, as seems reasonable, objectivist or so-called foundationalist (or apriorist) views can be expected to be on the defensive and decline for some time to come, it hardly follows (so far at least) that the status of relativism would be or need be adversely affected by that fact alone, or that the attempt to support relativism would correspondingly decline or have to decline.

The interesting charge advanced (by Bernstein and similar-minded opponents of relativism), therefore, holds that, although it opposes objectivism, which is untenable in any case, relativism is or may or may not be committed to the thesis that *only* objectivism could preclude skepticism. Hence, relativism is committed to skepticism, possibly to a version of the (radical) incommensurability thesis (to the effect that claims drawn from different paradigms cannot be treated as cognitively competing claims). The counterstrategy is at once clear: construe relativism as (indeed) opposed to objectivism, disallow the skeptical reading (which the sanguine opponent of both objectivism and relativism—so styled—already contests), and reinterpret relativism as less than a rigid monistic thesis about science and rational inquiry. I see no reason to link the fates of objectivism and skepticism too tightly: even the defeat of transcendentalism—which is a kind of monism—yields a benign form of skepticism, in yielding to pluralism; it need not, however, address the question of relativism at all. It makes perfect sense to inquire whether, say, the interpretation of poetry or painting supports or favors some form of relativism (which I should say is reasonable—even true). But raising the issue in an ad hoc way has nothing to do with the independent prospects of objectivism. Bernstein has been misled. The importance of the relativistic alternative (thus reinterpreted) lies in this: theories of science and rational inquiry may (viably) oppose both objectivism (or foundationalism) and skepticism (or incommensurability or the like), and yet *they may still be usefully sorted as favoring or opposing a refurbished relativism.* Since a great many of the leading discussants of the issue regard themselves as opposed to relativism (if the bare list provided be reasonably accurate), the recovery of relativism promises to be of some significance. The larger strategy, then, is this: (1) show how relativism need not be parasitic on objectivism, and (2) show how a relativism in accord with (1) can meet the adequacy conditions already enumerated. The fact is, Bernstein never considers the question of defending relativistic theories opposed to objectivism—very few commentators do. (I shall, in a moment, apply these distinctions to a particular quarrel. Otherwise, the full force and charm of the issue might well be jeopardized. But we need to be careful as well about shaping the conceptual contest that Bernstein's account conveniently invites.)

Admittedly, to say this is not yet to say *what* might be meant by nonobjectivist "objectivity" with respect to science, but the implied burden surely falls on relativists and nonrelativists alike. Here, Bernstein is particularly helpful, because his own attempt at specifying the new objectivity both brings into focus essential aspects of the history of the issue and unintentionally highlights the decisive lacunae that his own effort shares with that of most of those who claim to oppose relativism. A closer look at Bernstein's argument is, therefore, invited.

Bernstein begins in this way: First, he identifies "the central cultural opposition of our time":[8] "Many contemporary debates are still structured within traditional extremes. There is still an underlying belief that in the final analysis the only viable alternatives open to us are *either* some form of objectivism, foundationalism, ultimate grounding of knowledge, science, philosophy, and language *or* that we are ineluctably led to relativism, skepticism, historicism, and nihilism."[9] He adds, "If we see through objectivism, if we expose what is wrong with this way of thinking, then we are at the same time questioning the very intelligibility of relativism."[10] So he rejects the search for "an Archimedean point" (Descartes's obsession); rejects "the Cartesian Anxiety" itself (that is, objectivism); views the "exclusive disjunction of objectivism or relativism" as "misleading and distortive," implausible and unnecessary, and tied to Cartesian anxiety; and urges us to "exorcise" the anxiety so that we can pass beyond objectivism and relativism to a viable, already-somewhat-articulated, "postempiricist," more "historically oriented understanding of scientific inquiry as a rational activity."[11]

What is fresh about Bernstein's approach is this: contrary to Richard Rorty's dismissal of epistemology (though in complete agreement with Rorty's rejection of objectivism and foundationalism), Bernstein invites us to consider how to characterize objectivity in science and rational inquiry, subject to the rejection of *both* poles of the "central opposition" and subject to the admission (in the Kuhnian spirit) of the indissolubility of science and the history of science. He goes on to salvage in a sympathetic way the essential focus and positive contribution of Kuhn's work on the theory of rational inquiry: "The shift from a model of rationality that searches for determinate values which can serve as necessary and sufficient conditions, to a model of practical rationality that emphasizes the role of *exemplars* and judgmental interpretation, is not only characteristic of theory-choice but is a leitmotif that pervades all of Kuhn's thinking about science." He adds that, in Kuhn's view (and in his own, of course), a paradigm is to be construed as "a concrete exemplar that is open to differing interpretations"—but in such a way as *not* to invite the mistaken inference that the contrast between "rules" and "paradigms" is "a contrast between the cognitive and the non-cognitive."[12] I agree with this much of Bernstein's argument.

Once these remarks are in place, the counterstrategy for defending relativism becomes remarkably simple: merely adopt the reconstructive views advocated and differentiate relativism along the formal lines already mentioned. In short, adopt at least the following:

1. Reject objectivism.

2. Deny the exclusive or disjunctive option of choosing between objectivism and either skepticism, nihilism, irrationalism, anarchism, or the like.

3. Separate relativism (along the lines already sketched) from all forms of skepticism, nihilism, irrationalism, anarchism, and the rest identified in the exclusive option mentioned in (2).

4. Construe subscribing to the Kuhnian paradigm or exemplar as an instance of subscribing to (1) and (2)—in particular, as subscribing to the view that the norms of rational inquiry are not separable from the actual history of inquiry.

Once matters are put this way, it is clear that the "exclusive option" is not in itself compelling; that the disjoined options may be separately opposed; and that the moderate relativism sketched earlier on is quite different from the so-called relativism of the "exclusive option," unaffected by the defeat or rejection of the latter and certainly compatible with its rejection.

Possibly, Bernstein owes *us* an explanation of why he so arbitrarily supposes that relativism cannot fail to take the absurdly stupid form it has so often been assigned (so-called Protagoreanism), or why it should be identified with such extreme views as skepticism and nihilism (which, in the sense intended, are utterly opposed to admitting the usual cognitive claims that relativism actually attempts to account for), or why or in what sense it should be linked necessarily, or merely adversely, with historicism and the concession of incommensurable, irreducibly plural conceptual schemes (taken as, or as entailing, alternative forms of skepticism and nihilism).[13] In the documentation Bernstein offers, the prejudice seems to be very widespread.

III

The prime strategy for redeeming relativism, then, rests with prising it apart from its allegedly symbiotic connection with objectivism. *No one has ever shown that the attempted defense of relativism must fail because objectivism fails (or its more familiar specialized versions fail).* That, after all, would be an extraordinary claim: first, because even the thesis about the stupid form of relativism need take no notice of objectivism, and second, because relativism itself has, whenever it has addressed objectivism, opposed it. (To imagine that in doing so it must make itself fatally indefensible for no apparent reason is certainly curious.) Hence, a decisive third option stares us in the face: Bernstein and similar-minded opponents of objectivism deplore and attack the argumentative strategy that would have it that the defeat of objectivism permits only a relativistic defense of science and rational inquiry. So there is an obvious gap in the argument that needs to be filled.

Consider, for example, that, contesting the import of Peter Winch's discussion of the challenge of Zande magic, Charles Taylor (who treats Winch as a relativist of a sort rather close to Bernstein's specifications) admits "incommensurable ways of life" (that is, activities that cannot be carried on at the same time "in principle" and not merely "in practice"—Zande magic and modern science, soccer and rugby football, possibly also pre- and post-Galilean science) but insists nevertheless (against the would-be relativist) that comparative judgments of worth or effectiveness or power (judgments of relative superiority) are not precluded for that reason:

> I entirely agree that we must speak of a plurality of standards. The discourse in which matters are articulated in different societies can be very different; as we can see in the Azande disinterest in explaining away the paradox Evans-Pritchard put to them in witchcraft diagnosis. The standards are different, because they belong to incommensurable activities. But where I want to disagree with Winch is in claiming that plurality doesn't rule out judgments of superiority. I think the kind of plurality we have

here, [regarding] the incommensurable, precisely opens the door to such judgments.[14]

The points to be noticed are as follows. First, Taylor's complaint has it that the relativist (*his* relativist) argues unjustifiably from the incommensurability of activities to the incommensurability of comparative cross-cultural judgments of such activities and from the impossibility of jointly performing certain activities to the impossibility of legitimating certain judgments. Fair enough. But the "relativist's" conclusion trivially follows from the putatively isolating or even imprisoning nature of different conceptual schemes, which he acknowledges. So the force of Taylor's countermove depends on its being the case that the non sequitur obtains *because and only because* "different" conceptual schemes are *not* incommensurable in all pertinent respects—in the sense that we and the Azande *can* understand one another's concepts and standards (which, as it happens, Winch always wished to maintain). Second, Taylor's relativistic opponent views matters entirely differently from the relativist (we have) already introduced, who denies *that* opponent's view of incommensurability and (also) admits that "judgments of superiority" *are* eligible. To put the matter as forcefully as possible in Taylor's terms: when he insists on "valid transcultural judgments of superiority" but admits that "there is no such thing as a single argument proving global superiority," what does Taylor have in mind (and what could he offer as support) in concluding "wherever the final global verdict falls, it doesn't invalidate but rather depends on such transcultural judgments"?[15] Can he possibly be reinstating a form of objectivism?

One should bear in mind that Taylor's theory ultimately must be squared with his own acceptance of the hermeneutic circle. For, as he says, "We cannot hide from ourselves how greatly this option [for admitting the hermeneutical sciences of man] breaks with certain commonly held notions about our scientific tradition. We cannot measure such sciences against the requirements of a science of verification: we cannot judge them by their predictive capacity. We have to accept that they are founded on intuitions which all do not share, and what is worse, that these intuitions are closely bound up with our fundamental options. These sciences cannot be '*wertfrei*.'"[16] But, then, his position *is* a relativism of the sort previously sketched; or is an undefended version of the paradoxical thesis that, in spite of the openness of history, of the hermeneutic circle, and of the interpretive fusing of horizons, human standards of rationality and value must in some sense remain essentially fixed, without depending on any form of objectivism;[17]

or else is an obscure form of objectivism itself. In the same vein, we may conclude that Kuhnian paradigms cannot ensure the defeat of a relativistic theory of science.

Taylor's argument against relativism depends on conflating two quite distinct charges: first, that relativism is committed to the incommensurability thesis, and second, that relativism is incapable of conceding "judgments of superiority." It is true that any relativism committed to what has been termed the exclusive option would be incapable of conceding judgments of superiority, but neither Taylor nor anyone else has shown that no pertinent form of relativism can escape the exclusive option or that any relativism that escapes or rejects the option nevertheless remains incapable of conceding judgments of superiority. Here is the fatal non sequitur. Furthermore, it is difficult to see *how* to exclude a relativistic account of such judgments (once objectivism is repudiated) without at least implicitly subscribing to some even-deeper form of objectivism. Such a tension is quite obvious in, for instance, Hans-Georg Gadamer's position, toward which both Taylor's and Bernstein's views noticeably converge. Thus Gadamer characteristically claims,

> That which has been sanctioned by tradition and custom has an authority that is nameless, and our finite historical being is marked by the fact that always the authority of what has been transmitted—and not only what is clearly grounded—has power over our attitudes and behavior. The validity of morals, for example, is based on tradition. They are freely taken over, but by no means created by a free insight or justified by themselves. That is precisely what we call tradition: the ground of their validity. tradition has a justification that is outside the arguments of reason and in large measure determines our institutions and our attitudes.[18]

Read correctly, this marks the unmistakable sense in which Gadamer comes very close to being a closet essentialist.

There appears to be absolutely no way, short of falling back to an explicit form of essentialism or universalism or foundationalism (which Gadamer resists), in which the thesis advanced could preclude a relativistic reading. Gadamer *does* wish to hold that the "authority" of tradition, changing more or less continuously in its historical process and subject to hermeneutic complexities, effectively fixes its instruction from one distinct phase of that process to another in such a way as to provide an effective, historicized analogue of essentialism. (I have dubbed this thesis *traditionalism*.) It is as if the authority of tradition remains recognizable through change *and* as if what it transmits (but does not otherwise legitimate) exhibits a suitably smooth and conservative transition from phase to phase, so that it insures a proper sense of what is being thus transmitted. The conceptual lacunae are clear enough. The objectivity of tradition is certainly not demonstrably incompatible with the relativist's thesis. The puzzle is generalizable for all materials subject to hermeneutic review.[19] Gadamer's hermeneutical "invariant"—perhaps then Taylor's and Bernstein's as well—seems to be discerned in the course of historicized change itself. But that is sheer self-deception.

A related confusion appears in Richard Rorty's claim that " 'Relativism' is the view that every belief on a certain topic, or perhaps about *any* topic, is as good as every other." Rorty adds at once, "No one holds this view." But he goes on to say, "If there *were* any relativists, they would, of course, be easy to refute" (since they would subscribe to the self-refuting Protagorean claim").[20] In any case, he says, " 'Relativism' only seems to refer to a disturbing view, worthy of being refuted, if it concerns *real* theories, not just philosophical theories"[21] (that is, "first-level," not merely "second-level," theories). But, of course, relativism *does* concern real theories of both sorts, once we recognize (contra Rorty) that there are no first-level theories without second-level theories or second-level theories without first-level theories. At long last he suggests, "Perhaps 'relativism' is *not* the right name" after all for the doctrine he really opposes—that is, "irrationalism," the doctrine (symbiotically but inappropriately) linked, as in Bernstein's account, to the rejection of the privileged grounding of cognitive claims.[22]

If our argument were conceded, we should be catapulted at once "beyond objectivism and relativism"—simply because relativism (the moderate relativism sketched) would then have been recognized as a stronger contender than it appeared to be when viewed as a mere parasite upon the back of objectivism. To that extent, we have justified the implied irony that the usual critics of relativism, who treat that doctrine as flailing away at an already hopeless thesis (objectivism), are themselves the self-appointed victims of that disorder.

But no one will be satisfied. After all, the appeal to Bernstein's original counterstrategy was made in the name of an economy; now, it might be seen as no more than a sly maneuver to gain an unfair advantage by way of a near irrelevancy. What more should be said? Certainly, the confusion between the two sorts of relativism should be accounted for. What may explain the confusion is this: in certain circumstances, the moderate relativist opposes the unrestricted admissibility of bipolar truth-values; somehow, this is converted into unconditional opposition to the admissibility of *any* use of bivalent truth-values (or truth-like values)—converted, then, into affirmation of a skeptical or anarchist or nihilist thesis. The relativist thereby becomes symbiotically dependent on objectivism. But, first of all, even mere indeterminacy of truth-value (at a given moment of inquiry or because of real-time constraints) is not an expression of skepticism: it is an affirmation of the cognitive standing of a given issue at a given time; findings of indeterminacy, after all, *are* assignments of truth-value relativized to the available evidence. Second, questions once thought to be "intrinsically incapable of determination"—that is, of being determined as true or false—may, over time, prove to be actually capable of such determination. Third, it is false to suppose that denying the unrestricted admissibility of bipolar truth-values (for relevant reasons) when logically weaker values are said to be admissible is just an expression of skepticism: it is itself a strong cognitive claim, presumably about the properties of a particular domain of inquiry. Thus, for instance, Quine's doctrine of the indeterminacy of translation is not merely a skeptical thesis; it is (meant to be) a benign relativist thesis: it holds that alternative (otherwise) incompatible ontologies *can* be empirically supported in given domains and that, because of the way ontological questions are addressed, stronger bipolar appraisals of candidate ontologies *cannot* be supported.[23] On the other hand, it may fairly be claimed that Paul Feyerabend (but not Thomas Kuhn) intended to hold a skeptical thesis *in* advancing various versions of the notorious incommensurability claim. For example, Feyerabend may have intended such a thesis in holding that "there exist scientific theories which are mutually incommensurable though they apparently deal 'with the same subject matter.' "[24]

The addition of these reflections pretty well settles the plausibility of all of our eleven conditions—at least as far as confirming the strong coherence and relevance of relativism is concerned. But we may round out the argument by collecting whatever substantive considerations may be expected to give relativism a genuine inning. First, then, wherever objectivism is denied or defeated, relativism is facilitated without actually being favored, for its rejection signifies that, in all domains affected, the strongest presumption in favor of bipolar values is disallowed. Nevertheless, the relevance of that rejection is often ignored or denied. For example, when Kuhn's incommensurability thesis is taken as a justified attack on objectivism, or at least on that strong form that holds that there must be a single, omnicompetent, "common, neutral epistemological framework within which we can rationally evaluate competing theories and paradigms or that there is a set of rules . . . that will tell us how rational agreement can be reached on what would settle the issue on every point where statements seem to conflict," it is sometimes insisted that the thesis "has *nothing to do* with relativism, or at least that form of relativism which wants to claim that there can be no rational comparison among the plurality of theories, paradigms, and language games—that we are prisoners locked in our framework and cannot get out of it."[25] Even Popper, who opposes Kuhn's incommensurability thesis, could allow that objection, although he would himself take the incommensurability claim to entail an extreme relativistic thesis.[26]

What is interesting, then, is this: both Kuhn and Popper, opposed on the incommensurability issue, insist on the "objectivity" of comparative judgments within science and on relativism's opposition to that constraint.[27] But, as already explained, their objection is curiously misdirected against (a moderate) relativism and depends on the altogether too easy conceptual slippage that links in one breath "irrationalism, scepticism, [and] relativism"[28] (doctrines labeled together thus in order to be discarded together). The opponents of relativism inadvertently impoverish its conceptual resources and thereby fail to address the challenge that it poses. They claim to support a form of scientific objectivity opposed to objectivism, always or characteristically or in the most important instances committed to the eligibility of bipolar values. Nevertheless, they invariably ignore the issue of legitimating such values against the relativist's option. That issue is almost never frontally addressed, and there is no developed argument that actually refutes or seriously weakens the relativistic alternative. In a word: there is no compelling reason why relativism should be restricted to incommensurability contexts.

The following distinctions may perhaps focus our findings in a compendious way: first, adherence or resistance to bipolar truth-values on purely epistemological grounds is a matter utterly distinct from the validation of truth claims such as those respecting any part of the encultured world; second, the repudiation of objectivism is as such entirely neutral, logically, both to assessing the formal coherence of replacing bipolar values with weaker truth-like values and to assessing the reasonableness of such a replacement in a particular context; third, the replacement of bipolar values, just as much as their advocacy, is as such opposed to skepticism, incommensurability, anarchism, irrationalism, and the like; and, fourth, rejecting the logical eligibility of relativistic truth-values solely on the grounds of repudiating objectivism and skepticism or incommensurability itself seriously risks an implicit appeal to an unacknowledged form of objectivism. It is true that objectivism (normally) adheres to bipolar truth-values. But that is no reason for supposing that the rejection of objectivism requires our continued subscription to bipolar values in all domains of inquiry.

IV

Repudiating the more determinate forms of objectivism, then, is bound to encourage even more determinate forms of relativism—for example, repudiating essentialism (say, in accord with Popper's well-known view) or so-called totalizing (against the program championed by Lévi-Strauss and other structuralists) or epistemological foundationalism itself.[29] In fact, if Popper's verisimilitude fails, then a scientific realism opposed to essentialism might well be driven to a relativistic position. Similarly, conceptual difficulties affecting univocal applications of the so-called principle of charity (for instance, as in Hilary Putnam's concessions regarding reference to theoretical entities) or difficulties affecting unique extensions of universals (for instance, in accord with Wittgenstein's reflections on the informality of rules governing natural usage or Goodman's strictures on resemblance) are bound to be favorable to forms of relativism, since they affect truth-values so fundamentally.[30]

The strenuousness of resisting relativism will be even more marked as we move on to the special complexities of linguistic and cultural contexts. Here, it is hard to see how the admission of intentional and interpretive considerations, of historicism, and in particular of the profoundly consensual (that is, reflexive) nature of objectivity in the human studies could possibly fail to strengthen the relativist's hand. Finally, wherever, under the accumulating burden of the themes here broached, questions of rational practice and policy cannot rightly claim to depend on the discovery of independent norms or ontologically "objective values," it is difficult to see how *whatever objectivity* may (reasonably) support moral constraints could preclude a relativistic interpretation of such objectivity.[31] Or, where conceptual issues are thought to require second-order inferences to the best account—noticeably, in speculations about what "there is," under historicized conditions shorn of any sources of apodictic certainty—it is difficult to see how relativistic considerations could be excluded or defeated merely as such.

The entire argument leads to two stunningly obvious questions: How, *if* "there is no single, timelessly adequate conceptual framework," and *if* "there is always an open-ended plurality of frameworks fitted to parts of the experienced world," and *if* objectivity under these conditions is conceded, can we demonstrate that the very choice of a proper framework for resolving particular disputes is invariably, predominantly, characteristically, or generally (for the important cases at least) made in accord with a strong bipolar model of truth-values? Or, how, assuming a rational choice fitting framework to question and question to framework, can we demonstrate that, *within* the contexts of inquiry thus provided, the resolution of particular disputes is invariably, predominantly, characteristically, or generally (for the important cases at least) made in accord with a strong bipolar model of truth-values? No answers seem to be forthcoming.

A final adjustment suggests itself. It has been argued that conceptual incommensurability, or "conceptual relativism"—the notion that there are different conceptual schemes recognizable as such but not translatable or paraphrasable into *our* conceptual scheme (either totally or partially)—"cannot be made intelligible and defensible." Donald Davidson, who presses the charge in what is perhaps the most strenuous and compelling way, straightforwardly declares, "the attempt to give a solid meaning to the idea of conceptual relativism, and hence to the idea of a conceptual scheme, fares no better when based on partial failure of translation than when based on total failure. Given the underlying methodology of interpretation, we could not be in a position to judge that others had concepts or beliefs radically different from our own . . . [and] if we cannot intelligibly say that schemes are different, neither can we intelligibly say that they are one."[32] Here, Davidson is attacking Kuhn's and Feyerabend's use of "incommensurable," which he takes (not at all unfairly) to mean what "not translatable" means.[33] This is not to say that "incommensurable" means "not translatable" on the best reading of the phenomena Kuhn and Feyerabend were examining— only that, with considerable uncertainty (and now, perhaps, with much less willingness to risk the issue primarily on the fate of a ramified theory of meaning), they did once favor such an equivalence. Davidson has, then, amplified very usefully F. P. Ramsey's very pretty point about mentioning, to another, one's own inability to pronounce *marmalade*.

Now, Davidson does *not* claim that we *can* actually translate into "our present scheme," whatever any natural-language speaker might say. He does confess, "I think our *present* scheme and language are best understood as extensional and materialist."[34] What, in effect, he shows is that, if conceptual schemes are to be individuated as radically different and if "failure of intertranslatability is a necessary condition for difference of conceptual schemes" (as he believes it to be),[35] then Ramsey's paradox obtains and the claim is no longer intelligible. Fair enough. But if actual translation efforts fail and if "failure of intertranslatability" is *not* a necessary condition for difference of conceptual schemes, then it may still be entirely reasonable to speak of different (even radically different) conceptual schemes without intending either a skeptical or irrationalist reading of Kuhn's rather unfortunate expression "different worlds" or a denial of conceptual relativism. One might (with Ian Hacking, for instance) speak of a "dissociation" of paradigms or exemplars rather than of a "failure of intertranslatability."[36] The fact is that Davidson has never shown that his own program of intertranslatability is even remotely promising for natural languages or that we have a good enough sense of what could effectively serve as criteria for intertranslatability (or for actual success of translation). Particularly with respect to theoretical terms (without either holding that their meanings are entirely determined by the theories in which they are embedded or that there are no such systematic constraints obtaining),[37] a dissociation of investigative practices, habits of thought, historical focus, beliefs, and the like might well encourage an inference to conceptual relativism. Under favorable circumstances, divergence would yield evidence for at least a robust or moderate relativism, and under no circumstances would it support (or need to support) a thesis of "radically different" conceptual schemes.

We can, therefore, have our cake and eat it too. We can admit dissociated, plural conceptual schemes in a logical space in which we *lack* a rule of global translatability and in which we *do not claim* the impossibility of translation. That is quite enough for a moderate relativism—and for a recovery of (what is defensible in) Kuhn's account of "incommensurable" paradigms. The question is, granting that much, how *could* the relativistic option be precluded or avoided?

Three

Science as a Human Undertaking

We analyze intentionality—say, our beliefs about the way things are and about how we should engage the world—with a sense that endorsing its puzzles is tantamount to challenging the hegemony of the unity of science, and we analyze the conceptual features of the human sciences with a sense of needing to reconcile the natural and the cultural. Technology straddles both concerns and is plausibly linked to the fortunes of both the unity and bifurcation models of science, so it affords a convenient economy as well as an important clue for any serious effort to picture the relationship between the natural and the human sciences. But we do all that with an imperfect mix of doubt and certainty that we never exceed. We seem incapable of unconditional indubitability. But we survive, as a race, within notable limitations, and we cannot abandon altogether the spontaneous imperatives of what appear to be our characteristic forms of cognition. We cannot assuredly identify the ultimate foundations of our knowledge—or, indeed, whether there are foundations. A fortiori, we cannot establish the hierarchical authority of our apparent resources, though we remain forever hostage to the question. So philosophy seems to be no more than a learned conjecture that cannot be entirely right or wrong—that may be better as a motley than as a unitary system, though our motley encompasses our provisional systems.

I

Insistence on the human standing of technology and the physical sciences may seem a wasteful reminder. There is, after all, no technology or science that is not a human undertaking, so the emphasis may be superfluous; technologies are essentially characterized in terms of facilitating specifically human interests, so the emphasis may be redundant; and the validity of the physical sciences is thought to mark the fortunate discovery of the lawlike regularities of an independent natural world, so the emphasis may be no more than intrusive. Insistence on these aspects of the matter would indeed be no more than a conceptual annoyance if they identified no more than the obvious themes of technology and science. Of course, we might query why these pursuits are uniquely human.

We might ask ourselves how human nature is affected by the technology it spawns. We might thus challenge the assurance that science simply discovers the structures of the independent world. We might explore the symbiosis of self and world, the indissoluble realist and idealist strands of our accomplishments, the incompletely penetrable and shifting preconditions of the life-world within which these other regularities are provisionally identified. Such exercises are hardly pointless. But they can be made to seem noticeably tired and tiresome if they have no more to say about technology and science than can be drawn by merely turning to examine the human condition itself. We should then have tricked ourselves by an inflated rhetoric. Are there findings about the principal features of science—about natural laws and causality and explanation—that we fail to grasp it we neglect the implications of the human face of science? Are there compelling distinctions regarding such matters that reflecting on the differences between human technology and the canonical picture of the physical sciences might reveal? Or, might they force a sizable revision in the canonical picture itself? Here, surely, is the sensible point of insisting on the theme of the human structure of science and technology.

The concessions eked out are already more than negligible. But they are as much illuminated by the study of the technological and the scientific as ever they illuminate science and technology. At any rate, it's the reciprocal benefit that we seek. We have in fact already managed to insinuate a double constraint on the review intended, one—so we may claim without demonstration—that represents the strongest convergent themes of the philosophical literature centered on the theory of the sciences: namely, first, that *all* would-be foundational, privileged, cognitively transparent, correspondentist, objectivist, logocentric, essentialist, apodictic, or totalized access to the structures of reality, phenomena, or whatever is said to be "given" in epistemically pertinent ways may be an indefensible presumption;[1] second, that, as a result, there are *no* discernibly different levels of cognitive *profon-*

deur, variably placed approximations to the "originary" sources of certitude or objectivity or necessary structures affecting our best theories of reality. The convergence of these two themes, though it may not be immediately obvious, may prove to be the point of intersection of the most promising forms, say, of naturalism, phenomenology, and deconstruction. Each of these orientations may, separately, harbor its own excessive claims, but the potential benefit of their intersection (even of their union) may rest with the issues we mean to pursue here. If we adopt both themes, however, we will effectively have refused any privilege to Kantian, Husserlian, or Nietzschean reflections regarding the legitimacy of such sources—supposing, in all candor, that the best vision possible requires a reconciliation of the master themes thus favored.[2] The resultant speculation would be unidimensional (however complex)—horizontal, so to say, in terms of the interconnections affected. A motley, as I say.

The upshot may be characterized in naturalistic terms, if we mean by that that no such speculation could be remotely pertinent if not reflexively addressed to whatever is most salient and least likely to be dismissed or denied or deformed within the consensual experience of an actual human community. It may, then, be characterized in phenomenological terms, if we mean by that that such reflection should disallow any fixities regarding the seeming order of the first and that we should nevertheless attempt to discern—within the historicized conditions of societal life that we cannot hope to penetrate except in accord with (to an unknown extent enabled by) the very aptitudes social history makes possible—whatever conceptual strictures or apparent necessities bear on the referential and predicative saliences of factual discourse. And it may also be characterized in deconstructive terms, if we mean by that that no conceptual schema (organizing factual claims) can be shown to be timelessly fixed or inviolate or comprehensively adequate for all possible evolving experience, and that we have, and in principle can have, no rational clue by which to assess the sense and extent to which our present schemes are approximations or partial fragments of such an ideally totalized conceptual vision. There is no doubt that such sanguine abstractions may be assigned to movements associated with Kant and Husserl and other figures. But our objective is to exploit their better natures (according to our lights) rather than locate them with perfect justice within the historical record.

If, then, we agree to treat the naturalistic, the phenomenological, and the deconstructive as no more than inherently one-sided concerns (when isolated from their fellows) within any minimally adequate reflection on the human condition and its cognitive relation to reality, we may well reconsider otherwise partial, potentially distorting views of technology or science generated more or less exclusively from one or another of such orientations—and gain thereby a surprisingly fresh picture of how an appreciation of what technology confirms about the human condition bears in a decisive way on the adequacy of (what we are here calling) the canonical theory of the sciences. That effort promises in fact a profound recovery of the sense in which science is a human undertaking. Once again, the point of the intended review is to isolate those respects in which such notions as lawlike regularity, causality, and explanation in the sciences—notably, in theorizing about the cognitive capabilities of the physical sciences—invite a contest of options usually neglected or dismissed or muffled in the literature favoring the canon, precisely because, there, the full role of the human inquirer is clearly deemed marginal for any explication of the powers of science (though of course it cannot be marginal). One might say, in the spirit of that canon: humans are the only scientists, but science is a well-formed cognitive practice adjusted to the way the world is—a practice that humans happen, contingently, not everywhere, to have fortunately hit upon. *If*, however, science were constitutively inseparable from technology, *if* technology were no more than a selectively focused study of pertinent human aptitudes (including, inseparably, the aptitude for science), then the properties of science could hardly be more than projections and proposals regarding how a person masters and comes to understand the world (and themselves) within the terms of their shifting life-world. The contrast thus formulated still seems bland enough. But the question arises (now more insistently), Is there a fundamental difference between a theory of science essentially linked to the concept of technology (here barely sketched) and the theory of science favored by the received canon?

II

Of course, there is no actual canon. There certainly have been attempts at formulating a canon, which in a fair sense may be characterized as a thesis bounded, for our own century, by such statements as Rudolf Carnap's *Logical Syntax of Language* and in overviews of the unity movement provided by Carl Hempel, Hans Reichenbach, and others—all counted as contributing to a developing canon.[3] There can be no question that the unity movement accommodates a variety of views that are occasionally incompatible with one another on a number of issues. There is no possibility of formulating a central set of doctrines to which all loyal adherents subscribe. So, for example, J. J. C. Smart would deny emergent laws and emergent properties of any kind—since, as Smart explains, "animals and men are [no more than] very complicated mechanisms."[4] Oppenheim and Putnam, on the other hand, are quite open to the prospect of emergent (empirical) laws and emergent properties. Hence, the partisans of unity are divided with regard to reductionisms of a very strong physicalist sort and views that tolerate various forms of emergence. In his later years, Carnap was himself drawn to consider what may be called pragmatist laxities, though this was not true at first.

In developing his argument, Smart is quite explicit about genuine laws of nature. They have "one very important feature," he maintains: "These laws are universal in that it is supposed that they apply everywhere in space and time, and they can be expressed in perfectly general terms without making use of proper names or of tacit reference to proper names." The trouble is that biology "does not contain any laws in the strict sense," the sense just given. The would-be laws of biology implicitly refer to the earth alone. Smart's view, of course, is hopelessly sanguine *if*, as it is currently fashionable to hold, science and the history of science are inseparable. For, then, on grounds quite neutral as between naturalism, phenomenology, and deconstruction, it would be impossible to obviate "tacit reference to proper names" (in Smart's sense); or, alternatively, the use of "perfectly general terms" would be no more than an idealized expectation of the lawlike standing of earthbound generalizations[5]—idealizations never actually confirmed as laws, possibly even incapable in principle of being explicitly so formulated.[6] Smart cannot do justice to the reflexive, earthbound nature of scientific inquiry itself.

Here, we come as close as possible to an essential requirement of the canon: the laws of nature must be *invariant* regularities. This way of putting matters is meant to remain neutral on the question of counterfactual and noncounterfactual readings of laws, on regularity conceptions of laws as opposed to views invoking nomological necessity, and on disputes between deterministic and statistical interpretations of laws—all of which obviously divide the loyalties of unity advocates. Wesley Salmon, for instance, admits counterfactuals in science, but Bas van Fraassen does not.[7] Hempel originally had not accommodated statistical laws but subsequently made provision for them, when he was able to reconcile their role with what he took to be the logical form of scientific explanations. Salmon offers what he terms an "ontic conception" of natural laws, which he puts in the following way (reviewing alternative readings of Laplacian explanation, although he himself rejects determinism): "*to explain an event is to exhibit it as occupying its* (nomologically necessary) *place in the discernible patterns of the world.*"[8] Convergence on the theme of invariance is impressively widespread.

One may therefore be reasonably disposed toward glossing the notion of the invariance of laws along the lines recently offered by Adolf Grünbaum—that, for instance, "explanations in physics are generically based on context-free, ahistorical laws"—except that Grünbaum actually offers the formula as an incorrect and utterly misguided view of physical laws fostered by both Jürgen Habermas and Hans-Georg Gadamer, who (on Grünbaum's reading) exaggerate the theme in order to bifurcate the natural and the human sciences.[9] The quarrel involving Grünbaum, Habermas, and Gadamer is worth tarrying over, because there is a great muddle involving all three and because its resolution actually bears in a decisive way on the contested views of laws and causality that were to be drawn (as promised) from contrasting the import of technology and the canonical view of the sciences. Let it be said at once that Carl Hempel had clearly espoused the doctrine that "there is no difference [in attempting the impossible task of giving a '*complete explanation* of an individual event'] between history and the natural sciences: both can give an account of their subject-matter only in terms of general concepts, and history can 'grasp the unique individuality' of its objects of study no more and no less than can physics or chemistry." When he wrote this, Hempel still held the view that a "general law" is "a statement of universal conditional form which is capable of being confirmed or disconfirmed by suitable empirical findings."[10] But, in conceding statistical laws, Hempel intended no concessions at all regarding a possible disjunction between historical and physical laws and explanations—which, of course, would have been inimical to the unity program. Certainly, historicity and exceptionless universal invariances are incompatible.

In that sense, Grünbaum's insistence is surprising: not because Grünbaum tolerates the bifurcation of the sciences—his own close study of the methodology of psychoanalysis is obviously designed to strengthen just the opposite view—but rather because he apparently believes he can reconcile the invariance or nomological necessity of scientific laws with the denial that they are "context-free" and "ahistorical."[11] But, of course, such claims, applied to the human sciences, formed the very basis on which Habermas and Gadamer had expected to disjoin the natural and the human sciences. It may be fair to say that Habermas and Gadamer are not altogether clear about the nature of the physical sciences, but it is equally fair to say that Grünbaum has somehow lost the thread of the pertinently challenging issue they raise (however weakly) and has, in addition, conflated two entirely different senses of *history* and *context*. On just such disputes as these depend, we may say, the entire contrast intended between the import of technology and the force of the canonical view of science.

Our question has suddenly become very complicated. For one thing, *if,* following Grünbaum, physical laws are not context-free or ahistorical, then it is difficult (if not impossible) to see how they can be genuinely universal or invariant. *If,* for another, following Smart, genuine laws make no use of proper names (or surrogate indexicals), then it is impossible to reconcile Smart's and Grünbaum's views of the logical properties of laws, and an intuitively necessary condition for the invariance of laws is placed at risk. *If* the "universal" scope of genuine laws does not require a strict universal form, then, on our two assumptions (the denial of cognitive transparency and the denial of a graded cognitive privilege favoring either naturalism, phenomenology, or deconstruction), it is difficult (if not impossible) to provide a theoretical basis for Salmon's and Grünbaum's insistence on nomological invariance. *If,* pursuing an additional complication, the invariance of laws is itself a posit or projection, within the historical context of an actual, practicing science, then the difference between the "canonical" view of science (which reduces technology to an application, in some sense, of the independent achievements of science) and a technologized view of science (which construes science as itself a disciplined idealization of human interventions in and within nature) cannot fail to be radically diminished. Finally, *if* that difference is erased, then the physical (or "natural") sciences cannot serve as an independent paradigm for the human (or "cultural") sciences, and their own rigor would be judged to be a function of whatever rigor might rightly be assigned the latter sciences. Differences among the different disciplines would remain, of course, and they might reasonably support the bifurcation of the sciences. But the decisive claim of nomological invariance would clearly have been systematically weakened (or altogether lost). In fact, it would then prove difficult (if not impossible) to deny that the human sciences (perhaps even the natural sciences) were under no *conceptual* obligation to admit that the phenomena they studied fell under invariant laws. They might even consider the option of treating the canonical explanation of such phenomena under invariant laws as entailing the use of a (useful) fiction. Why not?

Grünbaum is admirably explicit in his objections against Habermas and Gadamer. He introduces an example from classical electrodynamics, which yields the finding: "at ANY ONE INSTANT t, the electric and magnetic fields produced throughout infinite space by a charge moving with arbitrary acceleration depend on its own PARTICULAR ENTIRE INFINITE PAST KINEMATIC HISTORY!"[12] Grünbaum draws the general conclusion that, "though the individual histories of each of two or more charged particles can be very different indeed, the electrodynamic laws accommodate these differences while remaining general. The generality derives from the *form* of the lawlike functional dependencies of the electric and magnetic field intensities on the earlier accelerations, velocities, and positions of the field-producing charge. But the latter's individual history consists of the infinite temporal series of the particular values of these kinematic attributes (variables)," then applies it specifically against Habermas and Gadamer: "As against Habermas, I submit [says Grünbaum] that these electrodynamic laws exhibit context-dependence with a vengeance by making the field produced by a charge for any one time dependent on the particular infinite past history of the charge. And to the detriment of Gadamer, these laws are based on replicable experiments but resoundingly belie his thesis that 'no place can be left for the historicality of experience in science.'"[13]

The point of misunderstanding is simplicity itself. Whatever else may be said of their views, Habermas's and Gadamer's notions of "history" and "context-dependence" entail the denial of the kind of invariance strict (physical) laws exhibit (on the canonical view)—*when applied* to the regularities of human history. They do not deny the invariance of physical laws. Grünbaum is quite misleading, therefore, when he insists that, *if* Habermas's argument "were legitimate, it could *likewise* serve to establish the following absurdity: The elementary law of thermal elongation in physics [say, regarding the expansion and contraction of metals under changing temperatures] does not exhibit the nomic invariance of the causality of nature after all."[14] Habermas had intended (indeed, had explicitly stated) that there is a fundamental difference (following Hegel) between the "causality of fate" and "the causality of nature."[15] His argument may or may not work. But it's clear that Habermas intends to bifurcate the notion of causality (a fortiori, the sciences themselves)—dividing causality between the natural and the human sciences. It is a further irony that Grünbaum himself insists on the invariance of the laws of nature, just when he also insists on the historical and context-dependent features of physical phenomena. The fact is that, in Grünbaum's view (which, of course, endorses the unity canon), the historical and context-dependent features in question *instantiate the invariance of physical laws*—which is just the reverse of Habermas's express claim. They must also instantiate, therefore—in his argument regarding the would-be science of psychoanalysis—the *invariance* of any genuine psychoanalytic laws (if there be any). So it is clear that there is a profound misreading of the bifurcationist's thesis (however difficult it may have been to avoid) in Grünbaum's treatment of the temporal ordering of physical events (and the dependence of certain causal effects on such ordering) as conceptually equivalent to the notions of history and context dependence intended by Habermas and Gadamer. To have allowed the difference would have been to acknowledge the irrelevance of any of his analogies between cases in the physical sciences and cases in the human sciences (in particular, cases in Freudian psychoanalysis). So the champions and antagonists of the unity model are not really brought together in Grünbaum's account, though that is the apparent purpose of Grünbaum's extended review of hermeneutic conceptions of the human sciences. Grünbaum and Habermas cannot be sharing the same conception of history.

Now, it must be admitted that, for his part, Habermas bungles the required contrast—inviting the attack he receives—by attempting to distinguish between "invariance of nature" and "invariance of life history." Here is what Habermas says, interpreting Freud's remarks regarding the *causally* pertinent pathology of language and behavior: "Following Hegel we can call this the causality of fate, in contrast to the causality of nature. For the causal connection between the original scene, defense, and symptom is not anchored in the invariance of nature according to natural laws but only in the *spontaneously generated invariance of life history, represented by the repetition compulsion, which can nevertheless be dissolved by the power of reflection.*"[16]

It must be borne in mind that Habermas had remarked, just a moment before, that psychoanalysis "achieves more than a mere treatment of symptoms, because it certainly does grasp causal connections, although not at the level of physical events."[17] And it must be conceded that Grünbaum quite rightly perceives the radical nature of this reading of the methodological import of Freud's work—whether or not it correctly represents Freud (who, after all, subscribed to the main tenets of nineteenth-century positivism),[18] and whether or not the repetition compulsion may rightly be said to function in the manner assigned. Grünbaum offers an instructive (but argumentatively inappropriate) analogy between Habermas's reasoning and a similar form of reasoning that might be applied to the law of thermal elongation; he concludes, "In neither case can there be any question at all of 'dissolving' or 'overcoming' a causal connection between an initial condition I and an effect E on the strength of terminating E by a suitable alteration of

I." His point is that the effect actually instantiates and must instantiate the law in question and does not and cannot "dissolve" it *by* instantiating it.[19]

The "causality of fate," it should be said, is rather a nice notion. What it suggests is that there are contingent, identifiable causal complexes that function in a sufficiently regular way such that we may cast them in a form at least suggestive of genuinely lawlike regularities—so that we come to regard them as analogous in behavior and explanatory power when compared with genuine lawlike regularities. There is no logical or conceptual *need* to regard them as actually nomological; there can't even be a need (pace Habermas) to regard them as invariant. They merely need to be regular, salient, and reasonably congruent with familiar and effective sorts of explanation in the human sciences. "Fate" may be a trifle melodramatic, but we are usually not misled when, say, we speak of one's being "fated" by one's own gullibility—regularly disappointed (in causally relevant ways) by virtue of the trust placed in others. There is also no reason whatever for thinking that one could not dissolve or overcome such a tendency by exercising other pertinent aptitudes. There may be no sense in which thermal elongation exhibits a parallel case, but that is hardly a reason for thinking that a compulsion neurosis may not pertinently resemble gullibility (whatever Freud may have thought). Grünbaum's analogy is hardly Habermas's.

The trouble is that Grünbaum takes proper laws to be *invariant*—very much in the sense in which Salmon speaks of nomological necessity: they signify not merely the human formulation of some presumed regularity in nature but also the fact that there actually are such regularities in nature and that, for *any* domain that presumes to be scientifically accessible (in context: psychoanalysis), invariant laws (nomological necessities) will there obtain. But this is precisely what Habermas denies—and what Grünbaum never actually shows to be true or convincing. Habermas, however, commits the fatal blunder that *he* introduces "invariances of life history" meant to parallel "invariances of nature," so he cannot really dispute Grünbaum's objection. The only way—the only plausible way—to resist Grünbaum's argument is to *deny that causality must be invariant*: to disjoin, conceptually, causality and nomological necessity. Once that is done, then it becomes entirely possible to argue (regardless of whether it is true or not) that "dissolving" that regularity (not a strict invariance) in the life history of a patient—marked, say, as a repetition compulsion—*could* in principle effect a psychoanalytic cure. The compulsion, on that reading, would yield a sense both of the causal syndrome affirmed (separated from the issue of physical invariance) *and* of the replicability of the causal phenomenon adduced (within whatever limits are imposed in the absence of strict invariance).

The remarkable consequence is that there would then be absolutely no principled objection to raise against Habermas's notion that the compulsion neurosis—construed now as a relatively isolable causal syndrome that exhibits a certain sufficient regularity, uniformity, or loose or provisional "invariance" (justifying something like psychoanalytic "laws" or "fateful" regularities)—*could* be dissolved. Of course it could. One has only to think of it as a habit or a character trait or the like that is not unalterable by analogy with what is involved in speaking of social institutions, traditions, practices, styles, and so on. It is not merely that the compulsion neurosis is a causal factor instantiating a lawlike regularity (as Grünbaum not unfairly insists); it is also that it embodies lawlike regularities (if we favor the term) that are not invariant in the canonical sense. The proper quarrel concerns the question of whether there can be causality without nomologicality, or causality without nomological necessity, or causality without strict invariance; or whether such causality may be found in the human sciences independently of whether it also obtains in the physical sciences; or whether the meaning of *causal law* and cognate notions is simply equivocal, as between the natural and the human sciences.[20] Grünbaum does not address the question at all. For our part, particularly given the notorious difficulty of characterizing a genuine law of nature and the associated difficulty of providing a decisive sense in which would-be laws may be said to be confirmed or *pertinently* strengthened on empirical grounds, we may mark the fact that there is no known argument that conclusively demonstrates that it would be contradictory (or even without merit) to affirm causal processes and causal effects while denying strict invariance, nomologicality, or nomological necessity.[21]

There is, therefore, a theoretical option regarding causality and laws that is usually muffled, as already remarked, in the large literature addressed to the nature of science motivated in the spirit of the unity canon. Furthermore, given the suggested convergence between naturalistic, phenomenological, and deconstructive orientations already remarked, it is very reasonable to explore the bifurcation of the sciences—it may even be a logically inescapable finding—if physicalist and similar reductive programs regarding the analysis of the self (or eliminative programs, for that matter) collapse or fail to be suitably vindicated. In a word, it may well be that if one accepts the symbiosis of self and world, under historicized conditions that disallow any and all forms of cognitive privilege, one cannot then avoid admitting, at the very least, that the human sciences cannot be brought to heel in accord with the canonical view. Admitting its constructive effect on the physical sciences, as well, it may be that the canon will prove to be profoundly misguided even with regard to the physical and life sciences.

III

The essential pivot of competing intuitions about causality and laws that are drawn from the canonical picture of science and from reflecting on what may be called the technic (or technological) experience of humankind, the immemorial experience and activity of domesticating natural processes for human purposes—largely tacit, largely spontaneously apt, pretheoretical or only partially "entheorized,"[22] distributively successful—rests squarely with the issue of invariance. The Humean conception of regularity or constant conjunction cannot in principle be assigned any discernible or determinate invariance or necessity, except on the basis of prejudice, habit, nonrational disposition, or the like. Theorists of science, particularly those committed to the canon (since Hume did not assume its need), have tried one way or another to invest the *phenomenological* regularities of the various sciences (lawlike regularities, if you please) with the full import of the *theoretical* (or fundamental or explanatory) laws of those sciences: which is to say, they have tried to invest them with a strict invariance, an invariance applying to all possible instances of the empirically open-ended set of phenomena said to be governed by the laws in question, an invariance that just *is* nomological (or natural) necessity.

The difference between the two kinds of laws cannot be formulated in terms of a perceptual/nonperceptual disjunction or a theoretical/nontheoretical disjunction but depends, rather, on competing norms of methodological rigor and economy regarding what, in the indissoluble mixing of theory and perception *(and* experiment and technological intervention), would or would not justify pronouncements of the theoretically *implicated* strict invariance of given phenomenological regularities drawn from the human sciences. Those favoring phenomenological laws over theoretical laws, at least as far as inductive, experimental, and observational work is concerned, short of canonical explanations (though not necessarily incompatibly with the requirements of theoretical *explanation*), are not in any way logically obliged to treat phenomenological laws as nomologically necessary or strictly invariant—or. failing to meet that constraint, as laws only in a Pickwickian sense.[23]

The more-or-less standard view regarding physical sciences holds (paradoxically) that the very validity of treating phenomenological laws as approximative depends on their (reverse) derivability from fundamental (constructively universalized) laws (projected from them)—which, then, are taken to have a very strong, antecedently assignable realist character.[24] (Very odd.) But it is entirely possible to defend the realism of the "content" of phenomenological laws independently of the presumptive realism of explanatory laws and, therefore, to defend the standing of such laws without a commitment to nomological or natural necessity (the nomological necessity of the fundamental laws). In Nancy Cartwright's view, for instance, "the great explanatory and predictive powers of our theories lie in their fundamental laws. Nevertheless, the *content* of our scientific knowledge is expressed in the phenomenological laws." On the "ultra-realist" view of fundamental laws, the realism of phenomenological laws derives—causally or logically—from the realism of the explanatory laws. This is the usual reason (though it is not logically entailed) why a realism about fundamental laws is often closely linked with a reductionism regarding the world *of* our phenomenological laws (which includes all macroscopic objects, not the least of which are the very scientists who pursue these matters).[25] From the perspective of favoring fundamental laws, in the most generous view, phenomenological laws are said to have realist import because "the fundamental laws say the same things as the phenomenological laws which are explained"—only they say them better, more abstractly and more generally, and they say them in a way that permits the phenomenological laws to serve as "evidence" for the truth and realism of the fundamental ones.[26] (Once again, there is a benign equivocation here on the expression "phenomenological laws.")

If, however, we disengaged the grounds for the realism *and* nomic status of phenomenological laws from the standing of so-called fundamental laws, then (1) we would not need to presuppose that the two sorts of law say "the same things" (make the same affirmations of fact, have the same realist import); (2) we would secure a natural basis for holding that the validity and realist import of would-be fundamental laws depend instead on the prior validity and realist import of phenomenological laws; *and* (3) we would not need to concede that phenomenological laws either are (on inductive or experimental grounds), or need be, or even can be shown to be nomologically necessary.

This would suit the cultural or human sciences very conveniently. Once these themes are in place, it becomes reasonably clear that, because of the very process of inductive, experimental, and technologically inventive procedures for intervening in nature, phenomenological regularities depend essentially on generalizing (via whatever theories we employ) from discrete, individual cases that are observationally anchored and judged to have the realist import they do. It is more than reasonable to suppose that regularities among the candidates for phenomenological laws are confirmable without invoking arguments that justify construing such regularities *as* such laws—which is not to say that they can be confirmed on grounds that are theory neutral or empirical in any sense close to would-be empiricist economies. What the argument shows, then, in a particularly perspicuous way, is (1) that causality and nomologicality are logically and conceptually quite distinct notions, and (2) that their theoretical linkage (or the denial that they are so linked) is an artifact of competing visions of realism, of scientific realism in particular, and of the realist import of theoretical explanation. But to concede these findings is itself hospitable at once to (3) notions of causality *not* restricted to the Humean notion of constant conjunction or to the canonical notion of strict invariance or nomological necessity, and (4) analyses of empirical regularity, underlying any would-be laws, that heavily depend on notions of causality in accord with (1). To focus the argument in a very spare line: only a grasp of the technic, or technological, experience of humankind could possibly supply an alternative account of causality opposed to the Humean and canonical theories.

There is only one promising line of reasoning linking causality in accord with (1), empirical regularities in accord with (2), and a theoretical reliance on humans' technic experience: the exemplars of causality must be or must be drawn from (effective) human agency. Agency may well be attenuated in being extended from human exemplars to animals to inanimate forces, and, in that declension, the theme of agency may become vestigial and may be replaced (as the history of the theory of science confirms) by stronger and stronger notions of either Humean conjunction or nomological necessity.[27] Also, in admitting agency as a paradigm of causality, it is hardly necessary to disallow competing exemplars—that is, either the Humean or the strict invariance (the natural-necessity) view.

The essential point is that there is a natural and entirely viable model of causality that (1) precludes or at least does not require nomological necessity; (2) has strong realist credentials, or has them to the extent that human agents (selves or persons) cannot be ontologically eliminated; and (3) is capable of accommodating, on an adjusted view of the realism of science, whatever viable explanatory practices are assigned science on nonagential readings of causality. So seen, the presumptive *realist* import of experimental intervention and technological invention involving unobservable theoretical entities that are assigned causal efficacy is conceptually dependent on the interpretation of the very meaning of the deliberate and controlled exercise of human agency itself. In this view, it is a straightforward move (in an evidential respect) to assign a causal role to unobserved theoretical entities when, on a theory, a particular deliberate human intervention produces changes in these postulated entities, which thereupon produce observable changes of a technologically significant or successful sort. To produce for the first time a light bulb that actually works, for example, may be reasonably taken to involve the causal "agency" of pertinent theoretical entities operative in, or as a direct result of, the exercise of human agency. To turn on a light bulb in one's home is compellingly causal in nature—*not* because of any assurance that there is a lawlike invariance or nomological necessity covering the phenomenon (though there may be one), but because the very achievement of that technological marvel provides a natural basis for extending our familiar sense of ordinary human agency in routinized particular cases. Agency does not rule out nomologicality, but it does not entail it either. The point is captured in an admirably compelling way in Ian Hacking's formulation:

> The vast majority of experimental physicists are realists about some theoretical entities, namely the ones they use. I claim that they cannot help being so. Experimenters are often realists about the entities that they *investigate,* but they do not have to be so. Millikan probably had few qualms about the reality of electrons when he set out to measure their charge. But he could have been sceptical about what he would find until he found it. He could even have remained sceptical. Perhaps there is a least unit of electric charge, but there is no particle or object with exactly that unit of charge. Experimenting on an entity does not commit you to believing that it exists. Only *manipulating* an entity, in order to experiment on something else, need do that.[28]

In effect, Hacking offers a criterion of "ontic commitment" (rather than of reality *sans phrase*) in precisely the same spirit (though he hardly adheres to the same letter) as Quine famously favored.[29] That criterion (Quine's as well, if the truth be known) pretty well commits us to the reality of human agents (with whatever properties they exhibit—the power of causal agency in particular), even if they cannot be reductively streamlined in accord with the spirit of the unity canon. (Hacking does not explicitly address the question of entailments between causality and nomologicality, but he is distinctly sympathetic to Cartwright's account of intervening explanatory models and even indicates a reason for tolerating inconsistent laws.)[30]

The important point about agency is a dual one: first, persons are persons only in virtue of being effective agents (this is a paradigmatic notion of what it is to be a person—a notion entirely capable, incidentally, of accommodating difficult moral cases that do not happen to bear on our present issue), and apt persons are normally cognizant of being causally effective *as* agents through their deliberate, particular intervention in the world;[31] second, effective agency provides one of the principal grounds, possibly the most important, by which we fix what we take to be salient and real.

This, of course, is just the point of Hacking's insistence on "manipulation"—including the manipulation of unperceived theoretical processes and entities. The upshot is that to endorse the agency conception of causality is inevitably to admit a basis for reasonably detecting causal processes *in particular cases* without having to invoke causal laws at all and without being committed to any entailment between instances of actual causation and their subsumability under laws of any kind—fundamental laws, phenomenological laws because derivable from fundamental laws, or phenomenological laws *tout court*. Donald Davidson, it may be remarked, admits the reasonableness of ascribing causality in individual cases (even when agency, in the human sense, does not obtain, and even when no pertinent would-be covering laws are known to obtain); he nevertheless insists—without supporting arguments—that the concept of causality *is* nomological, is necessarily nomological (which, of course, is not equivalent to insisting that natural laws entail a certain natural necessity).[32]

The point of appealing to the effective intervention of human technology in clarifying the import of causality lies precisely here. For effective human agency or human technology—in whatever reasonable sense we concede a pertinent continuity between the most ancient human technology (largely tacit, hardly recognized, essentially pretheoretical) and the most up-to-date inventions and experiments of science—*proceeds largely by perceived similarities between particular cases or perceived analogies ranging over a small number of cases*. Effective technology and effective agency yield, upon reflection, a remarkably strong sense in which realism, real similarity, and causality are irresistibly linked as provisional saliences without ever presupposing or entailing invariance, universal scope, nomologicality, or nomological necessity.

It is the natural accessibility of this account, its coherence and economy, the unlikelihood of discounting it, and the difficulty of demonstrating that it cannot accommodate the most sophisticated work of the sciences that recommends it. It shows quite clearly that, once we prefer the phenomenological to the explanatory, once we key the phenomenological to an agential conception of casuality, we mark the very notion of uniform, lawlike regularities as a problematic one. We cannot simply convert the informal, analogically stipulated, case-by-case uniformities of technological intervention into nomological (or, more strenuously, naturally necessary nomological) regularities without a further argument. Such an argument may be ready at hand, but it is not logically entailed or presupposed in any way by (affirming) the reality of causally effective human agency *or* of what, in nature, is pertinently implicated in humans' successful technological interventions. There is no clear reason to suppose, *if* the phenomena of human existence cannot be eliminated or reduced to the phenomena of basic physics, that the paradigms of causality suited to the explanatory objectives of a realist physics could, in principle, obviate the agential conception of causality or the logical disconnection between causality and nomologicality. Furthermore, once we see matters this way—first, acknowledging agency as causality, and, second, disconnecting causality and nomologicality—we cannot fail to see that the very legitimacy of the Humean and natural-necessity readings of causal invariance presupposes an operative procedure for actually detailing the *uniform properties* of things that mere informal similarities (moving from case to case) cannot directly vouchsafe. The upshot is that, assuming the reductive programs of all those theorists who would eliminate the "human" or "folk" phenomena from the range of legitimate science (for instance, Sellars or Dennett or Stich or the Churchlands), it begins to *seem* possible to insist on the realism of the invariance reading of causal law. But the admission of the human along with the failure of reductionism (as opposed to eliminationism) places that exclusionary conception of causality and causal law in essential doubt—where it should be anyway. The point of the challenge is not satisfactorily perceived by theorists who regularly appeal to the invariance conception—for instance, Davidson and Grünbaum.

Causality, in the agential sense or in a technological sense bound to the agential (rather than keyed at once to the canonical nomological view),[33] has absolutely no need to insist on the strict detection of formulably uniform properties that strict nomologicality requires. A strong realist reading of natural laws cannot fail to be essentialist, in the sense Karl Popper has forcefully identified (perhaps too passionately in his vendetta against Aristotle):

> By choosing explanations in terms of universal laws of nature, we . . . conceive all individual things, and all singular facts, to be subject to these laws. The laws (which in their turn *are* in need of further explanation) thus explain regularities or similarities of individual things or singular facts or events. And these laws are not inherent in the singular things. (Nor are they Platonic ideas outside the world.) Laws of nature are conceived, rather, as (conjectural) descriptions of the structural properties of nature—of our world itself.[34]

What Popper's argument shows, however, is that a realist reading of laws (but not of causality) cannot be managed nominalistically;[35] that the conceptual linkage between causality and nomologicality (if preserved) need not be construed in realist or essentialist terms; that strict nomologicality cannot be demonstrated on inductivist grounds; and that there need be no conceptual entailment between causality and nomologicality.[36] The very enterprise of science, read in terms of the canonical view of causality—which (1) construes causality in realist terms, (2) construes causality in terms of nomological invariance, and (3) validates assignments of causality in particular cases on the grounds of their subsumption under such regularities—is completely stalemated without an independent provision for confirming the actual, strict uniformities of the properties in question. It is clear, therefore, that the canonical view gains an enormous advantage by stipulating that the uniformities of phenomenological laws, however informal and untidy they may be, can be satisfactorily corrected, regimented, brought into strict accord with the requirements of nomologicality just because the fundamental laws of any domain *fix*—*in theory*—the very uniformities that (would-be) phenomenological laws exhibit (otherwise indiscernibly or untidily). Hence, once the bond between phenomenological laws and fundamental laws is broken (with regard at least to denying the logical priority of the latter), once the bond between causality and nomologicality is broken, we are pretty well forced to retreat (or rather, to turn) to the paradigm of agency, *and*, in doing that, we are relieved at once of all essentialist pretensions regarding causal regularities and the need to defend a realist account of causal counterfactuals on either nomological grounds or essentialist uniformities or both.[37] (There is an instructive analogy, we may remark, between the alleged connection between phenomenological and explanatory laws in science and the connection between the grammatical structure of the uttered fragments of actual speech and the deep structure of the idealized sentences assigned such fragments in Noam Chomsky's theory of language.)[38]

Furthermore, if the canonical linkage between the phenomenological and the theoretical is broken, if the necessary linkage between causality and nomologicality is already broken, if the agential conception of causality is favored, then, if these notions are reconciled with our opening postulates (the rejection of transparency and the rejection of any hierarchized ordering of the privilege of scientific inquiry), it is but a step to concede that a human being's technological intervention extends to their linguistically formulated theories, to the competing conceptual networks they entertain, to their very thinking—to the artifactual structure of the real world they effectively explore, change, and manipulate. In a word, what counts as technology is radically different in the canonical and technologized views of science, and what science can accomplish is seen to diverge as well.

IV

It is important to grasp that in contesting the various loose and strict versions of the unity-of-science account of causality and nomologicality, we are breaching one of the most important *naturalistic* accounts of how a person discerns the properties of the real world. It is noticeably difficult to make the counterargument plausible—frankly, because of the longstanding professional hegemony of the canonical view. But it is very clear, on conceptual grounds, that such a countermove would be a reasonable one, once, as proposed earlier, the usual epistemic privilege of naturalistic science is discounted and naturalism itself is reconciled with moderate forms of phenomenology and deconstruction similarly shorn of their own characteristic presumptions. Such a policy (which would make no sense if realist forms of reducing or eliminating persons, human experience, and agency were actually open to straightforward validation) clearly encourages the view—within the terms of salience but not of privilege—that humans' technic or technological interventions count as the ineluctable channel by which they minimally discern, *distributively*, the real structures of the world. It is the *causal* effectiveness of human agency—of successful invention and intervention affecting the processes of nature, sensed and preserved pretheoretically (as in the manufacture of fire, doubtless) or improvised for reasons inseparable from theorizing about relations between unseen entities and processes and those we do perceive (as in producing the atom bomb)—that yields the most compelling and enduring stratum of what we take to be real. Notoriously, in all of his speculations about testing the sense of reality among alien speakers, Quine never once considers the role of species-wide technic experience in testing the so-called radical indeterminacy of translation.[39] If he had, he would perhaps not have given up ontological relativity, but he could not have secured it in "radical" terms unless (contrary to his own severe extensionalism) he subscribed to a comparably radical form of incommensurabilism.

Once we concede this, however, we grasp also the sense in which a strong disjunction between naturalistic and phenomenological views of reality (or a disjunction between ontic and preontic reflection) is merely contrived and unconvincing. Technology or technic experience (agency, intervention, experiment, invention—even observation, therefore) signifies the intersection of *all* humanly pertinent modes of discerning, contacting, affecting, and being affected by *whatever is real*. The technic, in short, is the principal way in which we move from a merely holistic sense of reality (since, after all, the race survives as a result of being somehow in touch with the effective structures and processes of things) to a distributive sense of such structures. The only warning required is that that transition must be confined to what is salient rather than privileged—hence, subject to phenomenological, critical, deconstructive (and further naturalistic) constraints. But that, precisely, is the essential theme of Heidegger's dualized account of technology, of *Zuhandenheit* and *Vorhandenheit*—which is to say (relative to *Zuhandenheit*, "readiness-to-hand") that the reality of worldly things is already centered in a global and nameless effectiveness of the worldly career of what Heidegger calls *Dasein*, and (relative to *Vorhandenheit*, "presence-at-hand") that the distributed real objects of the world, including explicit tools and more (human beings themselves, for instance), are thus articulated (and rightly thus articulated) within the global effectiveness of the other.[40] *Dasein*, for Heidegger, is never, of course, confined to any worldly articulation of the human, but there may be many ways of expressing the required intersection of the naturalistic and the phenomenological. At any rate, from both naturalistic and phenomenological perspectives, it is reasonable to insist on the peculiarly supple sense in which the technological provides a quite different vision of science—in particular, of causality and laws—from that afforded by the canonical picture. Recall Carnap.

The argument also shows that it is unlikely that this thesis can be given a fair inning without going very far afield of the narrow concerns of analytic conceptions of causality and laws. With an eye to argumentative strategies, the perceived weakness of the canonical picture depends on the difficulty at least of resolving the famous problem of universals.[41] Here, we need take note only of the fact that the importance of the problem of universals in resolving the further problem of natural laws, together with the importance of the agency conception of causality, confirms the profound sense in which the sciences are distinctly *human* undertakings, even when (as in the physical sciences) their domain is defined without reference to the distinctly human. The natural way in which this theme presents itself, consistently with a sanguine respect for the realism of science (in any of a wide variety of views), features—perhaps must feature—the salience of man's technic experience. It is a sense, needless to say, that cannot be easily discounted as merely picturesque or as the vestigial remains of a folk conception that is better exorcised than welcomed.

Perhaps a final word may be said about the problem of universals, not so much with the intention of settling that issue quickly as with the hope of affording a clearer sense of the relevance of technology and related ways of intervening in the world. We may first remind ourselves very briefly of one of Freud's characteristic claims, which Grünbaum (not at all unreasonably) takes Freud to have construed in terms of his own penchant for viewing psychoanalysis as a natural science. Grünbaum himself regards the following as a perfectly eligible scientific thesis the empirical evidence for which (on Grünbaum's account) Freud failed to supply—indeed, Freud apparently never got beyond a *post hoc, ergo propter hoc* argument: the thesis "that all parapraxes whose causes are unknown to the subject are the result of repressions."[42] The point of importance is that the *detection* of a string of instances that could rightly be characterized as parapraxes, in virtue of which a lawlike regularity may be adduced (or a regularity suitably linked to a covering psychoanalytic law, if it cannot be taken to be a law itself), requires an observational procedure by means of which to characterize a given string of instances *as* parapraxes.[43] It is important to notice that the vexed issue of whether psychoanalysis is a natural science (even if it is one without confirmed causal laws) depends on whether the conditions under which such distinctions as parapraxes and repressions are empirically detectable, are suitably congruent with the conditions under which empirically detectable regularities would support a natural science—a natural science addressed to strong invariance or nomological necessity, in the sense already supplied. (Grünbaum does not discuss the matter, which, it may be argued, is one of the decisive sources of contention regarding the disputed status of psychoanalysis.) For our present purpose, it is perhaps enough to indicate that it may be claimed that parapraxes and repressions are essentially intentional (and Intentional) in a way that cannot be straightforwardly matched in the physical sciences and, therefore, do not lend themselves to the enunciation of pertinent uniformities, as the simplest sensory similarities are alleged to do. This is not to deny, of course, that we may rightly speak of psychoanalytic uniformities, or that such uniformities may support the thesis that psychoanalysis is a natural science, or that intentional complications affect the uniformities of sensory perception as well.

The scientific standing of psychoanalysis rests, nevertheless, on being able to show that what is entailed in collecting a set of personal histories and anecdotes as a string of pertinent uniformities could or could not serve, in the psychoanalytic setting, as evidence for a causal law in just the sense in which the cognate connection is taken to obtain in the natural sciences. Furthermore, it is a reasonable conjecture that the intentional (and Intentional) complexities of psychoanalytically relevant attributions are bound to be very closely akin to the intentional complexities of the general agential life of humans. Hence, if the idiom of technological intervention both encourages a picture of science at odds with the canonical account and is essentially of a piece with the intentional idiom of psychoanalysis, Freud's (or Grünbaum's) sanguine views about the natural-science status of the discipline may still be misplaced (the matter need not be decided here), and how this status should be decided is bound to be affected, one way or another, by the methodological implications of first fixing psychoanalytically pertinent uniformities.[44]

Uniformities of sensory discrimination of the most elementary sorts indicate even more compellingly the pertinence of methodological links to agential and technological considerations. This may be shown most suggestively by considering Niko Tinbergen's well-known experiments with stickleback. Tinbergen has shown, of course, that the fighting and courtship behavior of the stickleback is decisively triggered by visual stimuli falling within almost-calibrated limits of variation (what Tinbergen calls the "dependence of innate behavior on sign stimuli")—as of shape, posture, abdominal swelling, proximity, "red belly," and "zigzag dance."[45] First of all, what, *behaviorally*, counts as uniformity with respect to pertinent visual discrimination cannot be decided in terms of uniformities adduced on the basis of purely physical laws (as of light frequencies) but depends instead on an intentional model of stickleback courtship and aggression—even though Tinbergen is expressly opposed to intruding, in a "scientific" study, any reference to "subjective" phenomena in animals and any "phenomena that can be known only by introspection."[46] Therefore, the pertinent sensory uniformities are conceptually dependent on analogies between the agential behavior of stickleback and that of humans.

What is particularly pretty about Tinbergen's work is that it shows us how a science such as ethology can function as a natural science despite such conceptual features and, at the same time, helps us understand why success in at least this range of ethology cannot ensure, in principle, a similar success in psychoanalysis. Furthermore, fixing the intentional behavioral model for stickleback—in particular, with regard to the innate releasing mechanism. Tinbergen has refined as the key to instinctual functioning—depends in a crucial way on the technological manipulation *of* the releasing mechanism (theoretically postulated), by means of experiments keyed to observing the behavior of the fish in the presence of a variety of ingenious dummies Tinbergen has fashioned. Here, we cannot escape the ubiquity of technic experience with respect both to the canonical conception of a natural science and to the possible bifurcation of the sciences.

Finally, it is clear that, according to the theory of the releasing mechanism itself, creatures exhibiting innate responses must be taken to have discriminated a relatively invariant, abstract uniformity, as of shape or color or behavior, ranging over a finite spectrum of graduated changes in particular instances—when, that is, an animal responds uniformly in those particular instances.[47] So the perceptual uniformities pertinent to Tinbergen's ethological studies are complex universals of some sort that *cannot* be specified (not merely not detected) except in a way that conceptually depends on the intervention and technic experience of the human investigator. If this is true in the ethological case, it is bound to be true in the psychoanalytic (a matter Grünbaum never addresses), and there (and elsewhere) it may force us to concede that the relevant universals will not support a unity-of-science model.

In general, one may argue that a conceptual linkage obtains between the methodology of a science and the nature of the properties of the phenomena the domain collects. It is a notorious fact, for instance, that, in strengthening his account of linguistic universals in natural language, Noam Chomsky retreats increasingly from his original close-grained empirical study of actual linguistic *performance* to *postulating* underlying universals of *competence* relatively indifferent to the conditions of contingent behavior. Roughly, this means that Chomsky's account shifts from the description and interpretation of sentences actually produced in the natural contexts of human discourse to the context-free generation of sentences in accord with the underlying theory. Terry Winograd, for instance, has rather tactfully insisted on the point in his own attempt at a computer model of English, observing, "A program for parsing language is as much a 'generative' description of the language as is a set of rules for producing sentences. The meaning of 'generative' in Chomsky's original sense . . . is that the grammar should associate a structural description to each permissible sentence in the language."[48] The upshot is that Chomsky is able to *present* his linguistic theory in a form intended to accord closely with the model of causal laws and causal explanation favored in the canon without really attending in a close way to the surface conditions—the conditions of cognitive pickup—under which *linguistic invariances in the contexts of actual use* are detected and tested. It is one thing, however, to model language in accord with the canon; it is quite another to confirm that natural languages actually exhibit structures—in contexts of use—suited to canonical explanation or to the unity of science.

In general, we may claim that, insofar as the uniformities essential to this or that would-be science critically depend on intentional considerations that *do not yield in a lawlike way* to physical reduction or elimination or even to approximative mapping, the technic experience involved in fixing such uniformities tends to favor a bifurcation of the sciences invoked, more than a unity-of-science reading. The technological straddles both options. But to grasp the fact is to appreciate why it is that the broad similarities of agential intervention, invention, manipulation, experiment, and observation do not automatically support the methodological uniformity of science and why it is that, by exaggerating the privilege of theory and explanatory rigor, one can easily mask—in the direction of favoring the physical sciences (as, in a way, Chomsky's speculations do)—decisive discrepancies among the methods suited to the different sciences themselves. The fact remains that the agency conception of causality provides (in different but compatible ways) for both the bifurcation and the unity thesis, for both the denial and affirmation of a strong connection between causality and nomologicality, and this dualized articulation of agency signifies the very role of technic experience in fixing our sense of what is conjointly real—according to both models applied in the same actual world.

V

One immense, enormously important final topic needs to be broached here, a topic that is quite naturally linked to the agential conception of causality—that is in fact quite naturally linked to what is shared between the agential notion and the notion of universals introduced in discussing Freud and Tinbergen. This is the right place to mention it, but we can do little more than make room for it, without at all supposing we are doing justice to the topic. If we acknowledge the agential model as one of at least two basic models of causality—in particular, the modes separately but compatibly favored in the human and physical sciences—we are bound to apply it in cultural contexts in intensionally encumbered ways. The most unguarded sort of case in which this way of speaking is invoked occurs when we explain what we mean when we say we wanted this or that and, wanting it, we acted to acquire or achieve it. The sense intended concedes that wanting plays a causal role in our acting as we do. This much, at least, accords completely with Donald Davidson's well-known, influential example of alternative descriptions of what is putatively one action:

> I flip the switch, turn on the light, and illuminate the room. Unbeknownst to me I also alert a prowler to the fact that I am home. Here I need not have done four things, but only one, of which four descriptions have been given. I flipped the switch because I wanted to turn on the light and by saying I wanted to turn on the light I explain (give my reason for, rationalize) the flipping. But I do not, by giving this reason, rationalize my alerting of the prowler nor my illuminating of the room.[49]

Davidson characterizes such descriptions within rationalizations as "quasi-intentional" and marks the feature in a formal way thus: "C1. R is a primary reason why an agent performed the action A under the description d only if R consists of a pro attitude of the agent towards actions with a certain property, and a belief of the agent that A, under the description d, has that property."[50] But why, we may ask, is the characterization said to be "quasi-intentional"; why not just intentional? Davidson compounds the mystery by acknowledging "C2. A primary reason for an action is its cause."[51]

In fact, we may reasonably claim that, if I flip the light switch (which, as an action, is identical with, or causally responsible for, illuminating the room), and if the event of the prowler's being alerted is not identical with the action I perform, then my flipping the light switch *causes* the prowler *to be alerted to the fact* that I am home. On any plausible reading, that causal connection would have to be independently specified. Davidson insists, of course, that "my unintentional alerting of the prowler" is not different from my flipping the switch, is not "just its consequence."[52] But he nowhere explains why this is so or why we should take it to be so. Furthermore, it would be very easy to adjust the example to make it out that alerting the prowler to the fact in question *was* a consequence of what I did: for instance, my flipping the switch (and illuminating the room) might well have caused the prowler (under various scenarios) to infer that I was home. The intensional feature of the causal sequence would not then be so easily tamed. But in any case, on the face of it, if my primary reason for flipping the switch was to turn on the light, then my *reason* (the reason I had) for acting as I did was the *cause* of what I did, whether described as turning on the light or as alerting the prowler—even though the latter could not rightly be specified as the reason I had, *within* my rationalization.

What is important to appreciate here are the alternative strategies that recommend themselves, not the final solution of the puzzle. Davidson makes one much-debated suggestion (which he calls "anomalous monism") regarding these cases: he insists, as already noted, that causal sequences fall under covering laws even if those laws are unknown; now he adds, "The laws whose existence is required if reasons are causes of actions do not, we may be sure, deal in the concepts in which rationalizations must deal. If the causes of a class of events (actions) fall in a certain class (reasons) and there is a law to back each singular causal statement, it does not follow that there is any law connecting events classified as reasons with events classified as actions—the classifications may even be neurological, chemical, or physical."[53] Davidson's solution clearly depends on his independent advocacy of a form of token identity (or, by analogy with provisional functionalist strategies) on narrow-gauge type identities facilitated by distributed token identities.[54] We need to take notice here only of the fact that, if type and token identities fail (if, in particular, Davidson's "anomalous monism" tends to form "inconsistent triads")[55] and if construing actions as no more than "primitive actions" token identical with simple "bodily movements" (such as moving one's finger)[56] falls with the general failure of token identity to escape such triads, then we should have to admit that there is no effective way of barring intensionally complex causes from obtaining within the space of the human sciences. But the protases mentioned are more than plausible.

The agential model of causality confirms the reasonableness of admitting that "we are usually far more certain of a singular causal connection than we are of any causal law governing the case."[57] This is Davidson's own wording—against a possible reading of Hume's view. But Davidson comes to Hume's rescue in maintaining that, even if it is wrong to hold that "'*A* caused *B*' entails some particular law involving the predicates used in the descriptions '*A*' and '*B*,'" it is nevertheless right to hold (and that alone would vindicate Hume) *that* "'*A* caused *B*' entails that there exists a causal law instantiated by some true descriptions of *A* and *B*."[58] But the agential model also confirms the reasonableness of holding that, in some contexts, causality does not entail nomologicality at all; at any rate, there is no conceptual incoherence in so affirming. Furthermore, the option might be strengthened if causes in agential contexts were prominently or characteristically intensionally complex. So the viability of Davidson's claim (clearly, the canonical and conventional wisdom) that causality entails nomologicality depends on independent evidence that intensionally specified causes—notably, reasons "had" or "primary reasons"—*can* be reduced token-wise in physical terms, so that "true descriptions of some relevant *A* and *B*" can replace the unwelcome descriptions of the *admitted* causes mentioned in our rationalizations. But, as we have already argued, there is no satisfactory demonstration that token identity obtains (let alone type identity): on the thesis that causality is (ultimately) invariably extensional, identifying reasons as singular causes is identifying what, qua reasons, can be specified extensionally—which is incompatible with Davidson's view of the holism of the mental; and, on the thesis that causality entails nomologicality, what are identified as singular causes can, as such, enter (type-wise) into lawlike generalizations—which is incompatible with Davidson's anomalous monism.[59] If intensionally complex causes prove irreducible, then it is a foregone conclusion that causality cannot assuredly entail nomologicality. So, at the very least, Davidson has steadfastly turned his back on a clear (if unpleasant) option that his own cases force us to consider.

In fact, Elizabeth Anscombe was very frank to admit, reviewing Davidson's paper "Causal Relations" shortly after its original appearance, "I have no sure insight into the sources of the conviction that causal statements are extensional."[60] She offered an interesting and helpful example of causality of the agential sort—although, quite instructively, she herself pursued the extensional question only in terms of causal contexts. *If* it were the case that contexts of causality and contexts of causal explanation could not be segregated, then of course (as Davidson himself implicitly acknowledges), since explanatory contexts are nonextensional, causal contexts could not but be intensional as well. But there seems to be no reason to deny that causal contexts are separable from explanatory contexts—particularly if we may know that "*A* caused *B*" without the least inkling of its would-be covering law.

Anscombe's example involves three causal statements differing only in the substitution of codesignative expressions identifying the putative causal agent:

> There is an international crisis because "moi, de Gaulle" made a speech.

> There is an international crisis because the President of the French Republic made a speech.

> There is an international crisis because the man with the biggest nose in France made a speech.[61]

Her reasonable point is that the explanatory use of "because" is affected by the intensional differences among the descriptions (including the epithet) offered. True enough. But what Anscombe fails to mention is that the referential use of the expressions in question does not clarify and does not transparently address the nature of the causes in question (no such uses ever would) and, hence, that the solution of the extensional puzzle of fixing causes within explanatory contexts does not directly bear on the solution of the extensional puzzle regarding the individuation of particular causes. It is notably difficult—in fact, it seems impossible—to bring Anscombe's example into line with Davidson's view that causality entails nomologicality *and* with Davidson's further view that, in accord at least with the strictures of token identity (and of the narrow-gauge type identities that might be discovered thereupon), the relevant covering laws "may even be neurological, chemical, or physical."[62]

This is simply to say that Davidson is here adhering (in however ingenious a way) to Hempel's conception of covering laws.[63] To see this is to see as well how the admission of the agential model of causality threatens the unity conception of science. To admit that singular causes can be discerned without reference to covering laws favors the agential model. To admit that "primary reasons" are actual causes risks the irreducibility of intensionally complex causes. To confirm the irreducibility of primary reasons taken token-wise is to subvert the claim that causality entails nomologicality. Furthermore, to reject the entailment and affirm the irreducibility in question is to concede the bifurcation of the sciences.

It may be difficult to appreciate the enormous power of this conclusion. But perhaps one way of focusing its force is to remind ourselves of the misunderstanding of the puzzle of intensionality encouraged by Daniel Dennett's much-repeated question, "What sort of thing is a different thing under different descriptions? . . . Intentional sentences are *intensional* (non-extensional) sentences."[64] The point is that causes are not "different" under different descriptions. It's only that intensionally complex causes cannot be reliably reidentified extensionally under different descriptions. It is for that reason that they cannot be collected under covering laws. But, of course (since the matter must be put vacuously), a cause remains self-identical under whatever descriptions single it out—or, what serves as a cause in a causal or explanatory context remains self-identical under whatever descriptions single it out (whether as a cause or not). To know that "every thing is self-identical" is to know nothing, as yet, about how to reidentify "any thing." So, the admission of intensionally complex causes does not lead us to support the absurd thesis Dennett rightly rejects; it also makes one wonder why Dennett offers it as a likely interpretation of the intensionality thesis. In any case, the admission of intensionally complex causes need not be taken to preclude causal explanations in the human sciences, or the scientific standing of particular human studies, or a plausible sense of objectivity for those same disciplines. It does mean, however, that, whatever we make out to be the objectivity of causal accounts in the human sciences, such objectivity will have to be construed in terms of consensually developed interpretations. This surely is the minimal consequence of admitting intensionally qualified causes within a space of inquiry in which the subjects observed and those who observe them are one and the same—that is, members of one and the same society (by way of bilingualism and biculturalism) of an extended and enlarged society that could acknowledge diverging, even alien, forms of life within its compass.[65] The objectivity of the human and social sciences presupposes a sufficient range of such common practices: a Quinean field linguist, for example, *simply has no basis at all* for claiming a pertinent or basic form of objectivity.[66] The issue also bears in a decisive way on the pretended ease with which culturally pertinent universals can be regularized for the purposes of inductions within the human sciences—for instance, as in Grünbaum's assessment of the validity *and* testability of Freud's hypotheses. In any case, it makes more sense to adjust our theory of causality to what appear to be the saliencies of the human sciences than to tailor our theory to antecedent prejudices drawn from entirely different sources (the physical sciences) that have not yet vindicated (and appear unable to vindicate) their exclusive rights to the field at stake.

Finally and very briefly, if phenomenological laws or lawlike regularities are disjoined from and take precedence over explanatory laws, if an agential conception of causality is disjoined from an invariance conception and given empirical primacy over the other with respect to both the physical and human sciences, if the agential conception with respect to both the physical and human sciences cannot be freed of intentional and intensional complications affecting the very formulation of similarities, regularities, uniformities, invariances, universals, then we *have* all but installed the general thesis of the praxical reading of science itself.

By the *praxical*, I mean here, at least minimally, the insistence (1) that a person's cognitive aptitudes and achievements are continuous with and incarnate in their technic or technological interaction with the environing world; (2) that a person's interventions in this regard incorporate to a significant extent activity that is tacit, pretheoretic, keyed to quotidian survival;[67] (3) that conceptualizing the regular features of the world is an artifact of a person's technic experience; (4) that such conceptualizing is itself tacitly preformed in a way that cannot be entirely or undistortedly exposed by any critical reflection via the praxically grounded beliefs and formative structures of the environing culture in which, in a historically contingent way, each generation masters the language and societal practices of preceding generations; (5) that the abstractions and generalizations of any viable science or rational inquiry or explanatory theory or descriptive classification are projections incorporating (always tacitly) dispositions of the species (and, within the species, particular, divergent, subspecies-wide cultures) to detect similarities, uniformities, causal mechanisms, and the like; (6) that, therefore, the effectiveness of social (possibly but not necessarily revolutionary) action depends on the extent to which idealized, ideologized, programmatic undertakings are actually in touch in a causally effective way with the effective technic forces that produce and sustain the (perceived) social structures viewed as needing to be altered; and (7) that the very condition of human existence commits one to an active, practical, interventionist orientation with respect to favorably altering or sustaining the conditions of social life, regardless of how such activity is reflexively or ideologically represented.

It is very much in this spirit—in an explicitly Marxist idiom—that Roy Bhaskar rather prettily remarks that "philosophy [and of course if philosophy, then science as well] is . . . soiled in life."[68] In fact, it may fairly be claimed that (1)–(7) afford an orderly articulation of Marx's *Theses on Feuerbach* shorn of any doctrinal privilege dividing "substratum" from "superstructure" or favoring the revolutionary role of the proletariat or anything of the sort (also, of course, not skewed in such a way as to preclude the defense of any such thesis). Marx is sufficiently Hegelian to oppose the eighteenth-century—particularly the Enlightenment—conception of the faculty of reason. He is sufficiently anti-Hegelian to oppose (the abstractionism of) Hegel's locating the effectiveness of rational analysis and rational action in the idealized *Geist* of an age. In the first regard, he treats reason and its conceptual proclivities as an historical formation; in the second regard, he treats a historicized reason as capable of much more (both in analysis and action) than an abstract or utopian exercise. He opposes, for instance, whatever may reasonably be collected in Edward Gans's Hegelian pronouncement: "Whatever is produced by a people at a determinate epoch is produced by its force *and by its reason*."[69] But in opposing (this version of) the Hegelian formula, Marx means to preserve the sense in which thinking is fundamentally practical—that is, directed to fulfilling projects, to altering one's life and the conditions of one's life, to being or becoming what one is or becomes through practical activity, and to being committed to and formed for such activity as the "essential" but structurally or historically entailed purposiveness of human existence itself.[70]

Nevertheless, although there can be no doubt that the modern conception of *praxis* has been most sustainedly explored in the Marxist tradition, the key notion itself is by no means absent in various partial forms from antiquity to Hegel. In our own time, it may fairly be ascribed, without prejudice, to such widely different thinkers as Dewey, Heidegger, and Foucault—which is to say, to the historicized currents of naturalism, phenomenology, and (Nietzscheanized) poststructuralism. (The radical difference between Foucault and Derrida must not be ignored, of course, but one can make out a reasonable case that something like a praxical orientation—admittedly a thin one—can be found in Derrida, despite or perhaps because of his disagreement with the French Marxists.)[71] In any case, the point of pressing the praxical in the present context is primarily to afford a sense of just how radical is the growing repudiation of the unity-of-science model and its characteristic abstractionism (notably regarding the supposed invariances or nomological necessity of causal processes). It affords, therefore, a sense of the profound import of insisting that the sciences are human undertakings and that the physical sciences themselves depend in an ineluctable way *on* the discipline of the human sciences.

Four

Reclaiming Naturalism

I

All the threads of contemporary Eurocentric philosophy come together in a fractious way to define the meaning of *naturalism* for our time. Definition, however, cannot now be read as a search for incontestable essences: too much depends on meeting the running puzzles of our inquiries while fending off rival challenges doing much the same—all with an eye to possible defeats and reconciliations on the way to the scattered unity of a shared world. The process cannot be easily completed or made to serve a single purpose. We are not likely to find our own intuitions adequately represented in the options the ancient and early modern accounts collect—for example, in matching the rationality of the human mind with the intelligible order of nature in the large. The ancient inclusions are only partly congruent with present philosophical purposes and convictions. There's no question the phrase "the natural world" is decidedly privileged in much of twentieth-century analytic philosophy, partly at least as a result of an enormous swell of confidence in mathematical or rationalist models of objective discourse applied to physics and the seeming sufficiency of extensionalist descriptions of the physical and biochemical world (still inadequately secured).[1] I say straight out, however, that the history of philosophy pretty well confirms that the answer to the question "What is the nature of *nature*?" was never a matter of factual discovery but of competing conceptual posits intended to capture (fairly enough) the high ground among competing philosophical systems vying for descriptive and explanatory hegemony, inclusive coherence, and more than plausibility in addressing the most disputed questions of our own or any age. In that sense, *naturalism*—the would-be analysis of nature, the "natural world"—is not a well-formed, settled, freestanding, autonomous, uncontroversial "first" question: it is instead a dependent, strategically defined proposal meant to identify the key to conceptual convictions chiefly about what is thought to be actual or real and, thus construed, advanced as a reasonably valid picture of "all there is." The question need never be finally answered: we treat the matter dialectically, diversely, open-endedly within our effectively endless inquiry. The uncompromising extensionalism of the logical positivists, for instance, has clearly and decisively receded.

Aristotle's match between the powers of nous and the intelligible structure of the physical, biological, and astronomical worlds once counted as a model of the naturalistic kind, but it can no longer do so. The aporiae of first causes, the presumption of one or another essential telos in all that belongs to nature, the very necessity of a changeless order embedded in or embedding a changing order of reality, the facultative competence of our cognitive powers assuredly fitted to grasping the inherent structure of the world, the primacy of a teleologized biologism are altogether too problematic and divisive for what we would now allow to fall within an acceptable naturalism, although to resist on all these fronts at once may entangle our best efforts to resolve other difficulties that now seem more important. Frankly, we are prepared to tolerate certain stubborn antinomies that threaten all otherwise-promising versions of naturalism alike, provided that what we now view as our most pressing puzzles can be satisfactorily met for the time being. Unresolved antinomy, for example, may be preferable to confidently accounting for the big bang ex nihilo or to conceding an infinite causal regress—whether according to Stephen Hawking or Thomas Aquinas.

The least distorting and most adequate pronouncements on naturalism in our time must rely, I would say, on a distinction the ancients never directly considered—possibly one of the few modern contributions of its scope to the ancient philosophical questions of the West—a metaphysical distinction, but hardly a disjunction, within nature itself, between physical nature and human culture and what that may entail. That essential difference was never explicitly formulated before the latter half of the eighteenth century, not before the time of Kant's, Herder's, Humboldt's, Goethe's, and Hegel's inquiries, and, truth to tell, it has not yet been made sufficiently clear. Nevertheless, Kant and the other figures mentioned are among the very first to begin to define the truly modern preoccupation with the issue, though Kant himself never succeeds, in the *Critique of Judgment*, in formulating more than the barest counterpart of Aristotle's account of rational freedom—in which the modern distinction of the cultural pointedly fails to appear:

> Among all [man's] ends in nature there remains [Kant says] only the formal, subjective condition, namely the aptitude for [one's] setting himself ends at all and (independent from nature in his determination of ends) using nature as a means appropriate to the maxims of his free ends in general, as that which nature can accomplish with a view to the final end that lies outside of it and which can therefore be regarded as an ultimate end. The production of the aptitude of a rational being for any ends in general (thus those of his freedom) is *culture*.[2]

Imagine being thus constrained only a short time before the appearance of Hegel's *Phenomenology*!

To understand Kant's limitation, you must consider what could possibly be meant by his construing human freedom as the pursuit of an end "that lies outside of [nature]." Kant signals a difficulty in his own doctrine that the post-Kantian idealists (including Hegel) never managed to resolve perspicuously, though they had a far better grip on the problem than Kant did. In the *Critiques*, Kant is all but incapable of formulating a coherent picture of the specifically *human* subject or self—a fortiori, he fails to define the cultural world as well. His transcendentalism collects what "lies outside of [nature]." (This will seem heresy to many.)

Naturalism at its most farsighted sets itself the problem of accounting for the human being entirely in terms of the natural world, though in a way that still collects the subsidiary distinction between the natural and the cultural. But "the natural world" means very different things to different theorists. Problematically, for Heidegger, for instance, no merely naturalistic treatment of *Dasein*, which humans in some sense incarnate, could possibly suffice, since what exists or is beyond nature is precisely whatever captures the uniqueness of the existentialia of *Dasein*—which apply to nothing else; for Kant, the powers of *Vernunft* define certain subjective conditions of empirical cognition but cannot themselves be captured by the empirical or natural world we thereby come to know; and, against Kant, Hegel assigns *Vernunft* to actual human beings, but then it appears that the inherent power of philosophical Reason—according to which "the truth of Reason is but one" ("absolute knowing")—cannot be captured by any familiar conception of finite nature. In particular, if "being," the theme with which

Hegel begins his *Science of Logic* (*Wissenschaft der Logik*), is in its "simple immediacy" "unanalyzable" qua "simple," then it seems clear that its being simple (also, what Hegel makes of that) is itself a constructive posit that depends on passingly persuasive arguments within the then-current fashions of philosophical thought and, thus, becomes an artifactual simple within the complexities of thought.[3] All three accounts are remarkably tenuous.

Hegel's *Geist* is a blunderbuss that hides even more than it explains, though we must admit (in hindsight) that it collects in the most compelling way available to its own age the conceptual threads of any viable resolution of our question. My own suggestion is that we must begin with Hegel but cannot round out an adequate analysis of the cultural world without conjoining Hegel's immense innovation with the new conceptual possibilities made manageable by Darwin's discoveries. That is in fact the relatively inchoate, thoroughly naturalistic intuition of the classic pragmatists. It's also the point of acknowledging that there is indeed a confirmable evolutionary continuum that joins the prehuman primates, the extinct hominids, and the sole surviving species of the genus *Homo* (*Homo sapiens*) to which we belong, within which biological evolution makes possible for the first time a convincing account of the difference between physical nature and human culture (within nature itself).

My sense is that the human version of the *cultural* (in all its manifestations) presupposes and depends on certain late biological developments but cannot be analyzed perspicuously in biological terms alone. Hegel grasped that much (in his accounts of *Geist* and *Vernunft*); he lacked a crisp distinction between biological and cultural evolution, though he obviously viewed beauty in the fine arts ("born of *Geist*")—a fortiori, the world of human culture—as, ontologically, "higher than nature." In fact, his own philosophical impulses were, I should say, distinctly naturalistic, though we cannot rest with his extravagant account of *Geist*, which is as much a mythic placeholder for a theory as an incipient guess at an adequate theory itself. There's the promise of the most fruitful post-Hegelian undertakings: notably, though still only incipiently, the promise (according to my own persuasion) of the classic pragmatists.

My own solution is that, now, the most convincing view of naturalism, addressed to the analysis of the human world, construes the human self as a "natural artifact,"[4] an evolutionarily new form of being that depends on the sui generis emergence of true language and the capacity to use language (and the cognate resources it makes possible) along lines that can no longer be explained in terms confined to strictly physical and biological processes—

in accord with which, in truth, *we* actually constitute ourselves (developmentally), both individually and species-wide, as selves. In this sense, the recovery of naturalism cannot fail to be essential to the kind of rapprochement within the Eurocentric world that I've been hinting at. The principal evidence in its favor is the sheer impossibility of fashioning an exclusively biological analysis of language, speech, and enlanguaged thought—a fortiori, the deep novelty of defining the human "self" itself. Slim though they are, such discoveries mark a mode of argument that cannot have appeared earlier than the middle of the nineteenth century.

By Darwin's time, an evolving naturalism had in effect discerned that the world of human culture can no longer be identified with physical or biological nature alone; the self's mode of being and activity calls into play descriptive and explanatory categories that cannot be explicated in physicalist terms alone; and, nevertheless, the cultural world evolved completely within an encompassing larger space of physical nature and was in fact indissolubly incarnated in physical and biological processes. You see the endless innocence of our opening question.

Yet even this much regarding the sui generis attributes of specifically human culture has often been conceded only weakly and grudgingly in our time. Francisco Ayala, for example, a well-known biologist who admits the requisite difference freely enough and who effectively acknowledges much the same argument that Richard Dawkins favors—that is, that "human beings are not gene machines" (here, Dawkins introduces the "cultural meme")—nevertheless can go no further than to say that "a distinctive characteristic of human evolution is adaptation by means of 'culture,' which may be understood as the set of non–strictly biological human activities and creations."[5] But that effectively papers over all of the important conceptual issues or falls back to unacceptable equivocation: what exactly are these "non–strictly biological human activities and creations"? They undoubtedly feature adaptation by one or another form of social learning, but that alone is not enough to distinguish between primate learning and the unique form of learning and creation (assigned to selves) that is penetrated by language and the cultural resources the mastery of language makes possible. To my way of thinking, the upshot is plain enough: proceeding thus, we cannot yet overtake the "continental" challenge of theorists like Husserl and Heidegger or confront the reductionisms of "analysts" like Sellars and Jaegwon Kim—or, for that matter, Carnap's *Logical Syntax of Language*.

Aristotle's naturalism is incapable of providing conceptual resources apt for resolving disputes of our contemporary kind between naturalists and antinaturalists or between different kinds of naturalists: say, between Rudolf Carnap and Martin Heidegger, or between W. V. Quine and Jaegwon Kim, or between Wilfrid Sellars and Edmund Husserl. The fact is, Aristotle's faculty of reason, nous, has no biological roots of its own. But the essential distinction between the natural and the historical or cultural may be said to have been already implicit in the Greek world, as Aeschylus's *Oresteia* and Sophocles' *Antigone* confirm. The Greeks might indeed have anticipated what must be the most distinctive philosophical contribution of the modern world. You may glimpse the reasonableness of such a claim by reflecting on the poverty of Aristotle's formulation, in the *Physics*, of the meaning of *nature* developed along the following lines, which are obviously of the wrong gauge for what our contemporaries would make of *Antigone*, supplemented now by what may be developed from their own larger cultural resources: "[Nature] is the primary underlying matter of things which have in themselves a principle of motion or change, . . . [or] nature is the shape or form which is specified in the definition of the thing. For the word 'nature' is applied to what is according to nature and the natural in the same way as 'art' is applied to what is artistic or a work of art."[6] Plainly, Aristotle anticipates no difficulty in the analysis of what it is to be human, or of the contrast between the physical and the cultural, or between the objective and the subjective; although, of course, the *Physics* leads ineluctably to its own problematic reflections, like that (in book 7) of resolving the paradox of the continuum of motion and causes. In fact, Aristotle's own naturalism leads inexorably to a kind of super- (or extra-) naturalism that became the rule for much of the medieval world.

According to a well-known argument, nature must have had (in the medieval sense) a beginning. Since the power that originally created nature must have been beyond nature, medieval "naturalism" (if I may call it that) was already dependent on supernatural sources. Our contemporary forms of naturalism would refuse such an extension—would need to reinterpret in a drastic way the usual causal questions posed by the whole of physical nature. Here, the meaning of *nature* obviously changes—avoids the supernatural and what, in cognitive terms, I am calling extranaturalism—namely, what implicates certain privileged but completely derivative human competences capable of discerning something of the changeless verities (of nature) by way of participating in the divine order itself.

In any event, the most up-to-date naturalisms now begin with the rejection of all such extravagances. The required adjustment is remarkably simple: admit the unresolved antinomies and move on! As far as naturalism is concerned, stalemate about the first cause, for instance, is *not* an endorsement of the necessary existence of any originative power either in or beyond nature.

The associated lesson regarding the distinction between physical nature and human culture—the threat of conceptual insufficiency more than of metaphysical extravagance—is largely unmarked even in contemporary debates. You will find the threat revived, for instance, in the difference between Alvin Plantinga's regressive return to the supernatural grounding of the natural and Heidegger's sense of the impoverishment of any merely naturalistic account of *Dasein*. Recent pragmatists have emphasized, in more modest ways, the promising convergence between, for example, George Herbert Mead and Maurice Merleau-Ponty (between pragmatism and phenomenology) and between Karl-Otto Apel, Jürgen Habermas, Charles Peirce, and John Dewey (between pragmatism and Kantian transcendentalism), but they tend to ignore the question of naturalism's conceptual adequacy.[7] There's the issue before us now.

What I have in mind is the prospect of demonstrating that currently central disputes about the boundaries of naturalism, whether defended or attacked, tend to dissolve in a surprisingly congenial way (not entirely without repercussions, however) when reconfigured in terms of the biological/cultural divide made possible by, but hardly derived from, Darwin's account of evolution. For instance, privileged cognitive faculties (as in Descartes's rationalism) might count as naturalistic within the terms of seventeenth-century philosophy, but they could never be more than insurmountably problematic (affecting, say, the standing of Husserl's faculty of pure phenomenological inquiry) within twentieth-century discussions. Husserl treats pure transcendental phenomenology as exceeding the competence of any merely natural or naturalistic form of understanding, but he means, in part at least, to dramatize the contrast between the supposed scope of empiricist or psychologistic accounts of experience and what he defines as altogether different, functionally, even if not actually separable from the psychological powers of the mind (as in reflecting on the muddled intuitions of the mental advanced by Descartes and Kant, whom he seeks to salvage or supersede). I shall return to Husserl's phenomenological claims later in this chapter.

Darwin's longitudinal picture of the emergence of a gifted species (*Homo sapiens sapiens*) provides the essential ground for a deeper conceptual innovation that has still to be fully grasped: the idea of a creature that is "naturally artifactual,"[8] a hybrid of biological and cultural development whose "second-natured" competences evolve in tandem with biological maturation but cannot be explained in biological terms alone or primarily; in short, the constitution of an artifactual self biochemically sustained but capable of functioning in linguistic, lingual, semiotic, and related ways that appear to be largely irreducible biochemically and are even incommensurable (though not incompatible) with the descriptive and explanatory treatment of the latter. If you permit the idea to count as the proper focus of an adequate naturalism in our time, then the most daring claims of Aristotle, Kant, Husserl, Heidegger, and others about exceeding the bounds of nature, about gaining necessary synthetic truths regarding cognitive privilege and apodicticity and the like, suddenly begin to appear extravagant, entirely arbitrary, impossible to validate, no longer relevant or plausible or legible in terms of the self's artifactual origins.

Darwin brings into play for the first time the robust possibility that the members of *Homo sapiens* might be evolvingly transformed over short periods of time in ways impossible to explain or foresee in terms of the extremely slow processes of biological evolution, manifested in socially stable transmitted practices—all the while remaining open to further, endlessly novel such changes. The entire process is completely sui generis, unmatched anywhere in the animal world: the achievement of a creature whose hybrid nature is its own history, causally efficacious in immeasurably powerful and unpredictable ways, unlikely to be regularized under causal laws capable of achieving a measure of closure at an enlanguaged level.

It's obvious that the apodictic pretensions of Husserl's phenomenological *epoché* are likely to be defeated as easily as Descartes's insistence on rational indubitability, in virtue merely of being relocated within the terms of external *Bildung* (the upshot of the invention and mastery of language). The philosophical advantage of admitting the full import of the Darwinian achievement is nothing short of breathtaking: it sweeps out Aristotelian essentialism and teleologism and Kantian transcendentalism at a stroke! I am, I concede, constructing before your eyes a Darwinized reading of Hegel's extravagant innovations trimmed down as far as possible to capture the incompletely explicit nerve of classical pragmatism's naturalistic vision. That is indeed the very engine of Dewey's (and Peirce's) best efforts.

All too plainly, this now exposes the inherent limitation of John McDowell's small but adventurous first step (in *Mind and World*) in the direction of reconciling Hegel and analytic philosophy (by way of Kant and Aristotle, if you can imagine that).[9] Even so, McDowell appears as the exceptional voice of a potential vanguard. The pivot of the needed innovation, however, was, for different reasons, never perceived (or if perceived, never adequately perceived) by figures as grand as Aristotle, St. Thomas, Descartes, Hume, Kant, and the analytic reductionists of the twentieth century (certain leading members of the Vienna Circle, for instance). In fact, it was scanted even among those post-Kantian philosophers who caught the deeper innovation of Hegel's critique of Kant's innovation: Hegel himself falls short in some measure, as do Marx, Dilthey, the classic pragmatists, the Husserlian phenomenologists, the Romantic and Heideggerian hermeneuts, the Frankfurt School, and even such splendid but self-isolating figures as Kuhn, Wittgenstein, and Foucault.

The boldest conjecture here relies on the coherence and viability of the stunning idea that the cultural world of humans is a sui generis, irreducible, emergent, biologically dependent, artifactually self-constructed, endlessly evolving world set in motion by the fateful evolution of *Homo sapiens* and the incipience of true linguistic communication, the primate mastery of which entails the full development of the powers of what we now call persons or selves. It is indeed the discovery of the hybrid, artifactual existence of the self that, in my opinion, is the ultimate and decisive innovation that the nineteenth century made accessible just prior to the advent of American pragmatism, which flourished at just the right time to seize the idea's advantage. But the pragmatists slighted both their Hegelian and Darwinian sources even as they joined them productively in their new undertaking.

All this constitutes an utterly new chapter within the bounds of what appears to be the endlessly alterable run of nature—sparked by "plain facts" rather than philosophical ideologies. Aristotle's biologism, Kant's transcendentalism, analytic philosophy's scientisms are dismantled at a stroke by the unique, emergent, immensely effective presence of language, culture, history, and an artifactually autonomous mind or agency formed by evolution and continually transformed by the reflexive processes of cultural history. For nothing is more completely confined to the natural world than the artifactual, and, there, nothing is more spectacular, conceptually, than the constantly confirmed truth that the artifactual maturation of the self outruns at an accelerating pace the conventional span of the biological maturation of the human creature itself. We have become the continual re-creation of our own technologies. I must add, therefore, that Darwin himself appears not to have fathomed the deepest innovation of his own theory of evolution, involving the transformation we call the self.

The naturalist's reply to Husserl insists that the empirical (or empiricist or phenomenal) and the phenomenological (including whatever Husserl might suppose comprises "pure transcendental phenomenology") are not only continuous at their source (that is, located in nature in some generous sense that spans the physical and the cultural) but inseparable in function as well (and, as a consequence, impossible to treat as incorporating any specifically privileged powers, whether read conjointly or separately). Husserl, it needs to be said, is never more than arbitrary (and inexplicit) in providing a suitable rationale wherever he claims to identify the would-be powers of transcendental reason. Furthermore, no up-to-date reading of Husserl has (as far as I know) found any textual basis for supposing that he ever abandoned his apodictic claims, which the admission of the artifactual self would have contested in the deepest way. Bear in mind that the emergence of the mundane human self of post-Darwinian evolution can now be approximately dated, on factual grounds (available to human selves themselves). I think that means, effectively, that the operative powers of Husserl's transcendental "I" must make sense in terms of the enabling and sustaining powers of what we now regard as the natural artifact we name *self* or *person*. We cannot meaningfully dismiss the existential powers of the mundane self vis-à-vis the ideal reality of the apodictic "I" that Husserl requires, *if* the mundane self is (rightly said to be) no more than a fiction or heuristic posit *of the other*. No doubt, it's a clever trick on Husserl's part, but Husserl fails to guide himself by anything akin to Kant's more sanguine scruple (regardless of the ultimate fate of the claims Kant makes in his Critiques). The argument requires a robust and unbreakable bond between the natural world and pure phenomenology. Otherwise, Husserl's posit cannot but be a self-serving solipsistic fantasy. No responsible naturalism could fail to disallow Husserl's ultimate proposal. There is at least that much rigor in the current debate.[10] The mundane and transcendental "I" must share a "common" or "overlapping" world.

My sense is that claims of cognitive privilege are now routinely dismissed, though they may still count in some notional way as natural or naturalistic. They cannot possibly be recovered, however, given Kant's own argument against the seventeenth-century rationalists and dogmatists and the outcome of post-Kantian objections to Kant's own transcendentalism turned finally against the idealists as well. Indeed, whatever Hegel's grandiose temptations may have been, his having historicized inquiry and cognition (against Kant) and his having removed all presumptions of privileged competence from his account of what is "given" (in *Phenomenology*) surely apply to speculative *Vernunft* as readily as to what, in the 1931 preface to the English edition of his *Ideas* (1913), Husserl defines as pure phenomenology.¹¹ The key to Hegel's revolution rests with the fact that *Vernunft* is not a *faculty* of cognition at all but an autonomous, culturally informed interpretive and appreciative aptitude (or functionality), which presumptive knowledge cannot do without.

Husserl hardly provides a convincing argument for recovering transcendental privilege: his affirmation is little more than an obiter dictum, and Hegel's emphasis on historicity and presuppositionlessness strengthens the thrust of contemporary naturalism, though Hegel's effort appeared too early to have considered the Darwinian lesson. Hegel's radical critique of Kant,¹² therefore, raises the question of whether Kant's transcendentalism (a fortiori, Husserl's) may not rightly be assigned some sort of extranatural standing. It does not oblige us, of course, to adopt a favorable reading of Hegel's extravagant system, though it entails or entrenches a distinct change in the analysis of the logic of predicates and categories, which, to my mind, marks the best possible reading of the sweep of Hegel's influence on contemporary thinking. Nevertheless, Hegel does not fit easily within naturalistic limits.

In any event, the definition of naturalism with a human face is both historically grounded and historicized—and is meant to accommodate within reasonable limits (and without privilege) whatever philosophical solutions addressed to pertinent, now-salient puzzles may strike the champions of contending factions as being sufficiently compelling. Certainly, the very idea of deciding the relative strength of contemporary movements like those of pragmatism, analytic philosophy, and the principal varieties of continental philosophy—preeminently, of phenomenology, in the sense in which Husserl and Heidegger must be jointly featured as being in opposition to Hegel, who is of course a very different kind of phenomenologist—could hardly be relevantly explored without redefining naturalism for our time. I suggest that the assessment of naturalism's prospects is the master theme of every pertinent reexamination of what it would take to restore a reasonable sense of the underlying unity of contemporary philosophy, without prejudice to the state of play of its most important disputes. Once we admit that Kant was not a naturalist at all, that Aristotle was a naturalist of a kind displaced by Galileo and Darwin, that Hegel was at best a modern naturalist in the making, you see how difficult it is to draw the lines of naturalism correctly from the conceptual resources of such very different pasts.

We cannot make progress here without grasping the essential discontinuity between the truly modern analysis of naturalism (that has come to dominate—was, indeed, largely developed in—the post-Hegelian nineteenth and twentieth centuries) and its more usual puzzles in the rest of philosophy's history, running from ancient times up to the prescient stirrings of the modern (in Vico and Herder).

I suggest the apparent discontinuity is itself rightly perceived as a deeper form of continuity, provided we realize that the older tradition unquestionably failed to distinguish what (by a term of art) I have already characterized as an encultured or enculturing conception of human nature. Metonymically, the contrast may be neatly focused in the differences between Aristotle's and Hegel's conceptions of humankind's second nature (the one biologized, the other historicized and encultured) in the tendency, in influential contemporary quarters, to conflate the two accounts in unhelpful ways.

Here, we learn from our mistakes, for what is meant by historicity and enculturation is incommensurable with Aristotle's biologism and Kant's transcendentalism, and the distinctive mark of truly "modern" modern philosophy depends on the new conceptual unity made possible (but not yet achieved) by conjoining Hegel's theme of *geistlich* history and Darwin's discovery of the evolutionary process that culminates in the appearance and uniquely hybrid development of *Homo sapiens*. No mere improvement of Aristotle's or Kant's (or Hume's) characteristic philosophical rigor even begins to approach the larger vision of naturalism McDowell leads us to suppose he wishes to draw from Hegel's innovations—but cannot formulate in terms of the conceptual resources he draws from Kant and Aristotle.

The essential clue is perfectly straightforward. The cultural world (of humans) emerges from the biological by sui generis processes—primarily by way of the incipient invention of true language (from the forms of primate communication) and its continually improved powers, which, reflexively, entail the matched transformation of the biologically evolved competences of the primate members of *Homo sapiens* into those normal to the artifactually hybrid, enlanguaged and encultured agents we call selves or persons—in such a way as to sustain the orderly transmission of the new competences from generation to generation (linguistic, psychological, agential) as well as their continuing evolution under the conditions of cultural history. You cannot fail to see that if the human person is an artifactual transform of the human primate (by way of the invention and mastery of language), then the "things" that belong to true language will henceforth count as natural (encultured) things, and, *then*, extensionalism and physicalism will prove inadequate to our conceptual needs. Our naturalism will have to change: the unity of science will either fail or yield a suitable parity between the human and physical sciences. (Certainly, the maneuver defeats Carnap's *Logical Syntax*.)

The process requires two very different modes of evolution and development: one, accounted for in terms of genetic, biochemical, epigenetic, and related interactive factors collected in our best inquiries along neo-Darwinian lines, however adjusted by continuing inquiry; the other, embodied and manifested in the first or, further, artifactually, in the *materiae* of the physical and biological world (as in our technologies, arts, and histories) but accounted for by the transformed, causally efficacious, culturally "penetrated" powers attributed to selves and to whatever they characteristically produce, collected in accord with the paradigm of linguistic meaning or of evolving analogues (symbolic, semiotic, significative, institutional skills), which, by a term of art, I call Intentional (whether fully linguistic or lingual—that is, not actually verbal but impossible without linguistic competence: as in baking bread, dancing, committing murder, engaging in war, making love, promising, worshipping, pursuing a career), and which, by various conceptual economies, are able to reclaim (for our best versions of naturalism) whatever of Hegel's exuberant *geistlich* world contributes to a reasonable picture of the human condition.

The pivotal issue concerns the definition of the metaphysical differences between the biological and the cultural: the specification of the emergent, novel, sui generis, irreducible processes and attributes of the cultural world that nevertheless remain causally efficacious in distinctive ways. And, indeed, if there *is* such a world, which includes societies of selves and what they are said to be capable of uttering (as by the skills just mentioned), then we will have already succeeded in providing a rationale for the strategic (straightforwardly naturalistic) innovation of distinguishing between the biological and the enlanguaged cultural: for example, we will have accounted for the natural artifactuality of selves or persons, and we will have replaced the classic reductionist forms of the unity-of-science program with an entirely new unity conception that prioritizes the executive role of artifactual selves and their cultural world. I cannot imagine a philosophical change of comparable power, except a successful reductionism or eliminativism. But there are no convincing essays of the latter sort. (Treat this as a response to McDowell's first step.)

II

Whatever is decisive for the definitional question, looking forward to the recuperation of the unity of Eurocentric philosophy, lies with the difference between two versions of the relationship between two distinct conceptions (the biological and the cultural) of humankind's second nature. I'm persuaded that the three-legged opposition dividing so-called pragmatists, analysts, and continental philosophers may be greatly simplified—defanged as a source of insurmountable difference—merely by interposing the distinction just tagged and by redefining in its terms those troubling suspicions that have divided Eurocentric thought against itself: that is, by investing them with the transformative resources first put in play by Kant's innovations and by Hegel's profound critique of Kant, because each introduces a new conceptual channel for canonical philosophy.

Kant's transcendental questions loom over the whole of epistemology and metaphysics even after their privileged pretensions have been completely discredited, and Hegel's radical historicizing of a vastly enlarged *geistlich* interpretation of what Kant had unconvincingly restricted to his own privileged questions of transcendental possibility now redefines what might be meant by a merely human grasp of the actual structure of the world we claim to inhabit—and to know, under the condition of our being first formed by an enlanguaged *Bildung* and continually altered historically. This is perhaps as close as we may come to Hegel's conception of "Absolute Knowing," which is itself no more than the infinite asymptotic limit that we forever invoke in our finite attempts to grasp the posited concrete unity of the whole of reality. In any case, it's what McDowell has yet to fathom, what figures like Aristotle and Kant never envisioned, and what Husserl believed he had satisfactorily tamed.

The cunning of history shows the way here because, in spite of its presumed argumentative skills, analytic philosophy remains, paradoxically, weaker than pragmatism or continental inquiry in its grasp of the conceptual revolution wrought by Kant and Hegel. All this affords an ample confirmation of just how far—and yet how far short of what is needed—the most perceptive (and courageous) *analytic* forays into the uncertain ground all "three" movements share have dared to penetrate. I've singled out (opportunistically, for the sake of an instructive economy already bruited) the helpful candor of John McDowell's intention, centered in his John Locke Lectures (collected in *Mind and World*), to coopt Hegel's concept of *Bildung* in the service of correcting Kant's transcendental extravagance within the largely ahistorical inquiries of the best of contemporary analytic philosophy. McDowell fails hands down in the Locke Lectures to capture the central theme of Hegel's *Bildung*.

But I read the verdict in a generous way, because McDowell succeeds (by failing in his own venture) in drawing our attention to the flat impossibility of benefiting from Hegel's critique of Kant and pre-Kantian philosophy (reaching back to Aristotle)—that is, *if* the analytic movement (or we, philosophers of any stripe) fails to incorporate into our conception of naturalism the full meaning of historicity and the difference between a biologized and a hybrid conception of human nature that concedes metaphysical differences between the biological and the cultural. We lose the decisive contrast between the two conceptions of humankind's second nature—implicated in the splendid (but still-inadequate) paradigms offered in Aristotle and Hegel, now dubiously conflated by McDowell. I admit the matter has its comic side because neither Kant nor Aristotle could have addressed, perspicuously, the Hegelian and post-Hegelian contrast between biology and culture and because Hegel's account, often drowned in the excesses of Absolute *Geist*, never rightly isolates the difference needed (though it collects whatever distinctions might yield that difference).

I hesitate to plunge in without providing more preparation for what needs to be said. But perhaps I'll not be misunderstood if I draw a perfectly obvious small clue from McDowell's reflections on naturalism (well, ethical naturalism) that nevertheless falls short of what I have in mind. Here's the argument: in "Two Sorts of Naturalism," McDowell notes that in the *Nicomachean Ethics* Aristotle "stipulates . . . that he is addressing only people in whom the value scheme he takes for granted has been properly ingrained" (as by "ethical upbringing").[13] There's the point! (McDowell offers nothing more expansive.) But *he cannot mean what he says here* unless either he means to legitimate what I call Aristotle's *Bildung*, by way of Hegel's usage, which would rightly require introducing the modern distinction between biology and culture, *which Aristotle lacks* and Kant all but lacks, or he means that Hegel's *Bildung* is essentially the same as the Greek *paideia*, which would be false, since *paideia* construes the normative issue as essentially biologized and conventionally drawn (though idealized) from the prevailing *Sitten* of Aristotle's world. That is, McDowell construes *Bildung* in the same sense in which Aristotle invokes "upbringing," but *Bildung* poses the question of the origin of selves in a way that *paideia* never intends. Failing to mark the difference, McDowell fails in a decisive and telling way.

Hegel's sense of *Bildung* entails the dialectical challenge of the evolving *Sitten* of one's own society and of other encountered societies—still internalist, I concede, in a way that might yet be confused with Aristotle's narrower notion, though it also requires a running assessment of competing norms, however provisionally they may arise, *within* the flux of history (in effect, of historicity).

Aristotle's doctrine involves no more than an appeal to upbringing, ordinary instruction, and indoctrination fitted to prevailing practices that are simply not construed in terms of any historicized or emergent challenge. Even Hegel's account fails to come to terms with the artifactual standing of all possible *Sitten* viewed in terms of a Darwinized picture of "external" (enlanguaged) *Bildung*: that's to say, the very process of transforming primate into person.

McDowell's failing is clear confirmation of the profound inertia of the best of analytic philosophy: of its remarkably late awakening to the need to bring a command of historicity and historied culture into the space of its most salient forms of naturalism. More than thirty years earlier, Carnap had already expressed his admiration for Thomas Kuhn's draft of *The Structure of Scientific Revolutions*.

Kuhn's *Structure* had originally been massively rejected in analytic circles, but it has surfaced once again, insistently, in a new philosophical surge that bids fair to enlarge current accounts of naturalism along broadly Hegelian lines. In any case, I dwell on McDowell's initiative because, hard as it is to believe, there is at the moment no more centrally placed analyst committed to reconciling Hegel and analytic philosophy! (The trouble is that there's almost nothing in McDowell that could possibly serve the purpose.)

According to McDowell, Aristotle conveys the sense—the sense McDowell champions—in which the ingrained spontaneity with which we learn to respond to ethical matters identifies (our) second nature entirely *within* the resources of (our) biology. McDowell says, "Any actual second nature is a cultural product, a formed state of practical reason . . . not something that dictates to one's nature *from outside*." He then adds: "[Where we apply] the rhetoric of ethical realism, second nature acts in a world in which it finds more than what is open to view from the [merely] dehumanized stance [that is, more than what it could possibly gain from the disenchanted, naturalistic, Humean world we treat as 'viewed from nowhere'—as lacking human meaning altogether] that the natural sciences, rightly for their purposes, adopt. And there is nothing against bringing this richer reality under the rubric of nature too."[14] Fine. But McDowell does not explicitly account for the cultural (or specifically enlanguaged) transformation of the human that makes "practical reason" and "ethical upbringing" normatively meaningful at all, open to genuine normative validation—naturalistically—that is, in the sui generis sense that marks the unique emergence of an encultured world. (Unless, that is, second nature is no more than a selective strand of an ethic identified only in the anthropological sense, which is certainly less than Hegel would require.)

The legitimation of ethical norms cannot be gained by any improved naturalism by merely "reenchanting" nature: that is indeed Aristotle's (and McDowell's) limitation. Think of the matter this way. Aristotle nowhere assures us that the relationship between potentiality and actualization in encultured and enculturing processes behaves in the same way the paradigmatic processes of human biology do, or that the relationship can be shown to be governed by biologically specified norms of any kind. McDowell could never offer the requisite assurances, since he lacks the conceptual distinction between biological nature and human culture. He does not offer any clue regarding the original focus of ethical norms: in effect, he cannot explain the force of Hegel's or Gadamer's use of *Bildung*.

They, too, lacking or ignoring the import of Darwin's discovery, fail to grasp the longitudinal significance of the prelinguistic achievements of the nonhominid primates, perhaps even the achievement of early humans brought to the very threshold of true speech. But then we, too, have delayed two hundred years too long. McDowell presumes too much in supposing he can accommodate Hegel's *Bildung* by merely reenchanting nature by way of Kant's account of the difference between reasons and causes joined to something akin to Aristotle's ethical instruction.

There's an enormous conceptual gap here, all but invisible to McDowell, that seems likely to miss completely the metaphysical difference between physical nature and human culture (within nature in the large). I'm prepared to risk the entire argument on a single challenge: if it were possible to redescribe all the distinctive features of true speech and language in physicalist terms alone, I would be persuaded that the difference I now take to be essential to the definition of naturalism could be refused without philosophical penalty. We are at a crossroads here because the very existence of human selves, history, the entire cultural world of humans is artifactually inseparable from the emergence of true language by way of a sui generis mode of evolution that depends on but is altogether different from any narrowly conceived biological evolution of *Homo sapiens*, which we now explain canonically in terms of one or another form of neo-Darwinism.

I'm not concerned to provide a satisfactory analysis of the huge distinction I have in mind. (I admit it's absorbed most of my energies over an entire career.) But it bears in a decisive way on the rapprochement of the principal movements of Western philosophy that I'm recommending.

I intend only to map in the briefest way the most important conceptions of naturalism struggling for hegemony at the present time, which come together in the nature/culture distinction.

There are, I suggest, three master strategies of the naturalistic kind that have occupied us chiefly through the second half of the twentieth century and the opening decades of the twenty-first: first, a reductionism of various kinds, perhaps most compellingly those associated with the classic unity-of-science program but open to accommodating the emergence or supervenience of the mental and the cultural—perhaps then, also, the stopgap measures of dualism and epiphenomenalism (think here of Jaegwon Kim); second, an emergentism of various kinds, perhaps most promisingly those associated with some form of biologism (narrow-gauge or wide) opposed to any mere physicalism as far as the human world is concerned but hospitable to subsuming the mental and the cultural (including linguistic behavior, intelligent action, cooperative commitment, creative and purposive production, and the like) within the terms of a teleologized reading of biological processes (think here of an updated Aristotle); and third, an emergentism involving cultural entities and processes, at once hybrid and sui generis, complex and irreducible, inseparably incarnate or embodied in physical and biological nature, instantiating novel forms of causal efficacy (preeminently, the agency of selves) and subject (for that reason) to causal explanations incommensurable with the classic unity-of-science canon though compatible with empirically confirmed forms of physical causation shorn of all pretensions of nomological necessity and the causal closure of the physical world (think of Peirce's evolutionary initiatives).

These very large options collect the most inclusive varieties of naturalism in our day, but they also make provision for supernaturalisms and anti- and extranaturalisms. I've listed them in order of descending professional support—and increasing conceptual resilience. Jaegwon Kim's supervenientism rightly counts as a strong contender of the first sort of naturalism; I've already mentioned John McDowell as a contemporary advocate of something close to the second; and I confess I'm committed to the third, which I judge to be the most resourceful of the three, congenial, especially, to the fortunes of contemporary pragmatism.

McDowell is certainly right in thinking that there cannot be any discontinuity between our grasp of truth and explanation respecting physical nature and legitimated norms and reasons applied to human action. Yet the project fails if McDowell will not or cannot press further in the direction of Hegel's very different conception of *Bildung*. For what is natural or naturalistic, as we now understand matters, must account for the radical difference between physical nature and human culture—without meaning by that to prejudge reductionism's prospects. For if reductionism fails (as I believe it must), then what falls within the bounds of nature will need to be sorted in such a way as to admit sui generis cultural properties and processes (which I collect as *Intentional*). McDowell's Kantian sympathies and Aristotelian convictions betray him here.

About "acquiring a second nature," McDowell ventures no more (in *Mind and World*) than this: "I cannot think of a good short English expression for this, but it is what figures in German philosophy as *Bildung*."[15] But *that*, precisely, stops short of the deeper theme of *Bildung* or second nature (external *Bildung*, as I call it) that McDowell needs but has not probed at all. It's the same naturalism that accounts for the causal efficacy of encultured agency (the self's distinctive causal powers) and the would-be objective norms of theoretical and practical life (the norms of science and morality, say). It's precisely what I mean by "Darwinizing Hegel."

You cannot fail to see that McDowell is aware of the problem since, on the very next page of his text, after remarking that "we need to recapture the Aristotelian idea that a normal mature human being is a rational animal, but without losing the Kantian idea that rationality operates freely in its own sphere," he explicitly says, "Modern naturalism is forgetful of second nature."[16] (Here, he means internal *Bildung*.) Of course, he's right: that's just the point of mentioning the need to recover a full-blooded sense of naturalism adequate to reuniting all the threads of Eurocentric philosophy. But that sense (the *second* sense of second nature, external *Bildung*) *cannot* be drawn from Aristotle, Hume, Kant, or the "modern naturalism" (the disenchanted version) McDowell discounts—or, indeed, McDowell's own proposed improvements. It needs our restoring at least Hegel's innovations regarding history and culture. Quite literally, McDowell brings his own inquiry to a halt by endorsing the very doctrines Hegel dismantles. McDowell never crosses the metaphysical divide.[17] And we, too, cannot cross, unless we produce a suitable account of the metaphysics of the self, but we cannot do that unless we oppose McDowell's regressive reliance on the completely contrived, universally assured, utterly abstract use of the faculty of reason Hegel had already dismantled in Kant!

You have only to remember that Wilfrid Sellars (whom McDowell admires but finds it necessary to improve on) had already supposed that we could (if we wished) simply add the norms and rational functions assigned to persons (the language of reasons, meanings, explanation, and justification) to the language of disenchanted science (the language of bare physical causes) to capture, in effect, all that McDowell might require.[18] Sellars's maneuver utterly fails: persons are already existent hybrid entities, in the sense I've been sketching, and thus are already implicated in Sellars's speculation (a fortiori, in Kant's). Ethical values are second natured, *for selves and for selves alone*.

It's hard to believe that Sellars could have meant his "addition" to be taken literally. McDowell keeps to his own improvement: "The right contrast for the space of reasons," he says, "is not the space of causes, but [echoing Kant] the realm of law." It's true, he adds, "that a *merely* causal relation [which nature 'as the realm of law' already exceeds] cannot do duty for a justificatory relation," but "it is also disputable that the idea of causal connections is restricted to thinking that is *not* framed by the space of reasons. The contrast leaves it possible for an area of discourse to be in the logical space of causal relations to objects without thereby being shown not to be in the logical space of reasons [for 'reasons might *be* causes']."[19] Of course (or, perhaps better, with due care for the unexamined complexities of Kant's own doctrine).

Still, all this skirts the essential issue: what, finally, are the boundaries of the domain of nature that could include and join disenchanted causes and justificatory reasons without yielding to such problematic extremes as reductionism, dualism, or the tinkering of a philosophical bricoleur?[20] The answer depends on a naturalistic account of the hybrid nature of human persons and human agency,[21] because *if*, following Jaegwon Kim's version of the unity-of-science argument, we agreed to the doctrine of "the causal closure of the physical domain," we would find it impossible (as Kim himself would say) to extricate ourselves from a reductionism of the unity kind. But if you see the conceptual link between causal closure, nomological universals, and reductionism, you will have grasped the sense in which to attempt to reconcile Hegel and analytic philosophy may well entail concessions regarding the realist status of the cultural world potent enough to oblige us to consider radical changes in the canonical picture of science itself.

McDowell is aware that he must reconcile the causal treatment of physical events with the causal treatment of human actions, say, that incarnate meanings in causally efficacious ways tethered to "explanations by reasons," where, as McDowell adds, "reasons might be causes." In Kim's view, only something like a unity-of-science reductionism could possibly be reconciled with "causal closure," and even causal efficacy.

I argue, therefore, that there can be no convincing way of escaping Kim's trap if we cannot provide a compelling naturalism of the third kind sketched earlier, for only such a naturalism could possibly vindicate our modifying the closure doctrine in a respectable way: an insult, for example, may cause another's anger and the usual reddening of the face and change of pulse and the like; the closure doctrine may then be admitted to hold for the whole of nature, but that could never validate the presumption that if it held, it must hold in adequately physicalist terms alone or, indeed, in terms that entail strong nomological necessities. Kim, therefore, cannot defend his own position any better than McDowell defends his. Culturally emergent but physically embodied actions—speech acts, for instance—may in principle be made to conform with some as-yet-unformulated version of the closure doctrine while at the same time it resists reductionism.[22] McDowell nowhere bridges the divide or explains what he means by *Bildung* in a way that might answer a critic like Kim.[23] Strict causal universality and nomological necessity are decidedly contestable.[24]

III

In chiding McDowell, I mean to draw your attention to the even more baffling truth that pragmatism has almost completely ignored the frontal analysis of the twin themes of historicity and enculturation, even though, as a "Hegelian" movement, it was always subterraneanly informed by both. Apart from Mead and Royce, chiefly among the continentals, these themes are rarely far from center stage.

At the close of his 1997 Woodbridge Lectures, almost entirely given over to tracking the Kantian import of Wilfrid Sellars's work, McDowell remarks, "[Sellars] is unresponsive to the Hegelian conceit of incorporating receptivity within Reason, and I have tried to display this as a blindness to a more soberly describable possibility. Given his conviction that the transcendental exercise must be undertaken from outside the conceptual, Sellars's responsiveness to Kant gives him no alternative but to construe the transcendental role of sensibility in terms of guidance by 'sheer receptivity.'"[25] This is, to be sure, the key to Hegel's objection to Kant.[26] But it's a lesson McDowell himself cannot rightly draw. McDowell's critique suffers from the same poverty of analytic philosophy's naturalism that he wishes to overcome, for it requires a theory of active reason originally informed by the transformative powers of *Geist* applied to what (in a Darwinian sense) may be called "primate" intelligence at the human level: McDowell exposes the inadequacy of Sellars's option on internal grounds but has next to nothing to say about the other matter, the issue I've been calling external *Bildung*—within the terms of which alone internal *Bildung*, Aristotle's doctrine of upbringing (according to McDowell's reading), makes any sense at all, as the historicized formation of a self rather than as the mere indoctrination of an already fashioned self.

Hegel enlarges our account of *Vernunft* immeasurably by incorporating the distinctive metaphysics of history and culture within a conceptual space that we might easily reclaim as "natural," but Kant could never have made such a move—and never made the attempt: it would have utterly subverted the assured closure of his transcendental system and the would-be standing of the changeless categories of the understanding (*Verstand*) Kant claims to have discovered. Historicity and universalism (a fortiori, transcendentalism) are finally incompatible. There, for instance, lies the key to Ernst Cassirer's profoundly Hegelianized Kantianism, which McDowell might have consulted. (It's also the key to the failure of Husserl's *Crisis* volume.)

My own view is that Kantian transcendentalism is a species of extra-naturalism that might have passed for naturalism in its own day but hardly in ours; so are all the forms of cognitive privilege: Descartes's clear and distinct ideas as well as Aristotle's nous. (They make us out to be minor gods, though still exceptional.)[27] Invoking constructivism under the condition of historicity, however, entails the complete dismantling of the Kantian a priori and any principled disjunction between transcendental concepts (or categories) and empirical concepts (transiently formed). Hegel's myth of Reason, therefore, profoundly alters the metaphysics of *Bildung*: outflanks at a stroke whatever, by apriorist means, might have stalemated the redefinition of *naturalism* in the conciliatory spirit I've been advancing.

You realize there's no settled picture of *Vernunft* in Hegel's entire account: Hegel cannot quite free himself from the heady thought that human reason is a fulguration of something akin to the Stoics' divine fire; at the same time, he cannot abandon the thought that knowledge is no more than a human achievement bounded by finitude and horizonal history. Hence, he favors the safety of a certain amount of bombast (benignly in touch with the distinction of the *geistlich*); all the while, we glimpse the impossibility of abandoning a thoroughly naturalistic economy.

The appearance of Darwin's innovation and of the data confirming the immensely slow evolution of the various species of the genus *Homo* leading to *Homo sapiens* and (doubtless) to Neanderthal as well (now extinct) forces us to concede that, in acknowledging that the invention of language and speech accounts for the enculturing transformation of the primate capacities of the species—hence, for the emergence of the artifactual self—we find ourselves obliged to abandon Descartes's and Kant's cognitional mythologies and to streamline the extravagances of Hegel's *geistlich* rhetoric. The best first steps in this direction lead through the work of the classic pragmatists and figures like Dilthey and Cassirer, since Marx and Kierkegaard appear too early to have incorporated Darwin. Pragmatism has surged again, so it might well return to the unfinished business of reclaiming its Hegelian heritage within the agon of contemporary philosophy.

The classic pragmatists never completely lost sight of the Hegelian corrective, though their analyses were often remarkably meager, until thinkers like Rorty, Brandom, Davidson, Sellars, Quine, Frege, Wittgenstein, and Heidegger had all been puzzlingly treated, at one time or another, as exemplars of the best work of pragmatism itself! In any case, the classic pragmatists were made stronger by such associations, although they were never drawn to Kantian disjunctions or transcendental privilege—all inimical to a viable naturalism: neither Peirce nor Dewey ever hesitated along these lines. In a curious way, then, the pragmatists and continentals have been waiting for someone like McDowell to come along to attempt to bridge the gap between themselves and the analysts, from the analysts' side. Accordingly, McDowell confirms the depth of analytic philosophy's estrangement and the vagueness of the pragmatists' reading of Hegel.

There are obvious constraints—some oblique, some straightforward—that may be incorporated at once into naturalism's larger proposal. For example, Kant's entanglement with noumena is a blunder that must be completely set aside: it has no useful life at all; it has nothing to do, for instance, with supporting the sensible admission that things may exist even if completely unknown to us or that what things we claim to know we may have good reason to believe exist in the way we claim they do, though independently of all our claims. There is no way to defend the thesis except by constructivist means—by positing (for good-enough reasons) a known thing's existing (as we claim to know it) independently of knowing or claiming to know it.

Simply put: noumena literally cannot be discussed at all, and the concept of an independently existing thing is not the same as the concept of a noumenon. But if you see that, you see as well that representationalism in the epistemological sense favored in the seventeenth and eighteenth centuries, favored in the first *Critique* (and, once again, in twentieth-century analytic thought), is little more than the obverse side of noumenalism—a doctrine, therefore, unacceptable to a rigorous naturalism. This is the implied lesson of Kant's admission to Marcus Herz (in his famous letter of February 21, 1772) identifying the fatal link between transcendentalism and noumenalism. To see this is to mark the burden of any viable post-Kantian forms of transcendental inquiry. Transcendental categories (Kant's categories) cannot be shown to fall (for epistemological reasons) within the bounds of nature: *they never*—they are never made to—bear directly on what is "given" in experience, or is subject to empirically generated concepts, or depends on the psychologically accessible data on which alone we could possibly build our claims to know the world. (Their a priori necessity depends on a higher, would-be-autonomous faculty of reason.)

Kant's transcendental distinctions are antipsychologistic: hence, finally, antinaturalistic. The only way to recover their specifically naturalistic advantage requires the defeat of Kant's actual system: "transcendental" categories would have to be empirically generated—dialectically favored, revised from time to time, serially idealized wherever holistically or systematically promising—meant only to provide (by constructive guesses) a provisional a priori regulative rule of objectivity fitted to our present inquiries but ready to be replaced where needed. (In this sense, Kant's system cannot be defended without being displaced.)

This is indeed akin to Hegel's master clue regarding the error of Kant's extraordinary effort to secure the objective standing of the natural sciences.[28] Kant could never have countenanced Hegel's revision of the transcendental undertaking. Hegel insists on it; in his account of "symbolic forms," Ernst Cassirer provides more than a sketch of how a Hegelianized version of Kant might actually work.[29] But the correction requires that the a priori be, finally, an a posteriori projection; that transcendental necessity be no more than rhetorical contingency; and that, strictly speaking, there simply are no demonstrable transcendental categories of Kant's sort. Here you gain a sense of the price of an adequate naturalism for our time.[30]

You realize that realism and idealism cannot be more than contingent regulative assumptions—articles of rational hope perhaps, in Peirce's pretty sense—never quite constitutive in the sense Kant examines (and Hegel advances in his own problematic way). Idealism cannot persuade us to accept the thesis that the physical world is somehow constructed or constituted, in part at least, by the mind's activity; nor can Kant's argument persuade us that empirical realism must be construed conformably.

Kant's transcendental innovations introduce the inescapable constructivism of epistemology. But Kant goes too far—fails to grasp the thoroughly constructivist nature of his own postulated faculties and categories. Kant is too early to benefit from Hegel's revisions just as Hegel is too early for the revisions that Darwin makes possible. They are, in a way, already anticipated by Marx and the classical pragmatists even before the endorsement of the argument of *On the Origin of Species*.

Constructivism remains in force, so long as epistemology is needed and so long as it is a priori. But, then, there cannot be a principled disjunction between the empirical and the transcendental or between the psychological and the phenomenological. If you grant the force of Hegel's argument, you see that it must lead as well to the defeat of Husserl's regressive attempt to identify an even more unyielding form of transcendental apodicticity than Kant proposes. All this bears directly on the definition of an adequate naturalism. (I shall return to Husserl.)

Indeed, C. I. Lewis, somewhat in sympathy with Dewey, affirms, in accord with his own "conceptual pragmatism," that "*a priori* truth is definitive in nature and rises exclusively from the analysis of concepts. [Nevertheless,] that *reality* may be delimited *a priori* is due . . . to the fact that whatever is denominated 'real' must be something discriminated in experience by criteria which are antecedently determined. [Yet] the choice of conceptual system for . . . application to 'particular given experience' is instrumental or pragmatic, and empirical truth is never more than probable."[31] Lewis never risks going beyond the bounds of nature (naturalism) in defining the a priori, or what might count as transcendental "certainty" or the "independence of the conceptual" from the empirical: "The reality of possible experiences in which any interpretation would be verified—the completest possible empirical verification which is conceivable—constitutes [Lewis says, almost repeating Peirce] the entire meaning which that interpretation has. A predication of reality to what transcends experience completely and in every sense is not problematic; it is nonsense."[32] This is a *reductio* of Husserl's phenomenology.

Murray Murphey has recently offered the following congruent summary of Lewis's conceptual strategy: "Lewis emphasizes that our categories are historical social products and, although they are prior to any given experience, they nevertheless can, and do, change over time. The test of the *a priori* is pragmatic, and the *a priori* is just that element in [systems of knowledge that can be changed for pragmatic reasons."[33] This catches up, very nicely, more explicitly than does McDowell or Putnam, the themes that serve to reconcile analytic philosophy and pragmatism in the strongest possible naturalistic terms: it demonstrates, in effect (per Dewey, Royce, and even Hegel and, by anticipation, even Kuhn, though hardly in Kuhn's terms), the historical replaceability of "conceptual systems" and an underlying commitment to the flux of experience.[34]

There simply is no determinate autonomous space of mind in which transcendentalism can actually distinguish between a priori and a posteriori ("synthetic") truths; hence, the decisive option affecting the definition of *naturalism* in our time rests with the force of Hegel's critique of Kant and the implied "pragmatist" critique (in Hegel's name) of Husserl's phenomenology (read in the standard way). I see no reason to believe (against the apparent views of McDowell and Putnam) that the achievements of science and logic cannot be reasonably recovered in accord with the flux of experience—or the flux of history (historicity)—if they can be recovered at all; accordingly, I see no reason to believe that objectivity in science is, as such, incompatible with one or another coherent form of relativism,[35] if objectivity can be recovered in the constructivist way.

Necessity, Peirce affirms, obtains only in deductive logic: where more is needed, metaphysically, we must fall back to constructivist devices. Conceptual truths, Hilary Putnam has persuasively argued (in a way that shows us how to harmonize pragmatism and analytic philosophy), are inherently revisable under historically pertinent conditions (as, contra Kant, with the first mention of viable non-Euclidean geometries). What Putnam demonstrates surely suggests a beneficial paraphrase of Hegel's treatment of the notion of historicity, although I doubt Putnam would welcome any such phrasing. Similarly, what he says accords with Dewey's somewhat undeveloped acknowledgment of the flux of history, though he roundly condemns relativism as conceptually irretrievable. Putnam is disposed (mistakenly, I would say) to believe that realism and relativism are incompatible and that (very possibly) the admission of a strong form of historicity or the flux of experience may threaten (as Lewis seems at times to suppose) the quasi-foundational function of scientific knowledge.[36] (They seem to signal pragmatism's continuing weakness.)

Once we abandon cognitive privilege and disallow "necessities of reason" (in accord with Putnam's excellent argument)—otherwise canonically disallowed in spite of evolving experience (think here of non-Euclidean geometries)—we shall have to concede at the very least, vis-à-vis Kantian questions, that objectivity in the sciences is bound to entail the a posteriori reading of a priori posits (C. I. Lewis's strategy). Furthermore, if that be allowed, the compatibility of realism and relativism (within naturalistic bounds) will, wherever relativism proves to be coherent and self-consistent, follow at once. Viewed this way, Dewey's pragmatism confirms the relativistic proclivities of the Hegelian correction of Kant—and thus enlarges the resources of naturalism. It is also, perhaps, part of the perceived advantage of a post-Darwinian critique of teleologism—applied to selves rather than primates.

I mention these qualifications for a number of reasons: partly to illustrate the systematic coherence of certain proposed constraints on a form of naturalism fitted not merely to analytic philosophy but to the whole of Eurocentric philosophy—where, that is, other options, even if equally naturalistic, are demonstrably not nearly as congenial or resourceful, partly because they suggest the considerable difference between pragmatist and analytic versions of naturalism as well as the ease with which they may be reconciled; partly to confirm that the debate about naturalism need not adversely interfere with the undistorted treatment of other important issues—realism and objectivity, for instance; and partly to hint (before addressing the matter in a frontal way) at how important a decision it is to ground (without involving privilege) the naturalism debate in one or another version of phenomenology—where Hegel's conception starts us off on the right foot. When all is said and done, I suggest, phenomenology (read in Hegel's rather than Husserl's way) begins to define the minimal conditions of an inclusive Eurocentric naturalism. But if you think back to Hume's and Kant's impoverishment of the cognizing and active "I" of eighteenth-century philosophy, you see at once the sense in which the culturally transformed Cartesian ego or Kant's "Ich denke" (the puzzlingly weak posit of the passage marked as §16 of the first *Critique*) is the assured *artifactual* mate (the self-constituting evolving agent of linguistic and allied fluencies) on which naturalism finally rests—the same "self" that remains invisible (but present) in Hume's *Treatise of Human Nature*, as a consequence of a mistaken application of Hume's own rigor.

IV

It would not be unreasonable to claim that the philosophical motley that includes Descartes, Hume, Kant, Herder, Hegel, Peirce, Marx, Nietzsche, Heidegger, Husserl, James, Dewey, Mead, Kierkegaard, Merleau-Ponty, Sartre, Gadamer, Austin, Wittgenstein, and Foucault depends on one or another version of phenomenological reportage. There is no single model that could possibly fit all of these figures perspicuously, but the collection is worth pondering. The lax use of the term *phenomenology* is not deemed a weakness, therefore; it's a concession to an important consideration that may be met in endlessly different ways and for different purposes: namely, that every effective philosophical thesis that has any epistemological or metaphysical pretensions (regarding "what there is") must begin by acknowledging some initial (some admitted but not the "first" or any "originary") set of data or données or "givens" of reportable experience.

Here, a grander conjecture is in order. We may think of Eurocentric phenomenology as having evolved along two distinct, separable, often opposed tracks that yield options not quite congruent with the actual theories of any well-known discussants of what is said to be given to, or spontaneously constituted by, a cognizing subject (a "self" or "I") in any pertinent mundane or transcendental science or cognizing episode. One track, call it existential, features a mortal, post-Darwinian self lacking any and all apodictic powers. Nevertheless, it's uniquely endowed, contingently, more or less naturally—successfully, it appears—in cognitive and agentive ways. It exhibits a historicized and self-motivated career, informed by natively acquired experiential gifts, however culturally modified or transformed: a seemingly ineliminable but uncertain channel into the world. The other track, call it transcendental, reflexively posits its own necessary presence and form of being, including apodictic powers, in order to account adequately for the acknowledged success of any ascribed sciences or agentive competences.

Neither doctrine escapes circularity. And yet, the substantive issue is thought to be worth debating.

According to the first model, phenomenology rightly accounts for our actually accessing all sensory, experiential, ratiocinative and related "appearings" (or "appearances-of-things") that serve as the initial, completely unprivileged but irreplaceable data (the givens of sensory and other forms of awareness) deemed essential to any form of human knowledge of what we name the world. According to the second model, phenomenology accounts for our ultimately grasping, understanding, even disclosing or constructing whatever synthetically necessary structures need to be cognized (as it's alleged) in order to achieve an objective grasp of "what there is."

Suitably applied, I associate the use of the first model with the most important contributions of figures like Hegel, Peirce, Heidegger, Gadamer, Merleau-Ponty, and Foucault—that's to say, figures that tend to expand the play of phenomenology along specifically experiential lines, which confirms our possessing an accessible channel in coming to know the world—without, however, ensuring the conditions of cognitive validity itself. The second, which I associate with Kant and Husserl, especially, but also (perhaps surprisingly) with the Carnap of *Logical Syntax*, defines what (quarrelsomely) is to be regarded as the privileged necessary myths on which our empirical sciences depend. I take Sellars and McDowell (in our day) to have been notably unsuccessful in uniting the contributions of the two models in naturalistic terms.

I'm speaking loosely here—and must—because any prior, determinate, systematic or reasoned limitation on what to include or exclude from the salient givens of experience would violate the spirit of what is provisionally thus collected. The only possible way Husserl (say) could have construed phenomenology in the methodological way he does requires yielding to antecedent privilege of some kind—thereby subverting the whole point of phenomenology, as Peirce very neatly puts it, as "a preliminary inquiry," for Peirce was an exceptionally effective (admittedly controversial) phenomenologist in the pragmatist mode.

Peirce follows Hegel—criticizes what he takes to be Hegel's "errors" and arbitrary restrictions (in the *Phenomenology* and *Encyclopaedia Logic*) but follows Hegel faithfully nevertheless—even to the point of idealizing Hegel's "three stages of thinking" in terms of the would-be "Universal Categories" of Firstness, Secondness, and Thirdness. Peirce exceeds his own insight here; his pass at a short list of universal categories—in the sense in which he finds Aristotle, Kant, and Hegel all bent on the same effort "to bring out and make clear the *Categories* or fundamental modes [of things or experience]"—is at best a problematic undertaking if we acknowledge the informal boundaries of the phenomenological and the elastic nature of Peirce's would-be categories. Peirce adds, "Hegel was also right in holding that these *Categories* are of two kinds: the Universal Categories all of which apply to everything, and the series of categories [which Peirce calls 'particular categories'] consisting of phases of evolution" (that is, developments that are salient in one phenomenon or one kind of phenomenon but not in another).[37]

If you allow the distinction, then "Universal Categories" are *also* provisional, though ubiquitous enough (among whatever "appears" to us) to justify being so construed in contrast with "particular categories." In any case, we cannot vouchsafe their necessity, exceptionlessness, apodictic objectivity, or their confirmation as uniquely valid within phenomenology's inescapable informality, unless vacuously, for instance, as a formal consequence of one of Husserl's "discoveries" regarding "transcendental intersubjectivity." Husserl affirms: "Concrete, full transcendental subjectivity is the totality of an open community of I's—a totality that comes from within, that is unified purely transcendentally, and that is concrete only in this way. Transcendental intersubjectivity is the absolute and only self-sufficient ontological foundation [*Seinsboden*], out of which every objective (the totality of objectively real entities, but also every objective ideal world) draws its sense and its validity."[38] Peirce might easily have favored something of the sort, though, fallibilistically, Husserl could never have spoken thus: it would have precluded all his transcendental claims at a stroke.

The Danish phenomenologist Dan Zahavi admits that Husserl "never gave a clear answer to the question of whether constitution is to be understood as a creation or a restoration of reality."[39] More to the point, Husserl never gave a satisfactory explanation of the privileged standing of the transcendental factors themselves. There's the *pons* of Husserl's entire project—because necessity and apodicticity are nowhere needed and nowhere assured! Contra Kant, there is no science of science, and contra Husserl, there is no transcendentally assured philosophy of transcendental (or pure phenomenological) philosophy.

I concede that Husserl arrives at a plausible schema here. But I cannot see that it escapes being more than the immensely quarrelsome posit of an objectively discernible world—a "transcendental nonego" that, as Husserl himself holds, "presupposes an element of *facticity*, a passive pregivenness without any active participation or contribution by the ego."[40] I suggest we are back at Kant's fatal invention of the synthetic a priori. I concede that Husserl effectively rejects *that* form of naturalism that disjoins subject and object epistemologically. But so do the pragmatists, the Hegelians, the post-Kantian idealists, and indeed Heidegger—speaking of different subjects and different objects, and Husserl may not really have escaped Kant's decisive problem, since he introduces the "passive pregivenness" of the world within the space of transcendental intersubjectivity. Since Husserl admits a world inseparably bound (in the constituting sense) to coordinately constituted subjects ("I's") and their intersubjectivity, I cannot see how his exertions could convincingly capture anything necessarily objective or apodictic here—frankly, anything bordering on the noumenal—except by circularity or sheer fiat. If we take Zahavi's admission seriously, we realize we cannot confirm the dividing line between subjective passivity and the active autonomy of whatever is implicated in what constitutes world, self, and intercommunicating selves, or indeed what accounts for any such constituting power.

The following is as good as one can find among pertinent efforts (apart from Hegel's own efforts) to clarify the ineluctability and special scruple of his phenomenology, regarding its "neutrality": that is, bearing on the scope or amplitude Hegel accords the given, on his avoidance of all pretensions of privileged standing, and on his admission of the continuing influence of natural experience, his rejection of facultative or subjective certainty or any principled link between such certainty and the supposed objectivity of science, metaphysics, or methodology. Peirce affirms, as a rather freewheeling Hegelian phenomenologist,

> Before we can attack any normative science, any science which proposes to separate the sheep from the goats here [Peirce "names three normative sciences: Ethics, Esthetics, and Logic, 'the three doctrines that distinguish good and bad' representations of truth, . . . efforts of will, . . . (and) objects considered simply in their presentation"], it is plain that there must be a preliminary inquiry which shall justify the attempt to establish such dualism. This must be a science that does not draw any distinction of good or bad in any sense whatever, but just contemplates phenomena as they are, simply opens its eyes and describes what it sees; not what it sees in the real as distinguished from figment—not regarding any such dichotomy—but simply describing the object, as a phenomenon, and stating what it finds in all phenomena alike. [Hegel made this his "starting-point" in the *Phenomenology*,] although he considers it in a fatally narrow spirit, since [Hegel] restricted himself to what *actually* forces itself on the mind. I will so far follow Hegel as to call this science *Phenomenology* although I will not restrict it to the observation and analysis of *experience* but extend it to describing all the features that are common to whatever is *experienced* or might conceivably be experienced or become an object of study in any way direct or indirect.[41]

Peirce confirms the good sense of the main thrust of Hegel's unconditional informality, although what Peirce adds surely casts *science* as no more than an honorific category.

I have also touched very briefly, earlier in this chapter, on Hegel's problematic use of the notion of "being" at the start of the *Science of Logic*. Any such beginning must explicate the role of *Geist* in isolating whatever we take to stand at the beginning of any pertinent metaphysical inquiry. But it needs to be said that there is no single or most salient way of beginning and that any solution comparable to Hegel's is, like Hegel's, dependent on its own myth of how to validate its findings.[42] For present purposes, our concern lies with querying whether, in the most generous sense of phenomenology, what we find in experience obliges us to acknowledge the conceptual insufficiency of naturalism. (I say, emphatically, that it concedes no such thing.)

That lesson begins straightforwardly enough: in contests between pragmatism and analytic philosophy, the motto I recommend is "natural but not naturalizable"—reading the second term in the scientific way associated with the proposals of figures like Quine, Davidson, and Rorty;[43] in contests between pragmatism (or analytic philosophy) and continental philosophy (represented in the strongest way by Husserlian and Heideggerian phenomenology), the motto might be "naturalism but neither supernaturalism nor extranaturalism," where the second term is liberalized to include transcendental subjects and transcendental worlds manifesting privileged attributes. I take the first motto to be already vindicated, and I take the second to be well on its way within late Eurocentric philosophy. Both mottos preclude *any* disjunction between the empirical (or natural) and the a priori (or transcendental): they build instead on an intuition that joins Hegel, Peirce, Lewis, and Cassirer in the critique of Kant's transcendentalism and the confirmation of the a posteriori status of the a priori. (That is to say, the mottos are meant to preclude any strict transcendentalism.)

A few initial constraints congenial to naturalism suggest how we may separate the least doubtful forms of phenomenology from those that are plainly indefensible or seriously problematic—for example, (1) the given cannot be fixed or shown to be indubitable or cast in terms of separable subjective and objective sources, can only manifest whatever saliences it is said to exhibit (phenomenologically) as the-way-things-appear-to-us-to-be, cannot invoke or entail or explicitly affirm any second-order facultative privilege, cannot pretend to free any such reports or avowals from the contingent contamination of whatever enters into the natural formation of any human agent's ability to report the same, and, hence, cannot be originary or more than contingently posited in the middle of our engagement with the world; (2) the given cannot be shown to be merely passive or undistorted or uninfluenced by whatever is alleged to enter actively or from the side of reflexive avowing, *in* whatever is said to be thus given, and cannot, conversely, be shown to be a pure active contribution from any subjective vantage, as if by way of reason opposed to sensation or by way of experience unalloyed in any such way; (3) whatever is taken to be given in senses (1) and (2) includes elements of experience, perception, feeling, emotion, thought, conception, or reason that, as given, appear to be inherently enlanguaged and penetrated by language, belief, theory, and the like—that is, given as linguistically and reflexively reportable but not decomposable into subjective and objective elements, paradigmatically human in the most ordinary ways; so that (4) all speculation or inference regarding what is given in the experience of sublinguistic animals and children is ineluctably anthropomorphized, meaning that such characterizations are informally modeled on the human and uttered from a human vantage—speaking in the name of sublinguistic creatures, with whatever degree or kind of qualification may be needed, to preserve a semblance of objectivity; and (5) phenomenological reports and avowals, often transient and accidental, are not inadmissible for that reason or diminished in any sense in conveying what is given. In short, what Husserl (or Heidegger) treats as phenomenologically constituted (whether cognitionally or existentially)—that is, as what "shows itself as what it is"—is not entitled to privileged standing but gains whatever standing it may claim contingently, provisionally, by diverse and divergent means, replaceably, constructively, and by second-order reflections on what is admitted to be given.[44] But if *that* is true, then, faute de mieux, even Peirce's "Universal Categories" cannot be more than provisional.

Arguably, Kant advances a phenomenologically indefensible option, because he treats what is given through the senses as entirely passive—contra (2); and Husserl's mature version (or at least the standard version of his mature account) is similarly indefensible, because he treats pure transcendental phenomenology as capable of yielding certainty or essentiality regarding the analysis of concepts; that is, because he fails to explain the bearing of the contingency of whatever such putative certainty depends on, or how pure phenomenology escapes the effects of such contingencies—contra (1)–(3).

The point of these caveats is to suggest—perhaps to demonstrate—that versions of Hegel's phenomenology are bound to be more easily defended, more congruent with naturalism's project, than any alternative that might favor Kant's or Husserl's classic options (as just construed). In any event, the economy brings us to what may reasonably count as a first pass at reconciling the entire sweep of Eurocentric philosophy ranging over pragmatist, analytic, and continental undertakings. But if so, then the entire diversity of the Eurocentric world may yet prove to be manageably convergent along naturalistic lines.

V

There are decisive consequences to be drawn from all this. As already suggested, the best phenomenological paradigm must be closer to Hegel's model than to Husserl's. Hegel's emphasis is not centered on a preferred philosophical method of analysis or reportage or methodology of any kind (though Hegel has his preferences) or on the selected findings of any such method or methodology.

Instead, it features *Erscheinungen*: that is, whatever may be reported or avowed as perceived or experienced—"lived through," as Husserl often says—by subjects or agents, naturally, second naturally (as we may now say), subjectively—as conscious subjects capable of reporting the appearings-of-the-world-to-us without invoking antecedent presumptions of any kind regarding what, finally, is given and what inferred, what subjective and what objective, what first order and what second order, what perceived or experienced or felt or thought or imagined and what the meaning of any of that may be, what transient and what essential, what a priori and what a posteriori, what accidental and what universal, what reality may be thought to require and what conforms or does not conform with the same, or anything of the sort.

The phenomenological is relatively innocent then, but not (for that reason) determinately neutral or certain in any assuredly objective regard: the given is changeable, often ephemeral, subject to diverse and uncertain influences of all sorts, valuable in that it includes what, as best we can tell at any moment of judging, we are least likely to ignore or deny as salient or familiar or persistent in the way of what "appears"—as well as what we would not exclude (if queried) however marginal it may seem. This is, in fact, very close to Hegel's notion of being (*Sein*) invoked at the start of the *Science of Logic*;[45] it also confirms the sense in which Hegel's phenomenology—straddling the *Phenomenology* and the *Logic*(s)—is essentially naturalistic in the most problem-free way. It's the key to the daring scruple of what Hegel means by "concrete" actuality.

In emphasizing what is reportable, we implicate the provisional saliencies of the verbal and reportorial skills of what we ordinarily call selves, persons, agents, second-natured subjects, ourselves—without prejudice to what we may theorize *is* a self or subject (or, for that matter, without prejudice to whether such entities actually exist or are only formally or functionally posited); without prejudice to what may be counted as the range of experience of prelinguistic animals and children; without prejudice to individual, aggregated, intersubjective, or historically diverse avowals at the level of ordinary human competence; and without prejudice to what is thus avowed or reported and to what may be sorted as empirical or sensory or simply experienced *as* thought. I take these to be the characteristic, most preliminary features of a Hegelian phenomenology.

In *Logical Investigations*, Husserl constrains any egologically determinate account of subjective experience as merely empirical (stream of consciousness), contrary to what he himself features as belonging to any genuinely a priori analysis of consciousness and experience. But he risks violating any naturalistic continuity between the empirically or experientially a posteriori and any higher-order analysis in a way that invites comparison with Kant's own problematic disjunction between the empirical and the transcendental. Hegel's account in the *Phenomenology* makes it impossible to process Kant's and Husserl's principal distinctions in a comparable way.

Once we admit, effectively with Hegel—or even if we assume (mistakenly, in my opinion) that Hegel was seriously tempted to find a way of escaping the flux of historicity—that the a priori is an a posteriori posit (artifact or construction) meant to accommodate the demands of evolving experience, we cannot distinguish, except horizontally, between the contingent and the necessary. Whatever we there concede also affects the pretensions we invariably find in Husserl and other phenomenologists (in Scheler, for instance, in Heidegger, in Sartre) that cling to the methodological reliability of a disjunction between merely natural or empirical and a priori faculties of analysis, even where disputes arise regarding what the a priori reveals.[46]

Husserl, in *Logical Investigations*, *Cartesian Meditations*, and *Ideas 1*, plainly views phenomenology as a discipline that claims to analyze a recovered range of primordial experience that cannot be disclaimed within the competence of human reflection, though it exceeds the bounds of any naturalistic inquiry. I see no compelling evidence that recent "corrections" in the reading of Husserl in the direction of reclaiming a robust sense of intersubjectivity (notably, in Dan Zahavi's accounts) qualify Husserl's apriorism in any significant respect. The decisive key is not intersubjectivity itself, however holistically joined to plural subjects and world, but the import of any such complex viewed as implicating the inseparability of the empirical and the phenomenological at *any* level of reflection. Husserl, I suggest, is a philosophically regressive figure, viewed in terms of transcendental privilege—just as Kant is, viewed from the vantage of Hegel's critique. We lack convincing evidence confirming the assumed validity of Kant's and Husserl's essential claims. They appear to be entirely stipulated.

In the interests of textual accuracy, we must distinguish between Husserl's views regarding the subject of experience in his own early and later works and his views about the difference between empirical (or naturalistic) and transcendental reflection vis-à-vis the structure of experience itself. Zahavi makes a convincing case textually (but hardly philosophically) for construing the ego of transcendental phenomenology as nonegological (that is, as not identical with the empirical self or subject of any naturalistic reflection or the "owner or bearer of experiences, but simply [as identical with] the experiences [themselves] in their totality"). Regarding this extraordinary claim (which obviously risks incoherence), Zahavi reports Husserl as holding, in the introduction to the second part of the *Investigations*, "that when we engage in a phenomenological description of experiences we should seek to capture them in their essential purity and not as they are empirically apperceived, namely as the experiences of humans or animals." Zahavi glosses Husserl's theme as follows: "We should not focus on sensory physiology or neurology, that is, on the empirical conditions that must be fulfilled in order for *Homo sapiens* to be conscious; rather, we should aim at analyzing the fundamental structures of consciousness, regardless of whether it belongs to humans, animals, or extraterrestrials. In other words, when investigating the experiential dimension, we should aim at essential descriptions of the experience, and . . . such descriptions will precisely exclude any reference to their empirical bearers."[47]

To be candid, I see no way to construe Husserl's *epoché*—in effect, the rejection of the adequacy of the "natural attitude"—as anything but conceptually ungrounded, vacuous, utterly arbitrary, inescapably self-serving, and impossible to reconcile coherently with any of the givens of (egological) experience on which transcendental reduction is said to work its separate magic.[48] I understand the correction intended: the world transcendentally encountered is said *not* to be encumbered egologically, remains accessible nevertheless for objective description without reference to any empirically generated distinctions. But I find this impossible to take seriously: every would-be pertinent test would seem to be privileged in a circular and question-begging way. Husserl has no grasp of or interest in the import of what I have labeled external *Bildung*. What could Zahavi mean by "analyzing the fundamental structures of consciousness [among] animals or extraterrestrials"?

I cannot see how the structure of consciousness could ever be effectively disjoined from mundane experiential considerations about how consciousness is itself embodied—the entire discussion of "other minds" and "intersubjectivity" (in Husserl and Zahavi—and Wittgenstein, for that matter) depends on it; I can't see how the consciousness of infants, animals, or extraterrestrials could possibly be studied, except under the constraints of anthropocentric reflection and theoretical cues drawn from the developmental history of such organisms; I can't see how the phenomenological or "pure" analysis of consciousness could be distinguished, in principle, from empirical or naturalistic inquiries.

Surely, the transcendental must be relativized to what is said to be given in experience, and, surely, what is thus given is continually qualified (reportorially) by whatever (for a time) is thought to be operative a priori. (Recall Putnam's discussion of "conceptual truths.")[49] Nevertheless, I don't deny that there is an important difference in reporting what we experience and in conjecturing about what makes such experience conceptually possible, and I don't doubt that Zahavi presents Husserl's views accurately—perhaps more accurately than accounts that rest entirely on texts like the *Investigations* and the *Meditations*. But Zahavi's qualifications are not meant to weaken the standard transcendental claim (may in fact make it more problematic and resistant to revision), and they seem to entrench the cognitive privilege of consciousness's "content" (not weaken it) without strengthening the grounds for any such confidence. Notice, also, that Zahavi's line of thinking has nothing to do with establishing Husserl's nonegological view of consciousness, as expressed, say, in Husserl's fifth Investigation (in *Logical Investigations*); on the contrary, the nonegological view *presupposes* the distinction between the empirical and the transcendental mode of the phenomenological itself (through all the classic variations of the latter).[50]

On its own showing, transcendental phenomenology must be aware of the empirically generated categories that apply to the givens it claims to analyze in its privileged way. I take that to be a *reductio*. Put in the briefest terms: wherever we admit action and responsibility (as well as perception and the intelligent use of perception in directing action), we admit agency; wherever we admit agency, we must (as far as anyone has argued) admit the individuation and reidentifiability of individual agents; and wherever transcendental agents reflect (or must reflect) on what is empirically given, such agents and the egological agents of experience must, in effect, be one and the same. *Any* principled disjunction here must, accordingly, be incoherent, but to admit the formal point is not yet to say what the nature of empirical and transcendental egos is.

It's entirely possible—even convincing—to suggest that effective agency depends on more than can be assigned to any ego (any single mind or brain, for instance), since what among second-natured agents depends on information—accessible in some ambient cultural space (as, in different ways, Hegel, Husserl, and Heidegger all admit)—may require, or concede, informational sources external to the consciousness of any particular ego. The complications of *Geist, Lebenswelt, Mitsein* surely implicate a plurality of human agents, but what these categories collect also includes what, whether biologically or culturally, qualifies the nature of the selves or agents we admit.[51] Furthermore, except for resurrecting privilege, it is difficult to see how to avoid a constructivist account of objectivity: but, surely, that means favoring some form of naturalism.

My point is a double one: First, if the phenomenological description and analysis of conscious experience (pure or transcendental) cannot be disjoined from the empirical or naturalistic description and analysis of egological experience, then Husserlian phenomenology will finally depend on something close to Hegelian phenomenology (whether it admits the fact or not). In that regard, the Hegelian conception will be more fundamental and (in my opinion) less doctrinaire, less problematic, in fact superior and more inclusive. And, second, if that be admitted, then the entire project of transcendental phenomenology will be placed at considerable risk vis-à-vis a naturalistic phenomenology, whether one admits the existence of a determinate subject of experience or not (that is, regardless of what our options are or may be). As I've already remarked, the entire counterargument can be made absolutely clear by simply reading Husserl's preface to the English edition of his 1913 German original of *Ideas*, which betrays the completely regressive, undefended nature of Husserl's enterprise—regardless of the fortunes of the analysis of such categories as experience, ego, or intersubjectivity.

Consider the following extraordinary lines, therefore, meant to explain transcendental subjectivity, without holding Husserl to his own early idealism or his tendency to disjoin the contribution of the transcendental (or "philosophizing") ego from the supposedly inseparable contribution of the nonegological world, though these and similar considerations do indeed belong to the preface to *Ideas*, where Husserl affirms:

> Transcendental Subjectivity does not signify the outcome of any speculative synthesis, but . . . is an absolutely independent realm of direct experience that becomes available only through a radical alteration of that same dispensation under which an experience of the natural world runs its course, a readjustment

of viewpoint which, as the methods of approach to the sphere of transcendental phenomenology, is called "phenomenological reduction."

In the work before us transcendental phenomenology is not founded as the empirical science of the empirical facts of this field of experience. Whatever facts present themselves serve only as examples. In this book, then, we treat of an *a priori* science ("eidetic," directed upon the universal in its original intuitability), which appropriates the empirical field of fact of transcendental subjectivity with its factual (*faktischen*) experiences, equating these with pure intuitable possibilities that can be modified at will, and sets out as *its a priori* the indissoluble essential structure of transcendental subjectivity, which persist in and through all imaginable modifications. . . .

I am no longer a human Ego *in* the universal, existentially posited world, but exclusively a subject *for* which this world has being . . .

I now also become aware that my own phenomenologically self-contained essence can be posited in an *absolute* sense, as I am the Ego who invests the being of the world which I so constantly speak about with existential validity, as an existence (*Sein*) which wins for me from my own life's pure essence meaning and substantial validity.[52]

I cite this well-nigh-unbelievable passage partly to assure you of Husserl's extraordinary hopes for phenomenology; partly to suggest that, although he changed his views about realism and idealism, about the status of the egological and transcendental subject, and about the inseparability of "I's," world, and intersubjectivity in both naturalistic and transcendental space, Husserl does not seem to have retreated from his strongest transcendental presumptions under the terms of later doctrinal revisions; and partly to confirm that the arbitrariness of Husserl's entire undertaking changes hardly at all through his enormous output and unpublished reflections. But if so, then, at least so far, phenomenology is not likely to withstand a thoroughgoing naturalistic challenge—along, say, Hegelian, if not pragmatist, lines.

In all of this, I find an insuperable vulnerability in Husserl's conception. I have always been struck by the peculiar but philosophically prudent impoverishment of the "I," the subject or self of Hume's and Kant's reflections. My own conjecture about the self suggests that the reflexive functions we nominally assign the individuated human self evolve as the artifactual (second-natured) powers of the equally artifactual, emergent (but genuine, all the same), socially formed and entrenched subject that the well-formed aggregated cohorts of selves of different societies come to recognize as they come to recognize themselves as selves.

To speak this way is, effectively, to recover George Mead's dialectic of the "I" and the "me" in terms of the overlapping but very different processes of formation that belong to instantiations of the different kinds of emergence made possible by the mechanisms of biological and cultural evolution that I sketched earlier in my argument. Hume and Kant could not have answered in the biologized and enculturing terms that were hardly accessible before Darwin's contributions (and, of course, Hegel's contribution). But Husserl could not have proposed his doctrine of the transcendental ego without being aware of the need to explain its provenance. There's the point. Husserl's confidence regarding the apodictic possibilities of the phenomenological *epoché* depend completely on the standing of the ego itself. But if the mundane ego is already a culturally contingent (though regular enough) artifact, as I argue, then it's child's play to mount a *reductio* of Husserl's thesis. But if so, then Husserlian phenomenology can hardly hold the line against a naturalism of the third kind (already introduced). In fact, the gathering argument makes it perfectly clear that the single most decisive thesis in favor of contemporary forms of naturalism—collecting Darwin and Hegel along the lines I've termed external *Bildung*—is indeed the doctrine of the culturally generated artifactuality of the self.[53] The most daring—the single most doubtful—premise of Husserl's doctrine is his posit of "an absolutely independent realm of direct experience" assigned to "Transcendental Subjectivity." Here, Husserl exceeds Kant's extravagances about the powers of transcendental Reason. But if the mundane self is already (factually, uniquely, reflexively affirmed) to be an artifactual transform, then Husserl's theory betrays at least two degrees of heuristic conjecture that *cannot* possibly be regarded as plausible without conceding the reality and conformational role of the mundane ego that is itself originally unaware of the priority and operative presence of the other.

VI

As far as I can see, the contest between pragmatism and analytic philosophy on the one hand and between pragmatism and continental philosophy on the other pretty well comes down to the question of the adequacy or inadequacy of a naturalistic account of subjectivity—and the form that subjectivity must therefore take. Such a summary is already an extraordinary economy. Nevertheless, there's a price to pay for endorsing naturalism's adequacy, though its gains are entirely straightforward. Let me offer a small tally of what would be essential to any satisfactory account of naturalism, drawing largely on what has already been admitted or confirmed or is obviously entailed by what has been confirmed.

Consider the following items as part of a reasonably well-formed, hardly strenuous compendium:

1. Subjectivity (in all its graded variety) may be ascribed sui generis to whatever "is" or "has" a mind, the content of which is directly reportable at some paradigmatically human level of functioning or is taken, by plausible analogy, to be reportable, where attributed to sublinguistic animals.

2. Experience, in the phenomenological sense, is, or is embedded in, what is intentionally structured, whether reported at the human level or imputed to human or animal manifestations of mind.

3. Paradigmatically, the human mind is also profoundly encultured or Intentional (my preferred term, meaning its being profoundly enlanguaged and encultured, "penetrated" and "transformed"), so that the whole of human experience functions significatively, bears its own burden of determinable significance, and is, for such reasons, also perspectived (or horizoned), second natured (or hybrid or artifactual), inherently and fluently reportable, and publicly intelligible among similarly encultured subjects (who share a common ethos as their aggregated second-natured nature).

4. The mental appears to be irreducible in current physicalist terms (though it may indeed be treated—in a mongrel way—as completely physicalist), preserving all of its (Intentional) exceptional distinctions, and would then be conceptually intolerable among the sciences if characterized both physically and Intentionally; it must therefore be biologically emergent (as well as prone to cultural transformation by way

of the contingent penetration of its own natural competences, as in infancy), or, qua emergent, it must be indissolubly embodied or incarnate in one or another suitably developed, possibly quite diverse physical or biological processes.

5. The admission of sentient organisms, human or subhuman, to which suitably graded, suitably qualified experiences are aptly ascribed, even if not linguistically or reflexively reportable, requires, faute de mieux, admitting a relatively unitary site of internal common reference (in effect, the paradigmatic human self or some suitable sublinguistic analogue) regarding intentionally qualified subjective awareness, understanding, purpose, a measure of rational coherence fitted analogically to the distinct aptitudes of this or that species, purposive and experientially informed action, and the like—apart from whether the site thus acknowledged is merely formally or functionally assigned (grammatically, as it were) or construed in some more substantive way.

6. Experience, responsibility, and rationality are all holistically interrelated, appropriately affirmed or denied or analogically imputed along graded lines among the different species, normatively qualified, and predicatively ascribed at each such site. Furthermore, regarding such attributions, there seems to be no competing model of comparable flexibility and adequacy.

7. Encultured human beings, second-natured as selves, serve as the Intentional paradigms of the sites admitted in (3) and are even more robustly construed when treated as the sites of specifically enlanguaged thought and experience or of rational response and purposive action. In fact, being a self or agent is actually experienced phenomenologically in continually entrenched self-referential thought or awareness (though not phenomenally or sensorially, as Hume observes), regardless of what we may think to be the true nature of the self.

8. As encultured or second-natured, selves share, through their own artifactual careers, historically formed, concrete,

collectively predicated practices and traditions that define their Intentional competences.

9. The Intentional world (which includes, as in painting and architecture, parts of mere physical nature transformed, made hybrid by one or another form of human utterance) is encultured and enlanguaged at a level adequated to the powers of agency (or creativity) of its member selves or subjects, through intelligent responses, purposeful action, feeling and emotion, perception and thought, concern and commitment, choice and deliberation, creativity and openness to evolving experience—in the sense in which the former (practices and traditions) constitute the second-natured public niches within which the equally second-natured aptitudes of the latter (thought and action) are first formed and, as a result, function suitably and well. Consequently, each changes coordinately with changes in the other, and, as a result, human selves may be said to have histories rather than natures (or to be histories) or to have hybrid natures that are no more than histories.

10. Selves (or agents) must be capable of being denumerably individuated and reidentified as the operative sites of perception, thought, action, and rationality, at every level of functioning at which such competences are ascribed.

11. There is no reason to think that the items tallied as (1)–(10) and others like them need exceed the conceptual resources of any plausibly ample naturalism.[54]

It is certainly true that we do not yet understand the biological conditions under which consciousness and the prelinguistic modes of sentience, perception, and mentation arise. It's also true that the paradigmatic features of human subjectivity are sui generis, however suggestive the protocultural and communicative competences of sublinguistic creatures may be. But nothing so far admitted exceeds (or need exceed) the conceptual space of naturalism, and the insistence that what is paradigmatically human, or what human selves may be thought to share with possible "higher" beings (as yet unknown), viewed (still) as sui generis at its most advanced level of manifestation—which may indeed qualify Heidegger's conception of *Dasein*—has yet to demonstrate that no such admission could be accommodated or reasonably paraphrased within the space of nature.

I fully admit that "natural*izing*" (that is, physicalist reduction) and dualism (construed naturalistically) are philosophically problematic and, thus far at least, entirely unconvincing options. But it is one thing to say that scientism is a failed or inadequate naturalism and quite another to insist that the human *Dasein* cannot be satisfactorily construed in naturalistic terms. Regardless, Heidegger's phenomenology may be the best-known specimen of what may be counted as the final objection to a thoroughgoing naturalism. My sense is that, in meeting its challenge, we are greatly favored by arguments mustered against all the forms of cognitive privilege; a priori powers; and extravagant or impossible, extremely vaguely defined or mysteriously potent, uncanny or even quasi-divine competences. For instance, Aristotle's account of nous in the *De Anima* (which suggests no biological basis) exceeds nature as we understand it. So does Plato's account, in the *Phaedo*, of the immortal psyche. So does Levinas's prioritizing existential encounters with *l'Autrui* before the applicability of rational categories of individuation and identity.[55]

Heidegger's phenomenology of *Dasein* (for instance, in *Being and Time* and *The Basic Problems of Phenomenology*) I find more illuminating, less abstract, more compelling than Husserl's various accounts of subjectivity, though the convergence between Husserl and Heidegger, once given the reclamation of Husserl's reflections on intersubjectivity, is striking enough. Still, Heidegger writes in a way that favors the existential uniqueness of *Dasein* more than the confirmation of the apodictic necessities of aprioristic inquiry. He remains an antinaturalist, of course, but he speaks primarily against scientism and the treatment of selves as mere objects. That is surely the point of Heidegger's "onto-ontological" doublet that is *Dasein*; the point of speaking of *Dasein*'s "existing"; the contrast between the universal "categories" of ontic analysis (applied to the human *Dasein*) and "existentialia"; the rejection (at the existential level) of the separability of one's own *Dasein*, the *Mitdasein* of others, and the world they share existentially and collectively; the meaning of "care" and the anticipation of death.[56]

Let me, therefore, place before you a specimen passage from *Being and Time* that catches up the spirit in which Heidegger offers his characteristic account—which confirms, almost instantly, the "protected" sense in which he distinguishes between categories and existentialia, the methodologically soft sense in which he means to feature the "primordial" standing of *Dasein*, and, as a result, the ease with which his entire intent may be captured naturalistically, if we but admit the uniqueness and unique openness of human existence.

The decisive adjustment favoring naturalism belongs to the Hegelian, post-Kantian, and pragmatist corrections of the excessive pretensions of Kantian apriorism (as promisingly sketched in Ernst Cassirer's and C. I. Lewis's proposals). It belongs also to countering scientism. I cannot see how Heidegger could possibly mean more, or, if he does mean more, why his findings would not be as problematic as Husserl's or Kant's alternatives. At his best, Heidegger is a naturalist manqué: in effect, once we accommodate Heidegger's existential themes (according to our own lights), it no longer matters whether we favor naturalism or what I've dubbed extranaturalism—they come to the same thing substantively, though they diverge rhetorically.

Here is the passage from *Being and Time*: "The disclosedness of the *Mitdasein* of others which belongs to being-with means that the understanding of others already lies in the understanding of being of *Dasein* because its being is being-with. This understanding, like all understanding, is not a knowledge derived from cognition, but a primordially existential kind of being which first makes knowledge and cognition possible."[57] No more than three small observations are needed here. First, "knowledge and cognition" at the paradigmatically human level of comprehension presuppose the mastery of a language and home culture, which cannot (then) be "primordial" or innate or independent of the natural rearing of human infants; at best, they presuppose the enculturing (natural) transformation of the infant members of *Homo sapiens* into fully formed second-natured selves (external *Bildung*). The aprioristic rendering of this condition as primordial is simply the tautological elevation of a known part of the natural history of selves *as* (problematically) a sui generis, nonnaturalistic, necessary, transcendentally existential condition of whatever is characteristic of the empirically describable lives of humans (in effect, the ontic) *and* of what is valued *there* (by Heidegger) as what is most essential and most arresting in the human world (in effect, the ontological). Second, psychological studies of neonates amply confirm that the linguistic achievements of infants presuppose innate, remarkably determinate prelinguistic social aptitudes of a communicative and playful nature that facilitate the rapid mastery of a home language (and associated culture) *and* the coordinate formation and maturation of an entire population of artifactual selves.[58] This, too, supports the adequacy of a naturalistic rendering of Heidegger's (as well as Husserl's) formulaic extravagances. Third, once we grasp the strategic importance of the fact that Kant's transcendentalism effectively revives an oblique version of the same Leibnizian and Wolffian rationalism Kant had already justifiably rejected, *our* continuing to invoke the "transcendental possibility" of any form of human cognition or understanding (under any guise) must be a constructivist (now, a naturalistic) posit drawn from the actual saliences of human life and experience.

The fate of Kant's view of the transcendental necessity of Euclid's geometry affords the classic confirmation (contra Kant) of the a posteriori standing (of any seemingly privileged version) of the a priori.[59] But then, all three considerations either defeat or achieve a provisional stalemate affecting the antinaturalistic pretensions of the entire play of Husserlian and Heideggerian phenomenology. You have only to bear in mind that the term *a priori* is pertinently used in two entirely different, irreconcilable ways in relation to our reading of the transcendental: in one, we admit—with Kant, the post-Kantians, Hegel, Husserl, Heidegger, Cassirer, Sartre, Lewis, Apel, Habermas, and others—that *any* speculation about the conceptual conditions (the possibility) of our powers of knowledge and understanding may be fairly called *a priori*, that is, as no more than what we are prepared to posit or postulate or presuppose as *their* "prior" enabling conditions, but without affirming any supposedly necessary synthetic truths about the matter; in the other, we are to believe—with Kant and Husserl preeminently, but not with Hegel and not with the Cassirer of "symbolic forms" or the Lewis of the "pragmatic *a priori*"—that the first sort of a priori leads inexorably to the discovery of what is said to be apodictic, unconditionally necessary, universally binding on the correct use of certain of our privileged powers of cognition, understanding, or reason. Here, neither Kant nor Husserl—nor Heidegger, Sartre, or Apel—offers any reason (beyond an obiter dictum) to treat the second sense of the a priori as demonstrably valid in any regard that compares favorably with the supposed validation of the first.

There is no such argument to be had: all known efforts are plainly arbitrary, vacuous, and self-serving. On the contrary, if we grant the advantage of Hegel's way of construing phenomenology over Husserl's, that is, conceding the complete informality and lack of privilege regarding what "appears"—or refusing to favor (in Husserl's way) any extranatural method or criterion for first identifying what is genuinely "given" relative to Husserl's *epoché*—we cannot fail to see the completely question-begging nature of the transcendentalist form of the a priori. There is no knockdown argument confirming necessary synthetic a priori truths within the space of nature. (All of Kant's specimens in the B introduction to the first *Critique*, for instance, are either demonstrable mistakes or affirmed by fiat.)

Furthermore, along these same lines, let me offer two additional naturalistic constraints (touched on in passing) that greatly strengthen the argument at stake. The first relies on the reasonable conjecture that the self begins, conceptually, so to say, as a mere grammatical surd (the use of which children learn to mimic uncomprehendingly), which then evolves as an artifactual construction, through iterated self-reference and maturation, as the site of awareness and self-awareness of all the forms of interior mental life, perception, agentive commitment, and the like. Somehow, Hume failed to grasp the fact that the *awareness* of the self's presence does not (and need not) involve any particular perception (except relationally, in being specifically aware of having a perception). The second notion depends on acknowledging that human cognition is not entirely autonomous or self-validating but rather depends on the existential conditions of human life itself—which, then, requires some form of reasoned interpretation of particular truth claims. Prominent among these conditions is the historicized nature of discursive judgment and belief: we become aware that, as historied creatures, we are forever subject to a benign form of skepticism that renders indubitable and apodictic cognition impossible.

Accordingly, presumptions or premises like Husserl's "a priori of history" and Kant's Copernican turn cannot rightly claim to acquire their respective forms of transcendental certainty. Historicity, I say, is an existential fact constraining the enlanguaged life of selves, and historicity and transcendentalism are incompatible. There's the key to pragmatism's advantage.

I foresee no additional barriers of comparable importance against the prospects of reinterpreting the whole of the Eurocentric tradition in naturalistic terms. I find the intuition entirely persuasive, but it's also true that the argument in its favor is surprisingly straightforward. The human is not less than unique for all that, nor less impressive in its distinction. Yet what I find even more intriguing is that the philosophies of the Asian world—which we must surely join with our own in some relatively near future—have also been exploring in their own ways other forms of naturalism's economy. Given the example of the history of the physical sciences, I see no reason to doubt that the acceptance of naturalism may require an enrichment of what we should mean by the *natural*, partly at least because it will also require an enrichment of what we should mean by the *physical*.

PART TWO

Five

Change and History

The essential feature of Aristotle's metaphysics lies in the skill with which he admits all forms of change or motion (*kinēsis* or, better, *energeia*) within the encompassing terms of invariant reality. Aristotle's was the first and most resilient reconciliation of change and changelessness the ancient Western world achieved. The work of the pre-Socratics, most notably Heraclitus and, later, Democritus, though all of his work is lost, and Plato's great effort (regarding the eternal Forms) have remained altogether baffling, from Aristotle's time to our own, so that they cannot really count as fully explicit alternatives. (Of course, they have inspired all sorts of alternatives.) More important is the intriguing and remarkable fact that history, although plainly a form of change, cannot be reduced to (that is, explicated, without significant remainder, in terms of) any other forms of change (those, say, that Aristotle admits). Not only that, but what we now mean by *history* had hardly dawned on the Western world until a philosophical review of the import of the French Revolution was seriously attempted. The significance of this single fact can hardly be exaggerated.

The conceptual link between theorizing about history and contingent history itself is probably unique in the chronicles of philosophy. That very fact bears in a most instructive way on the puzzles about legitimization aired in chapter 8 of *Historied Thought, Constructed World*.[1] I claimed there that the rationale for legitimation could not be satisfactorily supplied except in historicized terms and that this signified a certain profound contingency regarding what we should understand by *reason*. It now begins to appear that the theme of history is an unusually large one, not in any sense a mere adjustment (adding a species of change) to an otherwise more or less adequate account of reality. The modern form of the theory of history was hardly pursued in the ancient world. (You have only to read the few lines Aristotle spares history in his *Poetics*.) This is not to say that Thucydides' history was not a genuine history. But Thucydides' history was itself conceived in full accord with the common theme of classical philosophy: that is, the archic theme that change is ultimately constrained by the changeless order of nature.

Of course, if nature is a changeless order (nomologically fixed, for instance), then historicity is an illusion and history no more than a narrative of local change within that order. I associate historicity, however, with the invention of discursive (or enlanguaged) meaning—effectively, with the invention of the reflexive human self and hence, also, with the punctuated sequence of contemporaneities applied to the evolving praxis, technology, and conceptions caught up in local histories. In this sense, I treat the human person, uniquely, as existentially historied: confirmed—if capable of being confirmed at all—by the historied history of their own culture (which includes their own speculations about the invariant order of nature). No doubt there will be antinomies lurking here. But there is no compelling argument that affirms that nature or reality must be ordered in an invariant way; and the artifactual nature of the self (in effect, the obverse side of the invention of true language) is itself the most compelling evidence of the historicized career of the human being that we could possibly advance. If, for instance, it forces the stubborn antinomy of freedom and determinism upon us (or a stalemate), so be it. It is easily added to a well-known number of benign antinomies that belong to every account of nature. Its stalemate is no longer treated as fatal: we cannot expect more if we cannot escape the *petitio* of cognition. Let me add, however, that historicity, as an existential attribute of persons, introduces a benign form of skepticism and thereby precludes all the forms of apodicticity; hence, it is itself fatal if applied to any form of transcendentalism. There's an unforeseen confrontation that cannot be ignored.

What I am claiming is admittedly open to dispute. You may insist that the theme of history *was* discovered by the Greeks: that the difference between modern and ancient notions of history is *not* due to the appearance of a radically different notion of history (a sui generis form of change) but only to changes in our conception of the world in which histories and change obtain and, hence, that since the Greeks had in fact considered (and rejected) the conceptual viability of denying invariance, they may (or must) be said to have, at least implicitly, rejected the radical (modern) sort of history I am alluding to (the form of change featured in my *Historied Thought, Constructed World*, which has proved to be unavoidable).

I regard this last sort of resistance as a grand mistake, one that utterly obscures the distinctive features of human history. The Greeks did not theorize about history, because they did not consider the possibility that history was a sui generis form of change entirely unlike whatever forms of change might be found in physical nature.[2] They theorized instead about generic change (in nature), they subsumed history under that, and they admitted no essential distinction between mere (temporal) change and (Intentional) history. They supposed the chronicles of human life present us with information about change, about events that take time—in a sense of generic *change* suitably uniform for physical events and human affairs alike. Simply put, their view was that the temporal process (*whatever* its variety) was uniformly constrained, both epistemically and ontically, by the changeless order of things.

That is precisely what I mean to deny: both (a) the *necessary* link between history and changelessness and (b) Greek *indifference* to history's real structure in the analysis of change itself and, hence in the analysis of the nature of the things that change in the way of history. History, I say, is a sui generis form of change that qualifies only things of a certain nature apt for such change. The Greeks believed that temporal change (in effect, what they conveniently called *history* in certain accounts) applied in a uniform way to anything in (sublunar) nature—a fortiori, to humans. Much of the modern discussion of history agrees with this part of the Greek view: that is, with item (b) of the tally just offered. (I mean to replace it.) Plato's formula, in *Timaeus*, declares that "time is the moving image of eternity"; Aristotle's formula, in *Poetics*, holds that "poetry is more philosophical than history." Neither touches the essential issue.

The Greeks do not theorize about history, then, because they do not see the global significance of history as a conceptually distinctive kind of change affecting only distinctive kinds of entities (or the entire world because of that). They do not see that the analysis of history bears on the distinctive metaphysics of human existence and the corresponding features of human knowledge.

They theorize about human existence and knowledge all right—in terms of a generic relationship between (natural) change and changelessness—and *then* they admit history as a record of sequentially ordered changes from which, as in Thucydides, we may even glean political and ethical wisdom. *Kinēsis* and *energeia*, in Aristotle's sense, are certainly ample notions. But the heart of Aristotle's account—which is no different in this respect from that of any other ancient theorist—concedes that the exemplars of change may be freely or indifferently drawn from the inanimate and subhuman worlds; that, I say, betrays the Greek blindness to the distinction of history.

In any event, considering theorem (2.1) outlined in *Historied Thought, Constructed World*—the denial of the necessity of invariance[3]—I now safely affirm that

> (9.1) history does not presuppose—it precludes—a changeless order of reality.

Theorem (9.1) trivially recovers the large theme of (2.1) within the terms of reference that began to surface in *Historied Thought*. More provocatively, I claim (but cannot yet show) that, within the scope of (2.1),

> (9.2) history is a sui generis form of temporal change.

In this sense, the idea of history is perhaps the single greatest philosophical discovery of the nineteenth century. I shall come to my argument in a moment, but let me make clear its full intent. I mean to argue that

> (9.3) history is the sui generis (Intentional) structure of human existence and of whatever belongs intrinsically to the world of human culture;

hence, that, at the very least,

> (9.4) histories are real predicables.

Theorems (9.1)–(9.4) make a tidy set that captures the modern notion of history—what accounts for all the fundamental differences between the modern and the ancient treatments. *History*, as I use the term, signifies (predicatively) (a) a unified sequence of temporal change that (b) is paradigmatically manifested in human careers and also (only) in the careers of the artifacts of the human world, (c) is intrinsically meaningful (Intentional) in a sui generis way, and (d) is attributable to existing things without entailing any telos in the sequence of changes that it unites (qua history)—that is, without entailing a final cause somehow immanent and effective in the phases of an actual history. Chapter 7 of *Historied Thought* shows how the term *career* functions equivocally as a predicate and as a referring (or individuative) expression; we should not find it unreasonable to acknowledge, by the same equivocation, that

(9.5) a history is a kind of career.

Histories, we may say, are either predicables or individuated entities of some kind or both ([7.22]–[7.23]). Theorems (9.1)–(9.5) are noticeably modest, therefore, although they do indeed introduce a new theme—particularly (9.3). As they stand, except for (9.3), the set of theorems (9.2)–(9.5) hardly poses difficulties for Aristotle. It is of course (9.1) that radicalizes the rest of the set.

I have been inching forward here in a distinctly hesitant way. The obvious reason is that I take the philosophical significance of history to be of the grandest scope, to have been neglected or fundamentally misperceived by the entire Western world up to the period just preceding the French Revolution, and to have been inserted into the running account of my primer without adequate grounding. I *have* shown the indispensable role of historicity in resolving the puzzles of legitimation in (8.30), (8.31), and (8.34), and I regard that gain as vindicating the theorems so far introduced in this chapter. I have also shown that the doctrine of symbiosis leads, ineluctably, to the impossibility of disjoining the cultural and natural worlds—succinctly expressed in (8.35). That leads on (as I have shown) to historicizing thinking, in (8.26) and (8.32).

But I have certainly not prepared the ground (in any pertinent metaphysical sense) for the full use of such terms as *Intentional, cultural, human,* or *historicized*; theorem (9.3) might be (wrongly) suspected of having assumed that more was safely in place than has actually been worked out. Have patience, please. I should not want to give the impression, having opposed Aristotle on the archic issue, that I had (also) somehow justified (or thought I had justified) the newer issues I (now) take (9.3) to implicate (but not to have established). These are clearly meant to explicate theorems (8.34)–(8.35), which, in effect, identify the cultural world as inherently historicized. That is the radical theme I have in mind. I do invoke and use the pertinent terms, but I cannot claim to have defined the world they designate. (That is the liberty I must still redeem.)

In short, I have not yet directly addressed the question of the very nature of history's structure. But if it were confined to the temporal processes of the human or cultural world (or if it were at least paradigmatically first located there), and if thinking and cultural phenomena *are* in general Intentional ([8.37]–[8.39]), then the argument would also surely require that

(9.6) history has an Intentional structure.

This, too, cannot be more than a purely verbal formula as yet.

Intentionality, then, is the linchpin of the entire account. You cannot fail to see, however, that Intentionality is already implicated in the earlier discussions of reference and predication, of identity and individuation, of world and universe, of text and context, of symbiosis and social construction. All that has gone before leads inexorably (but conditionally) to the promissory note that is theorem (9.6).

We are poised, therefore, for a fresh beginning. I mean to explain the distinction of history in terms of Intentionality, and I radicalize its lesson by construing *history* in terms of historicity—that is, the thesis that thought is itself historied, subject to what I shall call *horizonal* constraint ([8.35]). Now, then, from an entirely different quarter—from my account of symbiosis, theorem (4.11), which, clearly, need not in principle be historicized—we cannot fail to see that combining symbiosis and historicity will yield a distinctive philosophy, one that could not have been available before the period of the French Revolution. I call it *historicism*, and define it simply as the doctrine that (or whatever doctrine) results from interpreting symbiosis in historicized terms.[4] Any attempt to recover invariance or cognitive privilege within its terms is bound to be self-contradictory ([8.31]–[8.41]). Ranke's historicism is self-contradictory—or else it is saved by God's benevolence in epistemic matters (for God is hardly confined in the horizonal way). Foucault's historicism (what Foucault means by "genealogy") is not self-contradictory at all (although it is relatively inexplicit philosophically).

As I see matters, the thread of thinking in Western philosophy that best captures what I am calling historicism runs from Fichte's Jena *Wissenschaftslehre* to Hegel's *Phenomenology*, from a mere post-Kantian symbiosis to Hegel's remarkable, fully historicized achievement. Foucault, in various stages of his own work, recovers what may (perhaps) be consistently redeemed of Kant's apriorism (the "historical a priori") within the larger terms of the "genealogy" of truth. In short, I am leading my primer's argument in the direction of a thoroughgoing and consistent historicism.

The schema is now very trim—and rather powerful. The trick is that I apply historicity to both constructivism and symbiosis. That yields (what I call) historicism. At the risk of an oversimplification, I should say that transcendentalism (a) logically precludes symbiosis, (b) accommodates constructivism (or constructionism), but (c) opposes historicity; as a result, (d) transcendentalism is a form of archism that treats the subject of (phenomenal) constructions as not itself constructed or historicized. My sense is that Kant *is* a transcendentalist in the first *Critique* and that readers of the third *Critique* attempt to escape condition (d)—Cassirer perhaps, Dilthey perhaps, certainly Habermas, possibly Putnam (at a considerable remove). They cannot succeed, I believe, if they are progressivists or teleologists (as Peirce and Habermas clearly are), if they hold that there is a uniquely correct account of the possibility of a would-be science or otherwise pertinent inquiry (as Kant and, in a sense, Husserl hold), if the categories of the understanding (and related structures) are not abstracted from empirical inquiry but are (somehow) presupposed by or innate in such inquiry (as Kant's letter to Herz affirms), or if our reflexive findings regarding the possibility of a would-be science *are*, when true, necessarily true, although synthetic (in Kant's sense). Externalism, as I say, precludes constructivism. Kant is hardly an externalist, therefore. But Kant interprets the epistemic pretensions of externalism within the terms of his own transcendentalism, and that is precisely what encourages externalists like Moore in their analytic reduction of Kant's own transcendentalism.

In what he calls *genealogy*, Foucault is (in my terms) committed to historicism. I should say that Hegel was as well—as a critic of Kant's transcendentalism. But if readers of Hegel insist that he is an absolute idealist (meaning by that that even his historicism is internal to a larger teleologism addressed to the universe), then I must part company with Hegel and charge him with a peculiar form of incoherence, since under no circumstances can a historicized or horizoned understanding confront the universe in a cognitively competent way. (That would be to reinstate something akin to transcendentalism.) But, then, I confess I find such a reading, offered as a serious reading of Hegel, quite preposterous.

I shall proceed by very small steps: it is much too easy to go astray. The history of the concept of *intentionality* may itself be flawed. It was introduced in modern times by Brentano, from a reading of its original use in medieval philosophy, and it was greatly improved by Husserl. That is the form in which it largely now survives: psychologized (by Brentano) and phenomenologized (by Husserl), with almost no attention to the collective dimension of cultural life or to history or historicity—themes which I have hinted at drawing together by a historied reading of Wittgenstein's *Lebensform*. In that form, it has nevertheless proved well-nigh ineliminable, despite Quine's notorious recommendation that it be eliminated from science and philosophy on the grounds that it is philosophically negligible as far as the descriptive and explanatory functions of the principal sciences are concerned. Quine was wrong, as the record shows, although I cannot stop to explain the sense of the intentional in Brentano's and Husserl's inquiries. (I will return to it, you may be sure. Quine himself never collected the telling evidence for his own claim.)

What, as I say, we need to notice about Brentano and Husserl is that *their* usage makes no explicit provision for forms of intentionality that cannot be analyzed in (or reduced to) whatever versions apply *first* to psychologically or phenomenologically apt agents (taken singly or as externally related aggregates). Brentano and Husserl treated the intentional (or the psychological or phenomenological) somewhat solipsistically,[5] although that was not their intention, in the sense that (a) Brentano defined the psychological, and Husserl the phenomenological, in terms of the cognitional aptitudes of individual agents (that is, subjects) without essential reference to any societally embedded, irreducibly collective structures and (b) characterized the societal dimension of thought and language as, in some inexplicit way, dependent on the prior cognizing powers of the merely psychological or phenomenological. The argument that follows is intended to support a very different—largely neglected—finding:

> (9.7) The Intentional cannot be reduced to or derived from (anything akin to Brentano's concept of) the intentional, construed solipsistically (in either psychologistic or methodological terms).

Put more provocatively,

> (9.8) the intentional, whether treated psychologically or phenomenologically, cannot be adequately analyzed without construing its own paradigmatic structure as Intentional (enlanguaged), emergent, and irreducible.

The upshot of theorem (9.8) is to disallow transcendental subjects—a fortiori, transcendental constructionism ([2.13]). This explains the sense in which the transcendentalism of Kant and Husserl, although they are hardly externalists, has been viewed congenially by analytic philosophers drawn to their particular forms of constructionism. (That is, always assuming that the transcendental may be empirically displaced.)

An important corollary for studies in animal psychology and artificial intelligence is tendered by the following theorem:

> (9.9) The intentional in nonhuman animals, machines, and the phenomena of physical nature is anthropomorphized: metaphoric, heuristic, or otherwise encumbered by the prior analysis of the human world.

By *anthropomorphized*, I mean no more than that feature of our discourse about *anything* characterized as a subject (anything that is *not* paradigmatically human in the way of cognition and Intentionality) that is described, defined, or explained in terms that ineliminably implicate the Intentional. Theorem (9.9) follows fairly obviously from (9.7)–(9.8). So we have made an easy and interesting gain. But that gain features the controversial possibilities of (9.3), which I acknowledged a moment ago.

Let me, therefore, now define the *Intentional* (*not* the intentional), as a frank term of art:

> (9.10) The Intentional is a collective predicable ascribed to individual human persons, selves, or subjects (in virtue of their culturally acquired competences) or to whatever artifacts or acts are conformably endowed (that is, Intentionally) by virtue of their use; hence, the Intentional implicates a model, or models, of rationality in agents, deeds, or artifacts, drawn from the collective life of their enabling society.

Language, for instance, is a *collective* practice, whereas speech is ascribable only (aggregatively) to individual speakers. The structure of meaningful speech implicates the rationality of speakers, and the rationality of speakers is a holist projection of legitimating norms drawn from the collective life of a historical society. (I return to the question of norms in "Values, Norms, and Agents," the final chapter of *Historied Thought*.) Against both the Francophone structuralists (Saussure, Greimas) and the Chomskyans,[6] we may say that, paradigmatically, in natural-language contexts, there can be no disjunction between the collective (or systematic) aspects of language and the individuated (improvisational and context-bound) aspects of speech (or the token instantiation of speech acts) or prioritizing of one over the other. Models of rationality are themselves historicized.[7]

Linguistic utterance is at once the activity of individual agents and of agents endowed with collectively qualified (linguistic) powers. By the *collective*, I mean (a) a predicable, (b) qualifying any of a range of phenomena that includes the mental, the psychological, the subjective, the linguistic, the lingual, the active, and the cultural, (c) that is not reducible to the solipsistic or to aggregative relations among solipsistic referents and (d) signifies the symbiosis between individual agents competent in terms of (b) and whatever social conditions account (by way of natural acquisition) for their actual competence. In effect, as we shall shortly see, the collective = the *lebensformlich*. I use the notion, therefore, Intentionally. I may perhaps add that I shall retire somewhat the use of the term *lebensformlich* in favor of the *Intentional*. I relied on the first chiefly because it was already familiar in the context of Wittgenstein's *Investigations*. But its use in a historicized spirit is clearly contrary to Wittgenstein's profoundly ahistoricist intuitions. Some, therefore, may have found my freewheeling use annoying. In any case, the *Intentional* is a term of art that has gained an advantage from association with the *lebensformlich*.

Saussure's distinction (or what passes for Saussure's distinction) between *langue* and *parole* is a disaster; Chomsky's hypothesis about hardwired "species-specific" grammars biologically prior to all forms of linguistic utterance is a completely arbitrary posit that has never been coherently explained. In particular, *if* "nomological necessity" proves a dubious concept, then the entire Chomskyan strategy is placed at risk for reasons more fundamental than any empirical (or a priori) local claims Chomsky might care to advance. Hence, if, as I recommend,

> (9.11) persons or selves are, inherently, linguistically competent humans,

then

> (9.12) persons or selves possess Intentional attributes that cannot be reduced to the biology, neurophysiology, or biologically emergent psychological capacities of the individual (primate) members of *Homo sapiens sapiens*.

From this, it follows that

> (9.13) persons or selves are not numerically identical with the members of *Homo sapiens*, since the first possess, whereas the second do not (unless derivatively), Intentional attributes.

Furthermore, recalling the promissory intention of (7.22)–(7.23), we may now begin to reclaim the earlier debt by affirming that

> (9.14) persons or selves are histories and consequently have Intentional natures, or, lacking natures, are Intentional careers,

and

> (9.15) persons or selves are not natural-kind entities, though they are natural entities ("natural artifacts"),

in that their natures do not accord (as such) with, or directly instantiate, *any* strict, universal, exceptionless law of nature (in particular, any law imputed to the "mere" things of the physical [or biological] world). None of this precludes, of course, our matching, as a matter of normal practice, individual persons and the individual members of *Homo sapiens*. They are related, but not by formal identity. (I address the question in "Mind and Culture," the next chapter.)

The import of all of (9.7)–(9.15) may now be conveniently summarized thus:

> (9.16) All and only persons or selves are subjects,

that is to say, (a) collectively enabled; (b) individually competent; (c) rational; and (d) apt for language, cognition, reflexive awareness, choice, and purposive action. We may now say that

> (9.17) subjects are self-interpreting texts,

and that the individuated artifacts of their cultural world (artworks, words and sentences, machines, preeminently) are also texts, since they possess Intentional properties but are not (normally) *subjects*.[8] Thus, to attribute expressive properties to Michelangelo's *Pietà* is hardly to construe that sculptural text as a person or as possessing a psychologically or cognitively competent nature, but the ascription does oblige us to answer the adequational question, which is normally ignored. Theorems (9.16)–(9.17) help to focus once again the peculiar failing of naturalisms that function only as physicalisms (as, say, with the Vienna Circle).

I conclude from this that Davidson (for one) is quite right to affirm something very close to this:

(9.18) There can be no strict or exceptionless (a fortiori, no deterministic) psychological or psychophysical laws.

However, I also believe Davidson is wrong to suppose that, nevertheless, the mental or psychological can be subsumed under universal physical laws, simply because either the mental or psychological can be reduced in principle in physicalist terms (which Davidson actually denies) or can be treated in terms restricted to a nonreductive physicalism or to a version of the supervenience theory (which he affirms).[9]

By these last terms, which are thought to yield equivalent truth-value assignments (speaking disjunctively in terms of the mental and the physical), Davidson advances the thesis (a) that the concerns of reductive and eliminative physicalisms (or similar doctrines) are to be treated agnostically; (b) that, nevertheless, it is modally (necessarily) true that there can be no change in the mental or psychological without a corresponding change in the physical; and, as a result, (c) that wherever a truth-value may be empirically assigned to reports about the mental or psychological (taken "token-wise"), *equivalent* truth-values can always be assigned their physical counterparts. Davidson's point is that we cannot rightly speak of correlations between the mental and the physical taken type-wise—that is, in such a way as to invite a search for genuine psychological laws. The reason, apparently, is that the mental is "intentional" whereas the physical is not. What Davidson means is that the mental implicates a model of rationality that is holist in the epistemic context of rationalization ("holist$_r$"), as introduced in *Historied Thought*, chapter 5. But *if* causal truths about the mental *can* be discerned token-wise, in individual cases, then there can be no a priori or principled grounds for ruling out psychophysical laws or type-wise generalizations. The supervenience theory is, therefore, completely arbitrary (in Davidson's presentation), for, *absent* identity, there is no reason (and none is ever offered) for believing the modal claim being advanced. No one, in fact, has ever shown its truth or plausibility; hence, one may even suspect that it is no more than a cryptic version (perhaps computationally motivated) of the very identity theory it is said to avoid (or replace). Furthermore, on substantive grounds, supervenience is a dubious doctrine, because it both (a) advances a modally necessary connection between the mental and the physical (or analogous relations in epistemic or moral or other contexts) and (b) is hardly as plausible, empirically, as the "many-many" principle Feigl formulated (but feared might be true).[10] The modal claim cannot be confirmed ([2.1]). The "many-many" principle holds, with respect to the mind/body problem, that, say, for any physical movement (a hand's waving), it is in principle possible that, in context, the movement may designate any of a variety of actions (signaling a turn in an automobile, pretending to signal thus, or acting the part of so signaling, among more elaborate possibilities); that, say, for any action (making a chess move), the action may, in context, obtain through or as a result of any of a variety of physical movements (a hand's pushing a pawn across a chessboard, a hand's writing a line of script [interpreted as a move], or a hand's motion flipping a switch on an electronic chessboard, among other more exotic possibilities); and that there is no algorithmic rule for determining or delimiting such linkages. (They are only Intentionally or interpretively related, not nomologically. They are more [loosely] paraphrastic than [strictly] translational.)

For the moment, consider the following four features of the Intentional (or cultural) drawn from what has already been said in (9.10): it is (a) inherently collective rather than solipsistic, (b) holist ($holist_r$) rather than extensional, (c) emergent rather than supervenient, and (d) historicized rather than naturalized. At the very least, no effort (in Quine's sense) to naturalize history and culture can claim to be conceptually responsible if it fails to come to terms with all four features mentioned. Davidson addresses only one: the sense in which the mental is "$holist_r$"—but that feature cannot stand on its own; it leads at once to the unsupported supposition that all $holist_r$ idioms are a mere *façon de parler*. Perhaps they are. But where is the argument?

This is a very large matter. I can afford only a few remarks. For one thing, when Davidson speaks of "types" and "tokens," he means nothing more than particular causal occasions not (yet) subsumed (or examined) under a causal law: mere "members" of an informal "set." (In the next chapter, I shall introduce an entirely different type/token idiom suited to cultural entities.) Second, when he speaks of "supervenience," he means a "dependency" (the term hearkens back to Moore's account of "natural" and "nonnatural" properties in the moral context, although Moore does not mention supervenience there). Hence, when he says the connection between the "mental" and the "physical" is a *necessary* one (in the direction of favoring the "dependency" of the mental on the physical), Davidson reads supervenience in terms that are non-Intentional, noncausal, and (logically) nonanalytic.

At this point, I need warn only that wherever the psychological cannot be satisfactorily characterized in non-Intentional terms (frankly, already at the level of human language and thought), supervenience cannot be a convincing doctrine, for, surely, the Intentional *cannot* be shown to be supervenient on the physical (in Davidson's sense). No view of the mental shorn of Intentional qualification can bear the weight of providing an analysis of the cultural world ([8.39]), and the Intentional is holistic (modeled in terms of rationality rather than extensionality) ([9.10]). In general, the relation between the mental (linguistically qualified) and the physical is and must be mediated by suitable interpretive schemes—what Rorty has dismissed as "*tertia*." The only other possibilities are the reductive and eliminative options that Davidson rejects.

In the same spirit, we may say that *if*, indeed, the psychological is Intentional ([8.37]), then (on the argument being favored, which is still largely inexplicit),

(9.19) the psychological cannot be "naturalized" (in Quine's sense),

which is a theorem that catches up the gist of (8.25) *and* at least part of the gist of Davidson's own claim about the mental (being not nomological as such)—*if* (also) supervenience fails. (Of course, Davidson does not believe supervenience fails.) So the complexities of our topic cannot be hidden, although I must concede again that what I have so far constructed still looks a little like a house of cards.

For related reasons, I take Popper to be right in holding that

(9.20) there are no laws of history,

if he means, by law, exceptionless or modally necessary (nomological) universals ranging over causal and cognate relations, regardless of whether we ever discern or can confirm them. But, against Popper, this is not to say that laws or lawlike regularities need be, or ever are, necessary *de re* ([2.6]) or exceptionlessly universal.[11] At the present time, there is a decided retreat from the once-favored dictum that the true laws of nature *are* nomologically (or ontically) necessary—contextless and exceptionless. Insistence along such lines now tends to be viewed as idealized (not strictly confirmable), possibly distorted for imagined explanatory gains, or relativized to assumptions that are hardly necessary themselves. Theorems (9.13)–(9.20), therefore, invite an entirely new set of decidedly empirical questions. As long as analytic philosophies of science (notably, in Hempel) persuaded general philosophy to regard the high constraint of nomological necessity, the bare admission of

Intentional complexities was judged to threaten a fatal departure from the canon of rational science. The general failing of positivism and the unity of science has changed our perception of all that.

Davidson's "anomalous monism," for instance, is a theory that could only have surfaced in the historical space between the decline of the nomological (the nomologically necessary), the extensional, and the physicalistic and the increased accommodation of all forms of intentionality. I am not saying a realist reading of the "laws" of nature is impossible, but its usual modal presumption is now surely problematic. The decline in nomological modality varies inversely with the star of Intentionality—and, with that, the rising need for an altered vision of what a science *is*. (For the reverse reason, the rise of interest in the supervenience doctrine is directly proportional to the decline in the fortunes of nomological necessity.)

The single most important and most strategic theorem in this process of conceptual change, bringing the attack on modal necessity ([2.1]) to bear on the archic reading of nomologicality, affirms that

> (9.21) every science, being a human construction, is itself a human science and, as a consequence, is Intentional in structure.[12]

Theorem (9.21) is the result of applying (9.10) to the terms of symbiosis, once the strictest determinism proves difficult or impossible to defend. The consequence is a deep suspicion regarding the theory of scientific law and explanation, even where (as with van Fraassen and Cartwright) new hopes spring up about the prospects for reforming the unity of science. The consequence for scientific realism, when historicity is permitted to affect law and explanation, is the clear loss of a methodological core and a clear drift toward relativism (as in Kuhn and Feyerabend). We simply do not know what restoration is possible now, but, in the interim, Intentionality cannot be put back in the genie's bottle. I say, therefore, that

> (9.22) science and philosophy are inherently folk-theoretic undertakings that function only top-down.[13]

It is reasonably clear that a theorem like (9.22) falls within the competence of any philosophical strategy that (a) features the *lebensformlich*, or (b) favors the post-Kantian reading of symbiosis, or (c) construes either of these in historicized terms. What I have been pursuing, therefore, is the enormous advantage (for such strategies) of the developing philosophical uneasiness about the universality reading of nomologicality, the last of the great archic themes of Western thought. That is what it means to have brought all my arguments within the ambit of Intentionality. (The structure of intentionality needs still to be made explicit.)

I do not say that (9.22) is itself a (true) archic claim. I say that it is the best philosophical bet any of us can now foresee. It is of course very widely opposed in current analytic philosophy. (It is part of the motivation for invoking supervenience.) There is, however, no (known) compelling refutation of (9.22) or even a strong alternative at the present time. That in itself I take to be a distinctly telling sign of certain errant tendencies in analytic philosophy—for instance, in eliminationism (or eliminative physicalism), which simply insists (without any argument that I have been able to find) that Quine's (and Sellars's related) rejection of the bare (ontic or realist) eligibility of any and all forms of intentionality in bona fide scientific or philosophical inquiries is unqualifiedly compelling.[14]

Eliminationism (which, of course, is itself a posit intended to subvert the supposed relevance and adequacy of any folk-theoretic [Intentional] thesis within the sciences) depends for whatever appeal it has on the canonical standing of strong nomologicality. This is as true in Churchland as it is in Quine and Sellars—and signifies a deficiency of argument for the same reasons. I should add here that by the *nomological*—taken in the strongest sense—I mean (a) that exceptionless attribute of the structure of the real world, (b) in virtue of which changes in the world are, rightly, causally explained, which (c) signifies that the changes that thus occur in nature occur deterministically.

Reichenbach allows nomological necessity only as an idealization, essentially on grounds of the impossibility of empirical confirmation (and its inapplicability at the microtheoretical levels of investigation). He replaces causal necessity with a carefully crafted notion of high probabilities of suitably regulated diversity.[15] The *nomological* may, consistently, be interpreted in various weakened ways.

By the canonical picture of science, I understand any theory, for instance the unity-of-science program, that holds that first-order description and explanation of what exists, as well as prediction and technological control, are pursued and formulated in nomological terms at least, as just explained.[16] (Science itself is inevitably more informal regarding the nomological and the complexity of what exists or functions causally, as we shall see. Effectively, any inquiry reasonably committed to the predictive, explanatory, and technological objectives of the canon, with or without the canon's modal presumptions, may claim to be a piece of science. There cannot be a strict canon once we yield on modal necessity. Also, one cannot then fail to ponder the parallel fates of nomologicality and supervenience in the larger context of naturalism.)

In any case, if we treat the expressions *folk-theoretic* and *top-down* as epithets signifying that worlds are texts (4.14), because the symbiosis and holism within which we function are themselves Intentional, then it follows that

(9.23) the entire universe is interpreted, textual, historicized, constructed—in a word (or two), Intentionally labile.

The closest anticipation of (9.23) may be found in Peirce's doctrine: namely, that the triadic structure of (what Peirce calls) signs "perfuse" the (symbiotized) universe. What Peirce calls triadic I call Intentional: whatever, predicatively, is (a) collective, (b) culturally emergent, and (c) interpretively significant ([8.32]–[8.35]). (I depart from Peirce in rejecting a "cosmic mind" and its implications for a weakened reading of symbiosis.)

I have permitted certain intriguing clues to surface as a consequence of having introduced the notions of historicity and Intentionality, but I have not yet analyzed them directly or essentially in metaphysical terms or justified any inference from them except conditionally. I have, therefore, put the entire argument at risk. (I may as well concede that this is the consequence of the strategy of this primer.)

I have, however, given a partial analysis of history in a tally a short while ago, (a)–(d), explicating the sense of (9.4), of *history* used predicatively. (I ask you to have another look at that.) We have only to add to that tally a further item—(e) the qualification of (9.6) (Intentionality)—to round out the general lines of a fair account. That is certainly tidy, although it obviously adds to the baggage of an already heavily burdened conditional argument. I don't believe it adds any untoward difficulty, however; it brings together difficulties already broached, and it actually facilitates their (joint) resolution.

I can make this quite clear through the following combination of brief summary and slight advance: (a) history = Intentionally ordered change ([9.6]); (b) the Intentional = the cultural (8.38); (c) symbiotized worlds are texted, socially constructed, and intrinsically interpretable ([4.9]–[4.16], [9.23]); and (d) constative discourse interprets our (interpretable) worlds ([4.15]). Treat this as a refinement of the earlier tally at (9.4)—hence, now to include item (e). Given that, it is no more than a terminological adjustment to add to the former tally, the one begun at (9.4), as item (f):

(9.24) Interpretability = intensionality.

I now draw—from, say, (8.34) and (8.45)–(8.47), which concern the historicizing of truth claims and legitimation—as item (g) of the same tally:

(9.25) Intentionality = interpretability.

Theorem (9.25) is, in a way, the middle term for everything that is locally at stake: all the pertinent linkages involving Intentionality, intentionality, intensionality, history, historicity, interpretation, horizonality, contextedness, symbiosis, and intransparency, at least.

Theorems (9.24) and (9.25) are extraordinarily useful. They serve to isolate the essential puzzle confronting every serious attempt to construe science in a thoroughly extensional way, along two lines: first, by admitting the realism of Intentionality itself (the world of human culture); second, by admitting the ontic and epistemic dependence of scientific objectivity on the conditions of reflexive human understanding (symbiosis). These are just the themes standardly neglected in analytic philosophy.

A bit of explication may be helpful. The term *intensional* is standardly used in philosophical contexts in two ways: (a) intensional = nonextensional, in that sense in which (in as generous or restricted a reading of *logical* as one wishes) logical (syntactic, formal, truth-functional) relations between terms, between sentences, between arguments are said not to behave extensionally (with regard to the assignment of truth-values)—as in accord with a logic in which, for instance, love, not designating a transitive relationship, is said to behave nonextensionally, or intensionally; and (b) intensions ≠ extensions, in that sense in which (in as generous or restricted a reading of *semantic* as one wishes) the semantic function (meaning, significance, semiotic import, or the like) of linguistic utterances (or of what may be abstracted as proper parts of such utterances, terms, sentences, arguments) yields the intension of such utterances, whereas what such utterances (or terms or sentences) designate, denote, refer to, or otherwise are rightly (perhaps veridically) applied to—particular things in the actual world or in possible worlds—form the extension of those utterances. (For instance, these or those actual horses form part of the extension of the term *horse*, whereas "equine quadruped" is the dictionary rendering of its intension.)

There are of course famous questions about the relation of intensions and extensions in sense (b).[17] Plainly, an archic reading (Aristotle's) would claim a regular, even rule-like connection between intensions and extensions, but *any* drift in the direction of the an-archic (for instance, the post-Kantian) will (as Putnam saw) call into question the supposed regularity championed by the archist. I have no need to pursue these matters here. The main thing is this:

(9.26) The Intentional is inherently intensional.

Theorem (9.26) shows at a stroke, therefore, why the (solipsistic) accounts of intentionality offered by Brentano and Husserl cannot but fail. The reason is this:

(9.27) The intentional, although conceptually distinct from the intensional, is paradigmatically intensional.

Brentano and Husserl both understand the intentional to designate—irreducibly—the puzzling relationship of aboutness. For the moment, I merely wish to emphasize that sentences used to describe inten*t*ional phenomena exhibit a characteristically complex (indissoluble) structure, which is or appears to be irreducible to noninten*t*ional structures such that those sentences behave logically in inten*s*ional ways (in accord with the first sense of *intensional* given above—for instance, "Tom has an irrational fear of horses" and "Tom believes that horses are dangerous and unpredictable" are sentences that, on a not-unreasonable theory, are *both* inten*t*ionally structured and behave inten*s*ionally—*and* behave intensionally *because* they are intentional. Thus, "Tom believes that horses are dangerous" may be true whether "Horses are dangerous" is true or false and whether there *are* horses or not. There you have a paradigm of the nonextensional.) The charm of this way of analyzing the phenomena before us is simply that it does not require taking sides, as between Brentano and Husserl, and postpones the need for a ramified analysis.

By *aboutness*, then, I mean no more than intentionality: that aspect of thought or speech in virtue of which a mental state is (as we say) directed to, intends (in the original medieval sense), is about (in the sense Brentano sketches) some (intentional) referent or content said to be internal to, inseparable from, significantly informing *that* particular state. Whenever, in linguistic and cultural contexts, we attribute aboutness to phenomena that are neither mental nor linguistic in any obvious sense (for instance, the lingual *tristesse* of the Swan Queen in Tchaikovsky's ballet), we automatically construe the intentional as Intentional (in the sense introduced). (I take the slippage to be philosophically unavoidable but usually not acknowledged.)

On this reading, the inten*t*ional is inten*s*ional for several reasons: (a) because the aboutness structure (in the mind, in the sentences appropriately affirming that structure in the mind, or, by a reasonable enlargement, affirming such structures in artworks or in the cultural world at large) is not reducible or detachable in any way that would permit an extensional treatment of *that* structure (in the first sense of *extensional* given above); (b) because the aboutness structure is inherently what it is, in virtue of the significant or interpretable content it encompasses—in effect, the meaning of the grammatical accusative of that structure—hence, what is specified intensionally, whether it is or can be specified extensionally (in the second sense of *extensional* given above); and (c) because aboutness may be assigned a realist function. Quine concurs in this: it is the reason he outlaws intentionality.

There are of course other important considerations: for instance, what sort of reality should be accorded the intentional structures of mental states (or artworks) thus characterized, or whether the sentential representation of the intentional would be best managed by an objectual idiom or by a propositional idiom. (For instance, should we say that Tom fears horses [possibly, nonexistent horses] or that Tom is in a mental state such that the [internal] intentional content of that indivisible [monadic] state is accurately represented by a proposition like "Horses are dangerous and unpredictable"?)

Granting the relevance of this much, I claim, confirms (9.27) and (9.9) (if propositional modeling is the better or at least a viable policy, as I recommend)—and, now, confirms the methodologically more pointed theorems (9.21) and (9.22). For, surely,

> (9.28) symbiosis entails the Intentional structure of our worlds and (mythically, our) universe, which is itself entailed by (9.21).

Hence, also,

> (9.29) the admission of the real world cannot preclude the (semiotized) agents (selves) by which it is constituted as intelligible and interpretable;

(9.30) the real world (or worlds) cannot fail to include real Inten*t*ional—inten*s*ionally qualified inten*t*ional—structures;

and

(9.31) the intentional and the intensional obtain only as abstracted within the space of the Intentional.

I take (9.31) to confirm (9.21) and (9.22) in a straightforward way. I also thereby obviate the need to raise (as with Meinong) the question of the reality or existence or "subsistence" of the "objects" (or internal accusatives) of intentional discourse, although I certainly do not preclude the possibility that intentional discourse may be addressed to what is actual.

If, now, you consider the discussion in chapter 3 of *Historied Thought, Constructed World* of reference and predication, you will not fail to see that the present review of the varieties of intentionality was adumbrated there. For, on the analysis of the inherent informality of reference and "real generals," I was led to the conclusion that the structure of effective discourse is (on its constative side) "entrenched" in the structure of the consensual practices of its enabling *Lebensform*. But that *is* what I take *Intentionality* to signify (on its discursive side):

(9.32) Intentionality = the consensual (collective) structure of our *Lebensform* (or something akin).

Theorem (9.32) bears in a profound way on the analysis of selves, but I must postpone the reckoning. I take the liberty, however, of focusing a little more sharply the meaning of the collective; that is, that feature designated by predicables that (a) are Intentional, (b) describe societal structures of meaning and signification as such, (c) apply to the aptitudes (behavior and thought) acquired by persons and their artifacts in virtue of enculturation, (d) are not reducible to the precultural aptitudes of *Homo sapiens*, and (e) are expressible (Intentionally) in rule-like ways, as in traditions, institutions, or practices.

I come, finally, to the bearing of this gathering argument on the matter of history. If history is indeed Intentional ([9.6]), and if history is a sui generis form of temporal change ([9.2]), then

(9.33) the time of history ≠ mere physical time.

Theorem (9.33) has a special importance. It distinguishes between "physical" and "historical" time, it's true, but, more than that, it poses the entire question of the conceptual relationship between the (real) worlds of (physical) nature and (human) culture. *That* bears directly on the metaphysics of history and Intentionality, and that is precisely what was missing in the conditional liberties I had taken (earlier) in airing a number of issues involving the analysis of change. It's what I had in mind, in fact, in challenging Aristotle's short account of history—as well as the classic unity-of-science doctrine.

You will remember that I argued that it was not enough to *add* a further *species* of change to the schema Aristotle offered. What was needed was a reinterpretation of how, *metaphysically*, the structure of history affects the analysis of change in *both* the natural and cultural worlds. Of course, Aristotle's archism precluded any adjustment of the sort I had in mind. But once one subscribes to (2.1)—the denial that the world requires invariant structures—and symbiosis, it becomes quite implausible (perhaps even impossible) to treat history in ways that do not ramify through the entire universe of discourse. I regard this intuition as the fruit of the "cunning" of philosophy itself: for the puzzle of history in the modern sense was first perceived to have been posed only at the time of (or a little before) the advent of the French Revolution—just in time, so to say, to permit history to be interpreted in Kantian terms and (consequently) to permit Kantian constructivism to be historicized (in the symbiotized post-Kantian manner that links Hegel and Nietzsche and Gadamer and Foucault).[18]

In short, the significance of (9.33) is barely adumbrated in the distinction regarding time; theorem (9.33) is, after all, little more than a special case of the following theorem:

> (9.34) Cultural, but not physical, entities intrinsically possess Intentionality, but both the physical and cultural worlds are, as the cultural artifacts they are, jointly affected Intentionally.

Obviously, if (9.33) and (9.34) and similar theorems are admitted, then

> (9.35) Intentionality affects the conceptual space of physical and cultural worlds in distinct ways; in ways that need not be alethically, epistemically, or ontically uniform; but in ways (nevertheless) that confirm their belonging to the same universe of discourse.

I need to make explicit the general theorem that links (9.4), which admits histories as real predicables, to the interlocking relations holding among history, Intentionality, interpretability, and the like (collected in the tally given a moment ago regarding the varieties of intentionality)—following (9.26) and (9.27). That theorem affirms that

> (9.36) Intentionality and interpretability are real attributes of existing (discursible) things.

In a more than merely terminological sense—but in that sense at least—I should add:

> (9.37) all and only cultural entities and phenomena intrinsically possess Intentionality.[19]

But then, speaking loosely, everything discursible may be treated Intentionally (for instance, Olduvai Gorge).

Theorem (9.37) brings before us all the puzzles that have been collecting in this chapter. For one, if cultural entities are real—in that they exist—then the theory of such entities will have to accord with the analysis of "exists" offered in chapter 6 of *Historied Thought, Constructed World* (where Peirce's treatment of Secondness served as the decisive clue). For another, that same analysis will have to come to terms with an argument (also in that chapter) involving theorems (6.16)–(6.21), to the effect that what exists has a material nature: hence, in a way that precludes what (rather baldly) is usually termed *Cartesian dualism*. (The standard interpretation of Cartesian dualism holds that Descartes subscribed to it, but some interpreters claim that he did not.)[20]

By *Cartesian dualism*, I understand a metaphysical doctrine that claims that there are two (or at least two) disjunctive *materiae* in terms of which (a) particular existing things are "composed" and (b) they may be individuated (*res cogitans* and *res extensa*, in Descartes). I take that thesis to be unsatisfactory, because (a) it permits no compositional account of the nature of human persons to be more than merely conjunctive (as involving the different *materiae*), and (b) it makes a conceptual mystery of causal interaction between the parts of any such composition. Psychophysical interaction (just the issue that exercised Davidson so strenuously) proves utterly unmanageable on the dualist reading. I may perhaps add another weakness to this tally, namely, (c) whatever, in the disjunctive sense intended, is an individual thing composed (in part) of *res cogitans* (or a similar immaterial *materia*: a mind, say) appears not to accord with the strong sense of "exists" that I have already given. (Possibly, then, the dualist sense produces difficulties for individuation.)

In any event, in agreement with the arguments of chapter 7 of *Historied Thought, Constructed World*—those involving (7.33) and (7.34), particularly—a metaphysics must be supplied that eludes the Scylla and Charybdis of Cartesian dualism and reductive physicalism. The decisive strategy is as elegant as it is simple. In speaking of Aristotle's metaphysics, I was led to remark that Aristotle introduces *hyle* as an explanatory principle ("matter" or "stuff," that from which particular things are composed or formed in the way of individuation), in spite of the facts that individuation does not and cannot depend on *hyle* criterially and *hyle* itself is unformed and lacks determinate properties. If it were otherwise, *hyle* would itself be individuated, and then the need to account for the individuation of particular things would apply to *hyle* as well. We should be caught in a vicious regress. (Clearly, *materia* ≠ *hyle*.)

What this shows is that, although the question of the ultimate *composition* of particular things generates the classic metaphysical concern regarding the choice between dualism and physicalism and the like, that question is really a dummy question. In short,

> (9.38) questions of metaphysical composition are nothing but questions about the stock of predicables validly attributed to particular things but cast in individuative terms.

That is, *nothing* of a predicable nature can be reserved for "that" of which particular things are composed (*hyle*)—over and above what we do in fact predicate of *them* (or better, what, qua real, they instantiate). Alternatively,

> (9.39) the composition of particulars or individuated things cannot be detailed except in terms of ulterior particulars (things already predicatively qualified).

There need not be, in principle, any "infimate" particulars, but there also cannot be any viable sense in which what makes a particular thing intelligible[21]—(a) its being identifiable and reidentifiable as the particular it is, and (b) its possessing the attributes it possesses—is itself a distinct kind of composition.

By (metaphysical) composition, I mean, therefore, that feature of particular (material) things in virtue of which they may be construed entirely as the parts of larger integral particulars ("wholes") or may themselves be analyzable exhaustively into constituent particular "parts." Hence,

> (9.40) *composition* is, in some measure, predicatively redundant; predication itself is not a form of composition, but existent things may have basic or essential properties.

Aristotle's strategy, therefore, is either completely vacuous or completely misguided. Or, the compositional reading of Cartesian dualism is either a thesis about the conceptual relationship (in particular the reducibility relationship) between "extended" attributes and "cognitional" attributes or else it is similarly misguided. (One of the strangest doctrines in all of philosophy, I may add, is the theory of "bare particulars," which rightly perceived that composition cannot violate [9.40] but insisted nevertheless that "number" was a matter independent of descriptive predication.[22] My point, here, is to make reference to the findings of chapter 3 of *Historied Thought, Constructed World*, to the effect that reference and predication are indissoluble parts of the same constative activity. Furthermore, I do not assume that, in the real world, the part/whole relation necessarily takes a single or univocal form.)

It follows from all this that such philosophical choices as that between dualism and physicalism are really judgments about the reducibility or irreducibility of certain sets of predicables to others. The eliminationist, for instance, believes that there *are* no mental properties: whatever is predicatively real is physical only. The reductionist insists that the mental is just (a subset of) the physical. The dualist claims that the mental is as real as the physical but altogether different from it.

A number of extremely important matters hang on these distinctions. For one thing, to advocate materialism (*not* physicalism), as I have pointed out in (6.17), is not to theorize about the nature of (the compositional) *hyle* that existent things (somehow) distributively share, but to make provision for their actually being *existent*. According to the argument of chapter 6 of *Historied Thought*, only "material" things effectively exist, in that (as we now understand matters) only things that possess physical properties at least (the minimal run of material properties) can exert the required Secondness to count as existent. (I find this implicitly acknowledged in the use of what are called mass nouns [*water, coal*] and count nouns [*horse, a piece of coal*].)

But this does not mean that existent things possess physical properties only. That *is* the argument of eliminationism and reductive physicalism, but it is plainly a non sequitur. More than that, it is a non sequitur probably born of the dualist's own primitive notion—namely, that whatever is not (merely) physical must be altogether other than the physical. The dualist had invented a purely conjunctive form of composition, and a great many physicalists (for instance, Churchland and Parfit) have, in opposing dualism, somehow supposed that if dualism fails, then the conjunctive composition of the mental and the physical fails, and (as a consequence) the mental must be either illusory or nothing but the physical.[23] The motivation for construing the choice between physicalism and dualism as disjunctive and pretty nearly exhaustive (with whatever accommodations may be thought necessary regarding functionalism and the like) is straightforward enough: deny intentionality and Intentionality in all their forms, and there will then appear to be no other choices. It's the admission of the Intentional as real and *emergent* in a sui generis way that makes it possible to entertain other accounts of the mental (for instance, the theory favored in this primer). My own guess is that the mental is (more than likely) a run of related modes of functioning of primordial matter, evolving biochemically, not a distinctive *materia* of its own. The decisive feature of the mental, evolving as far as reflexive awareness and conscious agency are concerned, is that its forms of functionality are complexly incarnated as the functionality of living organs or (say) the provisional habitudes of biochemical processes enabling specialized muscles and joints to function spontaneously, when prompted by adequate cues (as with a baseball pitcher's perfecting various kinds of pitches).

The fact is, the particular *way* in which particular things are made numerically one is not touched on at all by attending to what is merely predicable of them. Here, I recommend a terminological convenience: I speak of the unicity of a thing in speaking of what makes it (conceptually) individuatable, hence denumerable, fit for numerical identity, reidentifiable, apt for reference—in terms, say, of its nature, its career, its history, its composition, or another mode of integral organization. I speak also of the unity of a thing in speaking of that aspect of it which, in virtue of being individuated, is thereupon effectively assigned *number and nature* and distinctive forms of functionality. (Individuation and identity are quite different issues.)

Things need not be completely unified in order to exhibit sufficient unity to allow for unicity. (This returns us to my use of the terms *unicity* and *unity* in chapter 7 of *Historied Thought*, where they were introduced intuitively.) Artworks, for example, may be individuated and reidentified, but it hardly follows that the unity artworks exhibit is of the same sort that mere physical objects exhibit. If, in fact, cultural entities exhibit Intentionality but physical objects do not ([9.34]), then (I am prepared to claim)

> (9.41) cultural and physical entities cannot but satisfy different criteria of unicity and unity.

Aristotle's *hyle* disappoints us with regard to both unicity and unity; so does the dualist's reading of Descartes's *res cogitans* and *res extensa*. (Methodologically, the latter have nothing to do with individuation; they concern only predicables.)

We must go further. We must acknowledge the following theorem as well:

> (9.42) Real predicables that are not physical (or not merely physical) and also not dualistic may still be material if they are *complex* with respect to the physical or if the physical may be *abstracted* from them.

By *complex* (in the way of predicables), I mean, drawing from (9.42), that feature of an Intentional predicable in virtue of which (a) a physical predicable may be *abstracted* from it; (b) it itself is (in some as-yet-undefined sense) indissolubly embedded in, or inseparable from, such an abstractable predicable; or (c) it itself is not reducible to such abstractable and embedding predicables.

I say that a predicable is abstracted from another if (a) the latter is complex or (b) it is such that the predicate that designates it analytically entails the predicate that designates the abstracted predicable. For instance, *square* analytically entails *rectangular*, and *being red* analytically entails *being colored*, but neither of the first members of the pairs mentioned is complex in any organic way. By contrast, I say that

> (9.43) the Intentional—a fortiori, the mental, the cultural, the historical, the textual—is a complex predicable.

Because the Intentional is complex, the physical may be *abstracted* from it—but *not* merely analytically. For instance, the significance or signification of a painting is usually grounded in its physical properties; its Intentional properties are distinctly complex in a way that defies dualism. I shall say, provisionally, that the physical may be metaphysically abstracted from the Intentional (a) because the Intentional is complex, (b) because it falls among the real properties of existent things, and (c) because it is in some sense indissolubly embedded, as such, in the physical.[24] (I shall, in this chapter, later introduce *incarnate* as a term of art to characterize this embeddedness of the Intentional and to account for metaphysical abstraction.)

What is most curious about complex predicables is the bare fact that there are real predicables that are complex. In this sense, physical properties are not merely abstracted from complex properties; they are also in their own right predicable as real properties of existing things. That is part of what it means to say that they may be *metaphysically* abstracted. (Call that item (d) of the tally just given.) Since, however, Intentional properties are (by that tally) not reducible to the physical, since the physical is real, *and* since there are real entities that are qualified in terms only of the physical properties they manifest, I say that both physical and Intentional properties are basic (in a sense remotely akin to Strawson's thesis—except that Strawson employs the term for individuatable entities, whereas I restrict it to predicables). Properties are basic, then, in that (a) they are possessed by existent entities, (b) they are themselves metaphysically abstractable from complex properties, or (c) they are properties from which other properties are metaphysically abstractable, and (d) the entities that satisfy (a) form kinds of things that play, as such, a relatively important role in science or the explanation of nature (physical objects, organisms, human persons). (Normally, then, basic properties will be specified in accord with some theory or other of the natures or sortal natures of classifiable entities. Remember, natures need not be constant [(7.6), (7.14), (7.29)].) I take the term *basic* to signify nothing in the way of a single compositional account of "all there is" or an endorsement of the unity program or a fixed hierarchy of some sort of the compositional levels of what is real. Nevertheless, properties possessed must be adequated to the nature of the particulars that possess them.

Now, the pretty thing is that although, speaking thus, pure (as distinct from physical) geometric properties are (certainly) able to be abstracted from both physical and Intentional properties, no distinct entities (pure geometric objects) *exist* in virtue of which such properties (the pure geometric ones) are basic. For the moment, I content myself with merely mentioning that the complexity of Intentional properties accounts for the sui generis form in which they and the entities they qualify may be said to have emerged.[25] Clearly, the biological is also said to have emerged in the course of natural events from what was once lifelessly physical—without being complex in the precise sense assigned the Intentional. Hence, there cannot be a uniform sense of emergence in which whatever is real has emerged from whatever we suppose to have been the original state of the world. (I shall shortly pursue this matter more pointedly. In any case, I restrict the pure geometric to the predicative, as I have already done with numbers.) The pure arithmetic and geometric are, then, predicative distinctions only: there are no existent entities answering to them; hence, also, they are not basic or emergent in any sense. The biological *is* emergent, because there *are* existent organisms, but biological properties need not be complex (although, in speaking of the informational, this may be disputed). The cultural *is* emergent, since there are cultural entities (persons and artworks), but cultural emergence takes a sui generis form distinct from the biological, since Intentional (cultural, culturally formed mental) predicables are complex. We speak of numbers and pure or ideal geometric forms as objects or references, by a *façon de parler*, but we cannot rightly say that they exist. Nevertheless, there are indeed "things" that belong to physical geometry (space itself, for instance) as well as quantities of things that exhibit material properties. But when we speak of pure arithmetic and pure geometry, we hypostasize symbolically the putatively referent sites of the functional uses of a language suited to other uses. Selves and artworks are not (as culturally emergent "things") basic particulars in Strawson's sense, but physical and Intentional properties may well be basic in determining what exists in our macroscopic world. Causality, for instance, as Reichenbach surmises, may be empirically restricted to our macroscopic world; it may not parse satisfactorily in the subatomic and quantum worlds.

By this general strategy, I avoid (for one thing) the fatal weakness of Strawson's metaphysics—namely, that, contrary to his own plan, different "basic particulars" (as he terms persons and bodies) *may* occupy the same place in the world at the same time, without being "parts" of one another. I think there is nothing troublesome about admitting that what Strawson calls basic particulars *may* occupy the same place—and *may* be parts of one another. (Strawson's account would regard that as contradictory. But Strawson himself cannot escape that consequence.) The point of interest is that

> (9.44) existent entities that possess complex properties are *emergent* with respect to entities that possess metaphysically abstractable properties (*basic* properties) as the existent entities they are.

The biological and the (merely) physical are metaphysically abstractable from the cultural or Intentional, and the Intentional is distinctly complex. *All* are basic and therefore enter into the explanation of different kinds of emergent phenomena. (For the moment, the term *embedded*, mentioned in clarifying (9.43), is no more than a place marker.)

Theorem (9.44) helps to focus the essential problem of the reductionism that the unity-of-science program has favored, for it is entirely possible that (a) primitive biological entities (may) be construed as emergent relative to the inanimate physical world without ever being Intentional in the mental way (a fortiori, without being complex) and that (b) the conditions (a fortiori, the explanation) of the emergence of the biological and of the cultural are utterly different from one another.

Intuitively, the reason is this: persons (and other cultural entities) are numerically distinct from the entities in which they are indissolubly embedded, but that seems not to be true of all biological entities. They emerge *from* the inanimate world, as more complexly organized or differentiated, but they are not numerically distinct from other (numerically distinct) physical entities in the same way in which cultural entities are distinguished. (They may not be embedded in other distinct entities.) In particular, cultural entities are inherently Intentional, whereas physical and biological entities are not or need not be; furthermore, cultural entities are complex in virtue of possessing Intentional properties. By contrast, primitive biological entities are not thought to be complex in the same way. Biological properties are often thought to be such that physical properties are analytically entailed in them; alternatively, the biological is often thought to be an emergent mode of functioning of the physical itself. (In the most optimistic physicalist accounts, the biological will be reduced to the physical. There is no reason to think that that could ever happen to the Intentional.) By any of these strategies, the biological would not be said to be pertinently *complex*.[26] (There are other possibilities, of course—the matter is still open. For instance, questions may be raised about informational properties and, of course, mental properties. I shall touch on these in a moment, but the picture is hardly tidy.)

I leave the matter of what is *analytic* (as in speaking of entailment) undefined criterially: any working distinction, however informal, will suit my purpose. Quine may have been right to reject a principled distinction between the *analytic* and the *synthetic*, but, in natural-language contexts, usage will always support some effective, if informal, distinction between the two. In any case, my argument requires only that, say, the mental does not, in any ordinary sense, analytically entail the physical, although the physical may (as I say) be metaphysically abstracted from it. I shall, therefore, treat the mental (where it is Intentionally qualified) as *complex*, in accord with (9.43). That alone completely obviates dualism and also, perhaps, supplies the ground for rejecting all the forms of mere physicalism.

Certainly, to characterize the *mental* (that is, the linguistically or lingually informed mental) as complex (in the sense given) is to go utterly contrary to the canonical view. That explains why it is usually supposed that the mental must be treated *either* reductively, eliminatively, dualistically, functionally, or heuristically. But there is absolutely no reason to oppose thinking that the mental is (a) biologically emergent and may (b) *either* be complex in the manner of the Intentional (the culturally emergent) or (perhaps) not complex in that sense but still inseparable from the physical in the manner of the biological—even if, there, it is anthropomorphically modeled: emergent within the natural, non-Intentional world. I am persuaded that the mental *is* equivocal in this way: in fact, mental phenomena that are complex in the way of the Intentional are, in our world, (c) emergent with respect to the *mental* taken in the biological sense. (Nor do I rule out the possibility that the mental in the first sense may also be emergent with respect to the electronic or something of the sort, as in artificial-intelligence theory, or that it simply does not require such a dependence. It may, for instance, be, as a *façon de parler*, entirely anthropomorphized [9.9].)

At the present time, both in the biological and cognitive sciences, reference is made to informational properties (not actually discursive)—in a way that clearly signifies that they are thought to be real. Obviously, they could always be employed heuristically—as no more than anthropomorphized (as defined in this chapter). But it is not clear, for instance, whether, in speaking of DNA codes, one means that the informational properties of the code, ascribed to living cells, are meant only as a stopgap measure against the time when those would-be properties will have been successfully reduced to biochemical properties analyzable in purely causal terms (whatever that may entail) or whether informational properties are complex properties in a sense similar to that just explained. (I strongly doubt that the latter is the right alternative.)

I do not find the matter examined in any straightforward or careful way among the philosophers (and scientists) who regularly invoke the informational. But this I can say: either the near-ubiquitous use of the informational jargon is a newfangled version of dualism or it plainly lacks any metaphysical backing at the present time. (The same is true of the functional, which I introduced in speaking of the biological and mental when confined to biological resources[27]—that is, by way of a [heuristic] redescription in purposive or otherwise anthropomorphized terms.) Noticeably, in speaking of computers and systems of artificial intelligence, the issue is regularly finessed.

If informational properties were real properties, then, of course, the biological might be said to anticipate the Intentional.[28] (I doubt that they are independent properties. They are more likely to be anthropomorphized ascriptions made of the biological.) It would be an extraordinary discovery and would raise an important question about the possible reducibility of the Intentional to the biological (the genetic, for instance), even though the biological itself may not be reducible to the purely physical. I believe that this *is* the gist of Chomsky's thesis regarding universal grammar. The essential barrier to this entire line of reasoning is simply that it looks as if the informational is in all cases anthropomorphized—possibly an Intentional redescription of the causal—although the biological may indeed (also) be irreducible to the terms of the physically inanimate. (It is difficult to see what else it could be.)

I therefore venture the following theorem:

(9.45) Informational predicates may form a subset of Intentional predicates, whether or not they designate (and, in designating, describe) real properties.

By *informational*, read as a term of art, I shall understand those predicables that include teleological, functional, feedback, purposive, and even certain cognitional predicables applied to phenomena that do not as such invoke aptitudes at the conscious level. Think, for instance, of plants "seeking" nutrients, or biochemical "habits" that form in a baseball pitcher's arm in perfecting the throw of a ball. Broadly speaking, I shall regard informational properties equivocally, either (a) as heuristic designations of real properties that they do not, in so designating, literally describe, thus modeled (anthropomorphically) on the Intentional, or (b) as a subset of Intentional properties, whether ascribed in a realist or heuristic way. One obvious benefit of admitting such an accommodation is that it helps to explain how it is that (certain) norms and values may be treated naturalistically—for instance, homeostatic norms. Here, naturalizing the normative is simply exposing the anthromorphized or "redescriptive" use of an Intentional idiom.[29] But that alone hardly shows that the normative can always be naturalized.

Nothing substantive follows from *this* terminological decision, except perhaps to draw attention to the arbitrariness of supposing that there is a clear sense in which the lawlike features of the informational can already be assigned (as in Dretske), or in which the functional and teleological can (with assurance) be completely naturalized (as in Millikan). I take these to be premature, rather unguarded pronouncements. *If* informational properties are taken to be causally efficacious, then, of course, the metaphysical analysis of such properties cannot be forever postponed. (I do see that the usual use of the *informational* in the cognitive sciences is meant to outflank any usage like that of my own *Intentional*.) The obvious critical question asks whether the informational is itself reducible to, or entirely derivable from, the Intentional, or whether the Intentional features of the informational can be assigned without implicating specific *lebensformlich* or agentive processes as the complex resource from which it is itself abstracted. Informational properties assigned to brain and body appear to be anthropomorphized and not autonomously ascribed.

I venture a further thought. *If* the intentional cannot be disjoined from the rational[30]—meaning, say, that the concept of intentionality bears, paradigmatically, on beliefs and desires and their role in motivating action—then, if the informational designates the abstracted content of (Intentional) mental states, the informational may be construed as either anthropomorphized in terms of the intentional (as in supposing that a rabbit reacts to the perceptually internalized representation of the silhouette of a predatory bird) or as a mere *façon de parler* (where *information processing* is no more than an idiom for modeling the functional aptness of the rabbit's biochemical response to perceptual pickup not first characterized in intentional terms). J. J. Gibson has observed that, characteristically, rabbits respond too quickly to the perceived would-be danger to have acted on the basis of first processing the supposed internal representation. *If,* however, we *introduce* the intentional as designating no more than the (informational or functional) content of the appropriate neurophysiological process where that process bypasses, or is disjoined from, the supposed processing of the first sort, then (and only then) will the intentional be able to be naturalized biochemically. But it is not clear that the second model is not already parasitic on the first. I confess I cannot see how the intentional (or the informational content of the intentional) can be detached from the model of rationally ordered mental states, unless it is already known that reductionism or eliminativism obtains. For *what* is intentional or informational in the second instance? In this sense, I regard the prospects for naturalizing intentionality as profoundly empirical but also as ineluctably question begging.

The *Intentional* remains, as far as I can see, the pivotal notion. I introduced it in chapter 8 of *Historied Thought, Constructed World*, equating it with the *cultural*, but, for purposes of clarity, I should offer a more explicit sense of what the principal manifestations (the would-be extension) of the Intentional include. Try this:

> (9.46) Intentionality signifies—paradigmatically—the constative ascribability of any of a family of predicables of an intrinsically interpretive sort: namely, those regarding linguistic or lingual meaning, significance, signification, intensions, signs, symbols, reference, representations, expressions, rhetorical functions, semiotic import, rule-like regularities, purposes, habits, propositional attitudes, intentions, and the like, capable of being manifested biochemically or agentively in functionally apt ways.[31]

The principal exemplars are all linguistic or lingual. By *lingual*, I mean (once again) those predicables ascribed in the cultural world that, although not themselves explicitly linguistic, presuppose linguistic aptitude and, because of such aptitude, acquire, by *lebensformlich* extension, functions analogous to those assigned the explicitly linguistic. For example, the performance of "La Marseillaise" in France after the defeat of the Nazis may have signified the liberation of France and may have referred to that liberation. Michelangelo's *Pietà* represents events in the death of Jesus and expresses feelings bearing on the original mourning of that death. Signing a check normally intends the act of disbursing one's funds and, again normally, performatively utters that disbursing. There is no need for greater precision at this point, except to emphasize that speaking in this way is not in the least figurative. (It has a realist import—at the level of what is culturally emergent.) Thus, perception, cognitively construed, is also lingual, inasmuch as it includes a propositional ingredient. (It is that ingredient that is anthropomorphically predicated of nonlinguistic animals.)

What still remains unanswered, what haunts this entire account, is the ontic question of the relationship between (physical) nature and (human) culture, between what is non-Intentional and what is Intentional. That was the question I had in mind in beginning, in this chapter, with theorems (9.2)–(9.4) regarding the metaphysics of history. The ensuing argument appeared to lead away from that original question. But now, curiously, we are actually closer to resolving both matters—and at a single stroke.

I had broached the issue of historical change and historical time as a way of exposing the peculiar limitation and distortion of Aristotle's theory of change—and, by association, the entire later history of Western philosophy and science that, down to our own day, has (largely in accord with some form of the archic vision) construed historical change and historical time as (no more than) narrative devices used in *redescribing* physical change and physical time in terms of our contingent interests. I should say that such conceptions mean to "naturalize" history, along the same lines I drew attention to in those well-known efforts (from Quine on) to naturalize epistemology (for instance, with regard to history, in Popper and Danto).[32] (By *redescribing*—introduced here as a term of art—I mean heuristically recasting predicates that function naturalistically, in Intentional terms, so that they appear to be complex although they are not.)

I have given the problem of history a strenuous form by characterizing histories as real, in (9.4), and as intrinsically Intentional, in (9.6). Admitting that much, I was obliged (complicitously) to insist on the distinction between the physical and the cultural and, at the same time, to begin to provide an account of the sense in which both *are real* ([9.41] and [9.42]). That is where we are at the moment—and that is where we were at the start of the present chapter. I think it would not be amiss, therefore, to return to the topic of historical time and change in order to claim (or reclaim) the clue by which to resolve the several questions that have remained unanswered.

Certainly, although physical time (the time of physical change) cannot be the same as historical time (the time of human history), it would be preposterous to suppose that the two were utterly disjoint. Surely, we may insist that

(9.47) historical time is inseparable from physical time.[33]

The "two" cannot be identical, because one manifests Intentional features, whereas, ex hypothesi, the other does not.

You can already see that the resolution of the puzzle mirrors the mind/body problem that has bedeviled dualism and physicalism, but it offers a much larger canvas: it now turns out that the mind/body problem (admitting the equivocation on the *mental* mentioned earlier) is little more than a special case of the culture/nature problem and that, as a consequence, the usual options tendered by dualists and reductive physicalists alike are too narrowly construed. That was the point, you remember, of introducing the puzzle regarding informational properties. (Informational properties may be regarded as biochemical analogues of solipsistic [and habituated] properties.)

Still, I need to cast the argument in even more inclusive terms, for the resolution of both problems (mind/body and culture/nature) concerns itself not merely with the issues of unity and unicity already broached (and with what must be the nonconjunctive [nondualistic] composition of the mental and the cultural) but also with reconciling any would-be answer to either issue with the independent resolution of a further paradox that infects every speculation about the nature of the real world and our place in it. (We are close to the end of our labor; it will take a little more patience.)

The paradox in question is generated by the following two intuitions, neither of which we are prepared to reject: (a) that there must have been a time (in the physical world) when the world of human culture did not exist, and yet (b) that what we posit as that physical world must in some measure be an artifact of our symbiotized culture. To insist on both truths is what it means, roughly, to acknowledge the indissoluble union of realist and idealist conceptions of the world ([5.4]). The physical world, we say, *is* independent of the posits of our science, but its independence is itself a scientific posit ([7.41]). (This is very close to Thomas Kuhn's conjecture, except that Kuhn does not subscribe to symbiosis.) The first collects what, in first-order discourse, we hold true (holistically) of the things of the natural world; the second legitimates, in second-order discourse, what we affirm (distributively) in the first. And, of course, first- and second-order discourse are inseparable ([1.1]–[1.4]). Consequently, there need be no self-defeating paradox there. There is indeed a puzzle, but it resolves itself rather nicely on our admitting the symbiosis of world and language ([4.8]–[4.9]), the distinction and interconnection between external and internal relations ([4.11]), and the further distinction between the constative and mythic uses of language ([8.17]).

I claim that, within the terms of an an-archic vision, there is no plausible way of resolving the (last) paradox without subscribing to the doctrines just mentioned; I also regard the problem as the mate of the paradox of legitimation discussed in chapter 8 of *Historied Thought, Constructed World* (as the "antinomy of history"). In fact, taken together, the two puzzles offer the strongest possible rationalization for abandoning the philosophical programs this primer opposes. I shall call them *antinomies* for obvious reasons: the antinomy of legitimation (chapter 8) and the antinomy of ontic priority (this chapter). I insist, then, that

> (9.48) no philosophy is valid that fails to resolve the antinomies of legitimation (or history) and of ontic priority.[34]

My thought is that the two provide entirely fair criteria for assessing minimal philosophical success.

Now, if we allow ourselves to come this far, we begin to glimpse in a fresh way the gathering force of the entire argument applied both retrospectively and prospectively. Retrospectively, it falls out at once that

> (9.49) physicalisms of every sort are untenable summaries of the whole of nature

and

> (9.50) all naturalizing philosophies (not naturalism itself) fail.

The reason is simply that

> (9.51) the antinomies of legitimation and ontic priority are, for naturalizing strategies, inadmissible, or, if admitted, intractable.

This *is* the reason constative discourse is folk-theoretic (9.22). But it is also the reason theorem (9.22) imposes no restriction on science or inquiry of any kind—except, of course, to debar archic presumptions. If true, this would be a windfall, for it would confirm that

> (9.52) an-archic philosophy can absorb any or all of the resources of archic philosophies, except for presumptions of self-evidence, privilege, strict invariance, and the like.

To put the same point prospectively—that is, in a way meant to resolve middle-range problems that require a favorable answer to our antinomies—I recommend (for the local question of historical time and change that has been before us through this entire chapter) that we adopt the following characterization:

> (9.53) Time is an attribute or predicable—in particular, an adverbial qualification of any of a range of predicables implicating change or persistence among things that exist.

Theorem (9.53) accords rather well with Aristotle's view of time (time as the "measure" of motion or change) as well as with contemporary views that acknowledge the difficulty of rendering its adverbial feature in accord with the resources of first-order logic. For instance, to say that Brutus stabbed Caesar is *not* to say what, at least in Davidson's rendering, comes out as "(∃ x) (Stabbing x & At-time-t x)": no, the temporal structure is clearly an indissoluble part of (an adverbial qualification of) what it is to be the continuous event or career that is a stabbing. Nothing about the extensional behavior of predicates regimented in accord with a prior syntactic policy tells us anything about the internal structure of the predicables they are said to designate. In general, I should say that

(9.54) predicates ≠ predicables,

for one cannot say for certain how we should construe *time* as a predicable, from a study of the entrenched conveniences of a certain logical treatment of temporal predicates. The matter is no longer pressing, of course, if we abandon extensionality as a realistic ideal for the analysis of all natural-language discourse.

A much more important matter lies elsewhere. I suggest that we shall find it both economical and philosophically promising to concede that

(9.55) historical time is *incarnate* in physical time.

What I mean by *incarnate* is this: A predicable is incarnate in another predicable if (a) it is real; (b) qua real, it is complex—that is, Intentional and indissolubly bound to some real physical predicable (metaphysically abstractable from it); (c) it is emergent with respect to that (incarnating) predicable—that is, not reducible to, or explicable solely in terms of, the causal role of its incarnating predicables; and (d) it is basic. Hence,

(9.56) cultural (or Intentional) attributes are incarnate attributes.[35]

This is a very strong proposal. It affords, I think, the *only* reasonable general way of construing historical time and change as real, as Intentional, as coherent, and as in accord with an an-archic view of the world. It steers a middle course between reductive physicalisms and irresponsible dualisms—with respect both to the mind/body problem and the culture/nature problem. It is in this sense a fair specimen of a very large family of cognate solutions, including those bearing on the ontic relationship between persons and organisms belonging to *Homo sapiens sapiens*, actions and physical movements, machines and (assembled) materials, speech and (uttered) sounds, paintings and (applied) pigments, cathedrals and ordered stones, mental states and neurophysiological states, history and physical change, and the like. I claim that, granting whatever logical differences may arise among these and similar pairings, they all require the admission of the *incarnating* relationship: that particulars of the relevant kinds (all and only "culturally emergent") exhibit their characteristic unity and unicity through and only through their possessing incarnated (Intentional) natures.[36] The solution, therefore, dares to invite comparison with Aristotle's account of *ousiai* and, as I say, is more directly responsive to questions of individuation and numerical identity than is Aristotle's solution.

I cannot pursue these developing lines of inquiry here. What I want to make clear, however, is that *incarnation* is only one among an array of possible modes of organizing the intrinsic, integral, and entire structure of entities of different kinds, with regard to their being individuatable and reidentifiable as the particular entities they are. (I shall, in the next chapter, introduce the term *embodied* as a term of art answering, in individuative terms, to what *incarnate* signifies predicatively.)

It is, I think, worth noting that, in current analytic philosophy, although the problems of numerical identity and reidentifiability have received considerable attention, much less attention has been given to what it is *to be* a particular thing and *how* particular things may be individuated if their natures are not (sortally) constant. The solution I have barely sketched is intended to meet both of those questions. The general lines of the argument have been laid out chiefly in chapter 7 of *Historied Thought*, but we now have a strengthened way of construing the *integrity* of particular things of certain kinds (cultural entities) that is congruent with what has already been said about reference and predication and individuation and identity.

For convenience and clarity, let me add a few terminological distinctions. By *integrity* I mean that feature of particular things in virtue of which their unity and unicity are (a) accounted for ontically and (b) preserved epistemically. I have also said, in clarifying the notion of *incarnation*, that incarnate (Intentional) predicables are emergent with respect to their incarnating predicables. I cannot at the moment do full justice to what I mean by *emergent*, because, in the usage I intend, emergence (like causality) cannot be applied to predicables alone—that is, without attention to the (existent) entities that exhibit them—and I have not yet introduced (I shall in the next chapter) an account of cultural entities that, as emergent, possess (suitable) emergent properties. But what I can say is this: in speaking of *cultural emergence*, I mean to speak only of things of certain kinds (and their properties) that appear in the same world in which physical and biological entities appear—that is, entities uniformly subject to all the resources of constative discourse.

Of these, I say that cultural or Intentional entities (possessing incarnate properties) are emergent, in that (a) their existence and generation cannot be accounted for, causally or in any other way, in terms of the existence and the causal (or other generative) powers of the (non-Intentional) physical entities with respect to which they are emergent (selves and artworks, preeminently); and (b) their existence and generation *can* be accounted for, causally (or in other ways), in terms of other entities and *their* causal (or other generative) powers, if and only if they belong to the same emergent level of reality. Intentional entities are culturally emergent, then, in that the mode of their emergence and generation is specific to *that level of reality* at which their integrity is and only is preserved, namely, the cultural. (I take the claim, of course, to be a bet, in the sense already explained.) Furthermore, its admission captures what is essentially meant in speaking of the *hermeneutic circle*. "Level of reality," of course, borrows, parasitically, the standard usage of the unity-of-science movement but rejects its presumption. All Intentional predicables belong to the same level of reality in being Intentional, for descriptive and explanatory purposes, and they belong to a "higher" level of reality than physical predicables, in the sense that physical predicables may be metaphysically abstracted from them. (These are meant as indicative distinctions fitted to a promising science.)

These categories are not terribly instructive as they stand. The reason, of course, is that we need to know just what the nature of cultural entities is in order to know specifically what mode of emergence is pertinent to their integrity and what peculiarities such entities actually exhibit, with respect to reference, predication, individuation, identity, and historical change. For example, I hold that a Dürer print (*Melancholia I*, say) exists in multiple token prints, each with its own local history (or career), and that it may acquire new Intentional properties as a result of its interpretive history, which may (over historical time) actually generate properties (in it) that could not have emerged at some earlier time. (Think, for instance, of the standard Freudian treatment of *Hamlet*.)

There is extraordinarily little discussion of such complications in analytic philosophy, and what there is in continental European philosophy (in

Gadamer, for instance) is, however intuitively instructive, almost indifferent to the resolution of the kind of question I am raising. I am persuaded that the enormous complexities of the cultural world have been pretty well ignored in analytic philosophy, simply because the archic temperament (as well as a strong externalism) has held sway for centuries and because, within its terms, the analysis of physical objects has long been deemed exemplary for everything that exists and is real. (All that is doubtful now.)

Even without a full account of cultural emergence, certain very strong findings may be drawn from what has already been said. The key notion regarding *emergence* is that of the limited explanatory power (of whatever kind of explanation we admit) of theories whose *explanantia* are restricted to whatever *level* proves sufficient for the description and explanation of (the non-Intentional) phenomena that form the (incarnating) ground relative to which emergent phenomena are acknowledged to be emergent. If so, then the sanguine hopes of the positivists and those who have supported the various forms of the unity-of-science program are doomed, for

(9.57) the sciences of the cultural world cannot, in principle, be modeled epistemically or methodologically on any science whose own epistemic model admits truth claims addressed only to a non-Intentional world; hence, they cannot be modeled on the physical sciences—as, in the unity-of-science program, they are.

There cannot be a unified science (in terms that permit every "higher-level" phenomenon to be explained in terms of the phenomena of the "next-lower" level and the *bridge laws* linking the two levels) if culturally emergent phenomena are genuine. (Bridge laws are rules of translation linking the phenomena of two distinct "levels" of reality by way of the nomological regularities at each level [or at least at the "lower" level]. The very admission of such laws requires adherence to something close to the unity program.) There are (I admit) more optimistic conceptions of emergence than mine (Bunge's view, for instance) that attempts to restore methodological unity in the unity theorist's way, but I know of none that admits anything like the strong sense in which I have characterized cultural phenomena as Intentional.[37] I am prepared, therefore, to construe (9.57) conditionally. (I pursue this question in the next chapter of this volume, "Mind and Culture," and in the last chapter of *Historied Thought*, "Values, Norms, and Agents.")

Still, *if*, on the account so far given, the world is indeed texted ([4.14]), if all conceptual schemes are indeed interpretive ([5.2]), if everything that may be said to exist or be real is indeed a social construction ([7.33], [9.21]), then it cannot fail to follow that

> (9.58) all the sciences are sciences of the human world,

in two senses: (a) in that what they examine includes phenomena that inherently possess Intentional attributes or natures and (b) in that whatever attributes or natures *are* ascribed the things the sciences examine (even things that lack Intentional natures) are ascribed *only* on the strength of what is ascribed in accord with (a). If one accepts (9.58) in this way, then (I say) one is committed to a folk-theoretic conception of science and knowledge in general—and, in particular, committed to the view that all that is real is socially constructed ([7.33]).[38] (I return to the folk-theoretic in the next chapter.)

The irony remains that, *if* the opponents of the an-archic vision are right in thinking that the model of methodological rigor they favor cannot be effectively fitted to cultural phenomena construed in Intentional terms but wrong in thinking that the Intentional can be reduced to the non-Intentional (or eliminated altogether), then, on the argument adopted, there is no viable model of science to be had, or else the opponents of the an-archic vision have seriously misrepresented the successes of the sciences and the rigor they actually require. It may even be true, for instance, that those successes have been gained by means of a careful simplification and idealization of the complexities of the Intentional; if so, that very fact would confirm (rather than disconfirm) the need for a new picture of methodological rigor. In short,

> (9.59) the physical or natural sciences are themselves inquiries *abstracted from and within* the scope of the human sciences,

and

> (9.60) whatever fundamental explanatory role the physical sciences may rightly claim *is* rightly claimed within and only within the competence of the human sciences.

This is because, of course, symbiosis requires the presence and input of inquiring selves.

The sense of *abstraction* in theorem (9.59) is clearly the conceptual counterpart of metaphysical abstraction ([9.44]). The nerve of the entire argument initiated in chapter 8 of *Historied Thought, Constructed World* and continued here, focused for instance at theorem (9.6), is plainly this: that

(9.61) real Intentionality cannot be naturalized in causal terms borrowed from the natural sciences.

I have made something of a campaign out of exposing the inadequacy of that reductive form of naturalism that (following Quine's) is commonly called naturalizing. But I urge you not to lose sight of the fact that I have also been trying to steer a course between naturalism, on the one hand, and transcendentalism, on the other. My thought is that human subjects, apt in the construction of the phenomenal world, are themselves part of that construction, as a consequence of symbiosis and historicity. (That was the point of the antinomies already mentioned). If, now, you consider the import of such strong theorems as (9.23), (9.32), and (9.37), which link these themes to the Intentionality of the cultural world and to the existence of selves or subjects, you cannot fail to see that we are entitled to draw the analogue of (9.61) for transcendentalism as well: namely,

(9.62) real Intentionality precludes transcendentalism, since the cultural world is committed, existentially, to historicity.

I must add two abbreviated thoughts to hint at how much more is needed to yield a proper account of history. For one thing, *history* is not a "cognitive *faculty*" (in Kant's sense), but a "*functionality* of mind," a mode of thinking or reasoning (undoubtedly in part innate), not attributable to languageless primates, intelligent animals, or human infants. Chimpanzees and house cats, for instance, master inferential skills in solving puzzles; they "think" but have no (propositional) "thoughts." This vouchsafes perceptual, as distinct from discursive, concepts. There must be an affinity between the two if infants are ever to learn language. For a second, "mind" and "mental" are "materialist" distinctions that signify specialized composites of ultimate physical matter suited, say, to the formation of stars, living tissue, light, water, thinking, and the like. (Aristotle wasn't far off here.) Ultimate "physical matter" is our modern hyle and the specialized composites of matter I name "material."

Six

Mind and Culture

It is a common and important failing of contemporary analytic philosophy to have misperceived, or neglected to explore with care, the conceptual relationship between the mental and the cultural. This may in part explain the perennial prominence of Descartes, Hume, and Kant, for there is hardly a suggestion among these extraordinary philosophers regarding the irreducibly social, cultural, historied, collective, artifactually constituted, and variable nature of the mental. These are, of course, the three most influential early modern theorists examined again and again by later Western philosophy, even after the advent of Darwinian evolution, which fails in its own way.

Beyond admitting the dialectical play of the profession, it would not be unfair to claim that philosophy has remained remarkably loyal to the thesis that the best account of the distinctly human and mental is bound to be cast in terms of whatever proves, individually and aggregatively, to be the endogenous, species-specific endowment of *Homo sapiens*—perhaps, then, even what may be called (however misleadingly) the solipsistic resources of our biological nature. By the *solipsistic*, I mean, here, harmlessly enough, that feature of any theory of cognizing competence that accounts for all relevant aptitudes in terms of an initial genetic, precultural, effectively innate endowment and whatever improved skills its exercise among similarly autonomous and similarly endowed creatures may yield.

I take this to be a fundamental mistake. It obscures, if it does not altogether deny, the simple truth that

> (10.1) the attributes of cultural life among humans, particularly those that bear on our discursive and cognitive powers, cannot

be adequately described or explained in terms of any mere innate biological or biologically generated mental or psychological endowment.

Theorem (10.1) is a philosophical bet directed against both naturalizers (Quine, for instance) and transcendentalists (like Kant). No doubt the gifted members of *Homo sapiens* do become persons, but it would be an obvious non sequitur to infer from that that it must also be true that the Intentional (or linguistically encultured) must be analyzable or explicable in terms of the biological alone or primarily. There's a grand mystery there, as well as an equivocation. The bet cuts both ways, challenging reductionists and antireductionists alike. Persons emerge initially, originally, by internalizing the linguistic and lingual aptitudes of their encompassing society (their *Lebensform*, let us say). *Homo sapiens* has the capacity for *that*, but I shall argue that the change is both ontic and emergent—a change, however, that entails no biological loss and no transformative (enculturing) gain that is not grounded in the biological.[1] (There's the mystery.) If you grant the point, then, of course, mere physicalism becomes impossible to defend; we would have no way of guessing at the historied possibilities of our conceptual and mental powers.

The telltale clue to the puzzle lies in the plain fact that the restriction of the initial resources of the human psyche—in Descartes, Hume, and Kant—never entitles us to disregard the enabling societal powers of our cultural world.[2] No, the latter is taken to be as rich and as complex as you please. It's only its ultimate provenance that is misconstrued. This accounts, for instance, for Locke's marvelously candid puzzlement at finding it impossible to discern in the sensory impressions that strike his tabula rasa a sufficient clue as to the source of the idea of *substance* (a certain je ne sais quoi) that he realized he could not do without.

The (solipsistic) impoverishment is barely perceived, it seems: for nothing that should be acknowledged in the cultural milieu is actually denied admittance. It's only its complex source that is misread. Whatever we discern in ourselves and the world is accounted for, epistemically, in terms restricted to the mind's endogenous endowment feeding (as cleverly as you please) on the incoming data of the surrounding human world. It wrongly supposes that the subjective can be analyzed entirely in terms of a biological (or nativist) model of the mental. By *endogenous*, I mean any putatively original source of the mental, the cognitive, the subjective, the rational that is species specific and characteristic of its aggregated primate members or otherwise native to human *subjects* (taken singly or in some sense prior to social or cultural learning or exchange). The endogenous, accordingly, ranges over naturalistic and nonnaturalistic claims—for instance, in Chomsky's as well as Kant's and Husserl's accounts.

In Locke and Hume, language is essentially a convenience for recording the prior work of pristine thought; in Kant, the intelligible structures of the world are imputed to it as the gift of a nativism ample enough for what we claim to discern; in Descartes, God, very much offstage, is taken to have endowed native human reason with whatever one requires for understanding the various parts of Creation. In analytic philosophy, there is almost no concern to secure a sense of any societal adequation between the native powers of *Homo sapiens* and what their exercise is said to reveal about the environing world or the cognizing self itself. You will find the exemplary evidence in Fodor's nativist analysis of concepts, which is a kind of Cartesian—even Platonist—recovery of Locke's failed project.[3] The admission of the actuality of the collective life of a human society is the decisive nemesis of all reductive physicalisms (notably: the physicalist reading of the unity-of-science program), although a materialist qualification of the mental, I should say, is unavoidable.

I must say also, however, that I favor two very different pictures of the human person. They are not semantically or theoretically equivalent, but I mean them to be extensionally comparable, as holistic paraphrases. In one model, persons are transforms of human primates; that accommodates the general lines of Darwin's evolutionary theory, though Darwin himself failed to grasp the uniqueness of the transformation (that is, that it exceeds the limits of biological and biochemical processes). The other model holds that persons are incarnate in the members of *Homo sapiens* (paralleling the sense in which words and sentences are incarnate in selected sounds and marks but are not (or at least need not be treated as) identical with them. Much the same is true, and for similar reasons, in speaking of paintings as incarnate in canvases selectively covered in paint: that accommodates the sui generis powers of Intentional or discursively qualified production that mark the insuperable difference between physical and enlanguaged cultural processes and sciences. The two models afford different readings of what we mean by those forms of emergence that require the entwinement of the biological and the discursively cultural. I find it useful to endorse both models, though I concede that the "incarnating" model suits speech and painting better than the "transformative" model. I may add that I first formulated my own account by analogy with the creation of artworks and only later in terms of evolutionary theory. But both draw on natural affinities I shouldn't want to lose, in view of the continued attraction of physicalism. The transformative model takes note of the ontological complexity of the unity-of-science program.

My point is this: on pain of paradox or incoherence,

> (10.2) the cognizing powers of the mind and the cognized features of the world must be *adequated* to one another (a consequence of symbiosis).

Analytic philosophy largely ignores this issue—which, in their separate ways, Descartes, Hume, and Kant ingeniously address. By *adequation* (both ontic and epistemic), I mean the specific matching (*equilibration*) between the conceptual powers we impute to ourselves (apt for discerning whatever may be discerned in the world) and whatever (we claim) we actually discern.

The formula is not as vacuous as it may appear, although it is quite true that different criteria of adequation are bound to be internal to the theories this or that particular philosophy favors. (It is precisely this menagerie of ideas that needs to be collected and displayed.) Thus, already in Plato, the theory of Forms (and the coordinate doctrine of the soul's recollection) "adequates" our actual discourse about justice and the good life and the conceptual resources said to make that possible.

Predictably, the more powerful the role of the Forms, the more impoverished the reckoning. Similarly, in Kant, once the phenomenal world is seen to be spatially and temporally organized, the cognizing mind (Kant thinks) must be natively endowed with the capacity to impose spatial and temporal structures onto inchoate experience and then to discern those same structures in the experienced world thus constituted. Neither in Plato nor in Kant, however, do *these* resources of collective cultural life play an executive role (*as such*) in the formation of our cognitive competence.

The telltale reason seems to be this: the cognitive powers of the human self or subject are assigned, in effect, to account for (or match) whatever we take to be the content of our beliefs and knowledge. Even where some genesis or biography is offered that apparently acknowledges the priority of epistemic considerations, as in Descartes's *Discourse* and Locke's *Essay*, the labor seems no more than an artful way of abstractly matching once again an account of what native, innate, mental powers are deemed adequate enough to account for science and intelligence. Admitting a few notable eighteenth-century exceptions, there is hardly a serious attempt, until we reach the post-Kantian idealists, to think of our conceptual and cognitive resources in terms of the particular culture and historied world in which our developing aptitudes first take form. The essential point may be put this way: there's no question that, moving from Descartes to Kant, cognizing selves or subjects are admitted to exist, but their existence as the historied agents they are is never really treated *existentially*, that is, in terms of the specific cultural (or bodily embedded cultural) forces they respond to in becoming (emerging as) the apt *discursive* agents they become. One finds the latter theme in Hegel, Marx, Nietzsche, Dilthey, Heidegger, Adorno, Dewey, Gadamer, and Foucault. You cannot find it in Russell, Moore, Quine, or Davidson, or in Brentano, Husserl, Frege, Carnap, Apel, or even Habermas. They might as well be pre-Kantian thinkers. In a way, they can be considered such—if you disregard their late-nineteenth- and twentieth-century projects. (By *existential*, incidentally, I mean no more than that aspect of the historical formation of our careers as cognitive and active selves in virtue of which our interests, convictions, and categories of understanding are what they are, however diversely.) Selves live in a historied way; primates do not. Philosophical modernity is decidedly historied and hospitable to the informality and contingencies of cognition.

Viewed abstractly, adequation must be trivial. It is only in the details of the match required that we mark the master philosophies of the tradition. We build our picture of the mind's or cognizing self's conceptual powers *by* adequating our theories of mind or self *to* what we say we know. Nothing could be simpler or more difficult. Thus, cleverly but disappointingly, Aristotle treats the highest powers of reason (nous) in a completely ad hoc and undeveloped way: *whatever* the changeless structure of reality is said to be, the intuitions posteriorly assigned as the exercise of competent nous cannot fail to be (trivially) adequate to its task. Nous has no interesting (existential) structure of its own. It mirrors (or, better, receives) the fixed forms of things: its actualized power is no more than its passive capacity to be undistortedly informed by those same forms.

Nous is nothing but a deus ex machina.

Aristotle's theory is certainly adequated in the formal sense but completely vacuous as far as its scientific function is concerned. Once we call the archic thesis into doubt, we cannot suppress the fact that Aristotle has even less to say about the themes of (10.1) than the philosophers I've mentioned. (I should add that, by *equilibration*—the term is borrowed locally from Goodman and Rawls and is now comparatively standard—I mean no more than a reciprocal adequation, a conceptual reckoning regarding what theorem (10.2) requires at both poles of the cognitive process, taken together.)[4] Equilibration makes very good sense if we accept the terms of a *lebensformlich* symbiosis; it makes no sense at all if the cognition of the world is construed in terms of an externalist competence alone. That is precisely what is so suspicious about Aristotle's and Plato's accounts. Both lack an internalist history of cognitive formation suited to the mastery of enlanguaged thought.

As I see matters, the most strategic (certainly not the only) puzzle adequation must address concerns whether the Intentional (especially its collective and interpretable features) can be adequated (as, in effect, Descartes, Hume, and Kant suppose), say, to the initial biological, or solipsistic, or species-specific, or endogenous, or transcendental powers they assign to cognizing selves. I should say straight out that I believe that this cannot be convincingly conceded without a supporting argument. The point is, it's the litmus for every viable theory of the mental and cultural. It marks the difference between the mind/body problem and the culture/nature problem.

One strategic question that cannot be satisfactorily addressed in terms of Aristotle's theory, but is nonetheless important in contemporary inquiries, asks whether the conceptual and cognitive powers of human beings can, with the acquisition of an enlanguaging culture, be *greater* than (that is, not reducible to) any of these supposed (essential or innate) powers or whether any supposed improvement or enlargement of such powers is anything but a skilled use of our first *fixed* biological (or subjective) powers combined one way or another, so that the mind may be taken to be a closed system. Innatism or nativism (sometimes also called rationalism), professed (in different forms) by Chomsky and Fodor *and* Descartes, holds that there is no increase in human conceptual powers beyond some original (modularly isolated) endowment (genetic or providentially assigned) and that, therefore, any apparent such increase can and must be accounted for by (what in effect are) the innate rules of the operation of the mind or reason or sensorium or computational powers of *Homo sapiens*. That is certainly close to what Descartes had in mind in speaking of the "natural light of reason."

Piaget, of course, opposed Chomsky's innatism (or appears to), arguing that the conceptual powers of maturing children actually change, develop, increase, become greater (*emerge* at a higher level) in virtue of their continual interaction with their environment (including their cultural environment). In effect, Piaget's argument (also Waddington's) holds that our conceptual powers *cannot* be accounted for reductively. Nevertheless, in his own structuralist theory, Piaget supposed that there was a necessary and invariant sequence manifest in the more and more powerful stages of the development of the conceptual capacities he mapped—which (as Chomsky rightly observed) do not really escape (as Piaget believed they did) the larger constraints of innatism. (For Piaget, unaccountably, the environment merely triggers an innate developmental capacity. This was just the point about language acquisition that Vygotsky pressed against Piaget. It anticipates my own theme.)

My own view is that *some* concession to innatism (but not transcendentalism) is entirely consistent with admitting the *social construction* of persons or selves. All that is needed is a division of labor, so to say: the admission (for instance, with Bruner) of some initial hardwired endowment open thereafter to alteration or enlargement in ways that cannot be convincingly assigned or accounted for only innately. The advantage of this option (which is *not* incoherent, as Piaget's may well be) is that it accommodates two essential intuitions: (a) that the mental *does* indeed belong to the biological endowment of humans; and (b) that man's conceptual and cognizing competence is culturally generated and varies in power and structure, at the level of consciousness and cultural emergence, from society to society and from one phase of human history to another. We may concede that humans have innate cognitive powers, but we cannot rightly say what they are, what limits they impose, what rules they function by. The truth is, whatever we claim about our innate (Intentional) endowment is itself an anthropomorphized conjecture viewed from the reflexive level at which we discover our actual aptitudes ([9.9]–[9.12]). Hence,

> (10.3) innatism and social constructionism are not in principle incompatible, but they cannot apply coextensively, everywhere;

and, of course,

> (10.4) the most advanced forms of the mental are, in any pertinent generative sense, jointly biological and encultured.

There is, I think, a very simple way to accommodate (10.3) and (10.4)—namely, by admitting

> (10.5) our culturally acquired (culturally emergent) conceptual and cognizing powers are incarnate in the biological structures to which our innate mental capacities are directly ascribed.

In that sense,

> (10.6) our culturally acquired aptitudes are incarnate in our innate endowment.

What we need to remember is that

> (10.7) our innate mental endowment is and can only be inferred from the vantage of our reflexive (linguistic) competence (anthropomorphically).

Since all forms of strict physicalism fail ([9.49]), and since we are committed to symbiosis ([4.9], [4.11], [4.12]), there is no independent way to fix our innate endowment (whatever that may be), except by inference from what we ascribe to ourselves as our linguistic, lingual, *and* prelinguistic competence. That is,

> (10.8) there is no direct perceptual access to our innate mental endowment.

We cannot query infants, and we cannot say what it is like to be a bat, except from the human vantage; bats have no idea.[5]

I may as well add that we cannot ask the historical past—those who lived in the past—what they thought or meant or intended *in the past,* except, once again, from *our* present vantage. That is the insuperable lesson of Gadamer's hermeneutics and (if I may press the point, for provocation) the unacknowledged lesson of the better part of Quine's notion of "analytical hypotheses."[6] For what Quine concedes, however thinly, is the ineluctability of contingent *tertia* (Rorty's term).

What all this means is this:

> (10.9) Our innate mental endowment cannot fail to be anthropomorphized.[7]

We must remind ourselves that our intuitions about the mental—items (a)–(b), presented just before introducing theorem (10.3)—are no more than special cases of the deeper antinomies of legitimation and ontic priority explored in the previous chapter. It is for this reason that cognitive psychology cannot be naturalized ([9.19]) or explained in transcendental terms ([9.62]).

We are moving rather quickly here. But, before I venture too much further, I should like to recover a connective theme (from what has already been said) that may easily be overlooked. The notion of *adequation* mentioned a moment ago has two foci, the significance of which requires that they be viewed together: one features the theme of the ontic resemblance between the conceptual powers of cognizing subjects and the cognizable features of the objective world; the other, the emergent *lebensformlich* (constructed, enlanguaged collective) nature of the uniquely human mode of cognition. The first is the theme common to Berkeley and the post-Kantian German idealists; the second, the effect of a late Hegelianized reading of themes in accord with Wittgenstein's notion of "forms of life" (as via Gadamer and Foucault). What needs to be emphasized is both that these two themes are nearly completely absent from the externalism of current analytic philosophy and that they are both serviced by the doctrine of symbiosis. I don't believe any philosophy can be convincingly fitted to the puzzles of our age that does not embrace some form of symbiosis.

There are several distinctions involving the analysis of mind that contemporary philosophy is plainly wrong about or scants. Theorem (10.1) marks the most important and the most neglected of these. It confirms that, if we treat the mental or psychological in terms restricted to some initial biological, genetic, or nativist sources confined to *Homo sapiens sapiens*, we cannot but fail to provide for the full range of the mental in *humans*. For what is essential to being competent in the human way unavoidably involves linguistic and lingual competences. But these are specifically *lebensformlich*, *collectively* defined, and, hence, impossible to analyze in terms of merely solipsistic or biological resources. There's the *reductio* of innatism. For,

(10.10) the *lebensformlich* is *ontically* distinct from the physical and biological (or biochemical), is tacitly historied, and cannot, as such, yield nomological exceptionlessness of any kind.

Wittgenstein would never have allowed this way of speaking, of course, or my treatment of related liberties. But it doesn't matter. In the same spirit, I can see how easy it would be to convert Plato's Forms into a metaphor for what I call the *lebensformlich*; I don't find the suggestion in Plato either.[8] I should add that this explains the ingenuity of Chomsky's general strategy: Chomsky converts the Intentional—the culturally emergent and interpretable—into the biological or nativist. He claims that there is "no other possibility" to consider, but he nowhere explains how the conversion is possible. (He eventually abandons his doctrine of universal grammar.)

I have already claimed—through the running argument of chapters 3 and 8 of *Historied Thought, Constructed World* and, explicitly, in the previous chapter of this volume, where I construe the Intentional as inherently collective, in (9.10), and relate it to the consensual life of aggregated humans, in (9.32)—that the cultural, the historical, the interpretable, the linguistic, the discursive, the intelligible cannot but be (or incorporate) the formative powers by which *we first emerge as persons or selves* ([9.11]–[9.15]). I inferred (in the same context) that solipsism was inadequate, in (9.7); that the intentional (in humans) was ultimately discursive and Intentional, in (9.8); that the intentional among nonhumans was anthropomorphized, in (9.9); and that, as a consequence, persons need not be confined to members of *Homo sapiens*, in (9.13). I must add here that I am not (in any way) committed (as yet) to affirming or denying that persons and selves are numerically identical. I'm inclined to believe our usage of such terms is decidedly labile: sometimes, for instance, the term *self* signifies a phase or special function of a person, and sometimes it has the same sense as the term *person*. I see no danger here.

I meant to introduce in this connection a range of distinct options regarding unity and unicity by which to ensure the integrity of the entities in question, including (a) bare numerical *identity* (as in Bernard Williams's identification of persons with human bodies), (b) *composition by mere conjunction* (as in Descartes's dualistic union), and (c) whatever, regarding entities, would be the substantive analogue of incarnation regarding predicables. For the moment, I merely mention that the counterpart of incarnation that involves entities I call *embodiment*. I don't say the tally just offered collects all possible modes of *integrity*, but it does indicate the truth of (10.1) and the reasonableness of (10.2). And that signifies that analytic philosophy has done poorly in its account of minds and selves.

Let me make clear the benign paradox of (10.1):

> (10.11) Persons or selves are (or may be treated as) numerically distinct entities possessing natures that exhibit collective structures.

By a term of art, then,

> (10.12) persons or selves are embodied in the members of *Homo sapiens*, just as their cultural natures (their encultured properties) are biologically *incarnated*; alternatively expressed: persons are artifactual transforms of human primates.

I do *not* hold that the individual members of *Homo sapiens* lack mental capacities. Far from it. (Although, as between Chomsky and Piaget, and between Chomsky and Bruner, there are numerous ways of reading the prelinguistic competence of infants and even prehistoric *Homo sapiens*.) My point is, rather, that

> (10.13) the Intentional (the discursive or discursively expressive) nature of humans marks what is *not* innate or merely biologically evolved regarding them—as well as what, by definition, *is*, cognitively, most essential to their being persons or selves.

As a consequence, in having failed to provide for the *adequation* between our culturally collective (discursive) powers and our biologically (or otherwise endogenously) solipsistic gifts, a considerable part of contemporary philosophy has utterly failed its calling. I implied (just above) that this failing may be manifested in distinct ways: (a) as in supposing that our *collective* powers may be analyzed and explained *solipsistically*, (b) as in supposing that our *lebensformlich* powers may be analyzed and explained in terms of the *innate* competences of *Homo sapiens* (or precultural subjects), and (c) as in supposing that the historically *horizoned* powers of human selves may be analyzed and explained in terms of the *ahistorical* powers of some precultural (or transcendental) state. Failure along these lines signifies a failure to have adequated our conceptual and cognizing powers to our nature and to what we affirm as the intelligible features of the world. Analytic philosophy, I say, has favored these impoverishing commitments within its various externalist programs.

If, now, you look back to the account of reference and predication offered in chapter 3 of *Historied Thought, Constructed World*—look back to theorems (3.8)–(3.12), which affirm that both sorts of act are entrenched in the *Lebensformen* in which they function—you will see at once the argument for supposing that if, indeed, world and language and cognizing subject and cognized object are symbiotized ([4.8]–[4.11]), then,

> (10.14) culturally enlanguaged entities intrinsically possess collective attributes.[9]

For instance, a painting by El Greco, said to be baroque in style, is an individual thing whose salient "style" belongs to it only in virtue of its being a variant of the collective period style (instantiated in other aggregated artifacts) of the same epoch. The style is horizontally real in accord with our interpretive prejudices ([8.35], [8.36]). (*Prejudice*, you recall, really means what is prejudged or preformed in terms of judgment before deliberate judgment itself obtains—but not before acquiring discursive powers. The point is Gadamer's: a clever reading of *Vorurteil*.)

But, of course, if (10.12) be admitted, together with the impoverishing discrepancies assigned a moment ago to the externalist programs of analytic philosophy, then it follows at once that persons or selves cannot be straightforwardly identical with the members of *Homo sapiens sapiens*. (I have already affirmed this thesis [9.13].) I have no wish to deny that we are both persons and members of *Homo sapiens*. I say only that saying that is profoundly equivocal. Since, for logical reasons, true identities are necessarily true, *we* need to make room for such possibilities as (a) individual members of prelinguistic *Homo sapiens* who are not or not yet persons (fetuses, perhaps); (b) nonhuman creatures that are persons (Martians, perhaps); and (c) the conceptual possibility, supposing the pertinent reductionisms fail (as I believe they do), that persons cannot be "merely" numerically identical with any of the individuated members of *Homo sapiens*. That at least is what was anticipated in introducing the strenuous idiom of cultural emergence, incarnation, embodiment—and, more subtly, unicity and unity, and symbiosis.

But I must remind you that I'm prepared to work with both the transformative and the incarnating models of emergence. I must, therefore, add that my use of the terms *incarnation* and *embodiment* is both provisional and heterodox. It's entirely possible that a simpler (ontological) idiom would serve as well or better. But if not, then fine. I've introduced the concept of an entity of one kind (an Intentional or cultural entity) incorporating an entity of another (arguably, a simpler or more basic kind) within the boundaries of a living organism—where one is an artifactual transform of the other: actions, words, artworks, selves, and the like, with respect to mere physical or material things. I have, in this way, acknowledged the novel ontological (evolutionary) change occasioned by the invention and mastery of language and a hint at the resolution of the puzzle of the relationship between the physical and human sciences (the unity-of-science question).

I favor examples drawn from the art world, I must say, because, like persons or selves, they too are culturally emergent and embodied, without yet admitting that they are minded or have mental or psychological attributes. In a word, artworks ≠ subjects, although it is possible that, rightly construed, some subjects are artworks (according to Nishima, if you care, for good or bad, or Nietzsche's *Übermensch*, or the God of the Christians according to Iris Murdoch).[10] This confirms, of course, that

(10.15) the mind/body problem ≠ the culture/nature problem,

although, in the human context, the first cannot fail to implicate the second—or (asymmetrically) the second, the first. In fact, on the argument offered, it is not possible to solve the first without also solving the second. It should be clear, then, that

(10.16) the Intentional is not restricted to the mental, though it presupposes it;

and

(10.17) the mental is either inherently Intentional or Intentionally modeled (anthropomorphized), as in analyses of animal intelligence and cognition.

In the same spirit, I now add that

(10.18) the cultural or Intentional (or collective) competences that define persons or selves are acquired naturally, within the boundaries of societal life, though they are artifactual, hybrid powers.

By "naturally" I mean only that newborn human offspring (*Homo sapiens*) aptly and spontaneously internalize one or another linguistic and lingual *Lebensform* merely by living and maturing among the mature (enlanguaged) members of a human society.[11] But to admit the (existential) achievement marked by (10.18) is hardly to admit that the Intentional can be adequately analyzed in terms of the prelinguistic (cultural) aptitudes assigned *Homo sapiens*: the process of effecting the change required ≠ the process of understanding the change produced. There is a lacuna there. *Homo sapiens* has a capacity to develop beyond its biological capacities. (Also, in introducing the term *naturally*, as I have, I mean to prepare the ground for saying, trivially but in a normative sense, that there is nothing that humans do naturally—by nature—that is unnatural—contrary to human nature. We may partition the natural abilities of humans in such a way as to approve and disapprove of different parts of the behavior of apt selves, but saying so confirms the artifactual standing of such approval and disapproval. I return to the issue in the "Values, Norms, and Agents" chapter of *Historied Thought, Constructed World*. Furthermore,

(10.19) the enabling *Lebensform* of particular societies changes continually with, and as a result of, its continual exercise.

Theorem (10.18) is an obvious empirical fact; by contrast, (10.19) is profoundly puzzling—it is perhaps the template for that family of doctrines developed by Hegel, Marx, Nietzsche, Gadamer, Foucault, and Bourdieu and largely absent from analytic philosophy. What (10.19) signifies is the dynamic nature of a living tradition—in which, that is, the aggregated use of a society's collective habits and practices changes those practices in a historically continuous way. (This is precisely what Gadamer means by a *tradition* and Bourdieu by a *habitus*.[12] I coopt these terms, therefore, although without subscribing to their authors' analyses of them.)

It is important to bear in mind that, although our Intentional aptitudes are formed by internalizing the enabling practices of a tradition (to speak metonymically of a *Lebensform*, a tradition, a habitus, an *episteme*, a practice, an institution), traditions are normatively idealized, abstracted regularities of cultural practices—not things of any kind. Discourse about traditions is entirely predicative. A tradition is (a) an Intentional structure and (b) a collective structure, (c) nominalized over the culturally enabling powers of a parental generation with respect to its offspring, (d) deployed historically, (e) entrenching prima facie norms of propriety or reflexive conformity, under historical change, and (f) characterizable, heuristically, by the apt agents (persons) it enables to emerge, by way of rules or rule-like regularities. A perspicuous clue is offered by Wittgenstein in *Philosophical Investigations* (§202): "'obeying a rule' is a practice." *There is*, however, no rule that is (or need be) obeyed. A rule, I should add, is (a) an Intentional uniformity, (b) ascribed to a tradition or practice, (c) imputed in either a realist or heuristic sense to (d) the behavior, action, work, or thought of apt cultural agents, (e) possessing normative import (as of cultural propriety or aptness), and (f) capable of extension under the conditions of evolving, open-ended societal life. In chess, the rules of play are genuinely constitutive and regulative of admissible chess moves—and are such as to form a closed system. In natural language usage, there are no actual, binding rules; nevertheless, apt discourse is rightly characterized in rule-like ways. (Wittgenstein notes this as well.) I should add, (g) rules are adequate to a model of rationality (holist$_r$).

Every parental generation, let us say, is altered and affected by its role in rearing its own successors, and every successor generation differs from its parent in virtue of the changed *Lebensform* it must internalize. This is the generic lesson of what Gadamer calls *Horizontverschmelzung* (fusion of horizons). It signifies that thinking is historical, that the cultural world is a flux, that the metaphysics of Intentional entities is sui generis.

The key is this:

(10.20) Paradigmatically, Intentional attributes are instantiated in the intentional life of persons and, hence, derivatively, in the artifacts they generate.

If we admit (10.20), we may infer

(10.21) cultural entities do not exist, as such, except in a cultural "world,"

from which it follows directly that

(10.22) solipsism is incoherent.[13]

The point of introducing (10.22) so abruptly (although the matter has come up before) is to gain a march on the resolution of the puzzle of the relationship between the mental and the cultural. There are, and can be, no solitary *persons*, except accidentally, as with Robinson Crusoe. (That was surely Marx's point, in the *Grundrisse*, where he ridiculed the "Robinsonades" of contemporary theorists. It is also part of Peirce's inspiration for denying that pure "Firstness" ever obtains.) In short, selves and enlanguaged cultural worlds entail one another ([10.21]). I can put the point quite briefly: *praxis* (I should say) marks the conditional aspect of human powers that obtain as a consequence of (10.19); hence, it signifies that aspect in which theoretical as well as practical life (or reason) gains its competence and bearings in terms of the collective practices of its enabling (historical) culture. If I now add that reference and predication (as discussed in chapter 3 of *Historied Thought*) are praxical, you can begin to see how radical (10.19) may be judged to be. The use of the term *praxis* hearkens back to Marx's use and critique of Aristotle's *Nicomachean Ethics* in the *Theses on Feuerbach*. (I return later in this chapter to other aspects of the notion.)

The extraordinary importance of (10.22) lies with developing a reasonable policy for individuating numerically independent persons—in accord with the line of thought (offered in chapter 4 of *Historied Thought*) that links external and internal relations between subjects and objects within a symbiotized (logical) space. Since Intentionality does not obtain in any merely physical world—it cannot be adequate to merely physical predicables if it cannot be analyzed or explained reductively—there is a danger of not being able to account for the reality of cultural worlds in a sufficiently robust way. I am trading, of course, on two themes that have already been secured: (a) the symbiosis of world and language and (b) the symbiosis of external and internal cognitional relations. We now find that, in the cultural world, a *third* form of symbiosis must be acknowledged, namely,

> (10.23) human selves are individuals only insofar as they effectively share the collective practices of a common *Lebensform*: individuality is itself a product of discursivity, whose unicity is savored only in the unity of societal life.

I recommend therefore that we hold that

> (10.24) persons or selves are, by definition, culturally (discursively) apt agents,

I remind you, further, in passing, that many of the higher animals at least (elephants, chimpanzees, whales, wolves) share nondiscursive (perceptually centered) cultures, in terms of which their members learn the practical habitudes of their home societies (within the bounds of their ecological niches). Human infants, of course, uniquely begin as such nondiscursive creatures attached to discrete, discursively apt societies. Normally, they learn to transform themselves into discursively apt members of such societies: they become selves themselves—and recognize and exploit the uniquely Intentional world they share. It's my contention that humans cannot function effectively as selves or persons if they do not regard their *lebensformlich* world as real, hence the immense importance of the unrestricted ubiquity of earthly bilingualism! The Rosetta Stone is already a monument to a fluxive metaphysics. There is and can be, for contingent reasons, no transcendental vantage that can successfully override the existential habitudes of *lebensformlich* practices, although, since habitudes are historied, they are themselves continually outlived by their own historied successors. Here, the insuperable provisionality of human science and the historied candor of its benign and reflexive skepticism come together as the ultimate premise of a post-Darwinian pragmatism (at least) that brings all the forms of rationalist and transcendental modernity or apodicticity (from the sixteenth and seventeenth centuries through the eighteenth to the twenty-first century) to a decisive end. Here, I daresay, the principal text to ponder—not, indeed, the strongest—is Husserl's *Crisis* volume, in which existential historicity and transcendental apodicticity finally collide. We find ourselves at a crossroads here, and we must choose disjunctively. On my reading, it's the factual continuity of Darwinian and post-Darwinian evolution that rightly decides the matter: discursivity itself arises out of prelinguistic primate intelligence; the spontaneity of the most advanced rational minds must be accessible, finally, to the native limitations of infantile (perception-centered) intelligence. There's the ultimate meaning of existential historicity. Our sciences and praxis must be grounded in the conceptual powers embedded in our perceptual abilities. This is already clear in the human infant's mastery of language among agents capable of constative and other linguistic or lingual acts. (In chapter 11 of *Historied Thought*, I return to the question of what an *agent* is.) I do not say the natures of human agents are nothing but their aggregated acts nominalized or assigned on the basis of such acts. (That would be close to the spirit of reductive behaviorism, except for the fact that Intentional predicables are anathema to thinkers like B. F. Skinner—although not, let it be said, to thinkers like Ivan Pavlov.)[14] My point here is that

> (10.25) persons or selves are individual entities only insofar as they are aggregatively symbiotized relative to the collective *Lebensform* they share.

Put more provocatively,

> (10.26) the very *existence* of persons cannot be construed, ontically or epistemically, in terms of a model of relations that intrinsically lack Intentional attributes.

To admit theorems (10.24)–(10.26) is to admit at a stroke that

> (10.27) the criteria for *objective* truth claims in the human sciences cannot be modeled on whatever naturalized criteria prove applicable to the "things" that belong solely to the physical sciences,

for

> (10.28) persons cannot be mere *spectators* of their own minds or of the cultural artifacts of their world, in anything like the way in which they function as spectators of physical or natural or non-Intentional phenomena.

Alternatively put,

> (10.29) persons are spectators of their cultural world only insofar as (*as* observers) they interpret the Intentional structures of whatever belongs to their (collective) world—that is, only insofar as they are competent agents in and of that complex world,[15]

and

> (10.30) there is no viable way of disjoining the (objective) *perception* and *interpretation* of cultural phenomena from the reflexive discernment of their own Intentional attributes.

A whole raft of troublesome puzzles confronts us here. I content myself with two claims only and their joint import: one, that

> (10.31) perception is linguistically modeled among selves;

the other, that

> (10.32) interpretation is perceptually or semiotically entrenched.

You will remember that, in this chapter and the previous one, I argued that Intentional predicables are *incarnate* in non-Intentional predicables, and that (earlier in this chapter) I suggested that (as existent particulars) cultural entities are *embodied* in non-Intentional material entities. (Embodiment and incarnation, I should say, entail a sui generis form of hybrid emergence, namely, *cultural emergence*—that is, a form of emergence that cannot be expressed in terms of the non-Intentional features and causal processes of the natural world alone.) I also indicated the need to confirm various forms of adequation: in particular, (a) the ontic adequation of cultural entities and (their) Intentional attributes and (b) the epistemic adequation of the conceptual and cognizing powers of selves and what they admit as the intelligible features of the "things" of their world. Grant that much, and it will be apparent, once you recall the third sort of symbiosis mentioned a moment ago (the aggregated sharing of a collective *Lebensform*), that

(10.33) relative to *perception* and *interpretation*, Intentionality affects the external relations between cognizing subjects and cognized objects in different ways.

Certainly, however, before going further, we should explicitly affirm

(10.34) persons or selves cannot be naturalized or reduced, though they are indeed natural entities.

Theorem (10.34) is already entailed by (10.1), (10.2), (10.11), and, trivially, (9.13)—as well as (I remind you) by (9.15) and (9.19)—but it is also the compendious sense of the entire foregoing argument.

I draw your attention to the stunning fact that the distinctive aptitudes (cognitive and active) of persons are accounted for and legitimated in precisely the same sense in which the viability of reference and predication is legitimated—namely, *in the real processes of collective life*. What this shows is that *if* the inherent informality of reference and predication (reviewed in chapter 3 of *Historied Thought*) presupposes, for their characteristic epistemic success, the consensual processes of our *Lebensformen*, then the same is bound to be true regarding the cognitive and active competences of persons. This is the reason the culture/nature problem cannot be subsumed under the mind/body problem—the same reason the Chomskyan option is no more than a placeholder for a theory never satisfactorily supplied.

I should say that I regard these phrasings as moderate ontic liberties—mongrel liberties, as I name them; that's to say, not literally true (or false) but, rather, adequate with regard to our conceptual needs. There are bound to be plural ways of invoking cognition and whatever is culturally cognizable—where there is no assured way of capturing their "true" structure. Perhaps all mundane truth claims have a touch of the mongrel about them: I see no reason to disallow the possibility. I have already hinted that this must be true of the ontic standing of selves and persons, which are functionally robust enough to claim existence but lack any discernible locus in the natural world. This more than matches the notably weak formulation of Kant's treatment of the "Ich denke" and the doctrine of transcendental apperception in the "Appendix to the Transcendental Dialectic," in the first *Critique* (A642/B630ff.), which (in my opinion), together with the existential standing of the historied nature of human life and cognition, effectively defeats Kant's transcendentalism and claims in favor of apodictic truth hands down.

There is an enormous puzzle looming here. On the one hand, persons, as has been argued, are not (or need not be) identical with the members of *Homo sapiens*; on the other hand, they are the emergent artifacts of a collective culture, functionally identified as competent agents, in virtue of their sharing the collective (discursive) practices of their enabling societies. There are other distinctive features of selves that I shall come to shortly, which bear on the relative indeterminacy and inconstancy of their natures as histories. These directly affect the precision with which we speak of persons as individual entities and specify the acts they characteristically instantiate. I don't deny that persons are individuals and that we treat them as such. But we are guided by different conventions in different milieux (law, medicine, biography) and even a certain informality regarding the unity of persons. Nothing untoward follows from this, unless one insists on a greater precision than the data will support—in fixing individuation, numerical identity, knowledge, effective action. In any case, examples drawn from the merely physical world cannot rightly serve us here. (One sees this very clearly in epistemic contexts.)

Consider perception. I use the term *perception* in various wide and narrow senses to signify (a) the exercise of a *cognitive* capacity that is biologically grounded and culturally empowered (as in sensory perception, sensation, memory, feeling, introspection, general awareness, and the like), in virtue of which particular truth claims may correctly express, report, or represent particular perceptions, and (b) the occasional exercise of a particular modality of (a) (as of vision, feeling by touch, fearing, being aware of, believing, intending, and the like). I take senses (a) and (b) to do general duty for nearly anything that may be said to be a distinct mode of cognizing. To this may be added further technical restrictions (c) to what is admissible regarding (a) and (b) (for instance, causal constraints on veridical vision or memory).

Furthermore, regarding the normal use of many of these modalities, we distinguish (d) between a nonpropositional and a propositional ingredient, both of which may (perhaps must, at times) be jointly instantiated in the paradigms of veridical perception.[16] Thus, in the matter of visual sight, exemplary cases admit the following paired sorts: "John sees a horse on the hill" and "John sees that there is a horse on the hill." These are essentially *matched in veridical perception*. Veridically, John sees a horse on the hill only if John sees *that* there is a horse on the hill and only if certain other conditions obtain nonpropositionally *and* noncognitively.

But there are also well-known asymmetries that hold in first- and third-person reports: for, if I merely *say*, "I see a horse on the hill," it may be correctly inferred that I simply believe I see that there is a horse on the hill, although I may not actually see *that* or anything pertinently, whereas if I say "John [veridically] sees a horse on the hill," one cannot normally then infer that John merely believes he sees *that* there is a horse on the hill. The point of interest in this muddy problem is this:

> (10.35) *knowledge* or *cognition*, which is at least lingual, if not explicitly constative, can be adequated only to persons or selves; otherwise, pertinent ascriptions are no more than anthropomorphized.[17]

That is, theorem (10.35) follows from admitting that, paradigmatically, perception is propositionally structured (or modeled). Hence,

> (10.36) knowledge is or (as with animals) is modeled as an Intentional state,

which catches up the argument of chapter 5 of *Historied Thought* against naturalizing strategies. (Quine's, for instance.)

Our tally about perception conforms, therefore, with what is affirmed in theorem (10.31), but that is hardly enough to ensure *veridical perception*. For one thing, in veridical perception (in the case before us), there must *be* a horse on the hill to *be* perceived; for another, John must (we say) *be* in the right state *to* perceive the horse on the hill (veridically); and, for a third, it must *be true that* John then perceives the horse on the hill (nonpropositionally) and also perceives *that* there is a horse on the hill. Furthermore, for the second of these conditions to obtain, there must normally have been caused to occur a specifically noncognizing form of (nonpropositional) perception in which veridical perception could rightly be incarnate (neurophysiologically, say). The clearest cases are afforded by sensory perception. Thus, *to* see a horse on the hill, John's eyes must have been suitably affected ("irradiated," says Quine) so that he appropriately *sees* it. It is certainly reasonable to suppose that a causal account may be given of the nonpropositional structure of perception (which, in addition, we suppose to be ingredient in perceiving in the cognitional way). But what should we mean by a causal account of events connected with the *propositional structure* of veridical perception or with the matching of the two?[18] (Certainly nothing nomologically manageable. I take the naturalistic maneuver to be a transparent dodge to avoid admitting legitimative questions.) Also, of course, these subtleties suggest a way of linking the biological and cultural aspects of perception and knowledge, but one that defeats our dreams of naturalized causal precision.

These busy qualifications go some distance toward explaining why *no* adjustments relative to the different senses of perception can automatically ensure veridical perception and why naturalizing strategies are likely to fail. I conclude that

> (10.37) ascriptions of knowledge and truth in epistemic contexts are standardly honorific, relativized to legitimate convictions—a distinctly pragmatist liberty.

By *honorific*, I mean only that the ascriptions in question are never cognitively privileged or adequately characterized in psychological terms. (To deny this is, in effect, to naturalize epistemology.) This is not to deny the importance of such ascriptions, but it does remind us that models of epistemic rationality (rationalization) are themselves contingent artifacts of our *lebensformlich* practices ([5.14], [5.15]).

Broadly speaking, an-archic strategies strenuously lower the philosophical importance of the role of truth and knowledge in the analysis of epistemic matters, resisting at one and the same time postmodernism and naturalizing. An-archism refuses to dismiss second-order questions, but it is unwilling to treat them (reductively) in first-order terms (causally or solipsistically, say) or in privileged (second-order) terms. This is the point of theorem (10.37).

In short—to risk a leap that I cannot stop to support with the care it deserves—it now appears plausible to suppose that

> (10.38) ascriptions of knowledge depend as much on presumptions of rationality as on evidence of the occurrence of the right causal sequences.

There are no ready ways of tracing causal sequences involving propositional perceivings: they already implicate the holism of our models of rationality. There is no way of overcoming the various sorts of indeterminacy affecting Intentional states and episodes, in terms of whatever precision we assign the description of non-Intentional states and episodes. Hence, a third consideration, individuated perceptions (beliefs, memories, sightings, even acts) are, more often than not, imputed rather than reliably discerned. In fact, there is here more than an inkling favoring a strong analogy between our policies in ascribing veridical perception and in ascribing moral validity to our actions and commitments. (I return to this theme in chapter 11 of *Historied Thought*). I am persuaded by the analogy.

There are at least two further senses of perception worth mentioning briefly: for one, there is no developed sense in which some noncognitive form of the perceptual modality in sensation, in feeling pain or tickles or aches, for instance, actually matches the fully cognitive form; for another, the pertinent modalities are distinctly intentional and either, as in the first option, no developed noncognitive sense obtains or, where it does, it does not match any cognitive sense in the required way. Thus, in Wittgenstein's reading of first-person reports of pain, there is no ready sense in which cognizing subjects can be said to *know* their pain, or that they are in pain, by perceptual means; they are said, rather, to avow (not to affirm constatively) what they say they feel. That which they avow (that is, their sensations) cannot be independently perceived by others.

Nevertheless, as in the dentist's chair or on the chiropractor's table, there *are* other causal and physical factors (rule-of-thumb correlations) that strengthen the sense in which avowals *are* cast as cognitively allowable facts.[19]

It is very much to the point, then, that although (felt) sensations are the internal accusatives of sensation-events, they are neither independent nor intentional (as Brentano realized).[20] Furthermore, as in Freud's account of the neuroses—in the unconscious fear of horses (said to be intentional, hence mental or psychological)—the use of "intentional" does not play a role paralleling the noncognitive role of perception that matches perception proper.[21] Still, Freud's use of the intentional modalities (fearing, suspecting, and the like) is not altogether distant from ordinary ascriptions of belief, although it is usually restricted to explanatory inferences and assigned a twilight area a cut below conscious knowledge. (Even normal belief is often only inferentially and conjecturally ascribed.)

The practice is also not very distant from the sense in which Chomsky claims we tacitly "know" the deep grammar of our natural language—not, however, in that way in which we normally make truth claims about our language. (But Chomsky nowhere pursues the import of the standard sense of *know*.) These considerations show once again the reasonableness of affirming (5.13) and (10.37). I mark our uneasiness about the honorific ascription of *knowledge* thus:

> (10.39) Knowledge is no more than a legitimated status publicly assigned perceptually incarnate states as well as states of other kinds.

Hence, knowledge is a dummy state: neither a physical state nor an incarnated state—not a bodily state at all. Theorem (10.39) precludes all forms of cognitive privilege. By *status*, I merely mean, here, some normatively graded attribution (linked to certain standard interests—those of successful technology, for instance) that may or may not be construed in realist terms. Here, I remain agnostic about the matter. (In the "Values, Norms, and Agents" chapter in *Historied Thought*, I raise the realist question directly.)

Wittgenstein's point, I should say, was valid against the externalist, but it is not in accord with his own notion of a *Lebensform*. The difficulty shows that Wittgenstein had not sufficiently thought out the import of his own doctrine. Probably, he was himself attracted to a form of externalism, although not to any as crude as Russell's or Moore's. There is a matter of immense importance looming here, of which we have only a glimmer. It is this: *since* knowledge is Intentional ([10.36]) and *since* the Intentional is collective ([9.10]),

> (10.40) states of knowledge (perception, memory, sensation, nondeductive inference, and the like) signify as much the favorable consensual conditions in an enabling society as they signify either or both neurophysiological (or other physical or biological) conditions or psychological belief or conviction (or other subjective or private conditions).[22]

That is, no one knows *anything* in the propositional sense, except as a competent agent:

> (10.41) Cognition is a *forensic* competence rather than a *bodily* competence of any sort.

Here, I take a leaf from Locke's theory of what it is to be a person. (*Forensic* means predicatively ascribable, said of states of competence and responsibility, in accord with consensually legitimated norms.) There's no question Wittgenstein had more than an inkling of (10.41). It is close to the master theme of the *Investigations* and *On Certainty*. But if he had seen it roundly, he should have seen that it would extend to reporting one's private pains as well. And if he realized that persons were themselves constructed in a *lebensformlich* way ([8.39], [10.23]–[10.29]), then he might have been led to a full acceptance of symbiosis. He was not so moved. At the very least, *knowledge* is a state paradigmatically assigned selves or subjects, open to realist ascription only if persons or selves may be construed in realist terms, and persons or selves may be said to exist only if their *lebensformlich* cultures may be said to be real. We see, therefore, the import of admitting the sui generis nature of cultural emergence: admit cultural emergence, and (as already acknowledged) naturalizing and transcendental strategies fail at a stroke.

To accept all that leads now to a momentous finding. Although the assignment of various forms of competence and responsibility to persons (as cognitive and active agents) may be distributed to them as individuals, their competence cannot be assigned solely on grounds drawn from whatever is internal to their subcultural nature—physically, biologically, solipsistically, causally. For,

> (10.42) agents are competent (and judged responsible) insofar as they instantiate the pertinent forensic (*lebensformlich*) practices of their enabling society.

By *responsible* (as a term of art), I mean judged (said of persons or selves) to be or to have been competent in the way of knowledge, of action, or of being the apt agents of an enabling or surrogate society.

This shows very neatly the strong analogy between judgments of cognitive and moral agency (laid out in the "Values, Norms, and Agents" chapter of *Historied Thought*). What is more important for the moment is that we grasp how assigning a nature to persons or selves opposes any strong (individuative) disjunction between denumerable persons, contrary to what our individuative practices may recommend—particularly if we take physical bodies for our paradigms. That is,

> (10.43) Intentional entities, having collective natures, are individuals only as instantiative sites of collective attributes: in particular, persons are so individuated only as *agents*; they are individuated Intentionally, only as Intentional agents.

Hence,

> (10.44) the objective description and explanation of the attributes of cultural entities (persons, artworks, words and sentences, and the like) cannot be disjoined from the description and explanation of the *lebensformlich* practices of an entire viable society.

This, for instance, explains at a stroke the validity of Putnam's notorious remark: "'meanings' just ain't in the *head*."[23] We individuate persons in a strong sense when we are attracted (with Williams, say) to the dictum "one person, one body," but we resist the strong analogy between individuating Intentional and non-Intentional entities when we feature the interpretable and collective—even horizoned—nature of cultural entities.

I can now also explain what I mean by speaking of perceptually independent physical things: I mean anything that (a) exists, (b) lacks Intentional properties intrinsically, (c) is in principle publicly perceivable in accord with exercising one or another of the modalities of sensory perception, and (d) may be confirmed as veridically thus perceived. Anything meeting at least conditions (a)–(d) is, I should say, perceived objectively. (This is the canonical sense favored by externalists: I have no objection to it.) I am also entirely prepared to extend these distinctions wherever needed, for instance, to account for the *objective* standing of theoretical entities: namely, those that, in addition to meeting conditions (a) and (b) but not (c) and (d), are (e) imperceptible (on some pertinent theory) and (f) posited for the purpose of causally explaining what is perceivable in accord with (c) and (d).[24] It was in this sense that I had earlier introduced theorems (10.27)–(10.30). Other adjustments may well be needed, particularly regarding the perception of Intentionally qualified attributes and entities (as of paintings and persons). All this may be reconciled with Peircean Secondness.

It is easy to lose one's way here. The relevant distinctions form a thicket that the advocates of the causal theory of knowledge (Goldman, for instance) and the naturalizing of epistemology (Goldman again, since the causal theory is the principal strategy of the "naturalizing" school) tend to discount too easily. My own strategy has been to show that knowing (perceiving, say) is a salient power of persons or selves and, since it is inextricably bound to legitimative concerns, cannot be disjoined from the complexities of the Intentional world. Very simply put, this means that

(10.45) the folk-theoretic account of knowledge is conceptually insuperable.[25]

This returns us to the existential primary of (historied) perceptions and the symbiosis of cognizer and cognized. The first factor obtains only in the discursive world; the second is essentially the same for honeybees and for human selves, however different their respective cognitive ranges.

Theorem (10.45) affirms (9.25) more challengingly. The relevant argument has been greatly strengthened, because, now, to deny (10.45) is to claim to be able to show that the symbiosis of language and world and of internal and external relations within the terms of the first *can* be effectively retired. I cannot see how that can be done. If the intended denial fails, then the folk-theoretic entails a third sort of symbiosis (mentioned before but not strenuously pursued): namely, the symbiosis that holds between the individuated integrity of persons and their aggregated sharing of some collective *Lebensform* ([10.23]).

I know of no self-described physicalist who opposes the folk-theoretic (Churchland, for instance) who has directly addressed this puzzle. I should perhaps add—recalling [9.25]—that, by a *top-down* methodology, I mean no more than this: that constative discourse cannot be reduced in any way not adequated to the resources of the folk-theoretic. I remind you once again that I have in mind the puzzles of reference and predication, which, as I say, seem to elude every conceptual strategy that is not folk-theoretic.

There are two striking objections to the reduction of the folk-theoretic (ultimately, the first is a version of the second): (a) the collective cannot be reduced to the solipsistic; (b) the Intentional cannot be reduced to the non-Intentional. I put it to you that if these barriers cannot be breached, then the essential thread of the entire foregoing argument cannot be effectively opposed. *That* is a very considerable advance. But if you accept it, then, I claim, you cannot fail to go on to acknowledge that the form of objectivity proper to the human sciences cannot be reduced to the objectivity said to be canonical for the physical sciences. We are being pressed, therefore, to admit that the canonical (externalist) picture of objective science cannot be right—or, better, cannot be enough *even for its own work*. The reason is plain: if all sciences are human sciences ([9.21], [9.58]) and if the human sciences cannot be modeled solipsistically ([9.7], [9.59], [10.1]), then neither can the physical sciences! QED. The physical sciences are, I claim, abstracted from and abstracted within the terms of objectivity appropriate to the human sciences ([9.60]).

Grant that, and a decisive corner will have been turned. The key is this:

(10.46) The elimination or reduction of the Intentional entails the advocacy of the solipsistic.

Theorem (10.46) is the essential pivot on which the dominant programs of analytic philosophy (the canon) founder. I can collect all of this now in a most strategic way:

(10.47) The normative function of epistemic appraisals cannot be reduced to, or replaced by, causal explanations of the psychological states judged to count as cognitions.

The first, of course, addresses what is incarnate, and the second, what is incarnating; also, the first incorporates second-order concerns and the second does not.

We need to be clearer, however, about the nature of the objectivity appropriate to the cultural world. Again, the key is surprisingly straightforward:

(10.48) Objectivity cannot but be consensual.[26]

Theorem (10.48) is a little startling but entirely straightforward. By *objectivity*, I mean no more than that condition of our constative powers in virtue of which our truth claims can be legitimated as veridical: justifiably judged true (or otherwise suitably judged). Remember, we are not bound to bivalence. Of course, by the *consensual*, I mean (a) entrenched in the *lebensformlich* way, but (b) not as such criterially. You have only to refer to the discussion in chapter 3 of *Historied Thought, Constructed World* regarding reference and predication to see that the matter was already implicitly decided by what we were there obliged to admit regarding our discursive resources. Under the various forms of symbiosis, consensual criteria governing the assignment of truth-values cannot but accord with our conjectures of what is rational in the way of validity and legitimation. Hence,

(10.49) objectivity, like truth, validity, legitimation, rationality, is little more than a consensual artifact.

But what does the consensual entail? Try this:

(10.50) In an Intentional world, consensus is reflexive;

that is, it (a) entails discerning what is collectively shared by aggregates of selves, (b) in virtue of which each is empowered in pertinent cognitive ways. Compendiously,

(10.51) in an Intentional world, objectivity is consensual, reflexive, and interpretive.

Theorem (10.51) is no more than a summary. But from it follows that

> (10.52) in an Intentional world, cognizer and cognized are, at least in part, the same,

that is, such that the observation of their objective attributes entails the interpreted perception of the *lebensformlich* structures *they share*. Hence, the observers of an enlanguaged cultural world are apt agents in and of that same (collectively qualified) world ([10.10], [10.29].) Alternatively put,

> (10.53) persons or selves are, at once, cognizing agents and cognized cognizers.

Theorem (10.53) signifies, in effect, that insofar as persons are the apt individuals they are, their aptitude instantiates the incarnate collective practices that constitute their *Lebensformen*. In short,

> (10.54) in an Intentional world, there is no exit from the interpretive consensus in virtue of which such a world is constituted and perceived.

Alternatively,

> (10.55) in an Intentional world, perception is inherently subject to the hermeneutic circle.[27]

Viewed more paradoxically,

> (10.56) Intentional structures are real only insofar as they are cognizable by percipients whose own cognizing aptitudes are suitably qualified and conformably constituted.

Theorem (10.56) supplies the deepest version of that benign paradox known as the hermeneutic circle. I take it to define the "circle." Its puzzle cannot be resolved except within a *lebensformlich* world in which cognizer and cognized are constituted as such and adequated to each other, as in (10.52). I may now say that I mean, by the *hermeneutic circle*, that constraint on our cognitive powers such that (a) our constative claims and perceptions are inherently informed by a more inclusive *lebensformlich* consensus, (b) the objective determination of *that* consensus presupposes an interpretive consensus, (c) every claim of interpretive consensus is an artifact of (a), and (d), namely, that there is no escape from conditions (a)–(c).

I trust it is clear that to admit the hermeneutic circle is to admit that cultural emergence must be sui generis and inexplicable in terms of whatever forms of emergence obtain in any world adequately characterized in non-Intentional terms. In effect, this means that, unlike biological or psychological emergence,

> (10.57) cultural emergence is at once natural and legitimative.

Theorem (10.57) is an extraordinarily important finding. I can suggest its subtlety by reminding you that, in the psychiatric nosology, schizophrenia is often characterized as involving a deformation in the veridical perception of the objective world. But, of course, in the account I have been developing, the natural phenomenon of schizophrenia cannot, in principle, fail to be inseparable from its legitimative status vis-à-vis objective knowledge. The taxonomic manuals do not accommodate that fact—or, for that matter, its methodological import regarding the scientific pretensions of psychiatry. Another subtle consequence is this:

> (10.58) Since they are Intentional entities and since the Intentional is collective and horizontal, the integrity (the unity and unicity) of persons or selves is itself a function of our horizontal interpretation of their (and our own) careers.

Theorem (10.58) begins to open up dizzying possibilities, which, though still manageable, are clearly completely alien to canonical views of individuation and numerical identity. (Certainly, it is completely incompatible with externalist models of cognition.) Any surprise here is a consequence of the failure of analytic philosophy to address the culture/nature puzzle adequately. I suggest that it *has* been anticipated in recent views regarding the objectivity of literary criticism. Furthermore, both physical and cultural emergence are posited only at that level of emergence at which linguistically apt agents are first able to broach the question. It is in that sense that science is invariably top-down.

I should perhaps add explicitly that, once you accept the general line of argument that leads to my reading of the hermeneutic circle, you cannot fail to grasp as well that it provides a similar treatment of *praxis* (in the general, Marxist sense, shorn perhaps of the particular model of social causation the Marxists have favored historically.)[28] I take Foucault's notion of power/knowledge (*pouvoir/savoir*), for instance, to be sufficiently materialist in this regard as to be Marxist. The idea is that the constructed standing of knowledge is a function of the historically contingent but practically effective scheme of institutionalized distinctions (power) that some viable society has entrenched. The thesis is meant holistically, not criterially. Hence, it cannot be equated with the specific effects of deliberate political power, although it accommodates them. (A *Lebensform*, we may say, is a site of power, and *knowledge* is the artifactual status of legitimated exemplars within its space.)

The hermeneutic circle, it's true, is normally not employed in the context of social causation, but it could be (and probably ought to be). In any case, I mean by *praxis* (adding to what has been said) (a) the defeat of the conceptual basis for Aristotle's disjunction between theoretical and practical reason, (b) the characterization of theory or theorizing (or language, for that matter) as itself a form of practical activity, and (c) the interpretation of a *Lebensform* in terms of praxis and of praxis in terms of the enabling powers of a *Lebensform*. In short, the *lebensformlich* is the middle term between *praxis* and the hermeneutic circle.

Of course, objectivity, according to the canon (among the positivists, the advocates of the unity-of-science program, those who would naturalize epistemology, those who would reduce the Intentional to the non-Intentional), (a) presupposes solipsism, (b) admits a cognizable world that lacks Intentionality, (c) denies theorems (10.51)–(10.55), and (d) regards cognizer and cognized as *epistemically* independent of each other. Call this view of objectivity *objectivity$_e$* (meaning that objectivity is confined to externalist relations) and the earlier view (in accord with [10.48]) *objectivity$_i$* (meaning that objectivity accommodates internal as well as external relations). The two versions are clearly distinct. But the standard unity-of-science primacies have been reversed: that is the point of (10.45). (It signifies that objectivity$_e$ is a deformation or delimitation of objectivity$_i$.)

Let me bring this discussion to a close with a final set of curious puzzles. Intentional properties are real only in the milieu of a viable culture ([10.56]), or only as the interpreted vestiges of a once-viable culture sustained by another that is still viable. Here and there, extraordinary conceptual bridges have been built between cultural worlds that no longer function reflexively and others that still do. (The Rosetta Stone is one of the most remarkable of these bridges.) Collective practices evolve through the effect of their actual exercise ([10.19]). I construe this to mean that

(10.59) cultural worlds are histories relative to which whatever things exist within them are also histories.

On the strength of (10.59), we may now add,

(10.60) existent histories are Intentional entities embodied in non-Intentional entities,

just as Intentional properties (now, *their* Intentional properties) are *incarnate* in non-Intentional properties. This is the condition on which the integrity of embodied entities can be ensured—that is, the adequation of their unity and unicity. I have argued, in chapter 7 of *Historied Thought*, that individuated things need not have constant natures ([7.6]). It turns out, as a consequence, that, since the *lebensformlich* sources from which the natures of embodied entities are drawn are themselves historicized ([10.19]), embodied entities cannot have constant natures ([10.58]).

Let us say, then, that

(10.61) all cultural entities are permeable.

By *permeable*, I mean that the nature of cultural entities is affected and altered as a direct consequence of changes in the *Lebensform* in which they are formed and within which they persist. Hence,

(10.62) selves are permeable because they have Intentional (consensually formed) natures, subject to continual change.

This explains the bearing of the internal/external symbiosis ([4.11]) and the open-ended nature of the hermeneutic circle on the methodology and objectivity of the sciences.

Furthermore,

(10.63) all cultural entities are porous because they are permeable.

By *porous*, I mean that cultural entities are capable of acquiring and losing Intentional properties as a function of the consensual practices on which their existence depends: that is, *that* their natures are intrinsically (Intentionally) collective and interpretable. For example, *Hamlet* has acquired psychoanalytic import as a consequence of changes in the ethos of Western society—attributes that were not salient (or not even possible) in Shakespeare's time.[29] Similarly, the recent development of the feminist critique of male-dominated modes of life has entered into contemporary social criticism in such a way that, for instance, the macho lifestyle has been perceptually (interpretively, *really*) altered. (Theorems like [10.62]–[10.63] oblige us to construe the hermeneutic circle in a historicized and relativistic way.)

This is not to say (as Dennett charges) that those who favor the "intentional" idiom hold that real things are altered as a result of mere redescription.[30] No, Dennett has misconstrued the problem. For one thing, non-Intentional entities are, in every view, completely unaffected by changes in mere description. (No respectable intentionalist has claimed otherwise.) It remains true, however, that, *in* intentional contexts ("opaque" contexts, as Quine calls them), it is not always clear whether one and the same entity *is* being referred to when descriptions change. Here, I claim only that theorem (10.63) is not incompatible with what I have just said about non-Intentional entities.

Finally, given the historicized symbiosis of world and language (for example, along the lines Kuhn stresses, in admitting that Priestley and Lavoisier lived "in different worlds"), the objective concepts (objective$_e$) with which the *non*-Intentional world is described and explained *are themselves* the artifacts of our *Lebensform* (of what is objective$_i$). In this sense,

(10.64) scientific objectivity is historicized.

Foucault was right. But I am also prepared to concede that

(10.65) whatever lacks Intentionality is impermeable and nonporous.

The *Hamlet* example is profoundly instructive in other ways. (I count *Hamlet* as a metonym for the cultural world.) Over time, *Hamlet* has acquired a psychoanalytic import—as has, also, *Oedipus Rex*. But the *Mona Lisa* smile still possesses, vestigially, a trace of Verrocchio's work.[31] Freud, by contrast, completely failed to see "in" Leonardo's *Virgin and Child with Saint Anne* the cultist meaning of rendering the two women equal in age: Freud *imputed* a sense to the painting that tradition has not sustained. Again, we *have* surely lost much of the semiotic import of the masks of West Africa, which have acquired traits born of being brought, in the museum world, into constant conjunction with mainstream European painting. And Dante's *Commedia* has obviously lost a great deal of the import of its putative Muslim exemplar (which may yet be restored). To the question of *where* the Intentional properties of these works are to be found and located, the best answer seems to be *in* the works themselves (Intentionally complex artworks, mind you) *as* discerned in or imputed to them by Intentionally apt (even matched) agents. By *imputed* (to them), I mean only that the consensual traits (the meanings, the representational properties, and the like) they have are *interpretively* discerned in them. They have the changing natures they have in virtue of the rigor (*naturans*) of such imputations; the imputed properties are objectively discernible *in* them, as a consequence (*naturata*). In this sense, artworks (as well as selves) are socially constructed and continually reconstituted interpretively ([7.33], [9.23], [9.37], [9.38]).

This helps to explain the objectivity of the cultural world—recalling, always, that the seemingly rigorous sense of objectivity in the physical world is itself dependent, epistemically *and* ontically, on just *this* objectivity.

I want to concede, however, that

(10.66) the individuation and predicated nature of cultural entities are labile.

By *labile* attributes, I mean attributes in virtue of which embodied entities cannot be located physically, except by an interpretive convention, inasmuch as (a) embodiment ≠ identity and (b) incarnated and incarnating attributes are fundamentally different. (Theorem [10.66] readily applies to persons, artworks, actions, histories, and sentences.) If you appreciate the Intentional or interpreted realism of the cultural world (regarding the characteristics of persons and the properties of artworks), you will see at once the sense in which Peirce's interesting view of real indeterminacy and real vagueness (Thirdness) has its best application among culturally emergent entities. (I had hinted at this in chapter 6 of *Historied Thought*.)

Where, for instance, does an action begin and end? or a war?[32] If, say, a particular act of flipping the light switch is embodied in a particular physical movement confined in some way to a certain (non-Intentional) causal event, then if (say, with Davidson) the action (or act) of flipping the switch = the action of alerting a burglar (who happens to be in the house), then how may we confine that action to its proper boundaries in terms of its unity and unicity—its integrity, in short?

Certainly not by appeal to *whatever* may be true regarding incarnating or embodying (non-Intentional) considerations. Furthermore, it is entirely possible that the practice of interpreting (a fortiori, individuating) actions according to the law may be very different from the practice of interpreting paintings. It is also possible that several different actions be embodied in the same physical movement. My schema is meant to accommodate all such puzzles. There is nothing quite comparable in our discourse about (mere) physical things.

I must press these gains a little further. I have already remarked that persons or selves are culturally apt agents ([10.24]). Let me add now that

(10.67) persons or selves are the only Intentionally apt agents there are,

in the sense that

(10.68) only persons or selves work or produce work.

(Remember, machines, prelinguistic infants, and animals may be anthropomorphized as agents.) By *work*, I mean no more than (a) acting in a way informed by an enabling *Lebensform* (as in speaking or weaving a carpet) or (b) the artifacts (or artifactual deeds) produced (or effected) by work in accord with (a). Furthermore,

(10.69) an act or action or piece of work is done or performed only by individual agents, even when collective action may be affirmed,

as when what is done or produced possesses properties that, as Intentional, are intrinsically collective, as in a conversion, or war. This explains why that which is, predicatively, culturally significant is interpretively such. The curious thing is that

(10.70) persons or selves are not only interpretable entities, they are also, uniquely, *self-interpreting* entities (texts).

(I have explored the notion of a *text* in chapter 4 of *Historied Thought, Constructed World*.) The important point here is that

(10.71) selves are the sole *agents* of history, though not the only *causes* of effective historical change.

Certainly,

> (10.72) collective agents are fictions or anthropomorphized causes (or imaginaries, as in a usage favored by Charles Taylor and Cornelius Castoriadis).

Braudel slights the role of particular human agents and favors instead the agency of large complexes of the Mediterranean world.[33] Certainly, for purposes of assigning collective responsibility, corporations are acknowledged in the law. By a *corporation*, I mean a collective agent (or person): a fictitious or anthropomorphized agent (said to be capable of work and artifactual deeds and of assuming responsibility). But it strikes me that the convention of introducing *corporations* is an acknowledgement of the truth of (10.69): corporations are collectively constituted individual agents, construed fictively or heuristically. I add, therefore, following Locke,

> (10.73) persons or selves are cognitively competent (forensic) agents capable of work and of assuming responsibility.

The account is quite tidy now. Nevertheless, before closing this chapter, I must draw your attention to the import of (10.70). Selves, I say, act in ways in which, interpretively (whether consciously or not), *they* are the very agents by which, through their permeability and porosity, they effectively alter their own natures (as well as, a fortiori, other artifacts of their own culture). Hence,

> (10.74) selves are self-interpreting texts, the continually reconstituted artifacts of their own reflexive agency.

I regard theorem (10.74) as capturing a good part of the strenuous but different doctrines espoused by Hegel, Marx, Nietzsche, Gadamer, and Foucault. It is a theme largely missing from analytic philosophy.

We are nearly at the end; a few more observations will round things out acceptably. Returning to a matter I treated too briefly before (but cannot do full justice to in this primer), I remind you that I introduced the notion of being *embodied* in order to have it play an ontic role isomorphic with that intended for *incarnate* ([10.60]). The ramifications of (10.60) are extraordinarily rich, but for the sake of the most minimal clarity I add only these summary remarks:

(10.75) By definition, embodied entities necessarily possess incarnate properties,

and, as a consequence, drawing on the entire foregoing account,

(10.76) Intentional, intentional, mental, cultural, linguistic, lingual, interpretable, historied, historical, artifactual, permeable, porous, labile, and similar properties are incarnatable properties.

I should say here that by *embodied* I now understand (a) a complex relationship between numerically distinct individuals, (b) one entirely different from that of instance/kind and member/class, in that only individuals may be thus related; (c) an indissoluble relation as far as the existence of pertinent entities is concerned, (d) such that their incarnated properties are emergent with respect to their embodying entities, (e) open to being affirmed in a realist, heuristic, anthropomorphized, or fictitious sense. (By *individuals*, I mean persons or selves. By *individual things*, I mean particulars, taken singly, usually in the sense of being apt for reference.)

There are a great many puzzles about the individuation and numerical identity of embodied entities. This is particularly clear when one thinks about plural (and differing) performances of the same Mozart sonata or plural utterings of the same word or sentence. I can just report that I have found that all of these yield perspicuously to the following distinction of art:

(10.77) All and only embodied entities are tokens-of-types.[34]

I hyphenate *tokens-of-types* deliberately. Particulars that are embodied particulars are token instances of a type that is itself countable. Brahms wrote one Fourth Symphony, we say, but that symphony has been performed innumerable times and in many different ways. We are not, however, obliged to think of *types* as abstract (existent) particulars of some sort that are (oddly) instantiated by (token) particulars. No, the token performances instantiate pertinent musical predicables, and we count those performances heuristically (nominalize them as events) as tokens-of-a-given-type for reasons of interest within our society (credits, permissions, royalties, and the like). The interesting thing is that the cloning and reincarnation of persons (regardless of the empirical facts) trade on the coherence of the same notion.

A further caveat is in order here:

(10.78) *Emergent* phenomena need not be embodied or incarnate.

By an *emergent* order of reality, I may now say, more precisely than before, that I mean to include any array of empirical phenomena that (a) cannot be described or explained in terms of the descriptive and explanatory concepts deemed adequate for whatever more basic level or order of nature or reality the order or level in question is said to have emerged from and (b) is causally implicated and cognitively accessible in the same world in which the putatively more basic order or level is identified. For instance, the order of biological phenomena is said to have emerged from a more basic order (or level) of inanimate physical things—without being incarnate in the sense here intended.

It is among questions of emergence that questions of adequation and reduction arise and are resolved. For example, Searle is prepared to make mental ascriptions of the brain, but the coherence and viability of doing so depend on the demands of adequation and the prospects of reduction.[35] Two puzzles arise, which Searle does not satisfactorily examine: first, whether, if the mental can be ascribed to biological organisms (including *Homo sapiens*), it follows that the mental can be ascribed to the brain; second, whether, if the first puzzle is favorably resolved, it follows that Intentional forms of the mental can also be ascribed to parts of the brain (neurophysiological processes, say).

You can see that there cannot be an end to these puzzles. The decisive point is that they all arise and are resolved within the terms of (10.48): the consensual nature of every sort of objectivity. It is curious, therefore, that conjecture about such puzzles as those just mentioned is so often insouciantly detached from the milieu of their very resolution. It is the irreducibility and sui generis features of the Intentional that, in the last analysis, are decisive.

Addendum

Here I depart briefly—must depart—from the essential plan of this collection of essays. I do so confessionally. My central concern, you understand, is to construct a reasonably adequate philosophical sketch of the nature and powers of what we mean in speaking of a human self or person. I add these (the following) remarks to the chapter titled "Mind and Culture" because the linkage signals the part of the theory required—bearing on the enlanguaged, artifactual, encultured, conscious, cognitionally unique competence of the human self—that I've made a fair start on: hence, the pairing of mind and culture, to emphasize the hybrid entwining of biological and cultural processes in forming what we call the mind. I make a few oblique remarks of a different kind (here and elsewhere in the book) to distinguish between the merely physical and the enabled part of the physical body that can actually incarnate that mode of bodily functioning that we call mind.

I call the modifications of the physical (which include the brain, certain specialized chemical streams, and a great deal more that I'm largely ignorant of) *material* rather than merely physical. In short, I require at least another chapter—perhaps "Mind and Body"—to address the biological (especially the neuroscientific) contribution to that mode of bodily functioning that I'm calling mind. I've made some progress here on my own: for instance, I see that mind must be a mode of functioning of variously specialized systems and subsystems of the body, capable of mapping and analyzing, from moment to moment, nonconscious (but functionally intelligible) as well as conscious, informationally qualified episodes that make the stable appearings of the experienced world stable enough to be interpreted and construed cognitively among creatures like ourselves. The network of the mind penetrates the entire system of the body; it cannot be restricted to the brain any more than the brain can be the sole center of the unifying interplay of whatever internal bodily processes contribute to our conscious and coherent grasp of the world we claim to inhabit. A baseball pitcher's habitudes of accuracy (monitored only partly consciously, in practice and play) are in good part monitored by chemical habitudes that guide the fine-tuned movements of the limbs and muscles that determine the quality of a given pitch. In that sense, the mind functions nonconsciously as well as consciously in the joints and subordinate acts that comprise a pitcher's throw.

I have no interest in contributing to neuroscience itself. But the complex relationship between mind and living body remains the most neglected part of the theory of the human self and mind. I'm inclined to think that what we require is a plurality of plausible models of the functional unity of the self in terms of the cognizing, feeling, and expressive functions we call mind. This much of the picture I'm prepared to defend, but it's still rather elementary—though hardly unimportant. It's only in the latter part of the twentieth century and the start of our new century that the resources that we collect as neuroscience have reached a level of precision and acceptance that may be reliably drawn on for philosophical gains. Hence, the confessional line I wish to add to the loose unity of the entire collection. I simply want to say that, in reading Antonio Damasio's *The Feeling of What Happens: Body and Emotion in the Making of Consciousness* (New York: Harcourt, 1999), I've found an approach to the unwritten chapter, "Mind and Body," that can reasonably call on the specialized literature of neuroscience that, at the same time, remains hospitable enough to my own fledgling effort. Other philosophers may find this a useful suggestion. I would only add that, given this much of the corrective picture, the most strategic question (for my purposes) remains that of the functional unity of the self and mind.

Seven

Selves and Other Texts

I

Paradigmatically, texts are the intrinsically interpretable utterances of (human) selves; derivatively, anything is a text if and when suitably anthropomorphized, modeled on the paradigm of human thought and behavior. This is the linchpin of my proposal bridging artworks and selves within the analysis of the cultural world. I shall allow it to expand a bit extravagantly at first, in order to suggest its amplitude and resources. But then I shall confine it to what is needed for a more limited purpose. The cries of a newborn infant, for instance, are not texts, except derivatively, in the sense in which infant behavior and psychology are heuristically described (as they must be) in accord with the model of the linguistic competence of self-conscious selves apt for reporting their thoughts, their intentions, their experiences, their undertakings. In this sense, too, the world is a possible text, or is texted, if we concede that its intelligible structure is inseparable from the symbiotized conditions under which we understand ourselves: even the realism of the physical sciences may be said to be texted, if realism is interpretively constructed (or constructivist), *not* if we claim to know the world neutrally, or to know it as it is independently, or to know it as it is invariantly structured. In any case, to say the world is texted in this sense—epistemically—is not to fall back to any form of idealism, only to concede (and to avoid thereby) the insuperable paradoxes of the Cartesianism that spans Descartes and Kant and is rampant once again in twentieth-century Eurocentric philosophy.

We ourselves are texts, if we view ourselves—our thoughts and deeds—as the individuated expression of the internalized enabling structures of the larger culture in which we first emerge, are first formed, as the apt selves we are, apt for discovering how the language and practices of our society course through our every deed. In this sense, selves are the paradigmatic agents of linguistic and lingual uttering; also, metaphorically (historically), they are the legible utterances of their age: Goethe, Napoleon, Rousseau, Goya, for instance.

One might say that every generation utters its own offspring, not in the sense of merely producing offspring but in the more pointed sense of facilitating their formation as second-natured (encultured) selves of this or that particular ethos. Formed thus, selves continue to utter and alter and transform themselves reflexively, by interpreting and reinterpreting and effectuating their evolving potentialities in speech and deed.

Viewed this way, Freud's and Marx's and Foucault's theories of the human condition converge on the texted nature of human life, but they do so by featuring the would-be mechanisms of change by which we understand life's meanings, not mere change itself. In this regard, their theories are very different from those offered by such figures as Lévi-Strauss, Gadamer, and Bourdieu, who pretend to isolate objective meaning without attention to the dynamics of societal life or who reduce dynamics to kinematics. *Text* is a term of art that may be made to do service for a very wide range of undertakings spanning the interpretation of artworks and human histories. What unites them is a common sense of the conditions under which meanings are generated and discerned and made effective in cultural life. The trick is to grasp how the epistemic puzzles of objective interpretation are indissolubly embedded in the causal forces of historical change itself *and* how change in the cultural world is inseparable from the play of those same epistemic puzzles.

I have in mind answering the interpretive puzzles—both epistemically and ontically—but only in order to bring my answers into functional accord with the question of how to understand and explain human history. I am aware that I am barely broaching the larger issue. Its answer, however, cannot avoid the dynamics of generated meanings. The analysis of meanings has also been distorted therefore, by urging an overly simple analogy between the predicative standing of Intentional attributes and the standing of physical attributes. Viewed that way, one can hardly grasp the sense in which the objectivity of interpretation mediates between the objectivity of the natural sciences and that of the judgments of practical life. Yet that *is* the key to bridging the lesser difference between our understanding of art and our understanding of ourselves. (I seize the occasion to add at once that by *lingual* I mean only to mark the various nonlinguistic or nonverbal forms of utterance that presuppose and depend upon linguistic competence and cognate powers and thereby manifest many of the same interpretable structures that language manifests—as in art and action—in making love and war and sculptures and food and clothes. Both lingual and linguistic utterance must be construed, of course, in bodily terms.)

I agree here somewhat with the spirit of Pierre Bourdieu's analysis of the habitus, except that I construe the mechanisms of enculturation and of the continuing transformation (and self-transformation) of agents and practices *dynamically*, in terms of cognitively effective powers (no matter how subterranean); whereas (according to my reading) Bourdieu tends not to venture much beyond Lévi-Strauss's *kinematic* strategy, as in his empirical sociology. In that sense, Bourdieu's analyses tend to be factorial, though not uninstructive. Still, the validity of the societal model must be supported dynamically. (I think, here, of the analogy of comparing Copernicus and Newton on the movement of the planets.) Bourdieu treats the habitus of a salient practice as "generative" *of* that practice through the "body's dispositions"—somehow without attention to the actual microprocesses of human behavior cast in causal and epistemic terms at once.[1] The result is close to the explanation of opium's inducing sleep by its dormative powers. (The explanation need not be vacuous, of course, but its dynamic factors must be properly supplied.) The analysis of what to make of the valid interpretation of art helps us, I believe, to see what is required (but missing in Bourdieu) in order to explain the automatic fluency of social life. Here, you begin to see the strategic advantage of formulating what to count as the objective description of the life of historical societies based on the requirements of validating objective interpretations in the arts. The two undertakings are, finally, very much the same.

To press the point: it would not be unreasonable to say that selves are self-interpreting texts, meaning by that that selves view themselves as perpetually interpreting subjects as well as tacitly interpretable, often problematic objects, each role reciprocally affecting and potentiating the other through an evolving history that is in part constructed by that same duality. Grant only that the temporal careers of selves and societies and what they do and produce have histories or are histories in this sense, and you have in hand the essential clue to the complex informality of interpretive objectivity. Canonical usage, I concede, does not favor such an accommodation. But if you construe speech and art and action as the interpretable utterances of culturally apt selves, then you cannot rule out the propriety of our speaking of selves as texts, by way of their interpreting their own utterances, which, being texts as well, are assignable to the cultural processes themselves capable of altering the potentiated powers of the very agents of cultural change (selves, of course). Ultimately, putting matters thus poses, but hardly answers, the question of the conceptual relationship between physical nature and human culture (as with reductionism, for instance).

Much that is suggested here in the way of enlarging the scope of the theory of texts may be thought extravagant, perhaps even flatly false. But you must bear in mind that humans are the only creatures that view themselves at once, ambivalently and intransparently, as both cognizing subjects and cognized objects: the only creatures capable of reporting and interpreting their own public utterances, the only creatures that acquire by enculturation a functional second nature as linguistically apt selves, the only creatures that address the world directly and discursively in terms that are inseparable from the theorizing and interpretive categories through which they understand themselves and what *they* utter and produce, the only exemplars of historical and creative careers. It is in this sense that selves serve as the paradigms of cognitive and mental life, for, of course, the bare question of how to analyze cognition and mental life arises only reflexively: only in a society of selves. We have no alternative option here.

It is entirely reasonable to recommend that we confine the principal work of understanding and interpreting texts to the most absorbing linguistic utterances we can identify—or (perhaps better) to the entire world of art, or (perhaps) to the world of history. But, as you consider such enlargements, you realize that, just as there is no strict demarcation between persons and their acts, there is none between a functioning self and that self's utterances. We scan even ourselves as the phased, significant, often mysterious or surprising precipitates of our own Intentional acts—that ineluctably embody the vagaries of our incompletely fathomed culture. Think of interpreting Beethoven or Alexander the Great or van Gogh or James Joyce or Jean Genet.

Beyond all that, the detailed theory of texts will inevitably remain hostage to a choice of seeming axioms of knowledge and reality—for example, to what, disputatiously, we are prepared to take as given in the way of objectivity, necessities, invariances *de re* and *de cogitatione*, cognitive privilege, universality, flux and closed systems, divergent and incommensurable conceptual schemes, communicative success, conditions of truth and understanding and legitimation, and norms of rationality and worth. It seems obvious that one cannot demonstrate the validity of a theory of texts, as if by way of a scrupulous analysis of a particular sector of the independent world—for instance, in the arts, with respect to poems and novels (literary texts), or, by analogy, with respect to paintings and the performance of notated music (visual and musical texts, say), or, more directly, with respect to human histories and social practices (historical and sociological narratives).

But the very idea of a study of texts as of determinate, stable, well-boundaried *objects* relatively unaffected by their undergoing interpretation is open to serious challenge: for one thing, because texts are the utterances of selves and are never completely detachable *denotata* of effective interpretation; for another, because, in the world of culture as distinct from physical nature, there is no entirely assurable disjunction between cognizing and cognized; for another, because whatever the interpreted structure of uttered texts may be, it can never be independent of the interpretive resources of the self-examining selves that undertake the task; for another, because the interpretive powers of individual selves are never completely known to those same functioning selves, who are (themselves) no more than a small self-conscious part of the tacit, collective, effective competence of one or another enabling society; for another, because the reciprocal historical influence of interpretive power and the palpable precipitates of prior interpreted structures (the work of historical memory) substantively affect the evolving interpretive resources shaped for subsequent utterance and interpretation; and, for still another, because interpretive scope and focus and fluency are always endogenously limited by the historically contingent horizon under which they are affected and made effective.

It is not as a theorem of the theory of texts but as a reasonable presupposition of it that we affirm that general practices cannot be cognitively fixed by way of universals or Platonic Forms or Husserlian *eide* or anything of the kind; nor, conformably, can meanings or what may be called Intentional structures (ranging over lingual as well as linguistic utterances) be objectively determined in any comparable way. For one thing, the cultural world is irreducibly subject to one or another form of the hermeneutic circle, meaning that one cannot, in interpreting texts, exit from our practice—the practice that first formed us—of imputing cultural significance and signification to the things we encounter and produce in our encultured world: Intentional structure is ineluctably sui generis, coextensive with the lives and interests of a society of apt selves. To have emerged as selves is to implicate a world in which, alone, we function as selves; but that *is* the theme of the hermeneutic circle formulated by other (ontic) means.

I mean by the *Intentional*, as I have said earlier, no more than the culturally significant—the linguistically and lingually meaningful, the representational, the expressive, the institutionally purposive or rule-like, the intentional and intensional as manifestations of cultural formation, the symbolic, the semiotic, the rhetorical, the stylistic, the traditional, the historical, the narrative.

For another thing, in the cultural world (also in nature at large, to the extent that cognitive resources are, paradigmatically, linguistic and reflexive), objectivity is never more than consensual—in a sense akin to what Wittgenstein favors, in the *Investigations*, as the *lebensformlich*, without ever being criterial (except derivatively), being (rather) tacitly permitted by ongoing social practices that yield to gradual and divergent change without epistemic dislocation. This is not to deny the possibility of testing the aptness of would-be objective categories; it is only to say that such testing is itself ultimately grounded not in self-evident propositions or assured cognitive sources, but in the entrenched practices of an actual enabling society.[2]

When Derrida notoriously declared "Il n'y a pas de hors-texte,"[3] he did not say (or intend) that there was nothing outside any particular text or outside *the* single inclusive text that is the entire intelligible world, but only that whatever is locally judged to be "outside" a specified text is itself a text or texted: that is, the *hors-texte* of any particular text is itself a text— alternatively, a context, the texted conceptual space within which texts, or even the various parts of physical nature, are (may be) relevantly texted. For, surely, *contexts* are human contrivances, perspectived and selective frames of reference uttered to enhance or make legible the pertinently interpreted structure of some particular part of the world. That is, Derrida need not be read as an idealist here, only as a beneficiary of post-Kantian discoveries. (Correspondingly, you may treat the thesis that selves are self-interpreting texts as a heuristic convenience by which to feature the Intentional life of human societies—hence, not as idealist in any familiar sense.)

If (with me) you construe the universe as the context of all contexts, you may agree that it is conceptually impossible (except on the presumption of a form of cognitive privilege equal to God's competence) to pronounce any textual order as the unique and total system of the intelligible world. I take that to be part of Derrida's meaning—to be, in fact, the master theme of deconstruction. But if that is conceded, then there cannot be an outer limit (an *hors-texte*) by which valid or objective interpretation can be determinately confined: the limits of objective interpretation are themselves interpretively constructed (critically, let us concede), but always contingently, endogenously, serially, divergently, by way of prejudice—the preformation of our power of judgment—if (as seems obviously true) the universe is never, as such, a datum for description or analysis. It is, I would say, the import of the leanest lesson drawn from the constructivism that, since the post-Kantian analysis of early modern philosophy (particularly Hegel's), shows us how to avoid the paradoxes of classical realism without abandoning realism itself.

So seen, the admission of the world's textuality is tantamount to the denial of first principles or First Philosophy.[4] For textualizing the world is tantamount to admitting the (epistemically) inseparable unity of cognizing subjects and cognized objects, the defeat of objectivisms of every sort, the impossibility of exiting from the hermeneutic circle, the insuperable dependence of meanings or Intentional structures on the historicity of selves, and the endless and endlessly divergent reinterpretability of given texts and their interpretations.

You see at once, therefore, that a generous theory of texts of the sort I suggest brings in its wake strenuous puzzles regarding the number and nature of denumerable texts—of the familiar sorts considered in professional criticism in the arts, in legal and scriptural disputes, and the like. I intend to address the most important of these puzzles, but in a way congruent with certain contested axioms (as I've called them) bearing on knowledge and reality in the largest sense. Frankly, I am convinced that canonical objections to such a theory are almost always ill founded, both because they insist on forms of privilege they cannot convincingly secure (*de re* necessities, for instance, or the noetic grasp of universals and essences) and because they insist that extreme departures from such constraints inevitably produce paradox and self-contradiction "somewhere." I have in mind such deviant options as the defense of the objective standing of incompatible interpretations (as valid, even if not jointly true) or the admission that the natures of interpreted texts actually change under interpretation (though without generating self-defeating paradoxes of any kind).

In any case, what discussants on all sides of the question wish to know is whether there are principled limits on what to regard as a text and what to regard as admissible in the objective interpretation of a text. Clearly, no one wishes to favor interpretive chaos. Nevertheless, it is quite surprising to discover that there are no compelling objections against unrestricted interpretation, except in conformity with the limits of brute memory, fluency, tolerance within habitual practices, pertinence regarding contingent interests or purposes, and what may be shown to be internally coherent and supportable in evidentiary ways. These, it turns out, are not particularly arduous constraints.

II

Having offered my preamble, I hasten to emphasize that, at the present time, there is no prospect of reducing language (or the lingual analogues of cultural life) to subcultural (biological or physical) processes, or, a fortiori, of eliminating language altogether. Many are sanguine on this last score, of course, notably the partisans of neurocomputational models of the mind.[5] But it would not be unfair to claim that they have not succeeded and have never explained how (apart from a conceptual wave of the hand) the trick is to be turned. I myself believe that the natural (but nonreducible) emergence of language and culture is reflexively posited at just that advanced level of enculturation at which we are able to consider, discursively, looking back at evolution: say, to grasp the fact that a threshold must have been crossed at some distant hominid moment close enough to our present competence to make sense of it constructively. I find the conclusion unavoidable if, for instance, reference is, as I have argued, impossible to capture algorithmically.

I see no significant difference here in judging when a human infant first begins to speak and when we suppose language first began. Both conjectures are necessarily anthropomorphized, modeled top-down on our own linguistic and lingual competence. But if that is so, then the proper parts of texts are themselves never less than texts or texted, even though the cultural world surely depends upon, incorporates, and is inseparable from physical and biological nature. That is the precise sense in which we cannot exit from the hermeneutic circle: for we cannot function as selves if we cannot function linguistically and lingually, but, of course, functioning thus, we cannot discern anything that is not a text either paradigmatically or by the courtesy of anthropomorphizing. Effectively, the world of human culture is both irreducible and ineliminable; hence, its emergence is sui generis and functional in *reflexive* (Intentional) terms rather than in terms only of the biological processes in which it is incarnate.

Here, we touch on quarrelsome and neglected matters that may seem remote from the question of the objective interpretation of texts but are really of decisive importance. If texts may be said to exist as individuated entities (*denotata*) of some kind, then, in accord with a robust sense of existence (eschewing abstract entities like concepts or kinds or universals or numbers) and applying the category (*text*) to linguistic utterances, actions, selves, artworks, and historical events, texts must be materially embodied in some suitable way, though not reducible to their embodying entities. For example, if Michelangelo's *Pietà* is, as a sculpture, a text (as I would say), then, although it is embodied in a block of cut marble, its representational and expressive parts (the interpretable details of the sculpture) must be similarly embodied. *They are not parts of the marble but of the sculpture.* That surely affects the individuation and numerical identity of the sculpture, as well as the objectivity with which we may analyze its Intentional structure or nature.

Similarly, to remind ourselves of another needlessly tormented issue, the expressiveness of music *is* musically perceptible, *is* incarnate in sound, *is* part of the predicable nature of music itself. Expressiveness belongs to a piece of music because a piece of music is a musical text. It needs no metaphor (in Goodman's sense)[6] in order to be objectively attributed. It needs no fictive human voice within the sound, no make-believe, to ensure its conceptual adequation.[7]

In saying that music *is* an interpreted text or utterance, I mean (1) that music (or painting) *is* created or Intentionally constructed; (2) that it possesses, as a result, Intentional properties (expressiveness among them); and (3) that it is in virtue of conditions (1) and (2) that its Intentional properties (expressiveness again) *can be* directly discerned by an informed percipient as easily as any merely sensorily perceivable property. The gain the theory of texts makes possible is this: to speak of the expressiveness (or similar properties) of a piece of music *does not* presuppose or entail that there is, or must be, some logically prior (real or fictive or otherwise contrived) emotional or psychological state *of which* the imputed property is the expression, or that we can only validate its objective attribution *when it is made to depend* (literally, fictively, metaphorically, by make-believe, or in some alternative relational way) *on* some posited psychological state. There's a clause too many there. Once you give up reductive materialism and admit the reality of culturally emergent phenomena, the entire mystery of expressiveness dissolves. (If you see the argument's force, you are bound to see the vacuity as well of treating habitus as subterranean generative structures, and if you reject the primacy of the inner generative view, you will be drawn to analyze the epistemic importance of explicit Intentional practices. It is there, in fact, that the effective power and structure of Intentional utterance are to be found.)

I hasten to add as well that, by *embodied*, I mean (as I have remarked earlier) no more than that texts are indissolubly complex entities, emergent under the sui generis conditions of enculturation, characterizable jointly in material and Intentional terms, where, conformably, the Intentional is complexly incarnate in material properties.[8] To exist, then, texts must be embodied; they exist in and only in the same cultural space in which selves exist—and no wonder, for they are deliberately uttered or produced by selves, who are themselves culturally uttered by the caretakers of their society.

By *utterance*, once again, I mean no more than the effective, Intentional, intrinsically interpretable activity of culturally competent selves. So texts are relatively freestanding individuatable entities (*denotata*). Our paradigms are unavoidably linguistic. But since, as I would argue, the linguistic is itself also lingual—language not being autonomous—the category, *text*, easily includes lingual entities like sculptures and music and even the most complex of texts: selves or persons.[9]

But, if what is meant by insisting that we cannot exit the hermeneutic circle is that whatever belongs to the cultural world is real, emergent, irreducible, sui generis, then, for one thing, texts cannot be individuated or identified by way of individuating or identifying their embodying *materiae* and, for another, their Intentional attributes cannot be specified in any non-Intentional ways. As already remarked, the physical sources of materially embodying entities lack and embodied (material) entities possess Intentional properties. That is why, for formal reasons, they cannot be one and the same.[10] Entities possess Intentional properties and are ontically hybrid for that reason—Picasso's *Demoiselles d'Avignon*, for example.

These are no more than tautologies, but they are hardly negligible. They affect not only our grasp of the peculiar ontology of texts but also the conditions of objective interpretation. They are animated dynamically by being informed by the processes of mutual understanding among selves.

Here, I must respectfully disagree with the forthright and otherwise attractive definition of texts offered by Jorge Gracia, who has in recent years formulated one of the few sustained analytic accounts of what it is to be a text. "A text," Gracia says, "is a group of entities, used as signs, which are selected, arranged, and intended by an author in a certain context to convey some specific meaning to an audience."[11] As it happens, all of Gracia's carefully worded conditions may be challenged along the lines I've suggested, but two (I think) are of signal importance for objectivity. Gracia clarifies his meaning at once, adding, "A proper understanding of textuality requires that we distinguish texts from the entities used as the signs that compose texts. This is important because . . . the distinction between texts and the entities that constitute them may account for the seemingly incompatible predicates that are often predicated of texts."[12]

It is easy enough to misread what Gracia intends here. One may be tempted to think that the expression "entities used as the signs that compose texts" signifies *non*-Intentional material marks of one kind or another that are first denoted *as* material marks, in order thereupon to identify signs, which are themselves nothing but the nominalized *denotata* answering to the sign-use of the prior marks—which, in turn, permit us to denote, by compositional means, true texts, distinguished by some further function different in principle from the function flagged by the sign-use of the original marks. That would be a double mistake, apart from the fact that it is certainly not what Gracia means: it would signify, first, that texts—artworks, histories, sentences—are identified by material, *non*-Intentional means (which would require supervenience at least);[13] second, it would signify that texts are a distinct compositional union of some sort of the sign-use of ulterior non-Intentional or nontextual marks.

Nelson Goodman is instructive here—apart from the exaggerated precision with which he believes scripts and scores may be identified, even characterized, by way of inscriptional marks and, by *their* use, the further properties of musical works (musical texts, as I would say) that (Goodman believes) are similarly perceivable in entirely non-Intentional terms. In fact, Goodman commits the error that Gracia escapes—or seems on the point of escaping. "Characters," or elements in a notational scheme, Goodman says, "are certain classes of utterances or inscriptions or marks . . . [and] an inscription is any mark—visual, auditory, etc.—that belongs to a character."[14] This sounds right, and it may be allowed on a suitable reading. But a closer study of his account confirms that Goodman conflates the physical (or, in Goodman's own sense, material) or non-Intentional perceptual element—which, given his own sense of *perceptual,* is "visual, auditory, etc."—with the culturally "perceivable," Intentional element designated by the (same) inscriptions in a script or score.[15] One simply needs to flag the equivocation on "perceive."

To fix what is essential, consider that the proper parts of a piece of music (analogously, the proper parts of a score representing the music) are *not* mere physical sounds (or marks) but musically (Intentionally) significant sounds embodied in some admissible range of physical sounds. Goodman loses the distinction, and Gracia does not quite explain the relationship between marks and signs, although it is perfectly clear that Gracia does not confuse the two: "strictly speaking," he says, "only the entities or features of entities that function semantically should be considered constitutive of a text."[16] But he does favor something like a two-story theory of texts. He tends to oppose admitting as textually significant what is not strictly semantic in the linguistic sense—what, for instance, may be semiotic in a lingual way (the expressive and representational attributes of a ballet or a symphony).[17] I cannot agree: texts are diversely cultural, not merely linguistic, artifacts. Marks and signs are relevantly related top-down, not bottom-up. Material things are already (in my usage) complex entities Intentionally contrived and embodied (as, say, a word or painting or melody)—hence, not merely physical.

The quibble is not unimportant, because it draws attention to a puzzle about denoting texts and, hence, given Gracia's definition, to a question about the two-story nature of a text. There's the point of my complaint. Gracia, I would say, cannot answer the denotative (or individuative) question (nor can Goodman); furthermore, since Gracia is inclined to treat texts only predicatively, he cannot fail to compound the difficulty.

My own sense is that, since predicative distinctions cannot replace genuinely denotative or referential ones, the failure to explain the denotation of texts adversely affects the entire matter of interpretive objectivity. (I shall come back to that.) Also, if signs are proper compositional parts of texts, then, as I say, *they* also are texts. At any rate, once the denotative issue is resolved, there is no need to insist on a two-story account of the Intentional structure of texts: the reason for doing so can only be for the sake of the erroneous doctrine that texts, and all Intentional artifacts, may be, and must be able to be, adequately denoted by way of denoting non-Intentional marks, or the equally erroneous doctrine that the identification of signs is interpretively reliable or privileged in some prior way in which the interpretation of texts is not. Certainly, Gracia means, by distinguishing (however benignly) between *signs* and *texts*, to justify restricting the admissible meaning of a text ("intended by an author in a certain context") in such a way as to disallow incompatible meanings (or interpretations) of the text in question: the distinction between *signs* and *text*, he says, "may account for the seemingly incompatible but inadmissible predicates that are often predicated of texts." You see how the complications begin to swarm.[18]

What we require is hardly more than a verbal convenience to mark an essential ontological distinction. I distinguish between the physical and material: the physical answers to the strictest physical sciences; the material, to this specifically hybrid functioning of the mental embedded in the physical. (I make no pretense of understanding the ontological status of the mental, except to conjecture that it ranges over a familiar run of functional powers that we take to comprise the mind that are rightly assignable to a suitably specialized part of the physical body [let us say, neuro-physiologically qualified, centered in the brain].) In this sense, the material signifies a certain (evolved) functionality of the body. A sign or gesture (best construed in Peirce's sense) is then a hybrid artifact that manifests Intentionality, mentally or behaviorally, naturally or by convention, linguistically or not.

III

I have already remarked that the theory of texts is bound to reflect the bias of prior epistemic convictions about our capacity to understand meanings and Intentional structures. I am entirely willing to be frank about my own persuasion. I am convinced, for instance, that it is quite impossible to fix the conditions of referential (or denotative) success as well as of predicative success (in particular, of interpretive success) criterially, by way of rules or algorithms, and I am equally convinced that there is no algorithmic way to fix the very contexts in which reference and predication succeed in natural-language discourse.

This is as true of nonfictional texts as it is of the fictional kind, a fact that colors in a decisive way the issue of the objectivity of discourse about literary texts; a fortiori, about texts in general. There is no gradation of objectivity here, along the lines Jonathan Culler has suggested: that is, that "Some texts are more orphaned [less encumbered, culturally, whether referentially or predicatively] than others."[19] There is also, then, no danger incurred regarding the prospects of objective interpretation by merely opposing the familiar canon that a literary work—rather than a mere text, in the labile sense the poststructuralists have favored (Barthes, notably) and I, by implication, also favor—has a determinate identity, a determinately bounded nature, and this also supports our sense of the definite contexts in which its meaning may be fixed with some precision. The canonical argument has been elegantly voiced by Meyer Abrams and echoed by many others. But I'm afraid it has no legs, simply because the puzzles of reference and predication and context plainly affect the presumption of every theory of objective interpretation.[20] (The distinction between *text* and *literary work of art* cannot be more than a verbal convenience.)

From my point of view, therefore, there is no conceivable gain to be had by supposing that texts may be (or may have to be) denoted by way of denoting physical objects first (along, say, Goodman's or Wollheim's or Danto's lines) or by way of privileged signs (as Gracia sometimes seems to insist). Referential and predicative success and the fixity of context are entirely consensual and epistemically inseparable from one another—in the noncriterial sense sketched so tellingly in Wittgenstein's *Investigations* and *Culture and Values*.[21] The referential (or denotative) question obviously requires a much closer look, inasmuch as its resolution cannot fail to influence our conception of the possible variety of viable interpretive strategies.

It is an incontestable fact that the linkage between the denotation of texts and the would-be objective description or interpretation of their meanings has been completely ignored (or, "solved") by virtue of assuming that there is no pertinent epistemic difference between the description of *denotata* possessing non-Intentional natures and those possessing Intentional natures. But to believe *that* blatantly presumes that there are no existent entities that have, or can have, natures that are *not* straightforwardly in accord with the familiar picture of natural things possessing strictly determinate physical properties and conforming equally strictly to a logic confined by the principle of excluded middle or (if initial decidability poses a difficulty) at least the principle of *tertium non datur*.[22]

Yet texts *have* only determinable, not strictly determinate, natures (in possessing Intentional structures), and the meanings that may be assigned them, objectively, are surely hostage to the historied nature of interpretive practice and the historied formation of the cognizing competence of the selves who undertake the effort. But that is not to say that texts are simply indeterminate or without structure. I put it to you that there simply is no compelling theory that demonstrates the supposed similarity—ontologically, epistemologically, methodologically, logically—between physical properties predicated of mere physical things and meanings predicated of materially embodied texts. All the evidence goes against the analogy. So that, *if* you admit texts as actual entities within a cultural space, you must concede the possibility that they may be entirely determinate denotatively (in fact, as determinate as physical objects are) *without*, as a result, being predicatively determinate as well (as physical objects are said to be). The history of the interpretation of texts—the history of philosophy, for that matter—has largely assumed the contrary. I take this thesis to mark the single most radical, most far-reaching feature of the theory of texts that anyone could claim.

Accordingly, I offer the following distinctions in the way of logical and epistemic presuppositions (or postulates) that any reasonable theory of texts must address somewhere. First, I reject all substantive necessities *de re* and *de cogitatione*, but I do not hold that that rejection counts as a necessary principle of the same sort. Obviously not. It is, I should say, a philosophical bet, to the effect that no one can show the unavoidability of such necessities (apart from uninterpreted tautologies and contradictions). Second, I would say that it was entirely possible (and noticeably advantageous, particularly in cultural matters) to concede that individuation, numerical identity, denotation, reference, and reidentifiability are all quite viable (without producing paradox) in dealing with entities that lack essences or fixed natures or that possess histories or careers instead of natures. In fact, texts lack natural-kind natures and have, or are, only histories; that is, their interpretable nature, their Intentional structure, is and can only be a genuine function of the history of the cultural utterances, the interpretations and self-interpretations, that obtain in the contingent cultures in which they are actually produced and discerned.

These two distinctions go entirely contrary to Aristotelian presuppositions, but, frankly, I take the modal form of the Aristotelian claims to be patently indefensible.[23]

I have two considerations to offer. The first concerns how, denotatively, we should understand the relationship between "marks" and "meanings."[24] I agree that one cannot be aware of spoken words and sentences without, in some sense, being aware of uttered sounds, but it hardly follows that one understands the meaning of uttered words *by* understanding that they are the meanings assigned the sounds (or marks) first uttered or used to signify some determinate, antecedent, objective, independent, intended meaning. The reason is simply that *meanings* (or, Intentional structures) cannot be "objects" that play "the same role [in understanding] as the object [for instance, the perceptual object] in the process of [perceptual] knowledge."[25] There is an insuperable disanalogy that counts against the thesis. The clue already lurks in expressions like "the meaning *conveyed*" by would-be signs, "the meaning *of the marks*"—or the meaning of the signs *constituted by* "the *use of* the marks" or by the "*intended use*" *of* the marks. There is no lexical order between marks and signs or between signs and texts.

If you grant that understanding language, texts, artworks, and the like are forms of reflexive understanding—understanding ourselves and what we utter—then there is no satisfactory sense in which when I understand what a poem means (or, by analogy, what a practice means), there is a separable meaning, independent of any interpretive effort, that belongs to the marks (or to the use of the marks printed on a page, or, analogously, to the movements of the body) that I discern and understand, in the same way in which when I see (and come to know by perceiving) that there is a horse on the hill, *there is*, apart from my perceiving the horse, a horse on the hill! Meanings are not objects in any such sense; they are objects only by way of nominalization, for what we discern (if we may be said to discern meanings at all) are the Intentional attributes of our own natures or histories or utterings—the reflexively assignable meanings of the interpretable texts of a common culture.

In genuine sensory cases, cases confined to the activation of our sense organs, we require a workable disjunction between cognizing subjects and cognized objects. But in understanding texts, there is no such antecedent disjunction, which is not to deny that understanding meanings may be judged to be objectively valid or invalid—or perceived. It's just that the ontology and epistemology can't be the same in the two cases. Both New Critical theorists (for instance, Monroe Beardsley)[26] and Romantic hermeneuts (for instance, E. D. Hirsch)[27] treat meanings very much like independent properties, though very differently from one another. (Gracia appears to hold a related view.) I take these variant views to commit the same mistake. There is no way to ensure the standing of meanings as analogous to that of the properties of independent objects (Beardsley) or to assign authorial intent or stylistic genres a determinate criterial role (Hirsch).

There is no way to fix the intention or intended use or meaning of any current text except in terms of the contingent linguistic (and lingual) fluency of apt speakers within a historical culture, who, from the vantage of such fluency, continually reconstitute (as they see matters) the intended meanings of texts produced in past phases of that same history. Objectivity cannot fail to be consensual (in the *lebensformlich* sense already suggested), and if it must be that, interpretive objectivity cannot be the analogue of sensory and allied forms of objectivity. The objectivity of texts is productive, not disclosive; interpretive, not sensory or merely sensory-like. But, of course, if that is so, the objectivity of sociology or practical politics will be affected as well. Bear that in mind.

Furthermore, if, as I have argued, texts may be determinately denoted and reidentified, even though their nature or history or meaning need not be antecedently determinate (but only diversely determinable), then interpretive objectivity cannot convincingly require that a text should possess a single or unique or fixed or independent meaning. If, also, our interpretive powers are continually reconstituted historically, or are horizontally perspectived as far as self-understanding is concerned, then the analogy between Intentionally structured and non-Intentional *denotata* will be put at mortal risk.

In short, to admit the sui generis realism of the cultural world is, effectively, to reject the analogy between texts that we *understand* and mere physical or natural objects that we *perceive* in the sensory way. But we cannot deny the existence of texts if we admit the existence of selves, and uttered texts cannot be more determinate than the reflexively determinable nature of self-interpreting selves. Ultimately, the theory of texts is a theory of selves and of their utterances.

The second consideration is one that should be credited to the logical empiricist Herbert Feigl (already mentioned), who, well before the current fashion favoring supervenience with regard to the mind/body problem,[28] realized that there was no known basis for insisting on an invariant relationship between changes or differences in mental (or cultural or intentional) attributes (or meanings) and matched changes or differences in physical (or material) attributes. What Feigl maintained—let me say again—was this: (1) that a meaningful action (or thought) could be performed (or conveyed) by indefinitely many different bodily movements (or neurophysiological processes), (2) that a particular bodily movement (or neurophysiological process) could convey (or embody, as I would say) indefinitely many different Intentionally distinct actions (or thoughts), and (3) that there was no known algorithm or rule by which changes in the one were necessarily matched with changes in the other. (This alone defeats supervenience [in Kim's sense], of course, which claims a necessary [however loose] correlation between the two.) But if so, then the individuation and denotation of texts are doubly Intentional and cannot be captured by our denotative strategies or, computationally, fitted to non-Intentional entities ("marks," in Goodman's and possibly in Gracia's sense).

Our finding is a double one: first, that of the sheer coherence of admitting the denotative determinacy of texts (comparing favorably with the numerical determinacy of physical objects) together with their interpretively determinable but not determinate nature (as opposed to the nature of physical objects); second, following on the first and admitting as well the historicized nature of the interpretive powers of self-interpreting selves, the impossibility of ensuring, evidentiarily, that the objective interpretation of texts (the utterances of self-interpreting selves) can ever yield a uniquely correct or fixed or singular or independent meaning.

Here, the ontology of texts reflects the essential cognitive difference between knowledge by mere sensory perception and knowledge by understanding (or, as we may say, interpretively informed "perception"). I take this to be very closely linked to the familiar Diltheyan distinction between *Verstehen* and *erklären*,[29] except that the cognitive powers in question cannot possibly operate independently of one another; sensory perception has its interpretive (or hermeneutic) side, and self-understanding entails sensory perception. What *does* follow, however, is that it is hardly necessary to subscribe exclusively to a bivalent logic and that it is decidedly unpromising to do so in the context of interpreting texts. The second finding seems a very natural one and neatly outflanks the usual heavy-handed insistence on the "logic of science." Both are, in fact, rather powerful findings for such a modest effort.

In short, what I am claiming is this: once we admit (a) that texts may be denotatively determinate but predicatively never more than determinable, (b) that all texts or culturally emergent *denotata* have Intentional natures that are inherently interpretable, and (c) that in the cultural world, provision must be made for the cognitively pertinent process in which cognizers and cognized are one and the same and culturally constituted, it becomes well-nigh impossible to deny that the objectivity of interpreting Intentional structures cannot disallow the full pertinence of historicism, relativism regarding the reasoned assignment of truth-values, and even the hermeneutic relevance of self-reflection among the physical sciences. There you have the single most contested thesis in the theory of texts made as plausible as a commonplace.

IV

The lesson I've been pressing about reference and denotation is simply this: that even the denoting of a particular physical object apt for reidentification is, apart from any general theory of language, a decidedly Intentional act; hence, it cannot be convincingly claimed that merely to admit specifically

Intentional entities is, effectively, to jeopardize more disciplined discursive resources restricted to physical objects. There is no such rigor to be had. The very idea bespeaks a false optimism that rests on the mistaken notion that predicative resources may, in principle, be counted on to retire our would-be referential and denotative devices, or that the predicative resources of the physical sciences may be segregated from those of the cultural world. I say that that's impossible. I have already taken note of a strong proposal favoring the failed conjecture (about reference and denotation, in Quine's *Word and Object*) that appeals to the limited resources of the first-order predicate calculus.[30] But there is absolutely no known argument to show that numerical identity can actually be captured, in real-world terms, by a mix of quantification and predication.[31] (The insight goes back, as I have also remarked, to Leibniz.)[32] And the indissolubility (or symbiosis) of the subjective and the objective in referential and predicative discourse completely obviates (unless constructively) the epistemic disjunction of inquiries into the natural and cultural worlds.

What this shows is that the *admission* of a physical world lacking Intentional properties presupposes (for epistemic reasons) a world of Intentionally (cognitively) qualified entities. (That is the supreme lesson of the post-Kantian ethos.) Otherwise, it would make no sense to speak of denoting, individuating, reidentifying, referring to one and the same entity. I mark this a considerable gain in behalf of a realism regarding texts. (Realism, I remind you, cannot, on the gathering argument, fail to take a constructivist turn.)

For somewhat different reasons, the same presupposition makes an appearance in predicative contexts. The two are bound to be connected, for, if (per impossibile) denotation could be retired by the joint use of quantificational and predicative devices, we should be driven to decide whether properties may be determinately fixed or epistemically managed in strictly extensional ways. The answer is no, absent Platonism.[33] But, of course, there is no known way to access universals by any form of human cognition. Furthermore, if that's not possible, then it follows at once that the very idea of an objective property belongs to the indissoluble space of cognizing subjects and cognized objects—certainly not to any merely objective (or objectivist) space; hence, it leads, once again, to the presupposition of Intentionally qualified selves.

Again, if texts are, as I suggest, the utterances of reflecting selves, reasonably nominalized or detached as separable artifacts apt for interpretation, then their meanings, predicatively construed, cannot possibly be managed extensionally, since general attributes (non-Intentional attributes in particular) cannot be. This confirms very trimly the coherence of admitting that texts may be determinately denoted though they lack determinate natures.

Both parts of the thesis are concessive with regard to the would-be determinacy of physical objects. I have no wish to press that issue here; I wish only to secure grounds needed for a cultural realism hospitable to texts. We have only to acknowledge that the similarities on which any predicates are justifiably extended to new instances depend (noncriterially) on some *lebensformlich* tolerance, in servicing one societal interest or another (predictive precision, for instance).[34]

If we wished to challenge the objectivist reading of physical nature, then what has thus far been said would be sufficient to carry the argument.[35] I may just add, however, that recent work in the history of the new technology of high-level physics—Peter Galison's study, for instance, of the rather local, somewhat fragmented, heterogeneous cultures of professional physicists variously centered on measurement, experiment, technology, and explanatory theory, often differing in incommensurable and even incompatible ways—does plausibly show that such societies do (or could) in fact manage, despite such discrepancies (which are never quite overcome and never need to be), to cooperate, piecemeal, within established behavioral patterns, without at all understanding one another in terms of a single overarching idiom or theory. I take this to be no more than a corollary of Kuhn's original claim against perceptual and scientific neutrality.

Galison sees an effective "trading zone" here, both in physics and the marketplace, between very different cultures that are neither incapacitated by such divergence nor obliged to overcome it by appeal to a neutral idiom in order to function effectively at all. He speaks of a trading zone in both settings: in effect, a congeries of ad hoc, temporary, behavioral accommodations good enough to coordinate "this" with "that" for the work at hand, so that "*despite* . . . differences in [practices of] classification, [assignments of] significance, and [commitment to] standards of demonstration, [different] groups can collaborate. They can come to a consensus about the procedure of exchange, about the mechanisms to determine when [they succeed]. They can even both understand that the continuation of exchange is a prerequisite to the survival of the larger culture of which they are part."[36]

I read this as an obvious analogue of my proposal about texts, extended to the work of the most advanced physical sciences. That is, practical judgment, logically informal though it must be (for example, regarding reference and predication and context and interpreted meaning), is able to work well enough, in terms of consensual practices, relative to any given undertaking, even though what counts as understanding and cooperation and success may never be able to be fixed in any unique, neutral, principled way. Such judgment is able to confirm a measure of constructed objectivity, but it can no longer claim to have simply "discovered" in a contextless way what the neutral truth finally is.

That fiction may well be gone forever. By parity of reason, in learning a social practice, there is (normally) no fixed or algorithmically defined practice that we learn. Our fluencies, here, are offered in the form of abstracted rules, but the rules are hardly ever more than heuristically advanced and continually recast—even though they may be helpful (for unspecified intervals) in informing spontaneous behavior in accord with the practices assumed. (The inertial life of a viable society changes, at different rates, through the different parts of its habituated practices. Needless to say, I offer Galison's view as friendly testimony regarding the advanced sciences—not as confirmation of my thesis.) But to admit the point is to confirm the need to understand just what is mastered in understanding a practice.

If, now, distinguishing between Intentional and non-Intentional predicates, you add (1) that sensory perception and the understanding of meanings are fundamentally different and (2) that the objectivity of meanings is inextricably bound up with the historical drift of our interpretive practices (in a way that is not pertinently matched by any form of mere sensory objectivity, though perceptual objectivity drifts as well), then the following doctrine, already elicited, cannot possibly be legitimated: the doctrine that holds that if we grasp, by interpretive means, the objective meaning of a text, then that text must determinately possess that meaning independently of our actually interpreting it.

Ironically, that *is* the canonical view. Only a Platonism could possibly save it. Otherwise, objectivity regarding texts is, first, thoroughly *lebensformlich* and (beyond Wittgenstein) historicized; second, objectivity cannot, as a result, disallow a priori the interpretive validity of divergent, even incompatible or historically evolving meanings, or meanings that depend on the prior history of interpretation (and *its* interpretation).

Here, the primary question is not one of coherence or mere possibility but of societal memory, tolerance, interest, perspective, prejudice—and the capacity to juggle reasonable attributions (in the way of sorting plural strands of each). That is an unexpected gain. For what it means is simply that relativism, for example—which I espouse but have no wish to defend just here—is grounded in the very same *lebensformlich* sources that we would need to enlist if we had simply insisted on there being no more than a uniquely correct meaning assignable to each particular text.[37] Once you admit the fundamental disanalogy between sensory properties and meanings, you cannot escape the slippery slope of historicizing meanings, in admitting the artifactual and historicized nature of selves. But then, once you admit the *lebensformlich* character of reference and predication, you cannot escape historicizing the conditions of objectivity for discourse about physical nature either. (This is simply to admit the symbiosis of the ontological and the epistemological and the *petitios* of First Philosophy.)

There is nothing in these adjustments that risks the regularities of cognitive practice. On the contrary, if the argument holds, then the perceptual and theorizing resources of our best sciences will be seen to be grounded in the same fluxive condition, for, here, *flux* means nothing more than the denial of necessities and fixities *de re* and *de cogitatione*. There is no reason to regard that as paradoxical.

You must turn to someone like David Hume to find a theory of the meaning of terms that actually defeats intelligibility. For Hume accelerates, in the *Treatise*, the effect of flux beyond manageable limits: Hume holds that the least change in a perceived quality signifies an utter change of quality—hence, an utter change of predicate.[38] The theory requires (in principle) an instantaneous, continual replacement of one entire vocabulary by another—which, of course, is impossible. Neither historicism nor relativism requires anything of the kind. The concept of a general predicate concerns no more than the notion of what may be judged to remain qualitatively the same *through* perceived differences or changes. Consensual practices are enough. If Hume were favored here, we would destroy the very possibility of linguistic communication, or deliberate cooperation for that matter. In fact, many critics of historicism and relativism fall back to similar (pointless) worries about rendering texts unintelligible, once it turns out that they cannot disallow either doctrine on grounds of internal incoherence. (But they do not understand the threat Hume poses.)

The main lines of the argument are now quite clear: texts are artifacts existing in cultural space, possessing real Intentional structures (meanings, if you wish) apt for continual interpretation. But if Platonism is indemonstrable, if reference and predication are historicized and *lebensformlich*, if selves and their cognizing aptitudes are similarly formed, then the conditions for understanding individuated texts are inseparable from the conditions by which we understand ourselves. But if so, then understanding the meaning of texts cannot fail to be objective (that is, cannot fail to provide for objectivity) since there is no viable notion of what it is to be a competent self deprived of such fluency. To interpret correctly the artifacts of human life (texts, if you please)—thoughts, actions, speech, artworks, histories, institutions—*is* simply to function as an exemplary self.

There remains, however, a double hermeneutic drift to be acknowledged, which Hans-Georg Gadamer has pinpointed most effectively: namely, that, as they change historically, enabling cultures change the cognizing horizon of functioning selves and, coordinately, change the potentiating range of meanings apt for subsequent interpretation (or cooperation).[39] (That, of course, is historicism pure and simple.)

If you bear in mind that selves cannot fail to be aware that they interpret themselves and the other texts of their world from the vantage of a transient horizon that must have replaced other such horizons in the past, you see that they cannot disallow similar further horizonal alterations, amplifications, revisions, even replacements, diverging and competing streams of interpretation—within the consensual limits of societal memory and interest and tolerance—within which they function.

Admitting all that entails two extraordinary complications that theorists of art and history generally avoid—but cannot justify avoiding.[40] One collects the fact that the meaning of the historical past belongs to the interlocking horizon of an evolving history (itself constructed) in which it is continually relocated and, hence, that the meaning of the historical past (*not* the physical past) must be a changing artifact of changing interpretations. The other complication is at least as strenuous: namely, that texts of every sort acquire ambient trails of interpretive history, always subject to further interpretive weighting, that tend (if undisputed) to define, inertially, the proper context of understanding the particular texts to which they attach. Such fixities can never be more than reportorial conveniences or local hegemonies, as Roland Barthes's interpretation of Balzac's *Sarrasine*[41] and George Thomson's interpretation of the *Oresteia*[42] very nicely confirm.

I must enter a warning here. I am quite aware that, regarding "intentional discourse," certain logical puzzles arise when circumstances affect the *truth* of what is believed, which may be wrongly believed to affect *what is actually believed*. This is what Peter Geach had in mind in speaking of mere "Cambridge changes." I grant the point. When, for instance, I believe that de Gaulle is the tallest Frenchman, and it happens, as time goes by, that someone else comes to occupy the status of tallest Frenchman, then the truth of what I believe may be altered but not my belief (which was true at a time but is no longer, or now, true). I do not, however, admit that changes in the meaning of texts as a result of continual interpretation and historical development *are* mere Cambridge changes! Not at all. You may oppose my view because you oppose my picture of the reality of the cultural world. But that's an entirely different affair.

V

It is in the sense intended that texts are assigned unitary careers. We grasp the meaning of a human life by understanding the sequence of its biological phases within the context of a culturally significant career. By analogy, literary texts, artworks, more amorphous histories—hardly lives, but utterances all—are cast as sustaining unitary careers, chiefly as a result of their interpretive histories. They have no closed form of their own, of course. Think of the career of the endlessly reinterpreted American Civil War (or Velázquez's *Las Meninas*, for that matter). There is no way, now, to interpret the war (or *Las Meninas*) responsibly, except through the scruple of preserving the history of its accumulating interpretations—without yet supposing that *any* interpreted part of it need ever be finally fixed or fixed within its encompassing career. The most interesting texts appear to be both protean and inexhaustible: the Bible, the Vedas, the American Constitution, the *Odyssey*.

Thus construed, the chief constraints on interpretation rest with a society's capacity to remember and bring to bear on new interpretations of a given text some part of that society's present sense of the text's entire history. Generally, much of this will be forgotten or interpretively rearranged or selectively discounted, and the unity of the text's predicated *nature* will be diversely imputed, always preserving *number* in the denotative sense. Just recently, in fact, the practice has been confirmed in a telling but circumscribed way by its deliberate restriction in the reading of an exemplary text, from a vantage that can hardly be called careless or uninformed—in Helen Vendler's important rereading of Shakespeare's *Sonnets*.[43]

An adequate theory of interpretive practice is bound to be far more generous (and more strenuous) than the rationale for any particular reader's practice. But, then, the *society* of the practice of all readers is bound to be more diverse and more tolerant than any individual theory of texts might ever proclaim. That is what I find so neatly illustrated by the absence of any justificatory rationale in what Vendler offers in explaining her own "commentary" as a modest "supplement" to certain important readings that she happens to favor.[44] It is surely worth an additional moment's attention. (The amplitude of a society's tolerance for different sources of interpretation is a soft analogue of a species' need for a diverse gene pool.)

I mean to draw from Vendler's example two strategic gains for the theory of texts: one concerns how naturally even a deliberately restricted commentary like Vendler's may be reclaimed by a more generous theory of reading (the sort, frankly, that I am recommending), which Vendler explicitly opposes; the other, how straightforwardly we may ensure the coherence and plausibility of the more accommodating radical theories of interpretation spawned from the first gain. The point is to soften the charge of arbitrariness and the fear of interpretive chaos that are so often brought against theories that deny that meanings are fixed in historical time, as by authorial intent or by essential genres or by whatever else may be thought to govern a determinate set of words, and also to assure us that the theory being championed is not likely (as a result) to be confronted by any intractable paradox or logical difficulty that only a more canonical (objectivist) view of interpretation could possibly save us from. I claim no more than the coherence and viability of the upstart theory and the incapacity of the familiar canons to guarantee more.

Turn, then, to Vendler's readings. I acknowledge the spare scruple of Vendler's commentary on the *Sonnets*. But she never ventures beyond the sense of the words that earlier authoritative commentaries have already entrenched; she also does not venture beyond certain very limited (antecedently approved) lines of interpretation that rely heavily on fitting just such established meanings. In this way, Vendler conveys an almost impregnable impression of the sheer objectivity of the entire exercise, of moving with precision toward a uniquely adequate, very nearly ordained reading of each poem. But she barely touches on the possible validity of entirely different strategies of interpretation or the threatening import of their potential validity on the right assessment of restricting interpretation in the way she favors, and she nowhere addresses the question of fixed meanings.

Speaking of her own effort, Vendler offers the following defense:

> I intend this work for those who already know the *Sonnets*, or who have beside them the sort of lexical annotation found in

the current editions (for example, those of [Stephen] Booth, [John] Kerrigan, or [G. B.] Evans. And why should I add another book to those already available? I want to do so because I admire the *Sonnets*, and wish to defend the high value I put on them. . . . Contemporary emphasis on the participation of literature in a social matrix balks at acknowledging how lyric, though it may *refer* to the social, remains the genre that directs its *mimesis* toward the performance of the mind in *solitary* speech. A social reading is better directed at a novel or a play: the abstraction desired by the writer of, and the willing reader of, normative lyric frustrates the mind that wants social fictions or biographical revelations.[45]

This seems to supply a fair reason for Vendler's deliberately restricted undertaking. But, if you think about it, there can't be any reason to suppose that conceding the lyric to be a genre committed to "the performance of the mind in *solitary* speech" adversely affects the propriety of interpreting *such* speech in terms of its supposed "social matrix." I'm afraid Vendler's argument—for it is now no longer an autobiographical admission—is a transparent *petitio*. By its own rationale, Vendler's forthright practice actually strengthens the reasonableness of opposing her essentialized division between appropriate and inappropriate readings of the *Sonnets*, for, in defending her own restrictions, she ineluctably betrays the arbitrariness of insisting on adhering to them!

Vendler offers two specific considerations, both of which backfire badly. For one thing, she says, "The true 'actors' in the lyric are words, not 'dramatic persons'; and the drama of any lyric is constituted by the successive entrances of new sets of words, or new stylistic arrangements (grammatic, syntactical, phonetic) which are visibly in conflict with previous arrangements used with reference to the 'same' situation."[46] Taken literally, this goes contrary to Vendler's insistence on "the performance of the mind in *solitary* speech." For one thing, it is a voiced performance; for another, it is, in Shakespeare's case, often cast in the form of an imagined address to one's beloved; and, for a third, its appreciation is expressly cast (by Vendler) in terms of a proper grasp of the novel language Shakespeare introduces in fashioning the lyric voice he offers. So it is not implausible to view the *Sonnets* as dramatic even if solitary (like the soliloquies), and, in any case, "words" cannot be "actors" by themselves: they must be uttered in a "performance of the mind." There *is* a theory (of sorts) implicated in

Vendler's practice, but it cannot justify the restriction she intends, and it cannot validate any ideal norm of exclusive interpretation. (It is, I may say, not altogether dissimilar to the views of Beardsley and the jurist Antonin Scalia, whom I've mentioned [in another setting] much earlier.)

The second consideration is at least as telling: it actually undercuts Vendler's treatment of the first. Here she relies on some plain talk from W. H. Auden (which she cites favorably). Auden offers the following: "The questions which interest me most when reading a poem are two. The first is technical. 'Here is a verbal contraption. How does it work?' The second is, in the broadest sense, moral. 'What kind of a guy inhabits the poem? What is his notion of the good life or the good place? His notion of the Evil One? What does he conceal from the reader? What does he conceal even from himself?'" Vendler glosses these remarks thus: "Like any poet, Auden knows that the second question cannot be responded to correctly until the first has been answered. It is the workings of the verbal construct that give evidence of the moral stance of the poet."[47] Yes, perhaps. But that has nothing to do with what may be called the lexical order of the two questions.

In fact, if you reread Auden's remark, you see how reasonable it would be to suppose that the voice or "guy" that "inhabits" the poem is quite inseparable from the "verbal contraption" itself: whether read as (as in lyric) the dramatic voice of the poem viewed as an imagined utterance *or* as the actual poet's creative utterance creating the voice of the other (which, of course, are not the same).

The interpretation of Shakespeare's moral stance is itself constructed (at least in part) *by* the very reading of the "verbal construct" that is Shakespeare's utterance of the original poem (thereafter read as an imagined lyric utterance). There is no principled disjunction between the two. But, if not, then Vendler's gloss on Auden is simply untenable. (There is, indeed, something of a structuralist predilection in Vendler's method of reading).

You may glimpse the intent of her practice in reading sonnet 9 ("Is it for fear to wet a widow's eye"), which is admittedly restricted and occupied with a great deal of word play, where Vendler remarks, "Whatever the charms of mirror-image letters [in the spelling of 'widdow' in the Quarto edition] and symmetrical words, the poem has to mean something too, and has to have a general shape."[48] Vendler supplies its meaning, finding in the octave and sestet the "theological contrast" between a sin of omission and a sin of commission.[49] But she confines the commentary (true to her own intent) to the formal structure of the sonnet. The question remains whether, even here, some more adventurous reading of the "theological contrast" (itself already adventurous enough) may be rightly pursued. The operative image is captured in the first two lines and assessed in the final couplet:

> Is it for fear to wet a widow's eye
> That thou consum'st thyself in single life?
>
> . . . .
>
> No love toward others in that bosom sits
> That on himself such murd'rous shame commits.

The verdict is too forceful to disallow conjecture.

For example—though I claim no expertise—could the poem be an insinuation of the waste of the celibate life of religious orders (analogous to the absurd waste of the young man's demurrer of marriage, alluded to in the sonnet)? That would show at least the impossibility of disjoining the questions Vendler claims to disjoin, as well as the impossibility of getting the first question right without locating would-be "stylistic arrangements (grammatic, syntactical, phonetic)" within the richer conceptual space of the moral and cultural world of human speech and agency. The second possibility shows how arbitrary it would be (and is) to restrict the reading of the *Sonnets* in Vendler's way. I cannot see how that can be denied. There are no easy outer limits to interpretation here.

I seize the occasion, therefore, to remind you of a more adventurous theory and practice among professional readers of Shakespeare (perhaps more usually focused on the plays than the sonnets). Here are some remarks of Stephen Greenblatt's that convey the intended rigor of the kind of criticism Greenblatt and his associates practice (what has been called new historicism), which supports a conception of the open-ended nature of denotatively determinate texts: "Works of art, [Greenblatt announces at the start of *Shakespearean Negotiations*,] however intensely marked by the creative intelligence and private obsessions of individuals, are the products of collective negotiation and exchange. Why should works of criticism be any different?"[50] (Commentators like Vendler have no answer.) Greenblatt glosses the announcement as follows:

> If there is no expressive essence that can be located in an aesthetic object complete unto itself, uncontaminated by interpretation,

beyond translation or substitution—if there is no mimesis without exchange—then we need to analyze the collective dynamic circulation of pleasures, anxieties, and interests. Art does not simply exist in all cultures; it is made up along with other products, practices, discourses of a given culture. (In practice, "made up" means inherited, transmitted, altered, modified, reproduced far more than it means invented: as a rule, there is very little pure invention in culture.)[51]

Obviously, interpretive practice and cultural ontology go hand in hand.

I shall close my remarks with a final claim that you may find entirely too extravagant. It is, however, the one I prize the most. I have characterized a *text* as any interpretable *denotatum*, either intrinsically such, as being Intentionally qualified (selves or sentences or artworks or histories), or suitably anthropomorphized or modeled on the human paradigm (the utterances of languageless infants, animals, machines, and the like, even physical nature viewed under one or another explanatory theory). In this sense, texts are relatively independent *denotata* apt for interpretation, but their interpretation is inseparable from the reflexive interpretation selves practice on themselves: for texts are, after all, the utterances of selves, whether linguistic or lingual (in the sense already supplied)—or conformably anthropomorphized.

Now, if we give up the forms of privilege and modal necessity, we see that all questions of referential, predicative, contextual, and interpretive fixity and objectivity depend, finally, on the consensual tolerance of the fluxive practices of the fluxive society in which our discursive powers were first formed and are sustained. I have already insisted that there are no criterial or algorithmic rules by which any of the cognizing competences associated with interpretive objectivity can be vouchsafed. But if you grant all that, you must see that the peculiar nature of Intentional attributes cannot be counted on to justify any principled constraints (Vendler's, for instance) said to override our local and variable interests, the construction of our capacity to recover past phases of our admitted history, and our spontaneous willingness to enlarge and alter the interpretive resources of our culture.

Already in Schleiermacher, the hermeneutic tradition was forced to admit that authorial intent could not be confined psychologically; furthermore, Romantic hermeneutics discovered that, once the historicity of cultural life was admitted, there was no way to assign Intentional fixities to historical "horizons" or genres in any criterial sense suited to fixing interpretive objectivity.[52] Given that Intentionality is sui generis, utterly unlike physical properties, emergent only in the sense in which human selves are themselves emergently second natured, there simply is no neutral or assuredly unique way in which linguistic and lingual meaning can be fixed objectively. There *is* objectivity to be found—in the sense in which the apt members of a society *are* tacitly prepared to treat, as a continuation of their usual practices, some *further* modification of what can be consensually sustained as still within the objective recovery of the meaning of particular Intentional *denotata*.

If you grant all this, you cannot fail to grant also two further, distinctly heterodox proposals: one, that every particular text owes its determinability in part to the shifting family of related texts whose meanings its own changing interpretation affects but which (in turn) affect its own interpretable potentialities; the other, that there are no clear boundaries to the nature of a particular text or to the horizon of a self-interpreting culture, and that even Intentional structures imputed to the historical past or historical origin of a particular text are subject to being continually altered in accord with the present and future saliencies of its evolving ethos.[53]

These are simply corollaries of a realist reading of cultural entities—under historicity, for meaning or Intentional structure has no locus apart from the ongoing consensual life of a viable society, and, there, there are no fixities *de re* or *de cogitatione*. There is no interpretive objectivity apart from the collective tolerance of a society's grasp of its own historical saliencies through change, and there are no such saliencies that do not automatically provide a ground for a constructed objectivity. There is no unique telos toward which responsible interpretations tend, and the ongoing contest between different interpretive currents simply confirms the sui generis nature of objectivity in cultural matters.

Roughly speaking, the diversity of interpretation tends to mirror the diversity of cultural life. Seen that way, it is very likely an elementary blunder to insist that the strong convergence among the natural sciences must be canonically matched among the interpretive disciplines. There is no compelling rationale for insisting on such norms. In fact, recalling the puzzles of reference and predication and context, we may suppose that the model of objectivity in the natural sciences (possibly even plural models) is itself confirmed through the same cultural sources by which we are prepared to test the outer limits of interpretive objectivity. Inquiries of these two sorts answer to different interests. But they are interests of the same inquiring agents, and they are sustained in one and the same culture.

PART THREE

Eight

The Definition of the Human

If you take the long view of the career of Western philosophy, you may be forgiven for yielding to the fiction that its continuous history confirms a legible thread of discovery spanning the speculations of the Ionians and Eleatics and our more baffled inquiries at the start of the twenty-first century. It hardly matters whether you believe the tale or trust it as an economy that cannot finally be toppled. In either case, I shall need your patience. I have the pieces of an imaginary history that yields a more than plausible sense of the entire human world by way of a sequence of conceptions that were never construed in quite the way I recommend. I *trust* that history, though I don't believe it to be strictly true.

Canonical history has it that Plato and Aristotle sought to reconcile changing and changeless being in the spirit of the Ionians and against the excessive strictures of Parmenides' dictum, which appears to make no allowance for the changing world, though it addresses it insistently. If that dictum had never been contested, the whole of science and our grasp of the human condition might have remained hopelessly paradoxical—in the Eleatic way. I accept the usual reading, therefore, as the sparest narrative (fiction or not) that might be true. Except for two caveats: the first, that the actual lesson of the best work of classical philosophy could never have been formulated within the horizon of the Greek world anyway; the second, that what Plato and Aristotle accomplished in their heroic way remains distinctly uneasy, unfinished, uncompelling in their own time, just at the point they manage to harmonize the opposed notions of the changing and the changeless—that is, the point at which they simply compromise with Parmenides.

The intuitive evidence is this: If there are two distinct worlds—the one changing, the other changeless—it is hard to see why the changeless world would ever be needed to ensure the presence of the other, and if its own intelligibility presupposed that change *is* necessarily what it is only relative to what is changeless, then how could that be demonstrated if we ourselves are confined within the changing world? If our world is a fluxive world, and we have no inkling of the changeless world—beyond Parmenides' dictum, or conjectures like those spawned in the *Republic* (provided by disputants who admit they do not know the changeless world), or Aristotle's faulty paradoxes ranged against those who affirm the fluxive world—then the classical contribution must be more limited than history affirms. Otherwise, read more generously, the matter may have required conceptual resources the Greek world never dreamed of—possibilities discovered only in a later age.

If the changing world were not (not known to be) in need of a changeless stratum, we would hardly need to admit that human nature must itself be changeless or depend in some ineluctable way on a changeless world. That would already be a gain sizable enough to challenge two thousand years of quibble effectively. The world of the arts and culture in general, bear in mind, makes no sense except as a historied world, and such a world hardly appears in a legible form much before the end of the eighteenth century. Imagine that!

Plato and Aristotle seem to recognize Protagoras as the arch-foe of Parmenides—Plato in the *Theaetetus*, Aristotle in *Metaphysics* 4—and their arguments against Protagoras's relativism are singularly thin and uncompelling, though they are, it should be said, very nearly the whole of contemporary objections to modern forms of relativism.[1] At this point in my story, it's not the championing of relativism that counts but defending the coherence of the flux—*not* chaos, not the sheer absence of all order, but the discursibility of the changing world itself. Here Protagoras is surely more interesting than Heraclitus; read anachronistically, "man is the measure" is very much ahead of its time, an idea at least as advanced as any the post-Kantians hit on—except for the small fact that, like Plato and Aristotle, Protagoras lacked our modern conception of historicity, the historied nature of thought itself. But I admit straight out that to remedy the lack harbors no subversive intent at all: nothing that would undermine, for instance, the splendid achievement of the natural sciences or the coherence of the unnumbered single world in which we live our hybrid lives. The recovery is meant only to provide a picture of a wider spread of conceptual resources than are usually acknowledged—an account, so to say, in which the theory of the arts and the sciences will be seen to be closer cousins than the usual idioms would be willing to admit.

I want to suggest that the narrative outcome of the classical phase of Western philosophy lies more with abandoning Parmenides' constraint altogether—placing it under a charge of irrelevance and arbitrariness—than with reaching a verbal compromise (any compromise) in the way Plato and Aristotle seem to have found impossible to avoid.

The truth remains that their best compromise could never reach what was needed to catch and hold the minimal distinction of the human world. You'll say that's hubris, but it's not, though to admit it signifies that we live in a conceptual desert deprived for more than two thousand years of a proper understanding of the sui generis history of the human being. Of course, *we* see (ontologically) the human world *in* Plato and Aristotle and Protagoras—and even Parmenides. But, strange as it may seem, the Greeks never understood what it was they saw, if what emergently was always metaphysically present in the human way was first made conceptually palpable at the end of the eighteenth century and the start of the nineteenth, in the work shared by Kant and the idealists, especially in the work of Hegel. I think it is no accident that the discoveries I have in mind are coeval with the fledgling labor of the philosophy of art, which, in Kant, shows every prospect of losing its way, even as Kant turns from nature to art,[2] until the philosophy of art moves on from Kant to Hegel. The change requires two distinct moments: one, to displace invariance with the flux of history—which means displacing Kant himself; the other, to fill the space of change with the specific resources of cultural constitution—that is, language, *Bildung*, self-consciousness, freedom, effective and creative action—which means embracing Hegel's dialectical intuition (if not his actual doctrine). There's the point of the story.

In short, the upshot of the contest between Plato and Aristotle and Parmenides is not so much the classic compromise they wrest from Parmenides (which has dominated Western philosophy down to our own day) as it is to experiment with the complete abandonment of the invariances of thought and being by exploring the new vision that begins to find its voice (and conceptual adequacy) in the late eighteenth and early nineteenth centuries—in, say, its first full incarnation in Hegel's encultured and historicized empiricism, that is, in Hegel's phenomenology.[3]

The Greeks were simply disadvantaged, struggling in Parmenides' shadow, because they lacked the conceptual resources that might have helped them escape—as those resources helped Hegel in his own attempt to escape the corresponding fixities of Kant's transcendentalism. They lacked what we now realize is a novel conception of the regularities of ordinary cultural life—with which perfectly ordinary people are now acquainted, without exceptional training—just the reverse of what would be true of the Platonic Forms; or "what is," in Parmenides' sense; or the essences of natural things directly grasped by nous; or the powers of transcendental understanding or of pure phenomenology, in Husserl's sense;[4] or anything else of such a crazy kind. Hence, I suggest the Greeks were literally unable to construct an adequate account of what it is to be a human being—beyond, say, the rather comic biology Plato offers in the *Statesman* or, more earnestly, though by the same sort of fumbling, the quasi-divine biology of Plato's psyche and Aristotle's nous.

We learn that if we mean to define what a human being is, we must somehow settle first the ancient question of the conceptual or, more grandly stated, the ontological linkage between the changing and the changeless. For, of course, Parmenides' conception of thinking is inseparable from his conception of being (or reality), as is true in a more ingenious way for Kant and the post-Kantians. I need to assure you here that in speaking of the *ontological*, I have no intention of invoking any privileged sources of knowledge or assurances about any secret changeless order of reality indiscernible by ordinary means, without a knowledge of which we could never confirm the validity of our beliefs. Once we give up all such baggage, *metaphysics* or *ontology* is little more than a benign abstraction from the world we claim to know. Nothing quarrelsome hangs on the term.

If this line of thinking leads us well enough out of the ancient labyrinth, then we may claim to have grasped the defect of classical philosophy: the fact that, for the Greeks, faute de mieux, human nature must embody a changeless (or necessary) structure of its own that could account, in principle, for the intelligent grasp and application in thought and act and productive labor of the changing world. The Greek solution is no more than a deus ex machina that falls back to its compromise with Parmenides. It misperceives the sui generis nature of the human, which is fluxive and artifactual or hybrid. That, at any rate, is my charge.

If this is a fair assessment, it is a stunning truth that affirms that an adequate conception of the human—in a sense we now think impossible to ignore—cannot have been philosophically available before (or much before) the end of the eighteenth century and the beginning of the nineteenth.

Alternatively put: the concepts of *historicity* and *enculturation*—on which, as I suggest, the very prospect of grasping the unique features of human being and the whole of the human world (including the arts) depends—may be, indeed *are*, the gift of a very small interval of discovery confined within the span of Western thought, fashioned a mere two hundred years ago. By now these notions belong to the entire world, of course. But I draw your attention to their first appearance to remind you that the definition of the *human* is itself a historicized undertaking subject to the evolving conceptual resources and saliencies of human thought and to feature the radical difference between the immense flexibility of Hegel's dialectical picture of human history and the stubborn rigidities of Eleatic influence on both classical philosophy and our own.

Plato is surely the best of the ancient critics of the ideal Forms and what we take to be the Parmenidean claim. The discussion (in the dialogues) of the soul has very little point, for instance, if separated from the theory of the Forms. Aristotle's conception of *nous* seems to have no biological basis at all and is little more than a transparent device designed to shore up the Eleatic theme; in both his biological and ethical tracts, there is a noticeable slippage from the essentialized invariances of science and morality.[5] All this begins to explain the deeper joke of the *Republic* as well as Plato's patience with the inconclusiveness of the early dialogues and the question-begging fixities never completely dispelled in the best work of Aristotle's attractive empirical rigor.

I am moving here, I assure you, in the direction of defining the *human*. I have chosen an oblique route partly to dramatize the fact that the Greeks did not understand the human in the same way we do; though, reading them, we instantly translate into our own idiom what they actually say, so we often fail to see the enormous difference between our respective views. If you doubt this, just consider, closer to our own world, that Kant very nearly abandons the human altogether in the strenuous analysis of his "transcendental subject." There actually is no sustained analysis in Kant of what is merely or essentially human, although, of course, Kant's rational agents are forever occupied with human concerns! Literally, Kant's transcendentalism makes it impossible to define the specifically human, though there's evidence enough that he anticipated returning to some sort of reconciliation between the mundane and the transcendental aspects of the human mode of being.[6] Certainly, in his *Aesthetics*, Hegel pointedly takes note of the alien quality of what Kant offers as his abstract picture of a "human agent," which, Hegel suggests, cannot fail to disable the entire undertaking of explaining the creation, criticism, use, and appreciation of the entire world of art.[7] He's right, of course. We lose our grasp of the arts if we lose our grasp of history and the artifactual formation of the human.

My own impulse is to infer by association that Aristotle's treatment of the polis as the proper setting for grasping the philosophical import of more than Greek ethics and politics is instantly imperiled by Alexander's attempt to extend the normative role of the classical ethos to an empire meant to bring the Greek and Persian together in a new way, with no attention to those historicizing consequences that Alexander (under Aristotle's sway) could never have understood. Considering the Aristotelian temptations of our own time, the same disquieting lesson, I'm afraid, must surely haunt, say, Martha Nussbaum's Aristotelian account of Henry James's novels as well as her United Nations–oriented attempt to universalize Aristotle's conception of the virtues.[8] You cannot, however, determine the normative in practical life by empirically statistical methods of any kind. You begin to see the need for an important correction here. A place must be found for historical forces. There are no such forces in Aristotle's *Ethics* or, conformably, in Nussbaum's.

Moral judgment, like the exercise of taste and the practice of art criticism, is not a discipline that can be convincingly pursued on the basis of abstract descriptions: it requires the engaged perception and experience of the very specimen phenomena that are to be judged. Kant and the Kantians, therefore—and at least the Aristotelians, if not Aristotle himself—are plainly wrong. There you have the essential clue to the difference between the natural and human sciences—a fortiori, the paradigmatic lesson of the logic of the fine arts. (Allow this anticipation, please, to count as a piece of earnest money against the small liberties I've been taking.)

I see no way that Kant's hoped-for reconciliation between the empirical and the transcendental could possibly succeed, unless Kant would have been willing to abandon the quasi-divine powers of his own transcendental subject. He was, finally, unable to historicize his account of the human condition along the lines, for instance, that Johann Herder recommended and Hegel found congenial. It is, in fact, in Hegel's innovations that a truly modern conception of the enculturing formation of the human subject (self, agent, person) begins to dawn in a way that still fits contemporary intuitions. Yet a very large swath of twentieth-century philosophy actually opposes the adoption of the defining themes of historicity and enculturation, which, beginning approximately with Hegel, are inseparably tied to every philosophically viable account of the human.

The speculative theme I am pursuing has been battered, throughout the history of philosophy, from the vantage of at least two profoundly opposed strategies of analysis. One favors appropriating the divine, or what seems close to the divine, in our earthly world: what belongs to Parmenides,

Plato, and Aristotle; the medieval world; Kant and the post-Kantians; and, more recently, thinkers as diverse as Husserl, Heidegger, Levinas, and some of the British idealists. The other prefers description and explanation in terms restricted to the inanimate physical world: what belongs to the reductive and eliminative convictions of the unity-of-science program, positivism, the radical forms of neo-Darwinism, computationalism, and other manifestations of what may, not unfairly, be called scientism.[9]

The first is persuaded that the human *cannot* be defined in terms restricted to the natural world; the other, that an adequate definition *can* be rendered in terms sufficient for the entire inanimate and subhuman world. So, one way or another, language, culture, history, agency, creativity, and responsibility are rightly seen to be, in principle, no more than complexifications of basic states and processes that need no conceptual supplementation drawn from the cultural world itself.

Both strategies fail, in the plain sense that the human is entirely natural, as natural (or naturalistic) as anything we might otherwise specify; yet, in being natural, the human is also uniquely competent in ways that cannot be conceptually captured by categories that initially refer to anything less (or more) than what the distinctive processes of history and culture immediately display. That is what the Greeks and Kant lacked or largely lacked, although, of course, they were able to refer to (but not to analyze) what was uniquely human in a naturalistic but sui generis way. If you think of natural language as the exemplar of the cultural, you see the problem at once—although the protocultural among subhuman animals may be reconciled with the protolinguistic forms of animal communication.

Let me change direction here. I don't really believe Plato ever championed the doctrine of the Forms. He was not, in my opinion, a closet Eleatic or Parmenidean—or a Platonist—of any kind. On the contrary, his best work, which I associate with the Socratic elenchus, shows very clearly that he was fully aware—was perhaps worried, puzzled, enchanted all at once by the fact—that the "Socratic" inquiries, paradigmatically addressed to the definition of the virtues, proceeded in a fluent way without relying on strict invariances or necessities of any substantive kind. But they did so, apparently, without ever achieving their appointed purpose. I take Plato's continually testing and retesting the powers of the elenchus to be a sign of his interest in the possibility of abandoning the Parmenidean constraint altogether, but it's the classical world itself, of course, that makes any breakthrough impossible.

The Forms are never featured in the early dialogues, and when they begin to appear—at first, as one says, under the mode of absence, in fact even more strikingly in the *Statesman* than in the *Republic*—they are perfunctorily dismissed in a burlesque of the elenctic process itself. In the *Statesman* (a dialogue never easily placed), Plato pointedly returns to the elenchus, once it is explicitly conceded that we don't know the Forms at all—though we admit we must decide (there's the point) on a rational way to rule the featherless bipeds we know ourselves to be! Hence, Plato reverses or replaces the inquiry begun in the *Republic*: he assigns the instructor's role to an Eleatic stranger, under the terms of an expressly diminished elenchus, though Socrates remains in attendance. This way of reading the *Statesman*, of course, goes completely contrary to Gregory Vlastos's influential ordering of the dialogues.[10] But it makes perfect sense.

Plato, I suggest, returns repeatedly to test the mettle of Socrates' subversive practice, which is itself a daring transformation of the original Parmenidean elenchus. It seems he cannot discharge the Greek longing for invariance, but he obviously sees that invariance is neither required nor accessible in a fruitful discussion of the moral/political virtues. Still, Socrates never really succeeds in defining any virtues. If only Plato had had Hegel's conceptual resources, say, regarding the *sittlich* nature of the virtues themselves—in effect, a full conception of what a culture actually is—he might have penetrated to the heart of his own fascination with those ordinary modes of discourse that begin to yield a grasp of valid norms and encultured competences without invoking any changeless order whatsoever. *That* I take to be the convergent meaning of Plato's perseveration and Hegel's conceptual breakthrough. Both depend—the first, uncomprehendingly; the second, with stunning clarity—on a conceptual strategy that draws on the prephilosophical fluencies of ordinary practical life. Hegel seizes the advantage, but Plato seems forever baffled. Both abandon Parmenidean fixity— whatever Parmenides' true intentions may have been.

Plato's scruple leads him to an impasse, which he reenacts again and again without apparent comprehension. But he surely senses that the secret of the human world, which eluded Western philosophy for more than two thousand years, must lie somehow in the elenctic process itself. Plato *has* an inkling of its exemplary importance, but he has no idea of what he's found. So he clings somewhat dysfunctionally to the remnants of Parmenidean fixity. Hegel, of course, invents a dialectical model of a conversational critique bridging opposed (so-called contradictory) tendencies within, or between, the salient options of historical life. He appears to resolve the

Platonic impasse by an evolving series of transformative reconciliations that preserve as well as possible the normative claims of the contending customs and traditions that confront us. Hegel accepts the initial validity of the norms of *sittlich* life within the flux of history; he therefore has no need for invariances of any substantive sort or for any changeless ground of normative validity. He finds the elenctic mechanism already in play in the human reconstruction of human history. There's the grand solution that eluded Plato, the breakthrough of the most daringly modern of modern conceptions. It also explains, of course, why Hegel has no need for the contortions of Kant's *Critique of Judgment* in ensuring the linkage between the play of imagination in artworks and the intimate bearing of art on the formation and direction of moral sensibility: Kant was obliged (in the opening passages of the third *Critique*) to disjoin altogether the judgment of aesthetic taste (or beauty) from any contamination of conceptual subsumption (that would have directly associated the aesthetic with the scientific and the moral) and then reversed himself regarding the relation between art and moral sensibility in the second part of the third *Critique*. Hegel saw at once that the aesthetic and the moral were inseparable within the *geistlich* holism of the cultural world.

At times, Hegel seems almost besotted with his own device. He invents his "discovery" of the rational self-understanding of the whole of endless history: at its best, it's a heuristic instrument of the supplest possibilities; at its worst, it's the march of God in the world. But *we* need not pretend to grasp Napoleon's or Alexander's "world-historical role," as Hegel claims to do, in order to appreciate the novel advantage of his conception of history. Both the Socratic elenchus and Hegel's dialectic must be fitted, *in* evolving time, in essentially the same way, to emerging history. Plato senses the goal but never masters the process. Hegel masters both but loses something of the reflexive sense of the human limitation of just such an understanding. The briefest overview of the continual near chaos of the actual evolution of the modern state—for instance, according to something not unlike Michael Oakeshott's well-known summary[11]—would soon persuade you of the completely contrived nature of Hegel's picture of the entire course of history, whether in politics or the arts. Hegel confronts us with the profoundest contingencies as if they were all ineluctable necessities of Reason. Doubtless, he knew the difference.

Hegel knew he was transforming Kant's entire vision in a radical way—by historicizing it, by reading Kant's system as less than necessary. He knew he was completing Plato's elenctic dream. But he had no patience with the piecemeal scatter of a merely human understanding of history. No more did Jean-Paul Sartre, of course, more modestly—as Foucault complains.[12] Hegel relies, as does Plato, on the entrenched stabilities of societal life. But viewing them in terms of the distinctive explanatory structures of cultural history, he takes them at once to provide a ground for normative validation as well, whereas Plato, viewing social practice as mere convention and contingency, never finds a sufficiently strong reason to replace the Forms by human practices as such. Plato never realizes that what is provisionally normative in our practices is not merely discernible but actually part of the formative forces that determine the very mode of human being.

In any event, I view the elenchus and the dialectic as two closely related strategies of inquiry that are (1) presuppositionless; (2) *sittlich* (in a generous anthropological sense); (3) free of Parmenidean infection of any kind; (4) lacking any formal or criterial method; (5) cast as forms of discursive reason; (6) inherently incapable of claiming or validating any uniquely correct analysis of whatever sector of the world they choose to examine; (7) committed only to what, as a practical matter, is adequate to our salient interests from time to time—or committed in such a way that theoretical inquiry is seen to be dependent on, or derivative from, or internal to our practices of discursive inquiry; (8) applied to what is intrinsically interpretable without end; (9) unable to discover in any simple or direct way the objective (or telic) structures of the independent world; (10) hence, applied to what is culturally constituted or constructed relative to our evolving experience of the world; (11) applied to what is local, contextual, not strictly universalizable, and validated in *sittlich* ways; (12) historicized and known to be such; and (13) insuperably phenomenological—that is, grounded in and restricted to our encultured experience of the world (in something closer to Hegel's than to Husserl's sense).

All this counts as a summary of the sense in which I view Plato's use of the elenchus (more in promise than in fact) and Hegel's dialectic (viewed as more tentative, more plural, more provisional, more contested at every turn, and more discontinuous, too, than Hegel may have supposed at times) as bearing in a decisive way on the definition of what it is to be a human being or what counts as the human world.

If the tally holds firm, then two important lessons may be drawn from it without delay: one, that both the Greek and Kantian accounts have almost no grasp at all of the metaphysics of the human or cultural world as such; the other, that the cultural world, however embedded in physical nature and for that reason not adequately described or explained in physical terms alone, has no fixed structures of its own of any kind, is subject to the flux of history at every point of interest, and yet confronts us (contrary to Plato's worry) with all of its evolving, perfectly legible stabilities—the regularities of *sittlich* practice. Both Plato and Kant retreat to the safety of proposed invariances, Plato possibly less tendentiously than Kant, since Kant requires fixity in order to secure his conception of the closed system of the first *Critique*, whereas, paradoxically, Plato sees no way at all to save the elenchus he assigns Socrates.

There's the abiding failure of the first two thousand years of Western philosophy! Bear that in mind, please. For the saving lesson *is* the conception of historied culture, which surely generates the principal part of any valid moral theory or valid theory of the arts—very probably, also, any valid theory of science. Viewed from our own vantage, the force of the entire clue makes itself felt in the *recency* of Kant's failure to have hit on an adequate inkling of the historicized and artifactual nature of human being. The extraordinary distortion of philosophy's canonical history begins to dawn.

Before I press any part of my own answer to the secret of the human (a perfectly open secret by this time), let me add to our elenctic company a third voice closer to our own than either Plato's or Hegel's, which catches up the intuitive directness of the first (without Eleatic temptations) and yields to the historicizing effect of the second (without properly acknowledging the explicit role of history). This third voice illuminates, obliquely again, certain inherent limitations in the "method" of cultural analysis, which counts as little more than an improvisational meander shared by the apt members of a particular culture in a way that entrenches (consensually but not by criterial means) their collective understanding of the world they share.

In this way, they (that is, we) become aware of the determinable—never fixedly determinate—*geistlich* ground on which all their inquiries and commitments ultimately depend: especially what, by various strategies (elenctic, dialectical, now meandering), prove to be legible and capable of supporting diversity, extension to new cases, correction, transformation, opposition, sheer scatter, and normative standing. Sophocles' *Antigone* offers an elenctic example at least as telling as the Socratic practice, perhaps even closer to an understanding of cultural history than the dialogues could claim, since, in the play, one and the same society acknowledges the valid but contingently competing priorities of throne and family.[13] *Antigone* may be the clearest specimen text we have, against the backdrop of which Socrates and Hegel may be seen to subscribe to the same conceptual resources. For without an incipient sense of history (better: historicity), the central conflict would have had to be assigned to the cosmic order itself—a palpable scandal. At any rate, that is a judgment we find ourselves drawn to, viewed from a contemporary vantage.

Plato fails because he neither vindicates nor overthrows the Parmenidean dictum. Strictly speaking, the Socratic elenchus is not a method or a rule or an algorithm of any kind. It is only an informal practice that comes out of the fluencies of ordinary conversation. But Plato never seems to fathom (*or* he grasps but cannot defend) the power and sufficiency of elenctic informality against the Parmenidean prejudice that defines rational rigor. That informality will help to define, in turn, precisely what *human being* means.

The same tolerance for transient opposition marks the nerve of Hegel's dialectic, though Hegel, of course, presents his account of history in a much too high-blown way. Hegel was obviously enchanted by the brilliant applications of his method to the whole of the *geistlich* world, but historicism could never have assigned his interpretive tales a principled advantage without actually cheating. Any such bias would surely go contrary to Hegel's immense grasp of the contingency of cultural change itself.

Perhaps the theory of Forms began to seem as feasible to Plato as the rationality of *Geist* may have seemed to Hegel—incipiently in the *Meno*, say, where the dialectical play of the elenchus begins to evolve in a new direction. But Plato surely senses the distinctive power of culturally formed debate, though he cannot see how to free the force of the elenchus from the fixities of Parmenides' strategy. He obviously considers yielding. Yet, as in the *Republic* and the *Statesman*, he never betrays the insuperable contingencies of the cultural world. That is his instinctive scruple. But what of Hegel?

For the moment, I suggest that, within the tale I'm telling, Hegel's dialectic is effectively the historicizing analogue of the Socratic elenchus, productively applied to the entire *geistlich* world. Plato has no *geistlich* categories, though he knows the human world as well as anyone. In that same sense, Kant plays a sort of Eleatic role in Hegel's work rather like the role Parmenides plays in Plato's, and both Plato and Hegel share a distinct sense (less than actually incipient in the one, more than fully formed in the other) of how, through its sui generis resources, we may analyze the process of self-understanding in the cultural world. In fact, there actually is a first-rate Kantian who reinterprets Kant's "fixities" along the lines of Hegel's historicizing reform—namely, Ernst Cassirer, who applies the strategy in nearly every sector of scientific and philosophical work,[14] replacing transcendental invariances with provisional (but seemingly fundamental) "symbolic forms" so that we begin to see how an analogous elenctic reading of the Forms might have been available to Plato.

Here, then, is the gist of the argument thus far, cast in a more familiar light. The ancient quarrel—the quarrel between *physis* and *nomos*—has almost nothing to do with solving the puzzle the elenchus poses. It leads, rather, to stalemate, as the dialogues confirm. More than that, the disjunction it offers actually precludes any fresh option that might have construed the relationship between those notions differently. The issue before us has little to do with specific preferences among the virtues of human-made laws or norms: it concerns, rather, the right definition of the human as such—at a deeper level of reflection. Once you see that, you see the promise of the modern conjecture that the human is an artifact of cultural history. That is precisely what the *physis/nomos* contest never broaches—in effect, actually disallows.[15]

To this expanding conjecture I now add, as a third exemplar, the voice of the Wittgenstein of the *Investigations* and related texts. Plato, as the author of the Socratic elenchus, confirms the stalemate the Eleatic constraint imposes on the resolution of our puzzle regarding the practical problem of choosing a right form of ethical discipline and political self-rule. It's as if Plato realized we cannot abandon these normative concerns if we are to be the human beings that we are, yet the Parmenidean dictum proves completely powerless—in fact, unsuitable—in helping us find our way. Plato *exhausts* its possibilities! The elenchus seems to have a grip on resolving normative disputes that still remains completely unexplained (as far as Plato is concerned), since it secures (or might secure) its objective without ever invoking the canonical Forms. Plato, we must suppose, grasped the paradox but had no idea of what to make of it. Of course, our understanding of politics and art hangs in the balance; there's the pivot of the matter.

Hegel offers an incomparably richer sense of how to apply the categories of cultural life to cultural life itself—to grasp what Plato misses: that is, the fact that the objectivity and validity of every such application are *reflexive* and culturally constructed, at once empowered and constrained by the historicized conditions that account for the construction of the *human* as well. Plato loses the very possibility of sharing anything akin to Hegel's insight—which, in its own age, goes well beyond the Kantian and Fichtean lessons—wherever Plato invokes the myth of recollection. That alone, I would say, is a frank admission of failure. Recollecting, of course, is also in its own way a myth of self-understanding—except that, as in Chomsky's Platonism, the self that we finally fathom (if we do) is never the familiar creature of historically formed habit and practice—ourselves! In the dialogues, the myth of recollection is simply a philosophical wave of the hand, a capitulation to Eleatic fixities. In Chomsky, it has proved to be the admission of a failed (perhaps impossible) analysis and the return of the still-opaque encultured world to the distant visions of contemporary scientism.[16] For what Plato, Kant, and contemporary scientisms lack is precisely Hegel's phenomenology of culture—that is, what moral theory and the theory of art cannot afford to be deprived of.

None of this entails, for Hegel, the recovery of the changeless or the strictly necessary. Hegel, I would say, is the first philosophical master to map a comprehensive account of our understanding of human culture and ourselves along historicized lines. Hegel's dialectical resolution of evolving, *geistlich* "contradictions" provides a sort of abstract template (an elenchus of sorts) for identifying the freewheeling interpretive possibilities that cultural history requires. Hegel's interpretive practice is a better and more adequate instantiation of any would-be mode of self-examination than the Socratic elenchus, although, by virtue of the tally given a moment ago, I treat Plato and Hegel as fellow investigators of the sui generis distinction of human being.

Only when we have such a tally firmly in mind can we see what Plato was attempting to capture. Plato confirms the inherent limitations of classical thought, which he sometimes seems on the verge of breaching. Certainly, the *Theaetetus* introduces, within the Eleatic milieu, the possibility of analyzing and explaining the nature of our world in terms that eschew every form of invariance. But the analysis founders on too easy a refutation of Protagoras: Plato is forced back to the Eleatic constraint.

Hegel masters in a particularly commanding way the main themes of the advance required, although he also encumbers his study of the essential categories in a way that makes it difficult to free his innovations from the peculiar architecture of his own huge vision. Our world is admittedly Hegelian because we can hardly claim to recognize the human condition if we refuse the fine-grained distinctions of historicity and enculturation. But contemporary philosophy would never be willing to be governed by Hegel's extravagances: the prospect of a fresh analysis of the arts and sciences hangs in the balance.

Wittgenstein is particularly instructive here—remarkably spare—because, by an unexpected turn of events, his self-trained intuitions recover important strands (unwittingly) of the Hegelian conception of cultural life, without addressing history at all and without (it seems) an actual acquaintance with Hegel's texts—*and*, indeed, against his own mentor's (Bertrand Russell's) deliberate effort to erase all evidence of Hegelianism from British philosophy!

Wittgenstein's notions of *Lebensform* and *Sprachspiel* seem to have developed partly in tandem with his continuing attention to the *Tractatus* (say, from 1929 to the work on the second edition).[17] But a good part of the motivation for these later conceptions has more than a little to do with the paradoxes and limitations of the *Tractatus* itself—and with what Wittgenstein took to be the misguided labors of the academic philosophy that actually spawned his earlier effort. The fact is that Wittgenstein's "method" in the *Investigations* was never a method at all: it was a gifted, even brilliant, meander (a kind of elenchus, if you please) that worked its spell very quietly—plausibly, transiently, always in surprisingly effective and untried ways, always informally, without the use of any academic armature, and never in search of any fixed structures of thought or world. Russell and Frege may have been poor substitutes for Parmenides, but they proved to be Wittgenstein's philosophical demons.

All seems to be in flux for Wittgenstein within the human *Lebensform*:[18] the conceptual concatenations he identifies in his surefooted way plainly follow no preappointed path. Indeed, many seem as much invented as discovered. What he offers is peculiarly congenial to practical life itself. We find ourselves heartened by the discursive resources of the unanticipated meander he leads us through. Put another way, Wittgenstein never finds fixed structures in our language games, though he remains confident that we can find our way easily enough to the bedrock of our form of life: we are supported by the human pace of the variable rate of change we find among our habituated practices. There is no settled conceptual path that leads from one example to another. Curiously, the same is true of Hegel's grander dialectic, though, of course, Wittgenstein's meander is sparer in terms of disturbing our cultural ecology. But it's also true that Wittgenstein has no theory of the flux of the cultural world—and Hegel does.

If you press the point, you see at once the sense in which Kant *couldn't* have been an incipient Hegelian: the insistent claims made by the author of the second preface to the first *Critique* require a conceptual closure among the set of his transcendental categories that could never have honored the historied status of every would-be set of such categories. By parity of reason, Hegel could never have been the right-wing Hegelian he is made out to be. And Wittgenstein's *Lebensform* must be a Hegelianized version of Kant's transcendentalism if we insist (with Newton Garver, for instance) that it is a Kantian thesis.[19]

Our complicity, our validation, in effect, of what Wittgenstein offers is essential here because, of course, we are as well informed as he, being apt speakers of the language. (Construe all this as a sign of a more spontaneous elenchus to replace the uncertain Socratic original, informed by its own reflections on our *sittlich* ways without any reference at all to Hegelian convictions.) We are made agreeably aware that we simply never noticed certain discursive linkages in thought and action, which Wittgenstein brings to our attention, which often help clarify otherwise intractable academic puzzles, and which define unexpected conceptual alignments that promise to extend their application (without apparent artifice) in ways we sense will doubtless keep us from many a philosophical blunder. (But we do all this without the pretense of applying rules.)

We begin to grasp the *plural* possibilities of our habits of thought and action and, as a consequence, a fresh sense of the adequate stabilities of our prephilosophical discourse—a contingently evolving culture that reciprocally spawns and responds to Wittgenstein's meander. We realize that we've been relieved of the least Parmenidean twinge! We need only replace an outmoded conceptual fixity with the discursive fluencies of encultured self-discovery. The key to recovering Socrates lies through Hegel—a Hegel shorn of his own excesses, as by way of the critique offered by figures like Marx, Nietzsche, Dilthey, even Dewey and Heidegger, that brings us back to the *geistlich* world Plato and the Sophists explore in their tantalizingly innocent way. In this sense, Wittgenstein is himself an artifact of the "cunning of Reason."

What I mean is that we are never sure—in fact, we are inclined to doubt—that what Wittgenstein displays *are* actual structures he's discovered in our language or associated practices of thought, at least. What he shows us, rather, is that our form of life builds on, supports, incorporates, and abandons by pieces the transient, potentially useful, not-altogether-ephemeral concatenations of the kind he tracks. He shows us by unexpected example the determinable possibilities of having mastered our cultural resources, not any determinate structures in any parts of that culture. There seem to be no fixed structures at all. He shows us by his own assurance how far we might go in envisioning the whole of our everyday world as a tolerated flux of graded stabilities that have no need of fixity! (Plato might have found in this an incipient answer to his own worries.) Nevertheless, in admitting that, we are not bound to concede that there's no use in formulating different theories—many throwaway theories—of the conceptual order of our actual world.

Wittgenstein's improvisations provide the key to how such theories begin to take form. They even show us how the grandest philosophical visions tend to become too fixed, too abstract, too intolerant of change—they even show how they stray too far from the bedrock of societal practices—too far to be relied on without risk. Read this way, Wittgenstein's innovation deepens the import of recovering the Socratic and Hegelian strategies. *That* I take to be as close as we can possibly come to an indispensable philosophical discovery about the right way to view morality and the arts and sciences because, of course, it's no more than a corrective, therapeutic warning rather than a rule or foundational doctrine. Wittgenstein shows us that our practices are entirely reliable but not entirely determinate. There's the profound puzzle that haunts our every attempt to link the analysis of physical nature and human culture indissolubly. (I take instruction here.)

Wittgenstein is hardly an adequate guide in a post-Hegelian world. But it is Wittgenstein, more than anyone else in the recent Eurocentric world, who shows us how to simplify in the most stripped-down way the superfluous complexity of Hegel's necessary innovation—centered now in terms of our *lebensformlich* second nature. In short, Wittgenstein provides what amounts to a version of the Socratic elenchus enriched by a Hegelian transformation and then brought back, more comprehendingly, to its original spontaneity.

Wittgenstein intuitively hit on the tactic of *Entfremdung* amid what was completely familiar to his audience: the fluxive world of ordinary language and ordinary social habits and activities, viewed reflexively as the public sharing of a contingent cultural practice within whose terms we rightly count on answering all our quotidian philosophical questions about the meaning of what is said and done, our choice of norms in practical and theoretical matters, the continuing coherence of our engagement in a changing world, and what it is to be a human being. Wittgenstein almost never admits the play of history or historicity. Yet, in perfecting what I am calling his philosophical meander, in the untendentious way he does, he fashions a kind of moderate elenchus under an attenuated Hegelian sense of the *sittlich* and the *geistlich*—which he never subjects to explicit analysis.

In all its forms, the elenchus is the resource par excellence of conceptual improvisation, cast as discovery, within and about the everyday world. It can always be overridden for cause, but it cannot be bypassed or ignored. It fixes the sense in which what is given, as by a kind of *geistlich* phenomenology, cannot be derived from any deeper facultative competence; on the contrary, it affirms that all precision and exactitude derive, consensually, from the very stability of our practical world. (That is precisely what allows us to outflank the Eleatic scruple.) Wittgenstein celebrated the same fact—in a way, uncomprehendingly—that is, the Hegelian theme of his entire elenctic meander. For instance, in what may be one of its best-known expressions, Wittgenstein offers in the spirit of his method, " 'So, you are saying that human agreement decides what is true and what is false?'—It is what human beings *say* that is true and false; and they agree in the *language* they use. That is not agreement in opinions but in form of life [*Lebensform*]."[20] I cannot see how this could exceed the cultural flux that eluded Plato.

Wittgenstein is, then, a bit like the author of the Socratic elenchus: he is not entirely aware, it seems, of the full range of the sui generis contingencies of cultural life. Certainly, his characteristic specimens are of a narrower gauge than those of the large world Hegel addresses—or than those the more radical post-Hegelians might advance along the lines of historicity and the open logic of interpretation. But what is most compelling in Wittgenstein is the sheer simplicity and intuitive force of his method: it is as open to counterinstance as it could possibly be, even against his own occasional metaphysical preferences. Plato, you recall, was probably more conservative than the elenchus required, and Hegel was probably more daring than the dialectic could actually endorse. We need these diverse practitioners—and more—for it is hard to deny, even now, that we are only at the beginning of a proper inquiry into the human.

Very pretty, you say, but you've missed the mark. What then *is* the human? Let me venture a few clues in accord with my own account of the elenchus—and what I have in mind in what follows. The human is artifactual; socially constituted; historicized; enlanguaged and encultured; second natured; real only within some culture's collective life; embodied through the cultural transformation of the infant members of *Homo sapiens*; originally or externally *gebildet*; sui generis; emergent through mastering a first language and whatever aptitudes such mastery makes possible; indissolubly hybrid, uniting biological and cultural processes and powers; capable, therefore, of hybrid acts or utterances (speaking, making, doing, creating) incarnate in the *materiae* of any part of physical nature; self-transforming or internally *gebildet* through its second-natured powers; empowered and constrained by the collective history it shares with similarly emergent creatures; capable, thus, of functioning as a self, a person, a subject, an agent, within an aggregate of similarly formed selves—that is, free, responsible, and capable of causally effective (incarnate) initiatives, of self-reference, of reporting its inner thoughts and experience in a public way, and of understanding the utterances and acts of similarly endowed selves; inherently interpretable and subject to change through being interpreted; not a natural-kind entity but a history, or an entity that has a history rather than a nature, or a nature that is no more than a history—a history determinable but not determinate. All in all, the human is a unique sort of being, you must admit, but an individuated being nevertheless: emergent in part by natural (biological) means and in part by artifactual or cultural transformation—possibly, then, a conceptual scandal or even the living refutation of many a convention of canonical philosophy. Is that enough?[21] Perhaps not quite.

We do not understand ourselves well enough—philosophically—and I cannot hope to put my conception in a more compendious way, given the kind of narrative I've been airing. It would require an entirely new beginning, which may strike you, of course, as a strange complaint. But I can indeed collect some useful questions here, linked to the tally just offered and keyed to what I've been suggesting about elenctic thinking—which may now serve as a place marker for a stronger analysis that I'm about to venture. The single most important question that must be settled concerns whether human being—the mode of being of human beings (if you don't mind this way of speaking)—is itself, in belonging to the natural world, a natural-kind distinction or something else. There's an equivocation there and a puzzle to be resolved.

Heidegger pointedly affirms that human beings, the plural manifestations of the "human *Dasein*," exist. They appear to be the only beings that do exist in Heidegger's sense; mere "things" (of whatever complexity) do not.[22] Heidegger means by this that *Dasein* is *not* a part of nature, for to be entirely a part of nature is, it seems, to be a mere thing. For my part, what Heidegger says here cannot persuade us if he cannot, or will not, specify some feature or other of being human that could never, without paradox or incoherence or inconsistency, be admitted to be distinct or unique when compared to all else that is found in nature—while remaining natural itself, subject in every respect to the forces of the natural world. I daresay Heidegger never meets the challenge. Nor, within my reading, does anyone else who follows a similar intuition.[23] Heidegger flirts with the notion that *Dasein* is a kind of ontological presence that is not a countable entity at all. But that must be a false lead if he (or we) intends to speak of *Dasein*'s ever acting in its own right—doing or making anything in an intentionally effective way. All speech, art, responsible commitment would have to be abandoned.[24]

I myself take persons or selves to emerge from biological nature—naturally but not by biological means alone, hence not in the way of natural-kind change. The equivocation is resolved by admitting sui generis cultural processes within the bounds of nature. I concede that *Homo sapiens* is a natural-kind kind, but I hold that (human) selves or persons or subjects are not, though they exist, entirely in the natural world. I mean by this that *language, history, culture, art*, and similar distinctions are not natural-kind distinctions of any kind—which is to say, they are not reducible in natural-kind terms. Persons are not the mere members of any biological species, though in our earthly world there seem to be no other kinds of persons (unless we admit fictions: legal persons, corporations for instance, that are not human in the precise sense that qualifies the members of *Homo sapiens*).

If I understand him rightly, Heidegger may be forced to admit that *Homo sapiens* isn't human; or that the strictly numbered members of that species do not exist; or that, in existing, *Dasein* manifests a mode of being beyond all biology and nature. I don't understand this way of thinking, unless it's just an expression of extravagant respect. In my opinion, this signifies that Parmenides and Kant and Husserl and Heidegger (and Levinas, if you allow a lesser addition) may at times be practicing philosophy beyond the pale, and if selected extravagances on the part of Plato, Aristotle, Aquinas, and Schelling must be read literally, then they need not apply, either.

No, what I offer in the way of a direct challenge to any theory of what it is to be a human being is this: that all the available evidence points to the fact that the members of *Homo sapiens* are, shall we say, spontaneously transformed into selves or persons in the process of acquiring a natural language and the culturally formed aptitudes that that makes possible. *Homo sapiens* harbors, as such, no selves, in the plain sense that languageless creatures, including wild children, are incapable of self-reference and reporting their inner mental states. *That* extraordinary ability, unmatched anywhere else in nature, fully justifies our speaking, uniquely, of selves as second-natured hybrids—ontological transforms, if you don't mind. By this, I mean no more than that the emergence of human selves obtains in a perfectly natural way—is a sui generis process, not at all like mere biological evolution or growth. The emergence of selves is, rather, an artifactual process in that it occurs only through acquiring a natural language and a natural culture—where language, having evolved at least incipiently from sublinguistic skills, cannot then be explained in any merely biological or other natural-kind terms.[25] There is no algorithm, for instance, that accounts for the emergence of language in the way in which self-replicating proteins are said to have emerged for the first time.[26]

Furthermore, what holds for embodied second-natured selves holds (for logically trivial but momentous reasons) for all the incarnate utterances and acts and creations of such selves. Hence, if selves are sui generis, so are the arts and the sciences and language and history—as well as the descriptive, interpretive, explanatory, and logical resources that we judge to be required in each domain. Most particularly, it means that human perception is culturally altered, transformed, penetrated—as in the perception of paintings: it is itself a cultural artifact that cannot be reduced in neurophysiological or phenomenalist terms.

It's for these reasons that I characterize a human self as a hybrid creature whose native biological gifts are startlingly transformed through a human infant's internalizing the ability to speak the language of its home society. In that sense, a self is itself a cultural artifact. But to say only that is to be prepared to explain in sufficient detail the natural (not natural-kind) process of cultural emergence (enculturation, the second naturing of *Homo sapiens*). I see no difficulty there—no more than a familiar sort of empirical ignorance. Furthermore, *hybrid* is meant to signify our successfully obviating both dualism and reductionism with regard to selves and their characteristic forms of utterance. It is, in short, the simplest, perhaps the only viable alternative we have. Even a confirmed neo-Darwinian like Richard Dawkins admits he sees no way of explaining cultural transmission in terms of genetic processes and any variant of environing physical conditions.[27]

There are, of course, endless questions that would need to be answered if the thesis of the hybrid being (or nature) of human being were adopted. But there is no a priori barrier against its general coherence or the coherence of cognate solutions applied to problems in the theory of science or mind or language or art or morality. I have addressed a good many of these smaller questions elsewhere, and I see no crippling paradox in the offing. I concede that adopting this single theorem requires altering in considerable depth the entire canonical picture of nature and science. But that's hardly a reason for opposing such a change.

Let me add another consideration from another quarter touched on earlier. I am persuaded that the constructivist solution to the paradoxes of early modern philosophy—the paradoxes of Kant's magnificent innovation as well, which reached its strongest and most original form (against Kant, of course) in Hegel's historicism—is essentially the same achievement as that of explicating the concepts of historicity and enculturation. Surely, the first counts as one of the most decisive advances in the whole of the history of Western philosophy; the second counts as the single most important modern contribution to philosophy's conceptual resources and, as a result, to its most radical reinterpretation of the general problem of human knowledge and self-understanding: the key to the elenctic puzzle itself.

But if that is so, even the natural sciences are *constructive posits* of, and within, the constituting forces of history and enculturation—all this is in spite of the alleged fact (the canonical view) that the natural sciences need never, in their descriptive and explanatory work, invoke the sui generis categories alleged to be essential to our understanding of the cultural world.

On the admission of cultural emergence, however, both vocabularies take form within (and only within) the terms of a constructive realism (drawn as economically as possible from Kant's and Hegel's analyses). If so, then we cannot defend *any* principled disjunction between the natural and the human sciences, and every science will be a human science: the vocabulary of the physical sciences will then be read as an economy imposed on a more inclusive inquiry, *not* as an independent idiom independently achieved or validated—or validated prior to cultural inquiry. Indeed, I take this to be the neglected lesson of Thomas Kuhn's ill-fated *Structure of Scientific Revolutions*.[28] You begin to see, therefore, just how and why the elenctic process in any of its forms is bound to color the definition of the human. I think this catches the deeper meaning of Kuhn's profound reflection, which (if I dare suggest) Kuhn himself was unable to fathom sufficiently or analyze without inviting conceptual disaster. It marks the sense in which the human is natural or naturalistic without being naturalizable in the reductive sense that runs through so much of analytic philosophy's penchant for scientism— fixed in the very title of W. V. Quine's well-known paper "Epistemology Naturalized" and feared (for that sort of insufficient reason) by so much of contemporary continental philosophy.[29]

The lesson of the elenchus is still too elliptical as it stands. Let me put it another way. Parmenides, who originates its dialectical economy, does so in the name of his supposed necessities of thought and of the truth about being. Plato's brilliant stroke lies in his converting the original strategy into the Socratic elenchus: which is to say, first, that Socrates applies the elenchus only to the changing world, never to "what is" in Parmenides' sense; second, that its argumentative resources are confined to *sittlich* beliefs, whether in logic or method or experience or convention; third, that it centers on questions of normative conduct and character, just those that are likely to yield (we may suppose) to a society's accumulated wisdom; and, fourth, that whatever success it achieves is never more than consensual, persuasive, provisional, endlessly open to revision and diverse conviction and application, grounded in whatever may be given in the practical life of a viable society.

I take that to be the deeper meaning of Socrates' "ignorance"—as pertinent a lesson under the changed circumstances of modern thought as it ever was in its original setting. That is, all our powers of cognition and intelligence are finally, however critically refined, artifacts of cultural history and consensual tolerance. (Socrates knows he has no knowledge, because he knows he has no knowledge of the Forms!)

Modern philosophy since Hegel (as distinct from Kant and Fichte) transformed in a new way (but never abandoned) what we should understand as the grounds of knowing. Hegel may rightly be thought to have anticipated Wittgenstein in holding that the ground of knowledge is not a proposition (or opinion) of any kind but a form of life.[30] The world of absolute and infinite *Geist* is, finally, the presumptuous daring of a contingent creature transformed into a being that invents its own realm of freedom, which it treats as a discovery! Hence, knowledge no longer requires foundations or a source of certainty; it requires just what moral and political objectivity require—namely, a constructive grounding in historical life itself. That is precisely what the Greeks could never penetrate, but also what Plato (to his credit) saves in the Socratic elenchus.

It would be a mistake to infer from all this, however, that the post-Hegelian world rejects the possibility of knowledge. Hardly! Its entire purpose is to outflank any such skepticism. It shows, rather, that human knowledge and understanding must take a constructivist turn if they are ever to escape the Cartesian (and Parmenidean) paradoxes. It is in just this sense that, through the "cunning of Reason," Hegel's dialectic has become the perfect clue to the larger lesson of the Socratic elenchus—which, of course, Plato could not have fathomed.

If you concede this lesson, you see the sense in which to admit the role of enculturation in the construction of the human self is tantamount to admitting the inescapability of a constructive and historicized realism; that to admit that is to abandon every form of fixity and privilege in, say, science and morality; *and* that to admit all *that* is to admit that we have lost the a priori right to oppose the compatibility of historicism and/or relativism and a constructive realism—if, that is, it should prove true, independently, that either option of the first pair *was* coherent and viable in its own right.

There's no need to apply these radical options everywhere: it's more reasonable to invoke them wherever they fit best. But once we gain the high ground of the post-Hegelian world, we can afford to let Plato's philosophical stone roll down its hill for the last time. For to be able to bring relativism and historicism within the pale of knowledge *is* to have superseded the Parmenidean constraint once and for all! In that sense, even Wittgenstein's meander may be viewed in a different light. We may ultimately have no other resource than elenctic reason. I think that's true. But the elenchus runs much deeper than we ever supposed. For example—though it counts as more than a mere example—the elenchus introduces an inherent and insurmountable logical informality and provisional diversity that must color every dream of extensional rigor and determinacy of analysis that (up to the present time) has furnished the most admired moments of the whole of Western philosophy. (We are closer, now, to escaping the old hegemonies.)

There remains a considerable gap in the argument nevertheless, a gap that must be filled: not so much in the way of what we might wish to add as a fuller account of our elenctic powers, more in the way of explaining the conceptual relationship between agents capable of such powers (selves, ourselves) and the members of *Homo sapiens* from whom they somehow arise. In the modern world, any tenable answer would implicate some form of evolution or emergence that would avoid the defeated options of dualism and reductionism and therefore would need to admit formative processes ampler than the merely biological. As far as I know, the Greeks never sought to explain the relationship between selves and *Homo sapiens* in evolutionary terms of any kind; they spoke primarily of education and maturation within the telic cycle of the natural creature, though they were attracted very early, of course, to the meaning of cosmic order, which they took human intelligence to resemble.

When Aristotle speaks of man as the "political animal," he obviously treats the political as a fully biologized process, though biology is for him a much more generous category than it is for us. There's the difficulty: the biological or natural is so expansive that it proves impossible to speculate, in classical terms, about the difference between "our" conception of biology and what we regard as cultural process. Ultimately, both *physis* and *nomos* are subsumed within the pale of nature so that even our being governed by *nomos* (or convention) is, finally, read as being governed by nature. (Compare Vico.) If you insist that the distinction between the two still preserves our distinction between nature and culture, you place yourself under an obligation to deliver an analysis of custom or justice (or language or art) that would support your claim. It can't be done in Aristotle's terms!

Furthermore, where Aristotle may have been nonplussed along related lines, where he needed a concept of reason (nous) adequate to his theory of knowledge, as in the *De Anima*, he simply invents out of whole cloth an ad hoc faculty, more divine than human, for which he never deigns to offer a biological clue—although it is true that he weaves the powers of nous (so conceived) together with the powers of biologized perception in an interesting way. Aristotle never regards his device as a sign of failure, although its obvious epistemological compromise would never pass muster within the precincts of Socrates' elenchus.

This entire line of thinking anticipates the sense in which the theory of the fine arts is bound to match the theory of human being: Aristotle's mimesis, for instance, is the perfect counterpart of nous. Hence, if we accept the declension of the elenchus along the lines I've sketched, we begin to see the near inevitability with which we must abandon necessity and fixity, begin to view the human world as a hybrid and constructed world, and thereupon find it impossible to avoid exploring the distinction between the physical (or natural) and the cultural—even if in a more radical setting we choose to reclaim the whole of this new unity for nature once again. For we will have done so only within the sparest limits we imagine we could ever imagine.

In fact, there is a very pretty rendering of a cognate thesis formulated in evolutionary terms by Marjorie Grene, drawn from Helmuth Plessner's ingenious theories, which Grene also presents as her own "basic [biological] intuition"—that is,

> the principle of the *natural artificiality* of man. We become human not just by being born *homo sapiens*, but by relying on a complex network of artifacts: language and other symbolic systems, social conventions, tools in the context of their use—artifacts which are in a way extensions of ourselves, but which in turn we actualize in our personal lives. It is our nature to need the artificial, art in the broadest sense of that term, or, indeed, poetry in the broadest sense of that term: making and the made.[31]

The breathtaking intuition behind this lovely finding, which Grene shares with Plessner, is that, much as with human birth itself, *Homo sapiens*, phylogenetically conceived, is already profoundly *incomplete* in a moral sense, already in "need" (Grene's term) of the forms of cultural transformation. "All" that is missing is the theory of art and cultural artifacts. But that, of course, *is* the whole of what we need. If we isolate the differences between the biological and the cultural and reinterpret Grene's intuition (if I may co-opt her notion thus) in terms of an actual theory of the self, we would find it very natural to treat the self as hybrid and second natured, along the lines already sketched—and along additional lines that have still to be introduced (involving the arts particularly)—*and* we would also find (I daresay) the remarkable flexibility and power of the elenctic theme confirmed and vindicated. Bear that in mind, please. It's the motivation of the argument that follows. I capture the entire thrust of this last adjustment by speaking of human utterance, that is, what it is that human selves—but not the members of *Homo sapiens*—do and can do by exercising their encultured second-natured powers.

Nine

What, After All, Is a Work of Art?

It is incredible—but true enough—that, if you ask professional aestheticians what a work of art *is*, they will not be able to find a compelling answer in the whole philosophy of art.¹ Theorists are skittish on the question, for a variety of reasons: (a) they have been burned too many times; (b) they are aware some ingenious artist will make a point of producing a work theorists will be uneasy about excluding, though it will defeat their definitional darlings; (c) they find it so difficult to say, in the face of art's baffling variety; and (d) would-be answers tend to be too ambitious and too abstract. Behind the scenes, knowledgeable theorists mutter that artworks are obviously not natural-kind entities, hence not definable in the way camels and gold are, or else these theorists pointedly remark that the question has no explanatory interest if, after all, it's essentially a matter of convenience or discursive fiat. But if we abandon the hapless idea that there's no point to empirical definitions or broad generalizations along definitional lines that are not meant to be essentialist or concerned with capturing the necessary and sufficient conditions of every admissible specimen, we may well discover much that would otherwise hardly be mentioned.²

The fact is that artworks are very strange entities, if your best specimen of an entity is a stone, a tree, or a camel—or even a carving knife or a pencil or, anticipating more-notorious cases, a urinal, a snow shovel, or a Brillo box. I am not concerned in any strenuous way with official definitions of art. I have tried my hand at that and see no harm in it, but its benefits are regularly misread as a result of a certain literal-mindedness about definition itself.

I am quite sure about two constraints at least in making any definitional effort: (1) the would-be definition should be offered against the backdrop of a reasonably clear-cut range of central specimens and for the sake of answering a specific question about them—no more than that; and (2) we should abandon all pretensions of a modally necessary, essentialist, or invariantist sort regarding art and freely admit there is bound to be a use for endlessly many alternative such definitions relative to other questions and other runs of core specimens. It's almost never the definition that matters: it's more likely to be one or another contested theory about the arts that a would-be definition serves to focus in a certain felicitous and systematic way. Seen thus, the comparison of entirely detached abstract definitions really has no point, since it risks all connection with the living parts of the tradition of the arts that probably called the effort into play in the first place.

I have, in this regard, favored the generic (not yet specific) formula "artworks are physically embodied and culturally emergent entities," which has drawn a certain amount of controversy.[3] However, in offering it, I agree many questions should be answered if we are to credit it properly. In any case, we should want to know what it is about art thus construed that draws our interest and how the definition serves it.

For example, it is often remarked that a poem is *not* physically embodied since it is composed of words. It is also remarked that poetry often belongs to an oral tradition and so may be neither clearly individuated nor physically (or materially) embodied, hence not an entity at all. One also hears that artworks in the performing arts are not entities or objects but, rather, events.[4] The conceptual picture is murky, I admit, once you go down the road of physical embodiment and cultural emergence (and even if you don't). I have no wish to pursue the minutiae of the definition I offer here. (I have done so a number of times in the past.) Nevertheless, a clarification or two may serve a deeper objective.

First of all, I treat *entity* in a sense that signifies *any* individuated, reidentifiable *denotatum* in the world of existing things. I rule out at a stroke, therefore, numbers, predicables, types, universals, kinds, and the like: none of these exist, though they may well be real. What I say in this regard is that what is real but does not exist is—at a first approximation—real, *if true*, predicatively, of what exists.[5] This rules out at once all theories pretending that artworks (of whatever kind) are kinds, types, or universals. (There are in fact a number of prominent theories of this sort.)[6]

The reasons against the option are straightforward enough. If artworks are kinds or types, they must lack perceptible properties. But that is plainly false. If the perceptible properties of their earthly instantiations—performances of a Mozart sonata, say, or prints pulled from one of Dürer's engraved plates—are derived in some way from the prior properties of some corresponding kind-entities, then artworks possess certain everlasting properties (as Nicholas Wolterstorff is prepared to claim), even if those properties answer to the historically contingent features of the human world. (Wolterstorff considers the properties of Gogol's *Dead Souls* as involving a contingent "selection" by Gogol—somehow—from the everlasting properties of the kind DEAD SOULS that belong to God's providential plan. Wolterstorff says nothing about the contingency of nineteenth-century Russian history here.)[7] But the most important objection rests with the obvious fact that no one from Plato to the present has ever been able to say just how we might discern such changeless forms, kinds, or universals. Surely it is a mad extravagance to go that way.

Again, I don't deny that what we carve out of an oral tradition as the particular artworks (entities) we mean to count will undoubtedly be reconciled (will have to be) with our practices in the gallery, concert, museum, and library worlds. I see no difficulty with this, though I admit a certain degree of freedom here. It's the same freedom we find in admitting differences between the numbered performances of a Mozart sonata for which we have a score. There are technical difficulties here, but (I believe) they are all easily resolved by introducing the notion of a token-of-a-type (solely for individuative purposes). Nevertheless, there are no types (in the sense explained), and where the token instances are reasonably collected as admissible instantiations of types, the usage is merely heuristic and meant only to service our critical practice.

Artworks are individuated as entities, but critical discourse may appeal to scores and notations that subtend a run of would-be instantiations. Think, for instance, of Kenneth Branagh's film version of *Hamlet*, which is said to use Shakespeare's "complete entertainment"—that is, the entire text of the play—which cannot be said of any important theater performance of *Hamlet* in recent years.

The point, of course, is that criticism and history are largely occupied with predicative questions and therefore require an individuative strategy applied to objects and events alike. Explicit ontologies range all the way from firm assertions about "what there is" to reasonable ontic commitments under given circumstances to convenient idioms that service our referential and predicative practices but admit a wide range of taste and preference and heuristic tolerance. Certainly, we mean to include various shortened performances of *Hamlet* among the admissible instances *of Hamlet*, though to do so requires a somewhat-flexible notion of numerical identity. The evidentiary considerations are worth an effort, and additional complications need to be addressed. Nevertheless, I set all that aside here by suggesting that the salient puzzles cannot be managed by any known extensional treatment of performances via scores and scripts (Nelson Goodman's allographic proposal, for instance).[8] These are not negligible puzzles, I admit, but neither are they the most interesting complications.

Finally, in my own view, language, like thought, is an abstraction from the life and behavior of encultured selves—ourselves—as the apt members of a particular society. Our fluency is such that we imagine too easily that language is an autonomous, abstract, communicative medium of some sort only contingently bound to the physical and perceptible properties of sounds, bodies, actions, institutions, histories, and the like. I take all that to be utterly mistaken, utterly wrongheaded: for instance, thoughts are often characterized propositionally, hence abstractly, though it seems to me that thinking is complexly incarnated in a way that includes the neurophysiology of the brain *and* the culturally habituated behavior of our society (assuming, of course, that the latter cannot be reduced to the former). I draw the same lesson from language and, accordingly, find no serious difficulty regarding my original definition. On the contrary, the point of that definition—"physically embodied and culturally emergent entities"—was, precisely, to feature art's most puzzling attributes as a preparatory step in confronting and testing the adequacy of the most important theories of art in our day.

I

So much for preliminaries.

I should add immediately that I don't at all wish to discount the importance of the formal analysis of reference and predication—or of individuation and reidentification, for that matter, or of the mode of existence and the nature of an artwork. Far from it. Interest in the peculiarities of art criticism and art history obliges us to ask ourselves how best to render the defining features of artworks in such terms. For instance, if (for argument's sake) the interpretation of artworks favored a relativistic logic (as I believe it does), then we should have to ask ourselves how that might be reflected in our theory of what an artwork is—unless, of course, it could be shown on independent grounds that such a theory could not possibly fail to be incoherent. But there is no such argument. As soon as the challenge is voiced, an extraordinary fact glides into view. For it must dawn on us that there is simply no criterial or algorithmic solution to the problems of reference and predication—or, a fortiori, to the problems of individuation and reidentification, which depend on a solution to the first set.[9] General injunctions against avoidable incoherence and inconsistency remain completely vacuous, in any case, until they are suitably interpreted in terms of what is actual or real—and then we are back again to the details of criticism and history.

But if all this is so, then we will have made an enormous gain without much conceptual exertion, certainly without yielding to any unfriendly canon. For, on the argument—that is, granting the logical informality of referential and predicative success—there cannot be any advantage in adopting essentialism or modal invariance, or in insisting on modeling the metaphysics of artworks on what may be thought canonical in speaking of physical, natural, or natural-kind entities. For instance, it is not necessary to favor anything as unyielding as Aristotle's ontology, in *Metaphysics* 4, or indeed any contemporary approximation. The point is that we should be entirely within our rights in equilibrating our choice of a metaphysics and our choice of a logic for critical and historical inquiries. (Disputes about the definition of art are bound to accommodate such informalities.)

Notice, for instance, that if we supposed a critical reading of *Hamlet* could never rightly disallow plural, nonconverging, otherwise-incompatible interpretations of the play—which we should then want to say were jointly valid (no longer contradictory: incongruent, I prefer saying, in accord with a relativistic logic, as I explain in the first chapter of this volume)—such a possibility would never be admitted on Aristotle's model, for Aristotle holds to an omnicompetent bivalence fitted to what is antecedently invariant in reality.[10] Aristotle claims that the denial of bivalence instantly produces self-contradiction. But his argument depends not on bivalence itself but on the modal fixity of reality (at least in the argument at stake), on which (he supposes) the bivalent injunction relies.

Nevertheless, Aristotle nowhere secures that fixity; at no point does he demonstrate that ontic fixity cannot be coherently denied. No one has ever shown that, for it cannot be done. (No evidence exists, for instance, proving that the denial of invariance violates the principle of noncontradiction. Only if particular things had fixed essences would the doctrine of flux produce contradictory truth claims. But essentialism, of course, is what Aristotle would have had to demonstrate. It's hardly a logical principle in its own right, but it is indeed the basis for Aristotle's exposé of Protagoras.)

It's perfectly possible to construe artworks—coherently—as lacking a fixed nature (frankly, I should say the same of physical nature), if doing so accords with the salient features of a critical practice we wish to favor and violates no other logical constraints. If we can secure that much, we can easily turn the tables on familiar canons said to govern current practices in criticism and history. It is, I admit, a standard assumption that individual entities possess crisply determinate properties and boundaries. This may be true of purely physical entities (though I doubt it), but I know of no argument that convincingly demonstrates it must be true of artworks or other cultural entities, and I take the modal claim to be demonstrably false. In any case, the counterargument goes against the familiar canon—but does so coherently: it holds that the activities of identifying entities numerically and describing their natures may be no more than loosely or informally linked with one another, without producing paradox. After all, *denotata* cannot, for logical reasons, be captured by predicative means alone.

The logical flexibilities that this single distinction makes possible have been very largely neglected. In fact, if you allow the two distinctions I've already mentioned—one to the effect that Intentional properties are determinable (on interpretive grounds) but not antecedently determinate, the other to the effect that the numerical identity of artworks can be fixed with as much precision as physical entities but without seriously constraining the relative indeterminacy of Intentional properties or (as a result) the logical peculiarities of the interpretive history of a given artwork—you will have in hand the principal premises favoring the viability of a strongly historicized and relativized account of interpreting art (in effect, the intended benefit of my generic definition of art).

If the argument goes through, you see at once it is no more than an elementary mistake to suppose that, if an otherwise numerically distinct artwork *may* rightly be ascribed Intentionally determinable (but not determinate) properties in interpretively incongruent ways, the would-be singular entity must yield (for logical reasons) to a set of numerically different *denotata* (under the constraint, of course, of a bivalent logic that refuses to countenance incongruent attributions).[11]

Let me remind you here of Monroe Beardsley's theory of literary criticism. His thesis may be the best-known contemporary statement by an English-language philosopher of art. While it is certainly as uncompromisingly committed to bivalence as is Aristotle's metaphysics, it proceeds by a different route. Beardsley's argument is genuinely instructive and, for all its brevity, not without force or subtlety.

Beardsley writes in defense of what he regards as a fair extension of New Critical policies, and he faithfully recommends (in its spirit) what he calls "the principle of 'the Intolerability of Incompatibles,' i.e., if two [interpretations] are logically incompatible, they cannot both be true."[12] You see how sensible this sounds, if you suppose (with Beardsley) that artworks are entities, more or less in the same sense in which physical objects are.

Of course, what Beardsley says *is* true enough: incompatibles cannot both be true. But what Beardsley implies is that at least one of a pair of apparent (but more than apparent) incompatibles must be false, and *that* hardly follows—or, it follows only if a bivalent logic is inescapable.

As far as I can tell, Beardsley offers two very different arguments in favor of his thesis. One is somewhat concessive: if we are prepared to go contrary to the intolerability principle, then we must be admitting superimpositions rather than interpretations proper. For example, if I construe Jack and the Beanstalk as a Marxist fable or *Alice in Wonderland* as a Freudian tale, then, though it may be coherent to admit such a reading even where others dispute it, I should have exceeded the tolerance of interpretation proper. Here, Beardsley develops a two-story account of what, informally (but then, incorrectly), may be called *interpretation*: the first story belongs to interpretation proper; the second, to so-called superimposition. This is because superimposition presupposes and rests on the prior work of valid interpretation—it simply goes beyond interpretation's limits, adding a further externally associated sense of how the story might be treated.

Here, the restrictions of bivalence are not really called into play (though, I should add, they are not really violated either); superimpositions are rather like the contingent idiosyncratic appearances of things viewed under variable circumstances. (Aristotle had already conceded such a possibility, even in nature.) You see, therefore, that Beardsley's first strategy requires a clear disjunction between interpretation proper and superimposition *and* a view of the metaphysics of literary entities such that interpretation proper must conform with the fixed nature of literary works. But the fact remains that Beardsley nowhere supplies even a rough criterion of the boundaries of a literary work in virtue of which interpretations and superimpositions can be demarcated in the way he favors. I say it cannot be done.

The reason, of course, is that the Intentional attributes of artworks are interpretively determinable but not determinate in anything like the sense in which physical objects are said to have determinate properties. For, if meanings (or the Intentional significance) of artworks change (very likely in a variety of ways) and cannot be reliably fixed (let us say, in terms of the sheer meaning of the uttered words or of original authorial intent), then the distinction between interpretation proper and superimposition founders, and the relative indeterminacy but interpretive determinability of artworks will have been conceded. Even beyond the world of art, one has only to think of the renewed controversies in our time regarding the correct meaning of the texts of the Bible to realize that the fixity Beardsley requires is ineluctably open to great swings of interpretive conviction and historical perspective. The fact remains that Beardsley nowhere addresses the determinable nature of meanings and Intentionality, except when dismissing any threat to a strict bivalence.

This first strategy may be fairly viewed as the analytic counterpart of the (Romantic hermeneutic) theory offered by E. D. Hirsch, which, for altogether different reasons, also affords a two-story distinction: this time, between the proper "verbal meaning" of a literary text and its secondary "significance" relative to some external or special perspective.[13] Thus, for example, "La Marseillaise" came to acquire, among the French, the symbolic import of the national shame of the Nazi occupation of Paris during the Second World War. Beardsley would, I'm certain, characterize that as the musical counterpart of a literary superimposition, not a proper interpretation of the song at all. But Beardsley neglects to explain how to tell the difference in a principled way (that is, supposing music has representational powers). Hirsch also fails, but he has an answer of sorts.

Beardsley secures his theory in a way very similar to that in which bivalence is secured in Aristotle's view. Beardsley offers (in effect) a pair of metaphysical principles. About the first, he says, "everyone must agree on [it]." He calls it "the Principle of Independence" and formulates it in the following rough way: "literary works exist as individuals and can be distinguished from other things, though it is another question whether they enjoy some special mode of existence, as has been held."[14]

It is worth mentioning that, in Hirsch's view, literary works are imaginatively constructed in the process of reading and interpreting a string of words (or signs): a text. In effect, Hirsch violates Beardsley's "Principle": literally nothing constituting an existing literary work (according to Hirsch) *can* be said to exist independently.[15] What exists (the verbal signs) permits us only to reconstruct what we should take the (thereby constructed) poem or story to mean. The question of existing poems (poems as entities) does not arise.

You must appreciate that if Hirsch were entirely consistent here, he would have to concede that words and texts do not exist either—all we have are sounds or marks, which, arranged as they are, may be imaginatively constituted or reconstructed as a text (that is, interpreted, construed, transfigured) in accord with the original author's intent. This comes very close to the disastrous doctrine (favored by many in our own time) holding that artworks and texts are posited as what answers to a certain use of purely physical entities.[16]

However, if you adopt the doctrine literally, you will be faced with the need to treat selves (who make such posits) in the same way, and then you will find yourself confronted by a vicious regress (or a doubtful reductionism). Admit the reality of cognizing selves—ourselves as culturally formed entities apt in whatever way you care—and you cannot then deny the existence of the artifacts (artworks) they create. (Otherwise, you must demonstrate the reducibility, in physicalist terms, of our linguistic and creative competence. I say it cannot be done.)

That, at any rate, is a reasonable bet. There is no known successful reduction of the intentional, or Intentional, to the physical; art and language are themselves obviously uttered by human selves. The Intentional structures of art and language cannot, therefore, be different from the conditions of reflexive understanding among encultured selves.

Hirsch is every bit as insistent on bivalence as Beardsley is, but he does not concede the independent existence of a literary work. He does insist on an alternative notion of invariance, however, and in doing so comes close again to Aristotle's model. In particular, Hirsch insists on the invariant features of literary "genres" (abstracted from a society's cultural life) in terms of which a poem is first uttered (authorially) and by reference to which (the sentences uttered) the intended poem can be recovered.[17]

The truth is that Beardsley and Hirsch subscribe to very different models of the human sciences. Both of their theories about literature are untenable because each requires a form of metaphysical invariance its proponent cannot defend—and nowhere does defend—and each supports a bivalent canon on the strength of such presumed invariance. Furthermore, each concedes a certain two-story tolerance for incongruent interpretations, which is to say that each admits that the practice of favoring incongruent interpretations need not be self-contradictory.

Hirsch's theory is the more adventurous of the two since it secures all the advantages of referential and predicative success without succumbing to anything like Beardsley's entitative model. The fault in Hirsch's theory lies with the practical impossibility of ever discerning the supposedly changeless structure of the literary genres governing a society's poetic utterances. Hirsch means to show why, admitting genres, valid interpretations must rest on a bivalent principle and why a two-story practice linking "meaning" and "significance" may be regarded as theoretically benign.[18] But, of course, Hirsch is candid enough to admit that the fixity of genres is a myth, approximated (if we may speak thus) by probabilizing their entelechies, which, strictly speaking, genres cannot possess, since they are hardly living organisms. This proves to be little more than a tortured way of admitting that genres are open-endedly subject to innovative revision under the terms of the hermeneutic circle. Hence, they cannot possibly play a strict criterial role governing interpretive objectivity.

Beardsley offers us a second principle, which he admits is disputatious—incorporating, as it does, the notorious doctrine of "the Intentional Fallacy."[19] The second principle, which he calls "the Principle of Autonomy," affirms that "literary works are self-sufficient entities, whose properties are decisive in checking [the objectivity of] interpretations and judgments."[20] Of course, if his Principle of Independence fails, so must his Principle of Autonomy. Hirsch suggests a counterstrategy he does not himself pursue.

The local difficulty with Beardsley's theory is simply that it nowhere explains how meanings could possibly be treated as properties intrinsic, or internal, to the independent and autonomous *entity*, the poem or story—the literary work—or in what sense meanings are changeless. Here Beardsley supports too literal an analogy between poem and physical object: much more needs to be said about how to secure referential and predicative success in the case of poems. In fact, Beardsley concedes, "The boundaries of textual meaning . . . are not all that sharp. Some things are definitely said in the poem and cannot be overlooked; others are suggested, as we find on careful reading; others are gently hinted, and whatever methods of literary interpretation we use, we can never establish them decisively as 'in' or 'out.' Therefore whatever comes from without, but yet can be taken as an interesting extension of what is surely in, may be admissible. It merely makes a larger whole."[21] This is all that Beardsley has to say on the matter.

I shouldn't want to force the argument on textual grounds alone, but this last passage is a very large admission. Beardsley's concession points the way to a deeper challenge—namely, that he cannot supply (even if he tried) a principled disjunction between interpretation and superimposition or between what is "in" a poem and what is not. But if he cannot do that, he cannot vindicate his bivalent logic either. I am not concerned so much with the argument against bivalence or with what may coherently replace bivalence in the practice of criticism and history as with the inherent informalities of number and nature. Here I assume the validity of the argument against bivalence. (I've barely hinted at it but have addressed it earlier.) The more interesting question asks us to consider what kind of entity an artwork is if its description or interpretation eschews bivalence, admits incongruent truth claims, and admits even-stranger features answering to the practice of criticism and history—for instance, that the meaning of a poem may change under the very practice of interpretation, or that we can defend no principled division between putatively admissible and inadmissible sources of interpretation.

Of course, if these adjustments were conceded, both Beardsley's and Hirsch's theories would be subverted at a stroke. The curious thing is, neither attempts to show that the reverse of his policy is more unreasonable or more unworkable or less fruitful. My guess is that both believe (quite wrongly) that the violation of bivalence is *pro tanto* the violation of inviolable *de re* invariances. But that is Aristotle's failed doctrine all over again.

II

We are now on the edge of certain interesting concessions regarding artworks as entities. Let me offer a specimen theory that is really a halfway house to the radical options that are beginning to dawn. I can think of no better exemplar (for my purpose) than Wolfgang Iser's reader-response theory, which draws inspiration chiefly from Roman Ingarden's version of Husserl's phenomenology. "The phenomenological theory of art," Iser says, "lays full stress on the idea that, in considering a literary work, one must take into account not only the actual text but also, and in equal measure, the actions involved in responding to that text."[22]

You must catch the humor of the situation. Beardsley makes the literary work autonomous and independent; as a consequence, wishing to save the objectivity (and bivalent logic) of criticism, he is obliged to construe the meanings of a poem or story as the perceptual properties of an object in a way that permits no significant difference between the analysis of a poem and the analysis of a lump of coal. This is the inflated price of bringing the practice of criticism and history (a fortiori, the human sciences) under the tent of something like the unity-of-science program.[23] The whole idea fails at the very moment it is tested, for, as Beardsley himself agreeably concedes, there is no way to specify the criteria required for determining what is "in" and "out" of a literary work.

It is true that Beardsley makes this generous concession in the briefest way. It would hardly do to press the advantage too far. But it is also to the point to insist that he nowhere offers a theory for fixing the meaning of actual utterances, and he nowhere considers the essential question affecting literary theory of the import of the history of the reception and interpretation of particular works. It is not so much that artworks become enigmatic as the history of their reception lengthens; it's rather that our sustained interest in them, over time, invites continual reinterpretation in ways that are plainly not merely additive.

Hirsch avoids the reductive model by disorganizing at the start the very idea of a literary work's being an independent entity, or an entity at all. Hirsch manages to recover a form of objectivity (objectivism, in fact) that he regards as comparable in rigor to the work of the physical sciences. He does so by falling back to the hermeneutic (Romantic) model spanning the theories of Schleiermacher and Dilthey, among others, which claim resources sufficient for recovering authorial intent by invoking the objective genres (or analogues of genres) of a historical culture. Hirsch shifts, therefore, from the analysis of an entity's *properties* to the reconstruction of a linguistic sign's probable *meanings*.

Hirsch fails, nevertheless, because the supposed probabilities of meaning cannot be shown to converge toward any ideally fixed or independent meanings. Meanings are forever hostage to the drift of history, and the genres Hirsch invokes cannot fail to be constructions continually altered by the fresh pressure of inventions that depend in their turn on a continual revision of the would-be constituting genres by which they themselves are said to be grasped. This, of course, is the fatal weakness of the Romantic version of the hermeneutic circle.[24] (Not of the circle itself.) If reading and what is read belong alike to the movement of history, then we cannot exit the hermeneutic circle by fixing, in the objectivist way the Romantic hermeneut pretends is possible, original authorial intent. (This is, of course, no more than a restatement of Gadamer's objection to the Romantic view.)

Still, Hirsch does manage to provide an incontestably valid reason for distinguishing between the verbal signs of a society's linguistic and literary practice and the subjective complexities of anyone's attempt to interpret such signs within a larger critical space. Iser is onto a similar distinction. It is what he means (following Ingarden)[25] by the difference between an "actual [verbal] text" and the "literary work"—the latter being a "*Konkretisation*" (Ingarden's term) of the former by means of a reader's reading. (Ingarden's model of the entitative text that our aesthetic response is said to concretize is, as an ontology, conceptually monstrous but heuristically suggestive nevertheless as a guide to criticism. The ontology cannot be satisfactorily recovered by any likely adjustment.)

Iser outflanks both Beardsley and Hirsch, since authorial intent (however discernible from a reading of textual signs) cannot, he believes, account for the full "aesthetic" interest of a poem or story: "the literary work cannot therefore be completely identical with the text, or the realization of the text, but in fact must lie halfway between the two."[26]

This is promising—but hardly more—for reasons rather distant from Iser's own intention. What he says suggests the plausibility of even more radical options directed as much against himself as against Beardsley and Hirsch. For one thing, Iser is primarily concerned with a kind of empathy on the reader's part (almost an identification with the original author or with the author's intention) rather than with the criterial question of how, on his own bipolar assumption, an objective reading can actually be confirmed. In addition, although he recognizes the historied nature of creating and reading a literary work, Iser nowhere develops a sense of the role of history in testing the validity of particular interpretations—for instance, along the horizonal lines Gadamer features.[27] The neglect of this theme appears already in Ingarden and Husserl, for Husserlian phenomenology (as well as Ingarden's variant) is unequivocally opposed to any strong commitment to the historicality of thinking. Of course, if, in Iser's model, you admit the historicality of thinking (a fortiori, of meaning) and *also* admit the pertinent contribution to the meaning of the work made by a reader's response to a text, you defeat at once all the fixities theorists like Beardsley and Hirsch invoke. But how could we escape making such a concession, even if we did not subscribe to Iser's particular theory?

Iser's account contains an essential tension between a "phenomenological subject" realizing or "concretizing" a given text (along Ingarden's lines) and a human reader's historically formed response to an inherently "incomplete" (schematic) text.[28] This becomes apparent, for instance, in Iser's reliance on the following remark from Husserl's *Phenomenology of Internal Time-Consciousness*: "Every originally constructive process is inspired by pre-intentions, which construct and collect the seed of what is to come, as such, and bring it to fruition."[29] Actually, I object to such expressions as "bring it to fruition" and "complete": they suggest, without defense, that right interpretation is telically directed to the completion of a particular work (and thus, by suggestion again, there is a uniquely correct way to complete an artwork). That cannot be shown.

In Husserl's mind, the process is rationally ineluctable, ideally convergent, and uncontaminated by historical contingencies. Iser, on the other hand, wishes to accommodate the plurality of the forms of historical experience within the Husserlian vision. One cannot say for certain whether Iser believes the structure of a text places inviolable constraints on the "concretizing" practice of diverse readers or whether the contingent experience of readers rightly alters the supposed original textual structure that subsequent readers will have to address. You see, therefore, that the phenomenological model of interpretation generates a two-story puzzle that is the counterpart of what we have already noted in Hirsch's Romantic account and Beardsley's New Critical account.

My sense is that Iser never resolves the question satisfactorily. He appears to favor both directions at once—which would be self-defeating—but gets no further than this: "Text and reader no longer confront each other as object and subject, but instead the 'division' takes place within the reader himself."[30] It is possible to construe this line as anticipating Gadamer's notion of *Horizontverschmelzung* (the fusion of horizons), but that would be overly sanguine and completely out of character. If Iser actually favored such a reading, he would have brought the phenomenological account into line with that of such theorists as Gadamer, Michel Foucault, Roland Barthes (in *S/Z*), Stanley Fish, and the pragmatists of criticism and history. (That would be very unlikely.) But if his reader were governed by transcendental (phenomenological) constraints, Iser would be obliged to fall back to a two-story model of interpretation or response of his own; he would then have matched in a new way the objectifying (telic) strategies offered by Beardsley and Hirsch. You see, therefore, how extraordinarily labile the theorizing possibilities are. Textually, there is little reason to believe Iser would ever openly yield in the historicist direction.

For my purpose, it hardly matters whether Iser fails us here or does not. He brings to light a better sense of the conceptual possibilities: on the one hand, we begin to see the plausibility of historicizing criticism, whether we adopt a New Critical, Romantic, or phenomenological approach; on the other hand, we begin to see that a constructivist or historicist approach is bound to subvert any privileged—two-story or invariantist (or telic)—constraints on eligible interpretations (and, of course, definitions) of art.

Here, at any rate, is Iser's rather Husserlian account of the reading process: "each intentional sentence correlative [the phenomenological expectation of a sentence in a literary text] opens up a particular horizon, which is modified, if not completely changed, by succeeding sentences. While these expectations arouse interest in what is to come, the subsequent modification of them will also have a retrospective effect on what has already been read."[31] You see how easily this lends itself equally to a Husserlian (an ahistorical) and a historicist reading. In fact, a historicist reading (though certainly not textually indicated) makes very plausible the idea that the historical past (as distinct from the physical past) *can* be altered by the very concatenated process of reading Iser recommends. (Certainly, the historicist reading of Iser would not support the idea of asymptotically approaching any ideal or objective limit of interpretation.)

All that would be required is that, in an ongoing interpretive process, whether by way of a society's reception of a text or in the experience of an individual reader, a fresh conceptual resource appearing late (or unexpectedly) in the process may validate (but hardly in a merely cumulative or linear way) a significant reinterpretation of the meaning of *earlier* historical events or of a text's sentences addressed at an earlier moment in the interpretive process. The structure of interpreting history and literary texts, in this regard, is essentially the same. You begin to see the historicist possibilities of the hermeneutic circle and the analogous possibilities of its phenomenological mate. (Of course, the citation from Iser is meant to be Husserlian, not historicist.)

The important point here is that interpretive practice need not be all of a piece. It is a perfectly acceptable way of practicing criticism to offer a reading that collects plausibly relevant resources within an interpretive tradition without attempting (or even being able) to come to terms with the entire history of interpreting the work in question (or related works). Such an approach is entirely different from the practice—bordering on connoisseurship—that advances an interpretation that seeks to come to terms with the full interpretive history of the work in question. Roland Barthes's interpretation of Balzac's *Sarrasine* remains, for me, the most compelling specimen of the first practice. The second is likely to be practiced only on the most important works: Weitz's summary of the *Hamlet* interpretations suggests how the second might proceed. Stanley Fish's readings of Milton mingle the two sorts of effort in a spirit favoring the first, whereas Helen Vendler's reading of Shakespeare's *Sonnets* suggests the likely conservatism of the second.[32]

My intent is to urge you to consider the implications of admitting that, under interpretive conditions, artworks may change in nature without risking a change in number. Here you see the point of my insisting, earlier, on the sui generis nature of cultural entities: the conditions under which they are individuated (and reidentified) as particular *denotata* are informal enough to secure (without losing descriptive or interpretive rigor) the constancy of their numerical identity, despite debated (interpreted) changes in their nature.

I shall shortly say (as I have said before) that the distinctive mark of cultural entities lies in their possessing Intentional properties and that their natures, incorporating as they do Intentional properties, can (cannot fail to) change through the process of history and interpretation—but not in any simple telic way. What I have already shown is that theories like Beardsley's, Hirsch's, and Iser's are unable to defeat the need for (and the viability of) such an admission. I don't believe any comparably strenuous theories of art would fare better. But you can also see that admitting the ontic distinction of artworks goes a long way toward ensuring the plausibility of relativism.

III

Now, the serious philosophical question asks whether the extreme historicist alternative is actually coherent and manageable and, if it is, whether objectivisms like those already noted in Beardsley and Hirsch, and now Iser, can be convincingly championed against that option. I should like to persuade you that the radical possibility is indeed coherent and viable and that I have very good reasons for preferring it to more canonical policies. In fact, the objectivist options cannot (I claim) fail to be arbitrary and completely unworkable.

Bear in mind I am trying to explain something of the nature of a work of art by way of what makes sense when interpreting a literary text. All sorts of questions may be fairly raised about the similarities and differences among artworks of different kinds and of different periods. I concede the point. But I cannot believe that if a thoroughly historicist picture may be vindicated for a significant sample of literary texts (or paintings or histories, for that matter), it will then be possible to confine the claim in any narrow way that would relieve the partisans of invariance. That, for instance, is what I understand to be the true import of Foucault's challenge in interpreting *Las Meninas* and Barthes's interpretation of Balzac's *Sarrasine*.[33]

I argue, therefore, in favor of the following theorems: (1) there are no principled antecedent constraints on the cultural sources from which relevant interpretations of artworks or historical events may draw (as of time, place, or home tradition); (2) the consensual acceptance of interpretations in accord with (1) belongs to the open, ongoing practice of interpretation and affects subsequent interpretations of particular artworks and histories (including the historical past of given events and prior phases of the interpretive process itself); (3) interpretive and historical criticism in accord with (1)–(2) is open to as many diverse, even nonconverging, interpretations as memory and interest are able to sustain; and (4) there is no reason why, admitting (1)–(3), objective interpretation should be linear, cumulative, or approximative of some postulated ideal interpretation or that it should even be possible to collect an inclusive total history of interpretation that all responsible interpretations should have addressed.

It takes no more than a moment's reflection to appreciate the potential paradox of the proposal. But you see also that one cannot really oppose it without addressing the bare bones of the metaphysics of a work of art. That is normally avoided—as if to say it is irrelevant or too obvious for words. But, of course, it is neither irrelevant nor too obvious—notably neither—in our late age, when what we admit as artworks and interpretations departs so radically from canonical practices defined as recently as the writings of Iser, Hirsch, and Beardsley.

As it happens, a number of the strategic notions regarding the treatment of an artwork as an entity, more or less ignored in the standard literature or discounted without sustaining proof, are particularly hospitable to the interpretive practices I have been sketching. Rightly perceived, these notions invite us to consider whether the rest of the real world might not also be advantageously construed in its terms. I confess I am persuaded that it would. In that case, the master theme is *flux*: not chaos or the denial of intelligible structure, but, rather, the denial that any and all discerned structures—*de re, de dicto, de cogitatione*—cannot but be invariant or necessarily inviolable, on pain of incoherence or self-contradiction.[34] The global claim is not my concern at the moment. Although our way of understanding history and the arts may be quite instructive about what the natural sciences can actually accomplish, it is enough for my present purpose to draw attention to the need to match our ontic and epistemic conjectures in either direction. For instance, once you favor a historicist account of interpretation, you cannot then adopt the fixities urged by our specimen theorists. Alternatively put, the point of either line of speculation is to arrive at an equilibrated theory that fits our inquiries as well as the possibility of coherently enlarging the scope of any such practice. Clearly, there is no reason to suppose that if one such alternative metatheory proved promising, there could not be a larger family of similar but diverse options to consider. The telic reading of interpretation would thereupon fail.

So, flux is the decisive first posit. Admit only flux—admit the indemonstrability of modal invariance in any interpreted domain—and the arguments that run from Aristotle to Beardsley to Hirsch to Iser instantly tumble. That is surely a windfall, but it leaves us with a seeming vacuum. If not by the real and rational limits of necessity, then how, we wonder, should we be guided in science or literary interpretation? The minimal answer is plain enough: we must begin with the socially entrenched practices of the various inquiries that we habitually pursue, shorn (if possible) of the pretensions of invariantist philosophies. My own fanciful way of characterizing this economy is to fall back to an elenctic reading of Socrates' original mode of questioning: to take seriously Plato's instruction (in the *Statesman*) regarding the "second-best state" (or second-best science or philosophy) shorn of any knowledge of the would-be eternal Forms.

There are endlessly many models of successful societal life that you may prefer. What they have in common, I suggest, is the admission of consensual practices that do not rest on prior rules, principles, criteria, or algorithms, which we ourselves internalize by mastering (in infancy) the language and practices of our native culture—on which (alone) our would-be rules and criteria depend for their own effective use.

On my reading, the lesson is best limned in the company of such unequal thinkers as Thomas Kuhn, Wittgenstein, and Hegel. What I mean is that if every disciplined inquiry (literary interpretation, say) is second best in the elenctic sense, then the only philosophical strategy possible is to explore the most salient, most coherent, most manageable, most convincing, and perhaps historically most fashionable ways of pursuing the inquiries we inherit. You may wonder, Is that really all? I see no cause to probe further, for I see no reason to suppose that there must be some single supreme answer to these questions. There are bound to be a thousand viable answers. Whatever we offer can only be strengthened and enriched by acknowledging the interminable agon.

Beyond these plain-spoken adjustments, I am prepared to back a small number of contentious theorems:

1. Effectively fixing the reference and reidentifiability of the *denotata* of literary interpretation is relatively independent of

What, After All, Is a Work of Art? 307

and indifferent to the assigned nature of the textual entities that are thus fixed.

2. The conditions of successful reference and predication are logically informal, consensual but not criterial, *and* dependent—whether with regard to natural or cultural entities—on the linguistic tolerance of natural language discourse.

3. The properties of artworks—all cultural entities, in fact—include, most prominently, Intentional properties, that is, linguistic, semiotic, gestural, symbolic, significative properties—for instance, those that are specifically expressive, representational, rhetorical, stylistic, and intrinsically apt, as such, for interpretation.

4. Cultural entities have historied natures, or are histories, because Intentional properties, which form their natures, are themselves historied and alterable as a result of the ongoing practice of reinterpretation, under the condition of historically changing experience.

5. Objective interpretations need not conform to the constraints of a bivalent logic or preclude indefinitely many, nonconverging, or even incongruent interpretations.

6. The valid practices of interpretation are themselves consensual, collective (not merely aggregative or conventional in the usual sense), and effectively constrained by their own local histories but capable of drawing into their conceptual space indefinitely many diverse traditions—as additional interpretive resources—to whatever extent they can coherently incorporate such (historically opportunistic) options within their extended practice.

7. No natural telos or ideal asymptotic limit or singular range of tolerance is assignable to the interpretive process itself.

I set no particular store by the precise formulation of items (1)–(7). They are meant only as a reasonable first pass at a thoroughly historicist account of objective interpretation. Accordingly, they define a radical conception of a family of sui generis entities utterly at variance with familiar views about the nature of natural and physical entities but not incompatible with such views (once modal claims of necessity are set aside). I make no apologies for the contrast. On the contrary, in the argument I have in mind, if indeed reference and predication depend on the consensual life of creatures like ourselves—or selves, as culturally constituted entities that accord with the tally I have just given—then the objectivity of the physical and formal sciences must be a function of whatever objectivity belongs to the practices of societal life, for such practices, too, are culturally constituted competences. Moreover, I should argue, the historicist account of objectivity is coherent—in other words, viable and hospitable to the peculiarities of the globally interpenetrating cultures that now mark our current age. It strikes me as altogether plausible that the insular practices of science and literary criticism, formulated in an earlier age when the new technologies of our own age had not yet made it impossible to speak with assurance of the boundaries between different cultures, should be so easily baffled by historicist accommodations. In any case, in this argument, physical objects *cannot* be the exclusive or paradigmatic exemplars of what it is to be an entity.

You must think of a literary text as a denotative construct, reasonably well individuated so as to incorporate a particular string of sentences at least. Local puzzles about what precisely to include or exclude as the words and sentences of an interpretable text are normally not difficult to manage. For example, Emily Dickinson collected variant wordings of her own poems, and Shakespeare's plays have been recorded in different edited forms. In the performing arts, type/token distinctions complicate our notations of numerical identity in benign ways. None of this is troubling as far as the entitative standing of artworks or the logic of interpretation itself is concerned. The important point is that individuative and reidentificatory strategies trade consensually on whatever is already in place in the use of such measures in discourse about the natural world and about language. Nothing more strenuous is needed.

But the individuation and identity of artworks are hardly the same as the individuation and identity of the natural or linguistic entities upon which they depend (and which they incorporate). If, for instance, a block of marble, however cut, lacks Intentional properties, whereas a sculpture—say, Michelangelo's *Moses*, which incorporates the marble—intrinsically possesses Intentional properties, then the two *denotata* cannot be numerically the same.[35] So far, so good. It goes some distance toward explaining why so many theorists of art speak of artworks as a way of *using* natural or physical objects or the like, or of transfiguring them rhetorically by imputing all sorts of Intentional properties, which, in this argument, these physical objects could not logically possess. But that is hardly a defense.

Once you see that the individuation and numerical identity of artworks are relatively informal matters—need be (and can be) no more than that—and that they trade on whatever conveniences the practice of individuating natural and linguistic entities affords, you cannot fail to see how admitting all that enlarges our choices regarding what to count as the nature of such objects. For instance, when the numbered exemplars of a Dürer print are pulled from an inked plate, they normally count as instances of that engraving, even when they differ from one another in perceptual ways. But the bare metal plate (which is not, for individuative purposes, treated as an artwork itself) and the causal process by which the prints are produced are not, as such, sufficient for individuating or identifying a Dürer print in accord with one or another type/token convention. There's a conceptual lacuna here that must be overcome.

Now, within limits, a work's nature includes what we judge to be compositionally incorporated in the work (a certain painted canvas within a painting, a span of painted cement within a fresco—whether Rembrandt's damaged *Night Watch* or the nearly entirely replaced surface of Leonardo da Vinci's *Last Supper*, whether an abbreviated *Hamlet* or a Bach *Brandenburg* transcribed for modern instruments). The interpretable structure of the work counts as its nature, whether or not its Intentional structure varies over the span of its interpretive history and whether or not admissible interpretations of the same work assign plausible structures to it that may, on a bivalent logic (but not now), be incompatible (that is, incongruent, I should say) one with another. It's the relative (but not complete) independence of the conditions of numerical identity and predicable nature that is the decisive matter. If my argument is a fair one, then the puzzle before us should be possible to accommodate. (But it remains a strenuous puzzle.)

Familiar philosophical canons deny this, of course. (Think of Aristotle!) They prioritize nature over numerical identity because they presume that natures are fixed or nearly fixed in the way natural-kind discourse requires and that individuation presupposes a relative fixity of nature. But artworks, like human selves, are better thought of as histories—Intentionally structured careers deployed over time as individuated entities, subject, because of that, to considerable diversity and change of nature as a result of the vagaries of historicized interpretation.

Apart from natural-kind entities, cultural entities (preeminently, selves and artworks) are rather informally identified as particulars—certainly without prejudice to what may be offered in interpreting their (Intentional) natures. Since cultural entities are historied, possessing Intentional properties, I view them longitudinally as careers. They have sufficient *unicity* of career (despite lacking the boundaried or determinate nature of physical objects) to support objective interpretation, but their *unity* of nature (matching their unicity) is somewhat lax and ad hoc, inconstant, in fact—a revisable construct of an artwork's or text's own history of interpretation.

We secure numerical identity and reidentifiability because we regularly recover (hermeneutically, say) the longitudinal unicity of a particular artwork's career as entailing its numerical identity. By *unicity*, I simply mean the sense of the integral career of an artwork or cultural entity—in interpretive as in ordinary discourse—in virtue of which we are able to assign a relatively stable number and nature to such *denotata*, though their natures change.[36] This is often thought to produce an insuperable paradox, which I deny.[37]

The trick is to posit a historied continuum of an artwork's career (its unicity, *not* any random or irresponsible interpretation) by which we favor not only the relative constancy of its physical properties (though bear in mind da Vinci's *Last Supper*) but also the norms of interpretive practice. The matter is, I think, almost entirely neglected in standard accounts of artworks.

In this regard, it is entirely possible that the verbal text (the sentences) of *Hamlet* remain reasonably constant; hence, the individuation and identity of *Hamlet* also remain reasonably constant, without imposing prior Intentional constraints on the interpretive amplitude of the play itself (on what we should count as its content or nature). I have, for instance, always been attracted to the peculiar aptness of George Thomson's Marxist interpretation of Aeschylus's *Oresteia*, in spite of the dubiousness of the evolutionary thesis that lies behind its original claim.[38] The same holds true of Ernest Jones's rather more stilted Freudian reading of *Hamlet*.[39] Both are anachronistic (if you discount their scientific pretensions). But what does that matter? Their themes belong in a natural way to our transient ethos. Furthermore, their strength is such that they are not likely to be easily incorporated into, or reconciled with, alternative interpretations. They have a maverick quality and are not likely to be regarded as a connoisseur's reading. Responsible interpretation must consult the prior history of a work's interpretation to some extent, but it need not attempt to build linearly on that history or even know the whole of it.

To think of artworks and persons as histories or historied careers is to deny the conceptual priority of nature over number. A career is at once individuated and distinctive in its nature, so that to collect the diverse and alterable Intentional content of *Hamlet* is to collect such attributions as attributions rightly applying to one and the same play and as falling within the evolving nature of that play—at one and the same time. I see no logical difficulty in this practice, but it plainly departs from the canonical treatment of physical objects. You see at once, therefore, the procrustean arbitrariness of Beardsley's policy and the likelihood that the same may be said of Hirsch's and Iser's policies, though for different reasons.

The entire issue of what to make of the entitative standing of artworks obviously depends on what to make of the structure of Intentional properties. (I have, I concede, moved only a little distance from the genus to the specific difference of artworks. But I count that an advantage, since it ensures the greatest flexibility with respect to the baffling variety of artworks themselves.)

I capitalize the term *Intentional* (now a term of art) in order to distance my own use of it from the standard use of *intentional* in Husserl's and Brentano's philosophies and to permit their usage to be incorporated within mine. Broadly speaking, by *Intentional* I mean cultural, in the straightforward sense of designating something as possessing meaning or significative or semiotic structure in accord with the collective experience of a particular historical society. Think, for instance, of stylistic properties: the baroque in painting or music, say.

So, the Intentional includes the intentional (Brentano's and Husserl's alternative versions of the theme of aboutness) as well as the intensional (or nonextensional) treatment of meaning or meaningful structure. It departs from Brentano's and Husserl's narrower notions in a number of important respects: (1) it is used in a collectivist rather than a (methodologically) solipsistic (or aggregative) way, as when one says that a natural language is collectively (not merely aggregatively) possessed by a people; (2) it is inseparably incarnate in the physical or biological or similar materials of the natural world; (3) it is sui generis, neither reducible nor open to reductive explanation in terms of any of the processes of physical or biological nature, without being ontically separable from such processes; (4) it is intrinsically interpretable, which is not true of non-Intentional predicables; (5) it functions solely in a predicative way and so shares (doubly) the peculiar informality of general predicates; (6) the distinctions it collects are, peculiarly, artifacts of cultural history and subject accordingly to historical transformation; and (7) being alterable as a result of historicized interpretation, its attribution affects what we should understand as the nature of anything so characterized.

I find these distinctions forceful and well-nigh impossible to resist. But the convergent lesson they convey is simple enough: namely, any entity that has an Intentional nature cannot but be a history (or historied career) and cannot fail to have the curiously labile form I have been attributing to artworks. Roughly, I have been arguing that the inherent informality of predicative success is complicated, in the cultural world, by the admission of specifically Intentional properties; that the objectivity of predicables is a function of consensual life; that consensus itself, though not criterial, changes under the conditions of historical practice; that the nature of artworks cannot be rightly specified except in terms of Intentional properties; and that this forces us to acknowledge entities of a kind distinctly at variance with what we suppose holds true in a purely physical world.

Per contra, I have been arguing the following: the practice of interpretive criticism is increasingly hospitable to incorporating resources drawn from whatever cultural tradition may be coherently assimilated to the home tradition in which we first learn our linguistic and allied skills; Intentional restrictions imposed on would-be objective interpretations begin to appear conceptually arbitrary; also, we find ourselves plainly attracted to diverse and changing interpretive possibilities that reflect the history of prior interpretation and the new resources that an evolving and globalizing history begins to fashion. Such findings entail that the historical past cannot fail to be subject to interpretive transformation.

IV

The essential point of the foregoing argument is that the gathering account is quite coherent and immensely plausible. What is startling is how far the conception departs from standard philosophies and the usual philosophies of art. The history of the arts is itself a kind of experimental laboratory in which creative practices impose on us (as would-be theorists of art, criticism, and history) the plain fact that we must forever adjust our theories to the evolving work of fresh artists and fresh critics. What, for instance, can you make of Picasso's *Les demoiselles d'Avignon* if you ignore the deliberate freewheeling reinterpretation of the forms of West African masks as a way of suddenly redirecting the energies of Western easel painting? Neither the specialists of West African sculpture nor the specialists of nineteenth-century Western painting can make sufficient sense of Picasso's arch transformation of the admissible resources of interpretive objectivity in terms of categories already in place. Picasso's innovation cannot be routinely reconciled with any of the would-be canons of well-formed painting up to the intrusion of *Les demoiselles*, including most of Picasso's own previous work.

You find here two degrees of freedom: one, instanced by Picasso's inventiveness in suddenly incorporating within the Western horizon Intentional structures that were never there before, is still alien to a palpable degree but is now more nearly recoverable and open to further improvisation; the other comes from the usual freewheeling curiosity of any home culture that seeks to enlist categories of sensibility and understanding that belong to other ages and other cultures, which it seeks to reconcile (one way or another) with its own modes of sensibility. The truth is that we cannot understand any single sentence, thought, or Intentional structure apart from the *lebensformlich* "world" in which it is so discerned. That world is itself forever open to further diverging possibilities of change that, once made salient, draw in their wake innumerable threads of remembered and implicated histories through which they gain and lose interpretive influence—which, thereupon, affect our grasp of whatever else belongs to our past history.

It is normally supposed that physical objects are discrete entities. But cultural entities are never entirely such, since they share the Intentional structures of a common interpretive world (and therefore its collective fortunes). Nothing can be said to have Intentional properties, except in terms of stable assignments of what, through such a shared history, makes such assignments consensually acceptable. But such conditions already include the entire milieu of historicized structures that some ingenious mind may suddenly show us how to bring to bear in new ways on the interpretation of particular artworks (or ourselves). Barthes's reading of *Sarrasine* shows us quite clearly how the process works: every such entity trails in its wake an atmosphere of interpretive precipitates that confirm the objectivity of its reception. No Intentional fixities are needed, and none can be secured. We abide in the core stability of the historical process; change, for instance, cannot viably outstrip the conserving habits of natural-language usage.

The norms of Intentional order in literature and painting clearly follow—often at a considerable distance and always provisionally and improvisationally—the subaltern role of the changing world of art that reflective critics and theorists scramble to seize as well as they can. The intelligible unity of artworks is deeper than our would-be canons because, in moving from one exemplar to another, we are already convinced of the endlessly many possible variants of number and nature artworks generate by their own exuberance. It is not easy to see how Proust's *Remembrance of Things Past*, Joyce's *Ulysses*, Beckett's *Molloy*, or Rushdie's *Satanic Verses* take form as properly individuated novels—or to see what the proper interpretive milieu should be (hence the liberties of *unity* and *unicity*). Their singularity is itself a critical construction of how to interpret their assignable natures. When you judge that the notes to T. S. Eliot's *Waste Land* are an integral part of the poem, you recommend (by that act) a way of defining the poem's unitary career as a provisional boundary condition for the subsequent interpretation and reinterpretation of its Intentional content and that of the rest of the repertory.

You cannot merely be interpreting "the" poem—the poem *ante* (prior to an imminent interpretation). No rigidly fixed single entity need be in place (think of Dürer's prints). But also, there *cannot* be any interpretively fixed nature to discern: think of *Las Meninas* and *Sarrasine*. What we take the stable *denotatum* to be is proposed, revised, and entrenched in the interpretive process itself. The poem viewed as a numbered entity—whose compositional structure normally includes a certain string of sentences (and now the notes, in Eliot's case, though that may be argued without seriously disturbing our sense of the poem's reidentifiability)—is already a construction encumbered by a prior consensual tolerance (regarding the general practice of reading literature) that takes up the minimal verbal *text* into a reading of the postulated *poem*. That is why we are justified—both as relativists and antirelativists—in continuing to speak of interpreting one and the same poem (or painting): you cannot settle the ontology of art by imposing a priori constraints on the logic of interpretation.

Number and nature are defined together: first of all, their informality is no more and no less than the inherent informality of reference and predication in natural-language discourse; second, the identity of an artwork is affected by the sui generis peculiarities of Intentionally structured entities, when contrasted with natural and physical entities; and third, the informal play of defining a particular artwork's nature is specifically designed to accommodate its interpretive history. The important thing is the obvious viability of such a practice, for the plain fact is that we never need a precision cast in invariantist terms, and we could never secure it if we wanted one.

That's what the opponents of a relativistic model of interpretation mean to resist, but there is no compelling argument in their favor.

There is great prejudice against making concessions of this sort. You sense it obliquely in the proposals of theorists like Beardsley, Hirsch, and Iser—and, I should add, Danto, Goodman, and Wollheim, who happen not to have formulated any sustained account of interpretation. This entire company is persuaded that, whatever they may prove to be, the appropriate formal conditions of number and nature must be tethered to the minimal needs of physical objects.[40] But, of course, every such affirmation is committed, whether it wishes to be or not, to the *foundational* standing of the physical world—which is itself a noticeably doubtful doctrine.

You have only to think no principled disjunction exists between inquiries into the question of what we should take reality to be like and the question of what we should take the conditions for knowing reality to be to grasp the benign antimony that belongs to the post-Kantian world we cannot escape, for although physical nature is (doubtless) ontically prior to human culture, the cultural world is (in its turn) epistemically prior to the physical. Concede that much, and you will have freed up our right to make conjectures about the peculiar logical informality of the number and nature of artworks—without fear of paradox.

In any case, if, as I claim, reference and predication are profoundly informal—successful only in consensual terms that cannot be fixed criterially or algorithmically—the puzzles of number and nature will prove entirely benign, whether applied to physical or cultural entities. For example, it is widely appreciated in the sciences that, whether the theoretical entities proposed by competing accounts of the mechanism of genetic inheritance are or are not the same entities (about which we may dispute), when we move from one theory to another ultimately depends on the pertinence of what has been called the principle of charity. A theoretical biology would have no point if charity about reference were not conceded. But if it is admitted in the sciences, it is hard to see why it should be denied in the arts.

The truth of the matter is that what we grandly designate as the logic and metaphysics of entities are often a matter of quite local conceptual carpentry—even bricolage. Certainly, our interpretive posits need have no invariantist pretensions: they merely follow the developing needs of evolving experience and try to shape new conceptual habits that will serve us for a useful interval. I find confirming evidence even in the paradoxes of classical mechanics that invite (but still lack) an ontology for quantum physics—

which is to say, the evidence lies in various forms of nostalgia, oscillating (when it suits) between the old metaphysics and its rejection. But then, quite frankly, the interpretive theories of figures like Beardsley, Hirsch, and Iser are even more difficult to defend.

Once the practice of literary criticism begins to gather force in the way it plainly does in the work of Barthes, Bloom, Stanley Fish, Stephen Greenblatt, and similar-minded improvisators, there cannot be a principled reason for refusing to invent a congruent logic and metaphysics if such is wanted.[41] For, first, the invariantist conception of reality cannot be shown to be indubitable; second, reference and predication do prove, for their part, to be inherently informal; third, the logical puzzles of individuation and number can be shown to be easily reconciled with the Intentional peculiarities of artworks; fourth, it is not difficult to demonstrate the self-consistency of a relativistic logic or to reconcile its use with the use of a bivalent logic; and, fifth, there are already in play actual interpretive practices that favor the adjustments just indicated and do so in a rigorous and coherent way. What more ought to be demanded?

The decisive clue about what our metaphysical policy should be rests with the fact that the things of the cultural world—artworks in particular—are natural but not natural-kind entities. There are no natural-kind entities, if to be such requires conformity with invariantist constraints. If less is required—for instance, by relaxing our views of what a law of nature is—then it will be seen that no principled conceptual advantage accrues to natural-kind entities over those that are not thus classified. It is only necessary that entities of either sort should be accessible to one or another form of disciplined inquiry. But then, they differ only in possessing or not possessing Intentional properties.

My primary objective here has been to assure you of the coherence of endorsing the freewheeling possibilities of literary and art criticism along alethic, epistemic, and ontic lines. I trust it is reasonably clear that no terrible paradoxes lurk in the wings. But I should also like to collect the argument in a trimmer way, perhaps with an eye to suggesting a deeper analogy between artworks and human selves. For of course it is an important part of insisting on the conceptual peculiarities of the art world to expose the more wide-ranging conceptual distortions that infect our discourse about the entire human world.

We ourselves characteristically count as discrete material entities only when counted as members of *Homo sapiens*; as encultured selves, we are linked to one another by sharing a collective culture and Intentional history in ways that appear (to us) to override biology. Sentences, artworks, selves, histories are ascribed determinate meanings, or meaningful structures, only by way of suitable abstractions made within the shifting milieux of similar assignments made (or already made) of other such *denotata*. To read *Hamlet* now, for instance, is to read *Hamlet* within the practice (within at least the sphere of influence) of the remembered readings of *Hamlet* that have shaped our consensual habits (or simply within our own practice of reading—within our interpretive sensibilities). What should count as conformity here is bound to be as elastic and as variable as you please. But that hardly disallows the consensual formation of a constructed sense of what should count as interpretive objectivity.

The issue at stake is a triple one: first, there is no formal need for fixed meanings or fixed criteria of meaning; second, the individuation and identity of cultural entities are not bound in any way to the standard assumptions governing discourse about physical entities that lack Intentional natures; and third, the objectivity of interpretation (like the objectivity of science, of course) is ultimately grounded in the consensual practices of our form of life. No epistemic privilege exists there.

All this, I admit, holds within the fluxive space of physical and cultural reality. Epistemically, the saving theme is simply the self-monitoring pace with which societies tacitly permit the processes of history to alter their linguistic, cognitive, and institutional regularities. Practice cannot be so labile that it outruns the fluencies of memory and reasonable expectation, but it also cannot be so inflexible that experienced history is prevented from continually adjusting our critical resources to the latest in interpretive fashion. We move safely enough between these extremes, and neither science nor interpretive criticism needs anything more demanding. On the contrary, if objectivity in the epistemic sense is constructivist in the way I suggest, it cannot justify any greater fixity. Interpretation may be as local, tendentious, opportunistic, freewheeling, and idiosyncratic as you please. Or it may have pretensions of a connoisseur's authority. But I cannot see any reason to choose between such options, and I cannot see how admitting either disallows the construction of objectivity or the tolerance of historicism and relativism.

What, therefore, I recommend (minimally) is no more than what I began with: namely, that cultural entities are histories, are Intentional careers—whether artworks, words and sentences, actions, machines, or selves—indissolubly embodied in physical, biological, electronic, or other artifactual objects or events. By *embodied* I mean only that (1) Intentional and non-Intentional properties may jointly be ascribed to such entities; (2) Intentional properties are incarnate in (that is, complexly include) non-Intentional properties; (3) such entities and properties emerge in a sui generis way in the cultural space of human life; (4) such entities and properties are intrinsically interpretable as such; (5) interpretive objectivity is best served by a relativistic logic; and (6) the natures of such entities (their interpretable content or Intentional history) are open, without paradox or loss of realist standing, to all the diversity, variability, transformation, incongruence, and historicized novelty that cultural history is known to generate.[42]

If everything here holds, then to admit the interpretive *determinability* of an artwork's nature will be seen as admitting to no principled distinction between discerning and imputing a *determinate* nature to an artwork by interpretive means. That, of course, follows from the distinction between Intentional and non-Intentional entities and attributes. For to discern an artwork as something other than a mere physical object is already to assign it Intentional parts (the sentences of a poem or the steps of a dance) apt for interpretation, and doing so belongs to the same practice within which one or another determinate meaning is interpretively imputed to be an objectively defensible reading of *that* entity's (determinable) nature.

There is no paradox here: discerning something as an artwork is constituting some set of material elements as embodying an Intentionally qualified *denotatum*, and interpreting that *denotatum* is precising its Intentional structure. The first is the interpretive work of a collective culture (in which individual selves share) by which the very reality of the cultural world is sustained; the second is the work of individual inquirers who venture an interpretive claim about the meaning of Intentional entities thus constituted.

Some theorists pretend you cannot interpret what is not antecedently described or describable or that you cannot make an objective interpretive claim if what you claim does not already answer to what is describably present in the entity considered.[43] But that is simply the result of construing the ontic and epistemic features of artworks as if they were the same as the pertinent features of physical objects; accordingly, it is to claim (without argument) that the legible relationship between description and interpretation in the physical sciences (say) cannot fail to hold in the context of cultural interpretation. But, of course, that is to ignore Intentionality.[44]

Furthermore, in this argument, the denoted Intentional parts of a discerned artwork may be said to provide (if we wish to speak thus) the describable structures of the work in question; thereupon, the interpretation of its putatively determinate meaning will, if valid, be consensually supported within the same *lebensformlich* practice in which the first is confirmed. In other words, it's the same practice that discerns an actual artwork (a fortiori, something possessing an intrinsically interpretable nature) *and* provides for a disciplined way of determining how best, or acceptably, to construe its meaning. If you bear in mind that (1) Intentional properties are incarnate in non-Intentional properties, (2) the identity of artworks is managed as well as the identity of physical objects, (3) certain minimal Intentional structures (sentences, musical phrases, dance steps, painted surfaces) are, in practice, acknowledged to be reliably discerned in individuating Intentional entities, and (4) the very existence of an artwork and its Intentional saliencies lies within the *lebensformlich* practices of an actual society, then the ontic and epistemic disanalogies between artworks and physical objects will be seen to neutralize completely any would-be paradoxes drawn exclusively from the side of physical objects.[45]

I believe that all that is true, here, of artworks is true as well of human selves and societies. But that is a longer and much more difficult tale to tell.

Ten

The Eclipse and Recovery of Analytic Aesthetics

If we ask ourselves to explain the eclipse of analytic aesthetics, the short answer is this: time has overrun all its entrenched positions. I speak with some authority as a partial victim at least, spared (if that is the right term) by running before the flood. Nevertheless, to admit this much is hardly to judge what has been gained and lost and not quite to say where the high ground will eventually reappear.

The best way to catch the change is to note its effects on acknowledged exemplars, and the best economy is to link these effects jointly to the principal themes of analytic philosophies of art and analytic philosophy in general—for they should be the same. They are indeed the same, and with only negligible exception the essential themes may be drawn from the work of relatively influential members of the analytic community of philosophers of art. I select four specimens and four themes: Monroe Beardsley, Nelson Goodman, Arthur Danto, and Joseph Margolis (myself); and, but not coordinately, empiricism, extensionalism, nominalism, physicalism, and (what already in still another idiom is termed) presence (or perhaps foundationalism or cognitive privilege). All of this will need to be explained, of course. But, by the economy intended, what has happened to these four theorists effectively marks what has happened to analytic aesthetics over a period of somewhat more than one (the last) generation.

Each has made telltale adjustments, whether primarily in aesthetics or in philosophy in general, that signify (not always intentionally) accommodations favoring theses substantially subverting whatever may be fairly taken to belong to the analytic canon.

There is no explicit canon, of course, but there can be little doubt that analysts have always been strongly disposed to subscribe to one. Also, each of the four theorists mentioned has proceeded in a way that suggests an entirely natural enlargement and shift in their respective views: so that although analytic aesthetics has been effectively subverted, the changes favored in the views of each hardly justify a straight-line application of that finding to each of them. In fact, with the exception of Beardsley, the theorists in question have clearly evolved as frank and vigorous opponents of certain themes distinctly favored in the analytic camp. It needs to be said, also, that if we do not concede within analytic aesthetics a penchant for the canonical, there would be little point in speaking of its eclipse. Since this cannot fail to be a quarrelsome matter, there is bound to be a touch of fiction about the manner of reporting adopted here.

Two caveats need to be mentioned. For one, both the substantive themes indicated and the disciplined manner of working that the analysts favor have come under severe fire—precisely because they are so intimately related. For another, the recovery of something not very distant from the canon is promisingly joined with options linked to the critique of the original themes. The truth is that the original analytic themes and the assured method of analysis were always contested within the practice of analytic philosophy—and within analytic aesthetics. So the admission of the eclipse of analysis is already part of its anticipated recovery.

These are cryptic remarks, no doubt. But they may explode the fiction that we are facing the imminent collapse of a monolithic philosophical program because of essential mistakes that ineliminably define the dogmas of the entire movement (perhaps, some might suppose, something matching the collapse of logical positivism.) There are no such dogmas. In fact, *none* of the themes attributed to the canon were ever permitted to run uncontested, and no one can rightly claim to formulate *the* canonical method of analysis. Certain themes and methods have dominated the movement; their distinct pretensions were regularly punctured by the best and most powerful practitioners of that movement; but then, of course, those same practitioners went blithely on with their own favored projects—against their own instruction.

To lose sight of this fact is to exaggerate the meaning of the eclipse. To insist too casually on its recovery is to miss the extent of the transformation required. To yield up the executive authority of such doctrines as extensionalism, nominalism, and physicalism, the unity of science, and privilege

The Eclipse and Recovery of Analytic Aesthetics   323

is, quite simply, to recover forbidden (or at least officially opposed or discouraged) conceptual fruit. And yet the effective subversive strategies are all traceable, in an admittedly thin way, to the central work of Anglo-American analytic philosophy. Their recovery—and the recovery of analysis—signifies the need for a frank rapprochement between Anglo-American and continental European philosophical currents. For it is clearly among the latter that such themes as the historicist, the hermeneutic, the preformational, the structuralist and poststructuralist, the deconstructive, the genealogical, the praxical have been consistently and productively favored; and it is only by quite openly accommodating those themes (and the varieties of conceptual strategy that addressing them must subtend) that analytic philosophy and analytic aesthetics can be recovered at all.

The truth is that the analytic tradition has tended to impoverish itself by a kind of increasing neglect of the leading themes of cultural life—a fortiori, the leading themes that inform the world of the arts. It has also neglected the subterranean possibilities of its own best work. The irony remains that, with regard to the *pre*analytic period, both in philosophy in general and in the philosophy of art, the themes of intentionality, historical tradition, preformational history, discontinuity and incommensurability, the impossibility of conceptual closure, the symbiosis of the individual and the societal, the denial of cognitive transparency, the critique of critique, the emergence of human culture, the priority of practices, interpretive indeterminacy and consensual tolerance, and a thousand related themes had already been in place and had already been most vigorously dissected. The hegemony of the analytic has, quite unpardonably, done as much as it could to dismiss the full complexity of these matters in its zeal to install its own executive vision. And many, notably our specimen theorists, who by their own interest should have been alert enough to have resisted that tendency, have often been co-opted by it and, on occasion, have been quite pleased to lead compliant troops over the philosophical cliff.

So the point of the recovery is clear. The analytic represents a measure of discipline that, at least saliently, at least with regard to the work of the formal and physical sciences (and whatever may fairly be associated with such work within the study of language, history, practice, art, and psychology), clearly succeeded in displacing what was perceived to be the incompetence, confusion, informality, and sheer error of preanalytic philosophy. In aesthetics, the chief villain was idealism.[1] But it *was* (and still is) unpardonable to have impoverished the field of analysis as unconscionably and as carelessly as the vanguard of analytic philosophy was prepared to do—and did do. Now, the matter haunts its progeny, and, now, many of that progeny are simply too fixed in their own prejudices to reopen the case.

I

The most general picture of the span of analytic philosophy over the entire twentieth century—certainly of its last fifty years—is reasonably fixed by the conceptual linkage between W. V. Quine's well-known theory of the indeterminacy of translation and Richard Rorty's notorious recommendation that "epistemology-centered philosophy" is (or ought to be) at an end.[2] This is not to say that either Quine or Rorty has pursued his own theme in the most perspicuous or most irresistible way. Actually, neither has—which complicates the tale to be told. It is rather to say that what is most tenable in the account of each symbiotically entails that of the other and that, at their peril, analytic philosophers of art have (until recently) tended to ignore the implied lesson. The eclipse of analytic aesthetics may fairly be said to depend on ignoring that lesson; its recovery depends on accommodating it. The irony is that, both in general philosophy and in aesthetics, the incompleteness of Quine's and Rorty's arguments—their frank prejudices and disinclination to explore the options they themselves have very nearly prepared—promises to enrich both analytic philosophy and analytic aesthetics in ways that could not be easily foreseen from their own exertions.

Quine is essentially a holist, a pragmatist who rejects all forms of cognitive privilege and treats distributed claims as functioning only within the space of the preformational parsings of societally entrenched "analytical hypotheses"—hypotheses that are themselves reflexively specified only by way of more attenuated such "hypotheses."[3] From this and Quine's profound demonstration that there is no principled disjunction between analytic and synthetic truths, between distinctions of meaning and distinctions of fact,[4] the indeterminacy thesis ineluctably follows: "There can be no doubt [Quine affirms] that rival systems of analytical hypotheses can fit the totality of speech behavior to perfection, and can fit the totality of dispositions to speech behavior as well, and still specify mutually incompatible translations of countless sentences insusceptible of independent control."[5] The trouble is that Quine never satisfactorily explained how "sentence," "behavior," and "fit" between sentence and behavior could be managed or reconciled with his own severe theory; or what might be the *non*behavioral evidence of "incom-

The Eclipse and Recovery of Analytic Aesthetics 325

patible translations" fitting behavior "to perfection"; or what *truth* might mean under such circumstances; or, indeed, what constraints within holism itself might reasonably be proposed to facilitate the comparative assessment of rival analytical hypotheses. Quine never tells us whether "the totality of speech behavior" falls within or outside of our "analytical hypotheses."

On all of these matters, Quine is disappointingly silent—even though it is plain that he favors physicalism, favors the rejection of intentionality, favors extensionalism, behaviorism, and a general empiricist bent congenially but loosely committed to something like the unity-of-science program. The bearing of Quine's work on aesthetics rests with the double theme (1) that analytic aestheticians (influenced by the tendencies Quine has spawned and nourished) have themselves tended to favor physicalist, extensionalist, and behaviorist strategies with respect to puzzles about art and criticism and (2) that those strategies have proved to be peculiarly vulnerable in aesthetics because they were never satisfactorily secured in analytic philosophy in general and because they hobbled the chances of formulating any adequate analytic philosophy of art. Holism, in Quine's account, could easily (but was never intended to) be a bridge to cognate continental themes—the hermeneutic circle, for instance, and the indeterminacy of translation might have been generalized (though that was hardly Quine's intention) to range over the whole of natural-language discourse. Still, at this late date, both doctrines suggest an enlargement of analytic resources that have only rarely been pursued.

Rorty is more radical about the radical import of having taken Quine's lesson (and Wilfrid Sellars's lesson) to heart—even against the "failure" of those two worthies (in Rorty's reading) to understand that the traditional philosophy of the West is at an end as a direct result of their own labors:

> To drop the notion of the philosopher as knowing something about knowing which nobody else knows so well would be to drop the notion that his voice always has an overriding claim on the attention of the other participants in the conversation [of humankind]. It would also be to drop the notion that there is something called "philosophical method" or "philosophical technique" or "the philosophical point of view" which enables the professional philosopher, *ex officio*, to have interesting views about, say, the respectability of psychoanalysis, the legitimacy of certain dubious laws, the resolution of moral dilemmas, the "soundness" of schools of historiography or literary criticism,

and the like. I do not know whether we are in fact at the end of an era. Perhaps a new form of systematic philosophy will be found which has nothing whatever to do with epistemology but which nevertheless makes normal philosophical inquiry possible.[6]

Quine does not offer an explicit or satisfactory account of how we proceed with the distributive claims of any disciplined inquiry *within* his own holism, and Rorty does not satisfactorily explain what is entailed in his favoring the work of the sciences or other inquiries within that same constraint. Quine does not concede that *his* extreme holism disqualifies philosophy in the least; Rorty argues that it does but never shows us why. Quine never really uses his holism in an operative way, though he claims its advantage, and Rorty never really abandons epistemology and metaphysics, though he assures us that he has. And we, caught between these two lines of argument, insist on saving whatever may be saved of the empirical sciences and other first-order inquiries we believe deserve an inning. But we, too, need to explain what we have salvaged in salvaging that.

Quine simply disallows programs of analysis that go against the elimination of intentionality, for instance, as in his well-known attack on Brentano: "In the strictest scientific spirit we can report all the behavior, verbal and otherwise, that may underlie our imputations of propositional attitudes, and we may go on to speculate as we please upon the causes and effects of this behavior, but so long as we do not switch muses, the essentially dramatic idiom of propositional attitudes will find no place."[7] But if anything is clear about the theory of art, it is that we cannot make sense of the structure of artworks, their cultural status, their history, the detection and interpretation of their properties without featuring intentionality and what I call intentionality. Analytic aestheticians either have actually tried to restrict themselves to a deintentionalized idiom (Monroe Beardsley, for instance) or have been drawn in a distinctly divided way toward and against physicalism, toward and against an idiom congenial to the unity-of-science idiom (Arthur Danto, for instance). Quine's influence is unmistakable here.

Once we see matters this way, the radical incompleteness of Quine's program and the radical arbitrariness of Rorty's stare us in the face. Their joined claims—that is, the claims for which they are now regularly made the totemic bearers (holism with respect to the analytic penchant for rejecting transcendental arguments, for naturalizing epistemology, and for promoting physicalism and extensionalism [Quine]; and holism with respect to repudiating the viability of all epistemology and metaphysics, despite favoring, in first-order discourse, an inherited physicalism and extensionalism [Rorty])—signify what is popularly perceived as the eclipse of analytic philosophy (a fortiori, the eclipse of analytic aesthetics). On the other hand, the perception of the incompleteness and arbitrariness of their respective programs signifies the beginning of the best program for the recovery of analytic philosophy (and, of course, of analytic aesthetics). Rorty's claim—hardly restricted to analytic aesthetics—is that "epistemology-centered philosophy," philosophy in the Western tradition, analytic philosophy as it has been canonically practiced, is now doomed. On the Rortyan line, Quine's program of analysis is best reinterpreted as a contribution to a supposedly radically different model of philosophy, the model of the "*conversation* [of humankind] as the ultimate context within which knowledge is to be understood."[8]

But what does that mean? Certainly, it means that *any* inquiry—scientific, philosophical, critical, interpretive, historical—must (1) give up the pretense of the transparency of reality with respect to human cognition; (2) admit the preformational and pluralized historical contingency of the conditions of understanding under which the members of any society make inquiry; (3) concede the impossibility of drawing from the holist conditions under which we dwell in the world, and survive as a species, any direct, distributed consequences affecting the truth of particular claims made within the space of those conditions; (4) recognize that our critical speculations about the enabling conditions under which the strongest sciences prosper are themselves subject to the same tacit preconditions as all other inquiries; and (5) acknowledge that philosophical work cannot be apodictic, cannot be known to be universally binding, synthetic a priori, or formulated for all conceivable conditions. To accept constraints (1)–(5) is to embrace what is convincing and common in Quine's and Rorty's views—to embrace what is common to pragmatism and analytic philosophy and a good deal of continental philosophy. But it is not tantamount to disallowing an "epistemology-centered philosophy" at all—as Rorty's mentors (including Quine, Sellars, and Davidson) have either implicitly grasped or at least never denied.[9]

To embrace (1)–(5) is, effectively, to disallow what has disapprovingly been called the philosophy of presence.[10] But it is not—certainly it need not be—to disallow philosophy *tout court*, to disallow epistemology, metaphysics, legitimative argument in particular. It is only to insist that philosophy must henceforth confine itself within the terms of (1)–(5) or within the terms of other corollary constraints of the same sort. Quine nowhere supposes it is impossible to do so, and Rorty nowhere shows that it *is* actually impossible. The recovery of analytic philosophy—a fortiori, the recovery of analytic aesthetics—follows apace: merely proceed as before, or proceed as would now be congenial to how one proceeded before, under the new constraints. I should take advantage, here, of having offered the tally just given to say that by *preformation*, I mean specifically the historically pre-existing conditions of cultural formation by which the members of *Homo sapiens* acquire their first language and home culture and thereby come to function as selves. The idea threads its way through the European tradition that includes Hegel, Marx, Nietzsche, Dilthey, Heidegger, Gadamer, and Foucault. It helps to explain the inseparability of the ontology of selves and of artworks, since artworks will prove to be what only selves can utter.

II

Turn, now, to our exemplars. I am not concerned here to render a full and reasoned account of each of our four specimen figures. My interest lies, rather, in gauging the viability of analytic aesthetics in the face of certain philosophical challenges that appear to threaten its continued effectiveness—coming mainly from continental European sources, centering on what (it may be hoped) we now see to be the pointless extravagance of Rorty's dismissal of analytic epistemology and metaphysics.

There can be little doubt that Monroe Beardsley is, of the four, the most devoted objectivist. This is the entire point of Beardsley's most widely discussed book, *The Possibility of Criticism*—which is committed to the rejection of intentionalism in criticism and relativism in interpretation and committed to the affirmation of the stable objective presence of literary artworks (and artworks in general), on the admission of which depends the very "possibility" (in the Kantian sense) of a discipline of critical reading that could be said to function as a fair analogue of the characteristic work of the empirical sciences.[11]

Beardsley never wavered in these commitments, though his candor and inventiveness led him, first, to admit "we can never establish . . . decisively [what is] 'in' or 'out' [of a given literary work]"[12] and, second, to incorporate into his analysis of a poem a speech-act model that installed the strong intentionalism of speech acts themselves, although Beardsley clearly hoped that the device of illocutionary acts would ultimately be dropped from his account.[13]

"If there were no principles involved in criticism," says Beardsley, "I do not see how it could be kept from collapsing into something purely intuitive and impressionistic."[14] Apart from the questionable use of the phrase "purely intuitive and impressionistic," this quotation admirably fixes the sense in which Beardsley was a straightforward naturalist or objectivist;[15] it marks the point of his quarrels with E. D. Hirsch (about authorial intentions) and with me (about relativism in interpretation). The latter theorists, of course, may also be said to have exhibited a similar sort of objectivism, even if they disagreed with Beardsley's line of argument.[16]

The essential challenge to a strong analogy between artworks and physical phenomena construed as *objects* suitably stable and determinate for the purposes of description, interpretation, criticism, and explanation (wherever and in whatever way pertinent for the disciplines in question) rests largely with the bearing of the puzzles of intertextuality on the determinate identity and intentional structure of artworks. *If* artworks cannot be fixed as referents for continuing critical discourse stable enough that their reidentification entails that their internal structure (their nature, as distinct from their number) remains relatively fixed and finitely bounded through the very process of critical interpretation, then Beardsley's project must fail, and the extension to criticism of something like the unity-of-science model is doomed.

The theme of intertextuality (or holism), perhaps most floridly flaunted by Roland Barthes in the notorious manifesto "Every text, being itself the intertext of another text, belongs to the intertextual,"[17] has by this time largely undermined any simple objectivism of Beardsley's sort in the practice of literary criticism. Whatever may be the ultimate fate of Yale deconstructive views (notably, Harold Bloom's) or reader-response theories (notably, Wolfgang Iser's) or those of such maverick theorists as Stanley Fish, it is precisely the intentionality and historicized existence of artworks, both opposed by Beardsley, that have forced a radical revision in the conception of the methodology of criticism.[18]

In any case, although Beardsley pursued, particularly toward the end of his life, all the principal currents of European and continentally inspired aesthetics, he never saw the need to modify the strong objectivism he favored, an objectivism that clearly approached (however informally) the extensionalist severities of Quine's program and of programs associated with the unity of science.[19] Nevertheless, as has already been implicitly noted, Quine's notion of "analytical hypotheses" is itself a thin pragmatist counterpart to continental themes of preformation (and holism)—the key philosophical themes that eventually yielded increasingly radical notions of intertextuality.[20]

We must be clear that the limitation of Beardsley's form of analytic aesthetics is a dual one: it is partly the consequence of an excessively optimistic empiricism in the face of intentional, historical, interpretive, and productive complexities that have taxed the ingenuity of his New Critical orientation beyond its apparent resources; and it is partly the consequence, via those complexities, of his never having come to terms with the preformational, intransparent, conceptually discontinuous, and incommensurable features of discourse about art and culture (and, by extension, about science itself) or, indeed, the familiar puzzles about the determinacy of the ontological structure of artworks. Analytic aesthetics (like analytic philosophy) can no longer pursue such simplifications if it is to survive. That texts and artworks are *not* suitably similar to physical objects and that their intentional structure obliges us to reflect on what it means to affirm or deny that artworks *have* determinate or completely determinate structures are certainly the most important theoretical issues confronting all philosophies of art at the present time, as well as the practices of history and criticism.

The bare question makes no sense in terms of Beardsley's framework—or, indeed, in terms of any first-order work drawn from Quine's orientation. The pivotal issue is the one already identified: namely, that *every* form of truth-bearing discourse must accommodate the constative functions of reference and predication; that no such discourse can be committed for that reason alone to a form of cognitive privilege; and that no holism (of sense or experience or intentional structure or reason) makes any sense if it does not provide for determinate truth claims in the inquiries we wish to pursue—whether in physics or literary criticism. The upshot is that Beardsley's philosophical pursuit of objectivity is *not* a disabling weakness of his analytic aesthetics; it is only his particular way of securing it that is indefensible (inspired by empiricism and the unity of science and opposed to the holism of meanings and cultural preformation). He solves the holism and determinacy issues by a kind of reductive feat that he nowhere earns.

In many ways, Goodman's aesthetics, particularly when qualified along the lines of his *Ways of Worldmaking* and *Of Mind and Other Matters*,[21] appears to bridge the divide between the two sorts of inquiry Beardsley scants. But Goodman hardly has that in mind. As with Beardsley, questions need to be raised about Goodman's substantive views regarding the arts as well as about the general philosophical orientation of his most recent publications. The truth is that there is no clear way of reconciling the peculiar fixities—bordering on essentialism—of *Languages of Art* with the so-called irrealism of *Ways of Worldmaking*.[22] Those fixities are in fact particularly doubtful on internal grounds.

The most noticeable oddity about Goodman's general philosophy, which remains pretty constant from *The Structure of Appearance* and *Fact, Fiction, and Forecast* to the latest books (despite the incompatibility between the visions of the two pairs—that is, the books just mentioned and the books mentioned in the preceding paragraph), is that Goodman's entire effort is centered on epistemological puzzles although he never actually engages those puzzles in explicitly epistemological terms. For instance, he raises the question of the viability of nominalism,[23] but then he treats the matter in purely formal terms, without the least attention to biological or cultural constraints that should rightly bear on the effective, spontaneous use of discriminated resemblances or general terms in natural-language contexts, and he converts the nominalist issue into an exclusively logical matter regarding the (ontological) eliminability of nonindividual entities.[24] Again, he poses the seemingly methodological question of valid "projectibles" within the context of induction,[25] but he nowhere pursues it in cognitive terms. That theory depends inescapably on an account of entrenchment—which is clearly an epistemological matter and, equally clearly, nowhere discussed in Goodman.[26]

Furthermore, although the notion of entrenchment reappears in Goodman's later writings (in fact, in the context of his aesthetics),[27] Goodman's handling of it is utterly irreconcilable with the notion developed in *Fact, Fiction, and Forecast*: it remains completely undeveloped in epistemological terms now so urgently required by his own irrealism (that is, by the proliferation of plural, "made," actual worlds), and it is clearly at odds with the strong essentializing tendencies of *Languages of Art*. The matter is complicated, but it bears in a decisive way on the structure of Goodman's aesthetics.

An instructive clue may be gained by reminding ourselves of the stern once-and-for-all application of the (intended) testing of would-be projectibles in a world that appeared (once) to be so orderly that Goodman's new riddle of induction seemed almost to capture the methodology of the sciences. Entrenchment seemed so promising that Goodman could afford to announce, "The obvious first step in our weeding-out process in determining (true) projectibility is to eliminate all projected hypotheses that have been violated. Such hypotheses, as already remarked, can no longer be projected, and are thus henceforth unprojectible. On similar grounds, all hypotheses having no remaining unexamined instances are likewise to be ruled out. However, neither the violated nor the exhausted hypotheses are thereby denied to have been projectible at an earlier time."[28] Of course, all of this was meant by Goodman to be read in terms of "the passing of the possible": "Possible processes and possible entities vanish. . . . All possible worlds lie within the actual one."[29]

All of this is now forgotten, swept away, or reduced to an utter shambles inasmuch as (pertinently for his theory of art) Goodman now affirms,

> Irrealism does not hold that everything or even anything is irreal, but sees the world melting into versions and versions making worlds, finds ontology evenescent, and inquires into what makes a version right and a world well-built. . . . How, then, are we to accommodate conflicting truths without sacrificing the difference between truth and falsity? Perhaps by treating these versions as true in different worlds. Versions not applying in the same world no longer conflict; contradiction is avoided by segregation. A true version is true in some worlds, a false version in none. Thus the multiple worlds of conflicting true versions are actual worlds, not merely possible worlds or nonworlds of false versions. So if there is any actual world, there are many. For there are conflicting true versions, and they cannot be true in the same world.[30]

There is, however, no explanation in Goodman of how to individuate worlds or world versions, or what it means to say that something is true in one (actual) world but not in another (and yet not false), or what it means to say that what is false is false in all actual worlds (despite the fact that what is true in one world may be in conflict with what is true in another), or what it means to say that *we* can sort such different worlds, or indeed what the logical relationship is between *true* and *false*. All of this amounts to a complete abandonment of the epistemological questions of entrenchment.

My own gloss on what Goodman must have meant by his "made" worlds is that he realized (correctly) that (in both the arts and sciences) we must accommodate some form of relativism (in my own idiom, incongruent judgments: judgments that, in a bivalent logic but not in a relativistic logic, would yield incompatible or contrary judgments). Since that would, in any ordinary way, require yielding ground against certain canonical constraints, bivalence and extensionalism in particular, Goodman preferred the strenuous option of finding some analogue of possible worlds—his made and continually remade actual worlds—ample enough to admit a relativism of worlds while saving his canonical commitments.

Goodman has found a way of *suggesting* that he is accommodating antianalytic attacks on objectivism in the most ramified way. But it is extremely difficult to find any such accommodation, and it is frankly difficult to make the case that his theory remains coherent in this regard,[31] *and*, whatever its motivation, it is quite impossible to draw out of it—or reconcile with it—the salient claims of *Languages of Art*. The essential point is this: Goodman's irrealism and apparent historicizing of the construction of plural worlds (in *Ways of Worldmaking*) are *never* intended to make any concessions in the direction of radically intentionalizing the world of art (or the world of science, for that matter); they are simply a device for avoiding palpable infelicities in a Quinean unitary world (which he eschews) governed (as he sees matters) by a nominalist and extensionalist canon. Goodman uses the device of plural actual worlds in order to make nominalism and extensionalism succeed in the domain of art and culture. This is why it is important to note that Goodman fails to address the (apparently) historicized puzzle of entrenching projectibles in epistemic terms. If he had, he would not have been able to avoid the problems of textuality or of intentionality or of the limits of nominalistic models.

There can be little doubt that *Languages of Art* is written in a straightforwardly objectivist spirit. There is nothing in it that manifests the slightest qualm along phenomenological or deconstructive or genealogical lines—that is, concerns about preformational forces standardly admitted, say, in hermeneutic or phenomenological or other pertinent continental sources. On the contrary, apart from the extremely important development of a semiotic idiom for the handling of philosophical issues about the arts—which certainly can and ought to be redeemed by an analytic aesthetics—Goodman is peculiarly intransigent about the nature and properties of the arts, a matter that might seem at odds both with his nominalism and his (later, or at least more explicit) irrealism. Two doctrines are of particular importance. In one, he contrasts in a strongly disjunctive way what he calls allographic and autographic arts.[32] That is, he not only introduces the formal distinction, he surveys the arts and finds that music and literature are (it seems, essentially) allographic—that is, individuated and identified by purely extensional or notational means.

The ulterior reason for the distinction may escape our notice: it is simply meant to bring discourse about the arts into a satisfactory alignment with an extensionalist model. The autographic arts are ones in which "even the most exact duplication of an original does not thereby count as genuine."[33] So intentional complexities are disallowed by ensuring uniqueness of reference. And the allographic arts are ones in which all apparent discrepancies, variations, differences (as of performance in music and printing or etching) may be tolerated (and discounted) as far as numerical identity and individuation are concerned, provided only that the individuating marks preserved satisfy completely extensional scores or notations. Goodman struggles manfully with the notational informalities of the history of music, but he never quite comes to terms with its profoundly historical and intentional nature. He is ultimately driven to this obviously unnecessary (even intolerable) conclusion: "The innocent-seeming principle that performances differing by just one note are instances of the same work risks the consequence—in view of the transitivity of identity—that all performances whatsoever are of the same work. If we allow the least deviation, all assurance of work-preservation and score-preservation is lost; for by a series of one-note errors of omission, addition, and modification, we can go all the way from Beethoven's *Fifth Symphony* to *Three Blind Mice*."[34] If Goodman had but found "ontology evanescent" enough, he might have allowed intentional informalities to flower or, at any rate, cognitive fixities to go more informal. For example, if one concedes that the numerical identity of a dance (as in reidentifying one and the same dance in different performances) is a function of its stylistic features, and if its stylistic features are profoundly intentionalized, historicized, *incapable* of being captured by any strict extensionalized notation, then it may well be that all so-called allographic arts are ineluctably autographic—and, in being autographic, irreconcilable with the severe nominalism and extensionalism Goodman means to favor.[35] The truth is that Goodman nowhere actually analyzes the stylistic *properties* of artworks (with regard to their intentional complexity)—or the predicates purporting, in a logically relaxed way, to designate such properties; he never goes beyond merely insisting that any and all such properties *are* capable of being extensionally regimented. Clearly, the collapse of that claim would place Goodman's sort of analytic aesthetics in serious jeopardy. Symptomatically, Goodman nowhere discusses the logic of interpretation in the arts. But you may glimpse in this maneuver a possible clue to Goodman's notion of a plurality of "made" worlds. If so, then its defect augurs the defeat of the more general irrealism.

The other large issue that Goodman addresses—tied to the present one because there is, in Goodman's work, no actual discussion of the structure of artworks—concerns the notion of exemplification. It concerns the nature of artistic expression and so borders once again on the complexities of intentionality. Goodman's key is given by the following: "Expression [in a work] is not, of course, mere possession [by the work, of the putatively expressive property]. Apart from the fact that the possession involved in expression is metaphorical, neither literal nor metaphorical possession constitutes symbolization at all. . . . [But] an object that is literally or metaphorically denoted by a predicate or the corresponding property, may be said to exemplify that predicate or property. Not all exemplification is expression, but all expression is exemplification."[36] Once again, the essential point remains that Goodman treats expression (semiotically) as metaphorical because to treat the expressive property of an artwork as literally possessed by it would entail serious complications for any extensional treatment of art—hence, for the autographic/allographic distinction as well. Nevertheless, Goodman nowhere justifies the metaphorical ascription:[37] he literally *has* no ontology of art, and he nowhere provides a suitable clue about how philosophical inquiries regarding the arts should proceed. He has no genuine analytic aesthetics.

That is, Goodman practices a variety of analytic aesthetics, but he nowhere entertains questions about the nature of philosophical strategies in the large. As a result, it is impossible to gain from Goodman's work a clear idea of how analytic aesthetics should meet the challenge of antianalytic currents, although it remains both true and provocative that Goodman's notion of world making has been seen—for instance, by the phenomenologically and hermeneutically minded French philosopher Paul Ricœur—as promising a new view of fiction (Ricœur is thinking of Goodman's symbol systems: quite another matter), as a sort of "productive imagination" by which we "make and remake reality" in ways that would obviously defeat any straightforwardly objectivist stance.[38] But whether Goodman would, or could, accept Ricœur's adventurous suggestion is difficult to say. In fact, the essential irony is that Ricœur favors Goodman's view of world making because he sees it as a powerful concession in the direction of historically preformational forces that lay a proper foundation for the admission and treatment of the intentional or hermeneutic features of artworks, whereas Goodman's motivation is to extricate a strongly antihermeneutic (that is, a formal semiotic) conception of artworks for his own favored extensionalism. Also, Ricœur openly favors a form of idealism, whereas Goodman means to avoid canonical idealisms. There could not be a more curious marriage of ideas.

III

Of our four specimen analysts, Arthur Danto affords the most detailed sense of adjusting a theory of art to the actual phases of the history of contemporary art—chiefly painting. He is particularly attentive to modernist, postmodernist, and especially conceptual art. For that reason, he is sensibly disinclined to specify any essentialist definition of art. For instance, he is suitably brief regarding George Dickie's "institutional" conception of art,[39] and he ultimately dismisses Goodman's thesis of expression as metaphorical exemplification with the following rather nice piece of tact: "It would be unfortunate to conclude that expressive predicates are never literally true of works of art."[40] He is also noticeably hospitable to Hegelian and broadly phenomenological currents. Nevertheless, it is quite clear that his general philosophical orientation is uneasily—and unsatisfactorily—divided between his appreciation of the complexities of cultural phenomena, particularly historicity and intentionality, and his residual commitment to a relatively inflexible physicalism and extensionalism. In fact, in his discussion of the issue of expression, which in the context of the rhetoric of art occupies his principal attention, Danto actually concludes: "The philosophical point [of the discussion of some of Cézanne's paintings and other artworks] is that the concept of expression can be reduced to the concept of metaphor, when the *way* in which something is represented is taken in connection with the subject represented."[41] By this device, Danto recovers what Goodman does not quite accommodate—but in an ingenious way that preserves his ulterior convergence with Goodman's extensionalism and tendency toward physicalism.

This is a large and rather complicated matter, not easily grasped or conceded. My intention here, remember, is to draw the thread of analytic aesthetics from a number of its principal champions in order to weigh the prospects for its continuing along the same lines. Let it therefore be said of Danto's work (in the philosophy of art) that its fatal weakness lies with Danto's failure to have resolved the analysis of what he himself had memorably identified as "the 'is' of artistic identification."[42] The point to grasp is that Danto's difficulty with the "is" of artistic identification (not, of course, a difficulty Danto feels) is both the mate of similar difficulties that surface in all of his philosophical work—in his theory of history and in his theory of action, for instance[43]—and a clue to his essential philosophical strategy.

But, it needs to be said, most readers of Danto do not sense the conceptual strain in his aesthetics because they do not take seriously enough the bearing of the "is" of artistic identification on *all* of his perceptive discussions of artworks. That is, *most* readers accept Danto's straightforward account of the complexities of art without attempting to reconcile his critical and appreciative remarks with his fundamental philosophical orientation. It is not that Danto embraces the empiricism, physicalism, nominalism, extensionalism, and unity-of-science orientation so characteristic of the analytic tradition: it is rather that his theory is fatally encumbered by the traces of such affiliations; he is divided in his heart about the adequacy of those doctrines and their disciplined application to the world of action, history, art, language, and culture; *and* he fails (by reason of that divided allegiance) to resolve the puzzle of the "is" of artistic identification.

The objective of Danto's entire strategy (going well beyond aesthetics) is to marry two disparate projects: one, the articulation of an idiom ample enough for the entire span of cultural life—notably, art, history, action, knowledge; the other, adherence to an underlying ontology, more or less faithful to the inspiration of the unity-of-science program and of a strong physicalism. *That* is what the "is" of artistic identification is all about, and that explains why Danto takes such pains to distinguish it from the "is" of (numerical) identity.

If, however, what is constituted by the first "is" *is* real as such, then the second "is" *would* ineluctably apply to it. So the trick is that Danto manages to hold that artworks are constituted as artworks by the "is" of artistic identification, all right, but that that same constitution does not yield an entity or real phenomenon about which it may be said that it is both real (in the ontological sense) and self-identical as such. What is true of "it" is held at arm's length from what is real, kept from capturing the actual properties of "mere" physical phenomena (not quite the equivalent of what Danto calls "mere real things").[44] But the motivation for that maneuver is still not very distant from Sartre's insistence that art is "unreal"—that is, superior to what is "merely" real.[45]

All this comes out reasonably clearly in Danto's relatively recent objection to Susan Sontag's view of interpretation. Here is what he says:

> Hers [that is, Sontag's objections regarding the nature of interpretation] is against a notion of interpretation which makes the artwork as an explanandum—as a symptom, for example. My [that is, Danto's] theory of interpretation is instead constitutive, for an object is an artwork *at all* only in relation to an interpretation. We may bring this out in a somewhat logical

way. Interpretation in my sense is transfigurative. It transforms objects into works of art, and depends upon the "is" of artistic identification. [Sontag's] interpretations, which are explanatory, use instead the "is" of ordinary identity. Her despised interpreters see works as signs, symptoms, expressions of ulterior or subjacent realities, states of which are what the artwork "really" refers to, and which requires the interpreter to be master of one or another kind of code: psychoanalytical, culturographic, semiotical, or whatever. In effect, her interpreters address the work in the spirit of science. . . . Mine is a theory which is not in the spirit of science but of philosophy. If interpretations are what constitute works, there are no works without them and works are misconstituted when interpretation is wrong. And knowing the artist's interpretation is in effect identifying what he or she has made. The interpretation is not something outside the work: work and interpretation arise together in aesthetic consciousness. As interpretation is inseparable from work, it is inseparable from the artist if it is the artist's work.[46]

Now, the transfigurative "is" is meant to accommodate absolutely everything of interest that may be said about artworks, but it collects all of that only in a relational way. That is, it is the artist's initial intention with respect to a merely physical object (or, in a more relaxed provisional sense, with respect to a "mere real thing" that may even happen to be an artifact—a snow shovel or bottlerack, for instance) and, therefore, the viewer's (or aesthetic percipient's) subsequent recovery of *that* (or something like that) *constituting relationship* (the interpretation) that permits the viewer to see it *as* an artwork: "To see something as art requires something the eye cannot de[s]cry—an atmosphere of artistic theory, a knowledge of the history of art: an artworld."[47] The trick is that Danto does not believe that physical objects are relationally linked to our perceptual abilities in a way that is analogous (however different) to the relational connection between artworks and our ability to "descry" artworks. This is, I concede, a very large question, but I see no reason to deny that if realist standing can be accorded "mere real things," it can be accorded artworks as well. The two continue to be very different in nature, nevertheless.

This suggests the reason Danto is so comfortable in declaring (as we have seen) that "the concept of expression can be reduced to the concept of metaphor," after having dismissed Goodman's version of a related thesis. Danto has a better way of holding onto all the complexity of art while reaching for the same extensional and physicalist model Goodman is more explicitly attracted to. But it cannot be enough if, as seems plain, human persons themselves, the paradigms of culturally complex entities, are *not* similarly reducible (by the "is" of identity) to mere physical bodies.[48] After all, if persons were thus reduced, then there would be no independent entities capable of *relating* to other physical objects, by suitable interpretation or theory, in such a way that those objects would be imaginatively transfigured (but not ontically transformed) into artworks (or human actions or historical events or speech). Otherwise, Danto would merely be the stock figure of a reductive physicalism (would hold that artworks just are—by the "is" of identity—physical objects), whereas (in truth) he means to be a *non*reductive physicalist.[49] In fact, Danto's account provides no objective basis for valid interpretation (that he wishes to support). Interpretive objectivity would require a suitable realism, but the rhetoric of transfiguration strictly precludes realism.

Danto is never sufficiently clear, ultimately, about the relationship between the intentionally complex language of human culture and the language of physicalism—which is what the true physicalist (whether reductive or nonreductive) cannot permit to remain inexplicit. That is why his account fails.

More than that, his endeavor fixes the plain sense in which, for all his considerable ingenuity and perceptiveness, his version of analytic aesthetics remains essentially bound to the objectivism that we noted at the start in Beardsley's very much simpler aesthetics.

Nevertheless, it would be churlish not to admit the finesse of Danto's sustained discussion of the historical and intentional complexities of art. What Danto manages to show thereby—against his own intentions—is that, by a logically small adjustment, fatal to the older strains of analytic aesthetics, these exemplary observations could revive the analytic orientation by embracing just the kind of complication the older strains disallow. Danto is too well informed to disallow them; but he is also too loyal to those older strains to work out an explicit ontology fitted to the kind of critical remarks he himself regularly favors. Hence, he never skimps on the critic's role, but then he also never addresses the obvious theoretical pressure that that role imposes on a realism essentially committed to the constraints of physicalism. He has, in fact, never bridged the gulf.

IV

The fourth of our specimens, Joseph Margolis (myself, of course, if I dare speak in the third person), is the only one of the four to have attempted systematically to reconcile the strategies of analytic philosophy with the principal currents of antianalytic philosophy—chiefly, with those that appear in Husserl, Heidegger, Gadamer, Derrida, and Foucault, that is, with phenomenological and hermeneutic and poststructuralist currents. My general argument insists that, first (as already remarked), there is no way to avoid the constative function of discourse and, second, that all such discourse (whether first order or second order, whether intended to be descriptive of the world or intended to be legitimative with respect to what purports to be descriptive—there being no way to disengage the one from the other) must submit to some form of critique, that is, some way of attending to the preformational (culturally holist) conditions under which constative discourse functions as such.[50]

This has the effect of phenomenologizing naturalistic discourse, or of naturalizing phenomenological or deconstructive or genealogical discourse, for the absence of the first leaves the naturalistic vision blind, and the absence of the second leaves the phenomenological and the deconstructive pointless and empty. The point is that second-order *critique* is entirely internalist—preformed but not privileged—and viable as such, that is, restricted in the same way any first-order inquiry (science or literary criticism) would be. In short, despite being second order and legitimative, critique utterly eschews cognitive privilege.[51] There's the point at which analytic and continental philosophies must converge: the matter has nothing (necessarily) to do with avoiding holism or intentionality.

It is a very pretty and uncomplicated consequence that the postmodernist conception of philosophy—preeminently, Rorty's—simply fails at a stroke, that is, fails in the sense that there are no professional practices of cognitive inquiry that can escape the need for legitimative reflection, even if (or precisely because) the "loyalty" we may manifest with respect to such practices "no longer needs an ahistorical backup."[52] Rorty's point is that the metaphysical, transparent, cognitively privileged, essentialist, correspondentist, mirrored, objectivist, transcendental, presenced, logocentric idiom of Kant and Descartes is neither necessary nor defensible. Fine. He offers two options: one, a historicized and naturalistic but *not* philosophical or epistemological source of reasons and arguments for the practices in question (which he judges to be a version of a naturalized Hegelian line); the other (that of the "postmodernist bourgeois liberal," also "Hegelian")—which simply abandons at a stroke the entire need *for* a justification of practices—a contentment with the notion that "on a Quinean view, rational behavior is just adaptive behavior of a sort which roughly parallels the behavior, in similar circumstances of the other members of some relevant community."[53]

But this is simply intellectual bankruptcy. For one thing, we cannot eliminate (Rorty does not wish to eliminate) constative discourse. For another, the practice—any practice, the practice of any community of inquirers—must have a rationale regarding how to go on to new cases not included in the paradigms learned in learning the original language or practice. Therein lies the essential disability of Goodman's nominalism and of every nominalism construed in a cognitively pertinent sense; therein also lies the defect and defeat of the postmodernist maneuver. For the problem is not merely one of how to go on extending the scope of complex predicates in new circumstances but also one of how to go on giving rational or critical redirection to any sustained and disciplined inquiry. The first is the pons of nominalism; the second, of postmodernism.

If analytic aesthetics is to survive—if analytic philosophy or any philosophy is to survive, if any rational inquiry is to survive—then (1) it must be possible to bridge the difference between naturalism and the "more" continental currents (phenomenology, deconstruction, genealogy, hermeneutics, historicism, and the like) that are hospitable to the complexities of holism and intentionality and the profound difference between the physical and the cultural, and (2) it must be possible to provide for second-order legitimative discourse that does not fail in the Kantian manner Rorty is at such pains to dismantle. My entire philosophical effort is committed to working out the conceptual conditions for satisfying (1) and (2), with attention particularly to the metaphysics and epistemology of culture and art. This is at least a viable proposal regarding a *new* program and orientation for analytic aesthetics—again, of course, considered here only in the spirit of tracing the prospects of analytic aesthetics. It would put into question all the older doctrines of objectivism, physicalism, nominalism, extensionalism, and unity-of-science constraints, and it would embrace, at least as pertinent options, historicism, intentionality, preformation, intertextuality, relativism, cultural emergence, nonreductive materialism, critique, incommensurabilism, and legitimation. The vista is large enough.

Through a marvel of innuendo but not argument, Rorty declares and insinuates at one and the same time, "Analytic philosophy *cannot*, I suspect, be written without one or the other of these two distinctions"—that is, the two Kantian distinctions said to be repudiated by Quine and Wilfrid Sellars, respectively: namely, the "necessary-contingent" distinction and the "given-interpretation" distinction.[54] The juxtaposition of the italicized "cannot" and the coy "I suspect" permits Rorty to play the enormously pleasant game of agreeing with all his critics for the sake of the ongoing conversation while at the same time cutting philosophy (and science and criticism) off at the knees. So he adds, catching up the point of what we took note of before, "Behaviorism claims that if you understand the rules of a language-game, you understand *all* that there is to understand about why moves in that language-game are made. (All, that is, save for the extra understanding you get when you engage in various research programs which nobody would call epistemological—into, for example, the history of the language, the structure of the brain, the evolution of the species, and the political or cultural ambiance of the players.)"[55]

But that is just what one does *not* understand, unless one understands the rationale, the legitimate rationale, the second-order moves in accord with which we recommend—dialectically, historically, contingently, without foundations—how to go on rationally.[56] If we give up the Kantian position, which we must, then we need second-order legitimative discourse more than ever—not less—because we need the best rational guess about what the conditions of inquiry and truth claims are by which to guide ourselves in extending our practice. That's what philosophy is all about, and no one has ever convincingly shown that to be disposable. To be sure, *rational* (like *true* and *false*) also has a history, which complicates philosophy enormously. But it *complicates* philosophy, it does not rule it out. Even Foucault rather wistfully acknowledges the point in reviewing the threatening incoherence of his own poststructuralist efforts.[57] There *cannot* be a recovery of analytic aesthetics, now faced with its own stalemate, without a rational second-order redirection of its energies. Rorty's is simply a counsel of despair or irresponsibility. The solution must go in the direction of constructivism and historicism—but that would be enough.

I have, then, deliberately sought to reconcile what the objectivist and naturalistic idioms have correctly perceived—namely, that constative discourse is ineliminable and that first-order and second-order (legitimative) discourse are inseparable—with the best elements of nonnaturalistic (but not necessarily nonanalytic) philosophy while abandoning the objectionable logocentric or privileged discourse that continentally minded thinkers have rightly perceived to be entrenched in most of analytic philosophy. Thus, the famous subject/object relationship that theorists like Husserl (and Heidegger and Derrida) so much inveigh against cannot be eliminated, but, once it is placed in an appropriate preformational or critical context (*without*, then, reclaiming privilege on its own), the relationship affords a perfectly adequate and viable (and necessary) basis for recovering epistemological and metaphysical inquiry—in aesthetics as elsewhere. There you have the clue to what must be preserved regarding cultural preformation (or a holism of meanings) and the operative separation of cognizing subjects and cognized objects in any truth-bearing discourse.

It is true that I have come to this rapprochement somewhat later than to my characteristic accounts of the ontology of artworks, of the logic of interpretation, and of relativistic judgments in general.[58] The result is that there is a distinct vestigial objectivism in these early discussions that needed to be exorcised (and eventually was).[59] This may be a matter entirely local to my own efforts. They are of little consequence in the present context. In more recent work, I explore the threat of ontic indeterminacy, the historicized openness, the lack of essential fixity that artworks exhibit. The fact remains that the analysis of the nature of art and culture, of description and interpretation, of texts, of histories, of reference, of judgment, and of relativistic and nonrelativistic truth-values is entirely congenial to both the rapprochement sketched and the continuance of analytic aesthetics.

In fact, my themes have characteristically been hospitable to the full recovery of intentional phenomena; the irreducibility of culture to nature; the inadequacy of both reductive and nonreductive physicalisms; the admission of emergence; the replacement of the unity-of-science program; the abandonment of a comprehensive extensionalism; the acknowledgment of the complexities of historicism; the advocacy of something other than ontic determinacy; the acknowledgment of conceptual incommensurabilities, of divergent pluralisms, of relativistic values; the rejection of closed systems; the insistence on the inseparability of the psychological and the societal at the human level; the denial of the disjunction between realism and idealism; and the endorsement of constructivist concessions regarding selves and the world. These are all themes peculiarly favorably attuned to phenomenologizing naturalism and naturalizing phenomenology—meaning by that to accommodate all forms of critique (say, the Marxist as well as the Nietzschean) that seriously address the question of the pursuit of first- and second-order inquiry under contingently preformational conditions that, at the level of both first- and second-order discourse, we cannot fathom in a privileged way.

I am particularly known for my defense of the coherence and pertinence—in aesthetics and in general—of relativism and historicism.[60] But these doctrines are themselves called into play and legitimated by a deeper discussion of the metaphysical and epistemological differences between physical nature and human culture.[61] Here, the simple novelty of my approach rests with attempting to work out the conceptual requirements of a realism that spans *selves* (uniquely enlanguaged, second-natured human agents) and their Intentional *utterances* (intrinsically interpretable artworks, histories, deeds, speech acts), reconciled (as emergent) with whatever is required by any realism restricted to mere physical nature. Mine is one of a very few such efforts tendered within the practice of analytic philosophy—not wedded to the canonical forms of physicalism or extensionalism or naturalism. My governing intuition mongrelly and heuristically expressed is that cultural entities are as real as physical entities but possess inherently distinctive structures—Intentional, or culturally significant, intrinsically interpretable structures—that mere physical entities simply lack. This is the essential pivot of my challenge to the models of art offered by Beardsley, Goodman, and Danto alike.

The solution I offer requires the admission (1) that the cultural world has emerged in a sui generis way from the physical and biological world (probably by way of small changes that first made the evolution of natural language possible); (2) that the phenomena of the cultural world can be analyzed only Intentionally (say, in terms of their representational, expressive, linguistic, semiotic, symbolic, rhetorical, stylistic, historical, institutional, traditional, and rule-like properties); and (3) that the realist standing of cultural entities entails their being indissolubly *embodied* in actual physical (material) and biological entities (with respect to which they are emergent sui generis) and entails also their properties being indissolubly *incarnate* in actual physical and biological properties (with respect to which they are interpretively specified). The characteristic objectivity of interpretive criticism in the arts and history depends, in much the same sense in which discourse in the natural sciences depends, on the conceptual match (or adequation) between *denotatum* and attributes.

I offer a two-step strategy in support of my general constructivism (constructive realism), the contrast I draw between physical and cultural entities, and my advocacy of relativism and historicism. By the first, I argue that all truth-bearing or constative discourse relies on referential and predicative resources, but I add that success in these regards cannot rest on evidentiary or criterial grounds in any cognitively determinate way. Success never counts as *savoir* (the exercise of an adequate cognitive faculty) but only as *savoir-faire* (practical conjecture and matched action consensually tolerated as adequate). Thus, for example, reference (to individual *denotata*, whether stones or sculptures) cannot be gained by any predicative means (agreeing with Leibniz and against Quine),[62] and haecceity cannot be discerned in any cognitively—merely linguistically—determinate way at all (as Duns Scotus seems to have conceded).

Again, we are forced to admit that if (as is obviously true) we have no inkling of how to access Platonic Forms or natural essences epistemically, success in predicative matters cannot be anything but consensual, without their thereby being criterial; that is, predicative success cannot but accord (in an entirely informal way) with the collective tolerance of our predicative practices and interests.[63] Furthermore, there is reason to suppose that the pattern of such tolerance diverges among societies and changes over time, within any society, in accord with the drift of local history. If you grant that much, then every viable realism must be a constructivism and, in principle, relativistic and historicist considerations are bound to affect our sense of objectivity everywhere.

If you grant the point, you have in fact exposed the arbitrariness of Rorty's objection to philosophy. For, although it is true (as Rorty insists) that the philosopher has no privileged source of knowledge by which to take precedence over first-order inquiry (Kantian transcendental resources, for instance), it remains true (against Rorty's objection) that the second-order questions philosophy raises are both needed and answerable. My own claim is that they are answered by reviewing the conditions of know-how rather than of (a privileged source of) knowledge. The best attempts at such a review belong, as I see it, to the Hegelian tradition construed so broadly that figures like Dewey and Wittgenstein may count among its number. (That means, of course, discounting whatever Kantian vestiges cling to Hegel's own thought.)

The second step of the argument holds that the referential or denotative determinacy of cultural entities is on a par with that of physical objects but that the nature or predicative determinacy of cultural entities need not be (for that reason alone) determinate in the same sense in which physical objects are said to be. The reason is simply that cultural entities possess, and physical objects lack, Intentional properties. Thus, for instance, if a physical object is (said to be) red, we normally suppose that *that* red (determinate in being a particular red but determinable in being open to further determination as this or that particular red) can always be thought to be more determinate without supposing that there is any infimate red in any particular instance.

By contrast, in making a particular interpretation "more determinate" (say, in interpreting *Hamlet*), we cannot convincingly claim that the increased determinacy of what is interpretively predicated will be more determinate in the same linear sense in which, say, red might be. No. The situations are altogether different. We are forced to admit that (a) objectivity takes a constructivist form everywhere; but (b), in the physical world, it is largely limited by the inherent informalities of reference and predication; and (c) the Intentional attributes or predicables of the cultural world are determinable but not determinate in the same sense in which physical attributes are said to be. Once you grant this much, it becomes impossible to deny that a relativistic and a historicist treatment of objectivity cannot be disallowed a priori (if it can be made internally consistent and coherent) wherever, at the very least, Intentional properties are being addressed.

Add to this two further qualifications, and you have the nerve of my argument: first, that history is cognitively blind, so that historicism is invoked only retrospectively, from whatever cognitive vantage we suppose we occupy, in accord with which the norms and exemplars of predicative similarity may be expected to change under historical forces; and, second, that we are free to choose our logic, our range of truth-values or truth-like values, relative to whatever domain of inquiry we pursue, so that, where Intentional properties are at stake (but possibly also elsewhere, for other reasons), we may favor a set of many-valued values over a strict bivalence (though the two may be used, with care, in tandem)—where, that is, we wish to support contending interpretations (incongruent judgments) that, on a bivalent logic but not now, would count as contraries or contradictories or incompatibles.

It would take us too far afield to attempt to strengthen any of these proposals.[64] The point here is only to show that the option is entirely coherent and workable; opposed to the salient accounts in analytic aesthetics but compatible with analytic rigor; and hospitable to hermeneutic, poststructuralist, and related continental currents that abandon all necessities *de re* and *de cogitatione* and yield in the direction of holism, constructivism, relativism, and historicism.

In short, to return to the original premise: analytic philosophy—and analytic aesthetics in particular—cannot be expected to prosper without recovering (at least selectively) the questions raised here, within the subtler space of an inquiry that avoids the older forms of cognitive privilege and foundationalism, or without resisting altogether the siren attraction of a know-nothing postmodernism. But there is reason to think the imminent future will transform these implied recommendations into a prophecy—and a fulfillment.

In any case, the best prospects of analytic aesthetics depend on two adjustments: (1) the pursuit of all the themes just mentioned, which go entirely counter to the canonical tendencies of analytic philosophy but are not at all incompatible with its native discipline; and (2) the ability to steer a middle course between the older tendency toward ahistorical privilege and the newest tendency to disallow, within historicized conditions, suitably adjusted versions of philosophy's legitimate legitimative concern.

PART FOUR

Eleven

Life without Principles

I

I have singled out Aristotle and Kant as the great exemplars of the two master visions of moral philosophy. I have taken a considerable liberty in doing so, of course, since there are many lines of theory that are neither Aristotelian nor Kantian. But I trust it will be clear that most if not all of the alternative options are either unpromising from the start (moral intuitionism, for instance, because it invents or posits a special and privileged cognitive faculty)[1] or makes no serious pretense at having any demonstrably universal or necessary or lawlike or rationally obligatory bearing on determining what, finally, is morally right or good (Hume, for instance, though equivocally).[2] But I have shown that both visions suffer from the same mortal weakness: the inability to prove that there are any modal (moral) invariances at all and, a fortiori, the inability to specify invariances pertinent to confirming the conditions of moral objectivity. Roughly, what I have said is that, failing in that regard, moral philosophies, particularly those I have called second-tier theories (the views of thinkers like Rawls, Gewirth, Apel, Habermas, Sandel, Taylor, MacIntyre, Gadamer, Lovibond, MacKinnon, Dworkin), whether or not they explore third-tier questions as well, devolve into *moral ideologies*—by which I mean (in a nonderogatory sense) that those philosophies convey substantive convictions about what is morally prescriptive or authoritative or categorically binding but without advancing autonomously compelling legitimate grounds for the same. On the strength of this concession, the whole of Western moral philosophy never quite escapes being ideologically quarrelsome.

I see no harm in that. On the contrary, an essential part of the legitimative undertaking of what I am calling fourth-tier strategies may still be said to be occupied with explaining how (what are frankly) moral ideologies may be shown to yield objectively valid findings in something like the prescriptive sense at issue—and what that should mean in the way of altering our legitimative notions. I put it to you that none of the principal theories I've canvassed features this possibility. Where, particularly in English-language philosophy, the full failure of canonical legitimation is admitted—notoriously, in Richard Rorty's work, ranging over general epistemology as well as moral and political philosophy[3]—philosophy itself is all but summarily dismissed for that reason alone. This is the essential policy of what Jean-François Lyotard has called postmodernism[4] (which Lyotard himself does not ultimately favor). I trust it will be clear that postmodernism is (or at least risks being) a *petitio*, a non sequitur, or (I should insist) a completely incoherent policy. The reason is simply this: it makes no sense to admit that these or those beliefs, statements, judgments, commitments, and the like are valid or justified in the *sittlich* way without our being able to explain their legitimative contribution. This is nothing but a reminder of what, in the local setting of moral disputes, Mackie rightly distinguished· as first- and second-order questions. (The trouble, of course, with Mackie was that he did not consider that the skeptical questions he put to canonical moral theory applied with equal force to epistemology; he therefore undercut his own skepticism.) In any case, Rorty's postmodernism is little more than an incoherent analogue of Mackie's ill-formed thesis. I say the objectivity of moral and moral/political claims is indeed the objectivity of *Sittlichkeit* and its range of reasonable compromises and modifications in resolving disputes involving opposed ideologies, at least. This is largely a neglected matter, though possibly our most rewarding option.

But if Aristotle's and Kant's claims about modal invariance in moral matters fail, then we are bound to ask ourselves what, in addition, in a philosophically serious sense, *is* even relevant (in their work) regarding the viable grounds on which moral objectivity may be legitimated.

On the admission of their failure to secure modal invariance (essentialism in Aristotle's account, rational necessity in Kant's), Aristotle's *Ethics* dwindles to a very skillful summary of a version of the moral and political ideology of the Greek polis, well on its way (as Aristotle certainly knew) to being completely eclipsed by the consequences of Alexander's imperial vision; Kant's *Foundations* proves even less relevant to legitimative concerns since, in a way, there is nothing else to Kant's theory but the argument for adopting the transcendental option he advances.

Now, what is most instructive about the failure of both Aristotle's and Kant's undertakings in this respect is caught up in the thesis already cited from Lovibond: "It is only as a member of some community that I exist as a moral being."[5] The same thesis, sometimes almost identically worded, appears in Sandel, in MacIntyre, in Charles Taylor, and in Gadamer—to confine ourselves to figures featured in these pages. I have suggested that this single theme is the conceptual fulcrum on which the difference between third- and fourth-tier theories may be sorted. Read in a way that is (still) neutral as between such theories, this single thesis, properly construed, leads directly to our completely discounting (1) the need to "solve" Wiggins's puzzle about the "meaning of life" and (2) the need to vindicate a realist account of moral norms and values as strong as that intended (and thought to be required) by the moral realist's failed strategy for meeting Mackie's challenge. That is part of what I have been at pains to show. Both adjustments prove to be trivially entailed by a plausible reading of Lovibond's dictum.

That much of the counterargument is captured at a stroke by admitting that moral matters—all human concerns, in fact—arise in and only in a *sittlich* or *lebensformlich* world. (I regard that as a gloss on Lovibond's remark.) What, however, I wish to add to this quite reasonable adjustment is this: second- and third-tier theorists either never consider the inherent historicity of what is *sittlich* or *lebensformlich* (remember: Wittgenstein had almost no philosophical interest in the historical) or, if they do, fall back (at least implicitly) to some ahistorical invariance meant to help us escape the supposed dangers of relativism, anarchism, irrationalism, and sheer ideology, in accepting the constraints of historicism. That, in different ways, is patent in Habermas and Gadamer—notably, in their published disagreement. It is also for this reason that I characterized Lovibond, Sandel, and even MacIntyre as, ultimately, second-tier thinkers. (This classificatory schema is explained in *Life without Principles*, where this chapter first appeared.)

Fourth-tier theories are, by contrast, wedded to some form of historicism. In virtue of that, they cannot fail to have been influenced by Hegel—if (to be philosophically sensible) to admit that much is still entirely compatible with rejecting Hegel's own absolute idealism, historical teleologism, and forms of seeming necessity applied to history. I should say that, in English-language philosophy, John Dewey's pragmatism shows the coherence of such an option—though perhaps not much more.[6] The most radical possibilities of the Hegelian option—sans Hegel, that is—what may be called Nietzscheanized possibilities, surely belong to Michel Foucault.[7] These two figures (Nietzsche and Foucault) help to fix the parameters of Hegel's influence, although, in my opinion, the single most important theme in Hegel (apart from Hegel's own extraordinary work) is to be found in Marx's (admittedly fragmentary and often tendentious) clarification of what we should mean by *praxis* in a historicized world. For, once Aristotle (who, of course, introduces the notion of praxis) and Kant (who, of course, produces an insoluble paradox for the moral use of reason) are seen to fail on the matter of modal invariance, Marx's insights regarding praxis help us to understand the inseparability of theoretical and practical reason. I anticipate, therefore, that in accepting (at least provisionally) the coherence of fourth-tier thinking we grasp (1) the equivocal import of Lovibond's dictum, as between third- and fourth-tier options, and (2) the inescapability of conceding that if legitimative questions are to be honored (against the skeptic and the postmodernist), then moral legitimation is the legitimation of moral ideologies. QED.

The supreme clue is offered by Hegel himself. Hegel is a devastating critic of Kant's formalism. But, more than that (if I may say "more"), his critique of Kant ramifies through all the Kantian formalisms of our time—Rawls's, Gewirth's, Apel's, and Habermas's (and the formalisms of all those who follow the lead of these theorists, which constitute a not negligible part of the whole of current moral philosophy). Here, then, is the most famous passage (that addresses arguments from the second *Critique*) in which Hegel defeats Kant out of hand:

> I ask [testing the Kantian criterion] whether my maxim to increase my fortune by any and all safe means can hold good as a universal practical law in the case where appropriating a deposit entrusted to me has appeared to be such a means; the content of this law would be that "anyone may deny having received a deposit for which there is no proof." This question is then decided by itself, "because such a principle as a law would destroy itself since the result would be that no deposits would exist." But where is the contradiction if there were no deposits? . . .
>
> If the specification of property in general be posited, then we can construct the tautological statement: property is property and nothing else. And this tautological production is the legislation of practical reason; property, if property *is*, must be property. But if we posit the opposite, negation of property,

then the legislation of this same practical reason produces the tautology: non-property is non-property. If property is not to be, then whatever claims to be property must be cancelled. But the aim is to prove precisely that property must be; the sole thing at issue is what lies outside the capacity of this practical legislation of pure reason, namely, to decide which of the opposed specific things must be lawful. But pure reason demands that this shall have been done beforehand, and that one of the opposed specific things shall be. presupposed, and only then can pure reason perform its more superfluous legislating.[8]

This is a wickedly businesslike refutation of Kant. There can be no recovery, in the plain sense that the supposed rule of reason cannot possibly establish that the practices we are judging must be already in place or be "lawful," as opposed to any alternative practice, equally self-consistent, that might (in its turn) morally defeat the Kantian claim. For example, we could never, on Kantian grounds, prefer or reject slavery or abortion (or even suicide), although Kant might not agree. One can also easily see in Hegel's argument a possible basis for Marx's thesis that private property is theft.

But Hegel's argument goes very deep, well beyond the local convenience of defeating Kant. Rightly understood, I think it confirms (though I have no grounds for believing Hegel would agree) that (1) moral legitimation is the legitimation of moral ideologies; (2) reference and predication (a fortiori, the confirmation of truth) are inherently historicized and function only informally within the *sittlich* practices of actual societies; (3) theoretical reason is a form of praxis; and (4) moral legitimation (a fortiori, the validity of moral claims) cannot but be relativistic.

These are startlingly powerful—and provocative—claims. (I do not say they are confirmed here.) You will appreciate, of course, that they go some distance toward redeeming the theorems I've merely sketched in chapter 4 of *Life without Principles*. They are also characteristic of what I am promoting as fourth-tier theories. I need to remind you, as well, that nearly the whole of Western moral philosophy has avoided or actually rejected every one of the claims collected here as items (1)–(4); that is what I meant, earlier, in characterizing fourth-tier thinking as radical. It was for this reason that I tried to show how theorists like Gadamer, Sandel, MacIntyre, and Lovibond fall back from the brink of adopting options of the fourth-tier sort, all the while they are obviously attracted to some form of what is *sittlich* in the historicist sense.

I draw all this from Hegel—shorn of Hegel's extravagances—although I am not persuaded that a proper reading of Hegel's philosophy of history would not support my view. It does not matter, and it would be extraordinarily difficult to show, that the textual argument must go one way or another. I say instead that the failure of second- and third-tier thinking has brought us to a point at which my last set of claims, (1)–(4), appear to yield the most promising legitimative strategies we are likely to recover, which have not yet been sufficiently explored, and which may yield also a plausible interpretation of the point of Hegel's critique of Kant.

You must see the point of Hegel's critique as, also, an enormous compliment to the boldness of Kant's argument. For what it means is that Kant risked his entire thesis on the likelihood that the purely formal grounds provided by the categorical imperative would weed out all would-be rational policies that the usual interests of moral communities favor weeding out, without ever requiring *any* argumentatively relevant admission of the substantive content of those policies. Extraordinary! What Hegel shows is that the formal possibilities are more complex than any adherent of Kant's strategy may have supposed. What Hegel shows, convincingly, is that Kant places too great a burden on purely formal (universal, ahistorical) criteria. Kant meant to accommodate the entire range of human interests, provided only that those interests could be reasonably represented—in the way of a rational defense before the bar of the categorical imperative. In this regard, Kant may be treated as the champion of moral pluralism. The trouble is that, in the hands of an ingenious tactician, the Kantian test might conceivably be made to endorse a policy of anything goes. (I should also say that, although they deplore Kant's formalism, Apel and Habermas seem to me to be every bit as formalistic as Kant—which is noteworthy. Perhaps the novelty of their own approaches has it that the necessity or universality of moral principles must be drawn from the actual practices of living societies. Nevertheless, I cannot see that they conform convincingly with their own injunction.)

Before leaving the larger matter, however, which may be clear enough, I should like to confirm the stunning accuracy of Hegel's charge by bringing it to bear, without adjustment, on a central thesis of Habermas's "Discourse Ethics," written nearly two hundred years later. First, Habermas himself opposes Apel's "transcendental-pragmatic justification" of a Kantian ethics of "argumentation," largely because he anticipates difficulties in any apriorism. He says it is "even too weak to counter the consistent skeptic's opposition to *any* kind of rational ethics." But, second, he himself is quite sanguine about legitimating "the principle of universalization" a posteriori, "which alone enables us to reach agreement through argumentation on practical questions."⁹ Habermas then introduces two principles: one, (U), a "rule of argumentation" or "principle of universalization," and another, (D), the "principle of discourse ethics" that he means to recommend. The formulations go as follows:

> (U) *All* affected can accept the consequences and the side effects its [that is, "every valid norm's"] *general* observance can be anticipated to have for the satisfaction of *everyone's* interests (and these consequences are preferred to those of known alternative possibilities for regulation).

> (D) Only those norms can claim to be valid that meet (or could meet) with the approval of all affected in their capacity *as participants in a practical discourse*.¹⁰

Apart from the question of how one could ever test whether (U) made any sense at all or was viable or testable, or whether (D) could ever be shown to conform with (U), one can see at once that whether any claim in accord with (U) or (D) or both *was valid* would presuppose that the actual "interests" of "all [those] affected" were *already* in place and were such that they could be reconciled with the interests of all others pertinently affected. But that clearly runs up against Hegel's argument (cited above), for any number of reasons. I mention only three: For one, Habermas's program cannot distinguish in principle between the ethical admissibility of supporting or opposing property in Hegel's example; for another, it cannot justify choosing between the one and the other option (incompatible between themselves) on the basis of (D). If we insisted that (D) must conform with (U), and if we admitted that (U) precludes Hegel's case, then of course (U) would itself be a substantive moral principle—which would be contrary to Habermas's intent and arbitrary, in any case. (Habermas seems not to have thought of this; it is the analogue of Rawls's inability to accommodate Isaiah Berlin's dictum regarding the inevitable sacrifice of goods.) So Habermas's ambitious program—to which many are drawn at the present time—collapses at its inception, for reasons that Habermas must have been aware of.

The third consideration is more complicated. I take it to be quite important—devastating, in fact, when rightly understood—but hardly easy to vindicate. I regard it as Hegelian in inspiration, if we understand Hegel's sense of history to preclude any conceptual scheme that, at any time, incorporates every arguably pertinent point of view (the "interests of all" or "all affected," as Habermas is fond of saying). I take MacKinnon (as a feminist) to have pressed the point, though more in a Marxist spirit than a Hegelian one, and I associate the theme particularly (in very different ways) with Derrida's deconstructions, Foucault's genealogies, and Levinas's ineffabilities. At any rate, Habermas's formulation of (D) addresses only "all affected *in their capacity as* participants in a [particular] practical discourse" (italics mine). But what of those who are precluded from participating but not by way of being explicitly assigned a deprived role "*in* a practical discourse"?

Lyotard may be the best-known discussant of this matter, having introduced the idea of a *différend*. But, in drawing attention to Lyotard's usage, I frankly want to distance myself from his somewhat extravagant way of putting things. He characterizes the *différend* as a term of art in a perspicuous way, and I am happy to invoke it: "A case of *différend* between two parties takes place when the 'regulation' of the conflict that opposes them is done in the idiom of one of the parties while the wrong suffered by the other is not signified in the idiom."[11] Lyotard gives the example of a worker being obliged to treat his own labor (in the law) as a commodity traded by way of a contract. The point is that if Lyotard is right, then there cannot be an end to *différends*; systematic moral and political discourse will always invoke them, but, if that is so, then the appeal to universalizability (or, in the more usual idiom, universality) cannot fail to be exploitative, cannot overcome the condition everywhere. And where it overcomes a particular *différend*, it cannot be supposed that, with that being done, we are progressing toward a final elimination of *différends*. Habermas nowhere addresses the matter.

This, I should say, is the theme of a deliberately constructive postmodernist morality. I associate it particularly with the theme of the "Others" (*l'Autrui*) offered by Emmanuel Levinas and fleshed out more fully by Zygmunt Bauman. I mention the fact because, in both Lyotard and Bauman, you will find some convergences with my own line of argument against modernist moral philosophies—for instance, Habermas's appeal to a universalized criterion. But I reject both Levinas's ineffabilist reading of the Other (which affects both Lyotard's and Bauman's accounts) as well as any presumption of "finding" a moral ground inherent in that ineffable condition. These maneuvers are incoherent and little more than insinuations of ideological privilege.[12] Still, I appreciate the humanity of their protest.

II

I can think of no more than one conceptual picture that perspicuously fits all the arguments up to this point and remains viable and coherent and plausible in its own terms. That picture directs us in a natural way to enlist (what I call) fourth-tier strategies. The conception is this—I add it to the tally already mentioned because it is clearly the central theme of the Hegelian turn: (5) persons—human selves, agents, subjects—are socially constituted (constructed) as artifacts of the historically diverse and changing processes of an enabling form of enculturation. This is, admittedly, a controversial and difficult doctrine. But what I want to emphasize, which bears decisively on the narrow concerns of moral philosophy (as well as, of course, on the larger issues of epistemology, the philosophy of science, logic, and the arts and criticism), is that selves are artifactual in at least the sense that, whatever their biology, their conceptual powers—especially linguistic but also lingual, those that presuppose language but are not specifically exercised in speech or the like—are a function of, and function in and only in, the context of the *lebensformlich* practices of this or that (enabling) society. To show that (5) holds would help enormously to explain, for instance, why reference and predication are forms of praxis, why theoretical and practical reason are inseparable, why Aristotelian essentialism and Kantian rationality are indefensible, why legitimation must be the legitimation of ideologies, and why, as a consequence, *there are no modally necessary principles in moral matters*—as, indeed, there are (also) none in epistemology and the philosophy of science.

It may be helpful to remind you, here, that this was the basis on which I argued earlier that Putnam's appeal to truth as a *Grenzbegriff* (very much as with rationality, for Apel and Habermas and, indeed, for Putnam again) could not be reconciled with Putnam's "internal realism" or, independently, with anything short of a retreat to cognitive privilege or First Philosophy. But I also need to guard against an easy misreading of item (5). Let me simply say that I do not construe the artifactual (the socially constituted) as fictional in any way, and I do not deny that the cultural complexities of personal life are inseparable from the biological resources in which they emerge. But I also do not see how the self can be naturalized (in Quine's sense: reduced, biologically) if selves *are* culturally emergent. This profoundly affects the logic of moral claims.

Once you admit historicism as conceptually viable and a possible basis for legitimative efforts in morality (as in science and cognitive matters at large), you cannot fail to grasp the profound incompatibility of historicism and universalism (whether the latter is exemplified in the form favored in Aristotle's essentialism or in Kant's model of maxims said to be capable of functioning as universal laws of nature). Gadamer, I think, is among the clearest on this matter, particularly in his well-known dispute with Habermas. There is some irony in this because, for one thing, as I say, Gadamer tries (and fails) to escape the upshot of his own (crypto-essentialist) argument[13] and because, for a second, perhaps more interestingly, the quarrel between Gadamer and Habermas is, if you think about it carefully, a quarrel between two branches of the same Kantian tradition: the one (Habermas's) centered in the first *Critique*; the other (Gadamer's) centered in the hermeneutic tradition drawn from the third *Critique* and eventually historicized through Dilthey and Heidegger.[14]

Gadamer's intended lesson comes in two steps. In the first, he identifies the grounds for repudiating any presumption of a neutral faculty of practical reason by the use of which the universal validation of morally enlightened norms of conduct is supposed to be assured: "The overcoming of all prejudices [*Vorurteil*], this global demand of the enlightenment, [he says] will prove to be itself [an unjustified] prejudice, the removal of which opens the way to an appropriate understanding of our finitude, which dominates not only our humanity, but also our historical consciousness. If this is true, then the idea of an absolute reason is impossible for historical humanity. Reason exists for us only in concrete, historical terms, i.e. it is not its own master, but remains constantly dependent on the given circumstances in which it operates."[15] In the second step, Gadamer rehabilitates the cognitive and directive contribution of "prejudice" [*Vorurteil*] thus construed and links it to a source of deeper "authority" that takes priority over the presumptions of "neutral" reason: "History does not belong to us, but we belong to it . . . [and so] the real consequence of the enlightenment is different [from what it proclaims]: namely, the subjection of all authority to reason [which is itself prejudiced against 'legitimate prejudices, if we want to do justice to man's finite, historical mode of being']."[16] By the "authority" of history and tradition, Gadamer means the effective formative processes of a society by which we, as linguistically apt selves, are *first* made apt for all those activities that are usually collected as the exercise of theoretical and practical reason. This is not always clear in Gadamer: sometimes, it is true, *tradition* is meant not merely in the holistic sense in which specifically human life is lived in the medium of social traditions but also in the determinate sense in which traditional answers to moral and political questions are, effectively, the right answers. Needless to say, the latter is always arbitrary—or undefended; Gadamer never affirms it in so many words, but it lurks in his account of the "classical." Nevertheless, he stalemates Habermas.

I draw three important findings from Gadamer's account: first, that reason is an artifact of history, preformed in a variable way by the horizonal saliencies of one history or another; second (though Gadamer does not address the matter directly), that, as a consequence, our discursive powers (preeminently, reference and predication) function as they do only in terms of the concrete, historical habits of thought that are actually operative socially—which is what I mean by *praxis*; and, third, that, in the sense intended in the preceding two findings, we ourselves are artifacts of an enculturing history. (The summary is clearly Hegelian in spirit.)

Objectivity, therefore, is a construct of history; neutrality, a construct of prejudice. Reason cannot completely fathom its own competence; it has a changing history and inescapably reflects the tacit perspective (or horizon) of that history. History and tradition play no criterial role of any kind. The authority of tradition is purely formative (and holist). It is, so to say, the medium of distinctly human life: "we stand always within tradition," Gadamer says, "and this is no objectifying process, i.e., we do not conceive of what tradition says as something other, something alien";[17] "the abstract antithesis between history and knowledge must be discarded";[18] and therefore "it is senseless to speak of a perfect knowledge of history, and for this reason it is not possible to speak of an object in itself towards which its research is directed."[19] The cognitive fates of science and morality converge here.

There is no Hegelian telos to the whole of human history; there is no changeless *archē* of Aristotle's sort; there is no neutral power of practical reason such as Kant supposes.

Grant all that, and you see at once the importance of the quarrel between Habermas and Gadamer and the inherent untenability of Habermas's position. The quarrel concerns the supposed objectivity and neutrality of reason—its "universality," as Habermas and Apel are fond of saying. But Habermas concedes that *reason is a historically formed, historically emergent competence*. At a stroke, therefore, the neutrality of reason is put at insuperable risk: *not* the very idea of neutrality or objectivity when viewed as a reasonable (constructive) posit matching our best (constructive) conjectures about science and morality, but only as a supposedly autonomous, original source for such neutrality. If you grasp the point, you cannot fail to see that it cuts against Rawls and MacIntyre with equal ease.

The quarrel between Habermas and Gadamer has a certain slack quality, however, that threatens to be interminable and unhelpful. I have no wish to fuel it further. But I am afraid that if I do not provide fair specimens of their opposed views, you may not see the full hopelessness of Habermas's Kantian claim or the nearly complete lack of interest on Gadamer's part to recover what is to count (*now*), under the hermeneutic conditions imposed, as the marks of objective rigor in judgment. The point is this: once reason is acknowledged to be historically constituted—whatever we take to be our cognitive and active competences—we must abandon all second- and third-tier strategies. Fourth-tier legitimation will then be seen to be the legitimation of ideologies, but, more than that, it will be seen to be a form of ideology itself: the legitimation of legitimation. There's a paradox there, but I believe it to be benign.

In any case, here is Habermas's fatal concession:

> Moral universalism is a *historical result*. It arose, with Rousseau and Kant, in the midst of a specific society that possessed corresponding features. The last two or three centuries have witnessed the emergence, after a long see-sawing struggle, of a *directed* trend toward the realization of basic rights. This process has led to, shall we cautiously say, a less and less selective reading and utilization of the universalistic meaning that fundamental-rights norms have; it testifies to the "existence of reason," if only in bits and pieces. Without these fragmentary realizations, the moral intuitions that discourse ethics conceptualizes would never have proliferated the way they did. To be sure, the gradual embodiment of moral principles in concrete forms of life is not something that can safely be left to Hegel's absolute spirit. Rather, it is chiefly a· function of collective efforts and sacrifices made by sociopolitical movements.[20]

I now add, without further comment, a well-known remark of Gadamer's, which makes explicit the consequence of *Habermas's* concession to historicity (to hermeneutics, in effect):

> We say . . . that understanding and misunderstanding take place between I and thou. But the formulation "I and thou" already betrays an enormous alienation. There is nothing like an "I and thou" at all [that is, primordially, invariantly]—there is neither the

I nor the thou as isolated, substantial realities. I may say "thou" and I may refer to myself over against a thou, but a common understanding [*Verständigung*] always precedes these situations [an actual tradition that we share, that we emerge within, that actually forms us and mediates our understanding].[21]

My sense is that the secret doctrine—the one that dies so slowly but is hardly noticed in either continental European or Anglo-American thought, the one that controls the fate of the entire dispute—is the single notion that there must necessarily be a neutral language into which all intelligible languages may be translated because an intelligible language is a translatable language! The argument is a palpable non sequitur. For how can we possibly demonstrate that what, within the (incompletely fathomable) horizon of society *A*, is regarded as a translation of utterances generated within society *B*—or, for that matter, is so regarded by the apt bilinguals of *A* and *B*—is neutral in any sense other than the sense in which neutrality is itself a consensual artifact plausibly idealized by the speakers of *A* (or the speakers of *A* and *B*)?

Habermas's claim may be permitted to stand, therefore—though not its conclusion, namely, that "the trait that all traditional languages have in common and that guarantees their transcendental unity [is] the fact that in principle they can all be translated into one another."[22] There is, however, no sense as yet (and no demonstration supporting the sense) that Habermas has discovered a modal invariance (a "transcendental unity") of any sort. I remind you that when Rawls argues about the reflection of rational agents in "the original position," he is committing himself, in speaking of "reason," to an analogue of Habermas's thesis.

I also find no difference in this regard between Habermas's claim and the one Donald Davidson has made so famous in his attack on plural "conceptual schemes."[23] There, Davidson explicitly says, arguing against the conceivability of plural conceptual schemes (the analytic counterpart of Gadamer's notions of prejudice and horizonality), that "the failure of intertranslatability is a necessary condition for difference in conceptual schemes; the common relation to experience or the evidence is what is supposed to make sense of the claim that it is languages or schemes that are under consideration where translation fails. It is essential to this idea that there be something neutral and common that lies outside all schemes."[24] Davidson means that the advocates of plural conceptual schemes (Kuhn, Feyerabend, Whorf) contradict themselves and, in any case, support an incoherent thesis because, for one thing, they presuppose (and yet deny) a neutral "something" in merely formulating their own claims and, for another, the very idea of "a difference of conceptual schemes" makes no sense apart from admitting a neutral "something" in virtue of which that difference may be said to be (thus) identifiable (and hence defeated).

But Davidson's argument, like Habermas's, is a non sequitur and a *petitio*. In fact, it is the same argument. First, we have no operative criterion of translat*ability*—or translatability into a neutral language. Second, failure of translation does not signify a failure of translatability. Third, it is not true (as Davidson claims) that a "failure of intertranslatability is [in principle] a necessary condition for difference in conceptual schemes." On the contrary, "different" or "incommensurable" schemes may well be translatable; certainly incommensurable "schemes" are intelligible—a fortiori, translatable qua incommensurable, a fortiori, paraphrasable in commensurable terms even if initially incommensurable.[25]

And, fourth, the very success of translation and the determination of both incommensurability and a "difference in conceptual schemes" are themselves artifacts of discursive practice in precisely the sense in which objectivity and neutrality are. They cannot claim any independent privilege. Davidson's objection is a complete nonstarter.

I can put the counterargument even more compellingly, for, even if we concede, with Davidson, that there must be a "neutral something" presupposed in merely admitting a "difference in conceptual scheme," it hardly follows that, *in* judging that there is a difference in conceptual scheme, we must be invoking *that* "neutral something" to confirm that difference. No, the operative criterion may be no more than an artifact (*not* demonstrably neutral, therefore) regarding our consensual judgment. Wherever substantive claims of neutrality or objectivity are at stake—in science or morality—the burden of proof obviously falls to the partisans of neutrality. Not to put too fine a point on it: in their very different ways, Habermas and Rawls and MacIntyre claim a march on rationality that they cannot rightly defend. They cannot do better than Davidson here!

III

I must firm up my account on the Aristotelian side. Bear in mind: I am trying to establish the plausibility of invoking fourth-tier strategies—which is to say, strategies (often opposed or neglected) that favor the following doctrines: the historicity of thinking, the social (artifactual) construction of selves, the inseparability of theoretical and practical reason as specifications of praxis, the indemonstrability of our occupying a neutral stance or possessing a neutral language suited to science and/or morality, the linguistic grounding of morality and normativity, the rejection of any realist discovery of true morality, the ideological cast of moral objectivity (distinct from strict realism), and the viability of relativism. All that is now beginning to come into focus. I argue in favor of fourth-tier thinking (just sketched) by way of demonstrating the utter collapse of second- and third-tier thinking, the obvious coherence and viability of fourth-tier strategies, and the evidence that late third-tier thinkers have skirted the prospects of historicism but pulled back too quickly and without justification. (The formative schema is no more than a makeshift to collect differing approximations and modes of avoidance regarding fourth-tier speculation, which I favor.)

I have shown (on the Aristotelian side) that MacIntyre's treatment of reason in resolving incommensurabilities at points of crisis between rival traditions never quite explains how objectivity is actually confirmed. For example, there are incommensurable, as well as incompatible, accounts of the defensibility of abortion and euthanasia in American society today: how might we show that one or another rival tradition was indeed rationally superior to its rivals? It is difficult to see how *any* familiar argument could be advanced that would not be either partisan or arbitrary (in the way of claiming cognitive or rational privilege) or plainly opportunistic (in claiming a suitable congruity with the preferred tradition). If reason were an artifact of history, as MacIntyre affirms, then it would seem to be too parochial for the task, and if it were equal to the task, then either it would not be an artifact of history or else the puzzles posed by incommensurable (as well as incompatible) traditions would be so elementary that it would hardly matter which it was. I find none of these possibilities promising. I characterize the fourth-tier option as existential and pragmatist.

MacIntyre genuinely tries to steer a middle course between sheer historicism and sheer universalism. I have no doubt that such a course is possible, but I cannot see how it could fail to be anything but partisan and privileged. That would not be a defect in itself. But MacIntyre obviously believes, along the lines Aquinas develops in the *Summa* and elsewhere, that his middle course (not a policy of compromise) is in touch with the truth of the matter—that is, in the same sense in which Aquinas tries to discern *the truth* "through an overall work of dialectical construction" that "summon[s] up" what must provisionally pass as the truth "internal" to the "scheme of concepts and beliefs" that mark off, say, the rival Aristotelian and Augustinian "traditions" (which Aquinas actually seeks to reconcile).[26] MacIntyre believes that espousing the historicity of reason is not incompatible with "truth" being a final "outcome" at the end of "an essentially uncompleted debate."[27] How so? you ask. Here is MacIntyre's answer:

> In the construction of any demonstrative science we both argue *from* what we take, often rightly, to be subordinate truths *to* first principles (*Commentary on the Ethics*, loc. cit.), as well as from first principles *to* subordinate truths (*Commentary on Boethius' De Trinitate*, Qu. VI, 1 and 3). And in this work of coming to understand which premises it is that state what is the case *per se*, in such a way as to function as first principles, we continually deepen our apprehension of the content of these first principles and correct those misapprehensions into which everyone tends to fall.[28]

What this means, frankly, is that there is a unique truth about things per se and that uttering that truth requires grasping "first principles" and truths appropriately "subordinate" to them, despite the fact that *we* are forever caught in an unending debate aspiring in that direction but characteristically deflected by the historicity of our particular mode of reasoning.

It needs to be said that an uncompromising historicism regarding reason cannot fail to be incompatible with claims about truth "*per se*" and "first principles" under which what is true per se may be known to be such. The theory of truth (a fortiori, the theory of rationality that can capture truth) that I have just cited is quite different from the theory with which MacIntyre opens *Whose Justice? Which Rationality?* What MacIntyre says at the beginning of that account is this: "Acknowledgement of the diversity of traditions of enquiry, each with its own specific mode of rational justification, does not entail that the differences between rival and incompatible traditions cannot be rationally resolved."[29] True enough. But this second citation is incompatible with the rational resolution of differences in accord with the terms of the first. There cannot be any operative sense in which (1) first principles, truth per se, can be invoked in historicized inquiry, or in which (2) historicized inquiry can meaningfully be said to approach, by increments, what is true per se or what would be true under the appropriate first principles and pertinent "subordinate" truths. There's a lacuna in MacIntyre's argument. I take it to be unsatisfactory.

I have already shown that Aristotle's system of first principles and subordinate truths offered in *Metaphysics* 4 fails because Aristotle cannot demonstrate that the denial of the modal invariance he affirms necessarily leads to self-contradiction. MacIntyre makes no effort (in this or anything like this sense) to demonstrate that there are (or must be) first principles that historicized inquiry can (come to) know or reasonably assume. I insist, therefore, that historicism is incompatible with the admission of first principles, hence, that MacIntyre is not genuinely committed to the historicism he appears to espouse. There must be a deep equivocation in MacIntyre's seemingly straightforward dictum: namely, "rationality itself, whether theoretical or practical, is a concept with a history"—that is, rationality is always historically formed and effective only in settings that take due account of the original setting in which it was formed as it was.[30] The genuinely historicized reading of MacIntyre's formula is pretty close to a definition of *praxis*; the other signifies a very clever reinterpretation of apparent historicity ultimately reconciled with a Thomist (or Thomistic-Aristotelian) recovery of nous and the doctrine of the modal invariance of reality. You must bear in mind that the denial of modal invariance (what I call the doctrine of the flux) is not itself affirmed as a form of modal invariance. It is a philosophical bet, a pragmatic, negative conjecture to the effect that no such invariance *will be* successfully sustained. The denial that there must be first principles is similarly a bet: it is not itself a first principle.[31]

There is a cognate weakness on the side of the doctrine of virtue. The countermove that is in sympathy with historicism is plain enough. If the virtues and their proper order among themselves were local to particular traditions, then moral assessments of one tradition made in terms of the model favored by another would be no more than completely partisan, and if there were a universal model of the virtues, then, equally plainly, essentialism would be entailed. So MacIntyre finds himself confronted in the preface and first pages of *After Virtue*, for instance, with the need to strike a middle course (MacIntyre's kind of middle course) between historicism and essentialism. He says there that what struck him was the fact that "the nature of moral community and moral judgment in distinctively modern societies was such that it was no longer possible to appeal to moral criteria in a way that had been possible in other times and places—and that this was a moral calamity! But to *what*," he asks, "could I be appealing, if my own analysis was correct?"[32] You must see how carefully this is worded. The solution MacIntyre seeks is one that will be "correct," but such a solution will involve, he adds, some "*what*" that *cannot* be drawn from the apparent data or resources of most "distinctively modern societies"—which (of course) only baffle what, "in other times and places," once enabled us to grasp the moral truth! Once you appreciate MacIntyre's candor, you cannot be surprised when, on the very next page of the same preface, he says flat out—reflecting (in the sixties and seventies) on "the question of the basis for the moral rejection of Stalinism"—that

> the conclusion which I reached and which is embodied in this book—although Marxism itself is only a marginal preoccupation—is that Marxism's moral defects and failures arise from the extent in which it, like liberal individualism, embodies the *ethos* of the distinctively modern and modernizing world, and that nothing less than a rejection of a large part of that *ethos* will provide us with a rationally and morally defensible standpoint from which to judge and to act—and in terms of which to evaluate various rival and heterogeneous moral schemes which compete for our allegiance.[33]

The heart of MacIntyre's argument is clear enough: it is the anticipated link between what comes "after virtue"—"in other times" and in our own chaotic times—and the recovery of a First Philosophy hospitable (but "rationally and morally" correct nevertheless) to our historicized rivalries. In a word, what we have here is MacIntyre's statement of *his* original position—the mate of Rawls's. The clue is elementary: the judgment about how to begin is already characterized as "a rationally and morally defensible standpoint." So reason cannot be an artifact of history, whatever MacIntyre may have been led to say, later, in the book's sequel. The competence of reason (here invoked) must be invariantly suited to the first principles on which morality depends, for "moral philosophy" is not "an independent and isolable area of enquiry."[34] To be perfectly frank, my reading of this is that MacIntyre cannot possibly have succeeded philosophically, though he *has* indeed succeeded ideologically in reclaiming the Thomistic version of Aristotle's powerful conception (scattered through the *Nicomachean Ethics*, the *Politics*, and *De motu animalium*) by a melding of First Philosophy and historicism that permits MacIntyre to attenuate, if not to bypass, Aristotle's own essentialism. He reclaims the telos of human nature in terms of a supreme *archē*, by way of a dialectical contest embedded in the plural *sittlich* regularities of our rival histories. In this, MacIntyre improves on Gadamer (the Gadamer who himself recovers the "classical" from the scatter of historicity) by not leaving matters in a mysterious and unexplained state. MacIntyre appears before us, therefore, as a kind of Hegelian reader of Aristotle.

I think you will find this confirmed in the final page of *After Virtue*, where MacIntyre considers (for a new beginning) "the reconciliation of biblical theology and Aristotelianism" in terms of Aquinas's doctrine that "only a life constituted in key part by obedience to law could be such as to exhibit fully those virtues without which human beings cannot achieve their *telos*."[35] I have no doubt, for instance, that this Thomistic confidence in what must now be called the *science* of ethics (in a sense akin to Aristotle's notion of a science) is just what must have provoked Martha Nussbaum's strong objection to MacIntyre's reading of Aristotle.[36] She was right, of course, to remind us that Aristotle did not regard ethics as a science, but the issue between MacIntyre and Nussbaum is surely more than textual. Her own extraordinarily relaxed analogies between Aristotle and, say, Henry James more than risk the historicized irrelevance I have already said threatens *any* Aristotelian theory shorn of essentialist assurances. Nevertheless, what MacIntyre claims is certainly premature (as philosophy), although it is by this time quite conventional as ideology.

Turn, then, to MacIntyre's theory of virtue. MacIntyre catches up the idea of a moral telos once again:

> Unless there is a *telos* which transcends the limited goods of practices by constituting the good of a whole human life, the good of a human life conceived as a unity, it will *both* be the case that a certain subversive arbitrariness will invade the moral life *and* that we shall be unable to specify the context of certain virtues adequately. These two considerations are reinforced by a third: that there is at least one virtue recognised by the tradition which cannot be specified at all except with reference to the wholeness of a human life—the virtue of integrity or constancy.[37]

In a way I agree with MacIntyre, and in a way I do not. I agree that, thinking along Aristotelian but not Kantian lines, the absence of a human telos will threaten to "invade the moral life" with a "certain subversive arbitrariness," but I do not agree that the denial of a human telos leads inevitably to moral "arbitrariness" or to a "subversive arbitrariness" in either a pared-down Aristotelian or Kantian speculation or, indeed, in the fourth-tier mode of thinking I am recommending. Also, apart from that, to insist on the point is surely a blackmail argument, especially as MacIntyre's own speculation nowhere demonstrates that there is a human telos or that contemporary moral life is a "calamity." (I have no wish to defend Stalinism or Nazism, for instance, but I should like to know which age did not generate its own moral horrors—consistent with its technological capacity and our sensibilities.)

I say it is impossible to demonstrate that human existence or human nature has a true telos, that that is precluded by any constructivist account of the human self (including the doctrine MacIntyre favors in admitting the historical formation of the many forms of rationality). It is also precluded by any historicism. I do not infer from that that historicism makes a virtue-oriented morality impossible or "arbitrary." Historicized morality may seem arbitrary, I don't deny, to anyone who, like MacIntyre, believes in a human telos and in first principles that permit us to capture what is true and correct (in the way of a moral science). I say only that that conjecture is itself arbitrary philosophically, though certainly not, for that reason, not viable ideologically.

I agree with MacIntyre that "every moral philosophy has some particular sociology as its counterpart."[38] But I take that to mean that Aristotle's original conception of *praxis* is indemonstrable and that a human praxis is nothing if not historicized. When MacIntyre speaks of "the tradition of the virtues," he means two things: first, a tradition (like the Aristotelian or the Thomist) that may be confirmed sociologically; second, that *that* historically promising tradition appears, dialectically, best placed to lead us to approximate to the truth about the human condition! That is the reason (as I understand it) that MacIntyre invites us to consider the "history of [the] transformation [of that most promising tradition, in the modern world]; for we shall only understand the tradition of the virtues fully if we understand to what kinds of degeneration it has proved liable."[39] Extraordinary!

I am aware of only one line of theorizing about language that attempts to show that the very idea of classification (somehow) entails a telic element—that, rightly developed, it would recover the human telos. The idea is a caricature of the themes of the Socratic elenchus in Plato's early dialogues (where the assurance wanted is plainly lacking). It appeared in a relatively prominent way in an argument of Stuart Hampshire's. Hampshire claimed that "the notion of goodness . . . necessarily enters into every kind of discourse in which statements can be made," so that "we necessarily have the idea of 'more or less a so-and-so' as part of the procedure of classification itself, and therefore as intrinsic to any use of language in thought and in speech."[40] The plain fact is that Hampshire fails to distinguish between "being good as a recognizable specimen of a so-and-so" and "being good in the way in which a so-and-so may be good." That remarkable oversight—which surfaced in a chance conversation with Hampshire—led Hampshire to suppose that, however attenuated, virtues (or functions; remember Plato!) form part of the natural classification of things or, more pointedly, part of the *natures* of things themselves. But the argument is a bust: first, because the idea of "a good so-and-so" is not entailed in the idea of "a so-and-so"; second, because (as I imagine Socrates knew) not everything is such that it makes sense to say that, by consulting its nature, one can discover what its appropriate virtue is. Baboons are not good by nature, although sheepdogs are—in a sense that obviously turns victory into defeat. By the same token, human beings have no telic nature, though shepherds "do."[41]

Now, the bearing of all this on MacIntyre's theory is plain. For what it confirms is that the idea of a virtue cannot be shown to be entailed in the idea of what it is to be a human being, and that the idea of what the true virtue of human existence or human nature is is not internal to the idea of human existence or human nature itself—because human selves have no essential nature, are only what they are historically formed to be or to be capable of making of themselves. (In a way, this *is* the Nietzschean and Foucauldian theme.) Foucault has been credited with opposing every invented ontology that makes the world favorably disposed *ontologically* to any supposed human purpose and interest—a fortiori, favorably disposed to our essentialist ontologies of ourselves as well.[42] I should say that MacIntyre falls rather easily within the scope of that complaint.

I am lingering over MacIntyre's theory because it is, in my opinion, the most challenging late-Aristotelian exemplar we are likely to find that avoids a frontal acceptance of essentialism and that tries to reconcile an Aristotelian strategy with historicism. I say that it ultimately fails—in a knockdown way—but it is, also, the only exemplar that manages to unite a theory of reason (at once theoretical and practical) with a theory of virtue. I regard it, therefore, together with Lovibond's argument, as betraying the incapacity or unwillingness of all third-tier theories that admit the historicity of reason and tradition to go on to a full-blown reliance on fourth-tier strategies. (Habermas's argument is very nearly the only prominent specimen on the Kantian side that risks the historicity of reason. It does that only timidly, but Habermas's quarrel with Gadamer shows very clearly that the Kantians cannot really afford to admit the full artifactuality of reason.)

It is essential, from my perspective, that MacIntyre elects to read Aristotle in accord with Aquinas, although I concede that it might be very difficult otherwise to avoid the imminent relativism of the historicist option.

I see Gadamer and Lovibond as having invented alternative maneuvers, but their failure is even more transparent than MacIntyre's. In any case, MacIntyre makes a welcome effort to explain how we should understand a virtue-centered morality under historicized conditions. I need to pursue this issue before bringing my account of MacIntyre to a close. I invite your patience here.

The single most important feature of MacIntyre's account of the virtues and their relationship to institutional practices lies with the fact that that account *looks* entirely neutral and straightforward but is not. It may seem ungenerous to say so in advance of giving MacIntyre an inning. But I have already laid out a great deal of MacIntyre's theory, and what still needs to be said can be very much shortened by my warning you (in advance) of its particular tendentiousness. What MacIntyre says about the virtues does recover the ancient policy of bringing society at large (the *polis*, in the Greek world) into harmony with the condition of human existence (the *psyche*, in Plato and Aristotle). I should myself insist on that, although it does not affect the assessment of MacIntyre's thesis. Here is its principal premise: "By a 'practice' I am going to mean any coherent and complex form of socially established cooperative human activity through which goods internal to the form of activity are realized in the course of trying to achieve those standards of excellence which are appropriate to, and partially definitive of, that form of activity, with the result that human powers to achieve excellence, and human concepts of the ends and goods involved, are systematically extended."[43] MacIntyre adds at once—fatefully, as it turns out—that he is concerned only with "internal," not "external," goods: that is, with such goods (as he pointedly says) as "can only be identified and recognized by the experience of participating in the practice in question. Those who lack the relevant experience are incompetent thereby as judges of internal goods."[44] He goes on:

> A practice involves standards of excellence and obedience to rules as well as the achievement of goods. To enter into a practice is to accept the authority of those standards and the inadequacy of my own performance as judged by them. It is to subject my own attitudes, choices, preferences and tastes to the standards which currently and partially define the practice. . . . In the realm of practices the authority of both goods and standards operates in such a way as to rule out all subjectivist and emotivist analyses of judgment.[45]

Hence, finally, "A virtue is an acquired human quality the possession and exercise of which tends to enable us to achieve those goods which are internal to practices and the lack of which effectively prevents us from achieving any such goods."[46]

If you look carefully at these remarks, you will see that the virtues are defined in terms of goods internal to institutional practices and that the practices pertinent to moral review (as far as virtues are concerned) are limited to those that are at least "partially defined" by them. That means that MacIntyre does *not* include within the scope of his theory any practices for which goods and virtues can only be specified as externally imposed on them (by whatever theoretical means we choose). That is extraordinary, partly because, whatever may have been true in the past—for instance, for the periods MacIntyre favors (however disputably)—modern and contemporary institutions tend *not* to be definable by goods internal to themselves; their virtues tend not to be such, therefore, that could be defined by way of goods internal to their given practices. Possibly, the game of chess might meet MacIntyre's model, but certainly not a modern market economy. Does that mean that the market betrays the "kinds of degeneration" MacIntyre has warned us about? Apart from that, it's clear that MacIntyre's theory of virtue cannot be disjoined from his account of the human telos and moral principles already noted. The additional warning about those who have not participated in the requisite practices rings a little hollow, since it begs the question of just *what* is morally at stake. In short, the notion that the virtues are (1) internal to a practice and (2) conformable with the human telos strips historicism of its essential charge and reduces history to a play of (Aristotelian) appearances that confirm our constant nature.

IV

Nothing more need be said about MacIntyre's model. It pretends to be hospitable to historicism, but it is not. Everything that may now be added is bound to be colored by its ulterior commitment to the ahistorical invariances it acknowledges but never defends. I believe that this explains MacIntyre's peculiarly sanguine treatment of incompatible and incommensurable traditions. Of course, it also exposes in a serendipitous way Rawls's naivety, since Rawls makes no proper provision for the diversity of reason. MacIntyre admits the obvious about diversity, but he mutes its force through his overriding loyalty to St. Thomas. His concern with the catalogue of virtues also threatens (for related reasons) the continued relevance of Hume's immensely appealing *Treatise*, for how can we now be sure that Hume's account of eighteenth-century sensibilities can have much to do with twentieth-century moral concerns or with those of more exotic societies? One has only to scan what, in the *Treatise*, Hume terms "natural virtues" to realize that they are inseparable from the eighteenth-century praxis Hume was reviewing (meekness, moderation, clemency, and frugality, for instance).[47]

There's the important lesson to be drawn from MacIntyre as well—against MacIntyre's own use of it. What it suggests, what I believe is true but cannot stop to demonstrate,[48] is that the legitimation of morality is the legitimation of moral ideologies, because neither practical reason nor virtue nor any comparably large theme of moral theory is meaningful apart from the historical praxis in which it arises and has its primary application.

To concede the point is to raise anew the enormously baffling, unanswered question of what *is* "common" and what accounts for what is common in the repeated—valid—use of the same general predicates. It is to acknowledge, of course, nothing less than the bothersome conundrum behind the ancient doctrine of universals. What I say is that the solution to that puzzle is inseparable from the right assessment of the compared resources of third- and fourth-tier thinking. Grant that predication is inexplicable apart from the praxis of a linguistically apt society: you cannot then deny that reason (whether theoretical or practical) is a *sittlich* artifact of history. Grant that, and Rawls, Habermas, and MacIntyre are defeated at a stroke: that is, defeated in their presumption, however differently deployed, of an essential, universal invariance on which all moral objectivity rightly depends. So, the stakes are immense—and risked on an issue the full relevance of which is almost never perceived—the moral possibilities of what I call fourth-tier thinking.

Ironically, the theme is strengthened by Martha Nussbaum, who (rightly) opposes MacIntyre's arch reading of Aristotle; her own scruple, however, tends to confirm the increasingly marginal relevance of Aristotle's *Ethics* in much the same sense in which historicizing Hume affects the relevance of Hume's own program. Following a general recommendation offered by G. E. L. Owen,[49] Nussbaum maintains that Aristotle, speaking of *phainomena*, will be describing the world as it appears to, as it is experienced by, observers who are members of our kind: "The *phainomena* are drawn from Aristotle's own linguistic community and from several other civilized communities known to him to have recognizably similar general conditions of life, though with different particular institutions."[50]

It is true that, for Aristotle, "the human being is the only living creature who has experience of the good and bad, the just and unjust; and the other ethical concepts with which [the *Politics*] deals; in consequence only the human being has the capacity to express these conceptions in speech."[51] But if ethics is not a science and if, in any case, we are not prepared to subscribe to Aristotle's notion of a science, then the net effect of Nussbaum's adjustment is to strengthen our sense of the marginal relevance of Aristotle's normative views, both because the virtues and the other normative notions will then be historicized and because our own predicative distinctions and Aristotle's regarding these same notions will be embedded in their own historical praxis—in which they function first and have their proper meaning.

This is not to deny that we do (and must) generalize over different runs of phenomena. It is only to draw attention to the problematic nature of doing that—especially regarding *sittlich* and legitimative distinctions that bear on the normative. (That is indeed what I had in mind in reserving judgment on Mackie's insouciant skepticism.)

In any case, the concession utterly undermines the point of Nussbaum's analogies between Aristotle and, say, Henry James. For if what I have just said is true, then it is hard to see how reference to Aristotle's *Ethics* can serve to confirm the validity of James's moral assessment of a society entirely different from those societies that Aristotle examines, and if James's judgment rests on its own resources (as Aristotle's does), then we had better have before us James's moral theory before we assess the match in ways that go beyond the merely textual. But that is never rightly supplied.[52]

Nussbaum cites the *Ethics* (1141b): "practical wisdom is not concerned with universals only; it must also recognize particulars, for it is practical, and practice concerns particulars." According to Nussbaum, ethics "should not even *try* for [the] precision [of the natural sciences—that is, their final deductive closure]": the *phainomena* of ethics are marked by "mutability, indeterminacy, particularity" in such a way that subsumption under universal principles is not really possible.[53] Nussbaum believes she is paraphrasing Aristotle's meaning. If so, then the emphasis in both Aristotle and Nussbaum is on the peculiar features of the *practical* (as opposed to the theoretical or scientific), whereas it seems to me that the emphasis should rather be on *predicables* as such. Nussbaum herself says, glossing Aristotle, "Practical wisdom . . . uses rules only as summaries and guides; it must itself be flexible, ready for surprise, prepared to see, resourceful at improvisation."[54] Yes, of course, but that leaves completely unexamined Aristotle's presumption that, *in their proper place,* universals *are* fixed and determinate.

Most of those, in fact, who find satisfaction in insisting that ethics is not a science are also inclined to insist that the sciences *are* sciences in a sense akin to what Aristotle affirms. I oppose the idea: I say it cannot be defended. My point is that there is no known argument by which the invariance of universals can be assured and assuredly known. That adverse finding would be required, of course, by any consistent historicism, but historicism itself would be greatly strengthened by its independent validity. The issue is a vexed one: nothing less—as I say—than the entire question of what we should mean by general predicates (*red, round, hirsute, loved, just*). I cannot do full justice to it, but I mean to sketch how it can be resolved and what its resolution signifies.

The trick is this: if what makes general predicates genuinely general is their conforming with or corresponding to some real, common predicables (so-called universals) that inhere in the world (whether separately or not), then Aristotle's (and Nussbaum's) emphasis is the right one. But if, as I believe, it is impossible to supply any evidence (1) to show that there are such universals or (2) to show that there must be such universals if there are "real generals"[55] (shared properties), then, of course, two decisive findings will fall out at once: one, that all those moral theorists (and more) who insist on the normative invariances of reason or the invariances of real norms or first principles (Habermas and MacIntyre, say) will have no grounds at all for their particular doctrines; the other, that historicism itself becomes instantly more plausible, possibly even inescapable, on admitting the first.

There you have the deeper connection between the notion of praxis and the fate of third- and fourth-tier strategies. For my present purpose, it is enough to draw your attention to the fact that the theory of universals is *utterly useless* (epistemically) because it is impossible to prize predicates and predicables apart, although it is not unreasonable to hold that there *are* "real generals," even lawlike generals, and that not all predicates correspond to such predicables.[56] For, in any viable theory, real generals cannot be, and cannot be shown to be, anything but artifacts of our consensual practice.

I believe this to be the single most important theme in Wittgenstein's *Investigations* and *On Certainty*—formulated (by Wittgenstein) in terms that happen to ignore the historical dimension of societal life but that nevertheless remain compatible with historicity. I know of no more compelling approach to the analysis of general predicates than Wittgenstein's. On the one hand, there *must be* "real generals"; otherwise, the spontaneous fluency of natural-language discourse (and science) would be impossible. On the other hand, we cannot meaningfully claim that there *are* real universals, because predication makes no sense if it is not cognitively construed, and universals (on any testable view: a fortiori, leaving aside Aristotle's view of the powers of nous) are incapable of being demonstrably discerned. The only possible resolution requires that real generals be confirmed in and only in our linguistic and lingual acts. But *that* is tantamount to denying a principled distinction between theoretical and practical reason and to yielding in the direction of a historicized praxis and the artifactual diversity of reason. Predicable generals are *lebensformlich*, open to "family resemblances."

The great quarrel about universals will hardly be put to rest by this thin maneuver. I agree. You may even complain that I am nothing but a nominalist or a conceptualist. But that misses the most important point. According to the argument I am advancing, *there are no universals*. There are no predicative *tertia* (Rorty's term). So the ancient choice between nominalism, conceptualism, and realism no longer arises. That is the point of Wittgenstein's innovation and economy.[57]

The problem of universals devolves into the problem of real generals, that is, the problem of how general predicates function in the fluent way they do in natural-language discourse—servicing truth claims in science and morality. It doesn't matter (at this point in the argument) how you explain real generals, so long as you admit (1) that real generals no longer implicate universals and (2) that no explanation that will work can presuppose a principled disjunction between language and world—because to deny that would be to reinstate the mediating role of universals! I have my own solution to offer, but this is not the place to argue for it. I say only that there can be no principled difference between our languaged world and our worlded language—or, I say, language and world can be sorted only within the terms of that symbiosis.[58] The result is that real generality (in Wittgenstein's sense) is not simply criterial, in the sense (already introduced) of strictly following a rule. That is what undermines Habermas and MacIntyre.

Predication is a cognitive competence, but there is no straightforwardly epistemic resolution of its puzzle—the smooth and spontaneous extension of general terms, in natural-language use, from known exemplars to new instances. What, in effect, Wittgenstein makes clear is that the confirmation of predicative claims, like the confirmation of binding moral norms, depends (but not criterially) on the consensual tolerance of a society's *lebensformlich* practices. Criterial matters, at whatever point of critical or legitimative reflection we may favor, can never completely escape the logically and epistemically informal feature of our *lebensformlich* or *sittlich* habits. That means that theorists like MacIntyre, Habermas, and Rawls are committed (very possibly unwittingly) to some form of the theory of Forms. That, ultimately, is what historicism opposes.

With these distinctions in hand, you will find in Nussbaum a certain telltale confusion regarding reference and predication—or, particular things and their properties—that runs through most of the casual slippage of moral theory that would bring to bear on the assessment of *our* society what, say, Aristotle or Hobbes or Hume or Henry James says about the society he considers. Remember, Nussbaum was explaining the sense in which, according to Aristotle, practical reason cannot function in the way of a science.

Aristotle's point concerns the universal invariance of the predicative regularities of a bona fide science, whereas practical questions (Aristotle says—Nussbaum concurring) concern the particular—which is to say, not anything that has to do with predicative issues as such but only the extension of what general predicates rightly apply to. The failure of ethics to be a science does not entail that the particular lacks general properties. Nothing does that! It is only that the particulars ethics addresses (as opposed to the particulars the sciences address) do not form a suitable class of instances, a class that answers to a covering law or an essence. Nussbaum observes, correctly, that Aristotle is drawing attention to the comparative scope of ethical and scientific generalization, but she sometimes slips (or seems to slip) and construes what Aristotle says here to signify instead the absence of general properties as such. (That, of course, would be incoherent.)

Thus, for example, she says, "Aristotle suggests that the concrete ethical case may simply contain some ultimately particular and nonrepeatable elements. He says that such cases do not fall under any *technē* or precept, implying that in their very nature they are not, or not simply repeatable." But there *are* no "repeatable particulars." What is repeatable—or, better, iterable in the way of predication—is the use of the same predicate in discourse about different particulars. What Nussbaum concludes, however, is that "in love and friendship features of shared history and family relatedness that are not even in principle repeatable are permitted to bear serious ethical weight."[59] But that is flatly incoherent (in intent) or irrelevant (in application).

What she obviously means (but does not quite say) is that the "repeatable" (general) properties observed in the context of love and friendship are not repeatable in accord with (able to be subsumed under) an exceptionless scientific law. The equivocation is not meant to undermine Aristotle (although, as I have argued, Aristotle's modal invariances cannot be confirmed). What it draws attention to instead is, first, the problematic nature of *any* would-be laws or principles or norms or rules that pretend to rest on invariant universals rather than on consensually constructed generals[60] and, second, the increasingly marginalized relevance of applying norms or principles drawn from the praxis of one society to the moral concerns of another. Here, Nussbaum's discussion of the moral power of James's fiction cannot fail to be at risk—philosophically. What I suggest is that she does not quite grasp the weakness of her strategy because she is not clear about the predicative puzzle. It lies at the heart of historicism, the theory of praxis, and the constructed nature of human reason and human selves.

I can afford only a little more space for the confirming evidence drawn from Nussbaum's treatment of James, but the detour is worth the labor and the patience. You must bear in mind Aristotle's warning (in the *Ethics*): "All law is universal; but about some things it is not possible for a universal statement to be correct. Then in those matters in which it is necessary to speak universally, but not possible to do so correctly, the law takes the usual case, though without ignoring the possibility of missing the mark."[61] The point of Aristotle's warning is indeed that law, like science, "is universal" (necessary and exceptionless) despite the fact that the application of law to practical matters characteristically involves what cannot possibly support a "universal statement" (but may support a general statement).

Aristotle does not relinquish, for that reason, the truth of universal law or universal science, but Nussbaum fails to show that James invokes universal laws (or universal moral principles), or that there *are* universal laws or principles that Aristotle and James share or could share, or that she herself can confirm such laws or moral principles in justifying her bringing Aristotle and James together in the way she does:

> To juxtapose Aristotle and James is not to deny that in many salient features their conceptions of reasoning are not identical. They have relevantly different conceptions of consciousness, of the nature and taxonomy of the emotions, and all of this should be borne in mind. And yet the convergence of sympathies is more striking than these differences; nor is the convergence merely fortuitous. For one thing, numerous lines of influence connect James with Aristotle—from his own direct reading to indirect philosophical and literary influence of many kinds. But it is more important still to point out that if in fact, as I have suggested, this conception truly answers to deep human intuitions about practical reason, intuitions that recur in much,

though not exactly, the same form across differences of time and place, then it is no surprise that two perceptive writers about practical reason should independently converge upon them. The problems of choosing well have a remarkable persistence; convergence on a good response requires less explanation than convergence in error.[62]

But you will not find the evidence in Nussbaum of the common human essence or the valid universal laws and principles that James and Aristotle share. She skirts the issue.

Nussbaum does say straight out that Henry James's novels explicate Aristotle's treatment and conception of practical reason (or, better, "practical wisdom"): "if we want to know more about the content of the Aristotelian way of choosing, and why it is good, we cannot do better than to turn to James's novels, [where] the Aristotelian view is appropriately embodied."[63] She cannot offer more than similarities in their categories of description and analysis (regarding emotion and imagination, for instance), but she claims that James's novels "embody" the Aristotelian conception of practical reason—and that is neither demonstrated nor demonstrable (either in the sense that James subscribed to Aristotle's theory or in the sense that Aristotle's theory is true).

Hilary Putnam has observed, about Nussbaum's Aristotelian reading of James's *The Golden Bowl*, that her "view is in danger of collapsing into 'an empty situation morality' in which everything is 'a matter of trade-offs.' "[64] The point, of course, is that, without Nussbaum's possessing invariant principles, the comparison between Aristotle and James on treating "literature as moral philosophy" cannot fail to confuse similarities in descriptive technique or theme with similarities in moral philosophy. You can see for yourself the validity of the charge by weighing some sample remarks (of Nussbaum's) regarding James's treatment of Maggie Verver in *The Golden Bowl*. (I shall not belabor the point.) After mentioning some episodes in Verver's life, Nussbaum summarizes the Aristotelian import of James's treatment thus:

> In ethical terms, what [the episodes mentioned mean] is that the perceiver [Verver] brings to the new situation a history of general conceptions and commitments, and a host of past obligations and affiliations (some general, some particular), all of which contribute to and help to constitute her evolving conceptions of good living. Perception, we might say, is a process of loving

conversation between rules and concrete responses, general conceptions and unique cases, in which the general articulates the particular and is in turn further articulated by it. The particular is constituted out of features both repeatable and nonrepeatable; it is outlined by the structure of general terms, and it also contains the unique images of those we love.[65]

I believe Nussbaum never attempts a firmer comparison (than this) between Aristotle and James. Also, the citation reminds us of the problematic nature of the "repeatable" and Nussbaum's conceptual perseveration on the "nonrepeatable."

V

I shall resist adding the evidence confirming the ubiquity of the presumption of moral invariance under conditions of historical, fictional, and ideological contingency. I trust I have made a fair case for one finding of exceptional importance—which nearly everyone refuses to admit—namely, that there are no demonstrably valid moral principles, if by a *principle* one means an exceptionless normative rule legitimated by reference to some discernible modal invariance or necessity of reason or reality. Grant that all would-be arguments fail; you will not then be able to deny that moral objectivity cannot exceed the objectivity of moral ideologies. I do not draw the skeptic's conclusion here. On the contrary, the history of moral philosophy has gone completely wrong (I suggest) because it has never endorsed this verdict or shown how one may escape it.

Having come this far, however, I should like to round out the account with some small observations and a distinction of fresh importance. First, I cite, for the record only, what is probably the most entrenched aprioristic insistence on invariance that one is likely to find among contemporary moral theories of the Kantian stripe. I have touched on it before, but now that we know that contemporary Aristotelians have failed to recover Aristotle's sort of modal invariance, it may be useful to have in hand an actual text (of the Kantian sort) with which to conjure—particularly since Rawls and Habermas have proved so coy in the defense of their respective Kantian programs. Here, then, without comment, is Karl-Otto Apel's well-known statement of his own a priori moral principle, which he calls "the principle of a dialectics . . . of idealism and materialism" (by which he means the rationale for extracting an ideal or "utopian" principle from every "material" or historical praxis):

> Anyone who engages in argument automatically presupposes two things; first, a *real communication community* whose member he has himself become through a process of socialization, and second, an *ideal communication community* that would basically be capable of adequately understanding the meaning of his arguments and judging their truth in a definitive manner. What is remarkable and dialectical about this situation, however, is that, to some extent, the ideal community is presupposed and even counterfactually anticipated *in* the real one, namely, as a real possibility of the real society, although the person who engages in argument is aware that (in most cases) the real community, including himself, is far removed from being similar to the ideal community. But, by virtue of its transcendental structure, argumentation is left no choice other than to face this both desperate and hopeful situation.[66]

Second, again without sustained comment, I should like to cite a counterpart statement (regarding scientific explanation) offered by Wesley Salmon, to remind you that arguments in moral philosophy and the philosophy of science are often surprisingly similar. What I wish to emphasize here is that the appeal to modal invariance in science is just as much an undefended a priori assumption as it is in moral matters. Salmon distinguishes three models of explanation in the physical sciences, which he associates with Laplace's original conception, although Salmon is hospitable to causal explanations that are inherently indeterministic.[67] He favors what he calls the "ontic conception" of explanation, which he summarizes in this way: "to explain an event is to exhibit it as occupying its (nomologically necessary) place in the discernible patterns of the world."[68] The use of the expression "nomologically necessary" signifies that the "ontic conception" entails the "modal conception" (of explanation), which may also function as an independent model. According to the "modal conception," Salmon says, "there is a relation of *nomological necessity* between [explanandum and explanans]."[69] In this sense, "nomological necessity" is not any sort of logical necessity; here, explanation need not, as such, be taken to be an argument. For this reason, Salmon identifies a third model, the "epistemic conception," which regards necessity in terms of the logic of argument; here, Salmon speaks of "nomic expectability."[70]

What is especially of interest to us is that Salmon traces all three conceptions to Aristotle's *Posterior Analytics* (71b 14–16), to the dictum "the proper object of unqualified scientific knowledge is something which cannot be other than it is." Salmon supports the "ontic conception," but he does not do so in the strong modal sense in which (as already remarked) Aristotle argues in *Metaphysics* 4. (That is, he does not offer an argument *for* modal necessity that is itself modally necessary.)[71] The trouble is, Salmon has already linked the "ontic" conception to "nomological necessity"; hence, it is difficult to see in what sense explanation is supposed to assign (in a valid way) some particular explanandum "its (nomologically necessary) place in the discernible patterns of the world." I have no wish to generate extraneous puzzles at this late hour, but only to identify the a priori element in Salmon's account. You see, therefore, that the argument I have been mounting against the canons of moral philosophy should rightly be applied as well in the philosophy of science. But I shall forgo the effort here.[72]

The fresh distinction I promised at the start of this section I can now produce without ceremony. Once moral necessity is rejected, in the sense in which it is explicit in Aristotle—in Apel, in Salmon and implicit in Rawls, in Habermas, in MacIntyre, in Nussbaum—there is no longer any demonstrable necessity for hewing exclusively to a bivalent logic. I offer two corollaries: for one, there is no known argument that shows that a many-valued logic is inherently paradoxical, self-defeating, inconsistent, or self-contradictory; for a second, there is no known argument that shows that a bivalent and a many-valued logic are incompatible, if the scope of each is operationally segregated from that of the other and provided with relevance constraints.

I should argue that the choice of a logic (which may be informally construed) is itself a contingent matter that depends on our analysis of what a given domain of inquiry requires or is able to support or favors in the way of conceptual felicity. If you concede, for instance, that, although moral claims and judgments take truth-values (or truth-like values), it is arguable that a particular act of suicide or a particular euthanasian act may be validly defended and also validly condemned in the same circumstances—without contradiction, without falling back to appearances or the like (the pluralist's option), and without thereby being unable to offer pertinent or telling reasons for each such judgment—then it may be said that bivalence should there be set aside (or bracketed) and a relativistic logic put in its place. I am not saying that a many-valued logic is a relativistic logic, but I do say that a relativistic logic is a many-valued logic—one, in fact, that differs from other such logics in being willing to validate certain claims and judgments (properly segregated) that, on a bivalent logic but not now, would be incompatible or contradictory. I see no paradox there.

The paradigm for a relativistic logic is easily provided in the context of literary and art criticism: for instance, in the proliferating interpretations of *Hamlet*, where one is unwilling to deny that two expert interpretations, incompatible with one another but compatible with the text, may be judged reasonable or plausible (where *reasonable* and *plausible* are truth-like values in some many-valued run of alethic values)—where, that is, the alternative interpretations may, *now*, be jointly affirmed without contradiction. I should say that such interpretations were, on a suitable logic, *incongruent* (and thus valid) even though incompatible or contradictory on a bivalent logic. Clearly, they could not be jointly true.[73] (That is what distinguishes relativism from pluralism, for pluralism regards seemingly incompatible interpretations as valid [perhaps even true, viewed singly] when read as collecting the admissible appearances of the same text, whereas relativism would not proceed thus. Relativism retires the bivalent use of *true* and construes selected incompatible interpretations as plausible or apt or the like in accord with a many-valued set of truth-values or truth-like values that permit incongruent judgments to count as valid. Clearly, the distinction between pluralism and relativism must go beyond any purely formal choice between alternative truth-value schemes to theories about the ontic nature of different sectors of the world. The two accounts are not equivalent.)

The point, here, is that, for cognate reasons—for reasons that bear on (1) the indemonstrability of any doctrine of moral invariance or necessity, (2) the ideological aspect of practical life, and (3) the implications of historicism and cultural praxis—a relativistic logic is likely to be particularly useful in moral disputes. Many suppose that relativism is a form of skepticism or anarchism or even nihilism and that, in any case, it cannot help but be incoherent. I know of no argument that demonstrates that it is impossible to formulate a pertinent form of relativism that is self-consistent.

I offer the following as a set of consistent constraints on the alethic values of a relativistic logic: (1) it is not a three-valued logic that merely adds a third value (*indeterminate*) to what would otherwise be a two-valued logic; (2) it is a logic that treats truth and falsity asymmetrically, so that claims may be shown to be false without being able to be shown to be true; (3)

it is a logic that refuses to treat *true* relationally, as true-in-*L* (for different languages) or true-in-*W* (for different worlds) or true-for-*X* (for different subjects) or the like; (4) it is a logic that supplies additional, possibly graded truth-values (for instance, *plausible* or *apt* or *reasonable* or the like) in place of truth; (5) it is a logic that is compatible with a bivalent logic, if only suitably segregated and provided with suitable relevance constraints; and (6) it is a logic that admits questions of consistency, noncontradiction, relevance, and the like.[74] Thus, if, in demonstrating that a would-be interpretation of *Hamlet* is falsified by the text, one trivially affirms (by straightforward negation) what is true of the text (what interpretation must then concede), then, of course, one straightforwardly invokes bivalence again. But doing that is not tantamount to disallowing a relativistic assessment of the interpretations themselves and is not incompatible with such an assessment. It is true that our logic is extremely informal and piecemeal as a result, but that (I say) is in the nature of the world. Let our sanguine logics beware.

Beyond these constraints, I freely admit that relativistic *claims* must be located in some epistemic and ontic space; alethic considerations are never enough. Put this way, relativistic claims, like all truth claims, are (trivially) relativized to whatever is admitted as pertinent evidence. The trick is that, in relativistic contexts, no uniquely legitimated criterion can be convincingly supplied for testing (epistemically) the neutral and objective validity of competing claims. I have (you may remember) traced the failure to vindicate truth as a *Grenzbegriff* in Putnam (and, in effect, in Quine and Davidson and Rorty, as well). What that means is that pluralism (a pluralistic form of realism that pretends to capture the way the independent world is) is, ultimately, no different from a realism that refuses to admit such a pluralized realism: both claim a minimal form of epistemic neutrality that neither can satisfactorily ensure. (That, as I see matters, is the futile point of the entirely unsecured contest between Putnam and Davidson.) Relativism insists on the lesson. Hence, relativism never admits any Archimedean point in our deliberations—in principle or in practice. It is for that reason that it allows incongruent judgments to stand as valid, whether in science or morality, within a constructed and historicized world.

The argument is very tidy now. The trouble is that it is entirely formal—uninterpreted in moral terms. I agree. There's little point to an extended analysis of moral objectivity if all that results is a picture that, however coherent and self-consistent, has no particular bearing on the resolution of serious moral disputes. I have, of course, a conceptual picture to offer. But I could not expect it to be hospitably received if readers were committed to a belief that, one way or another, an objective morality must be based on a principle in accord with some discerned form of modal necessity, or that a bivalent logic was modally necessary in some sense, or both. In this spirit, the fundamental claim and argument I originally had in mind has now been brought into clear view. There are no independently discoverable moral principles, I say, just as there are no comparable laws of nature or rules of thought. Or, whatever we offer in the way of principles or laws or rules are artifactual posits formed within a changing praxis. It's the modal claim that fails, *not* the sense of indicative regularities. We risk no conceptual resources, therefore, that the canon dares claim—except the indemonstrable presumption of modal invariance itself. Principles are no more than the idealized necessities of the observed *sittlich* regularities of our world (or invented improvements of the same). They are the instruments of effective ideology.[75]

Twelve

The Nature of Normativity

I

During the mid-twentieth century, in the first wave of postpositivist Anglo-American analytic philosophy, the well-known British-born materialist J. J. C. Smart insisted that biology was not a proper science because it was earthbound: that is, because Earth was the only planet known to support life forms of any kind, the would-be laws of biology could not rightly claim to be approximative in the nomological way.[1] All our formulations, here, Smart claimed, would be indexed to a range of experience effectively confined to the merely empirical (or "indicative") regularities of the planet; they could never justify true nomological presumptions.

Smart's conviction had it that the limitation did not hold for physics and chemistry since, assuredly, within the contingent limits of our inquiries, we could indeed draw specimen observations from other parts of the universe capable of validating nomological claims. Of course, Smart discounted the obvious fact that all the sciences are entirely managed by investigators who cannot but proceed in accord with their earthbound experience and interests, which they cannot have overcome in any convincing way. In effect, Smart thought our work in physics approximated to the true laws of nature but biological research could not be so described. He got things completely *verkehrt*: to draw in any way on the experience and reporting ability of human persons *is* to be earthbound and historied. The problem of nomologicality must go deeper than Smart supposed. Our conception of science and the laws of nature cannot fail to be restricted locally. There is no ready escape. But that's to say, overcoming local or historied constraints itself entails a local redescription. Nomologicality, rationality, normativity in all their guises are as thoroughly artifactual, second natured, historied, *earthbound*, culturally diverse as are human languages and persons. Normally, we are ignorant about what (in good part) it is we are ignorant about.

More recent theories of the practice of science have proved more open to contesting the necessity of construing scientific explanation in terms of exceptionless laws and principles (or forms of strict determinism or transcendental reason). They seek a sparer, reportorially more accurate, tolerably adequate picture of how we arrive at the would-be laws of nature, especially in physics and chemistry (for instance, in approximating to the instrumental use of the ideal-gas law, which is itself part of a favored picture of the world rather than an assured approximation to the supposedly real nomological invariances of independent nature).[2]

I venture to say that all such efforts acknowledge, epistemologically and methodologically, the insuperable entanglements of the earthbound role of the human person, the investigative agent of every inquiry—to speak with Kant but against Kant's doctrine—in both science and morality. The change of emphasis has yielded a new sort of open-ended tidiness willing to come to terms with the general untidiness and historied limitations of the human mind and the opportunistic specimen glimpses we rely on in our efforts to understand and control the world we experience as well as to bring our own behavior (or conduct) into accord with whatever we believe we may have discovered.

This change in attitude about the would-be laws of nature (a fortiori, the would-be rules or principles or laws of human intention or commitment or conduct) is hardly a small adjustment: it's the difference between an ancient confidence in a closed and completely legible universe (God's providential order, say) and the daring of a modern reading of Protagoras's dictum "man is the measure," which renders the likelihood of nomological closure profoundly doubtful since it must rely on humanly constructed evidence (focused from a vantage we cannot completely fathom or fix). I see in this a clue to the rise and fall of Kantian and post-Kantian idealist philosophy and, if I may speak here as a partisan, a clue to the ulterior force of Charles Peirce's "correction" of rationalism's hubris regarding the reach of human inquiry. In fact, it's here that I've supposed that Peirce begins to grasp the potentially misleading import of his own early conception of the infinite "long run"—by way of a comparison with Kant's transcendental presumption or, further, with Fichtean and Schellingian speculations intended to capture rational systematicity beyond the Kantian transcendental. For Kant was unable to answer (robustly) the idealist question: What are the conditions of possibility of transcendental philosophy?[3] What are the evidentiary differences between transcendental and empirical claims? And Peirce, contrary to canonical readings of his own texts, was, from the very beginning of his career, deeply skeptical about Kant's transcendentalism—hence, also, uncertain of the validity of his own idealist proclivities. I take this impasse to provide the effective inspiration for Peirce's ultimate "abductive turn," and I take the abductive turn to apply to normative as well as causal claims, though in ways that cannot pretend to adhere to principles.[4] It's Kant's tidiness that betrays the insuperable implausibility of his Critical vision, something akin to the closure and systematicity of a rational Creation, the plan of which proves to have been imprinted in humankind's dependent powers of Reason, partly but splendidly in Newton's physics, at the very least.

Bas van Fraassen, one of the more recent theorists of science I have in mind, in reconsidering the conceptual fortunes of nomologicality (meant to apply to nature and human behavior and conduct alike), offers a very pretty cameo representation of the earthbound bricolage this new sort of scientific narrative depends on, applied (say) to Newton's speculations:

> Think of how Newton proceeds to deduce the laws of motion for our solar system. Keeping his basic laws of mechanics as foundation, he adds the law of gravitation to describe this universe, then he adds that there is one sun and six planets to describe our solar system, and he finally adds that there is one moon to describe the more immediate gravitational forces on our planet Earth. Newton demonstrates that from a very idealized, simplified description of the solar system, something approximating the known phenomena follows. . . . What's the point of deriving true conclusions from a false premise?

It leads, van Fraassen assures us, to noticing "this deep assumption at work": namely, that "if certain conditions follow from the ideal case, then approximately those conditions will follow from an approximation to the ideal case. . . . [And] this assumption is in force when we have recourse to any model that we do not presume to be more than approximately similar to what it represents, but especially in the case of laboratory simulation." Van Fraassen warns us that this cannot be regarded "as a context-independent methodological principle, given its phrasing": it relies on "similarity in certain respects, with other aspects ignored as irrelevant for all practical purposes—[that is, for] the purposes at hand." Elsewhere in his account, he reminds us that the descriptive and predictive power of the ideal-gas law (familiar under the names of Boyle's Law, Charles's Law, and similar formulations) gains precision with its subsumption under the kinetic theory of gases (as that theory itself matures), as well as with fortuitous improvements in thermometry.[5] But the earthbound, improvisational informality of the entire process remains the essential lesson. (I'd say van Fraassen relies on strategies akin to an abductive logic.) A method of this sort cannot possibly yield a conception of the empirical discovery of exceptionless, necessary laws of nature. Behind these contingencies, the question looms: Do we need the laws of nature at all?

Hence, if we abandon cognitive privilege and foundationalism, admit the artifactual nature of persons, and find no conceptual disadvantage accruing to the theory and practice of science wherever we yield up the assurance that the laws of nature must be (are) demonstrably necessary and exceptionlessly universal, then, at the very least, any categorical claim of normative duty à la Kant—by way of analogy with the laws of nature, say—is likely to be insuperably difficult (effectively, impossible) to confirm. Moral norms, in fact agentive norms of every kind, suddenly risk appearing as no more than culturally, perhaps even idiosyncratically entrenched. Remove Kant's argument from any pretense of rational autonomy, I say, and Kant becomes a local ideologue.

You see at once, therefore, how the addition of abductive liberties enhances our tolerance of conceptual informality and risk in fashioning acceptable explanatory models in the sciences (and elsewhere)—as in Cassirer's endorsement of Hertz's and Helmholtz's loosening of the "regulative" strictures entailed in Kant's "copy theory" of Newtonian explanation and in van Fraassen's (and Nancy Cartwright's) eclipsing the need for strict nomological closure (supported in different ways), against Carl Hempel's scruple, say. You see in this the telltale insecurity of Kantian determinacies and the streetwise confidence of pragmatist guesses. There's the nerve of the deepest contests of Western philosophy: the agon between invariance and flux qualified by the aporiae of epistemology.

I shall apply this line of reasoning in appraising Kant's famous argument in support of the paradigmatic role of the categorical imperative. But I must add at once that I'm not primarily interested in any closely reasoned textual criticism of Kant's moral philosophy, and I'm not interested in restricting the normative to moral questions or to featuring only moral applications. I address normativity generically, wherever it arises. But I know no account of the normative in any part of the philosophical canon that is as firmly, as concisely, as uncompromisingly and maximally committed to the obligatory, or as exclusively addressed to the power of rational judgment as is Kant's claim regarding moral choices.

There's an argumentative advantage to be gained here, at Kant's expense.

On the premise, then, that the telltale vulnerabilities of Kant's superb but unsuccessful effort may speed our grasp of the entire play of normativity, I venture to sketch the main objections to Kant's argument, with an eye to the prospects of logically weaker, diverse claims of familiar or plausible normative sorts ranging over any appropriate sector of inquiry: legal, political, medical, educational, artistic, athletic, civilizational, or the like. Here, for convenience and the advantage of its ample and confident application, I avail myself of Christine Korsgaard's overview of the Kantian claim, though I'm perfectly aware that Korsgaard's reading of Kant will be thought (by some, or perhaps by many) to be inaccurate, unorthodox, and not authoritative enough in any textual sense to be relied on. I don't believe the liberty I favor will adversely affect the reasonableness of my counterargument: I shall be using Kant and Korsgaard largely to gain a footing in favor of an entirely different treatment of normativity, so that if the general analogy I'm hinting at regarding normative constraints on causal explanation in the physical sciences and on obligation in the broadly Kantian sense seems reasonable (even if unexpected), we may have gained a quick march on the general analysis of normativity with very little labor.

We tend to forget the earthbound cast of the strongest sciences themselves as well as the significance of the principle and practice of approximation in the sciences. But if we bear in mind the implications of the artifactuality of persons (in addition to the artifactuality of science), we must realize that we've taken a very bold step toward grasping the completely vulnerable, earthbound contingency of the concept of normativity (and of nomologicality), although, I must remind you, artifactuality does not entail and is not the equivalent of fictionality. The three notions—normativity, nomologicality, and artifactuality—I take to be intimately linked. They count, conjointly, as a heterodox premise—utterly opposed to Kant's triumphal penchant for rationalist systematicity. Valuing, even the comparison of goods and values, surely has some application within the unlanguaged animal world, though it need not (and does not, among languageless animals) implicate normative judgment. (Think, for instance, of monkeys preferring the bananas of one tree to those of another or finicky cats' taste in canned cat food.) These distinctions are open to extreme empiricists and rationalists alike—hence, also, to realists and antirealists regarding science and morality.

Nevertheless, questions of normativity arise only among persons, because normativity (unlike valuing) entails discursivity and because the issue of normative choices answers to *nothing in the world prior* to the advent of language and the emergence of persons. There are no normative issues for chimpanzees or clams (in the wild), though there are (or may be) pertinent incipiences among pets and trained animals among the higher mammals.

It's generally acknowledged that only humans occupy themselves with specifically normative matters—let's say, with questions of grading and ranking goods and values along determinate scales of conventionally ordered degrees of worth. It may be usefully remarked, here, that the concession has almost no bearing on impugning the would-be objective validity or universal force of the most ancient of moral and legal norms, essentially (I surmise) because the thesis of the artifactuality of persons and the coupling of the emergence of persons and language (as being the obverse sides of the same process) is, even now, barely acknowledged in philosophy and the human sciences. I suppose the revealed status of the Mosaic law and the Code of Hammurabi is, at the very least, read as a metaphor for affirming the universal validity of such pronouncements.

I don't mean, in mentioning these impressive specimens, to suggest (let me say again) that normativity is essentially or primarily confined to moral matters. Not at all. The concept and practices of normative judgment undoubtedly infect every human activity that has any rational or intellectual presumption. It certainly plays an essential role in the theory of truth and objective knowledge in the sciences, and it will be part of my brief that the normativity question cannot be answered uniformly, as far as truth and objectivity are concerned, across all the kinds of inquiries in which pertinent judgments are made. For instance, in the setting of organized sports, normative appraisals of performance are often treated as effectively equivalent to determining causal (valuationally neutral) outcomes of compared performances; any attempt to construe the Mosaic Commandments in a similar way is bound to be resisted—at least for reasons that bear on conceptual differences among generically different kinds of norms.

There *seems* to be no way of positing a normatively neutral range of acknowledged facts the admission of which logically entails normative appraisals of a decidedly moral sort. That, at least, is the standard view. Normativity, like linguistic meaning, which may be drawn into a related quarrel (that I've hinted at in *Toward a Metaphysics of Culture*, in mentioning Donald Davidson's paper "Radical Interpretation"), is culturally (or Intentionally) emergent (*emergent$_I$*) in a sense (already noted) opposed to the emergence of the macroscopic physical world (*emergent$_m$*), itself open in principle to reductionism and inter-level physicalist identities or pragmatically supported "counterpart replacements" short of identity.[6] (Frankly, such replacements are mongrel, not straightforwardly inferential.) Nevertheless, questions of normativity *seem* to arise as readily as questions of discursivity—in linked ways and uniquely with regard to the competences of persons, say with respect to purposive reflection and autonomy.

Normativity is, admittedly, a relatively circumscribed topic, but its conceptual boundaries are in good part defined in terms of what has been gained in inquiries already ventured. It must be canvassed in conformity with what's gone before if we are ever to complete a rounded picture of the unique features of the metaphysics of culture: those, for instance, needed in launching (on some fresh occasion) an account of the complex relationship between the physical and human sciences; in opposing certain orthodoxies dominant in both scientific inquiry and moral judgment; in acknowledging the hybrid artifactuality of persons and the Intentionality of their enlanguaged worlds or cultures; in conceding the opposed sorts of emergence manifested in our macroscopic world that qualify and vouchsafe the intertwined compatibility of causality and freedom; in admitting the sui generis complexity of Intentional things; in coming to terms with the historicity of human inquiry; and in grasping the asymmetrical interdependence of anything said to be actual, as belonging among material and Intentional things.

In all of this, the need for a congruent theory of normativity proves essential, especially in delineating a fresh theory of the human sciences. Put more quarrelsomely, the argument is meant to outflank the principal agon of Kantian and post-Kantian philosophy down to our own day: that is, the contest between the strongest claims of transcendental apriorism (and idealist systematicity) and reductive materialism. I take both sorts of programs (standard models of the human and physical sciences) to be fatally flawed. My conviction has it that neither is, finally, viable or recuperable and that the defeat of either or both hardly disallows the recovery of temperate elements (of normativity) drawn from either extreme within the terms of a new conceptual constellation (that is now slowly taking form).

My intuition favors pragmatism. But, then, the inherent laxities of philosophy and science (which already count as an essential plank in pragmatism's platform) recognize that if there is one plausible way of conceiving the coherence of the human venture, there must be many ways of doing so, which, nevertheless, cannot be easily read as supporting the objective discovery of any noble norms of life telically fitted to the human condition.

The artifactuality of persons precludes their possessing (inherently or essentially, in any legible way) any determinate purpose or function in the world at large, including such permissives or obligatives as "be fruitful and multiply" or, more challengingly, "act only according to that maxim by which you can at the same time will that it should become a universal law,"[7] although it's also true that humans are unable to live without the conviction that they possess purposes firm enough to make persuasive sense of their own conative constancy. There you glimpse the pathos of the normative. But then, it is almost impossible to mention any self-consistent commitments, however bizarre, compatible with the survival of relatively complex societies, that have not been favored, somewhere or in some age, by one society or another. It's my conjecture that Kant never felt the pressing need, when writing the first *Critique*, to explain the supposed competence of the transcendental *Ich*. On the contrary, there's every evidence that Kant was aware that he ought not dwell on the matter in too detailed a way, lest he encumber (thereby) his theory with paradigmatic applications that might hobble his solutions of even more important puzzles of coherence in the process of pursuing the main lines of the theory. The *Ich denke* (as Kant says) simply accompanies his speculations. But then, the artifactualist thesis—a broadly empirical claim—must count as the pivot of the deepest challenge to Kant's apriorism (and any comparable rationalism seeking complete systematicity).

These are extremely lax reflections, and yet they lead ineluctably to the single most compelling finding about normativity that we could possibly muster. I mean the arresting fact that there is no objective sign, in nature, of the normative calling of the species, despite the further fact that the race has a huge archival history of competing visions and options of how humankind should live and has actually lived—morally, politically, religiously, educationally, civilizationally, economically, idiosyncratically—from the conceptual debris of which we seem to be able to construct just about any conceivably viable option, without being able to define any one or several such options that the preponderant part of the race can (or must) assuredly support—rationally or timelessly—at any given time. I think it entirely possible that the advanced technologies of our day (and others that have yet to be invented) may, in time, homogenize the world's "agentive" norms (as I shall call them), those that claim to posit the highest goals of human aspiration. But, then, such a uniformity may be no more than the effect of civilizational inertia or subtraction rather than of any essentialist confirmation of the true targets of human life. I need only remind you of Max Weber's thesis regarding the rise of "instrumental reason" and his interpretation of Friedrich Schiller's phrase the "disenchantment of the world," a theme whose apparent threat has provoked a recuperative response from John McDowell (a little late in the day perhaps) along distinctly Kantian lines. (I shall come back to McDowell's treatment of Weber's distinction.)[8] But it does seem fair to concede that a literal-minded realism or cognitivism regarding agentive norms—apart from the logically trivial import of *sittlich* norms (by no means a negligible matter)—is, admitting the artifactuality of persons, effectively impossible to defend.

I won't apologize for the scatter I'm inviting. It's an essential part of my argument that, for one thing, the concept of the normative hangs by a very slim thread on the artifactual nature of selves or persons and that, for another, to admit that that's true is to expose the unearned presumption of all our stalemated inquiries in search, especially, of the validating grounds of agentive norms, the would-be higher or highest norms of purpose and aspiration that the human race claims to have discerned as a matter of course.

I'm persuaded that, on post-Darwinian evidence, going beyond the arguments of the philosophical anthropologists (Helmuth Plessner, most notably), the human primate has no ecological niche in the world (as do all other familiar species fitted to Darwin's theory) suited to any sort of biologically defined agentive norms or agentive teleology—answering, in a way, to the import of Plessner's "ex-centric" notion of positionality. The human creature, as we say, bends the world to his changeable purposes: there is no sense in which he can bring his purpose into accord with his biology, except in the merely enabling sense, instrumentally, which, it may not unfairly be concluded, ignores the entire point of admitting autonomy with regard to agentive norms.

Persons, as I've argued, are artifactual creatures, functionally unique transforms (formed largely by the mastery of natural language and whatever local culture a local language subtends), who *find themselves* already *gebildet* along normative lines that are also artifactual transforms of primate dispositions. We are, I say, hybrid creatures in that sense. We think and act purposively—telically, if you wish—because we are uniquely reflexive creatures, but our agentive norms and normative goals risk being arbitrary or ungrounded because such goals engage us as reflective *selves* but fit legibly (if they fit at all) our physical and biological and encultured circumstances only in the enabling way.

There's a discrepancy there that we can never overcome conceptually, though in practice we are forever absorbed with one or another run of agentive goals. I call these *second best* (following a suggestion of Plato's) because they succeed surprisingly well, *motivationally*, though they can never escape their artifactual provenance and their radically changeable, diverse, profoundly contested mongrel standing. That is indeed the pathos of the human condition, affecting both science and morality. Kant simply overrides such concerns, but he could not have anticipated the relevance of the Darwinian discoveries in his appraisal of Newton's achievements.

If you allow this part of my theory to stand, then, I say, the analysis of the normative is not difficult to complete. The emergence of the normative is inseparable from the emergence of the transformed powers of rational reflection, purpose, capacity for choice and deliberate agency—and our susceptibility to the endless forms of second-best persuasion that Nietzsche, for one, never tires of obliging us to confront. Whatever doctrine we adopt here by which to justify our normative preferences is bound to be constrained, in societal ways, by the enabling boundaries of the causal order of nature, the biological saliencies of species life, *and* the entrenched habits of interpreted history, prudential interests, and envisioned possibilities of human intervention and evolving experience. What's missing—what cannot be captured—are any assuredly independent grounds on which, within such limits, the true norms of human life (cognitive as well as agentive) may be finally discovered. (I take this to collect the meaning of Sellars's arresting phrase "the space of reasons.")

I put my own answer before you now, near the start of this particular inquiry, because it would seem too weak a finding if it were postponed until the end of an extended search. For if I'm right at all, then the rest of this chapter's account cannot fail to include a confirmation of the aimlessness and arbitrariness of a great many discussions of objective norms that simply avoid the full force of the post-Darwinian exposé. I confine my efforts along these lines to little more than the Kantian tradition: to Kant himself, to the neo-Kantians, to the Pittsburgh School, to the Frankfurt School, to recent revivals of Kant's moral theory and its bearing on the "required" closure of legal argument and the like. My point is not, however, dismissive or negative or deflationary in any way. On the contrary, I'm prepared to argue that normative inquiry succeeds in its second-best way, though *not* (for that reason) by recovering any resource that might restore us to the presumption of a self-validating science or practice of a noncircular kind. It succeeds in the *sittlich* way—which is also true (though with a different force) among the natural sciences—and, in normative matters, the *sittlich* is indeed conceptually adequate to its task. It will not seem so, however, wherever we are tempted by the extravagance that our agentive norms are finally validated by the rigor of Reason or the nature of Nature (or something of the kind) but that is the deception I wish to expose.[9]

II

I return to Kant and Korsgaard, therefore, to gain a march on normativity, which I've suggested lies ready for the taking, if we read the clue that beckons from recent treatments of the laws of nature in the physical sciences. If I understand the arguments of Bas van Fraassen, Nancy Cartwright, Otto Neurath, and numerous other recent and current theorists regarding the logic of the laws of nature, then, first, we cannot demonstrate empirically or on grounds shorn of epistemic privilege that the laws of nature we approximate are, in principle, necessary a priori or necessarily universal; second, none of the confirmable advantages of causal explanation involving nomological regularities are put at risk by admitting that the *form* of a valid law of nature need not be either necessary or universal; and, third, there is therefore no compelling sense in which *reason* obliges us to construe would-be laws of nature as conceptually impossible (or self-defeating) if they prove to be less than necessary or less than universal. Cartwright argues that would-be physical laws, cast as strict universals, cannot fail to have deformed testable uniformities, as they reach for exceptionlessness; Ronald Giere redeems such laws, more as models than as truth-bearing claims, fitted to aspects of an observational field of inquiry—always with the caveat that though Cartwright's "laws" (qua models) need not be "lies," it remains true enough that "one can have scientific judgment without rationality"[10]—in a sense I'm on the point of introducing.

The Kantian account of normativity is, admittedly, immensely complicated, but I find nothing in it that obliges us to concede that causal laws are, if true, necessarily true or necessarily universal or that, if validly binding in practice (that is, not literally true or false), they are necessarily or universally binding (or binding on all rational beings, if that is not trivially construed). Furthermore, these and similar concessions hold as well for

Korsgaard's explications and glosses regarding Kant's texts, even where we may wish to question or challenge her particular extension, emendation, or application of Kant's express views (as in the *Foundations of the Metaphysics of Morals*). What, however, Korsgaard provides in the way of clarification both catches up the most salient and robust readings of Kant in recent years and, rather innocently, confirms the pertinence of pressing the analogy of "law" used in causal arguments in the physical sciences and in Kantian disputes involving moral norms—hence, in the all-too-easy slippage among the alleged demands of Reason.

Korsgaard correctly construes Kant's argument leading to the unconditional ("rational") obligation to act in accord with the categorical imperative—in the form cited just above, or in other versions of the same obligation, tendered elsewhere in the *Foundations*—as a matter of human freedom (or autonomy). In short, she pits freedom and determinism against one another—in effect, causality and autonomy—but resolves any worries about whether we can act freely or responsibly at all by arguments designed to demonstrate that "determinism is no threat to freedom."[11] She regards Kant's solution of the freedom/determinism dispute as relieving us of the notorious regress argument (the regress of causes), and, indeed, Kant's answer does put an end to the regress problem, though at the high cost of an impossibly strong disjunction (as far as mortal humans are concerned) between freedom and causality.

Now, I want to accord Korsgaard as much liberty as she needs, in order to present her version of the Kantian argument in a way that can withstand doubts about her textual fidelity to Kant. One reasonable way of ensuring the latitude needed is to characterize her thesis as a Kantian view, though doubtless not Kant's own: well, for one thing, Korsgaard very carefully avoids invoking any usual form of transcendental or apriorist necessity or self-evidence, whereas Kant's entire argument (in the *Foundations*) requires that Reason remain a faculty capable of manifesting freedom or autonomy, precisely *because* it *does not* belong to the causal (natural) order of the human body. But then Kant cannot claim any natural advantage for his agentive paradigm.

Here, I must admit, though I won't press the argument against Korsgaard, that I take the assumption to be an insurmountable weakness in Kant's claim (ranging over the whole of his Critical philosophy): effectively, Kant's rational agent or rational being is not entirely a human being! In my view, even if one opposes the artifactualist thesis, causality and freedom remain conceptually inseparable: humans exhibit autonomy because they come under certain favorable causal influences in their *Bildung* and because freedom and purposive choice and commitment entail the operative instrumentalities of bodily movement.[12]

Korsgaard explicitly acknowledges that "Kant says that" the version of the categorical imperative she cites from the *Foundations* (which I've cited above) "is equivalent to acting as though your maxim were by your will to become a law of nature, and he [Kant] uses this latter formulation in his examples of how the imperative is to be applied." She pointedly notes that Kant relies on the (would-be) logical properties of a "law of nature."[13] In any case, here is how Korsgaard explains Kant's Formula of Universal Law— the first formulation of the categorical imperative—cited in *The Sources of Normativity*, which, as it happens, was published in the same year as her *Creating the Kingdom of Ends*:

> "Reason" means reflective success. So if I decide that my desire is a reason to act, I must decide that on reflection I endorse that desire. . . . [But] how do I decide that? . . . Kant . . . describ ed this problem in terms of freedom. He defines a free will as a rational causality which is effective without being determined by any alien cause. Anything outside of the will counts as an alien cause, including the desires and inclinations of the person. The free will must be entirely self-determining. Yet, because the will is a causality, it must act according to some law or other. Kant says: "Since the concept of a causality entails that of laws . . . it follows that freedom is by no means lawless."[14]

Fine, although all of this is entirely obiter dictum. But then Korsgaard takes up Kant's problem as her own. *She* needs Kant's doctrine of autonomy in order to defend her own variant of the Kantian solution:

> Since reasons are derived from principles, the free will must have a principle. But because the will is free, no law or principle can be imposed on it from outside. Kant concludes that the will must be autonomous: that is, it must have its *own* law or principle. . . . [But] where is this law to come from? If it is imposed on the will from outside than the will is not free. So the will must make the law for itself. But until the will has a law or principle, there is nothing from which you can derive a reason.

Extraordinary! Here, she gives "Kant's answer," which she also adopts:

> The categorical imperative, as represented by the Formula of Universal Law, tells us to act only on a maxim which we could will to be a law. And *this*, according to Kant, *is* the law of a free will. . . . *All that it has to be is a law.* . . . The categorical imperative merely tells us to choose a law. Its only constraint on our choice is that it has the form of a law. And nothing determines what the law must be. *All that it has to be is a law.*

Therefore, the categorical imperative is the law of a free will.[15]

It's not at all clear what it means to speak of "all" rational beings acting together in any normal circumstance—except, say, in coming to the same judgment or conclusion (which doesn't bear on the problem posed); similarly, it's just unclear what might be meant by its being possible that "all rational beings" could act together on *anything* substantive, except (once again) in agreeing in judgment or verdict or something of the sort—which is improbable. I'm afraid Korsgaard has simply failed to see the conceptual danger in insisting on an agent's merely satisfying the condition of a maxim's *taking the form* of a universal law of nature, for, as Hegel and others have shown, the merely formal requirement can be met in a trivial way even where our moral intuitions disapprove. I see no way of saving either Kant's or Korsgaard's proposal.[16]

The formula, of course, is a disaster. Put another way: it's as apriorist as it can be, despite Korsgaard's deliberate avoidance of any explicit transcendentalism. The idea that all rational beings are essentially committed to maxims of action that can serve as universal laws (in no more than a purely formal sense) is utterly arbitrary or arbitrarily apriorist or simply mistaken. There is no substantive argument in Kant or Korsgaard to demonstrate that human reason is bound to adhere to formal maxims that can serve as universal laws of nature, and there is no known ground on which it can be shown that merely to adhere to any such formula bears in any pertinent way on ensuring freedom or autonomy or moral validity, or that there is any compelling inferential connection moving from universality to valid norms of any kind. Once you allow "indicative" or local conditions of application (Armstrong's concern), the form of law can be applied (without nomological or moral uptake) as generously as you please. (I think of the case of the Reichstag fire during the Nazi days. We are philosophical somnambulists here.)

Both Kant's and Korsgaard's arguments are non sequiturs; furthermore, there appear to be no signs of having chosen freely (in Kant's or Korsgaard's sense), apart from the universal form of the maxims we select—which seems preposterous. Or if there are moral criteria, then, for one thing, they need not (or cannot) disallow heteronomous causes that do not overwhelm one's having chosen as a free agent, and, for another, Korsgaard must be mistaken—and Kant as well, if her reading of Kant is correct—since, on the grounds mentioned, what is morally tenable is not (cannot be) sufficiently decided on evidence of mere agency (if, say, an evil act may or must also be freely chosen).

Kant's thesis is surely a house of cards: it continually requires emergency measures to salvage the doctrine of the autonomy (and necessity) of self-legislation—for beings (instantiations of Kant's *Ich*) that are hardly human. Concede the dependence of human freedom on the selective causality of human *Bildung*, deny the need for (perhaps even the practical possibility of) exceptionless causal laws (as among the sciences): Kant's immensely influential claim evaporates without a murmur. Furthermore, as has already been shown, the autonomy of human action is not essentially a causal but a conceptual matter: agents cannot be said to cause the actions they utter or bring about, consistently with the externality of causes; whatever causal factors prove to be pertinent belong to bodily movements that incarnate uttered actions or whatever incarnates the intentions and purposes of effective agents.[17]

There's little to salvage from either Kant or Korsgaard. But if Kant fails here, then the entire idea of demonstrating the validity of unconditional duty or obligation will seem more than improbable, and we shall be obliged to fall back to weaker, less ambitious forms of support, whether in morality or in another quarter in which normativity also obtains. And there, of course, other conceptual hazards are bound to arise—as Kant was well aware—which he wished to avoid, at least until he could establish sufficient grounds for acknowledging the primacy of the categorical imperative. Kant cannot permit autonomous action to be encumbered historically, culturally, psychologically, or in any other causally pertinent way, because that would violate the conditions of rational validity he imposes; but then, of course, to disconnect the validation of action from *all* such linkages is to make every effort to locate objective grounds for normative validity—apart from the formal considerations already discounted—impossible to invoke.

Normativity is as essential, ubiquitous, and unique a reflexive human concern as any that can be named: we cannot afford to place it in conceptual jeopardy in Kant's way. But the whole of our biology and cultural history fails to disclose any conceptually compelling grounds on which agentive norms (norms concerned with the exercise of what we regard as human autonomy or freedom or flourishing) may be objectively confirmed, as distinct from the confirmation of mere enabling norms (norms concerned with consistency of reasoning; success in acquiring non-value-laden information about the environing world; and possibly even improved conditions of strength, health, security, technical skills, and the like that may help, instrumentally, to complete any and all of our ventures, regardless of agentive merit).

The contrast between agentive and enabling norms is a functional one: I see no reason to deny that what may serve in one context as an enabling norm may, in another, count as an agentive norm. The difference is a logical one, in the elementary sense that the idiom of enabling norms can often be replaced, without yielding up any intended meaning, by a causal idiom (or operatively effective equivalent) that permits us to omit explicit reference to the normative itself. A similar replacement of would-be agentive norms is, however, thought to deprive us of the highest substantive distinctions of normative ordering (effectively: of grading and ranking practices of every conceivable sort), especially where judgment and commitment regarding the nobler concerns of human life are said to be at stake. Here, the issue takes an existential turn because, of course, it's subject to deep puzzles generated by what I've called the Darwinian effect—the abandonment of teleologism and the resultant aporia of attempting to provide objective norms under the condition of the artifactuality of the human person.[18]

Bear in mind, please, that the most telling finding, here, rests with the fact that enabling norms (as of logical reasoning or bodily fitness) tend to yield to nonnormative equivalences, but agentive norms (moral, political, vocational, civilizational) normally do not. The difference is decisive. For, for one thing, it confirms the objective parity of propositions invoking enabling norms and nonnormative (causal, arithmetic, logical, and related) equivalences drawn from well-entrenched natural and formal resources. And, for another, it marks the completely different logic of the normative reflection involved in any societal endorsement of specifically agentive norms—which, I daresay, is precisely Sellars's primary concern. If so, then the Pittsburghers have surely misread Sellars.

I treat equivalences of the first sort as pragmatic (and mongrel) rather than semantic or logical: hence, as validating tolerable replacements (in this or that context of interest—instrumentally) rather than as true (in the way of formal reductions or identities of the distinctly extensionalist cast). The point is that they depend on practical decisions in vivo rather than on the right application of a formal rule already in place—canonically. To adopt the distinction effectively confirms the inherently subaltern status of inferentialism itself because, of course, there literally *are* no pragmatic inferentiables in play (in normal agentive contexts) until agents (or onlookers) commit themselves to construing events this way or that. It's not the primacy of inference that counts, therefore; it's the complexity of pragmatic interpretation linking enabling and agentive norms. (But, if so, then Brandom and Rorty have got the cart before the horse, and McDowell has simply misjudged the innovative intent of Sellars's "space of reasons." It's more a matter of disciplining Dewey's themes than of relaxing Frege's.)

The ulterior question we shall come to concerns how the validation of the nobler or higher agentive norms can be managed (at all) within the terms of these findings. Part of my answer advises that we fall back to what I shall call second-best solutions, in the light of the historical contingencies of the artifactuality of persons and their enlanguaged cultures and the sheer vacuity of the mere form of universality. I see no prospect of a stronger recovery, but I do see the likelihood of at least that much of a gain. Here, I give fair warning that Sellars loses his way in trying to reconcile the "manifest" and "scientific images" and that Kant's agentive formalism becomes increasingly irrelevant in practical life. Still, it's worth remarking that Sellars seems to have discounted this side of Kant's would-be contribution.

III

There are no a priori constraints affecting the central core of agentive norms (ultimate norms, let us say, concerned with the meaning and purpose of human life) that are not projected—stipulated by sheer fiat (troublingly or benignly)—from the contingent interests of the artifactual, second-natured creatures we take ourselves to be, and, in truth, the very existence (the sheer emergence) of persons is, serendipitously, little more than the verso of the ancient invention of language (that is, diverse natural languages and the cultures they subtend)—a fortiori, the same stunning happenstance on the strength of which normative questions confront us pertinently all the time. Normative concerns obtain wherever persons evolve. But there is no rational necessity in that, in determining the true agentive norms of the species. The survival of the species hardly requires adherence to the categorical imperative or to any recognizably rational plan; formal universality cannot distinguish satisfactorily between admittedly moral and immoral conduct; and, under the contingent conditions of actual human life, a prudent accommodation of wanton agentive norms and heteronomous impulses may appear to be as rational, normatively, as any utopian adherence to the formal requirements of the categorical imperative.

Let me insert, here, a helpful phrasing of Wilfrid Sellars's that marks one way to construe the entire range of the discursive side of human life (whether thought or spoken—or danced, for that matter) as coextensive with the normative. We shall find reason to return to Sellars's reflections on the normative. Here, at least, is what he affirms: "the most fundamental principles of a community, which define what is 'correct' or 'incorrect,' 'right' or 'wrong,' 'done' or 'not done,' are the most general common *intentions* of that community with respect to the behavior of members of the group."[19] This is, of course, a frank admission of the primacy of the *sittlich*: it signals no criterial resources beyond the *sittlich*. On the contrary, the *sittlich*, as actually and pertinently *intended* within a living community, adequately determines (confers and confirms) the valid standing of some designated set of agentive norms. Sellars's formula is all but Rousseauesque. Kant, of course, is also effectively captured by the *sittlich* forces of his Pietist world, but *he* believes he's testing the validity of the supposed maxims of his (and our) actions by applying aprioristic criteria beyond the merely *sittlich* (the self-legislating powers of rational autonomy, say). Sellars acknowledges the normative validity of the (true) *sittlich* itself; the field anthropologist merely reports the pertinent practices and convictions of the society they're examining: the question of the objective validity of its *sittlich* norms never arises there.

McDowell excuses Kant's lapse into the transcendental: Kant, he concedes, was unwilling to place his philosophical constraints within the bounds of nature! An extraordinary apology. But then, McDowell does not reject Kant's argument: he simply applies a little of the oil of his Wittgensteinian quietism to it; he does not commit himself, pro or con. Sellars is speaking of the norms of flesh-and-blood persons. So is Kant, but *his* selves (his agents) are only distantly related to the human. (Here and there, in Sellars's sprawling oeuvre, there are hints that he may have been attracted to something akin to the Darwinian effect in reflecting on second-natured humans.) But the idea may not fit very easily with the rest of Sellars's general strategy. McDowell, who offers a rather severe critique of Sellars, is not inclined to yield at all. In any case, if you accept Sellars's formulation, then neither universality nor necessity rightly counts as assured marks of autonomy or agentive normativity. Quite simply, Sellars features no more than what is given in the contingencies of societal life. But then, nothing more *can* be rightly given, *if*, as I say, persons are encultured artifacts.

My own argument, therefore, proceeds faute de mieux. Normativity is thoroughly artifactual; hence, it cannot be more than *sittlich*, though we take it to be more, if the *sittlich* is read in the anthropologist's way. The only possible enlargement of the idea that I can see is that the *sittlich*, in a sense close to Sellars's usage, *is* entitled to claim an objective function of its own, even with regard to the revision of agentive norms. Still, as thoroughly artifactual (contingent, changeable, parochial, contentious, disputed), it cannot be more than second best—though it can be at least that, and that much appears to be sufficient for our purpose. Thus construed, the *sittlich* functions civilizationally, in all sectors of agentive flourishing or concern.

Kant grasps the inseparability of the concepts of normativity and discursivity, but that does not bear as yet on either universality or necessity. (Kant cannot think of discursivity as paleoanthropologically *dated*, regarding *Homo sapiens* and the contingent advent of persons: the admission would lead to the contingency of agentive norms themselves.) Furthermore, in the eighteenth century, Kant could hardly have fashioned a convincing conception of the self's adventitious artifactuality, which, once admitted, could not have failed to affect our notions of the right criteria of morality and other agentive norms. The entire force of the first *Critique* teeters on that limitation—hence, also, the fortunes of the whole of modern philosophy, if you can believe it. Kant has no defenses to offer once the apriorist presumptions of *Vernunft* are called into question. Post-Darwin, human reason is itself regarded as an artifactual and historied competence reflexively applied, especially with regard to agentive matters. The very idea that agentively informed reason, as distinct from the diverse forms of enabling reason (the use of logic or arithmetic, for instance), is likely to discern normative duties that are at once demonstrably and universally valid seems utterly indefensible—effectively, irresponsible—whether in Kant's or Korsgaard's hands, or in Jürgen Habermas's or Karl-Otto Apel's, for that matter, or in Peirce's or Frege's, *or in ours* (in our dangerous world).

The corollary I draw from all this is that normativity, both agentive and enabling, originates as a fait accompli, as no more than a *sittlich* (or anthropological) regularity reflexively discerned to have been already in place before we had the wit to grasp the fact, ranging over competing, usually narrowly circumscribed, often incompatible, even incommensurable, bizarre, and conflicting claims. But, also, let me add, in the spirit of philosophical candor, regularities that continue to serve—that must be very nearly the only adequate resource we have—by altering and adjusting which we process and rationally resolve whatever second-order quarrels about the grounds and sources of normative convictions may confront us. Of course, this will seem outrageous to the tribunal of philosophy's history spanning ancient beginnings and present times: there is barely a mention of the artifactuality of the self in the whole of philosophy's narrative. (Somnambulism run rampant.) But that *is* indeed the nerve of my brief: normativity is thoroughly *sittlich*, largely parochial; it can hardly be counted on to provide demonstrably privileged sources by which to validate our claims or legitimate our validative practices before any universal tribunal. Something of the same holds true of truth and knowledge in general—though I remind you that that need not spell disaster. It confirms, however, the intuition that the analyses of science and normativity *are* systematically intertwined.

There's the saving theme: namely, that the objectivity of agentive norms could never be more than second best—meaning that, although any would-be empirical or rational discovery of true or objective norms based, say, on the biology of the species will have been rendered all but impossible (as a direct consequence of the artifactual, historied, and contingent formation of agentive selves), it will nevertheless remain possible to construct a debater's space of reduced presumption regarding the ordered merit of artifactual norms or of proposals based on *sittlich* values.[20] We should, of course, have to rely on the discursive powers of the persons we take ourselves to be and on some reasoned selection of the *sittlich* norms we deem promising and congenial. I argue only that that must be essentially what we do, even now, in matters involving agentive norms of any and every kind. There is no antecedent account to show that the validation or objective standing of agentive norms (of any kind) must take a universal form or be open to independent discovery. (We cannot vouchsafe that the laws of nature must take an exceptionless universal or invariant form, and we cannot show that strict universality is required in moral and other agentive matters.) But if so, then the objective standing of such norms (governing or guiding human life) may be logically very weak indeed, however consensually compelling in one society or another. Hence, it cannot be incoherent for different societies (or the same society, at different times or in different circumstances) to claim and also deny the objective standing of the same candidate norms, if what they mean is that they construe the objectivity of agentive norms in broadly *sittlich* terms or in terms of duly (contingently) endorsed such norms. There can be no doubt that, in itself, such a state of affairs is bound to be a source of considerable strife. (Many societies are prepared to endorse cruelty and violence and otherworldly goals, and to revise such convictions in the most drastic ways, but they are not likely to endorse conceptual chaos.) Agency (at the human level) may be inseparable from normativity—ontologically, so to say—but the validation of any selected agentive norms is another matter entirely. There, rationally (or epistemologically), we cannot exceed second-best conjectures.

Operatively, normative and scientific questions yield profoundly, benignly circular judgments—question-begging, open to insuperable regress, tethered to the *sittlich* (and to the *sittlich*'s ability to revise its own norms in the light of actual application), never more than second best (that is, such that self-appraisal is subject to its own *sittlich* grounding, within the terms of whatever innovations it may propose). But that, I suggest, may be perfectly adequate to our needs. In any case, it's a viable possibility, as rational as and less encumbered than the Kantian alternative—and it begins to seem the only resource we have. The human primate, I remind you, is evolutionarily unique in lacking anything like an ecological niche—hence, lacking any plausible telic basis for its profoundest agentive norms. I suggest that, in matters of knowledge and normative judgment, would-be criteria of validity must accord with the conditions of cultural immersion. We are not without resources, but our resources are contingent, historied, disputed, hostage to interminable quarrel.

You realize, of course, that the whole of the philosophical tradition is put at mortal risk thereby, since it is temperamentally disinclined to acknowledge that all the inquiries of First Philosophy (reconceived as a result of Kant's probing innovations—regarding truth, knowledge, meaning, reality, confirmation, norms) remain insuperably question-begging—inasmuch as the issues they address cannot be answered without making an initial commitment of the same kind meant to establish the pertinence and viability of the inquiry poised to be launched, even when we concede that its own commitment is inseparable from that of the very venture in question. That is precisely what I mean by the accusatory epithet *earthbound*, for the issue of the earthbound, whether in science or morality, is the *sittlich*, and the *sittlich* is the original source of applied normativity and, one may conjecture, of the Kantian transcendental itself.

If you see the inevitable regress among such matters, you see as well the reason I seize the opportunity that dawns adventitiously in the very process of contributing to the resolution of the normativity question to apply its lesson at the same time to "lesser" matters (cognition, for example) that happen to become distinctly more tractable for that reason: in particular, because I intend the answer to any such lesser question to entail answers of a larger holist sort that (in featuring the resolution of the normativity issue) effectively contribute to confirming the diminished standing of the single still-most-powerful voice of modern philosophy—Kant's—that, long ago, had already placed the normativity question and other questions linked to it (the right analysis of rationality, discursivity, agency, cognition, judgment, and the rest of the conceptual powers of the human self) under the well-nigh-impregnable protection of Kant's transcendental defenses. Effectively, the transcendental, in Kant's first *Critique*, is the fruit of the search for the adequate conditions of possibility of any run of *sittlich* knowledge or understanding thought to regulate our grasp of the objective features of the world or the rational liens on thought and action. Hence, Kant's synthetic a priori truths are no better than his Newtonian vision or whatever might replace it. But whether the theory of science must rely on necessary or universal conditions of possibility is a question that forever eludes our cognitive competences as well as the limits of empirical evidence. It's in this sense that Kant's labors lead directly to some form of pragmatist reversal. (That *is*, in fact, the drift of Peirce's argument.)

My essential brief, then, which I dare sketch only in the slimmest way, holds that the analyses of the concepts just collected stand and fall together, so that to show, for instance, that Kant's solution to the problem of empirical realism cannot be recovered in a way that could possibly leave the thesis of the first *Critique* textually intact or demonstrably valid is, effectively, to undermine the Kantian answer to the normativity question as well—and, of course, to advance by such means against other targets of opportunity.

I'm persuaded that Kant's imprimatur is (even now) so important to the academy's reception of arguments meant to determine the true standing of contested concepts as fundamental as normativity that I freely concede we cannot ignore any potentially fresh argumentative surges deliberately deflected along Kantian lines (possibly launched for unearned advantage), even where such targets may in time betray themselves as ultimately fruitless or unproductive. There's the reason I'm unable to treat the question before us as a matter of ensuring autonomy: its resolution cannot fail to be a verdict on the fate and prospects of the whole of "modern" modern philosophy—especially of Kant's and of every contemporary effort to restore a Kantian-inspired solution—within the terms of our own experience.

Let me add a word, now, about how I mean to canvass the matter, a reminder of the original intuition with which I opened this entire study. I'm persuaded that we've been very slow to see that the answer to the question of the nature and validity of normative claims depends essentially on our view of the nature of the human person and that, as a consequence of (what I call) the Darwinian effect—by which I mean the import of the bare evolutionary continuum of the animal and human (post-Darwinian more than Darwinian)—the mounting paleoanthropological and developmental evidence tends to confirm that the distinctive functionality we collect as *self* or *person* arises from, and as, the artifactual (historied) transformation of the primate members of *Homo sapiens* and their particular form of communication, effectuated, collectively and distributively, through the cultural invention and mastery of true language. I take the Darwinian effect, which is essentially an empirical matter, to yield the single most important philosophical challenge to Western philosophy since the appearance of Kant's first *Critique*, which (on my reading) marks the advent of "modern" modern (or Eurocentric) philosophy—a label not intended to be pejorative in any way, though it hints at the possibility of a new beginning.

As I see matters, Kant fashioned an immensely influential argument to justify retiring the presumptive privilege of an earlier rationalism's and dogmatic philosophy's claims to be able to answer, objectively and compellingly, all valid questions of First Philosophy. In the process, Kant substitutes the unvalidated (*subjective*) resources of his own transcendental(ist) critique and becomes thereby a closet rationalist of a particularly formidable sort himself—the contingent gift of his own Copernican revolution.

The upshot of all this is that Eurocentric philosophy has never really escaped from the hegemony of Kant's splendid inventions, even as his strictest, most powerful claims become increasingly problematic. My conviction has it that the Darwinian effect shows the way to retiring (possibly the mortal need to retire) the entire Kantian undertaking: first, by construing Kant's would-be transcendental contribution as aposteriorist at best, and, second, by demonstrating that there is, then, no principled difference to be made out between transcendental discovery and broadly empirical conjecture, and that the would-be transcendental demands of universality and necessity are no longer compelling, even where confined—as, tellingly, in Ernst Cassirer's problematic reading of the "regulative" function of transcendental reason, once Kant's "constitutive" restrictions vis-à-vis the cognizable world are treated in empirically laxer terms. (Kant's essentialized faculty of reason has no place in any artifactualized, still-naturalistic theory of the human agent.)

A transcendentally "regulative" principle cannot continue to claim apriorist force where its "constitutive" mate fails to satisfy its own would-be transcendental constraints (as, arguably, it is meant to do, in both Kant and

Cassirer). The reason is elementary: if empirical conviction is forever finite (and adventitious) though it may evolve in unpredictable ways (as in the history of science), and if, in thus evolving, it prompts a change in transcendental discovery, then the would-be constitutive claims of transcendental understanding (respecting the need to posit new kinds of objects) are bound to become insuperably problematic—effectively, more than contingently regulative, in Kant's largest sense.[21] Kant's transcendentalism proves, then, to be no more than a misplaced reading of a series of heartfelt guesses of (dare I say?) "abductive Hope"! This would explain, obliquely, Peirce's remarkably early verdict that Kant was, finally, a "confused pragmatist." In any event, it explains the metonymy of reading the career of Eurocentric philosophy in terms of a contest between Kantian certitudes and pragmatist abductions.

It's worth remarking (in this connection)—well, it's worth reminding ourselves—that Cassirer specifically quotes Kant's solution to the puzzle regarding the "constitutive" and "regulative" uses of transcendental reason in his reading of modern physics as satisfying Kant's conception of the regulative (hence, normative) direction of the sciences:

> Reason really has as object only the understanding and its purposive application. Accordingly, I [that is, Kant] assert the transcendental ideas are never of constitutive use, so that the concepts of certain objects would thereby be given, and in case one so understands them, they are merely sophistical (dialectical) concepts. On the contrary, however, they have an excellent and indispensably necessary regulative use, namely that of directing the understanding to a certain goal respecting which the lines of direction of all its rules converge at one point, which, although it is only an idea (*focus imaginarius*)—*i.e.*, a point from which the concepts of the understanding do not really proceed, since it lies entirely outside the bounds of possible experience—nonetheless still serves to obtain for these concepts the greatest unity alongside the greatest extension.[22]

Kantian-inspired philosophies, down to our own day, still tend to demur on relinquishing the need for a regulative constraint, managed in very different ways among thinkers as diverse as Ernst Cassirer, Karl-Otto Apel, Jürgen Habermas, Charles Peirce, John Rawls, Christine Korsgaard, John McDowell, and even Hilary Putnam. As far as I can see, the counterargument wins hands down. Very few philosophers now believe that strict necessity, exceptionless universality, or a demonstrably totalized system of basic categories that accommodate every form of rational thought is the sine qua non of any and every minimally tenable philosophical proposal of the regulative sort. (Here, Cassirer retreats to Hegel—possibly on his way to pragmatism!)

The point is that I agree with Kant that philosophy is best pursued in ways that are holist and systematic but that need not require and may well not be able to support the determinacies and conceptual closure that Kant favors. I also agree that normativity is insuperably intertwined with discursivity, but perceptual experience and animal and infantile analogues of perceptual judgment may oblige us to make concessions that are, conceptually, distinctly untidy when viewed from Kant's vantage. I'm not at all persuaded that commitments of these sorts commit us to holding that *any* of the executive conceptions that serve in non-Kantian as well as Kantian ventures—cognition, judgment, truth, autonomy, rationality, the unity of inquiry—demonstrably require (or can support) an apriorist reading.

Now, then, if this (*my*) charge is worth weighing at all, then it suits my argumentative strategy to suggest, for one thing, that, assuming the systematicity of the Kantian argument, it should be possible to show the more-than-doubtful (transcendental) standing of such claims as that perceptual experience *must be* discursive (as John McDowell insists, though without a compelling argument, against animal cognition) and, for another, that perception itself must be bound by apriorist constraints that match every step in the formation of perceptual judgment (as McDowell also effectively insists). How could we possibly know that, a priori?

Bear in mind that Kant was unable to answer the metaquestion: How is transcendental knowledge possible? Without a satisfactory answer, all a priori certitude threatens to unravel into infinite regress: one either yields to skepticism or falls back to something akin to abductive guesses. Either way, systematicity will have been lost: McDowell's "quietism," conveniently drawn from Wittgenstein's practice in *Investigations*, may prove not altogether convincing, because it permits McDowell to hold fast to what he believes remains valid in Kant without needing to exact any sufficient, supportive evidentiary labor.[23]

I can easily imagine that there is no uniquely valid solution to the Kantian question addressed in McDowell's second Woodbridge Lecture, "The Logical Form of an Intuition," which yields a splendid dispute between McDowell and Sellars regarding the relationship between the right analysis of a perceptual judgment and the counterpart analysis of a perceptual episode (a seeing, say). (The matter, I admit, is far too complex, and even too tangential to our present concern, to attempt to do justice to it here, but I risk the aside in the interest of a deeper and more freewheeling issue.)

McDowell plays the role of Kant's champion (with respect to Kant's answer to the question, as broached in the first *Critique*): he demonstrates well enough that Sellars's analysis of Kant's question (and answer) does not square with what Kant intends, according to McDowell's reading of the relevant Kantian texts. But this way of proceeding effectively confines the would-be transcendental answer to his own reading of Kant's question (a fortiori, confines the validity of McDowell's and Sellars's transcendental conjectures) to purely internal textualist interpretations of both Kant's question and answer *and* of otherwise independently legitimate interpretations of the scope and point of contemporary treatments of the evolving question itself.

Sellars, I suggest, wishes to experiment with alternative readings of the Kantian problem (certainly one of the most central—and most troublesome—examined in the first *Critique*), although, if I understand his purpose correctly, Sellars actually wishes to strengthen a larger, more accommodating possibility that *he* finds obliquely favored in Kant's own texts. The result is that he clearly departs from what McDowell takes to be Kant's "evident" thesis, which (in McDowell's view) is indeed the best, the most economical, and the least contorted reading of Kant's actual texts. (Here, McDowell seems even more confident than Kant, though also more unyielding.)

Now, as it also happens, McDowell is distinctly opposed to concessions involving concepts or protoconcepts in animal perception (and, of course, in perceptual judgment among animals and human infants, *if* perceptual judgments may be allowed at all). The matter bears directly on the capacity of languageless human infants to perceive the same sort of objects that enlanguaged persons are said to perceive—and, even more significantly, to begin to master true language in accord with their merely primate talents.

I find that Sellars's thought experiment, applied to competent persons, happens to facilitate a more plausible speculation regarding animals and infants than McDowell contemplates. There are also, in fact, serious complications that cannot fail to affect the realist treatment of Kant's, Sellars's, and McDowell's accounts of perceptual objects, once we link the discursivity thesis with the acquisition of a contingent natural language and then proceed to treat realism—effectively, "scientific realism," in Sellars's argument—as a theoretical construction rather than a perceptual discovery. McDowell dutifully cites Sellars's notorious remark: "*speaking as a philosopher*, I am quite prepared to say that the commonsense world of physical objects in Space and Time is unreal—that is, there are no such things. . . . Science is the measure of all things, of what is that it is, and of what is not that it is not."[24] McDowell opposes Sellars here, favoring Kant's commonsensism instead. But, as I've tried to show in numerous settings, realism itself is something of an abductive guess: it couldn't be anything else, and this, of course, is a more compelling claim than that of Sellars's scientism. (McDowell misses the full force of the issue.) For his part, Sellars does intend to restore the primacy of Kant's decided emphasis on the exemplary structure of perceptual judgment. Nevertheless, since, in *my* view, we lack any satisfactory distinction between transcendentally and empirically valid claims in matters of this kind, the *transcendental* dispute between McDowell and Sellars is of very little importance; correspondingly, since the seeming empirical uncertainty regarding the actual structure of perceivings is more rewarding vis-à-vis larger issues, there's no point in favoring any strongly disjunctive finding. I take the entire episode to bear directly on the self-referential paradoxes of epistemology and to yield almost nothing on the question of agentive norms.[25]

Kant was himself perfectly aware of the dangers of drawing on limited empirical knowledge and on the overly easy formalism of universalized claims. It's the decisive issue of the "Appendix to the Transcendental Dialectic," in Kant's first *Critique*—that is, of both parts of this particular appendix, but especially the first (A642/B670–A668/B696)—the resolution of which could easily have been the key to Peirce's abductive turn, as that might be read in accord with Cassirer's neo-Kantian formula—that is, too liberally. I am indeed persuaded that what Peirce grasped—what Kant might have grasped before him—was the impossibility of fixing the secure difference between apodictic and problematic uses of reason in testing transcendental claims.[26] Given the signal importance of the history of the physical sciences, the appendix to the first *Critique* (just mentioned) may well provide the decisive clue to the ultimate failure of Kant's entire transcendental program, somewhat in accord with Cassirer's treatment of the physical sciences (and beyond)—or, to speak with Peirce, the clue to the "confused" success of Kant's prescient pragmatism.

I'm persuaded that such trials regarding would-be cognition confirm the likelihood that normativity cannot be reliably shown to be guided or governed by apriorist constraints. (Think, here, of Kant's cooked argument for the rational necessity of the categorical imperative.) It's Kant's transcendental dualism regarding autonomy and causality—which persists in

Cassirer, who nevertheless yields considerable ground regarding the supposed universality of causal laws—that obliges latter-day Kantians (of different stripes) to support forms of regulative apriority likely to license improvisations that may appear more promising than they really are, when cleverly defined.

IV

It's the transformation of the human primate—the Darwinian effect, the empirical inference from prehistoric evidence, the strong claim in favor of the primeval invention of language (external *Bildung*), the enlanguaged rearing of successive cohorts of human infants (internal *Bildung*)—that accounts for the original presence of normativity in the Intentional world, effectively, the "space of reasons." That alone explains the influence of *sittlich* norms in the formation of persons. It offers nothing, however, in the way of legitimating agentive norms objectively: at best, they are all equally *sittlich*.

Now, neither Kant nor the neo-Kantians nor the so-called Pittsburghers nor the Frankfurters convincingly address the implied puzzle posed by invoking the "space of reasons": namely, *what*, if the self or person is an artifactual transform of a natural-kind kind, could possibly serve (beyond the *sittlich*) to validate the norms by which we ought to guide and govern our lives? The usual answers depend on some form of privileged access (as with Kant himself) that cannot easily be reconciled with the self's artifactuality. The question that needs still to be answered asks, rather, whether there might not be another way, besides privilege or adherence to the merely *sittlich*, that we may draw on profitably.

There is indeed room for accommodation, though it hardly yields more than a diminished liberty. I therefore call it a second-best solution, which follows Plato's surprising charge (advanced in the *Statesman*) to the effect that the state must be governed (Plato's spokesman affirms) in spite of the fact that we ourselves don't really know how to find out what the laws should be—what the "space of reasons" requires! How would Sellars or McDowell answer? (Possibly, Plato meant the *Statesman* to be a joke at the expense of the *Republic*.)

Before we consider this final issue, however—the question of how to treat the matter of the objective standing of agentive norms—I must turn back briefly to the distractions produced by the tension between McDowell's and Sellars's interpretations of Kant's account of perception and perceptual judgment, since it deflects us from the decisive matter of the standing of agentive norms. As I say, I cannot take McDowell's complaint about Sellars's "misreading" of Kant's solution very seriously. Because it's Sellars who has decided to explore the possibility of plausible emendations of the Kantian contribution along naturalistic lines—an effort that hardly requires a specifically textualist answer regarding the play of spontaneity and receptivity in perception and perceptual judgment—on which, of course, McDowell and Sellars disagree: they disagree about precisely when and how (in any Kantian-inspired account) the concepts said to be transcendentally provided by the understanding can be emended in still-congenial ways, so as to test fresh options in capturing Kant's basic innovation regarding perceptual experience. Certainly, Sellars is tempted by the primacy of languageless perception, among humans, even within a Kantian framework. McDowell will not allow it at all. There is no assured way to appraise the apparent dispute between Sellars and McDowell, which issues, of course, in only one direction. Neither the perceptual nor the normativity issue seems to have gained any ground here. (I concede that there may be no ground to be gained.)

What I think McDowell correctly grasps (notably, in the Woodbridge Lectures) is that if he does not act decisively to cut off the possibility of perceptual concepts at its origin (lacking discursivity), the entire project of articulating the rational systematicity of science and cognition will have been mortally imperiled—and, with it, the rationality of moral and agentive concerns *and* the upshot of invoking the space of reasons. Here, I think of the near-pragmatist confrontation of Sellars's scientific realism mounted, already in the 1970s, by Bas van Fraassen, who is both an antirealist and an opponent of a truth-directed account of the rationality of science[27]—also, indeed, a former student of Sellars's. Van Fraassen's challenge, even if we oppose his antirealism and extreme empiricism, and anything like an attack on a Kantian rationale respecting a realist reading of theoretical entities, *or* the inherent vagueness and lack of fixity of perceptual experience itself, *or* a truth-directed defense of theoretical knowledge, exposes the problematic cohesion of Sellars's philosophical system—anchored in "Philosophy and the Scientific Image of Man" and "Empiricism and the Philosophy of Mind," as we shall soon see.[28]

When, therefore, McDowell declares, in the introduction added to the original text of *Mind and World*, "[The] relation between mind and world is normative . . . in this sense: thinking that aims at judgment, or at the fixation of belief, is answerable to the world—to how things are—for whether or not it is correctly executed,"[29] he (McDowell) simply paraphrases

Sellars's executive thesis ("the space of reasons"), which he gladly accepts but leaves completely undeveloped as far as the objective provision of agentive norms is concerned. I cannot find any pertinent argument in McDowell that actually tells us how, precisely, to draw out the transcendental conditions of our "answerability to the world"—in support of the objectivity of science or of rational practice, or of the valid norms of agentive life itself. The best I can find appears in the Woodbridge Lectures; there, McDowell simply opposes (and displaces) Sellars's reading of Kant with his own obiter dictum—a more strenuous apriorism (I would say) than even Kant espouses in the first *Critique*, in order to disallow (it seems) the barest possibility of "perceptual concepts" (Sellars's temptation) suitable for animal knowledge. I don't see how the "space of reasons" can be authoritatively *applied* to the analysis of perceptual knowledge or perceptual concepts *tout court*—either "constitutively" or "regulatively"—and I don't see how McDowell's treatment of perception clarifies how we should apply the resources of the "space of reasons" argument to determining the true norms of agentive life. (*What*, cognitively or rationally, is the analogy between perceptual and moral judgment, for instance?) I see only stalemate there.

In fact, if I may put the matter this way, McDowell presses the notion of the "space of reasons" in order to secure his version of realism, which extends to normativity, whereas Sellars, because he reads normativity in terms of the *sittlich* and has given his readers notice that his own scientism is meant to prepare us for the abandonment of a final realist reading of the reputed objects of perceptual experience (recall Sellars's opinion of the "manifest image," which McDowell takes to be a clue to the effect that Sellars has made a profound mistake)—I say only that Sellars construes the "space of reasons" to signify his provisionally irenic compromise between the two "images," which may be no more than a passing tolerance for a vestigial agentive code that will have to be abandoned or replaced when the scientific image effectively eclipses the manifest image. My own view is more opportunistic: if language and interior experience and thought resist reductionism and eliminativism (as, thus far, they do), then we need (as far as we can see) a third image capable of eclipsing Sellars's dual invention.

Given the post-Darwinian argument, the deciding fact is, precisely, that the provenance of the "space of reasons" is itself thoroughly artifactual—*in* being thoroughly discursive. McDowell was indeed prescient in sensing that the solution of the normativity puzzle lay with the question of the discursivity of perceptual knowledge. But he simply fell back to a regressive reading of Kant, just where it was Kant's transcendentalism that had (or might have had) to be overturned! What is even more interesting, *Sellars*, who saw the connection more clearly, was definitely tempted by the idea that the admission of prelinguistic "perceptual concepts" might well be reconciled with an adjusted reading of Kant's transcendental undertaking. That, I think, explains McDowell's prolonged attack on Sellars, in the Woodbridge Lectures. But the attack is essentially an obiter dictum; it never engages the deeper issue, and it leaves us thoroughly bewildered. You cannot find an adequate answer regarding the criterial application of the "space of reasons" in Kant or among the Pittsburghers, or the Frankfurters, for that matter. The best answer remains Darwinian, which, of course, favors abductive laxities and historical contingency.

Admittedly, I find McDowell's *Mind and World* baffling (rather than merely mistaken). Because, first, what McDowell insistently affirms (as far as I can see) is that the agency of persons is inseparable from the ubiquitous play of normativity ("the space of reasons") in everything regarding judgment applied to any part of the world. Thus far at least, I agree with McDowell, but then, that is precisely what Kant bequeaths us and what Sellars extracts from Kant. It's really a comment on the ontology of persons and a step in the direction of an inquiry into what's involved in making valid normative judgments themselves. But then, second, McDowell never takes the next step! (Sellars makes an attempt but breaks off too early. Brandom is even more preliminary than Sellars. And Rorty falls back to *sittlich* solidarity—ethnocentricity—but not as a reasoned philosophical option.)

To affirm that the agentive (in the human sense) entails the normative *is* an important discovery: I take it to belong, broadly, to sociology, because the invention and mastery of language is simply the verso of the formation of persons. So, the *sittlich is* a part of reality. Fine. But that leaves the question of objective norms (meant in some sense firmer than the merely *sittlich*) still to be addressed, because the *sittlich* (especially agentive norms) is ineluctably earthbound, historically contingent, radically diverse, oppositional, not in any obvious way open to legitimation, except circularly by further *sittlich* means. Do the Pittsburghers offer more? I don't think so.

McDowell grasps the aptness of Sellars's phrasing, "the space of reasons." But he spends his force in opposing the impoverished ("disenchanted") vocabulary of "bare" naturalism and scientism, which conflates two very different charges, both problematically managed. For, as Sellars makes clear (in "Philosophy and the Scientific Image of Man"), the very pertinence of the "space of reasons" does not answer *any* substantive questions about how to reconcile morality or agency with an account of the objective sciences. Sellars fails us there. So does McDowell, though for entirely different reasons. Bear in mind that Max Weber makes it perfectly clear that the "disenchantment" thesis *is already cast* in terms of the Kantian "space of reasons"—hence, has no need for either Sellars's or McDowell's recuperation. The disenchantment of modernity *does not challenge normativity at all*: it's a more or less empirical claim about the modern impoverishment of agentive norms. Nothing more. For his part, Sellars loses his way between the "manifest" and "scientific" images; he's apparently unable to find a way of attaching the normativity distinction *to* the "scientific image"; he cannot show that any agentive norms make sense in the space of the scientific image, although he's committed to applying the "space of reasons" argument just there. It's not clear what further role McDowell intends to assign to the "space of reasons." Kant's minimal view of the notion remains uncontested; it's the question of actually discerning the objectivity of agentive norms that's ignored. It's the most quarrelsome philosophical question ignored by the Pittsburghers. Sellars is the most responsive member of the school, but not in the passages that interest McDowell most.

McDowell explains, in the introduction to *Mind and World*, that the entire purpose of the Locke Lectures is to relieve certain "philosophical anxieties" that arise when one may be insouciantly drawn to wonder how freedom, perception, normative judgment, and the like are regarded as "possible" (in a sense akin to the most strenuous Kantian questions).[30] The matter remains unanswered, however, as to *how* to distinguish valid from invalid agentive norms, and it's ultimately addressed in an extraordinary burst of transcendental confidence (more rigid than Kant's), when, in the Woodbridge Lectures, McDowell "answers" Kant's question about the conditions of perceptual knowledge and rejects Sellars's answer: "As I have put it," McDowell remarks, activating his distinctive form of Wittgensteinian quietism, "we need to exorcise the questions ['how possible?'] rather than set about answering them."[31] (There's the end of McDowell's story.) But are these questions separable? And is the first adequate to our needs? (McDowell's endorsement seems unhelpful, the rejection of perceptual concepts seems arbitrary, and the relevance of all this for objective norms seems mislaid.)

In spite of his responses, McDowell provides an excellent rundown of why, since Kant has no notion of second nature and is not drawn to what he (McDowell) calls "bald naturalism," Kant was unable to "find a place in nature for [the] real connection between concepts and intuitions" and so was obliged "to place the connection outside nature, in the transcendental framework." Extraordinary conjecture—baffling in any case—but what exactly was it supposed to explain? We must not lose sight of the fact that McDowell is himself drawn to a seemingly transcendental alternative under the pressure of opposing Sellars; indeed, a finding that becomes completely uncompelling when rendered in naturalistic terms, against both Kant and Sellars.[32] McDowell's economies of argument seem unsatisfactory here. (How, for instance, does he know that there are no "perceptual concepts" and how could that be shown? It's hardly self-evident.) Sellars is drawn to the idea that the admission of perceptual concepts may be compatible with a version of Kant's treatment of discursivity, perhaps in the way (remarked in chapter 3 of *Toward a Metaphysics of Culture*) J. J. Gibson maintains, in accord with his reading of Aristotle. Perhaps Sellars is right about perceptual concepts but wrong about Kant. Is there a "philosophical anxiety" there that would marginalize the import of McDowell's dispute with Sellars and, at the same time, identify the resources from which agentive norms are rightly drawn?

McDowell comes upon the normativity question frontally, because he's struck by the aptness of Sellars's phrase "the space of reasons" ("the logical space of reasons," as Sellars's phrasing has it, in "Empiricism and the Philosophy of Mind") in orienting readers of Kant's first *Critique* to the profound import of Kant's grasp of the necessary conceptual linkage between normativity and discursivity. He's disappointed, however, by Sellars's reading of the first *Critique* with respect to perception and perceptual knowledge, and he's deflected, accordingly, from pursuing the normativity issue with the same zeal with which he examines perception and opposes Sellars's "laxity" regarding the conceptual significance of our intake of nonconceptual sensory impressions. But then, though he's interested in Sellars's treatment of the distinction between "second-natured" nature and "bald" nature, he's not particularly interested in Sellars's opposing the "manifest" and "scientific" images, which brings the normativity issue to bear on the concept of the formation of a person and the fortunes of what Sellars regards as the central philosophical agon between "perennial philosophy" and what amounts to a version of "scientism."

In effect, Sellars and McDowell view matters very differently, in spite of sharing a sense of the Kantian importance of featuring the space of reasons: both are alert to the conceptual economies afforded by linking a commitment to empirical realism with the need to embed the robustness of normative judgment within the confines of an adequate conception of nature. There's the nerve of their common Kantian sympathies. But Sellars is a maverick Kantian at best, prone to experiment with unforeseen possibilities drawn from Kant's own texts, whereas McDowell selectively presses Kantian orthodoxies as far as possible. Sellars is the more explicit of the two, since he's quite straightforward about his interest in the philosophical viability of perceptual knowledge (whether animal or human) somehow separable from the exceptionless onset of discursivity—as with the radical possibility that a realism provisionally cast in terms of a phenomenal or phenomenological given (the "manifest image," say) may be legitimately abandoned in support (ultimately) of a reductive scientism and in ensuring the *sittlich* embeddedness of agentive norms in the intentional life of actual societies.

McDowell explicitly opposes the first two of these three (just mentioned) Kantian experiments; both McDowell and Sellars are much vaguer about the objectivity of agentive norms, though (as far as I can see) both tend to favor a more fully biologized and encultured human agent then does Kant, but Sellars also bruits the possibility of a more radical philosophical economy that might well supersede Kantianism altogether, whereas McDowell tends to go quietistic about his final "correction."

My guess is that McDowell comes too late to a first reading of Sellars's "Philosophy and the Scientific Image of Man," which I view as more important than "Empiricism and the Philosophy of Mind" and which betrays the fact that, although Sellars specifies the common ground for Kant's analysis of science and morality ("the space of reasons"), he (Sellars) was ultimately unable to resolve—or, for some reason, simply left unresolved, or thought he had resolved—the contest between the two "images" of man, which he came to believe must be "fused" in one coherent vision and can be successfully fused, according to a formula provided in "Scientific Image." I take Sellars to have been seriously mistaken here and to have left the normative (or agentive) issue completely unsettled.

I admit that I find Sellars's discussion of the reconciliation of the two images an unmitigated disaster (a minor contest at best). But, in the debate that occupies him, Sellars is aware (we realize) that he has no compelling reason to abandon the crucial role of the concept of a person, no matter how difficult it may be to reconcile the functionality of persons with the main thrust of the program of analysis he assigns the scientific image (which he apparently believes—wrongly—is in the ascendant). The irony involving Sellars is that, although he identifies the normativity puzzle with the uses of "the space of reasons," he cannot find the right placement for an adequate theory of the self or person *as* the very agent that "gives and asks for" reasons—the spare theme that captures Brandom's attention. He fails to reconcile his two images—it's not clear that they can be reconciled; he cannot incorporate the self or person into the scientific image; he cannot explain the objective standing of any agentive norms within the terms of either image. What is the point of fusing the two images if the scientific image cannot account for the normativity of the intentional and if we cannot decide the validity of the manifest image's norms that the scientific image should passingly adjust and then ultimately reject? And what is McDowell's alternative? There's at least as much unfinished business among the Pittsburghers as there is among the classic pragmatists.

Here, now, is the extraordinarily brief, much-cited passage from Sellars's "Empiricism," which affirms, abstractly, though in the context of cognitive (a fortiori, perceptual) episodes—or claims or assertions about such episodes—the ubiquity of "the space of reasons" and the coextension of discursivity and normativity. It must be read as a loyal Kantian economy that affects McDowell as deeply as it does Sellars (though Sellars wishes to naturalize Kant, if he can): "the essential point," Sellars says, "is that in characterizing an episode or a state as that of *knowing*, we are not giving an empirical description of that episode or state; we are placing it in the logical space of reasons, of justifying and being able to justify what one says."[33] It's clear that Sellars's lines point to the grounding of cognition in the conceptual linkage between discursivity and normativity—and, through that linkage, to the definition of a person. Of course, Sellars has the entire conceptual architecture of the normative in mind, in "Scientific Image," but he spends his best labor in maneuvers wedded to the completely futile effort to fuse the two images. (It can't be done.) For his part, McDowell allows himself to be sidetracked, in the Woodbridge Lectures, into a quarrel with Sellars about the correct reading of Kant's view of perceptual knowledge, which cannot possibly be resolved by apriorist fiat or textual fidelity (or Wittgensteinian quietism). No doubt his argument also relies on the conceptual linkage between discursivity and normativity, but for some reason he wishes to present himself as a more strenuous transcendentalist than Kant—in effect, a transcendental naturalist. In the bargain, McDowell fails to advance a theory of the human person (much as Kant fails), which (as with Kant, whose noble arbitrariness on moral matters I've already remarked) deprives him of rendering a proper account of either discursivity or normativity. If you now add to this Rorty's penchant for premature philosophical stalemate and Robert Brandom's postponement of his promised arguments, you gain at least a cameo summary of the very short life of the Pittsburgh School. (The upshot is that we look in vain for a fresh account of normativity among the Pittsburghers.) They seem unable to explain what *they* finally mean by the primacy of the linguistic (over experience); they offer no new conception of the objective standing of normative claims, and their stalemate seems to reflect the latent opposition between McDowell and Brandom.

I retreat, therefore, to Sellars's original texts, which are worth pondering. The formula in "Scientific Image" provides as unassailable a sense of the objectivity of the normative as can be mustered—so long as a merely *sittlich* order proves sufficient for our purposes; whereas the formula in "Empiricism" provides a general sense of Kant's (and Sellars's) grasp of the philosophical *ground* on which all descriptive, explanatory, interpretive, and analytic discourse (bearing on belief and knowledge) is said to belong to "the space of reasons": that is, to function in a normative or justificatory way.

Of course, one must acknowledge the easily overlooked fact that the dictum is uttered, in "Empiricism," out of earshot of the "Scientific Image" piece, just where the very concept of functioning persons proves exceptionally difficult to conjure with in scientistic terms. The entire play—in Kant and among the Pittsburghers—all but neglects any query that might have been prompted by Herder's or Humboldt's speculations regarding the original *onset* of discursive thought. The persistence of Kant's primacy, even in the twenty-first century, may signal, then, a subterranean worry that the essential question regarding the validity of Kant's splendid challenge—bearing on the criterial function of the categorical imperative—has still to be effectively formulated. My suggestion is that it lies with what I've characterized as the pragmatist reading of the Darwinian effect. It makes no appearance in Cassirer, for instance; but I'm prepared to argue that it's implicated in Peirce (and Dewey) and in Sellars. Sellars, I should say, addresses the placement question rather lightly, all but perfunctorily; he links it to a society's "intentions" but does not raise any questions about agentive validity.

There are at least two distinct threads of speculation in Sellars's larger narrative: one collects his reading of Kant's treatment of perception in the first *Critique*, which accommodates (but marginalizes in advance) McDowell's disagreement with this reading;[34] the other confirms the obvious truth that objectivity among normative judgments is easily secured if we require no more than the *sittlich*. The first leads to the ultimate disaster (as I read Sellars) of the "Scientific Image" piece (regarding the operative placement of normativity), and the second leads to an exploration of the possibility of venturing beyond the merely vacuously *sittlich*. I have something to say on both counts.

On the first, I offer a second passage from "Scientific Image" that combines a sense of Sellars's experiments with Kantian options and his troublesome account of the would-be contest between the "manifest" and "scientific images." Sellars's mistake rests with his failing to see that the two images are neither well formed nor freestanding, nor independent of one another, nor the best options to have mustered. Both require the unique competence of persons—the same abilities—which are nowhere secured. Sellars himself believes the manifest image to be ineptly cobbled, philosophically unable to account for its own perceptual and experiential powers, and, though he explicitly favors the fortunes of the scientific image over the manifest, at the close of "Scientific Image," he confesses that the scientific image must ultimately borrow the concept of the enabling powers of selves or persons ("intentions") from the manifest image that it's destined to eclipse—and, there, only by "external addition." Confusion all around. Hence, *if* the scientific image possessed such resources, there would be no difficulty in reconciling the two images; the scientific image would remain a conjectured deposit of an improved version of the manifest image.

But to yield on just that scruple would effectively betray the essential weakness of the scientistic option. Sellars has deceived himself, perhaps, by his own suggestion that the two images are to be regarded as "bracketed" (in something akin to Husserl's sense)—that is, *not yet* accorded realist status (in the exercise he's engaged in). The images are, he says, "*two* pictures of essentially the same order of complexity, each of which purports to be a complete picture of man-in-the-world [which is false] and which, after careful scrutiny, [the philosopher] must fuse into one vision [which seems impossible]." They are to be combined "in one stereoscopic view."[35] (But how, if reductionism fails?) They are incomplete, incompatible, unequal in scope, incommensurable, subaltern, contrived, falsely forced options that must be abandoned anyway.

As a result, Sellars cannot actually advance the premises by which to secure his version of scientific realism and the objective standing of his account of agentive norms. The theoretical and practical arguments come together, fatally, in one of the most disputed passages in "Empiricism":

> *speaking as a philosopher,* [Sellars says,] I am quite prepared to say that the commonsense world of physical objects in Space and Time is unreal [a daring step beyond Kant, meant to decide the realist import of both perception and intention: a fortiori, normativity]—that is, that there are no such things. Or, to put [the issue] less paradoxically, that in the dimension of describing and explaining the world, science is the measure of all things, of what is that it is, and of what is not that it is not.[36]

My own counterthesis holds, quite simply, that, for one thing, the "myth of the given" cannot disallow *all* forms of what is "given" phenomenologically (without violating Sellars's defensible objections—opposing privilege, apodicticity, presuppositional advantage, and the like) if realism is to be responsibly secured by (say) suitable constructions; and, for another, scientism (scientific realism) cannot succeed, unless Sellars can demonstrate that a conceptually adequate causal analysis of linguistic behavior, intentional states, and the phenomenology of what is given in thought and perceptual experience can actually be mounted. Here, I must confess, Sellars's proposal (at the very end of "Scientific Image") to fuse the two images by (*external*) "addition" conclusively confirms that his proposal simply fails.

The images can't be *fused*. Sellars makes it clear that he's thinking of something "conceived" rather than "imagined": the idea of visual or auditory "images" may accommodate the instruction to "fuse" the ocular pictures that belong to each eye, but to think of these images as *conceptions* is to raise the threat of logical incompatibility: stereoscopic vision entails a form of fusing, but the "fusing" of the "two perspectives" (as Sellars calls the "manifest" and "scientific images") is a matter of formal or logical compatibility. The point is that the two images *are not compatible*—Sellars could not be more explicit: they *preclude* the solution Sellars himself advances—a verdict the second citation confirms. More than that, there's absolutely no reason to believe (and none that Sellars provides) to show that it's impossible to construct *another*, altogether different picture that includes, consistently, an acceptable account of the human person *and* whatever the pertinent sciences of the human can validly provide. It would, of course, have to be an improvement affecting the manifest image or a new alternative; the scientific image concedes no element of the intentional (or of the Intentional) life of persons, although it needs to capture such an option. How could they possibly be fused?

Well then, here is the second passage (from "Scientific Image"), which adds some detail to the first and confirms (by its actual phrasing) its belonging to the "space of reasons" (conceived naturalistically):

> to recognize a featherless biped or dolphin or Martian as a person [Sellars says] is to think of oneself and it as belonging to a community. . . . One thinks thoughts of the form, "We (one) shall do (or abstain from doing) actions of kind A in circumstances of kind C." To think thoughts of this kind is not to *classify* or

> *explain*, but to *rehearse an intention*. . . . A person can almost be defined as a being that has intentions. Thus the conceptual framework of persons is not something that needs to be *reconciled with* the scientific image, but rather something to be *joined* to it. Thus, to complete the scientific image we need to enrich it *not* with more ways of saying what is the case, but with the language of community and individual intentions, so that by construing the actions we intend to do and the circumstances in which we intend to do them in scientific terms, we *directly* relate the world as conceived by scientific theory to our purpose, and make it *our* world and no longer an alien appendage to the world in which we do our living.[37]

Of course, "a person can [also] almost be defined as a being that has [*perceptions* as well as] intentions" (or language, for that matter), which confirms that persons may already be obliquely implicated in the would-be "scientific image." (I don't see how this helps Sellars avoid the reconciliation problem: it's the nerve of his intent to naturalize Kant's argument.) It can only mean that Sellars has thrown up his hands on the question of what it is to be a person (from the scientistic side), although he's collected the disconnected pieces of the two images he claims must be fused. It's tempting to ramble on about Pittsburgher prospects. But I think we can safely conclude that Sellars simply never managed to break through the impasse of "Scientific Image." I honestly believe it was always a dead end, a false option. I'm persuaded that a robust emergentism is the only way to go. I cannot see the sense in which *anyone* can reasonably expect (now or in our envisaged future) to render—in reductionistic or eliminativist terms—linguistic meaning, intentionality, interior thought and experience, consciousness and self-consciousness, and the like, drawn from the most obvious paradigms afforded within the life of human persons. I see no reason to object to christening such phenomena "emergent," complex "manifestations of matter" (along the lines Noam Chomsky suggested some years ago). But then, I think that that would change nothing. I can't see the advantage of a line of speculation that ignores the *entire* role of the human agent (ourselves) in what we call our science. In that unblinking sense, we must wait to see what either McDowell or Brandom (or a newer Pittsburgher) may yet devise. For the time being, we must honor their promissory notes.

V

I recommend we turn back to Wittgenstein—perhaps, also, to Max Weber and Charles Peirce—since we seem to have come close to exhausting Sellars's and McDowell's principal contributions on normativity. Sellars does not venture beyond the *sittlich*, and McDowell does not venture beyond his criticism of Sellars. Wittgenstein captures the spirit (and limitations) of the *sittlich* in a particularly memorable way. For instance, at the end of a baffling stalemate regarding what had seemed at first a simple matter of explaining the notion of "following a rule," Wittgenstein finds himself obliged to admit (at the height of the impasse), "When I obey a rule, I do not choose. I obey the rule *blindly*."[38] The only sense I can make of this is that Wittgenstein means that one must fall back to conforming with the *Lebensform* of one's social world—*and* that the enabling practice accommodates the seeming paradox of stalemating the successful application of the would-be rules themselves (thereby stalemating the regress as well).

I cannot see how McDowell's quietism functions here, or how it avoids yielding to a frank admission that it has yet to penetrate the daunting puzzles that beset our barest understanding of rules said to govern judgment—or meanings, or truth claims, or alternative pictures of reality, or the practical or moral norms of life itself. Furthermore, when McDowell co-opts Sellars's phrase ("the space of reasons"), he clearly means to use it to *separate* those lines of reasoning that might relieve us of *illusory* philosophical anxieties from those that are rightly regarded as requiring resolution, as stubbornly metaphysical or epistemological (or axiological or methodological or phenomenological or logical or conceptual). McDowell makes his own division of the field—though it is not entirely clear how or how he validated it—the apparent point of his own Wittgensteinian quietism, even as he advances his notably strong reading of Kant's theory of sensory perception and the "spontaneous" onset of the would-be discursive conditions of understanding.[39]

Of course, that's just what McDowell cannot rightly do yet: he cannot proclaim that percipient persons are known to be constrained in just the way he believes corrects Sellars's "mistaken" reading of Kant: the onset of and conditions of acquiring the contested powers of discursively ordered perceptual knowledge or experience, *by way of* his own (necessary) "transcendental" solution (in the Woodbridge Lectures): in effect, the condition that ensures the normativity (the objective import) of mere perceptual experience construed as apperceptive judgment. That is precisely what Sellars challenges at the outset of the argument of his *Science and Metaphysics*. There's an empirical issue at stake (the onset of true language)—or, it's an issue we cannot convincingly characterize as transcendental. Or, *if* we conceded it to be transcendental, how would that help? Think of the perception of infants and animals *and then* of linguistically apt persons. (For Kant's own explanation—a most ingenious but to my mind utterly unconvincing defense—see the first *Critique*, "Of the Deduction of the Pure Concepts of the Understanding," second section, especially B144–45.)

If we allow all that, we will certainly not be able to distinguish reliably between illusory philosophical anxieties and bona fide philosophical disputes—say, whether nondiscursive perceptual concepts are accessible to intelligent animals and human infants (*and*, possibly, apt adult persons as well) or somehow count as an incoherent option. I cannot see how McDowell can escape the obvious difficulty.[40] (In a lesser figure, one might have charged a *petitio*.) Furthermore, there's a distinct impression of one's reading a desert literature in reading the Pittsburghers: they tend to retreat to relatively early philosophical efforts to come to terms with the flood of inquiries, particularly post-Darwinian, that, in the nineteenth and twentieth centuries, hoped to map the human world empirically, more in the name of science than of philosophy. Although, as I say, the best discussants belong to eclectic minds that no longer have to segregate conjectural philosophy and reportorial sociology: for instance, figures like Max Weber and Alfred Schutz.

The normativity question posed by the Pittsburgh School is largely confined to the proposals advanced by Sellars and McDowell. I won't deny that it surfaces in Robert Brandom's work as well: it arises, for instance, in Brandom's explorations regarding the extension of inferentialism to contexts of specifically pragmatic inference, on the straightforward assumption that inference is expected to meet pertinent normative constraints. But, to be perfectly candid, Brandom has yet to provide a convincing account of how, precisely, to capture the extraordinary complexities of garden-variety pragmatic inferences—particularly those we conjecture reveal the actual norms of quotidian inference. Instead, Brandom draws (very reasonably, I concede) on the analogy of artificial intelligence (AI) simulation, to give us an inkling of possible pragmatic algorithms (of rationality). But it hardly sets the stage for Brandom's would-be contribution—the one he promises to deliver. New forms of normativity may lurk in the joints of such inference, but what it would need to be coaxed into the open would, I venture to say, be a breakthrough model of pragmatic rationality itself. I don't deny that we are caught up (all the time) *with* pragmatic inference, but I see (as yet) no way to capture inferentialism algorithmically, along *pragmatist* lines—except in accord with the external, adventitious interests of random observers, which is plainly another matter. There's very little on the horizon (that I can see) that promises more. Sellars, whose views on "material inference" have greatly influenced Brandom, almost never delivers on the promised outcome of his extremely sanguine beginnings.[41]

That's to say, when Sellars characterizes a "rule" of "material inference" as "written in flesh and blood, or nerve and sinew, rather than in pen and ink," he effectively stalemates Brandom's inferentialism (before it can begin), because Brandom is essentially committed to formulating the best or an acceptable "pen and ink" algorithmic rendering (effectively, a propositional rendering) *of* the "material" rule Sellars says "exists" in just that guise. Because, of course, Sellars's qualification signifies that, here, demonstrably pertinent inference *presupposes and depends on* the prior analysis and interpretation of the would-be "pragmatic contexts" in which the inferentialist procedure is deemed to function at all. But to admit the point is to concede that inferentialism cannot be an entirely autonomous philosophical method in quite the way Brandom supposes, because it cannot stand alone: it must depend, in a way Brandom neglects to flesh out, on some more inclusive program of analysis.

Brandom must, I suggest, invoke some new complex amalgam of experience (or life) and language that might supply a fresh clue to the distinctive logic of pragmatic inference—say, with respect to the interpretation of intent and context: it cannot be merely a form of AI simulation (or anything similar), since AI simulation is itself parasitic on some prior practice or other that it means to mimic functionally. In the case of pragmatic inference, it may well be true—I'm inclined to believe it is—that the forms of inference involved are likely to be entirely standard but that the interpretation of the contextual premises of pragmatic arguments (which are bound to feature *non*inferential analysis) invites a significantly different approach than Brandom's.

Brandom's error—if I dare put the matter thus—rests on an equivocation (whether deliberate or inadvertent) on the meaning of *discursive*: his account of the inferential relationship between the conceptual and the discursive will be seen very differently depending on whether what expresses the inferential content of some uttered piece of speech or action is or is not taken to be *already discursively conveyed*. I read Sellars as emphasizing that pragmatic contexts of expression (and, thus, the *pragmatist* analysis of conceptually structured expression) must make provision for the prior interpretation (often called the ecphrasis) of nondiscursively rendered expressions of conceptual content that are nevertheless linguistically informed (what I call "lingual" expression: as in a gesture or action) in a way that may then be suitably paraphrased discursively. But Sellars's account (which we have been led to believe guides Brandom's fresh effort) breaks off just there! At any rate, I cannot see how Brandom's inferentialism can gain much ground without a sustained account of the ecphractic paraphrase of the seemingly nondiscursive content of action and behavior in discursive terms. Sellars is decidedly unhelpful regarding the logic of pragmatic interpretation—which must precede the discovery of anything algorithmic in the way of inferences in pragmatic contexts.

Brandom, I suppose, may not quite see that to admit the ordinary possibility that rendering the inferentialist import of the conceptual structure of *nonverbal* action normally requires a speculative, rather complex model of how we are to proceed (as pragmatists: think of Dewey's and Peirce's concerns) in mapping the kinds of cases Sellars pointedly mentions.[42] I'm persuaded that Brandom's confidence (in *Articulating Reasons*) in the theory that "see[s] language use as antecedently and independently intelligible, and so as available to provide a model on the basis of which one could then come to understand mental acts and occurrences analogously: taking thinking as a kind of inner saying,"[43] which Brandom finds in the views of Michael Dummett, Peter Geach, and Sellars, is simply too sanguine for the task at hand. I cannot see that the discernible import of nonverbal action takes a reliably algorithmic form or, if it does not, why discursively conveyed pragmatic expression will not also resist inferentialist resolution along algorithmic lines. Meanwhile, the analysis of the normative, though ineliminable, will have slipped from sight. Sellars's exemplary specimen belongs within the "space of reasons," but how, exactly? Inferentialism may not be the most accurate characterization of the kind of analysis that's needed. The decisive factors seem to be *pre*inferential.

The idea that inference can be extended to complex pragmatic contexts and to nonverbal actions is hardly debatable, but I cannot see how acknowledging only *that* strengthens the *inferentialist's* hand: the inferentialist needs not only the salience of inference in human thinking but grounds enough for capturing the specific inferential patterns thus generated, in more or less algorithmic form, accessible enough to support a significant extension of demonstrable forms of inference that may be added to the canon. I cannot see that that is likely at all. I cannot see how Brandom could possibly succeed, and I cannot see how various possible AI simplifications—for instance, paraphrasing causal generalizations (as in advertising and shopping) as inferential sequences—could serve Brandom's purpose. I'm inclined to think the results would be completely trivial or banal (or already largely and loosely mapped), though perhaps not unimportant sociologically. In any event, the discursivity of analysis can claim no privilege regarding the algorithmic structure of any patch of verbal or nonverbal human intelligence. (This counts against the Kantians and the Fregeans.)

I cannot deny that, despite being largely ignored by both Brandom and Rorty, Peirce was indeed attracted to inferentialist themes (say, in his theory of signs). Nevertheless, as I've already argued, abductive guesses are essential to Peirce's "inferentialism" and the analysis of knowledge. Hence, Brandom's inferentialism (that's to say, the sketches we've been provided thus far)—a fortiori, anything like an algorithmic reading of Sellars's sketch of material inference—could never function as the executive principle of a viable pragmatism of Peirce's sort, because *Peirce's* notion specifically precludes the idea of abductive *confirmation*, without denying that at least some abductively recommended inferences may be tested and confirmed by *other* inferential means (by induction, say). Ultimately, algorithmic regularities co-opting abductions would be something of an oxymoron; also, according to Peirce's argument, abduction is essential to the functional adequacy of pragmatic inference itself. There may then be no way to capture pragmatic inferentialism algorithmically without conceding that we proceed here ad hoc, opportunistically, heuristically, piecemeal, diversely in terms of idiosyncratic interests. But if so, then inferentialism (like deflationism—and naturalism, as usually practiced) cannot be more than a subaltern discipline.

Imagine, for instance, that Max Weber was entirely correct in pressing the necessity of our relying, in contexts of sociological (*verstehende*) interpretation, on what he himself names the "imputational" or "heuristic"—definitely not empirically or formally confirmable realist—import of the predicative "constructs" he calls "ideal-type" descriptions (which are definitely not average or normal simplifications of actual empirical patterns of societal life). Imagine that such devices are regularly needed in attempting to map the inferential patterns of pertinent, so-called pragmatic contexts of speech and action (of the kind Sellars features and Brandom adopts). It would still be all but impossible to support the primacy of the inferentialism Brandom favors, though the inferential nature of rational action would never be in doubt.[44]

There, at one stroke, Kantian transcendentalism, Sellarsian inferentialism, and Brandom's inferentialist reading of pragmatism ("analytic pragmatism") are stalemated or placed in jeopardy. Philosophy turns insuperably informal, conjectural, and empiric: systematic closure becomes cognitionally impossible, and, daringly, Peirce's insistence on the ineliminable role of abductive guesses continues to impress. We are indeed creatures apt for fathoming our world, but not, necessarily, for formulating the rules by which we are thought to succeed. (How does Brandom intend to cope with such a possibility?) If logic is, as Peirce assures us, a "normative science," it begins with canonical necessities but ends in inchoate guesses adequate for existential occasions. Brandom, I surmise, believes he will find Kant and/or Frege waiting for him at the end of his inquiry, but he may find only Peirce and Dewey.[45]

McDowell's contribution is more of a puzzle. Certainly, in lecture 6 of *Mind and World*, McDowell makes it clear that he's quite aware of the general problem of distinguishing between human nature and animal nature—that is, aware of the problem (in part, the problem of normativity) posed in speaking of "rational animals": "The threat is that an animal endowed with reason would be metaphysically split, with disastrous consequences for our reflection about empirical thinking and action. I have claimed that we can avoid the threat even while we maintain, unlike bald naturalism [which he claims 'extrude(s) reason from nature'], that the structure of the space of reasons is *sui generis*, in comparison with the organization of the realm of law [causal laws]."[46] The last clause harbors, I believe, a profound mistake. What McDowell says here seems to be the upshot of a decision to work within the terms of Sellars's dilemma (regarding the manifest and scientific images), though under another guise, or in accord with Kant's treatment of discursivity and rationality—which are very different matters. I cannot see the point of preferring either approach.

Abandon Kant's argument, acknowledge Sellars's updated reading of Kant and the current state of philosophical play, and the "disastrous consequences" simply disappear. Furthermore, if we follow Sellars in his treatment of "the space of reasons," the normativity issue threatens to become an external question (for both Sellars and McDowell) when applied to the agon of the two images. Contrariwise, if second nature is a part of nature (as McDowell rightly claims but does not consider in the post-Darwinian sense), then normativity cannot be extruded from nature even where we favor reductionism or instrumentalism, even where the latter doctrines are thought to fail. Scientism, as Sellars's argument makes clear, will itself be committed—perhaps no more than passingly—to the space of reasons. But the details are missing: it's not at all clear that the space of reasons will have a future in the scientific image; it's also not clear that scientism will have any future if the space of reasons is jettisoned. I should mention that Kant's account of apperception and empirical knowledge requires that we treat reason as a cognitive faculty of distinctive power (as already noted). Nevertheless, Reason (*Vernunft*) is not a distinct faculty in any sense akin to the sensory modalities (or faculties). But, of course, reasoning (as in inference) is a mode of functioning in a cognitive way.

The thread of McDowell's argument remains unclear. The space of reasons never needed to be reclaimed: it already ranges over explanations of both causality and freedom; Max Weber's "disenchantment" thesis already falls within the space of reasons; and the challenge of philosophical programs like those of reductive materialism and (what McDowell calls) "bald naturalism"[47] explicitly begin with an acknowledgment of the presumption of the space of reasons. The matter of the right mixture of spontaneity and receptivity, regarding concepts in perceptual processes, whether (say) Kantian or Aristotelian, already implicates normative issues. I cannot see that the perceptual issue that absorbs McDowell so completely (or allied questions) bears directly on the analysis of specifically agentive norms. Sellars seems to get only barely beyond the stalemated contest between his two images (of "man-in-the-world"), and McDowell permits himself to be deflected by an inconclusive quarrel regarding the scope of discursivity (as in perception) meant to explain "the way concepts mediate the relation between minds and the world,"[48] though without addressing agentive norms in any suitably focused way. I cannot see that McDowell answers his own question adequately. And I cannot see that the accessibility of the space of reasons *requires* any executive concession that would favor Kant's transcendentalism. The idea is no more than an artifact of McDowell's oblique strategy.

The provisional answer I offer regarding the locus of normativity is that its salient structures are given in the *sittlich* history of human agency. That's to say, as soon as we are transformed into articulate selves, we find ourselves already engaged with matters within the space of reasons—though *not yet* with an answer regarding the true (objective) source of agentive norms, and not yet with an answer regarding the criterial use of the space of reasons. The epistemological/metaphysical import of all of this rests, then, with the artifactual transformation of human primates into selves or persons.

The issue is simpler and more fundamental than the defense of Kantianism. I see no metaphysical split between agency and nature leading to "disastrous consequences" à la McDowell—unless McDowell insists we must follow *his* Kant, which is too heavy a price for either (or any) of us to pay. But what, precisely, *is* the penalty McDowell wishes to free us from? The entire speculation is off the mark: the advent of the normative is settled by the advent of the person! There's the essential lesson of the Darwinian effect—a fortiori, the upshot of both pragmatist and Weberian treatments of normativity.

If we grasp this much, however, we cannot fail to see that the threat of a disenchanted nature *is not* the extrusion of reason from nature but only the impoverishment (in a valuational sense) of the whole of the normative within the terms of Weber's reportage. Once again, we realize, we've been marching in place.

VI

We are very close, now, to a reasonable resolution of the normativity issue, though it will require another turn at least. I have in mind a final question (for this chapter), possibly the most important, or at least the most paradoxical and penetrating of all the scattered issues I've been collecting. I'm persuaded that it's a question that can be rightly answered only at the price of disallowing the intransigent presumptions of those I tag true normativists—that is, those who believe there are higher norms (agentive norms) discernible in some other way than by yielding to the always already effective primacy of the *sittlich*. The *sittlich* has no a priori import, is thoroughly historied and continually evolving. If, indeed, persons are artifactual transforms, if normativity (always inseparable from discursivity) is also ineluctably artifactual, then agentive norms (of whatever persuasion) cannot be more than second best—that is, *sittlich*, in the most banal of ways (say, in the field anthropologist's descriptions, or as projections from them).[49] Agentive proposals tend to be conservative—that is, conserving—modifications apt to be both viable and effectively endorsed within the practices of an actual society, the very opposite of the utopian, although the utopian also begins with *sittlich* inspiration. There, delphically, you have the answer to my final question: it waits only for a last distinction. It's meant to rescue the aimless meander of following the Kantian and Pittsburgher arguments. We have never been far from the decisive clue, which draws almost no benefit from Kantian sources.

I take this line of reasoning to be ineluctable, the constant theme of every naturalism attuned to our being, qua persons, second-natured artifacts. Agentive norms need not be confined to natural norms, of course. But if we are contingent artifacts (lacking an essential nature or telos), then our assigned purpose, quite apart from being cast in terms of the habits of ordinary life, will already be prone to yield in the direction of the customary. Indeed, this marks the notable appeal of the *Nicomachean Ethics*, viewed by so many as a noble ideal to be realized within the actual world—favored civilizationally, in the sense of human flourishing, *not* primarily moral in the modern Western sense but ample enough to include the moral. Nevertheless, to gain such standing is never a matter of discovering any independent normative or moral truth. There are no such discoveries to be had, and the *sittlich*, despite its endless variety, is neither problematic nor lacking in inventive powers.

What we *discover* instead is the willingness of human societies to live in accord with an almost-unimaginable diversity of conflicting codes of conduct and aspiration, condemned and applauded with equal zeal—sometimes breathtakingly altered, over small stretches of time, by the same societies. One can hardly deny, reviewing the twentieth century and even the small span of the twenty-first that's elapsed, that there are no formulable visions of agentive norms of any large scale that can, with confidence, be said to be genuinely approximative of the universal goals all societies are committed to achieving. (We have only to remember 9/11 and Paris after the attack on *Charlie Hebdo*.) The only agentive norms we could reasonably claim to validate objectively presuppose the passingly *sittlich*, which is generally thought to be defective in an essential way. It *is* defective according to the usual convictions of the societies affected. But that signifies no more than that we live (and hope) in the space (may I say?) of one or another form of strife. Neutrality among agentive norms is more than improbable. Which is to say that normative improvement cannot be more than second best: partisan, diverse, polemical, consistent only with a selective run of *sittlich* convictions and local possibilities relative to the pertinent options that confront us. Furthermore, if this has nearly always been true, then there's little need for increased alarm now. The hazards are no more than what we have always lived with, and in any case there is no viable alternative. Indeed, the marvel is that, on the whole, the race does not despair. What needs to be acknowledged is that we begin and end as ideologues and partisans. This is not to endorse the arbitrary. But we cannot fail to conjure with the possibilities of our actual history and prevailing convictions.

Sellars, I would say, has grasped an important clue regarding normativity (in "Philosophy and the Scientific Image of Man"): it's not merely that scientism lacks a conception of agentive norms; it has no obvious way of accommodating the functionality of agency and agents within its own vision. If, then, Sellars is correct in linking agentive norms with societal intentions, then he's hit on an excellent reason for doubting that his "scientific image" is any more resourceful than his "manifest image." Because, as things now stand, "intentions" can only be drawn from the manifest image. (Actually, both "images" are thoroughly unworkable.) Sellars has, however, successfully passed his idea of the "space of reasons" on to McDowell; or, perhaps better, McDowell espies the refutation of scientism in what he calls the "extrusion" of the normative—the extrusion of agentive norms—from nature. (Bear in mind, I should add, that, logically, the attack on scientism has nothing to do with Max Weber's diagnosis of the "disenchantment of the world.") This is because McDowell, who, unlike Sellars, does not favor scientism—in fact, regards it as thoroughly misguided—treats the "space of reasons" as a constant factor in everything that, in the real world, requires judgment. The irony is that McDowell, in following Sellars's formula here, which he cites from "Empiricism"—"Sellars describes the space of reasons as the space 'of justifying and being able to justify what one says' "[50]—*also* accepts responsibility for the explanation needed. But what will count? (It cannot be enough to begin by affirming "we believe these truths to be self-evident"!)

For his part, *Sellars* must consider that the space of reasons may have to be abandoned when the defective manifest image is itself abandoned (or suitably absorbed), or if that's not true, then perhaps, in conceding the actuality of judgment (and what that must entail) within the victorious scientific image, Sellars would be obliged to retain intentions and perceptual experience as well; hence, normativity and discursivity may continue to function in the completed scientific image—reconciled with, as Sellars might say, not merely joined externally to, the manifest image. (At best, a mongrel union.) As a consequence, it can no longer be assured that Sellars supports a coherent option. By contrast, McDowell's application of the same dictum might well remain trouble free, since, in addition to his rejection of scientism, he characteristically speaks of normativity (in the "space of reasons") when he speaks of judgment in the most general terms—which is to say, where reference to enabling norms is distinctly more compliant than the validation of agentive norms.

But then, when McDowell says, without hesitation, that "meaning and aboutness are 'ought'-laden,"[51] he places himself under an obligation to explain just how, objectively, one *can* justify (or confirm) *agentive claims*, which he airs very carefully and very sparely. The thing is that precisely because enabling norms *are* replaced (pragmatically, as I say, *not* by semantic reduction but) by *non*normatively described, instrumentally effective means, we rarely find it difficult to validate such claims, whereas nothing of that kind greets us easily when we attempt to validate categorical or ultimate agentive norms. There's a lacuna there that McDowell does not quite fill but that Sellars appears to fill very neatly wherever he yields along *sittlich* (Rousseauesque) lines.

As it happens, McDowell, in a perceptive reading of Hegel's *Phenomenology*, favoring *Sittlichkeit* and informed, I daresay, by his reading of Wittgenstein's account of what it is to "follow a rule," explains what it is to be "a free agent" (in Hegel's sense and, as it appears, also in his own) as follows: "Freedom is responsiveness to reasons. It is not a natural endowment. Rational agency is a normative status. Understanding it requires a social context. There is *nothing* outside our reasoning on which we could found confidence in its results. There is no ground, and it [would be] wrong to suppose there was any need for one."[52] This could not apply to enabling norms. The question remains whether it holds true of agentive norms. I think it would be a near disaster if it were read literally. Agentive norms cannot be loyal at the same time to both *sittlich* history and a priori necessity. Hence, causal determinism cannot be total.

I find myself obliged to say (to McDowell), "Very nicely turned, but still misleading and still distinctly short of the mark." What I mean is, we must be able to give a better answer, but McDowell's answer *is* a good one *if* you accept it as a stand-in for an answer closer to the mark! And there I mean the answer is tethered to the significance of one's having been effectively immersed in one's home language and culture, in precisely the same sense in which Wittgenstein, finding himself faced by a puzzle case that seems *not* to be "following the rule" he thought *he* was following but that is so persistently tendered (by others) as complying, compellingly, that he begins to doubt that it does not comply and finally confesses (I've cited the passage earlier), "I obey the rule *blindly*." I mean (as McDowell seems to mean) that one *can* give both right and wrong reasons for a judgment or for a rule on which a judgment depends; one can be baffled; one can run out of fresh things to say. That's not the point. The point is that *justifying agentive norms* can only proceed in the circular, seemingly question-begging way by which the self-referential paradoxes of epistemology help us to understand what "knowing what it is to know" means, so that we may say irenically (with McDowell) that our norms are "groundless." But they're not literally groundless; it's just that repeating what makes our agentive norms *our* norms—having to repeat them circularly—leads us to say, figuratively, that they are groundless. (The same, of course, is true of understanding the meaning of words.) In any case, McDowell's disinclination to answer leaves us uncertain about how, precisely, he construes the matter of legitimating our agentive norms, invoking "the right norms"—where we suppose the question is not a question merely of contingent convictions.

McDowell never tells us what legitimates the discursive use of the "space of reasons" in agentive matters or how its use relates to claims of objectivity. You see how far McDowell risks going astray—and how reasonable he is—when you see how important it is to his argument about freedom and agency to link the distinction between mere animals and "rational animals" (humans) to his endorsement of an unexpectedly rigid and regressive (Kantian) theory of perceptual experience (in the first of the Woodbridge Lectures). Agentive normativity begins to slip from sight.

I take it to be an empirical fact (the force of which McDowell sometimes scants) that human infants are brute animals of a gifted kind that happen to be able, incipiently, to master discursivity by means of their native animal talents and that, in mastering language, are able to transform themselves into rationally competent persons. The "spontaneity" of reasons, which McDowell mentions a number of times—his Kantian wording for our human facility with discursive norms and the categories of understanding that are said to give cognizable form to sensory perception—comes *into play* (McDowell maintains) with the gift of language. But he nowhere explains what to understand as the onset of the mastery of language or, specifically, agentive norms. For instance, in opposing Sellars, he discounts the bare possibility of perceptual concepts altogether (which, as he notes, Aristotle, Donald Davidson, J. J. Gibson, Gareth Evans, and Wilfrid Sellars are plainly drawn to, and which the evidence in the paleoanthropological record, regarding the rearing of infants, seems to support). He admits that the mastery of language cannot be accounted for on merely biological grounds, but he does not examine the artifactuality thesis (which, if adopted, would defeat Kant's and his own treatment of perceptual experience at a stroke).

The important issue here is that the treatment of agentive norms cannot fail to be profoundly affected by the factual standing of the artifactuality thesis: McDowell's failure to engage the matter of perceptual concepts (affecting our account of human infants particularly) ineluctably obscures the logic of agentive norms. Post-Darwin, *Sittlichkeit* no longer signifies merely second-naturing *Bildung* but the artifactuality of agentive norms as well. Once this is conceded, there can be no way of disjoining the original onset of normativity and the failure of Kant's (and McDowell's) treatments of the objective standing of perceptual and agentive validation. The validity of norms rests in their artifactuality! There is no other source to draw on. Here, I remind you again that Weber's preoccupation with the "disenchantment of the world" is no more than a historied matter: it has nothing to do with McDowell's rejection of "bald naturalism"; it's the expression of a worry about the loss of the putatively grander agentive norms of the past. In that same spirit, I suggest, the entire effort of the latter-day Frankfurt School meant to retrieve the true agentive norms of the human mode of life—in, say, the claims of Jürgen Habermas and Karl-Otto Apel (though Apel was never a member of the Frankfurt School)—is, apart from its philosophical presumption, simply regressive.

Habermas, I'm bound to say, never managed to resolve the cognitional question regarding whether his defense of "discourse ethics" was, finally, transcendental ("quasi-transcendental," "transcendental in a weak sense," as he says in various essays) or simply pragmatist (that is, antiapriorist). Failing there, he's been unable to lead us beyond Kant's original aporia: what is "rational in the transcendental sense" remains completely elusive, and what he proposes pragmatically is unable to exceed a merely arbitrary or utopian hope. Apel, Habermas's mentor, was entirely justified in exposing Habermas's inability to decide the matter. But then, Apel's own transcendental(ist) conviction remains completely unsecured and (perhaps) even more obviously threatened by utopian vacuity and absolutist objectives.

Apel is rather short with Habermas: "The Habermasian strategy," Apel ventures, "of avoiding a methodological distinction between philosophy and empirical testable reconstructive science seems to me openly inconsistent. I suspect Habermas will have to make up his mind one day whether he wants to persist in the inconsistency or give back to philosophy its genuine *justificatory function*, together with its *a priori* universal and self-referential validity."[53] Apel's argument, however, rests on shaky grounds. His transcendental proposals are as much obiter dicta as are Habermas's—and, of course, Kant's.

Habermas provides an inclusive pragmatic principle, possibly transcendental (in some sense) but, if it is, then not (or probably not) apriorist, a formal rule of impartiality said to be fallibilistically universalizable. He's obviously in search of a pragmatist analogue approaching the openness of Kant's categorical imperative but formulated, ideally, to satisfy the condition of everyone's being accorded the liberty of entering into "every discourse." Seen this way, Habermas's formal rules of fair-minded discourse are no more than the vacuous satisfaction of an ideal model in which all may speak and all may question every speaker and every statement. (Habermas's argument is, then, a liberal manifesto akin to that of the public square, not a philosophical defense: there's finally very little difference between his "dialogical" and John Rawls's "monological strategies." Both are ideologies rather than transcendental or rational discoveries.) The trouble is that Habermas's rule or policy is patently impossible to fulfill: there's no operative way to bring it into accord with the conditions of actual life, and where it is universalistic, it cannot claim advantages from approximations. It provides only a paper offer: it affords no justification for being satisfied with such arrangements; it's also difficult to see why one should brand anyone who opposed such principles irrational or unreasonable or simply uninformed or barbarian. (The counterargument is meant to apply to any Kantian-like proposal in any practically oriented sector of rational certainty.)

Apel may well be right to think that Habermas will, in turn, be forced to embrace a stronger form of apriorism if he holds to his picture of ideal discourse. But, recalling what has already been cited from Apel, one may well wonder why Apel supposes *his* replacement of Kant's moral position would fare better. The reason lies (it seems) with Apel's conviction that Peirce had actually hit on the apriorist imperative that "binds" every "language community" to the constitutive rules of rational argument or discourse.[54] Apel believes he's carried Peirce's argument involving the semiotic (a priori) conditions of discourse to completion, so as to retire Kant's own defective a priori posit and to secure Peirce's semiotic alternative. I think we need only sample a specimen passage to assess Apel's thesis correctly, which, at one stroke, confirms his position vis-à-vis Habermas's, Kant's, and Peirce's alternatives—*and* its own vacuously utopian enthusiasm:

> The *a priori* of argumentation contains the *claim* to *justify* not only all the "assertions" of science, but also all human *claims* (including the implicit claims of human beings upon one another that are embedded in actions and institutions). Anyone who takes part in an argument implicitly acknowledges all the *potential claims* of all the members of the communication community that *can* be justified by rational arguments (otherwise the claim of argumentation would restrict itself in subject matter). He also commits himself to eventually justifying all his claims upon other people through arguments. Furthermore, I believe that the members of the communication community (and this implies

all thinking beings) are also committed to considering all the potential claims of all the potential members—and this means all human "needs" inasmuch as they could be affected by norms and consequently make *claims* on their fellow human beings. As potential "claims" that can be communicated interpersonally, all human "needs" are ethically *relevant*. They must be *acknowledged* if they can be justified interpersonally through arguments. This necessary readiness to justify personal *needs qua interpersonal claims* represents an analogy to the "self-surrender" demand by Peirce in that the "subjectivity" of the egoistic assertion of one's interests must be sacrificed in favor of the "transsubjectivity" of the argumentative representation of interests.[55]

Here is utopian thinking run amok: very likely noble but quite impossible.

One cannot fail to see Apel's formulation (one of many) as a response to Max Weber's disenchantment thesis and the social reality it represents. One also sees what Apel finds so distressing in Habermas. Nevertheless, Apel's charge is the expression of a deep concern for the fate of humanity, *not* a transcendental demonstration of moral obligations entailed, a priori, in order to fulfill the constitutive conditions of some "ideal communication community," itself (as Apel argues) implicated in the discursive activities of all actual communities. Transcendental Reason is, and was from its inception, a fiction; and Peirce's theory of signs (on which Apel bases his assessment of Kant's proposal) was never an apriorist doctrine. Apel treats Peirce as a failed Kantian whose "transcendental insight" Apel claims to have rescued so as to restore a valid approach to First Philosophy. Apel fails to see that Peirce is, finally, an opponent of Kant's transcendentalism: Peirce was wary on this score from his earliest reflections but was finally free of Kant's excesses by 1903 at the latest.

VII

There's nothing more to be said in Apel's favor. I turn back to add a final word about the Pittsburghers. I'll add only a bit to signal that Brandom's inferentialism, inspired by Sellars's abortive account of "material inference" and his sense of the phrase "the space of reasons" is quite uneventfully tethered to the normativity issue. Brandom has much to say about normativity, particularly in *Making It Explicit*, but most of what he says is completely formulaic and abstract—not altogether useless, indeed poised for application—but almost entirely linked, verbally, to what he's borrowed from Sellars's account of the normative import of "practices" and "rules" and, from there, of "commitment" and "entitlements."[56]

We never actually learn how pragmatically complex judgments are objectively assigned their appropriate propositional import, wherever agentive norms are implicated "in flesh and blood." (I see no evidence that Brandom has convincingly penetrated fresh algorithmic possibilities of a *sittlich* logic.)

I see no way in which Brandom's distinctive views on normativity can be made explicit enough to warrant careful scrutiny, until he ventures beyond canonical logics into the complexities of pragmatic life itself, which he evidently has in mind, in venturing the possibility of a new strategy of giving and asking for reasons—what he calls "deontic scorekeeping"—in a sense drawn from analogies with standard inferential canons, AI simulation, and the like, where unsuspected normative proprieties of societal life may have a distinctive regulative role to play in pragmatic contexts. (Certainly, Brandom does not explore the complexities of Sellars's account of "material inference" in the careful way Sellars himself might have attempted.)

The best that can be said for Brandom's efforts here is that he provides a reasonable conceptual scaffolding for the account he promises but almost nothing of the account required. Most readers would concede, without ado, the clarity of his general account. But, as yet, he has not demonstrated anything like the primacy of inferentialism. On the contrary, Frege is of little help here, Sellars's efforts are abortive, and Brandom himself draws almost nothing from the classic pragmatists or from Wittgenstein. In fact, if there were a distinctive pragmatic logic, then, of course, there would be an AI simulation of *that*. But how could AI analogies apply if we still lack the algorithmic extension of canonical logic *for* the novel complexities of pragmatic contexts?

Here, for instance, is Brandom's most general statement on normativity and the space of reasons:

> Reason is as nothing to the beasts of the field. We are the ones on whom reasons are binding, who are subject to the peculiar force of the better reason.
>
> This force is a species of *normative* force, a rational "ought." Being rational is being bound or constrained by these norms, being subject to the authority of reasons. Saying "we"

in this sense is placing ourselves and each other in the space of reasons, by giving and asking for reasons for our attitudes and performances. Adopting this sort of practical stance in taking or treating ourselves as subjects of cognition and action; for attitudes we adopt in response to environing stimuli count as *beliefs* just insofar as they can serve as and stand in need of reasons, and the acts we perform count as *actions* just insofar as it is proper to offer and inquire after reasons for them. Our attitudes and acts exhibit an intelligible content, a content that can be grasped or understood by being caught up in a web of reasons, by being inferentially articulated. Understanding in this favored sense is a grasp of reasons, mastery of proprieties of theoretical and practical *inference* . . . Picking us out by our capacity for reason and understanding expresses a commitment to take *sapience* rather than *sentience* as the constellation of characteristics that distinguishes us.[57]

This much is indistinguishable from the views advanced by Sellars and McDowell—and by Peirce and Dewey and many others. What, we must ask, do the "proprieties" of "sapience" comprise? They cannot be merely semantically decoded: they require a command of the thicker resources of practical know-how and something of a reflexive cultural anthropology. Brandom's seeming disjunction between sapience and sentience suggests that there probably *is* an implicit logic peculiar to pragmatic contexts of thought and deed that we could recover, by way of something like the heuristics of score keeping, but I doubt it. I think it much more likely that an interpretive linkage between a particularly salient chanced-upon fact and its associated abductive guesses, in context, are likely to be more instructive as an inferential invention than any straightforward algorithm. But then such a *jeu* would outflank the disjunction of sapience and sentience.

These last reflections persuade me that the Pittsburghers and the Frankfurters yield much less than might be wished. But they yield a great deal in yielding *that* discovery, because they reveal much regarding normativity's state of play among the most salient discussions of our day. I agree with the drift of the accounts of both schools (and with Kant, of course) as far as the conceptual linkage between normativity and discursivity is concerned. But that hardly confirms that normativity is, primarily, a semantic matter—any more than truth is—or, independently, that normativity requires a transcendental review. The first worry counts heavily against deflationism. Neither the Pittsburghers nor the Frankfurters are deflationists, of course, but the late Frankfurters tend to be florid transcendentalists, and the Pittsburghers neglect the full import of their best scruple.

It's in this circumstance that I suggest we turn away (if we can, without scuttling the entire issue) from the grand forays we've been sampling: that's to say, *not* from the Kantian issue of the "space of reasons" but from the threateningly vacuous and arbitrary extremes favored by recent Kantian revivals of the transcendental wild card. I recommend, instead, something closer to the very sensibly focused, small-scale, sociologically informed, yet interestingly disputatious analyses offered by a figure like Stephen Turner, who, as it happens, examines the views of the Pittsburgh group at the same time he reviews some of the most pertinent puzzles (regarding the Kantian treatment of the "space of reasons") that arise in specific legal and broadly social contexts—fortuitously, with attention to one of the best-known disputes involving Max Weber's thesis of "the disenchantment of the world."

Turner contributes a telling sense of the normative/natural opposition (alternatively, the normative/nonnormative opposition) that is genuinely instructive when read along Wittgensteinian lines. He shows convincingly, for instance, how the puzzle of distinguishing (as well as of not being able to distinguish, disjunctively) between the normative and the nonnormative arises in familiar anthropological and sociological contexts—as in the well-known dispute between Peter Winch and Alasdair MacIntyre regarding paradoxical Zande notions of normativity; or in Marcel Mauss's account of the mysterious Maori notion of the "spiritual power" known as *hau* that imposes strenuous obligations on true believers, but which Westerners have great difficulty identifying; or, most pointedly, in the decisive stalemate between the partially opposed views on normativity (in the law) favored by Max Weber and Hans Kelsen regarding the justificatory grounds of would-be higher-order agentive constraints and obligations, including (say) constitutional grounds on which positive law is said to be validated.

Turner himself (I must add in all candor) is too easily deflected by the annoying (largely irrelevant though not uninstructive) contingency of being unable to discern just what this or that society *means* when specifying the sacred sources of normative (or agentive) force.[58] What Turner demonstrates very skillfully, however, is Kelsen's inability to confirm that we *ever* discern the normative "constitution" (*Grundnorm*) on which the entire body of positive law is pronounced valid. (The issue remains thoroughly Kantian, but the analysis is not.) As far as I know, McDowell never mentions this impasse, which lies very close to the challenge of Weber's disenchantment doctrine—which McDowell regards as a legitimate target of his core application of Sellars's notion of the space of reasons.[59] (I judge that to be a mismatch.) Qua sociologist, Weber registers a palpable change in agentive norms (within the modernity of the West): he is *not* contesting the relevance of the space of reasons at all. The entire kerfuffle is due to an elementary oversight, which does indeed betray how little progress we've made.

Here is a remark of Turner's, then, that explains both Kelsen's and Weber's failure to grasp the true force and one-sidedness of their respective views of normativity, the exaggerated Kantian disjunction between the normative and the natural, *and* something of the true force of Wittgenstein's reflections, at the start of *Investigations*, regarding the first steps of languageless children in learning a language, which will in time disclose (quite reliably) an entire Intentional world otherwise invisible to uncomprehending primates (human infants) about to be transformed into persons. Quite naturally, *they* come to occupy the space of reasons—but not, *for that reason alone*, with powers greater than a *sittlich* competence and whatever that makes possible. Turner offers a dawning insight into the unity of (what I'm calling) agentive and enabling norms, their different logics, and their placement in the natural world. He sees how they serve contingent interests and yield, or may be made to yield, higher-order strictures, degrees of distinction, even obligations:

> The idea of separating the normative element from the natural facts of social life has been an important motive in ethics, at least since Rawls. It was prefigured in Kelsen's idea of a pure theory of law. The project, however, makes sense only from the side of the normative. The normative-natural distinction used in this way is a normative distinction, depending on the definition of norms, or the normative theory, that supplies the normative elements that are supposed to be separated out and used to reconstruct the phenomenon free from naturalistic or causal considerations. It is not an explanatory distinction found in nature or social reality. It is visible only to those constructing a normative lens.[60]

This is not entirely perspicuously phrased, but it's the last line that's decisive. It disarms the sense of the sentence it follows. Kelsen believes that the normative element in valid positive law is conferred ("constitutionally") by an originating, sui generis *Grundnorm* that is utterly unlike any merely "natural" (causal) factor. Turner perceptively discerns the transcendental, Kantian nature of Kelsen's claim, which Kelsen seems to regard as the only conceivable way of defeating Weber's disenchantment thesis—the only way to bring the regress problem to a proper close (which Kant had already signaled, rather casually, in the first *Critique*, but which he *there* regards as troublesome only for those not fluent in grasping synthetic apriorist truths). What is even more intriguing is that Turner finds a trace of the same Kantian theme in Brandom, Sellars, and (most significantly) McDowell.[61] (I'm in his debt here.) Nevertheless, Turner himself slights the range of the space of reasons, which, as Kant (and the Pittsburghers) realized, affects causal explanation (a fortiori, the logic of truth and confirmation in the sciences) as much as agentive decisions about conduct and commitment. The distinction that we require does not contest the discursivity of the normative; it insists, rather, on the different logics of enabling and agentive norms. We are not obliged to deny the viability of agentive norms in, say, contesting Kelsen's notion of the *Grundnorm*, but Turner does not quite see that the concession that agentive norms are essentially *sittlich* need not be deemed a conceptual disaster. It may actually prove flexible enough to accommodate all the uses represented by Kant's practice and that of the Pittsburghers and Frankfurters, and also Weber's usage, a reasonable correction of Kelsen's claim, and, of course, whatever a naturalistic reading of norms requires. Turner is unnecessarily hasty here.

The vulnerability of Kelsen's variant is entirely due to Kelsen's extraordinary candor (and naïveté). But the argument shows that the quarrel between Kelsen and Weber ultimately challenges the advantage of resurrecting Kant's essential dualism in any reasonable attempt to legitimate the objective standing of determinate agentive norms within the bounds of nature (explicated, somewhat contortedly, in McDowell's invoking the second-natured standing of the human person). Kelsen's reasoning is absolutely transparent: "only a norm can validate a norm" (Turner's phrasing of Kelsen's reasoning), which, construed in a sense akin to that of the mystery of the Maori *hau*, "is visible only to those constructing a normative lens"—that's to say, the artifactually hybrid members of one or another enlanguaged society.

McDowell co-opts Sellars's "space of reasons" to explain what's at stake in bringing another person's thought into accord with ours by way of a certain hermeneutic "fusion of horizons"—in effect, bringing another person's thought into the "space of reasons" that defines *our* community, though in a way that confirms the fact that both of us happen to belong to the same community of thought (and speech). This is indeed the intent of the following well-known, otherwise-impenetrable remark of McDowell's, in *Mind and World*:

> In the innocuous sideways-on picture, the person we do not yet understand figures as a thinker only in the most abstract and indeterminate way. When the specific character of her thinking starts to come into view for us, we are not filling in blanks in a pre-existing sideways-on picture of how her thought bears on the world, but coming to share with her a standpoint *within* a system of concepts, a standpoint from which we can join her in directing a shared attention at the world, without needing to break out through a boundary that encloses a system of concepts.[62]

Well, yes and no.

McDowell appears to mean no more (and no less) than that when we find that we and some seeming stranger understand one another, we certainly belong to the same discursive community—and thus share the same "space of reasons" (the same norms). But if that's the way to read McDowell, he claims too much: we share a space of *meanings* (to some extent), the same competence in processing norms and meaning, but *not* necessarily the potentially contested, higher agentive *norms* of that space. (Think of Habermas as a Pittsburgher!) There's an elementary equivocation here regarding the "space of reasons." There cannot be any one (uniquely valid) space of reasons suitable for all—unless we mean something like serial bilingualism. If McDowell means by "second nature" anything like an anthropologist's reading of what Aristotle reports in *Nicomachean Ethics* (the rearing of already-acknowledged persons), then McDowell hasn't faced the normativity issue at all, and if he means more than this, then he hasn't defended the position he actually advances. Sharing meanings undoubtedly means that we share norms that bear on sharing meanings, but it does not mean we share agentive norms, in sharing no more than meanings. Norms, like meanings, are determinably contentious relative to pertinent practices, whether verbally expressed or not.

Now, I believe I have an absurdly simple solution to Kelsen's problem, which escapes the infelicities of both Pittsburgh and Frankfurt (I mean, of course, late Frankfurt—Habermas's or even Apel's) efforts to recover the main force of what each wishes to retrieve from the Kantian account of normativity: you have only to construe the normative (of the specifically agentive sort)—which allows for the normative of the enabling sort and even accommodates Weber's paraphrastic policy regarding modernity *as* a *sittlich* normative. That's all! Because, as we've seen, we cannot help but begin with *sittlich* norms, since (as argued) normativity is inherently artifactual and inseparable from discursivity.

Wherever the enabling forms of normativity lend themselves to causal and natural paraphrase (as in medicine and the pursuit of practical goals), absolutely nothing is lost by adopting the equivalences of the normative and the nonnormative (à la instrumentalism and disenchantment), but wherever we oppose such paraphrases among the higher agentive norms, still within the bounds of nature (say, "treat man as an end and not as a means only"), it's precisely the solidarity and conviction of our *sittlich* beliefs that ensure their irreducibility. The phenomenon of "disenchantment" has absolutely nothing to do with answering the philosophical question of what to mean by the cognitive or rational standing of determinate agentive norms of any kind, but it's bound to affect the content of the norms we favor in any particular space of time. Weber was addressing a form of putative moral decline: there was never a need to *recover* the space of reasons—only, if you insist, the restoration of past glory (the putatively nobler agentive norms of our past). But then, that is also the key to the gathering contest between Kantians and pragmatists.

All that's needed to clinch the argument is that we grasp the difference between physical nature and human culture. Paraphrasing Wittgenstein's famous question about the difference between a voluntary action and a bodily movement ("raising my arm" and "my arm's rising"),[63] we need to ask ourselves, What is the difference between uttering a sentence and uttering a mere string of sounds? The answer requires one's grasping the sense in which speech involves the utterance of sounds that have meaning—the effective competence of persons, the effective presence of the enlanguaged world of specifically human forms of life. So Turner's worries about discerning the normative import of a particular event or state of affairs, or legal pronouncement or the like, are bare contingencies that have not yet come to terms with the conditions of linguistic fluency (and thought), on which the force of Kelsen's *Grundnorm* itself depends.

That's to say, Kelsen is right to insist that something is missing (if we lack the *Grundnorm*), though he can't say where to look for it. But then, *Turner* is right to suggest that the *Grundnorm* cannot be convincingly construed as the target of a separate (rational) discovery, though he also cannot say how to make provision for its determination. The normativists—chiefly, Kant, Korsgaard, Sellars, McDowell, Brandom, Habermas, and Apel (among those I've canvassed), and (now) Kelsen—turn to discovery (cognitive, if what is compelling to Reason is cognitive; not cognitive, if norms must be constructed here, according to our changeable second-best interests). Sellars (as we've seen) insists on remaining equivocal: speech and conception, he affirms, always proceed in accord with rules, but rules are discerned through endlessly improvised, diverse, approximative, interpretive guesses and compromises among our *sittlich* practices.

There seems to be only one way of answering: the ratio of the normative to the valuational must be analogous to that of person and primate, or word and sound (or action and bodily movement à la Wittgenstein). That's to say, Sellars does not get things quite right when he speaks of the placement of human judgment in "the space of reasons." The idea is not that, in making provision for the evidentiary treatment of judgment (the recognition, say, of the rules of right judgment), we simply oblige our sense of rational responsibility to submit (as if by some original act or contract) to the a priori trials of an infinite regress—which would be to reverse the order of practical life. The placement issue is always already settled by life itself. To be a person *is* already to function within "the space of reasons" (which has no apodictic order of its own). Mention of the logic of reasons or normativity is a reminder of the genealogy of the human, not the recovery of any Kantian-like strategy for ensuring some supposedly objective form of rational certainty or argumentative closure. Kant succeeds in validating *his* moral program only by making his rational agents noumenal. When they turn human, they lose their apriorist advantage. They become *sittlich* creatures and seek out what they are willing to be governed by. They become intelligent partisans. Again, I offer *Charlie Hebdo* in evidence.

In short, an agentive *norm* is at least a *sittlich* norm or value that has been suitably endorsed (consensually, say) by its supporting community under the would-be authority of higher-order values, rules, principles, philosophies of the human *Lebensform*, or whatever of the kind we pertinently favor (Kelsen's *Grundnorm*, for instance), to occupy the functional role of justifying locally applied (lesser, dependent) norms for this or that practice. There need be no vicious regress here, because the entire affair is a matter of artifactual, second-natured construction, contrivance, commitment, conviction, and conformable behavior. The threatening—the rational—regress is antecedently resolved by an actual society's manifesting (in some way) its effective endorsement of its own interests already embedded in its *Sitten*. I don't deny that *that* is a recipe for endless dispute; I say only that it is not a version of the regress argument and that it does not require a society's abandoning its deeply felt sense of the adequacy of the resources of the *sittlich* or the supreme value of debating how we should live. It is not even confined to the moral; it applies with equal fluency to every form of human or civilizational flourishing that invokes agentive norms. We ponder improvement by weighing up the future possibilities of *sittlich* history itself, which has no telos of its own. But in practical life, we tend to settle quarrels verdictively—according to our lights.

In short, the answer, in the first instance, rests with what accords with the *sittlich* facts of the matter and, in the second, with what, precisely, among our *Sitten* accounts for the supposed legitimacy of the validating pronouncement itself. That's all! Any seeming rational or argumentative regress fails to come to terms with the deep informality, the contrived avowal—the mythic utterance, if you wish—of the *volonté générale* of a given community (in something like Rousseau's sense) that assures us of the standing of the would-be *Grundnorm* Kelsen means to invoke. If *that* is worrisomely informal, so be it.

The philosophical issue at stake has been met in the only way possible, in accord with the second-natured contingencies of the life of societies of selves.

The ulterior question—perhaps the most important—that inquires about the true merit of the agentive goals any would-be system of laws ought to meet, or that might quell all doubts about the validity of our "constitutional" practices (per Kelsen), cannot be more than another step in the validative or legitimative process itself. That process ends with the *sittlich* sense that it has come to an end: it comes to an end in the solidarity of its actual practice, even if it claims to come to a proper end by satisfying its rules and argumentative tests. Hence, if it fails to bring questioning to an effective end, then, of course, *it fails*. The urgencies of practical life cannot afford a mere impasse here, though the *sittlich* acknowledges the openness of history as well. Questions of ultimate norms, like questions of ultimate or absolute knowledge, do not end in privileged knowledge. But then, of course, if we have (for good reasons) abandoned cognitive privilege, we ought to have the courage of our convictions.

In any event, we have been led to see that an acceptable resolution rests with the difference between questions regarding brute nature and questions regarding human culture. And there, the gap that remains—the choice of agentive norms by which we mean to live—always acknowledges the (*sittlich*) norms by which we actually do live (in moral, political, civilizational, even aesthetic ways, if you like), reflexively adjusted as we continually probe our most deeply felt interests (adjusted as a result of historied and technological successes and failures, natural events outside our control, the sum of accumulating experience, the perceived limits of human tolerance and desire, the steadiest prudential objectives of the compared careers of every society that has ever flourished, and their utopian visions). The objectivity of agentive norms is no more than whatever consensual support and criticism the commitment of actual societies endorses along such lines. The outcome cannot fail to be diverse, transient, blind to future contingencies, open to continual correction, perspectivally earthbound, and forever risked. In short, the legitimating grounds are inherently and insuperably contested: constructed, contrived, collectively conveyed, interpreted by partisans, and guarded with their lives. But you will look in vain for any sort of privileged access.

What, then, have we achieved? We've come to see that normative objectivity is assured at least because our agentive norms answer, artifactually, to our artifactual interests. That's to say, *they* (our norms) have *sittlich* standing, and *we* (persons) are capable of discerning norms as objective only if they are at least *sittlich* or capable of gaining *sittlich* standing societally—adequated to our interests, just as our interests are adequated to them. But, in that case, reflexively, the *sittlich* is capable of endlessly revising its own norms by *sittlich* projection or posit or revision; hence, the *sittlich* is capable of generating higher-order ends for the appraisal of both agentive and enabling norms. We are bound only by the autonomy of our continual self-transformation and the historied memory of whatever evolves as *sittlich* gains. Normative objectivity, then, answers to our deepest bias in the agentive way—rational or naturalistic, if we restrict our norms conformably, and, in the enabling sense, in accord with whatever form of testing answers to the nonnormative paraphrases that we are willing to accept.

There is no other answer if we are indeed the artifactual beings I've claimed we are. But that's to say, we live in Hope (Peirce's usage), abductively, through historied reason, inventing and reinventing our own purposes. Freestanding skepticism is never more than a form of self-deception, wherever it is thought to be actually threatening—otherwise it's compatible with our cognitive presumptions: the confirmation of our highest agentive norms is always second best, keyed to our historied interests, logically internal to our own grasp of the *sittlich*, universalized only ideologically, rationally reconciled with the resources of our time, validated in terms of practical conviction among competing agentive visions. All that remains is the perpetual contest of competing interests and the continual need for a modus vivendi.

Thirteen

A Reasonable Morality
for Partisans and Ideologues

Events like the terrorism of 9/11, cushioned in the spreading efficiency of the violence and brutality and warfare of the end of the twentieth century and the fledgling beginnings of the twenty-first, lend an unexpected legitimacy to questioning whether what we call ethics or moral philosophy may not, after all, be deeply and terribly wrongheaded. I assure you that by thinking aloud in this way, I am not calling into question all the moral dogmas and political ideologies of the race. They are safe enough as far as I'm concerned. I wouldn't know what to put in their place; besides, they are bound to thrive in spite of any philosophical exposés. The question of efficient moral engineering—the question Plato and Karl Marx and the Ayatollah Khomeini share—is also very far from my concern and competence, and I have no illusions about serving as a philosopher-king. But I do have nagging misgivings about the entire assured practice of mainstream English-language and Eurocentric moral philosophy; I have had misgivings for years even about my own early efforts along such lines, and I am only now beginning to catch a glimmer (well, more than a glimmer) of how that practice might be more promisingly redrawn without trading rigor for imagined relevance.

When, for instance, I think of the stunningly simple point of Amartya Sen's compelling criticism of John Rawls's entire vision—I mean Sen's insistence on the need for an enabling provision ("capability" or "capacitation") beyond abstract entitlement, which suggests at a stroke at least one fundamental difference between morality and law and the inappropriateness of reading morality's practical concern in terms of the theoretical modeling of the law[1]—I am acknowledging a conceptual shift akin to the kind of vision I have in mind. Sen's undertaking, however, is not committed to the conceptual reform my own intuitions favor. It's the latter that I wish to lay before you—*my* intuitions regarding how to revamp moral philosophy in order to bring it into line with flesh-and-blood life. Presumptuous, no doubt, but there it is.

I

I start abruptly, therefore. What strikes me about the great struggles over Kashmir, Kosovo, Northern Ireland, the Palestinian/Israeli world, Afghanistan, and more is that they cannot be easily, perhaps even legibly, captured by any of the usually debated systems of philosophical ethics that we know so well. I concede at once that my charge may be turned aside by an adept professional maneuver (say, a utilitarian or liberal feint—one of the many varieties we know, possibly abetted by a brisk reminder that there's a great deal of evil in the world, don't you know). But that would miss the point by a country mile. The evil or deviance that would have to be admitted would be so massive, so widespread, that we would surely risk, in the very pronouncement, the advantage of our principled perch. For no one can expect, nowadays, to win a moral dispute in the global setting by claiming to belong to the loyal remnant, those who have remained true to the requirements of global well-being.

What strikes the eye in reviewing the whole of the last century and the troubling start of the new century is simply that all the great conflicts that have made it impossible to separate moral and political objectives—in the determined way analytic ethics has insisted on so energetically—now appear, if you allow a rough-hewn summary, to take the form of one incipient religious war or another. I am struck by the obvious sincerity, conviction, zeal, ferocity, and warrior loyalty of all the pertinently paired opposing forces. The announced evil, for instance, of the attack on the World Trade Center, an attack deemed an act of war by the Americans, seems to be the same act as the outraged, desperate, possibly misguided but heroic attempt by Muslim "freedom fighters" (against all odds, according to the story) to smash through the impenetrable blindness and perceived evil of the Americans' own role in perpetuating the debased condition of the Arab world (as in the deepening corruption of Saudi Arabia and the continuing occupation of Palestinian lands).

I see no way to deny the prima facie plausibility of *both* characterizations viewed from their opposed perspectives, each of which may claim, fairly enough, to be grounded in the moral sensibilities of the populations they serve. What I cannot see is how one such charge could win out over the other—objectively, disjunctively, free of ideological slant, or without regard to enlisting the actual energies and memories and aspirations of the affected peoples—by the straightforward application of *any* familiar moral principle. I don't mean by this to appeal for expert advice in resolving the contest between such opposed appraisals (by recovering the Moral Truth, for instance) but rather to suggest, as gently as I can, that that is no longer an obvious or reliable or even plausible resource for any such recovery.

In this regard, 9/11 is a philosophically oblique, still inchoate, but politically frontal attack on the conceptual hegemony of an entire run of Western moral and moral/political practices deemed responsible for grave injustices and unpardonable evil visited on a people unable (before now) to begin to right such wrongs. History is filled with the expression of such convictions, of course. But the present situation is widely sensed to have marked a change of deep significance, partly because the actual event is being read, metonymically, as a first countermove in a developing global confrontation requiring drastic changes in the very conception of moral and political justice; because the most pertinent competing conceptions appear to be irreconcilable and bound to collide in more and more intransigent and unpredictable ways; because the increasingly realist bearing of global strategies is itself evolving along unfamiliar lines; and because the technologies of war have been democratized and miniaturized in an extraordinary way. Moreover, the resolution of the gathering disputes between powers of the emerging sorts will undoubtedly require innovations in the forms of reasoning about normative matters that are hardly being examined now and cannot be counted on to proceed by merely adjusting the practices and conceptions that the West has traditionally favored. This is, in fact, no more than the blandest first step in coming to terms with a radically altered moral landscape.

To my knowledge, there is no standard theory that belongs to the philosophical lists that would ever (1) admit the prima facie validity of opposed claims in a standoff of the sort just mentioned; (2) act to resolve the impasse without overriding the seeming force of (1), as if by appealing to higher normative considerations not themselves subject to a similar stalemate; or (3) admit that the valid or objective resolution of the impasse would (and could) never exceed the dialectical resources of the partisans themselves (or the resources of similarly placed parties) or the advantages of moderate revisions or extensions of such resources, which need never be deemed uniquely or exclusively valid. Nevertheless, I think that is how we must begin. My own charge is simplicity itself. I say that if moral questions have any point at all, the salience, if not the out-and-out priority, of disputes of the sort just mentioned cannot be ignored. Such moral questions make no compelling sense except in terms of the prima facie validity of the opposed interpretations and moral/political judgments of the interested parties. They cannot be objectively resolved in terms of any bivalent principle (of what is true or right).

Their valid resolution is restricted to options that cannot presume to rely on moral principles, moral rules, or moral criteria alleged to be confirmed objectively by means that are neither similarly partisan nor encumbered by prima facie norms—say, by inspecting human nature, responding to the dictates of reason, exercising special cognitive faculties, drawing on self-evident moral truths, or the like. All of these easy assurances must be set aside.

If this much be granted, I then suggest that nearly the whole of Western moral philosophy—preeminently, Anglo-American moral philosophy—will find itself in jeopardy and may, in fact, prove completely wrongheaded. The clue may be weakly glimpsed in Sophocles' *Antigone*, except that in Sophocles, the argument is not confined to the prima facie and is thought to be resolved in a satisfactory way. It also appears in Plato's elenctic dialogues, except that Socrates never analyzes the kind of rigor possible (or, more likely, required) in examining matters akin to the question of justice in the second-best state bruited in the *Statesman*. And, to leap to our own time, it appears in the terrible, intractable territorial claims of the Palestinians and Israelis regarding the same small piece of land—the implications of which, we begin to see, cannot be merely local.

You will, of course, need to have firmer premises in hand to vindicate my brief at all.

Broadly speaking, I construe moral or moral/political disagreement as a dispute between ideologues or partisans who seek, as their best option under the circumstances, a form of objective resolution that, they suppose, both sides may view as reasonable—as manifesting as much rigor as moral matters permit—and that, above all, never invokes normative principles or criteria that claim to be validated beyond, or essentially independent of, the actual confrontations and shared capacities and distinctive moral habits of those same partisans. I take it to be a postulate, faute de mieux, that we cannot rely on any objectivist ground of the kind just mentioned (and set aside) and that an alternative form of reasonable resolution must be possible. But what would it be like?

We do need to warn ourselves that moral philosophy cannot be autonomous, cannot be completely separated from the results of good work regarding the analysis of knowledge and reality in general. The argued differences in moral vision are bound to reflect deeper realist, cognitive, and normative differences that will be judged inadequate or untenable by the partisans of an opposed conviction. Think, for instance, of Kantians and Aristotelians who cannot approach the question of moral virtue without prior attention to the proper mode of reasoning about moral matters as such. I see no difference, here, between such contests and those, say, between Iranian mullahs and Thomistic theologians. (I realize that you may protest.) This hardly means, say, that the representatives of sovereign states could never agree, *as partisans*, to anything as ambitious or explicit as occasional resolutions like the United Nations Universal Declaration of Human Rights. Of course they could—and have. It means only that the rationale for their agreement affords an important example of the kind of objective reasonableness that I am presuming is possible (indeed, is necessary) among ideologues arguing from the proprietary vantage of what they regard as their own interests and norms of conduct, which (like the UN Declaration), we may suppose, are not always compatible with the *sittlich* norms they themselves favor and would neither wish nor be willing to abandon. The Iranians, for instance, have made it perfectly clear that the severity of sharia bearing on thieves and adulterers and other evildoers cannot be expected to yield to the terms of the UN Declaration! And, of course, they don't regard themselves as inconsistent.

If philosophical ethics is to succeed, it must be able to propose specimen forms of moral advice that need never congeal in the way of canonical claims of normative privilege—running, say, from Aristotle and Immanuel Kant to figures like Alasdair MacIntyre and John Rawls (late followers of Aristotle and Kant, respectively)—although advice of the new sort will have to be able to be fashioned *and* favored in exchanges between "reasonable" ideologues. To come to the point: I cannot see that adherence to the conditions I've collected as items (1)–(3), which motivate my brief against familiar societal canons, could not—or would not—be supported by alert partisans in a wide range of specific disputes. In effect, items (1)–(3) define (at a first pass) and instantiate what, in a minimal way, it *is* to be reasonable in a philosophical review of legitimating moral claims. Hence, conditionally, they define what it means to behave reasonably *as* a moral partisan. Nevertheless, *reasonable*, here, cannot be already captive to any well-entrenched normative vision championed by the partisan forces of any of our familiar contests. If even this small advantage cannot be counted on to gain a significant measure of acceptance in serious disputes (and perhaps in the most serious disputes), then the whole idea of a philosophical ethics will prove to be nonsense. For it is part of the sense of (1)–(3) that there is no facultative or objectivist or privileged or universalized or revealed source of normative objectivity to fall back to in either theoretical or practical affairs. In fact, I would argue that objectivity regarding what is true or right can never be more than a reasoned or critical *construction* regarding questions of fact or questions of how we should live and behave. I deem it unreasonable, almost by definition, to suppose that moral partisans would perseverate forever in a prolonged dispute—one that would put their own concerns of life and death at increased and irreversible risk—by falling back to privilege or revelation when debating dangerous opponents who, as they surely know, do not share their privileged or revealed norms.

Think, for instance, of the dispute between Israelis and Palestinians regarding the right to control Jerusalem, their competing claims marked by privileged reference to divine authority. Of course, I don't deny that it is entirely rational to promote such claims in order, for instance, to muster the latent militancy of one or the other of the affected peoples. The fact is that negotiations between the Israelis and the Palestinians have, by and large, distinguished very clearly between what would be viable in the opinion of the world community and what is needed to maintain the internal discipline and solidarity of the warring parties themselves. I also admit that it is entirely reasonable that a religiously committed people, convinced of the overriding merit of their strict adherence to revealed obligations, might be willing to be annihilated rather than betray those obligations. But even the Jonestown massacre shows its unlikelihood—and surely the great powers associated with the United Nations are unlikely to be willing to permit such a slaughter. (But I acknowledge the inherent limitation of my middle way.)

A constructivist reading[2] of objectivity is, I submit, an important—even a decisive—finding, but it is *not* a specifically moral finding. It also rests on no more than faute de mieux considerations. I mean, by *faute de mieux*, literally to endorse forms of reasoning that we cannot escape inasmuch as a better (or best) discipline is simply lacking and would be impossible to legitimate anyway. Here, we find ourselves obliged to follow Socrates' example in Plato's early (elenctic) dialogues: we may, Socrates confirms, analyze

A Reasonable Morality for Partisans and Ideologues 457

piety or courage or justice if we wish, but we lack any assured method of discovering what such virtues essentially entail. Plato, I would argue, never exceeds this preliminary finding.

Certainly, the *Republic* supports the idea that he was well aware of the limitation. I shall venture only a hint, therefore, about the defense of a constructive realism—in science or morality. But I say at once that constructivism (or constructive realism) signifies at least that the philosophical analysis of science and morality cannot be disjoined and that, as a result, disagreements about objective norms in matters of practical life (of global and near-global sweep) need not be restricted to the settled ideologies of opposed partisans. (I think here of Brazilian deforestation.)

To pin matters down a little more securely, let me introduce the term *reasonably* (as in *acting reasonably*) as a term of art. Perhaps *rationaliter* is more apt than *rationabilis*, so as not to suggest any determinate facultative capacity having normative competence or any virtue construed as an essential excellence of human nature, but only to designate what accords with my first tally, (1)–(3), or what the tally may be made to yield (possibly something like the UN Declaration or ordinary treaties and agreements that convinced opponents show some willingness to accept). There can be no doubt that the Kashmir dispute is deeply colored on both sides by considerations *rationaliter*. What the concerned world worries about is that such constraints may not be capable of keeping Pakistan and India from some nuclear adventure.

I admit the tally has some normative (that is, some moral) import, but only derivatively or consequentially, and only prima facie, which means in accord with, within the tolerance of, the avowed practices of contending factions (with their respective *Sitten*, as I say, borrowing Hegel's term for a deliberately thin use), regardless of whether the disputes to which they are applied are intra- or intersocietal. The qualification must already be part of the *sittlich* competence of opposed partisans faced with the potentially disastrous consequences of adhering—implacably, under real-world conditions—to their own disjunctively valid and apparently entirely adequate norms. Also, defining *rationaliter* is not a specifically moral affair, although, when applied to the *sittlich* world, it does yield constructive (or constructivist) moral proposals. This is a somewhat tortured way of saying that it is a plain fact that societies *are* generally able to resolve practical or moral disputes involving norms and values in ways that converge on items (1)–(3), even where, frankly, they are embedded in other ideological, doctrinal values that are thought to be privileged one way or another, are intransigent there, and often stalemate the resolution of an actual dispute. (My suggestion has distant affinities with Thomas Hobbes's doctrine, in his *Leviathan*, in the sense of favoring prudence—but, contrary to Hobbes, not with the notion of a faculty of reason that may be said to yield invariant laws of practical life.) Such values may be affirmed in a dispute without being called into play as a privileged normative factor in reaching a resolution. On the contrary, whatever holds *rationaliter* plays its best part just where privileged (even would-be moral) norms seem inadequate to their task under real-world conditions.

I should like to think, for instance, that the abortion dispute in the United States could be resolved, in part, step by step, *rationaliter*, even though many among the "pro-life" cohort embed the entire question in church doctrines that claim (but can never actually validate, *rationaliter*) the authority to define, in morally pertinent terms, just what it is to be a person. I note also that, when all is said and done, Protestants and Catholics in Northern Ireland—and even Indians and Pakistanis in Kashmir—hold rather well, however problematically, to items (1)–(3) in their political deliberations and disputes.

In any case, *rationaliter* signifies a minimal procedure (or, perhaps better, a metaprocedure) for managing *practical* matters of normative importance, however doctrinally entangled, within the pale of (1)–(3), as in matters in which a contest between partisans threatens to be stalemated though it is seen to be unacceptably destructive. Moreover, this minimal procedure provides in an open-ended way for possible changes in *sittlich* practices, still in accord with partisan interests, that can provide no compelling grounds for claims to independent normative validity.

My general assumption is that something of this sort is almost always in play in the life of complex societies and has only to be regularized where it is wanted. Here, practical reasoning seeks a modus vivendi, rather than a theoretically (cognitively) valid finding, where the doctrinal defense of stalemated *Sitten* and the entrenched norms of opposed partisans threaten to be futile, dangerous, and used up within their shared world. I admit that some contests may never be resolved. But it is really quite difficult to mention bona fide cases—where, that is, sustained disputes are already in play. (As you may guess, I don't see why war must be outside the pale of moral resolutions developed *rationaliter*.)

Even this small part of my brief depends on the decisive lesson bequeathed us by the philosophical tradition that runs from René Descartes to Hegel respecting realism:[3] namely, that the Cartesian model is hopelessly aporetic because of its fixed disjunction between cognizer and cognized world and its representationalism. Kant, I should add, was aware (however problematically) that the aporiae of pre-Kantian thought had to, and could only, be overcome by a constructivist alternative. Against Kant, Hegel rejected all reference to the noumenal; confined valid judgment to the data of socially shared *Erscheinungen* (the various ways in which "the-world-appears-to-us," more or less uncritically); rejected any facultative division between the theoretical and the practical; claimed no privileged or transcendental powers; and realized in some measure that experience was itself subject to historicized change. The upshot of the entire lesson is that we cannot claim that inquiry is ordained to lead to any final form of human freedom or similar excellence, or to any perfect knowledge of the world. Reason and objectivity are contingent constructs. They take different forms in the lives of different societies, all within the evolving space of historical inquiry.

All I need add, at the moment, is that items (1)–(3) are meant to be in complete accord with this much of the Hegelian resolution and that they count, accordingly, as a methodological constraint, not a moral one. Put more narrowly, there is no viable ground on which the would-be norms of practical life could be legitimated in *theoretical* terms akin to whatever may be thought to be true about the world, or (failing that) in terms subject to the authoritative directives of some specific facultative competence (reason, let us suppose, in the Kantian sense, or moral intuition in one form or another). Therefore, objectivity in practical affairs, in moral/political affairs in particular, is, at bottom, constructivist in a deeper sense than (or in as deep a sense as) truth is in scientific inquiry. You see why, in practical matters, we must work with the initial data of what may be deemed valid prima facie in practical life (in our *Sitten*), just as we must rely, in theoretical matters, on what is "given" (as Hegel says, presuppositionlessly, in the *Phenomenology*) in the way of *Erscheinungen*. This is as close as I can come to endorsing what Hegel identifies as the *Sitten* of practical life, the customs and practices of viable societies that clearly exert some normative force on the members of those societies in a prima facie sense, one that accords with what anthropologists describe (but do not independently confirm) as rightly binding on a given society's behavior. If, however, in reviewing the *sittlich*, Hegel's account of first-order norms invests them with a deeper sort of legitimation—possibly objectivist, in some historical sense—then Hegel and I part company. (Here I concede, as well, that some contemporaneous societies appear to live in different worlds or different centuries.)

I appeal to Hegel chiefly to facilitate my own account of moral constructivism,[4] my account of the methodological conditions on which a second-best morality may be validated in a second-order sense. It's for this reason that I favor Plato's pronouncement in the *Statesman* to the effect that we are confined to conjectures about the second-best state. Though we cannot grasp the Good, we must still construct our laws in spite of our ignorance of the best state! Hence, I advance the idea that our prima facie norms are essential to our normative reflections *rationaliter*. By *prima facie*, then, I mean the familiar, habituated, first-order aspect of the normative functioning of our *Sitten*, which themselves need not (and normally do not) conform to any preferred second-order norms constructed *rationaliter*. In particular, if reasoning must be second best—if we cannot claim to know the Good, or any comparable surrogate—then moral partisans *cannot* justifiably rely on the assurance of *their* privileged norms vis-à-vis one another. But they cannot do without them either.

II

I turn to the philosophical record primarily as an economy—to remind you, first, that twentieth-century Anglo-American philosophy is, in analyzing theoretical and practical questions, largely pre-Kantian (that is, Cartesian) or Kantian in the sense in which Kant was himself Cartesian and, second, that there is a very clear alternative, initiated about two hundred years ago, that runs subversively, possibly ahead of its original mentors, from Hegel through Marx, Nietzsche, Dewey, Heidegger, and Foucault, at least. This alternative conception views the human world in constructivist and historicized terms—abandoning transcendentalism, cognitive privilege, teleologism, essentialism, invariant norms—and concedes the diversity, especially the incompatibility, among the executive values of different societies. In short, as I read it, the Hegelian tradition suggests the notably strong idea that objectivity in normative matters involving very large (even global) spaces is best captured by the model of partisans acting and disputing *rationaliter*.

Partisans, of course, may not and need not agree among themselves about the weight and decisiveness of particular arguments or norms or competing methodologies. This does not violate the spirit of my original tally. You see, therefore, how spare—and yet coherent—the idea is. Endorse it, and a huge library of humane longings that masquerade as undoubted moral truths collapses at a stroke!

In short, in the interval spanning the contributions of Kant and Hegel, early modern philosophy reaches its most decisive finding in coming to realize that the recovery of any defensible realist reading of the work of the natural sciences (as well as of human studies or human sciences) must yield in the direction of a constructivist, historicized, and rather freewheeling account of our cognitive competence. We cannot justify the idea Descartes originated (as we conventionally say)—namely, the idea that we confront the independent world directly and adequately in the realist sense. Rather, we must construct what we take to be the world we know—which is *not* to invent the world but to admit the limitations of what we may conceivably defend as true. That, philosophy finds, is the price of escaping the Cartesian paradoxes and pretensions of privilege. We can hardly claim to have improved on this part of the academy's splendid discoveries; on the contrary, it would not be unreasonable to say that we have been battling the same Cartesian demons down through the whole of the twentieth century. The point of mentioning this larger history is to flag the fact that, if all *that* is conceded, then it follows instantly that moral theory must yield as well in the direction of a constructivist and historicized, even experimental, account of the objectivity and legitimation of moral norms. It may be adequate for our needs, without being demonstrably true.

That is indeed the nerve of my reflection on 9/11—and, I hasten to add, my limited use of the work of the tradition that spans Hegel and Foucault. Put another way, moral philosophy is neither autonomous nor demonstrably discernible or apolitical. It is, in fact, hostage to larger philosophical inquiries regarding the competence and conditions of human knowledge anywhere. Because I judge the best prospects of philosophy to depend on Hegel's critique of Kant and on Kant's critique of Descartes, I see a powerful advantage in construing the import of 9/11 as touching in a coherent way on the lesson of that essential conceptual episode. But I don't pretend to resolve any substantive moral issues by doctrinal privilege. Moral disputes of nearly any society remain practical, *sittlich*, and improvisational.

In my view, the pivotal discovery lies with realizing that there *are* no moral/political (or normative) concerns apart from the reflexive inquiries of human selves *and* that there are no selves (or persons) apart from the transformative processes of enculturation.[5] Human selves are not natural-kind entities. They are not the mere members of *Homo sapiens*. If biology were thought to be explanatorily adequate, there would be no morality at all: there would be no conception of what to count as morally significant, except on some expressly privileged ("best") ground. Persons—selves, agents, subjects—cannot be defined apart from language and culture. They cannot exist, save as biologically embodied and indissolubly emergent through enculturing processes (internalizing linguistic abilities, say, in a manner comparable to the adult competence of the already-apt members of their home society). That is the decisive complication that sets the human being apart from the rest of the animal world—however close, biologically, its life is to the life of the sublinguistic primates. It's the sine qua non of our reflective powers: of our sense of responsibility, of judgment, of deliberation and choice and commitment. On my reading, it is also the ineluctable lesson of the philosophical inquiry that spans Descartes and Hegel. I insist on the point because it confirms the constructive nature of morality itself, confirms the impossibility of making progress in our understanding of moral matters without a modest grasp of philosophy's contribution, and confirms the deep importance of reflecting on the meaning of 9/11 within the historicized constraints of how our moral concerns arise at all. Discussants often suppose that we have only to return to the moral verities to secure our bearings in the practical world, but that, I say, goes entirely contrary to the initial intuitions offered at the very start of this essay. I regard all this as a Darwinian lesson, though not a lesson contemporary neo-Darwinians usually draw. Apart from the perfectly understandable courtesies extended to prelinguistic infants, fetuses, the permanently comatose, those who cannot function beyond (or much beyond) an essentially vegetative life, and so on, selves remain the encultured transforms of *Homo sapiens*, uniquely competent in terms of their mastery of a first language and of whatever abilities such mastery makes possible (notably, in terms of thought and action, on which moral agency depends).

Selves are, literally, artifactual hybrids, sui generis emergents somehow generated by undergoing the enculturing process of mastering language. They may be said to be distinct from *Homo sapiens* but surely not separable. They are, I suggest, culturally emergent but inseparably embodied (mongrel, heuristic, fictional) in one or another of the individuated members of *Homo sapiens*, in the plain sense that they exhibit competences that cannot be adequately acknowledged—described or explained—in biological terms alone but (once again) cannot exist if not indissolubly incarnated biologically or, conceivably, by other means.

Paradigmatically, selves are moral *agents*, in the joint sense of judging themselves and others and of being the distinctive kind of creature regarding which such judgments are rightly rendered—a creature who can judge and make commitments. If, of course, the way in which selves function *could* be described and explained in terms of the biology of *Homo sapiens* alone, then, to be sure, moral norms would be reduced to natural or Darwinian functions. Hence, the irreducibility of the specifically cultural world, which applies preeminently to the emergence of selves, *is* the single metaphysical condition on which the analysis of moral objectivity depends. It is this encumbering condition that I emphasize rather than any obiter dictum of the moral sort. (I shall treat rather lightly the metaphysical complexities I've just noted. But there can be no question that, in a suitably ramified analysis, I would have to acknowledge and give an account of the philosophical complications I've broached.)

What's needed here seems to be comparatively straightforward, in accord with my initial intuitions about moral theories and my attraction to the least controversial innovations of Hegel's thought. You begin to see, therefore, why we cannot presume to answer our own moral questions without considering what we take to be a philosophically adequate account of ourselves! Indeed, 9/11 forces us back to a question that the assurance of our own moral/political visions—in effect, our dreams of moral hegemony—would rather ignore. I need only mention that neither Aristotle nor Kant provides an instructive clue about the decisive difference between biological nature and human culture: *that*, I believe, accounts for Aristotle's essentialist leanings and Kant's transcendentalism. Neither could otherwise have supposed his theory of science and morality was objective at all. The admission of the cultural construction of the fully human (a fortiori, the moral) makes possible an entirely different conception of validity and objectivity. That is precisely what Hegel's innovation affords.

The ontology by which I choose to advance my thesis may of course be challenged. But the empirical facts about selves and the conceptual irreducibility of cultural attributes remain indisputable—and, with all that, the uniqueness of the human *and* the moral. I would be unwilling to allow the nerve of the argument to be lost in the quarrelsome subtleties of metaphysics. We need only affirm that selves, in acquiring language, acquire the ability to query their own behavior, to ask how, finally, they should behave—aware, as they are, that they will be able to act in accord with what they judge to be fitting. In this sense, they acquire a second nature (name it as you please). Only in this context do questions of objective norms and morally valid behavior make any sense at all. Yet, as soon as we ask ourselves what we should understand by *true* and *right*, we grasp the import of the profound asymmetry between the two questions. If, indeed, *we are selves*, then surely the cultural world is entitled to realist standing—every bit as much as the physical world. But it remains a hybrid and emergent world; the merely physical world is differently construed. In fact, according to the picture I've been sketching, our conception of the physical world or of independent nature—not the world itself—cannot fail to be an artifact of our own history, our encultured second nature. There's the entire lesson of the philosophical interval that spans Kant and Hegel. I believe that there can be no valid account of science or morality apart from that concession. That's precisely why I read 9/11 in the way I do.

Grant all that, and there are, then, no grounds for correspondentist or coherentist—or, simply, objectivist—presumptions regarding the norms of practical life and conduct (that is, regarding what is right in the moral way). The analogous presumption remains in play (that is, must be met or properly displaced) in determining the sense of *true*. I don't deny that presumptions of the latter sort may fail. But those presumptions will fail (if they must—and I think they must) for broadly Cartesian reasons: because objectivism must fail. Yet, when they fail, they fail in the process of attempting to answer the perfectly answerable question of how, finally, our beliefs and assertions relate to what can be known of the world. Presumptions of the former sort fail for altogether different reasons. They fail because to succeed (morally) in cognitivist terms we would first have to pretend to have discovered that the world actually harbored (in some ontically pertinent way) the independent practical norms we wished to consult, so that we might then consult them! There cannot be any independent norms that govern what exists only in the way of socially constituted (or constructed) artifacts. But that's to say that there cannot be any straightforwardly cognizable natural-kind norms governing the judgments and practical commitments of human selves. This radical idea—contested, to be sure, on all sides—fits rather nicely with the facts regarding the constructed nature of moral norms and the second-natured nature of moral agents. It offers the best metaphysics for construing the significance of 9/11 in the way I do. But it qualifies morality politically, prudentially, in *sittlich* ways, ideologically, experimentally, improvisationally—and yet objectively, by approximative compromise, realistically more than veridically.

The most favored option regarding the true—in effect, the Cartesian vision of the true—confuses an acknowledged paradox for a viable strategy; another, regarding the right, construes its own fictions as discernible features of the actual world, though it errs in different ways in Kantian and Aristotelian accounts. In the work of recent Kantians (John Rawls and Jürgen Habermas, for instance), the normative competence of reason is found in the human world.[6] Kant is more careful: he may be read to hold only that we may "think" of ourselves as capable of following the assuredly certain dictates of autonomous Reason (*Vernunft*), though we cannot know it to be apodictically so. Furthermore, in the sense in which a good part of twentieth-century analytic philosophy favors the first mistake, nearly the whole of Western moral philosophy favors the second—or, if it abandons cognitivism but still craves a version of objectivity beyond the resources of disputing partisans, it tends to fall back, with Kant or Rawls or Habermas, to some sort of inviolate Reason capable of vouchsafing the objective standing of the directives we need. Nevertheless, if Reason is a hybrid artifact of human history and cultural formation, as I believe, then this last alternative will be as feeble as the cognitivist option it would replace.

Once we give up appealing to supernatural, revealed, fictional, utterly utopian, indubitable, unrealizable moral resources, as well as obviously false and unconfirmable beliefs, preferring to proceed *rationaliter* (as among those who do not share our norms and values), there cannot be any compelling account of human interests that would ignore our hopes and fears regarding life and death in all its forms. These worries define the principal part of the content of our prima facie norms. They concern ourselves and those we are likely to hold especially dear. There cannot be a fixed list of them, for they vary from group to group, from one age to another, from the sensibilities and technological resources of one society to another. And, of course, they depend in good part on our organizing ideologies. Yet it is well-nigh impossible that some run of such interests will not play a decisive role in the moral vision of whatever society we choose to examine.

I call such interests prudential (*prudentiae*), though I do not mean, by that, to designate any determinate virtue essential to human nature itself. They are bound to include familiar worries about security of life and limb and property and family and community and reputation, as well as enabling arrangements of health and education and economic opportunity and food and shelter and care; worries about natural disasters and war and violence and opportunistic forays against our interests; and more-attenuated worries about equality and freedom and respect of person and the gratification of desires. The point is that these are *not* intrinsically legitimating norms but only the salient data that, cast prudentially, are collected in our *Sitten* and serve as the ground on which our corrective moral visions build—in accord, say, with items (1)–(3) of my original tally. Normally, our *prudentiae* are defended in a coherent and holistic *sittlich* vision. They are never initially collected as discrete values that may be found to be, as anthropologists often suppose they are, universally acknowledged within the human species. That sort of universalizing, not atypical among recent Aristotelians, is completely opposed to admitting the distinction of the cultural, historical, constructed, and partisan nature of the moral world itself. To reason *rationaliter* is to intend to address prudential concerns effectively—more or less in accord with worries like those just mentioned and, as well as possible, within the range of our *sittlich* constraints. It would not violate the spirit of items (1)–(3), therefore, to add, as item (4), that persons, functioning as the partisans they are, may be expected to be prudent—or, better, to make provision for their *prudentiae* by what they judge to be reliable means, their *providentiae*—where the sense of that accommodation is not meant to define an objective or essential virtue apart from our prima facie norms but, rather, to spell out the going concerns of particular societies, the determinate details of a determinable modus vivendi. By such means, societies form a more flexible, more informal policy of how to modify their practices and norms responsibly along lines that cannot easily be judged to be merely arbitrary or question-begging. Moral reflection, you realize, is insuperably informal and improvisational.

It may be the principal business of moral reflection to resolve conflicts between different prudential interests or between such interests and what (presumably) history and social custom have already entrenched as valid practices. Conflicts are bound to be common here, as with slaves affirmed and denied as property in antebellum America; unequal property holdings that make it impossible for sizable populations to gain a viable share of whatever is judged to meet their prudential needs, whether confined to a single society or not (as in the impoverishment of the whole of black Africa); or unequal entitlements deemed valid by custom or law when viewed through some local tradition or revealed doctrine (as in the recent treatment of women in Afghanistan, under the rule of the Taliban).

Nothing that arises here shows that proceeding *rationaliter* must be less resourceful or less stable or less balanced than what may be yielded by treating any of our prima facie norms as if they were already independently legitimated. It may also be prudent (in the sense supplied) to respect the *sittlich* practices of the society we inhabit. But the plain truth is that, whatever their prima facie standing, prevailing customs and even our determinate *providentiae* (slaves as property, for instance) are likely to be the principal sources of conflict within our evolving concerns.

Here, I offer three small lessons. Two of them bear on the sort of social engineering that moral/political concerns inevitably entail; the third

A Reasonable Morality for Partisans and Ideologues   467

bears on the radical cast of the conceptual reform I have in mind. The first conveys a bit of malice, though I admit I find it entirely convincing: namely, that there is, in general, a greater danger of producing widespread suffering and destruction through social changes confidently pressed into service on grounds said to be independent of our *Sitten* than there may be in conforming with whatever is historically entrenched in the prima facie way, almost without regard to its specific content. I'm thinking here of the Crusades and recent uses of jihad, the policies of Pol Pot and the Bosnian Serbs, and Hitler's vision of greater Germany. I say, quite frankly: beware those who regard themselves as persons of principle! (This applies to Hobbes as much as to those he feared—and ourselves as well.) The second lesson concerns a timing problem. It often requires no more than a glance to see a reasonable resolution of a deeply felt injustice or a conflict that threatens the entire fabric of a society. But it may well require an age or more—and discipline enough to match the patience needed—to set in motion all the *sittlich* changes that would produce the workable reform intended. In the process, patience and correction stumble; opposing factions find that they cannot, over lengthening time, keep their agreements with one another; small breaches often prove to threaten much more than was ever in place before. Think of the Indians and the Pakistanis in Kashmir. The sense of justice tends to be focused on verbal agreements, as if in a court proceeding, but the resolution of practical disputes is a matter of *altered practices*. In this regard, there can be no determinate principle of justice read in the moral way. To say that justice requires giving everyone their due (beyond prima facie considerations), for instance, signifies that potentially *any* of a range of practical resolutions congruent with our entrenched practices and their adjustment *rationaliter* (in accord with our partisan *providentiae*) may function as one or another tolerable resolution under the circumstances given. So *justitia*, as we may call the moral sense of justice—a care for the well-being of all relevant parties, according to our lights—is intrinsically never more than improvisational under historical conditions. (We may refer to *justitia* to distinguish the moral sense from any strictly legal alternative [*jus*], that is, the sense of a determinate jurisdictional space and its rules of competence and authority.)

Its effective defense, however, cannot be determinate, simply because *justitia* applies to a modus vivendi as a practical resolution, which, as such, is only determinable.[7] That is, *justitia* is validated as a general form of life that may be acceptably instantiated, in this contingency or that, in many different ways that are not set out antecedently or in a modally obligatory way. But for all that, *justitia* must be made determinately effective by way of one or another actual commitment or resolution.

Hence, for practical (not jurisdictional) reasons, when *justitia* is satisfied, it is always satisfied determinately. A great deal of Western moral philosophy falters on the confusion that lurks here: reasoning about legal propositions and reasoning about moral commitments (or actions) are, logically and conceptually, never the same, though they are normatively inseparable.

This same lesson inevitably colors our grasp of the social-engineering issue, for, on the argument being mounted, there is no uniquely determinate, assuredly principled solution to any moral/political dispute. There are only tolerable or effective commitments, and alternative ones at that (that is, determinate instantiations of a determinably acceptable modus vivendi). This is, in fact, the heart of what it is to live as a partisan contending against other partisans for the same goods or an acceptable division of entitlements, whatever they may include. But it also means that pertinent disputes may be interminable without being irrational, or that resolutions *rationaliter* may require means that one or another putatively higher canon would refuse to countenance—war, or terrorism, or torture, perhaps, where a perceived injustice appears otherwise insoluble. Here, all seeming contracts and treaties—morally and politically construed—are qualified by ceteris paribus considerations that cannot be defined in any formal manner *ante*. (Officials of the United States government, for example, have been willing, in connection with the action against the Taliban, to air in a public way the possible defensibility of using torture against captive al Qaeda terrorists—on would-be humanitarian grounds!)

In fact, a valid moral resolution, the resolution of a practical impasse, is hardly obliged (and may be unable) to solve, at the same time, any implicated theoretical or ideological claims thought to be inseparable from the practical matter before us. Think of the insoluble doctrinal differences that separate the very factions that would have to agree on a practical policy in order to resolve one or another part of the abortion impasse or the interminable theological disputes regarding the control of Jerusalem. The first leads to what is or would be right in the way of action; the second, to what, presumably, is or would be true or plausible in the way of belief. Both have their constructivist resources, but they normally apply in different ways. The first centers on the resolution of a practical (an actual) impasse; the second, on assessing the validity or the truth of a particular doctrinal claim. The first yields no more than an instantiated modus vivendi, not (or not necessarily) a judgment about the standing of a truth claim or

A Reasonable Morality for Partisans and Ideologues 469

a proposition. One can see the need for conceptual economies in both sorts of circumstance, applied *rationaliter*. (I concede that the model I am sketching may be characterized as a form of pragmatism. But then, on my own argument, that is simply to say that pragmatism may appear here as an attenuated form of Hegelian thinking.)

Moral/political issues are practical affairs, though they often arise for doctrinal reasons. The resolution of the first is bound to implicate the relevance and fortunes of the second. But there can be no principled or independent derivation of the resolution of practical disputes on grounds drawn *from* the presumed priority of any theoretical puzzle. There simply are no objectively discernible or determinable moral/political norms at all, apart from what may be identified as valid prima facie or constructively proposed—second-order—options drawn from a review of our actual *Sitten*.

To confuse the two is to risk confusing the moral and the legal (possibly even the moral and the factual) or to mistake what is common to both. The *legal* is never more than the result of a regularized convention to treat what might otherwise serve as an improvisational moral or political norm as a formal rule for theoretical disputes within a well-defined jurisdiction (*jus*). You may, if you wish, treat this as a solution to Socrates' philosophical question in the first two books of the *Republic*—a solution possibly less offensive and more interesting than Thrasymachus's answer (that justice is the interest of the stronger) but closer to Thrasymachus's sense of the doubtful standing of independent moral norms than to Socrates' mock essentialism. When we revise our prima facie norms in the direction of the supposed objective validity of the change intended, we mean the change to take its place (so to speak) within our then-altered *sittlich* norms, so that it itself acquires thereby a measure of prima facie force. But adjustments of these sorts remain forever improvisational (even where formal agreements may have been reached), simply because there is no principled way to decide, in moral/political matters, when such new constraints are themselves rightly open to further change. By contrast, in the legal context, the courts are authorized to decide questions of relevance, ceteris paribus questions, and questions of jurisdiction in addition to actual findings. In short, legal matters rightly arise within an antecedently defined closed space, whereas moral matters do not arise in the same way. Nevertheless, a closed space need not be forever closed: history and technological change inevitably defeat the idea that the law is changeless in normal circumstances.

Think, however, of Osama bin Laden's charge that the presence of American troops in Saudi Arabia defiles the sacred homeland, whatever may have been the formal treaty or agreement between the consenting sovereign powers involved. To see the point is to see that there can be, finally, no principled division between the legal and the moral. But consider this, too: to construe religious revelation in terms of the legal model and to treat that same decision as rightly defining the paradigm of acting *rationaliter* (as, apparently, the Iranian mullahs do and as bin Laden opportunistically insists is correct) is to disorganize the very possibility of rational dispute among opposed partisans and, of course, to fall back to moral and political privilege. Put more narrowly, the right or wrong of, say, abortion or suicide *cannot*, in a republican or, more restrictively, a democratic political order, admit the argumentative pertinence of any revealed truth about abortion's or suicide's moral standing. This is the case even where it remains morally (hence, rationally) admissible, and perhaps advisable, that local religious sensibilities be taken seriously into account in fashioning a valid modus vivendi. Contemporary American political debates about abortion and suicide and homosexuality, for instance, quite frequently risk being irreconcilable with our proceeding *rationaliter*. (Alexis de Tocqueville, you may remember, was struck by the American penchant for mingling republican, even democratic, themes with religious tenets.)

Furthermore, granting this much, you see as well that, precisely because of its practical nature, a moral/political impasse cannot preclude on principled grounds the relevance of the division of actual power (separating the contending parties) in arriving at a valid resolution of a pertinent dispute. This does not mean that anything goes, or that might makes right. But because moral matters are often also prudential matters, a would-be resolution that disregarded the actual sources of power that may be brought to bear on a matter at hand is not likely to have been arrived at *rationaliter*. Nevertheless, a moral/political commitment is not merely (really, not at all) a matter of brute force. The Polish resistance against the Nazis and the Finnish resistance against the Soviets make this abundantly clear. Both hoped to enlist the effective sanctions of important powers that were not directly involved, and both succeeded, but hardly in the way they themselves had hoped. Hence, in yielding to Thrasymachus's important theme, we need not yield to his actual thesis. Utopian thinking, we may say, is a would-be form of moral/political thinking that ignores practical or existential constraints in the here and now and, in doing that, construes valid judgment as essentially theoretical. (That, effectively, is the confusion Sen perceived in Rawls and, in a curious way, what Lenin supposed he saw in Trotsky's doubts about the proletarian nature of the would-be Russian Revolution.) But of course there can be a utopian strain in would-be practical decisions, and there may be valid theoretical questions that practical policies must consider.

The fact is that if a moral resolution means to be effective in practical terms, it must take existing imbalances of power into account. The relevant circumstances are, however, not always apparent. For example, the struggle between the Israelis and the Palestinians is surely being waged, increasingly now, in the international media. Similarly, in domestic American affairs, the power of an entrepreneurial press has changed the balance of effective political power so much that moral/political concerns, managed through the reporting of the news, have successfully brought down the Nixon and Johnson administrations and hampered the prosecution of the Vietnam War so thoroughly that it could not finally be won. But the powers of the fourth estate are also changeable and fickle, as the threat of a consolidation of privately owned news media in America now makes clear.

Again, we do not need to define the true nature of a person in order to resolve—objectively—the abortion dispute *as a moral dispute*; similarly, we do not need to demonstrate how a valid territorial agreement between the Israelis and the Palestinians *derives* from the supposed determinate entitlements and rights of either party. To reverse the order of resolution is to prefer the legal or the theoretical to the moral/political or the practical. Otherwise, in the moral order, the political resolution of a dispute may itself impose (though it need not) a further legal encumbrance on the opposing parties. This is an extremely useful distinction, constructively advanced as being entirely in accord with reasoning *rationaliter*. The division of actual power is almost always morally relevant in the cases in question. Stalin did not see matters altogether clearly when he asked how many divisions the Pope had at his disposal. Political power is drawn from collective sources, and no one can confidently anticipate how power will actually form. Think of 9/11, for instance, as the transformation of political weakness into a weapon of incalculable power.

Beyond that, among responsible peoples, to be committed in a moral way is, in some sustainable measure, *to bear witness to*—to preserve the memory and record of—all prima facie claims of great injustice and wrong that have not yet been adequately reviewed or righted, approximating to what I shall call *summum malum*. Ultimately, it is to inform the entire world, to enlist the power of every society willing to function as a living archive of shared opinion or a spontaneous tribunal of a remembered wrong—or possibly as an ally. In part, the formation of these effective memories constitutes a source of morally informed power, however partisan it may be; in part, too, these memories constitute and give direction to the moral world itself. It is not so much a question of ensuring *justitia* as ensuring the continual conversation of justice. Tiananmen Square serves as an excellent example of what I mean.

There may be a reason to be sanguine about would-be moral sympathies, sanctions, consensus, and influence, no matter how informal: they may, over time, produce effective centers of concern or outrage or serious assessment (self-appointed monitors, for instance, like Amnesty International, or even governments moved by such tribunals to inform the world about global warming, nuclear waste, environmental hazards, drought and famine, or incipient holocausts). There is no reason to suppose that such activities will not be the work of convinced partisans. But what does that matter? There is no alternative. And if we remain consistent with the analysis being offered, we may suppose that, where *summum malum* is least in doubt, consensus will be of wider scope and more in accord with our intuitions of a humane life than otherwise. You must think of the reciprocating horrors of the Tutsis and Hutus in Rwanda, for example, or of something of even greater influence (though not necessarily of greater harm), like the Nazi or Cambodian holocausts.

III

You will have noticed that I have made no reference to disputes about norms or virtues of personal life—that is, matters of life and death in which the moral import of what we do is confined to how we live our individual lives, without reference to the bearing of our acts on the lives of others—such as, with pertinent constraints, regarding suicide, physician-assisted death, homosexuality, self-development or self- realization, possibly prostitution as a profession, the exercise of personal choice, and the like. The reason is plain. Different codes of conduct appear among societies that spell out their different *sittlich* constraints defining admissible and inadmissible ways of living. For Jews, Christians, and Muslims, for instance, suicide is forbidden on grounds that include, at least, doing harm or wrong to oneself (*noxae, peccati*). But the Stoics recognized suicide as an honorable act.

Suicide cannot rightly be unconditionally forbidden unless we construe ideologies or legal rationales against self-harm as morally valid in the strictest sense. I see no possible argument there, *rationaliter*. But that is not to disallow protecting selves against the dangers of their own irrational behavior or calling selves to bear responsibility regarding the lives of others (children, for instance) who may be adversely affected, or regarding the *sittlich* practices of an entire society. If persons *are* indeed cultural artifacts (as I believe they are), then there simply can be no independently objective norms for forbidding suicide as such. It cannot be more than a prudential or practical or legal decision—or a moral decision suitably *sittlich* on prudential grounds, but, if that's true, then it must be hostage to the changing tolerances of a society's evolving history. To admit that much is not yet to address suicide's moral standing, but it points to a surprisingly powerful strategy.

Here, I suggest a normative policy going beyond the prima facie but congruent with the sense of reasoning *rationaliter*, which I call *nullum malum*. By that, I mean that there is and can be no changeless rule or principle applied to human nature or human reason that could possibly justify any moral injunction against living one's own life *rationaliter*—on the grounds of violating human nature or intrinsic reason or cognitively privileged norms. You cannot fail to see the radical possibilities that begin to loom once we regard moral norms as societal artifacts.

The point of *nullum malum* is to justify relieving a society of any of its former codes—or supporting its resistance to instituting new ones—that impose normative constraints on its members' personal lives, in the sense supplied. The upshot is to reconcile a society's *sittlich* vision with reviewing (in a distinctly stronger sense) its validity *rationaliter*, under the conditions of changing history. Any policy favoring *nullum malum* may be construed as morally generous *because* it applies a conceptually generous distinction morally. This makes vulnerable targets of all would-be norms regarding the choice of personal lifestyles, norms that speak of harming or wronging oneself. Moral generosity based entirely on conceptual generosity, as with *nullum malum*, I call *liberalitas*. Thus, it would be entirely appropriate, *rationaliter*, to hold that all societies should eliminate as far as possible the most egregious *sittlich* constraints imposed on personal life (female circumcision, for instance). Doubtless, it would be good to pursue such matters with patience, in accord with developing resources and changing history, in ways that preserve as well as possible the remaining *Sitten* of the affected societies—that is, with due consideration. But you have here a suggestive example of how a substantive moral change may be made compelling in terms that make no objectivist moral claims at all. You begin to see how such a strategy works even in restricted contexts—for instance, in the American experiment admitting gays in the military, or, more problematically, in the post-Taliban Afghan effort to restore the rights of women. Of course, you also realize that the argument works just as well in the opposite direction. Think, for instance, of converting, *rationaliter*, security at airports into a central system for deciding who may fly and who may not—and more. I think of the My Lai massacre construed as a condition for saving the village. Critics may be distressed to find that my proposal greatly diminishes the sense in which resolutions of moral/political disputes may be fairly treated as objectively confirmable claims, within *sittlich* bounds. Here, an apparent moral claim may be a deliberately ventured departure from our *sittlich* regularities. A modus vivendi of the moral sort may need to be experimental. Think, for example, of the slowly gathering support for the institutionalization of gay marriage.

Those same critics may be further distressed to find that moral resolutions are not likely to conform with the supposed requirements of a bivalent logic applied to mundane propositions. For what I am urging is (1) that validity regarding moral matters is primarily practical, not theoretical—a question of action or commitment or, better, *sittlich* change rather than a matter of propositional truths; (2) that it concerns a modus vivendi (and the particular acts by which that may be *made* determinate) rather than judgments of what *is* determinately true or right (for instance, regarding the virtues); (3) that valid resolutions are arrived at in a practical way, *rationaliter, liberaliter*, with due consideration, but not by consulting objective norms independent of our *Sitten*; (4) that the resolution of moral/political conflicts cannot be more than determinable, never strictly determinate, as in providing a modus vivendi, which may be realized in various determinate ways; hence, (5) that the logic of moral claims is bound to be relativistic in some degree, rather than merely bivalent or pluralistic; and (6) that the would-be rationale for such claims must be ideological and cannot be defended more rigorously than resolutions defended *rationaliter*. Standard propositional claims simply tend to lack the practical and objective import they require, *if* they are not already tethered to the resolution of a practical dispute about how we should live in the face of actual opposition. (Ideological dispute is entirely arbitrary if separated from a practical dispute, itself already grounded in *sittlich* practices that, arguably, should be preserved or possibly modified.)

The point of *nullum malum*, then, is this. If we cannot legitimate a code of personal life on the grounds of independent norms that we claim to discern objectively but not construct—which, indeed, cannot be done—then *nullum malum* is likely to be as good as any other moral policy that can be defended *rationaliter*, for it seeks no more than a second-best morality liberated as far as possible from whatever in practice and ideology (bearing on the choice of a life) cannot be easily reconciled, *rationaliter* (without reference to our *Sitten*). If you allow the argument, then every catalogue of human virtues can be no more than an abstraction from the *sittlich* practices of one historical society or another. No such catalogue can ever be universalized as normatively required. (This goes entirely against the Aristotelian conviction, whether ancient, medieval, or contemporary.)

In matters of personal and societal conduct, I take morality to be an improvisational art of practical reasoning that issues primarily in the resolution of actual disputes and conflicts—*never* independently in claims about what is true or right in any merely doctrinal or ideological sense. It cannot favor the latter, because there is no theoretical inquiry that *can* yield independently true moral claims and because there is no essentially fixed faculty of practical reason (whether natural or transcendental) that could possibly issue neutral or universally binding moral directives about how one should live. This is why thought experiments and hypothetical cases are so doubtful in moral contexts, as contrasted with legal and factual ones.

Faute de mieux, moral reasoning begins with the initial data of our *sittlich* norms and the contingent *prudentiae* and *providentiae* that our society favors—in effect, favors *rationaliter*. It is bound, therefore, to challenge its own prima facie values wherever they conflict with evolving prudential concerns or with items (1)–(3) of my original tally, now amplified in the direction of prudence—item (4). As a consequence, moral reasoning proves to be inherently improvisational, logically informal, and more likely to be defended in accord with a relativistic logic than a bivalent one.

I have attempted here to construct an argument that deliberately abandons any and all forms of cognitive and rational privilege or certainty regarding would-be moral norms and to demonstrate—without conceptual trickery or arbitrariness—that we can still (1) defend a viable conception of objectivity in moral matters, (2) begin with a thoroughly conservative view protective of the *sittlich* norms of our own society, and yet (3) draw out of such slim provisions a perfectly reasonable sense in which those same *sittlich* norms may be responsibly altered, without seriously weakening the objective standing originally accorded their validity. That is surely an important gain. But if my argument stands, if any one moral vision of the sort I've sketched is attractive or viable at all, there must be many different, even conflicting, visions that are as good as any other, on theoretical grounds, and certainly better than any of the allegedly best moral visions. (The "best" can never demonstrate its own legitimacy.) Yet, in saying all this, in suggesting the advantages of relativism, I am emphatically *not* saying that I construe relativism to hold that anything goes or that it is impossible to show that one judgment or commitment is better than another. (I address the question elsewhere.) In a way, my demonstration is meant to explain the good sense and force of Socrates' intuition in the elenctic dialogues (including the first two books of the *Republic* and the important joke in the *Statesman* about a second-best state): that is, to explain the sense in which we *can* reason objectively about moral matters, without ever calling on the prescriptive resources of a faculty of pure reason or cognitive competence in discerning the true norms by which we should live.

This is exactly what I do believe about moral/political matters. But if the argument holds, it shows, hands down, that Western moral philosophy has a hopelessly inflated view of what it can achieve. It cannot, for instance, legitimate any account of what is normatively necessary or essential to the moral life, or binding in any strictly exceptionless way, or categorically obligatory or forbidden, or morally objective in a way free of partisan or ideological preference, or morally right or good in a sense so strict that it cannot be made to yield in the direction of a relativistic tolerance for incompatible alternatives.

This means that in the real world—this world more fraught with peril than it has ever been—we cannot take for granted the optimistic hope that reasonably responsible antagonists are bound to converge on what *we* take to be the assured normative lessons of our own reflections. Not on your life! But if that is so, then what it is to *be* reasonable in moral/political matters will have to be defined in a way that almost no one is prepared to admit. Certainly, what it means is at least that speculating about moral matters *rationaliter* does *not* aim at the recovery of a uniquely valid moral norm. Rather—and only second best—such speculation hopes to achieve no more than a prototype of a reasonable paradigm of normative construction (among alternatives), on the expectation that prudent agents will keep in mind the ineliminability of such diversity and its bearing on legitimated disputes between seriously committed opponents.

Notes

Notes to the Preface

1. For an intellectual biography of Margolis, see *The Dictionary of Modern American Philosophers*, ed. John R. Shook (Bristol, England: Thoemmes Continuum, 2005), s.v. "Margolis, Joseph Zalman (1924–)."

2. The best autobiographical account of Margolis's estimation of the Columbia philosophy department during his time as a graduate student there can be found in Joseph Margolis, "Interview with Joseph Margolis," *European Journal of Pragmatism and American Philosophy* 6, no. 2 (2014). http://journals.openedition.org/ejpap/301.

3. See Joseph Margolis, "*Aesthetics: Problems in the Philosophy of Criticism* by Monroe C. Beardsley," review, *Journal of Aesthetics and Art Criticism* 18, no. 2 (Dec. 1959): 266–69; and the exchange between Beardsley and Margolis in Stephen C. Pepper, Monroe C. Beardsley, and Joseph Margolis, "Letters Pro and Con," *Journal of Aesthetics and Art Criticism* 18, no. 4 (Jun. 1960): 521–28.

4. For the culminating statement of Margolis's early positions in analytic aesthetics, see Margolis, *The Language of Art and Art Criticism: Analytic Questions in Aesthetics* (Detroit: Wayne State University Press, 1965).

5. See, for instance, Margolis, "The Point of Hegel's Dissatisfaction with Kant," in *Pragmatism Ascendent: A Yard of Narrative, a Touch of Prophecy* (Stanford, CA: Stanford University Press, 2012).

6. For a full accounting of this revival, see Margolis, *Reinventing Pragmatism: American Philosophy at the End of the Twentieth Century* (Ithaca, NY: Cornell University Press, 2002).

7. For an earlier statement of Margolis's relativism regarding aesthetic judgments, see Margolis, "Robust Relativism," *Journal of Aesthetics and Art Criticism* 35, no. 1 (Autumn 1976): 37–46. For a broader defense of relativism, see Margolis, *The Truth about Relativism* (Oxford: Blackwell, 1991).

Notes to Chapter One

1. Thomas S. Kuhn, *The Structure of Scientific Revolutions*, 2nd ed. (Chicago: University of Chicago Press, 1970); Michel Foucault, "Nietzsche, Genealogy, History," in *Language, Counter-memory, Practice: Selected Essays and Interviews*, trans. Donald F. Bouchard and Sherry Simon, ed. Donald F. Bouchard (Ithaca, NY: Cornell University Press, 1977).

2. See, for instance, Carl G. Hempel, "The Function of General Laws in History," in *Aspects of Scientific Explanation and Other Essays in the Philosophy of Science* (New York: Free Press, 1965); and Wesley C. Salmon, *Scientific Explanation and Causal Structure of the World* (Princeton, NJ: Princeton University Press, 1984).

3. See, for instance, Nancy Cartwright, *How the Laws of Physics Lie* (Oxford: Oxford University Press, 1983); and Bas C. van Fraassen, *Laws and Symmetry* (Oxford: Clarendon Press, 1989).

4. See Michel Foucault, *The Order of Things: An Archaeology of the Human Sciences*, translated (New York: Vintage, 1970).

5. For evidence of recent tendencies, see Robert Stecker, "The Constructivist's Dilemma," *Journal of Aesthetics and Art Criticism* 55, no. 1 (Winter 1997): 43–52. Stecker pretends to attack relativism by addressing its alleged ontic and epistemic implications, but that puts the cart before the horse. You will look in vain for any sustained discussion on Stecker's part of the peculiar "nature" of artworks that might invite a relativistic option. My own argument (which Stecker has in mind, at least in part) is, as I have said, committed to item (1) of the tally given. (I return more pointedly to Stecker's paper in chapter 9.) The weakness noted appears more egregiously in Robert Stecker, "Relativism about Interpretation," *Journal of Aesthetics and Art Criticism* 53, no. 1 (Winter 1995): 14–18. A more careful formulation (along related lines) appears in Stephen Davies, "Relativism in Interpretation," *Journal of Aesthetics and Art Criticism* 53, no. 1 (Winter 1995): 8–13. But see also Robert Stecker, *Artworks: Definition, Meaning, Value* (University Park: Pennsylvania State University Press, 1997), 227–31. The last two papers mentioned (from the *Journal of Aesthetics and Art Criticism*) were invited for a symposium on my own paper, "Plain Talk about Interpretation on a Relativistic Model," *Journal of Aesthetics and Art Criticism* 53, no. 1 (Winter 1995): 1–7. Stecker relies (in his book) on Davies's paper, but I cannot see how the argument of either counts at all. They fail for the following reasons: (1) they do not show that relativism is not viable, fruitful, or worth preferring; (2) they nowhere address the ontic peculiarity of artworks in virtue of which relativism might be tempting; and (3) they confuse what may be called biographical considerations with philosophical ones. I don't doubt it is unlikely a convinced interpreter of a particular artwork will concede that another's interpretation of the same work (incompatible with his own, on a bivalent logic) might be as valid as his own, but that seems to bear on vanity and bias and not on philosophy. The question remains whether a society (through its professional

practices) may be willing to concede the validity of competing ("incongruent") interpretations. One can surely offer evidence for that. If I understand Stecker and Davies correctly, both are guilty of the same mistake.

6. See, in this connection, Willard Van Orman Quine, *Word and Object* (Cambridge, MA: MIT Press, 1960), §§15–16; and P. F. Strawson, "On Referring," *Mind* 59, no. 235 (Jul. 1950): 320–44.

7. Roland Barthes, *S/Z*, trans. Richard Miller (New York: Hill and Wang, 1974).

8. The complication regarding description and interpretation is overlooked in Richard Shusterman, "Beneath Interpretation: Against Hermeneutic Holism," *The Monist* 73, no. 2 (1990): 181–204.

9. See Monroe C. Beardsley, *The Possibility of Criticism* (Detroit: Wayne State University Press, 1970); and E. D. Hirsch Jr., *Validity in Interpretation* (New Haven, CT: Yale University Press, 1967).

10. See Torsten Pettersson, *Literary Interpretation: Current Models and a New Departure* (Åbo, Finland: Åbo Academy Press, 1988).

11. See, further, Richard J. Bernstein, *Beyond Objectivism and Relativism: Science, Hermeneutics, and Praxis* (Philadelphia: University of Pennsylvania Press, 1983); and Joseph Margolis, *The Truth about Relativism* (Oxford: Blackwell, 1991).

12. See Quine, *Word and Object*, chaps. 1–2.

13. It is repeated, for instance, by Myles Burnyeat, a specialist on Plato, in "Protagoras and Self-Refutation in Plato's *Theaetetus*," *Philosophical Review* 85, no. 2 (April 1976): 172–95.

14. See, for instance, Hilary Putnam, "Why Reason Can't Be Naturalized," in *Reason and Realism*, vol. 3 of *Philosophical Papers* (Cambridge: Cambridge University Press, 1983), 235–37.

15. For a convenient summary, see Jitendra Nath Mohanty, *The Concept of Intentionality* (St. Louis: Warren H. Green, 1972).

16. For a sense of its bearing on the defense of relativism, see Joseph Margolis, *Historied Thought, Constructed World: A Conceptual Primer for the Turn of the Millennium* (Berkeley: University of California Press, 1995).

17. See, for instance, Paul M. Churchland, *A Neurocomputational Perspective: The Nature of Mind and the Structure of Science* (Cambridge, MA: MIT Press, 1989); and John R. Searle, *The Construction of Social Reality* (New York: Free Press, 1995).

18. See Arthur C. Danto, "The Artworld," *Journal of Philosophy* 61, no. 19 (1964): 571–84; and the meaning of *transfiguration* in Danto, *The Transfiguration of the Commonplace: A Philosophy of Art* (Cambridge, MA: Harvard University Press, 1981).

19. See Harold Bloom, *The Breaking of the Vessels* (Chicago: University of Chicago Press, 1982), chap. 1.

20. Since giving these lectures, I have read Barbara Herrnstein Smith, *Belief and Resistance Dynamics of Contemporary Intellectual Controversy* (Cambridge, MA:

Harvard University Press, 1997). There is much that Smith and I share (and have shared in earlier publications). But with due attention to her rhetorical intent, I must say she slights the recuperative side of the epistemological and methodological issues. This gives her account a cast that is more sympathetic with Rorty's postmodernism, Feyerabend's anarchism, or the claims of the Scottish sociologists of knowledge than I would favor. I concede that all of these options make their contribution, but I also find them all (finally) inadequate.

21. Compare Kuhn, *The Structure of Scientific Revolutions*, §10.

22. See Beardsley, "The Authority of the Text," in *The Possibility of Criticism*, especially page 36.

23. See Hirsch, *Validity in Interpretation*, chap. 5, §C.

24. See Danto, "The Artworld."

25. See Ludwig Wittgenstein, *Philosophical Investigations*, trans. G. E. M. Anscombe (New York: Macmillan, 1953).

26. See G. W. F. Hegel, *Phenomenology of Spirit*, trans. A. V. Miller (Oxford: Oxford University Press, 1977). The sense of the *sittlich* extends, I believe, beyond the ethical.

27. See Joseph Margolis, "The Politics of Predication," *Philosophical Forum* 27, no. 3 (1996): 195–219.

Notes to Chapter Two

1. See, for example, the essays collected in Martin Hollis and Steven Lukes, eds., *Rationality and Relativism* (Cambridge, MA: MIT Press, 1982); and Hans-Georg Gadamer, *Truth and Method*, trans. Garrett Barden and John Cumming (New York: Seabury Press, 1975), 308–09.

2. Paul Feyerabend holds that "Protagorean relativism is *reasonable* because it pays attention to the pluralism of traditions and values," in *Science in a Free Society* (London: New Left Books, 1978), 28; there is some reason to think he believes that Protagoreanism has universal application. Contrast this with Peter Winch's view in "Understanding a Primitive Society," *American Philosophical Quarterly* 1, no. 4 (1964): 307–24.

3. Richard J. Bernstein, *Beyond Objectivism and Relativism: Science, Hermeneutics, and Praxis* (Philadelphia: University of Pennsylvania Press, 1983), 9; cf. W. Newton-Smith, "Relativism and the Possibility of Interpretation," in *Rationality and Relativism*, Hollis and Lukes, 106–22.

4. Bernstein, *Beyond Objectivism and Relativism*, 8. It is worth remarking that Bernstein observes that "A more appropriate title or subtitle of the book [Gadamer's *Truth and Method*], and indeed of Gadamer's entire philosophic project, might have been 'Beyond Objectivism and Relativism.' Gadamer's primary philosophic aim is to expose what is wrong with the type of thinking that moves between these antithetical poles and to open us to a new way of thinking about understanding

that reveals that our being-in-the-world is distorted when we impose the concepts of objectivism and relativism" (115). Gadamer was favorably taken with Bernstein's account of his work, and a letter to that effect is included in Bernstein's book.

5. Bernstein, *Beyond Objectivism and Relativism*, 8.

6. Bernstein, *Beyond Objectivism and Relativism*, 10–11; cf. Edmund Husserl, *The Crisis of European Sciences and Transcendental Phenomenology*, trans. David Carr (Evanston, IL: Northwestern University Press, 1970), 145–46 (cited by Bernstein).

7. Bernstein, *Beyond Objectivism and Relativism*, 37. The charge accords with Gadamer's assessment.

8. Bernstein, 7.

9. Bernstein, 2–3.

10. Bernstein, 166–67.

11. Bernstein, 16–23 passim.

12. Bernstein, 57.

13. Bernstein, 11–12, for instance.

14. Charles Taylor, "Rationality," in *Rationality and Relativism*, Hollis and Lukes, 98, 105. This is not the occasion for attempting to correct standard misinterpretations of Winch's position—including Taylor's. But it should in all fairness be noted that Winch does not seem to have actually opposed cross-cultural comparisons or cross-cultural "judgments of superiority." On Taylor's view, cf. Charles Taylor, "Interpretation and the Sciences of Man," in *Interpretive Social Science: A Reader*, ed. Paul Rabinow and William M. Sullivan, (Berkeley: University of California Press, 1979), 25–71.

15. Taylor, "Rationality," 104.

16. Taylor, "Interpretation," 71. It is interesting to note that Bernstein cites the passage but leaves out the next-to-last line, which reintroduces the threatening relativism: cf. Bernstein, *Beyond Objectivism and Relativism*, 135.

17. One should bear in mind Gadamer's endorsement of Bernstein's basic claims—which in a way Taylor also shares; cf. "A Letter by Professor Hans-Georg Gadamer," appendix to Bernstein, *Beyond Objectivism and Relativism*, 261–66.

18. Gadamer, *Truth and Method*, 249.

19. It applies straightforwardly, for example, to the views of Clifford Geertz, "From the Native's Point of View," in *Interpretive Social Science*, Rabinow and Sullivan; and Peter Winch, "Understanding a Primitive Society."

20. Richard Rorty, "Pragmatism, Relativism, and Irrationalism," *Proceedings and Addresses of the American Philosophical Association* 53, no. 6 (1980): 727.

21. Rorty, 729.

22. Rorty, 730.

23. See Willard Van Orman Quine, *Word and Object* (Cambridge, MA: MIT Press, 1960), chap. 2.

24. Paul Feyerabend, *Against Method: Outline of an Anarchistic Theory of Knowledge* (London: New Left Books, 1975), 274. There is an extremely helpful discussion of the difference between Kuhn's and Feyerabend's views in Bernstein,

Beyond Objectivism and Relativism, 79–93; Bernstein mentiwons the remark just cited from Feyerabend.

25. Bernstein, *Beyond Objectivism and Relativism*, 92. Cf. Donald Davidson, "On the Very Idea of a Conceptual Scheme," *Proceedings and Addresses of the American Philosophical Association* 47 (Nov. 1974): 5–20; Gerald Doppelt, "Kuhn's Epistemological Relativism: An Interpretation and Defense," *Inquiry* 21 (1978): 33–86.

26. Cf. Karl Popper, *Realism and the Aim of Science*, From the Postscript to the Logic of Scientific Discovery, ed. W. W. Bartley III, vol. 1 (Totowa, NJ: Rowman and Littlefield, 1983), 156–57; also Thomas S. Kuhn, *The Structure of Scientific Revolutions*, 2nd ed. (Chicago: University of Chicago Press, 1970), 150. It is fair to say that Kuhn has muted the strong and distinctive thesis here advanced.

27. Bernstein, for example, reporting quite accurately the debate about incommensurability, explicitly says that "the incommensurability thesis has been rightly taken as an attack on objectivism (not, however, on objectivity)" and that, therefore, it "has nothing to do with relativism" (*Beyond Objectivism and Relativism*, 92).

28. Popper, *Realism*, 18.

29. See Popper, "The Aim of Science," in *Objective Knowledge: An Evolutionary Approach* (Oxford: Clarendon Press, 1972); Keith Lehrer, *Knowledge* (Oxford: Clarendon Press, 1974); and Rorty, "Pragmatism, Relativism, and Irrationalism." It should be remarked that Popper's opposition to essentialism does not signify that Popper himself has successfully escaped the charge.

30. See Hilary Putnam, "Lecture II," in *Meaning and the Moral Sciences* (London: Routledge / Kegan Paul, 1978), 18–33; and Nelson Goodman, "Seven Strictures on Similarity," in *Experience and Theory*, ed. Lawrence Foster and J. W. Swanson (Amherst: University of Massachusetts Press, 1970), 19–29.

31. Bernstein, it appears, agrees with Gadamer's attempt to reinterpret Aristotle's (so-called) natural-law doctrine in historicized but objective and antirelativistic terms; cf. Bernstein, *Beyond Objectivism and Relativism*, 156–57; and Gadamer, *Truth and Method*, 278–89, 248–49. It is worth noting how J. L. Mackie, espousing a special doctrine of "moral skepticism," nevertheless attempts to avoid moral relativism: cf. Mackie, *Ethics: Inventing Right and Wrong* (Harmondsworth, UK: Penguin, 1977).

32. Davidson, "On the Very Idea of a Conceptual Scheme," 11, 20. There is a rather freewheeling attack on relativism, from the Popperian camp, that rejects the incommensurabilist thesis from the point of view of "the unity of mankind"—construed not as "a literal truth of descent" but as "a program, a proposal for how to act and think": I. C. Jarvie, *Rationality and Relativism: In Search of a Philosophy and History of Anthropology* (London: Routledge / Kegan Paul, 1984), 14; cf. also 81, 102. Jarvie's discussion adds little to the argument, except that it regards incommensurabilism as "invalid." But it is useful to take note of it here, if only because it signals the loose convergence among such diverse thinkers as Davidson, Bernstein, Taylor, Gadamer, Apel, Habermas, Popper, Gellner, and Jarvie regarding the "irrationality," "nihilism," "incoherence," or "anarchy" of relativism (reduced to incommensurabilism).

33. Davidson, "Conceptual Scheme," 12. Cf. Thomas Kuhn, "Reflections on My Critics," in *Criticism and the Growth of Knowledge*, ed. Imre Lakatos and Alan Musgrave (Cambridge: Cambridge University Press, 1970), 266–67; and Paul Feyerabend, "Problems of Empiricism," in *Beyond the Edge of Certainty*, ed. R. G. Colodny (Englewood Cliffs, NJ: Prentice-Hall, 1965), 214. Both are cited by Davidson.

34. Davidson, "Conceptual Scheme," 10. Cf. also Davidson, "In Defense of Convention T," in *Truth, Syntax and Modality*, ed. Hugues Leblanc (Amsterdam: North-Holland, 1973), 76–86.

35. Davidson, "Conceptual Scheme," 12.

36. Ian Hacking, *Representing and Intervening: Introductory Topics in the Philosophy of Natural Science* (Cambridge: Cambridge University Press, 1983), chap. 5. See also Hacking, "Language, Truth and Reason," in *Rationality and Relativism*, Hollis and Lukes, 48–68.

37. Cf. Putnam, "Lecture II"; and Dudley Shapere, "The Structure of Scientific Revolutions," in *Paradigms and Revolutions: Applications and Appraisals of Thomas Kuhn's Philosophy of Science*, ed. Gary Gutting (Notre Dame, IN: University of Notre Dame Press, 1980), 27–38.

Notes to Chapter Three

1. The full argument is given in Joseph Margolis, *Pragmatism without Foundations: Reconciling Realism and Relativism* (Oxford: Basil Blackwell, 1986).

2. I address this extraordinarily complex issue straightforwardly in "Relativism and the *Lebenswelt*," chapter 2 of Margolis, *Science without Unity: Reconciling the Human and Natural Sciences* (Oxford: Basil Blackwell, 1987).

3. See Rudolf Carnap, *The Unity of Science*, trans. Max Black (London: Kegan Paul, Trench, Trubner, 1934); Carnap, "Psychology in Physical Language," trans. George Schick, in *Logical Positivism*, ed. A. J. Ayer (New York: Free Press, 1959), 165–98; Carnap, "Intellectual Autobiography," in *The Philosophy of Rudolf Carnap*, ed. Paul Arthur Schilpp (LaSalle, IL: Open Court, 1963), particularly 50–53; and Carnap, "The Philosopher Replies," in *Philosophy of Rudolf Carnap*, ed. Schilpp. See also Carl G. Hempel, *Aspects of Scientific Explanation and Other Essays in the Philosophy of Science* (New York: Free Press, 1965); Paul Oppenheim and Hilary Putnam, "Unity of Science as a Working Hypothesis," in *Concepts, Theories, and the Mind-Body Problem*, vol. 2 of *Minnesota Studies in the Philosophy of Science*, ed. Herbert Feigl, Michael Scriven, and Grover Maxwell (Minneapolis: University of Minnesota Press, 1958), 3–36; and Robert L. Causey, *Unity of Science* (Dordrecht, Netherlands: D. Reidel, 1977).

4. J. J. C. Smart, *Philosophy and Scientific Realism* (London: Routledge / Kegan Paul, 1963), 50.

5. Smart, 53.

6. This is the immensely important issue that hangs on Quine's account of "pegasizing." See Willard Van Orman Quine, *Word and Object* (Cambridge, MA: MIT Press, 1960), §37.

7. Wesley C. Salmon, *Scientific Explanation and the Causal Structure of the World* (Princeton, NJ: Princeton University Press, 1984), 148–49; see Bas C. van Fraassen, *The Scientific Image* (Oxford: Clarendon Press, 1980), 118, cited by Salmon.

8. Salmon, *Scientific Explanation*, 18; cf. p. 190.

9. Adolf Grünbaum, *The Foundations of Psychoanalysis: A Philosophical Critique* (Berkeley: University of California, 1984), 16. See also Jürgen Habermas, *Knowledge and Human Interests*, trans. J. J. Shapiro (Boston, MA: Beacon Press, 1971), 272–73 (cited by Grünbaum); and Hans-Georg Gadamer, *Truth and Method*, trans. Garrett Barden and John Cumming (New York: Seabury Press, 1975), 311 (also cited by Grünbaum).

10. Hempel, "The Function of General Laws in History," in *Aspects of Scientific Explanation*, 233, 231.

11. It may be remarked that Popper, whom Grünbaum generally opposes, effectively agrees with at least this much of Grünbaum's thesis; see Karl R. Popper, *The Poverty of Historicism*, 3rd ed. (London: Routledge / Kegan Paul, 1961). Popper, of course, is also a partisan of some version of the unity program.

12. Grünbaum, *Foundations of Psychoanalysis*, 17.

13. Grünbaum, 18.

14. Grünbaum, 14 (italics added).

15. Habermas, *Knowledge and Human Interests*, 271.

16. Habermas 271(italics added).

17. Habermas 271.

18. See Joseph Margolis, "Reconciling Freud's *Scientific Project* and Psychoanalysis," in *Morals, Science and Sociality*, ed. H. Tristram Engelhardt Jr. and Daniel Callahan, vol. 3 of *The Foundations of Ethics and Its Relationship to Science* (Hastings-on-Hudson, NY: Hastings Center, 1978).

19. Grünbaum, *Foundations of Psychoanalysis*, 14.

20. See Margolis, *Culture and Cultural Entities* (Dordrecht: D. Reidel, 1984), chaps. 4, 5.

21. For mutually opposing views on this matter, compare D. M. Armstrong, *What Is a Law of Nature?* (Cambridge: Cambridge University Press, 1983); and Norman Swartz, *The Concept of Physical Law* (Cambridge: Cambridge University Press, 1985).

22. I borrow the term from Arthur Fine, "Einstein's Realism," in *Science and Reality: Recent Work in the Philosophy of Science*, ed. James T. Cushing, C. F. Delaney, and Gary Gutting (Notre Dame: Notre Dame University Press, 1984), 106–33.

23. See Nancy Cartwright, *How the Laws of Physics Lie* (Oxford: Clarendon Press, 1983), "Essay 5: When Explanation Leads to Inference" and "Essay 6: For Phenomenological Laws," 87–127. See also Ian Hacking, *Representing and Interven-*

ing: Introductory Topics in the Philosophy of Natural Science (Cambridge: Cambridge University Press, 1983), chap. 16; Pierre Duhem, *The Aim and Structure of Physical Theory*, trans. Philip P. Wiener (New York: Atheneum, 1962); van Fraassen, *Scientific Image*. (It needs to be said that Cartwright is speaking of "phenomenological" laws in a sense that applies to the natural sciences. But this does not adversely affect the issue at stake in distinguishing between the physical and the cultural sciences.)

24. Cartwright, *Laws of Physics Lie*, 127.

25. Cartwright, 100–03. One of the boldest specimen views of this sort is certainly that espoused by Wilfrid Sellars, "The Language of Theories," in *Science, Perception and Reality* (London: Routledge / Kegan Paul, 1963).

26. Cartwright, *Laws of Physics Lie*, 126.

27. See Tom L. Beauchamp and Alexander Rosenberg, *Hume and the Problem of Causation* (Oxford: Oxford University Press, 1981), chap. 4. See also J. L. Mackie, *The Cement of the Universe* (Oxford: Clarendon Press, 1974); William Kneale, "Universality and Necessity," *British Journal for the Philosophy of Science* 12, no. 46 (1961): 89–102; Karl R. Popper, "A Revised Definition of Natural Necessity," *British Journal for the Philosophy of Science* 18, no. 4 (1968): 316–321.

28. Hacking, *Representing and Intervening*, 262–63.

29. See Willard Van Orman Quine, "On What There Is," in *From a Logical Point of View: Nine Logico-Philosophical Essays* (Cambridge, MA: Harvard University Press, 1953), 1–19.

30. Hacking, *Representing and Intervening*, chap. 12, particularly pp. 218–19.

31. See Joseph Margolis, *Persons and Minds* (Dordrecht: D. Reidel, 1978).

32. See Donald Davidson, "Causal Relations," "Actions, Reasons, and Causes," and "Mental Events," in *Essays on Actions and Events* (Oxford: Clarendon Press, 1980).

33. See, for instance, Mario Bunge, "Toward a Philosophy of Technology," in *Philosophy and Technology*, 2nd ed., ed. Carl Mitcham and Robert Mackey (New York: Free Press, 1983); also Joseph Margolis, "Three Conceptions of Technology: Satanic, Titanic, Human," in *Philosophy and Technology*, ed. Paul T. Durbin, vol. 7 (Greenwich, CT: JAI Press, 1984). See also Albert Borgmann, *Technology and the Character of Contemporary Life* (Chicago: University of Chicago Press, 1984), particularly pt. 1; and Jon Elster, *Explaining Technical Change* (Cambridge: Cambridge University Press, 1983), particularly pt. 1.

34. Karl R. Popper, "The Aim of Science," in *Objective Knowledge: An Evolutionary Approach* (Oxford: Clarendon Press, 1972), 190.

35. This is what is so puzzling about Nelson Goodman's account of induction in the context of a practicing science. It provides the key to grasping the peculiar vacuity of Goodman's notion of "entrenchment"—correct in a purely formal sense but utterly inoperable in quotidian scientific induction *when construed nominalistically*. This issue does not at all depend on Goodman's careful restrictions on the use of the terms *law* and *causality*. See, for instance, Nelson Goodman, *Fact, Fiction, and Forecast*, 2nd ed. (Indianapolis, IN: Bobbs-Merrill, 1965), 20–22; in the context of

Goodman, "Seven Structures on Similarity," in *Experience and Theory*, ed. Lawrence Foster and J. W. Swanson (Amherst: University of Massachusetts Press, 1970); and Goodman, *Of Mind and Other Matters* (Cambridge, MA: Harvard University Press, 1984), pt. 2.

36. It also shows, inadvertently, that Popper himself wavers considerably in his rejection of a realist reading of nomologicality—by way of his doctrine of verisimilitude: "although I do not think that we can ever describe, by our universal laws, an *ultimate* essence of the world, I do not doubt that we may seek to probe deeper and deeper into the structure of our world or, as we might say, into properties of the world that are more and more essential or of greater depth" ("The Aim of Science," *Objective Knowledge*, 196).

37. A similar theme is developed, however, in terms of possible-worlds semantics, in David Lewis, "Causation," *Journal of Philosophy* 70, no. 17 (1973): 556–67. See also Nicholas Rescher, "Lawfulness as Mind-Dependent," in *Essays in Honor of Carl G. Hempel*, ed. Nicholas Rescher (Dordrecht: D. Reidel, 1969), 178–97.

38. See Margolis, *Science without Unity: Reconciling the Human and Natural Sciences* (Oxford: Basil Blackwell, 1987), chap. 12.

39. See Quine, *Word and Object*, chap. 2.

40. See Martin Heidegger, *The Question concerning Technology and Other Essays*, trans. William Lovitt (New York: Harper and Row, 1977); and Heidegger, *Being and Time*, trans. John Macquarrie and Edward Robinson (New York: Harper and Row, 1962), §§15–16.

41. The connection is explicitly pursued in D. M. Armstrong, *What Is a Law of Nature?* (Cambridge: Cambridge University Press, 1983). There is an extremely perceptive account of causal laws, which construes natural necessity more in terms of pragmatic "resiliency" than of "real" necessity, offered in Brian Skyrms, *Causal Necessity* (New Haven, CT: Yale University Press, 1980), pt. 1. By *resiliency*, Skyrms means (roughly) the degree of invariance of some statistical probability; hence, "High resiliency can be thought of as a statistical notion of *necessity*" (11–12). But Skyrms does not here consider the question of the operative relationship between detecting relevant invariances and the solution to the problem of universals.

42. Grünbaum, *Foundations of Psychoanalysis*, 197; see also pp. 1–9.

43. Grünbaum, 198; see also pp. 10–15.

44. This, it should be noted, is (at least to the extent suggested) sympathetic with Grünbaum's own criticism of the "hermeneutic" confusion regarding the priorities of methodological and ontological speculation (and commitment) in Freud; see, for instance, Grünbaum, 5–9.

45. See Nikolaas Tinbergen, *The Study of Instinct* (New York: Oxford University Press, 1969), 37–43.

46. Tinbergen, 3–5.

47. Tinbergen, chap. 2.

48. Terry Winograd, *Understanding Natural Language* (New York: Academic Press, 1976), 22; see also p. 42. See also Noam Chomsky, *Syntactic Structures* (The Hague, Netherlands: Mouton, 1957) and *Aspects of the Theory of Syntax* (Cambridge, MA: MIT Press, 1965).

49. Davidson, "Actions, Reasons, and Causes," in *Essays on Actions and Events*, 4–5.

50. Davidson, 5.

51. Davidson, 12.

52. Davidson, 4n.

53. Davidson, 17.

54. See Davidson, "Mental Events" and "Causal Relations," in *Essays on Actions and Events*.

55. See Margolis, *Culture and Cultural Entities*, chaps. 4–5; also Margolis, "Prospects for an Extensionalist Psychology of Action," *Journal for the Theory of Social Behaviour* 11, no. 1 (1981): 53–64.

56. See Davidson, "Agency," in *Essays on Actions and Events*, 43–62. See also Arthur C. Danto, *Analytical Philosophy of Action* (Cambridge: Cambridge University Press, 1973); Alvin I. Goldman, *A Theory of Action* (Englewood Cliffs, NJ: Prentice-Hall, 1970); and Margolis, "*A Theory of Human Action* by Alvin I. Goldman," review in *Metaphilosophy* 5, no. 4 (1974).

57. Davidson, "Actions, Reasons, and Causes," *Essays on Actions and Events*, 16.

58. Davidson, 16.

59. Cf. Davidson, "Mental Events," *Essays on Actions and Events*.

60. G. E. M. Anscombe, "Causality and Extensionality," *Journal of Philosophy* 66, no. 6 (1969), 155.

61. Anscombe, 155. Anscombe adds rather prettily, "I owe this pleasing example, as well as the thought about temporal connectives, to P. Geach."

62. Davidson, "Actions, Reasons, and Causes," 17.

63. See Hempel, *Aspects of Scientific Explanation*, pt. 4. An extremely careful development of a theory of action that departs from Davidson's account is offered in Myles Brand, *Intending and Acting* (Cambridge, MA: MIT Press, 1984). Unaccountably, however, it simply does not address the issue of intensionality that Davidson's model forces us to consider. Brand takes "intention" or "intending" rather in a psychologically restricted sense—which, of course, is a perfectly pertinent ingredient of the phenomena in question.

64. Daniel C. Dennett, *Content and Consciousness* (London: Routledge / Kegan Paul, 1969), 28–29.

65. This, I believe, is the essential and basically correct (Wittgensteinian) insight of that much-maligned book, Peter Winch, *The Idea of a Social Science* (London: Routledge / Kegan Paul, 1958).

66. Quine, *Word and Object*, chap. 2.

67. See Michael Polanyi, *Personal Knowledge*, 2nd ed. (Chicago: University of Chicago Press, 1962).

68. Roy Bhaskar, *Scientific Realism and Human Emancipation* (London: Verso, 1986), 16; see, further, the whole of chap. 1.

69. Edward Gans, *Das Erbrecht in weltgeschichtlichen Entwicklung* (1826); quoted in Louis Dupré, *Marx's Social Critique of Culture* (New Haven: Yale University Press, 1983), 67. See, further, the whole of chap. 2.

70. See Richard J. Bernstein, *Praxis and Action* (Philadelphia: University of Pennsylvania Press, 1971), pt. 1; Richard Kilminster, "Theory and Practice in Marx and Marxism," in *Marx and Marxisms*, ed. G. H. R. Parkinson (Cambridge: Cambridge University Press, 1982); Nicholas Lobkowicz, *Theory and Practice* (Notre Dame: University of Notre Dame Press, 1967); Adolf Sanchez Vazquez, *The Philosophy of Praxis*, trans. Mike Gonzalez (London: Merlin Press, 1977); Joseph Margolis, "Pragmatism, Transcendental Arguments, and the Technological," in, *Philosophy and Technology*, ed. Paul T. Durbin and Friedrich Rapp (Dordrecht: D. Reidel, 1983).

71. See Jacques Derrida, *Positions*, trans. Alan Bass (Chicago: University of Chicago Press, 1972).

Notes to Chapter Four

1. Perhaps the single most sustained, uncompromising, near-contemporary account along these lines appears in Rudolf Carnap, *The Logical Syntax of Language*, trans. Amethé Smeaton (Paterson, NJ: Littlefield, Adams, 1959).

2. Immanuel Kant, *Critique of the Power of Judgment*, ed. Paul Guyer, trans. Paul Guyer and Eric Matthews (Cambridge: Cambridge University Press, 2000), §83, pp. 298–99 (italics in original). See also G. W. F. Hegel and F. W. J. Schelling, "Introduction on the Essence of Philosophical Criticism, Generally, and Its Relationship to the Present State of Philosophy in Particular," *Critical Journal of Philosophy* 1 (1802), in *Between Kant and Hegel: Texts in the Development of Post-Kantian Idealism*, ed. and trans. George di Giovanni and H. S. Harris, rev. ed. (Indianapolis, IN: Hackett, 2000), 272–91. The essay is generally taken to be the fledgling, as-yet-inadequate, but essential beginning of Hegel's effort to comprehend human reason as a manifestation of an all-inclusive power of Reason to grasp its own infinite career of self-knowledge. There is an extremely helpful essay by George di Giovanni introducing the collection, "The Facts of Consciousness," which effectively confirms the difficulty of characterizing Hegel's view as fully "naturalistic" in any familiar sense.

3. See Hegel, *Hegel's Science of Logic*, trans. A. V. Miller (Atlantic Highlands, NJ: Humanities Press International, 1990), pt. 1, pp. 55, 63. See the perceptive account in George di Giovanni, "A Reply to Cynthia Willett," in *Essays in Hegel's Logic*, ed. George di Giovanni (Albany: State University of New York Press, 1990).

4. See Marjorie Grene, "People and Other Animals," in *The Understanding of Nature: Essays in the Philosophy of Biology* (Dordrecht, Netherlands: D. Reidel, 1974), 458.

5. Francisco J. Ayala, "Human Evolution: The Three Grand Challenges of Human Biology," in *The Cambridge Companion to the Philosophy of Biology*, ed. David L. Hull and Michael Ruse (Cambridge: Cambridge University Press, 2007), 248. See also Richard Dawkins, *The Selfish Gene*, 2nd ed. (Oxford: Oxford University Press, 1989); and Edward O. Wilson, *Sociobiology: The New Synthesis* (Cambridge, MA: Harvard University Press, 1975).

It's worth emphasizing that the concept of the phenotype risks becoming increasingly vague and equivocal when invoked in accord with treating cultural phenomena as Darwinian adaptations—*without* any close linkage to the genetic. (Of course, Darwin himself was deprived of the opportunity to invoke empirical genetics.) For a sense of the inevitable slippage, which obscures the difference between biology and culture (and, therefore, biological and cultural evolution), see Steven Pinker, *The Language Instinct: How the Mind Creates Language* (New York: HarperCollins, 1995). Pinker wrote and published his book just at the time Noam Chomsky was beginning to concede that his doctrine of "universal grammar" was clearly mistaken; Chomsky never abandoned the innatist conviction, though he admitted he had no satisfactory clues about how to replace his former executive thesis. See Noam Chomsky, *New Horizons in the Study of Language and Mind* (Cambridge: Cambridge University Press, 2000). Consider the following specimen remarks from Pinker:

Because of the language instinct, there is something much more fascinating about linguistic innovation [than mere innovation: borrowing, say, from other languages and introducing variable forms of what is thus incorporated]: each link in the chain of language transmission is a human brain. That brain is equipped with a universal grammar and is always on the lookout for examples in ambient speech of various kinds of rules. (244)

Evolutionary theory, supported by computer simulations, has shown that when an environment is stable, there is a selective pressure for learned abilities to become increasingly innate. That is because if an ability is innate, it can be deployed earlier in the lifespan of the creature, and there is less of a chance that an unlucky creature will miss out on the experiences that would have been necessary to teach it. (242)

This is surely Lamarckian in spirit, offered without any promising link to genetic theory, whether conventional or revised in some new way. The upshot is that the idea of a distinct form of cultural evolution (catching up the logical difference between biological and cultural properties) begins to fail. (In effect, Dawkins opposes Pinker's lax conception of *adaptation*.)

6. Aristotle, *Physics* 2.2.193a28–33, trans. R. P. Hardie and R. K. Gaye, in *The Complete Works of Aristotle: The Revised Oxford Translation*, ed. Jonathan Barnes, vol. 1 (Princeton, NJ: Princeton University Press, 1984).

7. For an example of pragmatism's interest in congenial continental figures, see Sandra B. Rosenthal and Patrick L. Bourgeois, *Mead and Merleau-Ponty: Toward a Common Vision* (Albany: State University of New York Press, 1991). In the analytic tradition, Alvin Plantinga is well known for his strong efforts to demonstrate the inadequacy of a naturalistic epistemology (and cognate claims) in the direction of the necessity of a supernatural grounding (by way of "natural theology"). See, for instance, Alvin Plantinga, *God and Other Minds* (Ithaca, NY: Cornell University Press, 1967); and Plantinga, *The Nature of Necessity* (Oxford: Clarendon Press, 1974).

8. As already noted, I take the wording from Marjorie Grene, who shares it with Helmuth Plessner, but the sense is my own. Grene means that we become "artifactual" in the sense of learning to use the technologies we acquire, whereas I mean that "we" (originally natural primates/infants) *transform* "ourselves" into (artifactual) *selves*, in the process of "inventing" and mastering natural language (the impact of which Darwin never fully grasped). We remain "natural" beings, however, in both accounts.

9. See John McDowell, *Mind and World*, 2nd ed. (Cambridge, MA: Harvard University Press, 1996). At the time of the initial publication of this chapter, McDowell had just published two collections of papers, *Having the World in View: Essays on Kant, Hegel, and Sellars* (Cambridge, MA: Harvard University Press, 2009) and *The Engaged Intellect: Philosophical Essays* (Cambridge, MA: Harvard University Press, 2009). Unfortunately, these appeared too late to be consulted.

10. See, for instance, Edmund Husserl, *Logical Investigations*, 2 vols., trans. J. N. Findlay (London: Routledge / Kegan Paul, 1970); and Husserl, *The Crisis of European Sciences and Transcendental Phenomenology: An Introduction to Phenomenological Philosophy*, trans. David Carr (Evanston, IL: Northwestern University Press, 1970).

11. Edmund Husserl, preface to *Ideas: General Introduction to Pure Phenomenology*, trans. W. R. Boyce Gibson (New York: Collier Books, 1962), 5–22.

12. I explore this further in "The Point of Hegel's Dissatisfaction with Kant," in *Pragmatism Ascendent: A Yard of Narrative, A Touch of Prophecy* (Stanford, CA: Stanford University Press, 2012), 7–49. See note 16, below.

13. John McDowell, "Two Sorts of Naturalism," in *Mind, Value, and Reality* (Cambridge, MA: Harvard University Press, 1998), 192–97. McDowell is referring to Aristotle, *Nicomachean Ethics* 1.4.1095b–6 (which he cites).

14. McDowell, 192–94 (italics added).

15. McDowell, *Mind and World*, lecture 4, p. 84.

16. McDowell, 85.

17. The only other site among McDowell's papers that I am familiar with that seems to lean, ever so tentatively, in the direction I'm suggesting, appears in McDowell, "In Defense of Modesty," in *Meaning, Knowledge, and Reality* (Cambridge, MA: Harvard University Press, 1998), 87–107, which briefly links Herder's and Hegel's general views on Enlightenment thought in a running critique of Michael Dummett's theory of meaning.

18. See Wilfrid Sellars, "Philosophy and the Scientific Image of Man," in *Science, Perception and Reality* (London: Routledge / Kegan Paul, 1963), 1–40. For a sustained sense of recent efforts by many hands to liberate analytic philosophy's version of naturalism from the impoverishing constraints of scientism, see Mario de Caro and David MacArthur, eds., *Naturalism in Question* (Cambridge: Cambridge University Press, 2004). The unifying themes seem to affirm that science, rather than man, is the measure of all things. The disjunction seems infelicitous: first, because science is itself the work of human beings and, second, because, on the argument I've been pursuing, the human self is a cultural artifact, so that what naturalism must include cannot fail to be qualified by what being a self signifies. I'm afraid there's rather little of fresh promise offered here—and almost nothing ventured—on the theory of the human self or subject or regarding overlooked resources drawn from continental European philosophy or, for that matter, from Darwinian inquiries.

19. McDowell, *Mind and World*, 71n.

20. See McDowell, 5n4: "In much of the rest of these lectures, I shall be concerned to cast doubt on Sellars's idea that placing something in the logical space of reasons is, as such, to be contrasted with giving an empirical description of it." I agree with McDowell here. But it presupposes a deeper account that McDowell nowhere supplies.

21. I should add that I take the chapters that form part 4 of McDowell's *Mind, Value, and Reality* to confirm just how distant the transformative, post-Darwinian doctrine of *Bildung* is from McDowell's account of Aristotle's ethical naturalism, in chapter 2.

22. I've examined Kim's argument more closely in "Constructing a Person: A Clue to the New Unity of the Arts and Sciences"; see note 53. The decisive clue against Kim's strong form of supervenience, physical realization, and causal reductionism is clear at once from his own definition of the supervenience of the mental: "Mental properties *supervene* [he says] on physical properties, in that necessarily, for any mental property M, if anything has M at time t, there exists a physical base (of subvenient) property P such that it has P at t, and necessarily anything that has P at a time has M at that time." The definition appears in Jaegwon Kim, *Mind in a Physical World: An Essay on the Mind-Body Problem and Mental Causation* (Cambridge, MA: MIT Press, 2000), 9 (italics in original). It's meant to suggest a strong form of the unity doctrine. But if you consider that a chess move may be performed in any number of contingent ways (which depend on chess conventions and ad hoc practices), you realize that Kim's definition is invalid: we cannot even tell whether a particular "bodily movement" *counts* as a chess move except top down (that is, by a subfunctional analysis of the molar action that is admitted to be a chess move: in short, an interpretation of the action involved). Hence, the nomological uniformities adduced by Kim are never necessary (in that guise). There's the insuperable complication of the cultural world if reductionism fails.

23. For a sense of the puzzling features of McDowell's account of *Bildung*, see Nicholas H. Smith, ed., *Reading McDowell: On Mind and World* (London: Routledge, 2002).

24. See, especially, Nancy Cartwright, *The Dappled World: A Study of the Boundaries of Science* (Cambridge: Cambridge University Press, 1999).

25. John McDowell, "The Woodbridge Lectures 1997. Having the World in View: Sellars, Kant, and Intentionality," *Journal of Philosophy* 95, no. 9 (1998): 490.

26. See Joseph Margolis, "Point of Hegel's Dissatisfaction," 7–49.

27. That goes well beyond any plausible form of naturalism. Have a careful look, for instance, at the extraordinary account Aristotle offers of the cognitive powers of reason in *On the Soul*, trans. J. A. Smith, in *The Complete Works of Aristotle*, ed. Jonathan Barnes, vol. 1, §4, 429a13–28, 429b9; also, the account in René Descartes, "The Principles of Philosophy," in *The Philosophical Works of Descartes*, trans. E. S. Haldane and G. R. T. Ross, vol. 1 (New York: Dover, 1955), 239–40, 243–44, regarding principles 51–52, 60 (pt. 1).

28. See G. W. F. Hegel, *Lectures on the History of Philosophy*, vol. 3, trans. E. S. Haldane and Frances Samson (Lincoln: University of Nebraska Press, 1995), §3.

29. See, for instance, Ernst Cassirer, *The Philosophy of Symbolic Forms*, vol. 3, trans. Ralph Manheim (New Haven, CT: Yale University Press, 1957), pt. 3. The nerve of Cassirer's "idea of limit" appears as a clear summary at pp. 475–76.

30. This counts heavily against McDowell's "delay" in reclaiming Hegel and "reenchanting" nature—if we mean to recover a viable form of realism or the norms of moral and political reason that rely, *within naturalistic bounds*, on the resources of "second nature." Consider the following passage from McDowell (*Mind and World*, 91–92):

Aristotle's ethics contains a model of a naturalism that would not stand in the way of a satisfactory conception of experience (and of action, I can now add). The position is a naturalism of second nature, and I suggested [earlier] that we can equally see it as a naturalized platonism. The idea is that the dictates of reason are there anyway, whether or not one's eyes are opened to them; that is what happens in a proper upbringing. We need not try to understand the thought that the dictates of reason are objects of an enlightened awareness, except from within the way of thinking such an upbringing initiates one into: a way of thinking that constitutes a standpoint from which those dictates are already in view.

In my opinion, this threatens to lose the link between Aristotle and Hegel. See also McDowell's congruent reading of Wittgenstein (92–93).

31. C. I. Lewis, *Mind and the World Order* (New York: Charles Scribner's Sons, 1929), x (italics in original).

32. Lewis, 32. See Murray G. Murphey, *C. I. Lewis: The Last Great Pragmatist* (Albany: State University of New York Press, 2005), 32 (italics in original); and Lewis, "A Pragmatic Conception of the *A Priori*," *Journal of Philosophy* 20, no. 7 (1923): 236–49.

33. Murphey, *Lewis*, 139; see Lewis, *Mind and the World Order*, 23–27.

34. Lewis, "The Pragmatic Element in Knowledge," in *Collected Papers of Clarence Irving Lewis*, ed. John Goheen and John Mothershead (Stanford, CA: Stanford University, 1970), 257; quoted in Murphey, *Lewis*, 135.

35. See Joseph Margolis, *Pragmatism without Foundations: Reconciling Realism and Relativism*, 2nd ed. (London: Continuum, 2007), pt. 1.

36. See Hilary Putnam, *Ethics without Ontology* (Cambridge, MA: Harvard University Press, 2004), 60–63, for a brief but pointed account of "conceptual truths"; and Putnam, "Rethinking Mathematical Necessity," in *Words and Life*, ed. James Conant (Cambridge, MA: Harvard University Press, 1994).

37. Peirce, "The Universal Categories," in *Collected Papers of Charles Sanders Peirce*, ed. Charles Hartshorne and Paul Weiss, vol. 5 (Cambridge, MA: Harvard University Press, 1962), 37–39 (italics in original).

38. Edmund Husserl, *Psychological and Transcendental Phenomenology and the Confrontation with Heidegger (1927–1931)*, ed. and trans. Thomas Sheehan and Richard E. Palmer (Dordrecht, Netherlands: Kluwer, 1997); quoted in Dan Zahavi, *Husserl's Phenomenology* (Stanford, CA: Stanford University Press, 2003), 110–11 (translation modified by Zahavi).

39. Zahavi, *Husserl's Phenomenology*, 72–73. Zahavi paraphrases approvingly a remark of Putnam's: "[I]t is not that the mind makes up the world, but it doesn't just mirror it either," from Putnam, *Meaning and the Moral Sciences* (London: Routledge / Kegan Paul, 1978), 1.

40. Quoted in Zahavi, *Husserl's Phenomenology*, 73.

41. Peirce, "Pragmatism: The Normative Sciences," in *Collected Papers*, Hartshorne and Weiss, vol. 5, ¶37 (italics in original). To pit pragmatism against Husserl is not yet to pit pragmatism against phenomenology *tout court*, since Hegel is a phenomenologist and Peirce, a Hegelian phenomenologist. The caveat bears usefully on the strong argument offered in Scott F. Aikin, "Pragmatism, Naturalism, and Phenomenology," *Human Studies* 29 (2006): 317–40. See also Sami Pihlström, "The Naturalism Debate and the Development of European Philosophy," *Philosophy Today* 46 (2002): 102–11, quoted by Aikin.

42. For a particularly interesting specimen of how the argument might develop, see Daniel O. Dahlstrom, "Between Being and Essence: Reflection's Logical Disguises," in *Essays on Hegel's Logic*, ed. George di Giovanni (Albany: State University of New York Press, 1990), 99–112.

43. See Joseph Margolis, *Reinventing Pragmatism: American Philosophy at the End of the Twentieth Century* (Ithaca, NY: Cornell University Press, 2002); and Margolis, *The Unraveling of Scientism: American Philosophy at the End of the Twentieth Century* (Ithaca, NY: Cornell University Press, 2003).

44. Compare Martin Heidegger, *History of the Concept of Time: Prolegomena*, trans. Theodor Kisiel (Bloomington: Indiana University Press, 1985).

45. G. W. F. Hegel, "With What Must the Science Begin?" in *Hegel's Science of Logic*, vol. 1, book 1, pp. 67–78.

46. I find this compellingly confirmed (unintentionally) in Dan Zahavi, *Husserl and Transcendental Intersubjectivity*, trans. Elizabeth A. Behnke (Athens: Ohio University Press, 2001), see particularly chap. 6.

47. Dan Zahavi, *Subjectivity and Selfhood: Investigating the First-Person Perspective* (Cambridge, MA: MIT Press, 2005), 33.

48. Zahavi provides a very useful textual summary of Husserl's evolving treatment of these notions. But the need to vindicate the transcendental "recovery" of the real world does not appear as a serious problem. See Zahavi, *Husserl's Phenomenology*, chap. 2; *Husserl and Transcendental Intersubjectivity*, chap. 1.

49. See Putnam, *Ethics without Ontology*.

50. Sartre follows Husserl here. See Jean-Paul Sartre, *The Transcendence of the Ego*, trans. F. Williams and R. Kirkpatrick (New York: Noonday Press, 1957). On the distinction between the "egological" and "non-egological," see Aaron Gurwitsch, "A Non-egological Conception of Consciousness," *Philosophy and Phenomenological Research* 1 (1941): 325–38. For a specimen of the opposed analytic view, see Sidney Shoemaker, "Self-Reference and Self-Awareness," *Journal of Philosophy* 65 (1968): 555–67.

51. See, for pertinent conjectures, Susan Hurley, *Consciousness in Action* (Cambridge, MA: Harvard University Press, 1998); Alva Noë, *Action in Perception* (Cambridge, MA: MIT Press, 2006); and Robert W. Wilson, *Boundaries of the Mind: The Individual in the Fragile Sciences* (Cambridge: Cambridge University Press, 2004).

52. Husserl, *Ideas*, 5–11 (italics in original).

53. I offer a version of this thesis in "Constructing a Person: A Clue to the New Unity of the Arts and Sciences," presented in October 2008 at the conference La filosofía como ciudad de las artes y las ciencias in Valencia, Spain, and now included in Margolis, *Toward a Metaphysics of Culture* (London: Routledge, 2016).

54. This tally is, roughly, abstracted from my *Historied Thought, Constructed World: A Conceptual Primer for the Turn of the Millennium* (Berkeley: University of California Press, 1995).

55. See Emmanuel Levinas, *Totality and Infinity: An Essay on Exteriority*, trans. Alphonso Lingis (The Hague, Netherlands: Nijhoff, 1979).

56. For Heidegger's account of "facticity" and "exists" (or "existence"), see Martin Heidegger, *Ontology: The Hermeneutics of Facticity*, trans. John Van Buren (Bloomington: Indiana University Press, 1988).

57. Heidegger, *Being and Time*, trans. Joan Stambaugh (Albany: State University of New York Press, 1996), 116; pp. 123–124 in the German pagination.

58. See, for instance, Jerome Bruner, *Beyond the Information Given: Studies in the Psychology of Knowing*, ed. Jeremy M. Anglin (New York: W. W. Norton, 1973), pt. 3, for a number of pioneer studies in prelinguistic learning and thinking; Michael Tomasello, *The Cultural Origins of Human Cognition* (Cambridge, MA: Harvard University Press, 1999); and L. S. Vygotsky, *Mind in Society*, trans. A. R.

Luria, ed. M. Cole, V. John-Steiner, S. Scribner, and E. Souberman (Cambridge, MA: Harvard University Press, 1978).

59. See the discussion of "conceptual truths" in Putnam, *Ethics without Ontology*.

Notes to Chapter Five

1. Joseph Margolis, "Legitimization," in *Historied Thought, Constructed World: A Conceptual Primer for the Turn of the Millennium* (Berkeley: University of California Press, 1995), 154–77.

2. For an overview of the problem of history, see Margolis, *The Flux of History and the Flux of Science* (Berkeley: University of California Press, 1993).

3. The important theorems developed in *Historied Thought, Constructed World* are listed in that book's appendix, pp. 301–03.

4. Pared down to essentials, the key figures here are Fichte and Hegel (defining the trajectory of post-Kantian idealism) and Foucault and Dewey (as fair specimens of contemporary post-Hegelian historicism). For a sense of Fichte's "subject-centered" theory, however unsatisfactorily articulated, see Johann Gottlieb Fichte, *Science of Knowledge*, ed. and trans. Peter Heath and John Lachs (Cambridge: Cambridge University Press, 1982). Hegel's view is centered in the *Phenomenology*. See his *Phenomenology of Spirit*, trans. A. V. Miller (Oxford: Clarendon Press, 1977). But see, also, the discussion of Fichte in Hegel, *The Difference between Fichte's and Schelling's System of Philosophy*, trans. H. S. Harris and Walter Cerf (Albany: State University of New York Press, 1977). For a sense of Foucault's thesis, see Michel Foucault, "Two Lectures." It is difficult to find a short account of Dewey's Hegelian heritage. In fact, the issue is hardly developed in the "appreciative" literature. For a sense of this, see R. W. Sleeper, *The Necessity of Pragmatism: John Dewey's Conception of Philosophy* (New Haven, CT: Yale University Press, 1986); and Paul A. Schlipp (ed.), *The Philosophy of John Dewey*, 2nd ed. (New York: Tudor Publishing, 1951).

5. For contemporary résumés of Brentano's and Husserl's views of intentionality, see (on Brentano) Roderick M. Chisholm, *Perceiving: A Philosophical Study* (Ithaca, NY: Cornell University Press, 1957), chap. 11; and Linda L. McAlister, ed., *The Philosophy of Brentano* (Atlantic Highlands, NJ: Humanities Press, 1976); on Husserl, see Jitendra Nath Mohanty, *The Concept of Intentionality* (St. Louis, MO: Warren H. Green, 1972); and Hubert L. Dreyfus, ed., with Harrison Hall, *Husserl, Intentionality, and Cognitive Science* (Cambridge, MA: MIT Press, 1984). The most sustained recent attempt in the analytic literature to recover intentionality appears in John R. Searle, *Intentionality: An Essay in the Philosophy of Mind* (Cambridge: Cambridge University Press, 1983), which is, in principle, also solipsistic. The odd thing is that what I call the Intentional (marking the term with a typographical distinction) is, of course, familiar in modern hermeneutics, both pre-Heideggerian

(as in Dilthey) and post-Heideggerian (as in Gadamer), except that it is almost never brought into close accord with the debate about intentionality itself. See Rudolf A. Makkreel, *Dilthey: Philosopher of the Human Studies* (Princeton, NJ: Princeton University Press, 1975), chap. 7. See, also, Gadamer, *Truth and Method*, part 2, §2; and Joel C. Weinsheimer, *Gadamer's Hermeneutics: A Reading of Truth and Method* (New Haven, CT: Yale University Press, 1985). The same, I should say, is true of Wittgenstein. See his *Philosophical Investigations*. I find it quite curious that Wittgenstein's emphasis on the collective aspects of *Lebensformen* should have been as widely ignored by his admirers as by his detractors. The theme of intentionality is much less explicit in Kuhn, *The Structure of Scientific Revolutions*, but it is surely there. It is also present in Dewey but, again, in a muted form. See Sleeper, *Necessity of Pragmatism*, chap. 5. For a sense of Ranke's version of historicism, see Leopold von Ranke, *The Theory of Practice of History*, ed. Georg Iggers and Konrad von Moltke, trans. Wilma A. Iggers and Konrad von Moltke (New York: Irvington Publishers, 1983).

6. I take Chomsky to hold one of the most extreme forms of solipsism, namely, nativism or innatism, the doctrine that our cognitive (in particular, our linguistic) capacities are, initially and in a profound sense, genetically determined, fixed in a species-specific way. Chomsky advances his claim on the grounds that there is no other option that is viable. But he nowhere explains how natural language is empirically acquired or how our innate competence is actually triggered among infants—or even how we function epistemically *as apt linguistic agents*. He offers no sustained account of the actual process of acquiring a first language in terms of the utterances of learning children. Characteristically, he offers idealized specimen sentences, treated noncontextually, atomically, as instantiating his grammatical theory and as (somehow) capturing the process of initial human speech. See, for instance, Noam Chomsky, *Knowledge of Language: Its Nature, Origin, and Use* (Westport, CT: Praeger, 1986).

7. A very large part of Lévi-Strauss's polemical work has been taken up with opposing any and all forms of historicism, notably in the work of Jean-Paul Sartre. But Lévi-Strauss never explains the grounds on which he projects a timeless or transhistorically valid model of rationality. This is a point of considerable importance in assessing the plausibility of structuralism. As far as I can see, the thesis is entirely arbitrary. It leads directly to a descriptive deformation of the empirical facts about different societies. See Claude Lévi-Strauss, *The Savage Mind*, trans. Doreen Weightman and John Weightman (Chicago: University of Chicago Press, 1966), chap. 9; and Lévi-Strauss, *The Elementary Structures of Kinship*. Although (and with justice) Chomsky cannot be called a structuralist, his nativism is subject to the same large criticisms that can be brought against Lévi-Strauss. For an "exasperated" (original term), often naive, certainly unguarded, more or less Wittgensteinian, nevertheless useful, and thoroughly charming critique of Chomsky's sense of linguistic system, see Ian Robinson, *The New Grammarians' Funeral: A Critique of Noam Chomsky's*

Linguistics (Cambridge: Cambridge University Press, 1978). For a critique (of an altogether different sort) of Chomsky's conception of a "generative grammar," see D. Terence Langendoen and Paul M. Postal, *The Vastness of Natural Languages* (Oxford: Basil Blackwell, 1984). See, also, Terry Winograd, *Understanding Natural Language* (New York: Academic Press, 1977).

    8. If selves or subjects and the artifacts of their cultural world are construed in realist terms—and there is no viable argument by which a realism of selves (ourselves) can be decisively denied—then, arguably, it is coordinatively (analytically) impossible to deny a realist reading of the Intentional features of artworks, languages, artifacts, and actions. That is an extremely powerful finding. Its denial leads directly to a profound incoherence. Danto professes to treat art, history, and action "rhetorically" (that is, not in realist terms), even though, quite obviously, he treats selves, human persons, as real enough. I am persuaded that this leads to unresolvable paradox. See, for instance, Arthur C. Danto, "The Artworld," *Journal of Philosophy* 61, no. 19 (1964): 571–84; Danto, *The Transfiguration of the Commonplace* (Cambridge, MA: Harvard University Press, 1981); and Danto, *Narration and Knowledge* (New York: Columbia University Press, 1985).

    9. Davidson's thesis (the two notions are not quite the same) appears in Donald Davidson, "Mental Events," in *Essays on Events and Actions* (Oxford: Clarendon Press, 1980), 207–24. This single paper has enjoyed the most remarkable reputation and has exerted an equally remarkable influence. It is, without doubt, one of a very small number of key papers that give a sense of direction to naturalistic philosophies of mind. It offers a fairly ample account of "anomalous monism" (in effect, nonreductive physicism) but no more than a sketch of "supervenience" (which has now eclipsed the other, among naturalists). But anomalous monism is inconsistent, and supervenience is arbitrary and undefended. It is also true that the supervenientists regularly assume that Moore's account of "good" as a nonnatural quality somehow, successfully, introduces the supervenience thesis. That is a flat mistake, for, although Moore surely did believe that good depended on natural properties, he nowhere says (and I think he would never have said) that there was a determinate entailment relation between particular natural and nonnatural (moral or ethical) properties. But if not, then Moore's argument cannot help the naturalist who addresses the human sciences and is (in fact) opposed to naturalism. See G. E. Moore, "Reply to My Critics," in *The Philosophy of G. E. Moore*, 2nd ed., ed. Paul A. Schlipp (New York: Tudor, 1952), 535–677. See, for a clear sense of the supervenientists' tendency to depart from Moore's thesis—which Davidson plainly shares—Jaegwon Kim, *Supervenience and Mind: Selected Philosophical Essays* (Cambridge: Cambridge University Press, 1993).

    10. I have heard Feigl speak of the principle but have not found it laid out in any text. It is plainly implicated, however, in Herbert Feigl, *The "Mental" and the "Physical": The Essay and a Postscript* (Minneapolis: University of Minnesota Press, 1967).

11. Popper believes that there are laws of nature, but he thinks nature is fathomless for humans. They cannot directly discern any asymptotic approximation to progressively improved formulations of the laws of nature (inductivism). Nevertheless, we do have rational strategies by which we can judge the "verisimilitude" of the would-be laws we formulate. I believe (and have some evidence) that Popper was influenced by Peirce in a general way. But Peirce's optimism about the "long run" is frankly teleologized, whereas Popper pretends that verisimilitude can be defended on rational or methodological grounds that need not rely on any teleologism. I find the argument unconvincing. See Karl R. Popper, "Two Faces of Common Sense: An Argument for Commonsense Realism and Against the Commonsense Theory of Knowledge," in *Objective Knowledge: An Evolutionary Approach* (Oxford: Clarendon, 1972); and, also, Popper, *Realism and the Aim of Science*, particularly chap. 1. The *Realism* book is one of three that together comprise *Postscript to the Logic of Scientific Discovery* (1983, 1982, 1982). I take them to be largely committed (by somewhat different routes) to the defense of "absolute truth" as a "regulative idea" (*verisimilitude*). I have, I should add, already mentioned selected current views that call the realism of nomic invariance into question. On Popper's view of history, see Karl R. Popper, *The Poverty of Historicism*, 3rd ed. (New York: Harper and Row, 1960).

12. I should say that, among contemporary philosophers of the physical sciences, Feyerabend subscribed most completely to this theorem, in spite of the fact that he also strongly favored a form of eliminative physicalism. The truth is, he viewed eliminativism as a project for the dim future. See Paul K. Feyerabend, *Against Method* (Atlantic Highlands, NJ: Humanities Press, 1975); and Feyerabend, *Philosophical Papers*, 2 vols. (Cambridge: Cambridge University Press, 1981).

13. This goes against eliminativist (physicalist) tendencies in current philosophies of mind. As far as I can see, they are entirely undefended and utopian. Feyerabend, I have just noted, was frank enough to push the need to muster arguments in favor of its denial into a very remote future. The same is true of Stephen P. Stich, *From Folk Psychology to Cognitive Science: The Case against Belief* (Cambridge, MA: MIT Press, 1983). The same is true, for all its bluster, in Paul M. Churchland, *A Neurocomputational Perspective: The Nature of Mind and the Structure of Science* (Cambridge, MA: MIT Press, 1989). I cannot find a single specifiable argument in support of any of these accounts, except the bare claim that the folk- theoretic view must be mistaken. The same (physicalist) point had been made years ago by J. J. C. Smart, *Philosophy and Scientific Realism* (London: Routledge / Kegan Paul, 1963). But Smart had the "advantage" that the unity of science seemed (then) to be in the ascendent. That is no longer true.

14. The most extreme statement of eliminationism in the context of the unity-of-science program is the one offered in Wilfrid Sellars, "The Language of Theories," in *Science, Perception and Reality* (London: Routledge / Kegan Paul, 1963), 106–26.

15. See Hans Reichenbach, *The Rise of Scientific Philosophy*, (Berkeley: University of California Press, 1951), chap. 18.

16. There is, of course, no single canonical "picture." For a sample of the spirit of the unity program, see the first three volumes of the *Minnesota Studies in the Philosophy of Science* (Minneapolis: University of Minnesota Press, 1956, 1958, 1962), edited by Herbert Feigl and his associates. For an inordinately optimistic version of that picture (or something akin to it), see Mario Bunge, "Emergence and the Mind," *Neuroscience* 11 (1972): 501–09; and Bungo, "Levels and Reduction," *American Journal of Physiology* 103 (1977): 75–82. The unity theorists and their allies have been much occupied with the problem of emergence in nature—reaching, of course, to the mental and the cultural—in terms of its reconcilability with a strict methodological canon. My own emphasis is precisely on the methodological discontinuity entailed by the admission of Intentionality. In effect, Peirce precludes any such admission—though not for the unity theorist's reasons—by adhering to his doctrine of "objective" Thirdness (which obtains independently of the constituting work of human inquiry). Peirce's "cosmic mind" falls away from the post-Kantian constraint, but its evolutionism is obviously dated.

17. An extremely clear sense of the puzzles involving extensions and intensions—in sense (b)—once we depart from something like Aristotle's archism, is offered in Putnam's papers on semantics. See Hilary Putnam, *Mind, Language and Reality*, vol. 2 of *Philosophical Papers* (Cambridge: Cambridge University Press, 1975).

18. For a sense of Kant's treatment of history, see Yirmiahu Yovel, *Kant and the Philosophy of History* (Princeton, NJ: Princeton University Press, 1980).

19. The whole thrust of positivism, the unity-of-science program, and naturalism is to insist that it is unreasonable to construe the phenomena of the cultural world as not analyzable, ontically or epistemically—hence, also, conceptually or methodologically—in the non-Intentional terms thought to be apt for the physical sciences. For a somewhat overly optimistic (but revealing) specimen, see Smart, *Philosophy and Scientific Realism*. To press the point, I cannot see any fundamental difference in outlook, although I admit local refinements and variations, in the more recent specimen offered in Daniel C. Dennett, *Content and Consciousness* (London: Routledge / Kegan Paul, 1969).

20. For doubts about the standard interpretation, see Lilli Alanen, "Studies in Cartesian Epistemology and Philosophy of Mind," *Acta Philosophica Fennica* 28 (1982); and Alanen, "On Descartes's Argument for Dualism, and the Distinction between Different Kinds of Beings," in *The Logic of Being*, ed. S. Knuutila and J. Hintikka (Dordrecht, Netherlands: D. Reidel, 1986), 223–48.

21. Although modern atomic (and subatomic) theory is utterly unlike the original "atomic" theory of Democritus, there is much that links them still. Democritus, of course, meant his atoms (indivisible entities) to be construed literally as such. Hence, in Democritus's view, *all* perceptible change in nature is to be explained

in terms of the combination of unalterable and impenetrable (ultimate) atoms and the distinction between the perceptual appearance of any combination of atoms and what combinations actually obtain at the atomic level. Modern cosmologies have been forced to concede that subatomic structures (as presently conceived) cannot be ultimate, but it is clear that the search for microtheoretical entities is still largely motivated by the dream of capturing the ultimate compositional elements of physical nature. The present state of quantum physics has proved particularly baffling. The plot gets much thicker. Quite a number of theorists, who oppose the optimistic physicalism of the unity-of-science model, nevertheless do believe that a unity can be recovered. Some of these have been led to believe that there must be a deeper connection between quantum physics and the structure of the mind. I have never found these accounts convincing, although I see the motivation for them. But then, I have never found the unity-of-science model convincing either. For specimen discussions, see Roger Penrose, *The Emperor's New Mind: Concerning Computers, Minds, and the Laws of Physics* (New York: Oxford University Press, 1989); and Michael Lockwood, *Mind, Brain and the Quantum: The Compound 'I'* (Oxford: Basil Blackwell, 1989). The general strategy of these very different books is to urge us to appreciate the puzzling complexity of *matter*—which *is*, after all, a refreshing change. For a rather revealing set of reflections on the part of David Bohm, who has surely had as much as anyone to do with the attempt to link the mind/body problem to our interpretation of quantum physics, see David Bohm and F. David Peat, *Science, Order, and Creativity* (Toronto: Bantam Books, 1987). My sense is that these accounts tend to confuse the requirements of symbiosis with the dream of a unified science.

22. The doctrine is the unfortunate consequence of attempting to treat, within the terms of a Fregean or Russellian logic, the analysis of particulars essentially in predicative terms. Hence, it is attracted to a kind of Platonism (as in Russell), in that a "particular" is construed in terms of the site of a "bare particular" at which universals somehow are present. See, for instance, Edwin Allaire, "Bare Particulars," *Philosophical Studies* 16 (1963): 1–7. The thesis is the result of trying to conform with certain of Russell's constraints without adhering to Russell's views about their import for knowledge "by acquaintance." See Gustav Bergmann, "Russell on Particulars," *Philosophical Review* 56 (1947): 59–72.

23. It is a curious but undeniable fact that physicalists often agree, despite rejecting dualism, that dualism offers the only (or very nearly the only) serious alternative to physicalism itself. There's no doubt, for instance, that that supposition motivates the accounts of Churchland and Parfit. See, for instance, Churchland, *A Neurocomputational Perspective*; and Derek Parfit, *Reasons and Persons* (Oxford: Clarendon Press, 1984). The confusion is palpable in Parfit, for, in one of the earliest of his papers leading to Reasons and Persons, Parfit actually conjectures that the issues of the numerical identity of persons may be retired in favor of certain predicative continuities. See Parfit, "Personal Identity," *Philosophical Review* 80 (1971): 3–27.

But, of course, that deprives the predicative issue of any determinate application and leads (if psychological attributes are still to be invoked) to what Strawson calls (and criticizes as) the "no-ownership theory." See P. F. Strawson, *Individuals: An Essay in Descriptive Metaphysics* (London: Methuen, 1959). In any case, there's no point to debating dualism and reductionism without a firm commitment to the logic of reference and predication. Something similar (to Parfit's difficulty) appears in Dennett's *Content and Consciousness*, for Dennett, too, believes that the concept of persons can be retired. In principle, this would require that intentional predicates be reduced in some suitable way so that their replacements could be predicated of (non-Intentionally qualified) physical or biological entities. Dennett nowhere provides the required account. In fact, he has tried, more recently, to enrich the language of intentionality. See Dennett, *The Intentional Stance* (Cambridge, MA: MIT Press, 1987); and Dennett, *Consciousness Explained* (Boston: Little, Brown, 1991). But the original intent is plainly still in play. Parfit's is more problematic, because Parfit does not broach any explicit, comparable reduction.

24. Strawson's very promising intuition about the difference between persons and physical bodies was spoiled, I believe, by his implicit adherence to a dualism of mental and physical properties. See Strawson, *Individuals*. This explains the ease with which Bernard Williams was able to show that Strawson had not satisfactorily distinguished his account from the dualism he wished to avoid. See Williams, *Problems of the Self*. If I am right in this, then the only conceptual option that respects the realism of the mental and the avoidance of dualism and reductionism is the one I propose: that is, the view that the mental is complex. To enrich the notion for what else is needed, I say that one must also construe the mental as Intentional, historicized, constructed. But the key maneuver rests with admitting the (cultural) emergence of the complex. (More needs to be said, however.)

25. I offer a short overview of the various relevant strategies of emergence in Margolis, "Emergence and the Unity of Science," in *Science without Unity: Reconciling the Human and Natural Sciences* (Oxford: Basil Blackwell, 1987).

26. For a clear sense of the problem of reductionism and of distinguishing between the physical and the biological, see Marjorie Grene and Everett Mendelsohn, eds., *Topics in the Philosophy of Biology* (Dordrecht, Netherlands: D. Reidel, 1976), especially pts. 2 and 3. For a very fair-minded overview, favoring (nevertheless) what Schaffner calls "the general redirection-replacement model," see Kenneth F. Schaffner, *Discovery and Explanation in Biology and Medicine* (Chicago: University of Chicago Press, 1993), particularly chap. 9.

27. For a sample of the sense in which the *functional* is invoked in biological and related contexts, see Larry Wright, *Teleological Explanation* (Berkeley: University of California Press, 1976). The most sustained (relatively early) discussion of functional explanations occurs, I believe, in Charles Taylor, *The Explanation of Behaviour* (London: Routledge / Kegan Paul, 1964). (Taylor's work influenced Wright. Schaffner reviews the critical literature.) See, also, Marjorie Grene, *The*

Understanding of Nature: Essays in the Philosophy of Biology (Dordrecht, Netherlands: D. Reidel, 1974).

28. For a sense of the role of the informational in the development of contemporary genetic theory, see James D. Watson, *Molecular Biology of the Gene*, 2nd ed. (Menlo Park, CA: W. A. Benjamin, 1970). You cannot fail to see that the philosophical issue is nowhere present. The most recent sustained philosophical application (that I know) of the informational in ontic and epistemic terms congenial to analytic philosophy may be found in Fred I. Dretske, *Knowledge and the Flow of Information* (Cambridge, MA: MIT Press, 1981). It is, I think, wedded too obviously to notions of nomological necessity, which are not independently defended.

29. Broadly speaking, this is the gist of Millikan's strategy. See Ruth Millikan, *Language, Thought, and Other Biological Categories*. The strategy works wherever the function is merely heuristic or emergent in the way of biological phenomena. For a sense, for instance, of the "homeostatic," see Ernest Nagel, *The Structure of Science: Problems in the Logic of Scientific Explanation* (Indianapolis, IN: Hackett, 1979), chap. 12. It's only when the normative specifically implicates the Intentional that the naturalizing strategy fails. See, also, Allan Gibbard, *Wise Choices, Apt Feelings: A Theory of Normative Judgment* (Cambridge, MA: Harvard University Press, 1990).

30. See James J. Gibson, *The Senses Considered As Perceptual Systems* (Boston: Houghton Mifflin, 1966); and Gibson, *The Ecological Approach to Visual Perception* (Boston: Houghton Mifflin, 1979). Among philosophers, Fodor is one of the most determined of those who would oppose "meaning holism" (a fortiori, the holism of models of rationality) and, as a result, the conceptual (necessary) linkage between attributions of intentionality (and information) and such holist models. See Jerry A. Fodor, *A Theory of Content and Other Essays* (Cambridge, MA: MIT Press, 1990).

31. The methodological complications of the theorem, or of the general admission of the reality of the cultural world, are amusingly and interestingly explored in Richard Dawkins, *The Selfish Gene* (Oxford: Oxford University Press, 1976). Dawkins seems to have become increasingly impressed with the promise of his model, although, of course, the constraints he favors (that is, cultural analogies with the gene) are uncertain (that is, imposed without any independent analysis of the relevant cultural complexities: those of Intentionality). See also Dawkins, *The Extended Phenotype: The Long Reach of the Gene* (Oxford: Oxford University Press, 1982).

32. One can, without difficulty, see that Popper and Danto converge, however remotely and with whatever difference in results, on the guidance of the unity-of-science program, at least as far as history is concerned. See Popper, *The Poverty of Historicism*; and Danto, *Narrative and Knowledge*.

33. It is not surprising that both Danto and Popper treat time univocally in the context of history and science. It is more surprising that Ricœur does so as well, which actually generates insoluble paradoxes for his well-known account of history.

Ricœur cannot decide whether the narrative structure of history is real or merely rhetorical. Curiously, he seems to say that it is both! See Paul Ricœur, *Time and Narrative*, vol. 3, trans. Kathleen Blamey and David Pellauer (Chicago: University of Chicago Press, 1988); and Ricœur, *The Rule of Metaphor: Multi-Disciplinary Studies in the Creation of Meaning in Language*, trans. Robert Czerny, with Kathleen McLaughlin and John Costello (Toronto: University of Toronto Press, 1981).

34. I take it as symptomatic that neither Davidson's naturalism nor Rorty's postmodernism comes to terms with the antinomies. I cannot see how the antinomies can be responsibly dismissed. See, for instance, Donald Davidson, "A Coherence Theory of Truth and Knowledge," and Richard Rorty, "Pragmatism, Davidson and Truth," both in Ernest LePore, ed., *Truth and Interpretation: Perspectives on the Philosophy of Donald Davidson* (Oxford: Blackwell, 1986).

35. I am unaware of any sustained theory along these lines within analytic philosophy except my own. I have explored it in a number of places, usually linking the discussion of incarnate attributes with that of embodied entities (the latter topic to appear in the next chapter). For earlier discussions, see, for instance, Margolis, *Culture and Cultural Entities* (Dordrecht, Netherlands: D. Reidel, 1984); and Margolis, *Texts without Referents: Reconciling Science and Narrative* (Oxford: Basil Blackwell, 1989).

36. What is conceptually unique about the culturally emergent is, of course, that it is only at that level that epistemically competent reflection is at all possible; a fortiori, it is only at that level, conceding symbiosis, that the structure of physical nature itself can be discerned and specified as obtaining at a lower (or prior) level—from which the cultural is itself emergent. That was the point of the antinomy of ontic priority. But to admit cultural emergence as sui generis (since it is not reducible or explicable, causally, in terms of the generative powers of any known lower-level phenomena) is to admit a tacit, endogenous limitation in our explanatory powers. The admission of the culturally emergent is, therefore, tantamount to the defeat of the unity-of-science program.

Interestingly, the matter never really surfaced in this form for the strong advocates of the program. They were fearful that the mental might be emergent in the sense that it could not be explained in terms of the nonmental. I take that to have been weakly prescient about the larger issue: the sense in which the mind/body problem turns out to be a special case of the culture/nature problem. It is certainly clear that the problem of emergence was central to the work of the unity program. See, for instance, Herbert Feigl, *The "Mental" and the "Physical": The Essay and a Postscript* (Minneapolis: University of Minnesota Press, 1967); and Paul E. Meehl and Wilfrid Sellars, "The Concept of Emergence," in *Minnesota Studies in the Philosophy of Science*, ed. Herbert Feigl and Michael Scriven, vol. 1 (Minneapolis: University of Minnesota Press, 1956), 239–52. (The volume is mentioned above for another reason.)

37. I have already cited Mario Bunge's views, above.

38. Paul Churchland is among the most energetic recent champions of the thesis (eliminationism) that the folk-theoretic claim may be straightforwardly shown to be empirically false. I have not been able to find his argument (to that effect) anywhere, but I also have not found that he addresses the issues I have been collecting here. Frankly, I take that to be a sign of a certain failure to engage the relevant objections (which Churchland shares with a large company of like-minded theorists). See Churchland, *Neurocomputational Perspective* and *Scientific Realism and the Plasticity of Mind* (Cambridge: Cambridge University Press, 1979). See, also, Patricia S. Churchland, *Neurophilosophy: Toward a Unified Understanding of the Mind-Brain* (Cambridge, MA: MIT Press, 1986).

Notes to Chapter Six

1. This is a remarkably strenuous issue, largely neglected by analytic philosophers (and others as well). I have already suggested that Chomsky gives the matter very scant attention, intruding in effect a sense of "knowledge" of the deep structure of language (that we are unaware of) as an extension or analogue of the "ordinary" sense of *know*—which he does not bother to analyze. This, the most interesting part of his theory, philosophically, is nowhere explicitly defended, except to say that there is really no other alternative. Piaget, however, offers the sketch of an alternative that is not unreasonable in its general outlines, except that it is an eccentrically structuralist alternative. There is a very revealing exchange between Chomsky and Piaget, in a volume devoted to a debate between them, that exposes the arbitrariness of each. See Massimo Piattelli-Palmarini, ed., *Language and Learning: The Debate between Jean Piaget and Noam Chomsky* (Cambridge, MA: Harvard University Press, 1980), particularly the opening papers by Piaget and Chomsky. On Piaget's view, see, also, Jean Piaget, *Structuralism*, trans. and ed. Chaninah Maschler (New York: Basic Books, 1970), which confirms that Piaget mysteriously supposed that the sequence of the developmental phases of our cognitional powers is somehow triggered by the external environment; Piaget, however, does not explain why the developmental sequence is invariant (Chomsky catches him out in this). See, also, C. H. Waddington, *The Strategy of the Genes: A Discussion of Some Aspects of Theoretical Biology* (New York: Macmillan, 1920); and Waddington, *Evolution of an Evolutionist* (Ithaca, NY: Cornell University Press, 1975). On his side, Piaget effectively challenges Chomsky's assumption that there is a determinate disjunction between what is innate and what is acquired. Vygotsky criticizes the early Piaget in a telling way for the implicit solipsism of his account. See L. S. Vygotsky, *Thought and Language*, ed. and trans. Eugenia Hanfman and Gertrude Vakar (Cambridge, MA: MIT Press, 1962), chap. 2. In a rather subtle way, Jerome Bruner draws attention to the likelihood of prelinguistic socialized invariants on which first-language learning depends—which, if

granted, could easily admit forms of grammatical regularity short of the invariances of a universal grammar (a hardwired, species-specific grammar, the full meaning of which is hardly clear)—given that there is no obvious way to account for informational invariances of the sort in question. For a glimpse of Chomsky's view, see Noam Chomsky, *Rules and Representations* (New York: Columbia University Press, 1980). On Bruner, see Jerome Bruner, *Acts of Meaning* (Cambridge, MA: Harvard University Press, 1990), chap. 3.

2. An excellent recent specimen is provided in John R. Searle, *The Rediscovery of the Mind* (Cambridge, MA: MIT Press, 1992). It obviously admits social phenomena in its account but effectively construes social significance in terms of some prior psychological endowment, which is itself identified with the brain's mode of functioning. This is precisely what I call *solipsistic*. There is no convincing way to generate the social or collective (for instance, in terms of language) from solipsistic mental resources. Searle promises a new book on the "social character of the mind," but he does not acknowledge the anthropomorphized nature of his present speculations about consciousness. So he holds that the mental is a feature of the brain. At best, the present argument is premature. I should add that Husserl is, in my opinion, guilty of a similar mistake, although it is frankly never quite clear just how Husserl distinguishes between the psychological and the subjective. He clearly means to absorb the social in the (subjective) work of transcendental phenomenology. But it is doubtful that he succeeds; if he had succeeded, he would not be able to disjoin the psychological and the subjective, and then the search for the apodictic would have been compromised. See Edmund Husserl, *Cartesian Meditations*, especially the fifth meditation. The generic version of this trick appears already in Kant's first *Critique*.

3. Fodor's indebtedness to Chomsky's conception is apparent in Jerry A. Fodor, *The Language of Thought* (New York: Thomas Y. Crowell, 1975). See also Fodor, "On the Impossibility of Acquiring 'More Powerful' Structures," in *Language and Learning*, Piartelli-Palmarini, which confirms that the thread runs through all of Fodor's work. In effect, both Chomsky and Fodor are Platonists who have interpreted *recollection* as genetic invariance with respect to knowing.

4. I mean, by *equilibration*, a theorizing strategy, not an epistemic source. For its more-or-less-standard use, see Nelson Goodman, "The New Riddle of Induction," in *Fact, Fiction, and Forecast*, 2nd ed. (Indianapolis, IN: Bobbs-Merrill, 1965); and John Rawls, *A Theory of Justice* (Cambridge, MA: Harvard University Press, 1971).

5. The reference is to Thomas Nagel's well-known paper, "What Is It Like to Be a Bat?" in *Mortal Questions* (Cambridge: Cambridge University Press, 1979). Nagel has made a complete about-face on the analysis of mind, but his query does not improve our sense of the question. The reason, plainly, is that *only humans can know what it is like to be a bat!* Humans may make empirical mistakes about the matter, as perhaps they do in wondering whether lobsters feel pain on being boiled alive. But only humans can correct their conjectures, by interpolating within a range

of cases that are reasonably clear-cut. But if this holds for Nagel's conjecture, it holds as well for Chomsky's and Fodor's. The truth is, *their* conjectures presuppose (but nowhere establish) something like Hjelmslev's doctrine: that is, that for the *process* of natural-language discourse to succeed, there must be a closed generative *system* adequate to it. They do not show the modal necessity for such a supposition. Nor do they notice the anthropomorphic nature of their own speculation. See Louis Hjelmslev, *Prolegomena to a Theory of Language*, rev. ed., trans. Francis J. Whitfield (Madison: University of Wisconsin Press, 1961). Searle is at his most effective, in *The Rediscovery of the Mind*, in combatting Chomsky.

6. The essential pivot of Gadamer's hermeneutics is directed against the so-called Romantic hermeneuts, who claimed that the objective rule for determining the meaning of a linguistic (or literary) utterance was the speaker's (or author's) intention (in the intuitive psychological sense). Gadamer's thesis is simply that speakers' intentions can be reclaimed only in a constructivist sense—from the vantage of our present reflexive practice—and hence, that this recovery is subject to two conditions: one, that authorial intent is a function of what, from our present vantage, we determine to be the intentional ethos or tradition within which relevant utterances are uttered; the other, that the meaning or significance of what is uttered is tacitly affected by our horizonal interests and sense of significance. The first condition implicates the historicity of discerning authorial intent; the second implicates the historicity of discerning the significance of whatever is designated in accord with the first. Together, they mark the joint play of what Gadamer calls *Horizontverschmelzung* (the fusion of horizons) and *wirkungsgeschlichtliches Bewusstsein* (effective-historical consciousness). Together, they deny the possibility of closure and uniquely correct interpretations under the terms of the hermeneutic circle. See Gadamer, *Truth and Method*, trans. Garrett Barden and John Cumming (New York: Seabury Press, 1975). Gadamer's entire theory may be fairly construed as post-Heideggerian, meaning both that Gadamer was specifically influenced by the theory of time and history offered in Heidegger's *Being and Time* and that, as a consequence, Gadamer avoids metaphysical fixities (notably in the human sphere). The upshot is that Gadamer's theory, like Heidegger's, emphasizes questions of "authentic" existence rather than of methodological objectivity. This, however, leaves the question of objectivity unresolved but still relevant. Moreover, Gadamer's own themes require an answer that he nowhere supplies. See Hans-Georg Gadamer, "Interview: Historicism and Romanticism," in *Hans-Georg Gadamer on Education, Poetry, and History: Applied Hermeneutics*, ed. Dieter Misgeld and Graeme Nicholson, trans. Lawrence Schmidt and Monica Reuss (Albany: State University of New York Press, 1992), 125–32.

7. Rightly seen, the theorem is the essential pivot for the defeat of the entire classical tradition of epistemology, from Descartes and Locke, through Hume and Kant, up to Husserl—a fortiori, to all the naturalizing of the twentieth century. For (10.9) signifies that any and all accounts of the solipsistic or species-wide resources of cognizing agents are projected from within the terms of our *lebens-*

formlich competence. Applied to Quine, for instance, it raises a question (which Quine never addresses) of *why* "analytical hypotheses" are not called into play in *every* cognitive claim, why there is an *interval* reserved for certain "stimulus-meaning" or "holophrastic" utterances that are *not* subject to the influence of "analytical hypotheses." See Willard Van Orman Quine, *Word and Object* (Cambridge, MA: MIT Press, 1960); and Quine, *Pursuit of Truth*, rev. ed. (Cambridge, MA: Harvard University Press, 1992). This may be all the reassurance Donald Davidson needed for his claims in "A Coherence Theory of Truth and Knowledge," in *Truth and Interpretation: Perspectives on the Philosophy of Donald Davidson*, ed. Ernest LePore (Oxford: Blackwell, 1986). There is a loose analogy here between Davidson's use of Quine and his use, elsewhere, of Tarski.

8. I cannot find any clear version of the theory of Forms in Plato's dialogues, and I cannot find clear evidence that Plato is committed to the theory of Forms. There's no question that he broaches the matter and appeals to myths involving the Forms. But I also cannot find any evidence that he repudiates the doctrine or that Aristotle is mistaken in claiming that his own doctrine is closer to that of Socrates than is Plato's. See, for instance, Aristotle, *Metaphysics*. Aristotle says that Socrates "did not make the universals exist apart." By a similarly motivated reflection, I cannot see that Wittgenstein actually formulates his notion of the *Lebensform* sufficiently explicitly to answer relevant epistemic questions, although the clues he offers are more robust than Plato's with regard to the Forms. It would not take much to interpret Plato along lines not altogether distant from Wittgenstein's—if one cared. The conservative bent of Wittgenstein's thought is captured in J. C. Nyíri, *Tradition and Individuality: Essays* (Dordrecht, Netherlands: Kluwer, 1992).

9. The theorem draws attention, among other things, to two features of collective entities: one, that the (Intentional) predicables attributed to persons, artworks, and the like are, intrinsically, subject to changes due to historicity; another, that their "natures" are, accordingly, no more determinate than Intentional attributes can be. Notions like period style, for instance, are inherently informal. This bears on the fortunes of the various forms of hermeneutics. For an instant sense of the difference between the semiotic and Romantic views of style or genre, see Nelson Goodman, "The Status of Style," in *Ways of World-making* (Indianapolis, IN: Hackett, 1978); and E. D. Hirsch Jr., *Validity in Interpretation* (New Haven, CT: Yale University Press, 1967). Hirsch, in appendix 2, explicitly condemns Gadamer's "Heideggerian" innovation. For Gadamer's use of "prejudice," see Gadamer, *Truth and Method*. To grasp the sense of (10.14) is to realize (a) that the nature of any particular possessing collective, Intentional properties may be affected by pertinent changes in other particulars sharing similar properties (the tragic cast of Sophocles' *Antigone* may be affected by the later history of Shakespeare's *Hamlet*) and (b) that the cognitive competence of individual members of the same society to understand one another is a function of their sharing a common Lebensform, in a sense that parallels the mutual interpretability of artworks possessing any of a range of associated genres or

styles within a common cultural tradition. I have explored these connections further in my *Interpretation Radical but Not Unruly* (Berkeley: University of California Press, 1995). I should add, of course, that I certainly do not regard Goodman as a Romantic hermeneut; only that, like the Romantics, Goodman lacks a sense of historicity. (Goodman's theory is a kind of ahistorical semiotics.)

10. See Iris Murdoch, *Metaphysics as a Guide to Morals* (London: Chatto and Windus, 1992), chap. 4. See also Alexander Nehamas, *Nietzsche, Life as Literature* (Cambridge, MA: Harvard University Press, 1985).

11. I take the acquisition of a first language to be an empirical mystery. I cannot see how it can be analogized, as Chomsky does, to the acquisition of a second language. That is simply Platonism. The idea plays a large part in Chomsky's debate with Nelson Goodman and Hilary Putnam, for instance, who are noticeably flat-footed in response to Chomsky. But the image is the wrong one, for, in Chomsky's own view, "universal grammar" (which is said to be innate) cannot function apart from the acquisition of a first language in the usual intuitive sense. Chomsky nowhere discusses that, and the supposed possession of a universal grammar is nowhere convincingly shown to function criterially with respect to the acquisition of a "natural" language. The Wittgensteinian *Lebensform*, on the other hand, bears only on the fait accompli, not on the process of the acquisition. See the symposium on Chomsky's "innateness hypothesis" in *Synthese* 17 (1967), to which Noam Chomsky, Nelson Goodman, and Hilary Putnam contributed.

12. For Bourdieu's use of the term, see Pierre Bourdieu, *Outline of a Theory of Practice*, trans. Richard Nice (Cambridge: Cambridge University Press, 1977); Bourdieu, *The Logic of Practice*, trans. Richard Nice (Stanford, CA: Stanford University Press, 1980); and Bourdieu, *In Other Words: Essays Towards a Reflexive Sociology* (Stanford, CA: Stanford University Press, 1990).

13. I find Marx unwaveringly clear—implicitly—about this theorem. It is the key both to the joke about Robinsonades and to the criticism of Pierre-Joseph Proudhon. See Karl Marx, introduction to *Grundrisse: Foundations of the Critique of Political Economy*, trans. Martin Nicolas (New York: Random House, 1973). Marx's emphasis is invariably on the historicized nature of collectively enabled cognitive powers—what Marx clearly means by *"praxis."* The term is Aristotle's, originally; also, Marx does not discuss the notion in a sustained and systematic way. For what seems to me to be the most convincing elaboration of what Marx may have had in mind, see Karel Kosík, *Dialectics of the Concrete: A Study on Problems of Man and World*, trans. Karel Kovanda and James Schmidt (Dordrecht, Netherlands: D. Reidel, 1976). Here you have the clue regarding my deformation of Wittgenstein's *Lebensform* and Gadamer's horizonal sense of "tradition." For, of course, neither Wittgenstein nor Gadamer has anything to say about the dynamics of social history.

14. On the very different behaviorisms of Skinner and Pavlov, see B. F. Skinner, *Science and Human Behavior* (New York: Macmillan, 1953); Skinner, *About Behaviorism* (New York: Knopf, 1974); I. P. Pavlov, *Conditioned Reflexes*, trans. G.

V. Anrep (London: Humphrey Milford, 1927); and Pavlov, *Lectures on Conditioned Reflexes*, trans. W. H. Grant (New York: International Publishers, 1928). Of course, Pavlov is neither a reductionist nor an eliminativist regarding human minds or selves.

15. I draw attention, here, to two important themes: first, epistemology is inseparable from the metaphysics of persons; second, epistemology is inseparable from moral philosophy. Both issues are ignored in analytic philosophy. Within the terms of symbiosis, theorem (10.29) strengthens the artifactual standing of both truth claims in general and claims of moral objectivity in particular. This is the consequence of conceding that knowing is inseparable from what we are able to do as agents. I take this to be the most instructive consequence of endorsing something like Marx's notion of *praxis*. The issue is taken up in "Values, Norms, and Agents" chapter in Margolis, *Historied Thought, Constructed World*. I may perhaps say that Rorty's pretense to restore historicity to philosophy is nowhere more transparent than in his advocacy of Davidson's ahistorical epistemology and in his disjunction between the private and public spheres of interest among human agents. These moves are simply incoherent on the acceptance of anything like (10.29). See Richard Rorty, "Pragmatism, Davidson and Truth," and *Contingency, Irony and Solidarity*.

16. For a sense of various standard ways of distinguishing between the two, see Chisholm, *Theory of Knowledge*, 3rd ed. (Englewood Cliffs, NJ: Prentice-Hall, 1989); and Fred I. Dretske, *Seeing and Knowing* (Chicago: University of Chicago Press, 1969). I offer these as specimen views only. Chisholm's favors a foundationalism I cannot endorse, and Dretske's, an externalism I cannot endorse.

17. Hume, who is a very likeable and ingenious philosopher, is almost never taken to task by his analytic admirers for the hopeless muddle that lies at the very heart of his theory. He offers his "official" account in terms of sensory "impressions" and "ideas," but, in doing so, he appeals to our sensibilities in discerning *these*. Now, Hume nowhere develops the issue of how to understand the continuous perceptual and cognitive competence of selves in virtue of which (alone) his entire argument makes sense. One might suppose Hume had missed the question in some way or other. But I know of no empiricist who has seriously considered the bearing of Hume's doctrine on the existence and nature of selves! (If anything, they typically—and wrongly—take Hume to deny that there are selves.) By parity of reasoning, I find most analytic accounts of perception and cognition (however they depart from empiricism) to neglect in general (unless they are out-and-out Kantians) a theory of selves as cognizing agents apt for the perceptions attributed to them. In this sense, Hume's influence among analytic philosophers is clinically instructive. See Hume, *A Treatise of Human Nature*, ed. David Norton and Mary Norton (Oxford: Oxford University Press, 2000).

18. Causal accounts of perception and knowledge are very popular among analytic philosophers. Nevertheless, I know of no explicit, sustained, and convincing account that comes to terms with the ineliminable propositional element of cognitive states. Two points need to be stressed: the first, to the effect that the admission of

the propositional ingredient inevitably leads to the ineliminability of legitimate matters; the second, to the effect that naturalizing epistemology leads to a causal theory of perceptual (and similar sorts of) belief. The second seems to free matters for a causal theory, but it does not really do so. For we have no satisfactory account of the causal conditions of intentional states—certainly none that could be said to behave in nomologically regular ways. Clearly, a causal theory of belief is bound to implicate a model of rationality (along lines already sketched, to which I shall return in a moment). Also, the judgment that *suitably caused beliefs constitute knowledge* remains a nagging question that the causal theory cannot itself resolve. See, for specimens, H. P. Grice, "The Causal Theory of Perception," in *Studies in the Way of Words* (Cambridge, MA: Harvard University Press, 1989); and Alan White, with H. P. Grice, in "Symposium: The Causal Theory of Perception," *Proceedings of the Aristotelian Society*, suppl. vol. 4 (1961). On the most recent version of the naturalist's causal account of knowledge, see Alvin I. Goldman, "A Causal Theory of Knowing," in *Liaisons: Philosophy Meets the Cognitive Social Sciences* (Cambridge, MA: MIT Press, 1991); and Goldman, *Epistemology and Cognition* (Cambridge, MA: Harvard University Press, 1986), chap. 3.

19. I take Wittgenstein's account of pain avowal to betray the fact that he, too, is an externalist. This suggests that he does not construe his Lebensform in the way I have deliberately exploited. For, if he had, he would have construed persons and their perceptions as artifacts of our Lebensform, and then he would have had to be hospitable to the idea that avowals of pain *could* function reportorially (in their distinctive way) every bit as much as constative utterances about sensory perception. See Wittgenstein, *Philosophical Investigations*. For an appreciation of Wittgenstein's account, see George Pitcher, *The Philosophy of Wittgenstein* (Princeton, NJ: Princeton University Press, 1964), chap. 12.

20. On Brentano's view, see Franz Brentano, *Psychology from an Empirical Standpoint* (London: Routledge, 1995), bk. 2.

21. Freud treats the unconscious as a theoretical posit invoked in explanatory contexts. It plays no reportorial role in first-person contexts. See Sigmund Freud, "The Unconscious," in *Collected Papers*, vol. 4, trans. under supervision of Joan Riviere (New York: Basic Books, 1959). It helps, therefore, in clarifying the fact that belief often plays an explanatory role in ordinary contexts, where it is unconscious in a familiar sense. Chomsky's version of the unconscious (innate, species-specific) does no explanatory work that I can see. It has no variable or variably structured function in different linguistic contexts. It amounts to no more than a pronouncement en bloc that whatever we rightly claim are the invariant and exceptionless grammatical structures of natural language are innately present in the biological resources of humans. It does not explain how these structures work, and it does not confirm that there are any such structures. See Chomsky, *Rules and Representations* and *Knowledge of Language*.

22. Here I generalize in a way linked to Locke's theory, except that Locke (who is of course profoundly pre-Kantian) does not realize that construing persons *forensically* alerts us to the possibility that *both* persons and their perceptions may be artifacts of a deeper process. Locke treats persons as independent existents—but forensically, whereas I treat them as artifactual existents—*hence* forensically. This suggests why Locke has no difficulty reconciling his Cartesian view of natural rights with his empiricism. It also explains why, although Hume is cleverer, Locke is more solid and more plausible. That Hume is on his way to some sort of constructivism is clear, but Kant's example shows that it needn't have led to the doctrine of symbiosis or to that of historicity. So the novelty of (10.40) becomes clearer. See Locke, *An Essay concerning Human Understanding*, ed. Peter H. Nidditch (Oxford: Clarendon Press, 1975); and also Locke, *Two Treatises of Government*, ed. Peter Laslett (Cambridge: Cambridge University Press, 1960).

23. Hilary Putnam, "The Meaning of 'Meaning,'" in *Mind, Language and Reality*, vol. 2 of *Philosophical Papers* (Cambridge: Cambridge University Press, 1975), 227. I take Putnam to have had a strong disposition favoring the collective, *lebensformlich*, constructivist theory of persons the post-Kantian tradition has championed, without quite grasping the full import of that line of reasoning. Putnam's "Meaning of 'Meaning'" helps to explain the collapse of Putnam's epistemology and metaphysics in *The Many Faces of Realism* (Chicago: Open Court, 1987) while not yet abandoning the vestiges of a Kantian externalism. Kant, of course, advances a very improbable conjunction of internalist and externalist cognitional factors.

24. A very reasonable account of the need to posit theoretical entities is offered in Ian Hacking, *Representing and Intervening: Introductory Topics in the Philosophy of Science* (Cambridge: Cambridge University Press, 1983). For an account along different lines, see Nancy Cartwright, *How the Laws of Physics Lie* (Oxford: Clarendon Press, 1983). Van Fraassen, who is more of a purist in the way of positivism than Cartwright, tries to interpret the laws of nature in empiricist terms, except that, in his appealing but self-defeating candor, van Fraassen admits that there is no principled demarcation between theoretical and perceptual distinctions. See Bas C. van Fraassen, *The Scientific Image* (Oxford: Clarendon, 1980).

25. I am not certain how, precisely, the notion of the *folk-theoretic* became a term in the eliminationist idiom. I feel sure that it has its immediate sources in Wilfrid Sellars, "The Language of Theories" and "Philosophy and the Scientific Image of Man," in *Science, Truth and Reality* (London: Routledge / Kegan Paul, 1963); and in papers such as Feyerabend, "Materialism and the Mind-Body Problem," *Review of Metaphysics* 17 (1963): 49–66. But it appeared in what seemed an instantly established usage in Stephen P. Stich, *From Folk Psychology to Cognitive Science: The Case against Belief* (Cambridge, MA: MIT Press, 1983); and it is associated in my mind with the views of such figures and works as Paul M. Churchland, *A Neurocomputational Perspective: The Nature of Mind and the Structure of Science* (Cambridge, MA: MIT

Press, 1989); and Daniel C. Dennett, *Brainstorms: Philosophical Essays on Mind and Psychology* (Cambridge, MA: MIT Press, 1978). But to be able to affirm (10.45) on the strength of the foregoing argument is to expose the rather surprising laxness of the entire company of eliminativists, who fail to a man to explain precisely how they mean to dispose of the subject or self or cognizing agent. Feyerabend suggests that we should wait as long as the "folk" tradition has held sway; Churchland says that anything like (10.45) is simply "empirically" false; Stich says what he would replace the *folk* idiom with but admits he cannot see how to do so quite yet.

26. The double lesson of the theorem is that objectivity is an artifact of *lebensformlich* practices and, as such, belongs to the realism of the cultural, but only (or initially) in a holist way. I construe holism here in a sense akin to that of Wittgenstein's appeal to the *Lebensform* (or, a "language game" within the terms of a *Lebensform*)—that is, acts and utterances in which we are entitled to claim a sense of congruity with our enabling practices but not yet with rules or criteria in virtue of which our claims may be judged to be right or valid. We simply know how to go on within our form of life, and whatever we assign as the criteria of correctness will, similarly, conform with those encompassing practices. See Ludwig Wittgenstein, *Remarks on the Foundations of Mathematics*, trans. G. E. M. Anscombe (Oxford: Basil Blackwell, 1956); and Wittgenstein, *On Certainty*, ed. G. E. M. Anscombe and G. H. von Wright, trans. Denis Paul and G. E. M. Anscombe (Oxford: Basil Blackwell, 1969). The important point to bear in mind is that Quine's holism, in *Word and Object* and *Pursuit of Truth*, is altogether different—a heterodox and doubtful interpretation of Duhem's more interesting holism. Quine's, I'm afraid, is incoherent: it tries to combine the "indeterminacy of translation" doctrine (which looks at first glance like a generalization of Duhem's theory) with some sort of minimal empiricism (which is supposed to be metaphysically neutral, as in the way of "holophrastic sentences"). But Duhem's emphasis is applied only to the empirical testing of theories, without our being able to say precisely which propositions within those theories are being tested (and why that is so); whereas Quine's maneuver is meant to subvert the pretensions of something like a "folk" science and metaphysics. See Pierre Duhem, *The Aim and Structure of Physical Theory*, trans. Philip P. Wiener (Princeton, NJ: Princeton University Press, 1991).

27. The hermeneutic circle is the central theme of so-called hermeneutic philosophies. Originally, it was applied to the interpretation of texts for which canons might be claimed: sacred, legal, and, more recently, literary. In that form, in the tradition from Schleiermacher to, say, E. D. Hirsch, it simply signifies the part/whole relation of interpretable texts: the meaning of any part depends on the meaning of the whole, and the meaning of the whole depends on the meaning of its parts. In post-Heideggerian hermeneutics—Gadamer's, preeminently—societal life itself conforms with the terms of the hermeneutic circle. In that sense, the "circle" signifies the consensual nature of interpretation, the absence of ahistorical canons, the historicized and open-ended nature of interpretation itself. I simply

co-opt the term in that sense, in a way that, contrary to Gadamer's usage, permits us to reconsider what objectivity may mean within the human sciences and human studies. My own argument emphasizes, of course, that the objectivity accorded the natural sciences is also affected. (I shall come to this in a moment.) For a sense of the Romantic view, see Hirsch, *Validity in Interpretation*; for the post-Heideggerian, see Gadamer, *Truth and Method*.

28. I have isolated the hermeneutic circle for particular mention. But there are a great many different influential views of the relationship of interpreting agents and interpretable materials that trade on the same part/whole relationship. I see the same theme in Marx's notion of *praxis* and in Roland Barthes's semiotized (poststructuralist) literary criticism; also, of course, in Foucault's archaeologies. See Roland Barthes, *S/Z: An Essay*, trans. Richard Miller (New York: Hill and Wang, 1974); see also Michel Foucault, *The Order of Things: An Archaeology of the Human Sciences* (New York: Random House, 1970).

29. Ernest Jones's *Hamlet and Oepidus* (New York: Norton, 1949) is a well-known example, literal minded though it is. A more interesting case is offered by George Thompson, *Aeschylus and Athens* (London: Lawrence and Wishart, 1941), which shows us how to construe the *Oresteia* in Marxist terms. I view these examples both metaphysically and epistemologically. The idea that these plays are simply being cleverly interpreted misses the essential challenge. My thesis is that the cultural world *is* permeable, porous, and (as I shall say in a moment) labile—metaphysically—because of its Intentional properties, and that objectivity in the human sciences is affected—consensually—because, in the human world, perceiver and perceived may be one and the same ([[10.51]–[10.56]). I hold that persons and artworks are very similar, ontologically, with regard to the fixity of their natures.

30. I find it difficult to account for Dennett's blunder. See Dennett, *Content and Consciousness*. Dennett does not correct his mistake in *The Intentional Stance*. At bottom, Dennett is an eliminationist, but he is also put off by the crudity and haste of the usual eliminationists. Hence, he keeps lengthening the postponement of the "inevitable" eliminativist coup. But he never supplies the decisive argument.

31. For a remarkable disconfirmation of Freud's speculations about Leonardo da Vinci, see Meyer Schapiro, "Leonardo and Freud: An Art-Historical Study," *Journal of the History of Ideas* 17 (1956). See Sigmund Freud, "Leonardo da Vinci and a Memory of His Childhood," in *The Standard Edition of the Complete Psychological Works of Sigmund Freud*, trans. under the general editorship of James Strachey, vol. 11 (London: Hogarth Press / Institute of Psycho-analysis, 1957). Shapiro's superb command of the art-historical materials as well as what pertains to Freudian psychoanalysis shows, by example, something of the recoverability of a sense of objective claims within the human sciences. Here, I should say, somewhat against Schapiro's view of his own procedure, that where he disconfirms Freud's conjectures (about the import of treating Mary and St. Anne as being of the same age), the evidence leads to a more decisive finding than when he attempts to support his own affirmative

conjectures about the psychoanalytic import of further details (for instance, about the alleged homosexual import of treating Jesus and John the Baptist as children of about the same age). I don't mean this in a merely art-historical sense—that is, in a merely evidentiary sense. What I have in mind is that truth and falsity play asymmetrical roles in a relativistic logic (see chapter 4 of *Historied Thought, Constructed World*) and that art-historical arguments favor, in my opinion, a relativistic rather than a bivalent logic.

32. Actions and historical events are extraordinarily difficult to individuate—hence, difficult to reidentify through redescriptions. For one thing, they have Intentional identities; for another, there are no clear criteria for deciding the aptness of alternative descriptions for particular actions and particular historical events. Donald Davidson has offered a remarkably confident thesis, congruent with a moderate physicalism and sympathetic with supervenience, for identifying actions in terms of minimal physical movements ("primitive actions"). But this supposes that there is a legible relationship between actions and movements favoring the rule "one movement, one action" (rather like Williams's policy of "one body, one person"). If, however, cultural emergence is, as I have argued, a sui generis form of emergence, the thesis is at the very least question begging. See Donald Davidson, "Actions, Reasons and Causes" and "Agency," in *Essays on Actions and Events* (Oxford: Clarendon, 1980). Alvin I. Goldman has, in *A Theory of Action* (Englewood Cliffs, NJ: Prentice-Hall, 1970), constructed an alternative theory, rather on the extravagant side, one that threatens paradox here and there, that nevertheless allows for indefinitely many different actions to be conceptually linked to a single bodily movement. My own view is that neither of these accounts can be said to have isolated anything that is modally necessary. Neither is particularly plausible. And neither conforms very closely to the actual practice of natural-language discourse. The important point is that any policy falling between Davidson's and Goldman's options will upset the effectiveness of an extensional treatment of actions—a fortiori, an extensional treatment of historical events.

33. The cultural world, I am arguing, depends essentially on the role of individual persons as competent agents. I have shown how entities other than culturally apt human persons may be construed as agents. The most interesting extension involves collective agents: societies, classes, families, clans, peoples, and the like. The *Annales* school has, in its effort to make history a science, been attracted to the possibility that individual human agents may be marginalized or eliminated. But this is to misunderstand (in a way not altogether distant from the structuralist temptation) the conceptual relationship between individual agents and the collective features of the culture human aggregates share. See Fernand Braudel, *On History*, trans. Sarah Matthews (Chicago: University of Chicago Press, 1980). War, for instance, can only (in the usual theories) be fought by collective agents, but, in the argument, there are no collective agents; they are fictions (10.72). Hence, wars implicate ideologies

(or imaginaries) by which aggregates of individuals believe they are serving the interests of a collective agent.

34. I believe I have invented a unique relational notion, suited exclusively for cultural phenomena but comparable in an interesting way with the member/class and instance/kind relationships. I take it that classes, kinds, and types do not exist but may mark real attributes. The notion of tokens and types originates with Peirce, I believe. Peirce's account treats types as universals of some sort. I construe the relation as one between individuals—one that is heuristically introduced. See Joseph Margolis, *Art and Philosophy* (Atlantic Highlands, NJ: Humanities Press, 1980). The principal alternative interpretations appear in Richard Wollheim, *Art and Its Objects*; and Nicholas Wolterstorff, *Works and Worlds of Art*. Both of these views admit real universals.

35. See John Searle, *Minds, Brains and Science* (Cambridge: Cambridge University Press, 1984).

Notes to Chapter Seven

1. See, for instance, Pierre Bourdieu, *Pascalian Meditations*, trans. Richard Nice (Stanford, CA: Stanford University Press, 1997), 142–46. For my own part, I much prefer the less mysterious, less abstract kinematics of the account of cultural practices in Michael Oakeshott, *On Human Conduct* (Oxford: Clarendon, 1975), chap. 1.

2. See Ludwig Wittgenstein, *Philosophical Investigations*, trans. G. E. M. Anscombe (Oxford: Basil Blackwell, 1953); and Wittgenstein, *On Certainty*, ed. G. E. M. Anscombe and G. H. von Wright, trans. Denis Paul and G. E. M. Anscombe (Oxford: Basil Blackwell, 1969), for instance §§110, pp. 204–05.

3. Jacques Derrida, *Of Grammatology*, trans. Gayatri Chakravorty Spivak (Baltimore: Johns Hopkins University Press, 1974), 158–59. See also Geoffrey Bennington, *Derrida* (Chicago: University of Chicago Press, 1993), s.v. "context."

4. Contrast this with Aristotle, *Metaphysics* 4, in *The Complete Works of Aristotle*, vol. 2, ed. Jonathan Barnes (Princeton, NJ: Princeton University Press, 1984).

5. See, for instance, Paul M. Churchland, *A Neurocomputational Perspective: The Nature of Mind and the Structure of Science* (Cambridge, MA: MIT Press, 1989), chap. 1.

6. See Nelson Goodman, *Languages of Art* (Indianapolis, IN: Bobbs-Merrill, 1968), 86.

7. I allude here to a number of the leading discussions of musical expressiveness collected in Jerrold Levinson, "Musical Expressiveness," in *The Pleasures of Aesthetics: Philosophical Essays* (Ithaca, NY: Cornell University Press, 1996), 90–125. This is not the occasion for dissecting these theories at close range. They

all require a clause too many. They make a mystery of expressiveness and then resolve the mystery by some jerry-built construction that ignores the plain fact that it is already coherent, conceptually viable, and philosophically reasonable to say that *music and painting are intrinsically expressive!* Levinson, I'm afraid, makes the same mistake as the others he collects—it is an important mistake—which I shall have to make do for the error of the entire raft of similarly motivated theories. (It hearkens back to my analysis of Danto's and Goodman's theories.) It begins with the first sentence of Levinson's essay: "I will endeavor to say exactly what musical expressiveness is," Levinson says, he and promptly moves on to do so. But what he offers is "an analysis of what it means to say that a passage of music P is expressive of an emotion E or other psychological state" (90). (This, of course, is a narrower and very different issue.) Put more carefully, Levinson proposes that "a passage of music P is expressive of an emotion or other psychic condition E *iff* P, in context, is readily and aptly heard by an appropriately backgrounded listener as the expression of E, in a sui generis, 'musical,' manner, by an indefinite agent, the music's persona" (107). Levinson himself remarks that this agrees with the general approach he offers in "Hope in *The Hebrides*," *Music, Art, and Metaphysics* (Ithaca, NY: Cornell University Press, 1990). But if words are intrinsically expressive—and surely they are—then why shouldn't music and painting be, as well? They are also uttered by human beings. There's the crux of the error and the essential clue to the remarkably widespread misunderstanding of the ontology of art. That is precisely what the theory of textuality corrects. (Music is expressive—period; it may also be expressive *of* particular human emotions. Levinson does indeed oppose Hanslick. But he does not quite reach up to the general expressivity of music as such; if he had, he could not have featured the question he does.)

8. See, further, Joseph Margolis, *Historied Thought, Constructed World: A Conceptual Primer for the Turn of the Millennium* (Berkeley: University of California Press, 1995).

9. I view these formulations, if I may say so, as trimmed-down versions of Vico's master theme: that humans understand history best, since they create the events of history. See Joseph Margolis, *The Flux of History and the Flux of Science* (Berkeley: University of California Press, 1993), chap. 1.

10. Compare Arthur C. Danto, "The Artworld," *Journal of Philosophy* 61, no. 19 (1964): 571–84.

11. Jorge J. E. Gracia, *A Theory of Textuality: The Logic and Epistemology* (Albany: State University of New York Press, 1995), 4. See also Gracia, *Texts: Ontological Status, Identity, Author, Audience* (Albany: State University of New York Press, 1996), which is the complement of the first. I should perhaps mention the very different account offered in Jurij Lotman, *The Structure of the Artistic Text*, trans. Gail Lenhoff and Ronald Vroon (Ann Arbor: University of Michigan Press, 1977), particularly chaps. 3–5, interesting in spite of its structuralist commitment.

12. Gracia, *Theory of Textuality*, 405. The same definition is offered in *Texts*, 3.

13. For a brief sense of *supervenience*, see Colin McGinn, *The Problem of Consciousness* (Oxford: Basil Blackwell, 1991), 179–81.

14. Nelson Goodman, *Languages of Art: An Approach to a Theory of Symbols* (Indianapolis, IN: Bobbs-Merrill, 1968), 131.

15. See Margolis, "Perceiving Artworks: Farewell to Danto and Goodman," in *Selves and Other Texts: The Case for Cultural Realism* (State Park: Pennsylvania State University Press, 2003), chap. 2; see also Diana Raffman, "Goodman, Density, and the Limits of Sense Perception," in *The Interpretation of Music: Philosophical Essays*, ed. Michael Krausz (Oxford: Clarendon, 1997), 179–92.

16. Gracia, *Theory of Textuality*, 6.

17. This is the actual point on which Susanne Langer faltered in her defense of "symbolic forms" against an entirely reasonable attack by Ernest Nagel. But it was not necessary to yield. See Susanne K. Langer, *Problems of Art* (New York: Charles Scribner's, 1957).

18. I take special note, here, of the very strong difference between the account being offered and Richard Rorty's "disappointment" in Umberto Eco's analysis of "the universe of semiosis, that is, the universe of human culture." In effect, Rorty resists distinguishing "signs and texts . . . from other objects—objects such as rocks and trees and quarks." He insinuates into his argument the (admittedly) misleading *prior* disjunction between the "semiotic" and the "scientific." (Eco is careless on this count.) But that has nothing to do with the legitimacy of distinguishing between the "science" of semiosis and the "science" of the physical sciences—read as a consequence *of* rightly distinguishing between texts and rocks and trees and the perceived requirements of objective inquiry. Rorty's attack on Eco, whom he would have liked to recruit in the service of his "postphilosophical" (or postmodernist, or pragmatist) strategies, is a last-ditch effort to support a form of reductionism "by other means." See Richard Rorty, "The Pragmatist's Progress: Umberto Eco on Interpretation," in *Philosophy and Social Hope* (Harmondsworth, UK: Penguin Books, 1999), 139; and Umberto Eco, *Semiotics and the Philosophy of Language* (Bloomington: Indiana University Press, 1984), 83–84.

19. Jonathan Culler, *Structuralist Poetics* (Ithaca, NY: Cornell University Press, 1975), 133. I find myself in general agreement here with Stanley Fish, "With the Compliments of the Author: Reflections on Austin and Derrida," in *Doing What Comes Naturally: Change, Rhetoric, and the Practice of Theory in Language and Legal Studies* (Durham, NC: Duke University Press, 1989).

20. See M. E. Abrams, "How to Do Things with Texts," in *Doing Things with Texts: Essays in Criticism and Critical Theory* (New York: W. W. Norton, 1989), 269–96; see also Peter Lamarque and Stein Haugom Olsen, *Truth, Fiction, and Literature: A Philosophical Perspective* (Oxford: Clarendon, 1994), 276–81.

21. See Ludwig Wittgenstein, *Culture and Values*, ed. G. H. von Wright and Heikki Nyman, trans. Peter Winch (Oxford: Basil Blackwell, 1980).

22. See Michael Dummett, preface to *Truth and Other Enigmas* (Cambridge, MA: Harvard University Press, 1975).

23. See, further, Margolis, *Historied Thought, Constructed World*.
24. Gracia, *Theory of Textuality*, 2.
25. Gracia, 22.
26. See Monroe C. Beardsley, *The Possibility of Criticism* (Detroit: Wayne State University Press, 1970).
27. See E. D. Hirsch Jr., *Validity in Interpretation* (New Haven, CT: Yale University Press, 1967).
28. See Jaegwon Kim, *Supervenience and Mind: Selected Philosophical Essays* (Cambridge: Cambridge University Press, 1993).
29. See Wilhelm Dilthey, *Introduction to the Human Sciences*, Selected Works, ed. Rudolf Makkreel and Frijthof Rodi, vol. 1 (Princeton, NJ: Princeton University Press, 1989).
30. See Willard Van Orman Quine, *Word and Object* (Cambridge, MA: MIT Press, 1960), §§37–38.
31. See Max Black, "The Identity of Indiscernibles," in *Problems of Analysis* (Ithaca, NY: Cornell University Press, 1954), 80–92.
32. See H. G. Alexander, ed., *The Leibniz-Clarke Correspondence* (Manchester: Manchester University Press, 1956), Leibniz's fifth paper.
33. Fodor is the most dogged American Platonist that I know of, but even he attempts to defend Platonism in noncognitivist terms. It is, I venture to suggest, the master theme of his entire oeuvre. A manifestation appears in Jerry A. Fodor, *Concepts: Where Cognitive Science Went Wrong* (Oxford: Clarendon, 1998), chaps. 6–7, with respect to both nativism and the atomism of concepts. But see also Jerrold J. Katz, *The Metaphysics of Meaning* (Cambridge, MA: MIT Press, 1990), for a related Platonism of a very different sort. I shall return briefly to the Platonist issue.
34. See, further, Joseph Margolis, "The Politics of Predication," *Philosophical Forum* 27 (1996): 195–219.
35. For a sense of the philosophical background, see Richard J. Bernstein, *Beyond Objectivism and Relativism: Semantics, Hermeneutics, and Praxis* (Philadelphia: University of Pennsylvania Press, 1983).
36. Peter Galison, *Image and Logic: A Material Culture of Microphysics* (Chicago: University of Chicago Press, 1997), 803–04.
37. See Margolis, *What, After All, Is a Work of Art? Lectures in the Philosophy of Art* (University Park: Pennsylvania State University Press, 1999), chap. 2.
38. See David Hume, *A Treatise of Human Nature*, ed. L. A. Selby-Bigge (Oxford: Clarendon, 1958), bk. 1, pt. 4, §6.
39. See Hans-Georg Gadamer, *Truth and Method*, trans. Garrett Barden and John Cumming (New York: Seabury Press, 1975).
40. A very clear recent specimen of such avoidance is afforded by Robert Stecker in "The Constructivist's Dilemma," *Journal of Aesthetics and Art Criticism* 60 (1997): 43–52.

41. See Roland Barthes, *S/Z*, trans. Richard Miller (New York: Hill and Wang, 1974).

42. See George Thomson, *Aeschylus and Athens* (London: Lawrence and Wishart, 1971).

43. See Helen Vendler, *The Art of Shakespeare's Sonnets* (Cambridge, MA: Harvard University Press, 1997).

44. Vendler, 4.

45. Vendler, 1–2.

46. Vendler, 3.

47. Vendler, 10–11. The passage from Auden is from W. H. Auden, *"The Dyer's Hand" and Other Essays* (New York: Viking, 1968).

48. Vendler, *Shakespeare's Sonnets*, 85.

49. Vendler, 85.

50. Stephen Greenblatt, *Shakespearean Negotiations* (Berkeley: University of California Press, 1988), vii.

51. Greenblatt, 12–13. I find this close in spirit to the view expressed by Michael Baxandall, *Patterns of Intention: On the Historical Explanation of Pictures* (New Haven, CT: Yale University Press, 1985), in spite of the fact that Baxandall professes a more conservative approach.

52. See Gadamer, *Truth and Method*, 269ff.

53. See, further, Margolis, *Interpretation Radical but Not Unruly: The New Puzzle of the Arts and History* (Berkeley: University of California Press, 1995); see also Anthony Giddens, *Central Problems in Social Theory: Action, Structure and Contradiction in Social Analysis* (Berkeley: University of California Press, 1979).

Notes to Chapter Eight

1. Compare, for instance, Myles Burnyeat, "Protagoras and Self-Refutation in Plato's *Theaetetus*," *Philosophical Review* 85 (1976): 172–95; and Hilary Putnam, "Materialism and Relativism," in *Renewing Philosophy* (Cambridge, MA: Harvard University Press, 1992), chap. 4.

2. I offer a fuller account of this "contest" between Kant and Hegel in Margolis, "The Point of Hegel's Dissatisfaction with Kant," in *Pragmatism Ascendent: A Yard of Narrative, a Touch of Prophecy* (Stanford, CA: Stanford University Press, 2012).See also the epilogue to Margolis, *The Arts and the Definition of the Human* (Stanford, CA: Stanford University Press, 2009).

3. See G. W. F. Hegel, *The Phenomenology of Spirit*, trans. A. V. Miller (Oxford: Clarendon, 1977). John McDowell may be the most suggestive recent English-language analytic philosopher to broach the matter. But McDowell remains, on his own declaration, a Kantian and a Platonist (a naturalized Platonist). He

introduces what appears to be the Hegelian (or Gadamerian) *Bildung*, but he makes sure that it never exceeds the Kantian formula. See McDowell, *Mind and World* (Cambridge, MA: Harvard University Press, 1976).

4. See Edmund Husserl, *Ideas: General Introduction to Pure Phenomenology*, trans. W. R. Boyce Gibson (New York: Macmillan, 1931), §32; and *Cartesian Meditations: An Introduction to Phenomenology*, trans. Dorion Cairns (The Hague, Netherlands: Martinus Nijhoff, 1960), fifth meditation.

5. On Aristotle's biological tracts, see Allan Gotthelf and James G. Lennox, eds., *Philosophical Issues in Aristotle's Biology* (Cambridge: Cambridge University Press, 1987).

6. See John H. Zammito, *Kant, Herder, and the Birth of Anthropology* (Chicago: University of Chicago Press, 2003).

7. See Hegel, *Aesthetics: Lectures on Fine Art*, trans. T. M. Knox, vol. 1 (Oxford: Clarendon, 1975), 56–61.

8. See Martha C. Nussbaum, "Flawed Crystals: James's *The Golden Bowl* and Literature as Moral Philosophy," in *Love's Knowledge: Essays on Philosophy and Literature* (New York: Oxford University Press, 1990), 125–47; and Nussbaum, "Non-relative Virtues: An Aristotelian Approach," in *The Quality of Life*, ed. Martha C. Nussbaum and Amartya Sen (Oxford: Clarendon, 1993), 242–69.

9. See Joseph Margolis, *The Unraveling of Scientism: American Philosophy at the End of the Twentieth Century* (Ithaca, NY: Cornell University Press, 2003).

10. See Gregory Vlastos, "The Socratic Elenchus: Method Is All," in *Socratic Studies*, ed. Myles Burnyeat (Cambridge: Cambridge University Press, 1994).

11. See Michael Oakeshott, *Of Human Conduct* (Oxford: Clarendon, 1995).

12. See Thomas R. Flynn, *Sartre, Foucault, and Historical Reasoning*, 2 vols. (Chicago: University of Chicago Press, 1997, 2005), particularly vol. 1, chap. 7; and Michel Foucault, "Foucault Responds to Sartre," in *Foucault Live: Collected Interviews, 1966–1984*, ed. Sylvère Lotringer, trans. John Johnston (New York: Semiotext(e), 1989), quoted in Flynn.

13. See Hegel's account of *Antigone*, in *Aesthetics*, vol. 1, pp. 220–21.

14. See Ernst Cassirer, *The Philosophy of Symbolic Forms*, trans. Ralph Manheim, 3 vols. (New Haven, CT: Yale University Press, 1953–57).

15. For a compendious account of the pertinent literature, see W. K. C. Guthrie, *The Sophists* (Cambridge: Cambridge University Press, 1971), chap. 4.

16. See Noam Chomsky, *New Horizons in the Study of Language and Mind* (Cambridge: Cambridge University Press, 2000); and Margolis, *Unraveling of Scientism*, chap. 1.

17. See Georg Henrik von Wright, *Wittgenstein* (Minneapolis: University of Minnesota Press, 1982).

18. This merely identifies the single most elusive difference between the *Tractatus* and the *Investigations*.

19. For a sense of recent speculation about Wittgenstein's notion of the *Lebensform*, see Newton Garver, *This Complicated Form of Life: Essays on Wittgen-

stein (Chicago: Open Court, 1994). There seem to be very few clues about what, precisely, Wittgenstein intended by the idea.

20. Ludwig Wittgenstein, *Philosophical Investigations*, trans. G. E. M. Anscombe, vol. 1 (Oxford: Basil Blackwell, 1953), §241.

21. Contrast the view of Paul M. Churchland, *A Neurocomputational Perspective: The Nature of Mind and the Structure of Science* (Cambridge, MA: MIT Press, 1989), chap. 1.

22. See Martin Heidegger, *Being and Time*, trans. John Macquarrie and Edward Robinson (New York: Harper and Row, 1962), §12; see also Heidegger, *Ontology: The Hermeneutics of Facticity*, trans. John van Buren (Bloomington: Indiana University Press, 1999). Heidegger and Wittgenstein seem to me to be fundamentally opposed, even though both tend to focus on the analysis of the everyday world.

23. See Frederick A. Olafson, *Naturalism and the Human Condition: Against Scientism* (London: Routledge, 2001); Hubert L. Dreyfus, *Being-in-the-World: A Commentary on Heidegger's Being and Time, Division 1* (Cambridge, MA: MIT Press, 1991).

24. Consider, for example, the strange turn (the *Kehre*) of Heidegger's "Letter on Humanism," trans. Frank A. Capuzzi, in *Pathmarks*, ed. William McNeill (Cambridge: Cambridge University Press, 1998).

25. For a general sense of the argument, see Margolis, *Historied Thought, Constructed World: A Conceptual Primer for the Turn of the Millennium* (Berkeley: University of California Press, 1995).

26. See Jacques Monod, *Chance and Necessity*, trans. Austryn Wainhouse (New York: Vantage, 1971).

27. See Richard Dawkins, *The Selfish Gene*, rev. ed. (Oxford: Oxford University Press, 1989); and Dawkins, *The Extended Phenotype: The Long Reach of the Gene*, rev. ed. (Oxford: Oxford University Press, 1999).

28. See Thomas S. Kuhn, *The Structure of Scientific Revolutions*, 2nd ed. (Chicago: University of Chicago Press, 1970), especially §10.

29. See W. V. Quine, "Epistemology Naturalized," in *Ontological Relativity and Other Essays* (New York: Columbia University Press, 1969), 69–90.

30. See Wittgenstein, *Philosophical Investigations*, vol. 1, §§241, 481; compare Wittgenstein, *On Certainty*, ed. G. E. M. Anscombe and G. H. von Wright, trans. Denis Paul and G. E. M. Anscombe (New York: Harper and Row, 1972), §110.

31. Marjorie Grene, "People and Other Animals," in *The Understanding of Nature: Essays in the Philosophy of Biology* (Dordrecht, Netherlands: D. Reidel, 1974), 358. The phrase "extensions of ourselves" catches up the best of Merleau-Ponty.

Notes to Chapter Nine

1. For a fair sample of recent theories, see Stephen Davies, *Definitions of Art* (Ithaca, NY: Cornell University Press, 1991). My impression is that there's little

point in separating the question of defining art from the substantive analysis of the arts themselves.

2. Perhaps the best-known analytic discussant of the futility of defining *work of art* is Morris Weitz. Weitz holds, arbitrarily I fear, that definitions are defenseless against the "open" nature of the arts; thus, *any* definition would necessarily be defeated. (Weitz never demonstrates why this must be so.) He maintains, accordingly, that definitions thought to be true must be essentialist in intent; hence, they are invariably false unless restricted "for a special purpose." See Morris Weitz, "The Role of Theory in Aesthetics," *Journal of Aesthetics and Art Criticism* 15 (1956): 27–35; Weitz, *The Opening Mind* (Chicago: University of Chicago Press, 1977).

3. I draw here on Davies's summary of my own definition, since that is pretty well the way it is most briefly reported (*Definitions of Art*, 162). But see also Joseph Margolis, *Art and Philosophy* (Atlantic Highlands, NJ.: Humanities Press, 1980). My views have evolved considerably since this early formulation. I find it useful still, but I have explored more fully what we should mean by *entity* and, in particular, *cultural entity*. What I offer here accords with my earlier views but is leaner.

4. See, for instance, Nicholas Wolterstorff, *Works and Worlds of Art* (Oxford: Clarendon, 1980).

5. I give a summary of the pertinent arguments in Margolis, *Historied Thought, Constructed World: A Conceptual Primer for the Turn of the Millennium* (Berkeley: University of California Press, 1995).

6. The best-known recent specimen views include Wolterstorff's *Works and Worlds of Art*; Peter Kivy, *The Fine Art of Repetition: Essays in the Philosophy of Music* (Cambridge: Cambridge University Press, 1993); and, most problematically, Richard Wollheim, *Art and Its Objects*, 2nd ed. (Cambridge: Cambridge University Press, 1980).

7. See Wolterstorff, *Works and Worlds of Art*, pt. 3.

8. See Nelson Goodman, *Languages of Art: An Approach to a Theory of Symbols* (Indianapolis, IN: Bobbs-Merrill, 1968).

9. For the supporting argument, see, further, Margolis, *Historied Thought*.

10. See Weitz, *Hamlet and the Philosophy of Literary Criticism* (Chicago: University of Chicago Press, 1964). On Aristotle and bivalence, see, further, Margolis, *The Truth about Relativism* (Oxford: Basil Blackwell, 1991).

11. This appears to be, in part, the motivation of Robert Stecker's "The Constructivist's Dilemma," *Journal of Aesthetics and Art Criticism* 55 (1997): 43–52. Stecker applies his objection in a somewhat glancing way to my own theory. I return to the issue later. (It is an important matter.) But his direct target is the theory offered in Michael Krausz, *Rightness and Reasons: Interpretation in Cultural Practices* (Ithaca, NY: Cornell University Press, 1993). Krausz's theory is related to mine. But Krausz and I do not agree on the fundamental handling of the numerical identity of artworks or the logic of interpretation. Krausz has met Stecker's challenge in his own terms.

12. Monroe C. Beardsley, *The Possibility of Criticism* (Detroit: Wayne State University Press, 1970), 44. Beardsley offers this as an explicit objection to my own thesis, to the effect that interpretation exhibits a certain "logical weakness" (that is, that interpretation may go contrary to bivalence).

13. E. D. Hirsch Jr., *Validity in Interpretation* (New Haven, CT: Yale University Press, 1967), appendix 1, especially p. 216.

14. Beardsley, *Possibility of Criticism*, 16.

15. See, for instance, Hirsch, *Validity in Interpretation*, 48, 216.

16. I take this to be featured in the views of Arthur Danto and Nelson Goodman (which are, however, not the same). See, further, Margolis, "The Eclipse and Recovery of Analytic Aesthetics," the next chapter in this volume. See also Jorge J. E. Gracia, *A Theory of Textuality: The Logic and Epistemology* (Albany: State University of New York Press, 1995).

17. Hirsch, *Validity in Interpretation*, chap. 3.

18. See Hirsch, 173–80. And see, further, Margolis, "Genres, Laws, Canons, Principles," in *Rules and Conventions*, ed. Mette Hjort (Baltimore: John Hopkins University Press, 1992), 130–66.

19. See W. K. Wimsatt Jr. and Monroe C. Beardsley, "The Intentional Fallacy," in *The Verbal Icon: Studies in the Meaning of Poetry* (Lexington: University of Kentucky Press, 1954), 3–18.

20. Beardsley, *Possibility of Criticism*, 16.

21. Beardsley, 36.

22. Wolfgang Iser, "The Reading Process: A Phenomenological Approach," in *The Implied Reader: Patterns of Communication in Prose Fiction from Bunyan to Beckett* (Baltimore: Johns Hopkins University Press, 1974), 274.

23. See, for instance, the treatment of history in Carl G. Hempel, "The Function of General Laws in History," in *Aspects of Scientific Explanation and Other Essays in the Philosophy of Science* (New York: Free Press, 1965), 231–43.

24. It's the point of Hirsch's frontal criticism of Hans-Georg Gadamer's post-Heideggerian hermeneutics. See Hirsch, *Validity in Interpretation*, appendix 2.

25. See Roman Ingarden, *The Literary Work of Art*, trans. George G. Grabowicz (Evanston, IL: Northwestern University Press, 1973).

26. Iser, *Implied Reader*, 274.

27. See Hans-Georg Gadamer, *Truth and Method*, trans. Garrett Barden and John Cumming (New York: Seabury Press, 1975).

28. See Ingarden, *Literary Work of Art*.

29. Iser, *Implied Reader*, 277. The idea may be implicit in the usual distinction between *describing* and *interpreting*. It is implied in Stecker, "Constructivist's Dilemma." See also Edmund Husserl, *The Phenomenology of Internal Time-Consciousness*, trans. J. S. Churchill (Bloomington: Indiana University Press, 1964).

30. Iser, *Implied Reader*, 293.

31. Iser, 248.

32. See Stanley Fish, *Is There a Text in This Class? The Authority of Interpretive Communities* (Cambridge, MA: Harvard University Press, 1986); and Helen Vendler, *The Art of Shakespeare's Sonnets* (Cambridge, MA: Harvard University Press, 1997). See also Paul Thom's review of Michael Krausz, *Rightness and Reasons*; Joseph Margolis, *Interpretation Radical but Not Unruly*; and Robert Stecker, "The Constructivist's Dilemma"; in *Literature and Aesthetics* 7 (October 1997): 181–85. Thom is exceedingly clear and instructive here. If I disagree with him in certain details regarding his summary of my view of interpretation, it is largely in terms of the variety of interpretive practices I mean to accommodate. (Which is to say, we largely agree, but that may not have been apparent enough to Thom. I definitely do not favor the recursive, therefore linear and accretive, model he sketches.)

33. See Michel Foucault, *The Order of Things: An Archaeology of the Human Sciences* (New York: Vintage, 1970), chap. 1.

34. The encompassing argument appears in Margolis, *Historied Thought*.

35. This confirms the good sense of Danto's refusal to identify (numerically) artworks and "mere real things," but it does not, of course, confirm his thesis that artworks are a "transfiguration" of "mere real things." See Arthur C. Danto, "The Artworld," *Journal of Philosophy* 61 (1964): 571–84.

36. See Margolis, *Historied Thought*, p. 206 and chap. 7.

37. Stecker apparently believes that paradox cannot be avoided if, preserving numerical identity, one holds to a constructivist realism regarding the nature of artworks, but he nowhere provides a decisive proof, and he nowhere addresses my argument. His charge is a strenuous one, but he neglects the complications of Intentionality. See Stecker, "Constructivist's Dilemma."

38. See George Thomson, *Aeschylus and Athens* (London: Lawrence and Wishart, 1941).

39. See Ernest Jones, *Hamlet and Oedipus* (New York: Norton, 1949).

40. For a glimpse of the evidence, see Margolis, *Historied Thought*.

41. See Stephen Greenblatt, *Shakespearean Negotiations: The Circulation of Social Energy in Renaissance England* (Berkeley: University of California Press, 1988)

42. See Margolis, *Culture and Cultural Entities: Toward a New Unity of Science* (Dordrecht, Netherlands: D. Reidel, 1984), chap. 1.

43. This is the so-called constructivist's dilemma that Stecker, in "Constructivist's Dilemma," claims is insurmountable in my constructivist account of cultural entities and interpretation.

44. See, for instance, Richard Shusterman, "Beneath Interpretation: Against Hermeneutic Holism," *The Monist* 73 (1990): 181–204, which Stecker cites favorably.

45. Some may wish a more explicit reckoning of Stecker's charge in "The Constructivist's Dilemma." I am happy to comply. The "dilemma" Stecker finds in my account is supposed to run as follows: interpretation "completes" the artwork and, at the same time, "makes" an interpretive claim about it. "Both Krausz and Margolis believe that interpretations help to complete their objects. If they did not

hold this view, they would not be constructivists. . . . The problem is to understand how making a claim about an object . . . can give it a property claimed for it" (Stecker 50). For my part, I am unwilling to say that interpretations "complete" an artwork: the idiom is suitable to a phenomenological theory of criticism—for instance, to the views of Iser and Ingarden—but not to mine. I am, of course, willing to concede that interpretation imputes a determinate sense to what (interpretively) is constituted as an Intentional *denotatum*—determinate as a *denotatum* and, as such, determinable in nature. The distinction is critical and is ignored by those (Stecker, for one) who neglect the complexities of Intentionality or who see no fundamental difference between Intentional and non-Intentional properties. But, of course, that is precisely what is at issue. Once you concede the distinction, the validity of historicism and relativism cannot be put at risk by merely formal considerations—that is, by insisting on the preference of bivalence, or on the paradox of truth claims that merely posit what they claim is true, or on the absence of any need for relativism if the *denotata* that are in question are simply numerically different from one another. Nothing of the like will do.

Notes to Chapter Ten

1. See, for instance, William Elton, ed., *Aesthetics and Language* (Oxford: Basil Blackwell, 1954); and Joseph Margolis, ed., *Philosophy Looks at the Arts* (New York: Charles Scribner's Sons, 1962).

2. Richard Rorty, *Philosophy and the Mirror of Nature* (Princeton, NJ: Princeton University Press, 1979), 390.

3. Willard Van Orman Quine, *Word and Object* (Cambridge, MA: MIT Press, 1960), 15–16.

4. Quine, "Two Dogmas of Empiricism," in *From a Logical Point of View* (Cambridge, MA: Harvard University Press, 1953), 20–46.

5. Quine, *Word and Object*, 72.

6. Rorty, *Mirror of Nature*, 392–94.

7. Quine, *Word and Object*, 219.

8. Rorty, *Mirror of Nature*, 389.

9. See, further, Margolis, *Pragmatism without Foundations: Reconciling Realism and Relativism* (Oxford: Basil Blackwell, 1986).

10. See Rorty, "Overcoming the Tradition: Heidegger and Dewey," in *Consequences of Pragmatism: Essays 1972–1980* (Minneapolis: University of Minnesota Press, 1982), chap. 3. For an up-to-date assessment of Rorty's general approach, see Margolis, "Richard Rorty: Philosophy by Other Means," *Metaphilosophy* 31 (2000): 329–46.

11. See Monroe C. Beardsley, *The Possibility of Criticism* (Detroit: Wayne State University Press, 1980).

12. Beardsley, 36.

13. Beardsley, p. 14 and "Testability of an Interpretation," in *Possibility of Criticism*.

14. Beardsley, 14.

15. See Richard J. Bernstein, *Beyond Objectivism and Relativism: Science, Hermeneutics, and Praxis* (Philadelphia: University of Pennsylvania Press, 1983).

16. See E. D. Hirsch Jr., *Validity in Interpretation* (New Haven, CT: Yale University Press, 1967); and Margolis, *The Language of Art and Art Criticism: Analytic Questions in Aesthetics* (Detroit: Wayne State University Press, 1965). The latter volume was considerably reworked and enlarged as *Art and Philosophy: Conceptual Issues in Aesthetics* (Atlantic Highlands, NJ: Humanities Press, 1980), though it exhibits much the same orientation. I mention these texts to give some sense, in passing, of how my views have evolved.

17. Roland Barthes, "From Work to Text," trans. Josué V. Harari, in *Textual Strategies*, ed. Josué V. Harari (Ithaca, NY: Cornell University Press, 1979), 77.

18. For an early overview of mine regarding these and similar currents, see Margolis, "What Is a Literary Text?" in *At the Boundaries*, vol. 1 of *Proceedings of the Northeastern University Center for Literary Studies*, ed. Herbert L. Sussman (Boston: Northeastern University Press, 1984). This account needs to be compared with my *Interpretation, Radical but Not Unruly: The New Puzzle of the Arts and History* (Berkeley: University of California Press, 1995) to appreciate how my analytic account has evolved.

19. I should add that Beardsley read Roland Barthes's *S/Z* as a straightforward objectivist semiotics of literature (a form of structuralism, in short) and failed completely to appreciate the subversively deconstructive intent of Barthes's essay. That is, where he was able to assimilate the poststructuralist literature, Beardsley regularly read it as something like a continuation of New Criticism—which, indeed, it superficially resembles. Otherwise, just as Derrida serves as a straightforward (!) deconstructionist (*Of Grammatology*), Beardsley serves as a straightforward and uncompromising New Critic.

20. For a sense of the most uncompromising analytic reading of holism, see Jerry Fodor and Ernest Lepore, *Holism: A Shopper's Guide* (Oxford: Basil Blackwell, 1992).

21. See Nelson Goodman, *Ways of Worldmaking* (Indianapolis, IN: Hackett, 1978); and Goodman, *Of Mind and Other Matters* (Cambridge, MA: Harvard University Press, 1984).

22. See Goodman, *Ways of Worldmaking*, x.

23. See, for instance, Goodman, "Seven Strictures on Similarity," in *Experience and Theory*, ed. Lawrence Foster and J. W. Swanson (Amherst: University of Massachusetts Press, 1970), 19–29.

24. See Goodman, *The Structure of Appearance*, 2nd ed. (Indianapolis, IN: Bobbs-Merrill, 1966), chap. 2.

25. See Goodman, "Prospects for a Theory of Projection," in *Fact, Fiction, and Forecast*, 2nd ed. (Indianapolis, IN: Bobbs-Merrill, 1965), chap. 4.

26. Goodman, *Fact, Fiction, and Forecast*, 94–99.
27. See Goodman, *Of Mind and Other Matters*, 32–33.
28. Goodman, *Fact, Fiction, and Forecast*, 83.
29. Goodman, 57.
30. Goodman, *Of Mind and Other Matters*, 29, 31.
31. See Hilary Putnam, "Reflections on Goodman's *Ways of Worldmaking*," *Philosophical Papers*, vol. 3 (Cambridge: Cambridge University Press, 1983), chap. 9.
32. See Goodman, *Languages of Art* (Indianapolis, IN: Bobbs-Merrill, 1968), 113–22.
33. Goodman, 113.
34. Goodman, 186–87.
35. See Margolis, "The Autographic Nature of the Dance," in *Illuminating Dance: Philosophical Explorations*, ed. Maxine Sheets-Johnstone (London and Toronto: Associated University Presses, 1984); and Goodman, "The Status of Style," in *Ways of Worldmaking*.
36. Goodman, "Status of Style," 52.
37. See Margolis, *Art and Philosophy*, 12–14.
38. Paul Ricœur, "The Narrative Function," in *Hermeneutics and the Human Sciences*, ed. and trans. John B. Thompson (Cambridge: Cambridge University Press, 1982), particularly pp. 292–93.
39. Arthur C. Danto, *The Transfiguration of the Commonplace* (Cambridge, MA: Harvard University Press, 1981), 92–95.
40. Danto, 189–97, particularly p. 192.
41. Danto, 197.
42. The notion first appeared, unanalyzed, in Danto, "The Artworld," reprinted in Margolis, ed., *Philosophy Looks at the Arts: Contemporary Readings in Aesthetics*, 3rd ed. (Philadelphia: Temple University Press, 1987), 132–45.
43. See Margolis, "Ontology Down and Out in Art and Science," *Journal of Aesthetics and Art Criticism* 46 (1998): 451–60; also in Thomas Anderberg, Tore Nilstun, and Ingmar Persson, eds., *Aesthetic Distinction* (Lund, Sweden: Lund University Press, 1998). The relevant texts include Arthur C. Danto, *Narration and Knowledge* (New York: Columbia University Press, 1985), which is the enlarged second edition of Danto's *Analytical Philosophy of History* (1964); and Danto, *Analytical Philosophy of Action* (Cambridge: Cambridge University Press, 1973).
44. See Danto, "Works of Art and Mere Real Things," in *Transfiguration*.
45. See Jean-Paul Sartre, *The Psychology of Imagination*, trans. Bernard Frechtman (New York: Washington Square Press, 1966); see also Arthur C. Danto, *Jean-Paul Sartre* (New York: Viking, 1975), chap. 1.
46. Danto, *The Philosophical Disenfranchisement of Art* (New York: Columbia University Press, 1986), 44–45.
47. Danto, "The Artworld," 162.
48. See, further, Joseph Margolis, "Constraints on the Metaphysics of Culture," *Review of Metaphysics* 39 (1986): 653–73. Here and throughout this chapter,

I try to convey a sense of a number of early transitional pieces through which I first began to reconcile analytic and continental treatments of the metaphysics and epistemology of the cultural world.

49. For an ingenious version of nonreductive physicalism, see John F. Post, *The Faces of Experience* (Ithaca, NY: Cornell University Press, 1987). See also Margolis, *Texts without Reference* (Oxford: Basil Blackwell, 1989), chap. 6.

50. See Margolis, *Pragmatism without Foundations*, chap. 8; and Margolis, *Texts without Reference*, pt. 1.

51. On internalist strategies, see Margolis, *Pragmatism without Foundations*, chap. 11.

52. Richard Rorty, "Postmodernist Bourgeois Liberalism," *Journal of Philosophy* 80 (1983): 583–89; reprinted in *Hermeneutics and Praxis*, ed. Robert Hollinger (Notre Dame, IN: Notre Dame University Press, 1985), 214–21; the material quoted appears on p. 216 in Hollinger's edition.

53. Rorty, 217.

54. Rorty, "Epistemological Behaviorism and the De-transcendentalization of Analytic Philosophy," *Neue Hefte für Philosophie* 9 (1978): 114–42, quoted material at p. 122; reprinted in Hollinger, *Hermeneutics and Praxis*, at pp. 95–96. Rorty professes to follow Lyotard, of course, in characterizing his own view as postmodern. See Jean-François Lyotard, *The Postmodern Condition: A Report on Knowledge*, trans. Geoff Bennington and Brian Massumi (Minneapolis: University of Minnesota Press, 1984).

55. Rorty, "Epistemological Behaviorism," 98; italics added.

56. See Margolis, *Pragmatism without Foundations*, chap. 11.

57. See, for instance, Michel Foucault, "Questions of Method: An Interview with Michel Foucault," trans. Alan Bass, in *Ideology and Consciousness* 8 (1981); reprinted in Kenneth Baynes, James Bohman, and Thomas McCarthy, eds., *After Philosophy: End or Transformation?* (Cambridge, MA: MIT Press, 1987), 100–18.

58. See, for instance, Margolis, *Art and Philosophy*; see also Margolis, *Culture and Cultural Entities* (Dordrecht, Netherlands: D. Reidel, 1984), chap. 1.

59. See, for instance, Margolis, *Interpretation Radical but Not Unruly* (Berkeley: University of California Press, 1995).

60. See, for instance, Margolis, *The Truth about Relativism* (Oxford: Basil Blackwell, 1991); and Margolis, *The Flux of History and the Flux of Science* (Berkeley: University of California Press, 1993).

61. See Margolis, *Historied Thought, Constructed World: A Conceptual Primer for the Turn of the Millennium* (Berkeley: University of California Press, 1995).

62. See H. G. Alexander, ed., *The Leibniz-Clarke Correspondence* (Manchester, UK: Manchester University Press, 1956); and Quine, *Word and Object*, §§37–38.

63. I take this to be the master theme of Ludwig Wittgenstein, *Philosophical Investigations*, trans. G. E. M. Anscombe (New York: Macmillan, 1953).

64. See Margolis, *What, After All, Is a Work of Art? Lectures in the Philosophy of Art* (University Park: Pennsylvania State University Press, 1999), chap. 2.

Notes to Chapter Eleven

1. See P. F. Strawson, "Ethical Intuitionism," *Philosophy* 24 (1949): 23–33.

2. Hume is difficult and, of course, supremely interesting. I feel I must take a moment to explain my dismissing Hume from the rank that Aristotle and Kant achieve among first-tier thinkers. Hume is a naturalist about morality, in the straightforward sense in which he is primarily concerned to explain how moral judgment arises from our impressions and ideas, among which the sentiment of sympathy may well be the most important (for Hume). Accordingly, I find section 2 (bk. 2, pt. 1) of Hume's *A Treatise of Human Nature*, ed. David Fate Norton and Mary J. Norton, vol. 1 (Oxford: Oxford University Press, 2000), to afford the quickest grasp of his general moral theory.

There are two decisive constraints Hume imposes on the account he offers. One is inevitably muted in his enthusiasm for moral reflection—namely, his inability to trace the idea of "self" or "person" to "any one impression" (Hume 164); the other is, consequently, his inability to ensure its constancy and constant structure through cultural divergence. Hume has nowhere given a satisfactory account of our idea of self. In a fair sense, therefore, his entire moral theory is hostage to this weakness.

My own view, remember, is that the self is an artifact of constructive social processes (enculturation), historicized in accord with the variable practices of this society and that. But Hume, of course, speaks directly of the nature of persons or selves—in particular, of the "passions" on which moral systems depend—as, effectively, humanly invariant. This conforms with the pivotal importance Hume assigns the "simple and uniform impressions" (the "direct passions") of *pride* and *humility* in his moral system. As he says,

> Pride and humility, tho' directly contrary, have yet the same OBJECT. This object is self, or that succession of related ideas and impressions, of which we have an intimate memory and consciousness. Here the view always fixes when we are actuated by either of these passions. Accordingly as our idea of ourself is more or less advantageous, we feel either of these opposite affections, and are elated by pride, or dejected with humility. Whatever other objects may be comprehended by the mind, they are always consider'd with a view to ourselves; otherwise they wou'd never be able . . . to excite these passions. (182)

Here, you find both the general sense in which Hume sketches the constant nature of human beings relevant for moral judgment and the centrality of the idea of self. But Hume nowhere ensures (1) the numerical identity or constancy of self or (2) the constancy of what belongs to human nature. Therefore, for all the *Treatise*'s charm, I cannot see how Hume can be considered a moral philosopher of the same rank as Aristotle or Kant. (I am entirely willing to concede that he is at least as perceptive about human nature as Aristotle and that he is usually more perceptive than Kant.)

The second constraint arises in regard to Hume's analysis of *sympathy* and is explicit. The context of his account is, as always, that of "the combat of passion and reason" (266), which leads to the famous dictum "*first*, that reason alone can never be a motive to any action of the will; and *secondly*, that it can never oppose passion in the direction of the will" (265). (That is, "Reason is, and ought only to be the slave of the passions" [266].) Once you have this in mind and the corollary—namely, that "a passion is an original existence, or . . . modification of existence, and contains not any representative quality, which renders it a copy of any other existence or modification" (266)—you can appreciate the central importance (for Hume) of sympathy.

Sympathy is usually termed a passion but, technically and for Hume, it is the process or the effect of "an evident conversion of an idea into an impression. This conversion arises from the relation of objects to oneself. Ourself is always intimately present to us. Let us compare all those circumstances, and we shall find, that sympathy is exactly correspondent in the operations of our understanding; and even contains something more surprizing and extraordinary" (Hume 208). Hume then integrates his entire theory (or provides the essential clue for doing so): "We may observe that no person is ever prais'd by another for any quality, which wou'd not, if real, produce, of itself, a pride in the person possest of it." Hence, "nothing is more natural than for us to embrace the opinions of others in this particular [viewing oneself 'in the same light, in which he appears to his admirer']; both from *sympathy*, which renders all their sentiments intimately present to us; and from *reasoning*, which makes us regard their judgment, as a kind of argument for what they affirm. These two principles of authority and sympathy influence almost all our opinions" (208–09).

The important points are, first, that Hume's conceptual apparatus makes no sense if the concept of *self* or *person* is not rightly secured from paradox (which, of course, it is not) and, second, that there is no argument in Hume (and in a fair sense there cannot be) to show that human nature and existence *are* invariant in morally relevant respects. It is for this double reason that I demote Hume. But Hume, in his deficit, is every bit as perceptive as Aristotle and Kant in their failed efforts at legitimation. I cannot see how Hume can be recovered in his own terms.

3. See Richard Rorty, *Philososhy and the Mirror of Nature* (Princeton, NJ: Princeton University Press, 1979); Rorty, *Contingency, Irony and Solidarity* (Cambridge: Cambridge University Press, 1989).

4. See Jean-François Lyotard, *The Postmodern Condition: A Report on Knowledge*, trans. Geoff Bennington and Brian Massumi (Minneapolis: University of Minnesota Press, 1984).

5. Sabina Lovibond, *Realism and Imagination in Ethics* (Minneapolis: University of Minnesota Press, 1983), 85.

6. It is not at all easy to isolate Dewey's Hegelian tendencies except in the abstract. For an appreciation, see Elizabeth Flower and Murray G. Murphey, *A History of Philosophy in America*, vol. 2 (New York: G. P. Putnam, 1977), chap. 14. Perhaps a fair impression can be got from John Dewey, *Reconstruction in Philosophy*, 2nd ed. (Boston: Beacon Press, 1957). See also Richard J. Bernstein, *Praxis and Action: Contemporary Philosophies of Human Activity* (Philadelphia: University of Pennsylvania Press, 1971). James Campbell confirms my sense that there is almost nothing that is robustly Hegelian in Dewey; Campbell has located the following remark of Dewey's (from Dewey's *Individualism Old and New*) in James Campbell, *Understanding John Dewey: Nature and Cooperative Intelligence* (La Salle, IL: Open Court, 1995), 12: "Gradually I came to realize that what the principles [of thinking] actually stood for could be better understood and stated when completely emancipated from Hegelian garb"—that is, cast more in accord with the Darwinian model. I think this pretty well means that none of the early pragmatists really made anything of history in any sense strongly akin to what Hegel favored. That is interesting in itself because one often hears it said that the pragmatists—Dewey, at least—espoused a kind of historicism. I see little evidence of that, and I think Campbell has caught the essential point. See, further, my *Life without Principles: Reconciling Theory and Practice* (Oxford: Basil Blackwell, 1996).

7. See Michel Foucault, "Nietzsche, Genealogy, History," in *Language, Counter-memory, Practice: Selected Essays and Interviews*, ed. Donald F. Bouchard, trans. Donald F. Bouchard and Sherry Simon (Ithaca, NY: Cornell University Press, 1977), 139–64; see, also, Mark Poster, *Foucault, Marxism and History: Mode of Production versus Mode of Information* (London: Polity Press, 1984).

8. G. W. F. Hegel, *Natural Law*, trans. T. M. Knox (Philadelphia: University of Pennsylvania Press, 1975), 77–78.

9. See Jürgen Habermas, "Discourse Ethics: Notes on a Program of Philosophical Justification," in *Moral Consciousness and Communicative Action*, trans. Christian Lenhardt and Shierry Weber Nicholsen (Cambridge, MA: MIT Press, 1990), 43–44; italics in the original.

10. Habermas, 65–66.

11. Jean-François Lyotard, *The Differend: Phrases in Dispute*, trans. Georges van den Abbeele (Minneapolis: University of Minnesota Press, 1988), §12.

12. See Zygmunt Bauman, *Postmodern Ethics* (Oxford: Basil Blackwell, 1993), particularly the introduction; and Bauman, introduction to *Life in Fragments: Essays in Postmodern Morality* (Oxford: Basil Blackwell, 1995). See also David Theo Goldberg, *Racist Culture: Philosophy and the Politics of Meaning* (Oxford: Basil Blackwell, 1993).

13. See the discussion of this in Joseph Margolis, *Interpretation Radical but Not Unruly* (Berkeley: University of California Press 1995), chap. 2.

14. On the formal relationship between universalism and historicism, see Margolis, *Pragmatism without Foundations: Reconciling Realism and Relativism* (Oxford: Basil Blackwell, 1986).

15. Hans-Georg Gadamer, *Truth and Method*, trans. Garrett Barden and John Cumming (New York: Seabury Press, 1975), 244–45.

16. Gadamer, 246, 247.

17. Gadamer, 250.

18. Gadamer, 251; see also 249.

19. Gadamer, 253.

20. Jürgen Habermas, "Morality and Ethical Life: Does Hegel's Critique of Kant Apply to Discourse Ethics?" in *Moral Consciousness and Communicative Action*, 208, in the context of the entire essay. In "Discourse Ethics," Habermas says, "Because morality is always embedded in what Hegel called ethical life (*Sittlichkeit*), discourse ethics is always subject to limitations, though not limitations that can devalue its crucial function or strengthen the skeptic in his role as an advocate of a counter-enlightenment" (99).

21. Gadamer, "The Universality of the Hermeneutical Problem," in *Philosophical Hermeneutics*, trans. and ed. David E. Linge (Berkeley: University of California Press, 1976), 7.

22. Jürgen Habermas, *On the Logic of the Social Sciences*, trans. Shierry Weber Nicholsen and Jerry A. Stark (Cambridge, MA: MIT Press, 1988), 144.

23. For a sustained discussion of Davidson's theories, see Joseph Margolis, "Donald Davidson's Philosophical Strategies," in *Artifacts, Representations and Social Practice*, ed. Carol C. Gould and Robert S. Cohen (Dordrecht, Netherlands: Kluwer, 1994), 291–322.

24. Donald Davidson, "On the Very Idea of a Conceptual Scheme," in *Inquiries into Truth and Interpretation* (Oxford: Clarendon Press, 1984), 190.

25. See Ian Hacking, *Why Does Language Matter to Philosophy?* (Cambridge: Cambridge University Press, 1975), chap. 12; and Hacking, "Language, Truth and Reason," in *Rationality and Relativism*, ed. Martin Hollis and Steven Lukes (Cambridge, MA: MIT Press, 1982), 48–66.

26. Alasdair MacIntyre, *Whose Justice? Which Rationality?* (Notre Dame, IN: University of Notre Dame Press, 1988), 169, 172.

27. MacIntyre, 172.

28. MacIntyre, 175.

29. MacIntyre, 9–10.

30. MacIntyre, 9, read in the context of p. 10.

31. The counterargument I am resisting here is, of course, a classic ploy. You will find it trotted out most recently by Carl Page, *Philosophical Historicism and the Betrayal of First Philosophy* (University Park: Pennsylvania State University

Press, 1995). Page directs it against my own advocacy of historicism, but he fails to grasp the possibility that the denial of a modal invariance is not itself the affirmation of another. There is reason to believe that the oversight is essential to all the philosophical strategies of the Straussians (the followers of Leo Strauss). See, further, Margolis, *Interpretation Radical but Not Unruly*, chap. 2.

32. Alasdair MacIntyre, *After Virtue: A Study in Moral Theory*, 2nd ed. (Notre Dame, IN: University of Notre Dame Press, 1984), ix.

33. MacIntyre, x.

34. MacIntyre, ix.

35. MacIntyre, 278.

36. See Martha Nussbaum, "Recoiling from Reason," review of *Whose Justice? Which Rationality?* by Alasdair MacIntyre, *New York Review of Books*, December 7, 1989, 36–41.

37. MacIntyre, *After Virtue*, 203.

38. MacIntyre, 225.

39. MacIntyre, 225.

40. Stuart Hampshire, *Thought and Action* (London: Chatto and Windus, 1959), 223.

41. See Zeno Vendler, "The Grammar of Goodness," in *Linguistics in Philosophy* (Ithaca, NY: Cornell University Press, 1967), 172–95.

42. See William Connolly, "Beyond Good and Evil: The Ethical Sensibility of Michel Foucault," *Political Theory* 21 (1993): 365–89.

43. MacIntyre, *After Virtue*, 187.

44. MacIntyre, 188–89.

45. MacIntyre, 190.

46. MacIntyre, 191; italics in the original text.

47. There is a useful summary given in Annette C. Baier, *A Progress of Sentiments: Reflections on Hume's Treatise* (Cambridge, MA: Harvard University Press, 1991), chap. 9.

48. I show the full connection among the concepts of historicism, praxis, the artifactual nature of selves, the analysis of reference and predication along historicized lines, and the viability of relativism in Margolis, *Historied Thought, Constructed World: A Conceptual Primer at the Turn of the Millennium* (Berkeley: University of California Press, 1995); also, in Margolis, *Interpretation Radical but Not Unruly*.

49. See G. E. L. Owen, "Tithenai ta phainomena," in *Logic, Science, and Dialectic: Collected Papers in Greek Philosophy*, ed. Martha Nussbaum (Ithaca, NY: Cornell University Press, 1986), 239–51.

50. Martha C. Nussbaum, *The Fragility of Goodness: Luck and Ethics in Greek Tragedy and Philosophy* (Cambridge: Cambridge University Press, 1986), 245.

51. Nussbaum, 246.

52. See Aristotle, *Nicomachean Ethics* (1142a), a passage Nussbaum translates in *The Fragility of Goodness*, 305.

53. Nussbaum, *The Fragility of Goodness*, 302; see also pp. 303–05.

54. Nussbaum, 305; compare Aristotle, *Nicomachean Ethics* (1142a23), which she cites.

55. The term is from Charles Sanders Peirce, who plays an almost-unique role in American philosophy in attempting to clarify the logic of general predicates. I agree with Peirce's judgment that there must be "real generals," but I disagree fundamentally with his analysis of how that comes about. See Margolis, "The Passing of Peirce's Realism," *Transactions of the Charles S. Peirce Society* 29 (1993): 293–330.

56. See P. F. Pears, "Universals," *Philosophical Quarterly* 1 (1951): 218–27.

57. See, further, Renford Bambrough, "Universals and Family Resemblances," *Proceedings of the Aristotelian Society* 9 (1961): 207–22.

58. For the full argument, see Margolis, *Historied Thought, Constructed World*. I take this to be the right elaboration of Wittgenstein's essential contribution. It is also related to Peirce's semiosis. But Peirce never quite abandons the doctrine of universals. See, also, Margolis, "The Passing of Peirce's Realism."

59. Nussbaum, *The Fragility of Goodness*, 304.

60. See, for an interesting comparison, Bas C. van Fraassen, *Laws and Symmetry* (Oxford: Clarendon Press, 1989).

61. Aristotle, *Nicomachean Ethics*, 1137b. The translation is given by Nussbaum, in *The Fragility of Goodness*, 301.

62. Martha C. Nussbaum, "The Discernment of Perception: An Aristotelian Conception of Private and Public Rationality," in *Love's Knowledge: Essays on Philosophy and Literature* (New York: Oxford University Press, 1990), 85.

63. Nussbaum, 85.

64. Nussbaum cites Hilary Putnam, "Taking Rules Seriously: A Response to Martha Nussbaum," *New Literary History* 15 (1983): 193–200, in this quotation from Nussbaum, *Love's Knowledge*, 93. See also Nussbaum, "Flawed Crystals: James's *The Golden Bowl* and Literature as Moral Philosophy," in *Love's Knowledge*, chap. 4, which offers an improved version of the thesis Putnam commented on.

65. Nussbaum, *Love's Knowledge*, 94–95.

66. Karl-Otto Apel, "The *A Priori* of the Communication Community and the Foundations of Ethics: The Problem of a Rational Foundation of Ethics in a Scientific Age," in *Towards a Transformation of Philosophy*, trans. Glyn Adey and David Frisby (London: Routledge / Kegan Paul, 1980), 280–81. Compare Robert Nozick, *Anarchy, State, and Utopia* (New York: Basic Books, 1974), 157–58; also, Alan Donagan, *The Theory of Morality* (Chicago: University of Chicago Press, 1977), 65–66.

67. See Wesley C. Salmon, *Scientific Explanation and the Causal Structure of the World* (Princeton, NJ: Princeton University Press, 1984), chap. 9.

68. Salmon, 18; italics in original.

69. Salmon, 16.

70. Salmon, 16.

71. See Salmon, 18, 19.

72. See, however, Joseph Margolis, *The Flux of History and the Flux of Science* (Berkeley: University of California Press, 1993), chap. 4.

73. I give a full account of the general problem in Margolis, *The Truth about Relativism* (Oxford: Basil Blackwell, 1991), and an application, in interpretive contexts, in *Interpretation Radical but Not Unruly*. Ronald Dworkin considers the similarity between interpretation in literature and interpretation in constitutional law. He takes a very strong line (in "hard cases") even against pluralism, but this may have more to do with his view of the institution. In literary cases, he considers relenting, but, again, he views this more in terms of the nature of the institution than of the logic of interpretation. See Ronald Dworkin, *A Matter of Principle* (Cambridge, MA: Harvard University Press, 1985), chaps. 5–6.

74. I draw this from a recent paper of mine, Margolis, "Plain Talk about Interpretation on a Relativistic Model," *Journal of Aesthetics and Art Criticism* 53 (1995): 1–7.

75. You will find a noticeably slack account of principles in Robert Nozick, *The Nature of Rationality* (Princeton, NJ: Princeton University Press, 1993), chap. 1. The reason is plain: valid principles presuppose a valid account of rationality, but if rationality is itself artifactually variable from one historical society to another, then principles cannot, logically, be modally necessary. This is why decision theory cannot but be contingent—however valuable. The general enthusiasm for decision theory often does not concede the point.

Notes to Chapter Twelve

1. See J. J. C. Smart, *Philosophy and Scientific Realism* (London: Routledge / Kegan Paul, 1963), chap. 3.

2. Among the best of these efforts that I am familiar with, though my grasp of the essential issues is confessedly elementary, I include Bas C. van Fraassen, *Scientific Representation: Paradoxes of Perspective* (Oxford: Clarendon Press, 2008); and Nancy Cartwright, *The Dappled World: A Study of the Boundaries of Science* (Cambridge: Cambridge University Press, 1999).

3. Compare F. W. J. Schelling, *Ideas for a Philosophy of Nature*, trans. E. E. Harris and P. Heath (Cambridge: Cambridge University Press, 1988), 41–42; and G. W. F. Hegel, *The Difference between Fichte's and Schelling's System of Philosophy*, trans. H. S. Harris and W. Cerf (Albany: State University of New York Press, 1977).

4. See, further, Joseph Margolis, "Charles Peirce's Abductive Turn," in *Toward a Metaphysics of Culture* (New York: Routledge, 2016), chap. 3.

5. Van Fraassen, *Scientific Representation*, 51–53, 125–130.

6. See, for an abundance of illustrations, Kenneth F. Schaffner, *Discovery and Explanation in Biology and Medicine* (Chicago: University of Chicago Press, 1993); and Margolis, "Constructing a Person," chap. 2 in *Metaphysics of Culture*.

7. This is the first form of the categorical imperative, in Immanuel Kant, *Foundations of the Metaphysics of Morals*, trans. Lewis White Beck (New York: Liberty of Liberal Arts, 1959), 421 (in the pagination of the edition of the Preussische Akademie der Wissenschaften), cited in Christine M. Korsgaard, *Creating the Kingdom of Ends* (Cambridge: Cambridge University Press, 1996), 77. Korsgaard pointedly prefers the title *Groundwork of the Metaphysics of Morals*, which she offers even in listing Beck's translation, which, in her later books on Kant, she effectively retires, in favor of Mary Gregor's translation of the same work, which is indeed titled *Groundwork of the Metaphysics of Morals* (Cambridge: Cambridge University Press, 1998). I mention this slight oddity to avoid confusion, since Kant also wrote *The Metaphysics of Morals*, which Mary Gregor has also translated (Cambridge University Press, 1991).

8. For a fair sense of Max Weber's conjunction of the "rationalization" of modern society and the "disenchantment of the world," see "Science as a Vocation," in *From Max Weber: Essays in Sociology*, trans. and ed. H. H. Gerth and C. Wright Mills (New York: Oxford University Press, 1946), 129–56. The theme appears already in Max Weber, *The Protestant Ethic and the Spirit of Capitalism*, trans. Talcott Parsons (New York: Scribner's, 1930/1958). There is a suggestive reflection on Weber's thesis (without explicitly focusing on Weber in any textual sense, centered on countering its negativism) in Charles Taylor, "Legitimation Crisis?" in *Philosophical Papers*, vol. 2, *Philosophy and the Human Sciences* (Cambridge: Cambridge University Press, 1985), 248–88. Taylor captures the sense of the threat of Weber's thesis with regard to the legitimation of what I am calling agentive norms as distinct from "enabling norms." His own essay favors a Christian resolution, which, of course, is eligible but not necessary.

9. For what it's worth, I draw your attention (without analysis or argument) to a failed (but much admired) effort to raise the *sittlich* to a level of implied (but unsupported) independent normative validity that is explicitly indebted to Heidegger's intuitions about "being-in-the-world" and, perhaps more deeply, to Aristotle's teleologized naturalism. I mean Charles Taylor's *Philosophical Papers*, 2 vols. Taylor's effort, which is intended to be ontologically explicit, in advancing a "hermeneutic" theory of human agency, assumes, without argument, that the natural history of human *Bildung* harbors evidence enough to confirm that that history yields a reasonable sense of the telic or essential normative thrust of human life (accommodating the diversity of history itself). It's a theme Taylor strengthens in his more recent work, though he does not come to grips, satisfactorily, with the import of the post-Darwinian literature I've drawn on. With all due respect, therefore, I'm persuaded that Taylor fails, though I see the effort as inherently more promising than the Kantian intuitions I examine. The simple fact is that Taylor does not explain how his theory of agency or self-interpretation (in the hermeneutic sense) actually provides a ground for the gradual reclamation of what, finally, is most convincingly agentive in the way of human norms somehow extracted from the immense scatter and fundamental

conflict among the actual commitments of the human race. See, particularly, "What Is Human Agency?" and "Self-Interpreting Animals," in *Philosophical Papers*, vol. 1, *Human Agency and Language*, 15–44 and 45–76, respectively. Taylor fails, I say, for much the same reasons Kant fails, though as an Aristotelian.

10. Ronald N. Giere, *Science without Laws: Model Systems, Cases, and Exemplary Narratives* (Chicago: University of Chicago Press, 1999), 6. See, also, Nancy Cartwright, *How the Laws of Physics Lie* (Oxford: Clarendon Press, 1983); and Carl G. Hempel, "Deductive-Nomological versus Statistical Explanation," "Maximal Specificity and Lawlikeness in Probabilistic Explanation," and "Postscript 1976: More Recent Ideas on the Problem of Statistical Explanation," in *The Philosophy of Carl G. Hempel: Studies in Science, Explanation, and Rationality*, ed. James H. Fetzer (Oxford: Oxford University Press, 2001), 87–145, 146–64, and 165–85, respectively.

11. Christine M. Korsgaard, with G. A. Cohen, Raymond Geuss, Thomas Nagel, and Bernard Williams, *The Sources of Normativity*, ed. Onora O'Neill (Cambridge: Cambridge University Press, 1996), 95.

12. This, of course, is precisely the point of the analysis in Margolis, "Constructing a Person," of human action and of my objection to Cassirer's avoidance of the problem of reconciling freedom and causality in his otherwise admirably tempered effort at freeing his own Kantian innovations from Kant's transcendental excesses. But if the concession is *required* (as I've tried to show it is), then Korsgaard's reluctance to yield on autonomy is itself a full-blooded Kantian weakness—which is to say, the analogy between causal laws and moral laws poses a decisive objection against the would-be *rational* requirement that a moral law or principle or imperative must be universally binding as well as unconditionally obligatory; I think it would be fair to say, therefore, that neither Kant nor Korsgaard secures the essential premise. I don't believe there is any ground on which it can be secured. If that's granted, then the argument amounts to a *reductio*.

13. Korsgaard, *Kingdom of Ends*, 77–78. The rest of her chap. 3 confirms the strategic importance of the issue for Korsgaard's project, apart from Kant's own difficulties.

14. Korsgaard, *Sources of Normativity*, 97.

15. Korsgaard, *Sources of Normativity*, 98. Korsgaard goes further, here. She adds (pp. 98–100) a distinction that does not appear in Kant's text: she makes the categorical imperative depend on what she calls the moral law: "The moral law, in the Kantian system, is the law of what Kant calls the Kingdom of Ends, the republic of all rational beings. The moral law tells us to act only on maxims that all rational beings could agree to act on together in a workable cooperative system." She adds here, tellingly, that "any law is universal," which I think we may now say is simply false—or true by fiat alone. Furthermore, if "all rational beings" can "act on [any law] together in a workable cooperative system," then they can act on a moral law that accords with the form of a causal law according to the views of van Fraassen, Cartwright, Giere, and others, and then both Kant's and Korsgaard's moral programs

fail outright, and if they demur there, it will be clear that their claims are simply arbitrary. There's no reason that I can see that the rationality of normative concerns entails the determinacy and universality of objective agentive norms.

16. For an instructive critique of Kant's thesis that "people are valuable in themselves" and that "they are ends in themselves," see Joseph Raz, "The Amoralist," in *Ethics and Practical Reason*, ed. Garrett Cullity and Berys Gaut (Oxford: Clarendon Press, 1997), 369–98. See, further, G. W. F. Hegel, *Natural Law*, trans. T. M. Knox (Philadelphia: University of Pennsylvania Press, 1975), 75–78. I find it difficult to believe that Korsgaard would let these pages (Hegel's) go unanswered.

17. See, further, Margolis, "Constructing a Person."

18. See Margolis, "Toward a Metaphysics of Culture," chap. 1 in *Metaphysics of Culture*.

19. Wilfrid Sellars, "Philosophy and the Scientific Image of Man," in *Science, Perception and Reality* (London: Routledge / Kegan Paul, 1963), 39. See, further, Willem A. de Vries, *Wilfrid Sellars* (Montréal: McGill-Queen's University Press, 2005), chaps. 9–10. I mention de Vries since he is one of the best-informed readers of a notably elusive figure. (Sellars is difficult to collect.) This is not to agree with de Vries's reading of particular texts, but it would be unwise not to consult his views. Also, it becomes increasingly clear that Sellars is the most interesting member of the Pittsburgh School on the general normativity issue and that, one way or another, McDowell, Rorty, and Brandom tend to deform the most promising of Sellars's doctrines.

20. I've pursued such a possibility in Margolis, *Moral Philosophy after 9/11* (University Park: Pennsylvania State University Press, 2001). I would say we are led in this direction by the effectiveness of arguments like the one just mounted against Kant and Korsgaard and that to yield on the grounds given ineluctably requires concessions to relativism. (Pragmatism is the mortal opponent of Kantianism in our time.)

21. See Ernst Cassirer, *The Phenomenology of Knowledge*, vol. 3 of *The Philosophy of Symbolic Forms*, trans. Ralph Manheim (New Haven, CT: Yale University Press, 1957), 475–79. I should perhaps add that Hilary Putnam risks a similar entanglement (which he eventually abandons) in his well-known quarrel with Richard Rorty, when he speaks of truth as a *Grenzbegriff*. See Hilary Putnam, *Reason, Truth and History* (Cambridge: Cambridge University Press, 1991), 216.

22. See Cassirer, *Phenomenology of Knowledge*, 478. I quote the pertinent lines from Immanuel Kant, "Appendix to the Transcendental Dialectic," *Critique of Pure Reason*, trans. and ed. Paul Guyer and Allen W. Wood (Cambridge: Cambridge University Press, 1998), p. 591, B672; Cassirer quotes them from another translation. Cassirer's application is marvelously in accord with Kant's dictum, as far as proposed objects go. But there are serious difficulties that must be acknowledged: for one, the argument in favor of Euclid's geometry (regarding the form of space—as also, on other grounds, regarding time) cannot be assimilated to the treatment of objects; for another, the evolving construal of causal laws (nomologicality), already

briefly aired here, cannot easily be read in any convincing apriorist manner, cannot support a principled distinction between apodictic truth and empirical conjecture, cannot (in *that* spirit) "regulate" the understanding so as to lead "all its rules" to "converge at one point."

I'm persuaded that the ultimate "regulative" constraint is too thin to be read as transcendental rather than empirical and that, if, at any point in scientific inquiry, insistence on systematic unity proves unwise empirically (as it would be if it were better to favor approximative strategies of the sort theorists like van Fraassen and Cartwright—and even Thomas Kuhn and Paul Feyerabend—prefer or recommend), then the apriorist idiom might be construed as no more than a *façon de parler*. Here, it makes sense to read Peirce's "regulative" notion of the "long run" as itself Kantian in spirit. But then, precisely, Peirce's abductive turn signifies a more plausible (and more powerful) turn away from any explicitly cognitive resolution of the regulative matter.

23. See John McDowell, "The Logical Form of an Intuition," in *Having the World in View: Essays on Kant, Hegel, and Sellars* (Cambridge, MA: Harvard University Press, 2009), 23–43. This is the second of McDowell's Woodbridge Lectures, largely centered on a close reading of Sellars's reading of Kant in *Science and Metaphysics* (Sellars's own John Locke Lectures, 1965–1966).

24. The remark appears in Wilfrid Sellars, "Empiricism and the Philosophy of Mind," in *Science, Perception and Reality*, §42, but there is a similar warning in "Philosophy and the Scientific Image of Man," p. 14.

25. McDowell's lecture (the second Woodbridge Lecture) appears, of course, in *Having the World in View*. Sellars's argument, summarized and cited by McDowell, appears for the most part in Wilfrid Sellars, "Sensibility and Understanding," in *Science and Metaphysics: Variations on Kantian Themes* (Atascadero, CA: Ridgeview, 1967/1992), 9–32. The suggestive passage in Kant's first *Critique*, cited by Sellars and duly and fairly noted by McDowell, appears at A78/B103–A79/B105. Sellars's reading is congenial to Darwinian and post-Darwinian considerations. On that score alone, McDowell's view seems decidedly regressive. I cannot see the point of taking the dispute seriously if the Kantian problem is not to be judged in the enlarged setting I've recommended.

26. See, Kant, *Critique of Pure Reason*, A646/B674–A650/B678. I have found the discussion of this decisive matter in Henry E. Allison, *Kant's Transcendental Idealism: An Introduction and Defense*, rev. and enl. ed. (New Haven, CT: Yale University Press, 2004), chap. 15, to be especially straightforward, candid, courageous, but finally inadequate.

27. See Bas van Fraassen, "On the Radical Incompleteness of the Manifest Image," *PSA: Proceedings of the Biennial Meeting of the Philosophy of Science Association* 1976, no. 2 (1976): 335–43.

28. Though I have the highest regard for van Fraassen's ingenuity, I confess I cannot see any operatively clear disjunction between a would-be atheoretical phenomenology of experience (that scientific explanation would be expected to "save")

and a theoretically infected phenomenology that would concede the perceptual standing of theoretical entities (molecules and atoms, say) and the realist standing of such entities. Here, then, I tend to support Sellars's realism over van Fraassen's antirealism (though not the perspicuousness of Sellars's arguments, or his account of the "manifest" and the "scientific images," or his scientism). I find myself, therefore, inclined to favor the arguments advanced by figures like Cartwright in *How the Laws of Physics Lie*, chap. 5 and pp. 151–62 (the so-called simulacrum account of explanation, said to be based on Pierre Duhem's theory—from which van Fraassen also draws inspiration—that is, from Pierre Duhem, *The Aim and Structure of Physical Theory*, trans. Philip P. Wiener [New York: Atheneum, 1962]). See, also, Grover Maxwell, "The Ontological Status of Theoretical Entities," in *Minnesota Studies in the Philosophy of Science*, ed. Herbert Feigl and Grover Maxwell, vol. 3, *Scientific Explanation, Space, and Time* (Minneapolis: University of Minnesota Press, 1962), 3–27. A thorough (and sympathetic) analysis of Sellars's scientific realism is provided in James R. O'Shea, *Wilfrid Sellars: Naturalism with a Normative Turn* (Cambridge: Polity, 2007), chaps. 1, 2, and 7. O'Shea very tactfully admits his puzzlement in assessing Sellars's realist account of the fusion of the manifest and scientific images, a "fusion" I take to be completely unsatisfactory. I shall come back to this important issue.

29. John McDowell, *Mind and World*, with a new introduction (Cambridge, MA: Harvard University Press, 1994/1996), xii. For a revealing glimpse of Rorty's treatment of the Pittsburghers, see Richard Rorty, "The Very Idea of Human Answerability to the World: John McDowell's Version of Empiricism," *Truth and Progress*, vol. 3 of *Philosophical Papers* (Cambridge: Cambridge University Press, 1998), 138–52.

30. McDowell, *Mind and World*, xx, xxiv.

31. McDowell, *Mind and World*, xxiv. See, also, the following important papers: "Projection and Truth in Ethics" and "Two Sorts of Naturalism," both in John McDowell, *Mind, Value, and Reality* (Cambridge, MA: Harvard University Press, 1998), 151–66 and 167–97, respectively.

32. McDowell, *Mind and World*, 98–99. See, further, McDowell, "Intentionality as a Relation," the third of the Woodbridge Lectures, in *Having the World in View*, 44–65.

33. Sellars, "Empiricism," §36.

34. See McDowell, "Intentionality as a Relation," 46, for McDowell's objection to Sellars's interpretation of Kant's text. (McDowell finds Kant too lax on the issues.) My own sense is that Kant's analysis of perception cannot possibly pretend (any longer) to proceed fruitfully in the apriorist way and that McDowell is perfectly aware of the empirical complexities of describing the perception of languageless animals, human infants, *and* mature persons. Aristotle, it may be remarked, would not have agreed with McDowell's exceedingly assertive conviction. One begins to see, here, how far McDowell was deflected from Sellars's own themes, at the point

of Sellars's venturing the idea of "the space of reasons." See, also, the candid "Postscript to Lecture VI," in *Mind and World*, 181–87.

35. Sellars, "Scientific Image," 4–5.

36. Sellars, "Empiricism," §41 (p. 173 in the *Science, Perception and Reality* edition). This is, indeed, the passage O'Shea finds not a little baffling, though he's prepared to stand by Sellars. If I understand Sellars rightly, however, then the uncertainties (regarding the vague and the indeterminate) that arise within the phenomenology of perception and experience—*on which* scientific realism itself depends, an essential part of the argument against the "myth of the given"—explain Sellars's provisional eclipse or emendation of Kant's version of empirical realism. But, now, the botched fusion of the two images (in "Scientific Image") effectively defeats the final step in Sellars's claims in favor of scientism (scientific realism). It also explains why the scientistic variant of Protagoras's "measure" thesis cannot succeed. Sellars is perfectly aware of the conceptual daring of his proposal (see, particularly, "Empiricism" §§43–44).

37. Sellars, "Scientific Image," 39–40.

38. Ludwig Wittgenstein, *Philosophical Investigations*, trans. G. E. M. Anscombe (Oxford: Basil Blackwell, 1953), pt. 1, §219. See, also, John McDowell, "Wittgenstein on Following a Rule," in *Mind, Value, and Reality* (Cambridge, MA: Harvard University Press, 1998), 221–62.

39. See McDowell, introduction to *Mind and World*. Quietism, in the sense here indicated, is an essential but decidedly problematic (incompletely explicit) part of McDowell's philosophical practice, in *Mind and World*. I find it only very distantly Wittgensteinian.

40. See McDowell, "Logical Form of an Intuition." The Woodbridge Lectures (which include the essay just cited) comprise the first three chapters in the volume. See, also, Crispin Wright, "Human Nature?" (together with Wright's "Postscript to Chapter 8"), in *Reading McDowell: On Mind and World*, ed. Nicholas H. Smith (London: Routledge, 2002), 140–73, which rightly raises what amounts to the challenge of the Darwinian effect—that is, a question that is partly scientific and partly philosophical. Wright offers an ingenious alternative analysis of knowledge and "perceptual concepts." But I'm persuaded that the alternative is not strong enough, since it does not address the issue of conscious experience on the part of animals and human infants: processing information construed in the cybernetic sense—as distinct from nondiscursive but "perceptual experience"—does not quite account for animals' and infants' learning from perceptual experience. Issues of this kind press hard against the very idea of the use of the transcendental a priori—hence, against construing the discursive nature of the normative's requiring a priori grounds. There's the interlocking connection between cognition and normativity.

41. Brandom's discussion of the metaissues of "material inference" is extremely promising and sensible, but progress on actual propositionalized inferential schemata

remains extremely meager. What Brandom offers is pretty well confined, at most, to what discussants of the issue would concede without argument. See, particularly, Robert B. Brandom, *Making It Explicit: Reasoning, Representing, and Discursive Commitment* (Cambridge, MA: Harvard University Press, 1994), chap. 2; and Brandom, *Between Saying and Doing: Towards an Analytic Pragmatism* (Oxford: Oxford University Press, 2008).

Brandom's debt to Sellars rests with the shadowy implications of the famous line from Wilfrid Sellars, "Language, Rules and Behavior," in *Pure Pragmatics and Possible Worlds: The Early Essays of Wilfrid Sellars*, ed. Jeffrey F. Sicha (Atascadero, CA: Ridgeview, 1998/2005), 423: "the mode of existence of a rule [of material inference] is as a generalization written in flesh and blood, or nerve and sinew, rather than in pen and ink." Brandom follows Sellars quite explicitly, quoting Sellars (from the same essay): "the authority of these [material] rules [of inference, cast as material subjective conditionals] is not derivative from formal rules [that are not logically valid inferences, as they stand, but may be] indispensable [in deconstructing pertinently correct valid inferences]" (cited in *Making It Explicit*, 103). So there's a good deal of (justified) vagueness here. Sellars is always careful to emphasize the normative features of such inferential sequences. His texts, however, are not always easy to consult. I have found de Vries's *Wilfrid Sellars* to be a reliable and nearly indispensable guide; see particularly chaps. 2, 10.

42. Notice that, close to the start of his *Articulating Reasons*—Robert B. Brandom, *Articulating Reasons: An Introduction to Inferentialism* (Cambridge, MA: Harvard University Press, 2000)—Brandom says, straightforwardly enough (though, as I claim, equivocally), "The master idea that animates and orients this [Brandom's own] enterprise is that what distinguishes specifically *discursive* practices from the doings of non-concept-using creatures is their *inferential* articulation. To talk about concepts is to talk about roles in reasoning" (10–11). Brandon misleads us here.

Concepts (even if we suppose concepts to be primarily discursive, which I do not, and which—as I believe—Aristotle and both Dewey and Peirce do not) may, on an equivocal reading of Brandom's formulation, be, at once, (a) discursively structured, (b) inferentially articulated, and yet (c) expressed only in a nondiscursive way! In fact, this is, precisely, what Sellars says in speaking of "a rule of material inference . . . written in flesh and blood." (The difficulty we encounter here is the analogue of what, in the interpretation of paintings, is often called ecphrasis.)

So, there is a familiar sense in which a nonverbal action may indeed manifest a discursible content that may not be publicly expressed in the discursive way. Here, Sellars would say that we must (then) *interpret* the supposed conceptual content in an explicitly discursive way—which may thereupon compete in the marketplace of ideas against other such interpretations. What Sellars means here is not entirely clear. He seems to favor a realist view of competing discursive interpretations, but I'm inclined (particularly in pragmatic contexts) to favor a heuristic reading—in, say, the spirit of Weber's treatment of "ideal-types." Of course, to adopt such a stand is to reject the primacy of Brandom's inferentialism, though not its pertinence or usefulness.

But then, as I suppose, although the human agent (in Sellars's discussion and Brandom's theory) is indeed a person, a linguistically apt creature, interpretation will be needed, will have to consider the entire pertinent life of the creature before us, in order to determine how its expression may be cogently provided. I'm not persuaded that interpretation is likely to take an algorithmic form, such as would advance the cause of inferentialism or would be generated by applying algorithmic regularities already in place. In that sense, the model of what we require would *not* be adequately captured along inferentialist lines, though it would not disallow inferential ingredients either. That may explain why Brandom turns in the direction of AI simulation, discounts Dewey's so-called assimilationist tendencies, and moves so quickly to characterize his own method as a form of "conceptual pragmatism" (p. 4). See the entire introduction to Brandom's *Articulating Reasons* and *Between Saying and Doing*.

43. Brandom, *Articulating Reasons*, 5.

44. See Max Weber, "'Objectivity' in Social Science and Social Policy," in *Methodology of the Social Sciences*, trans. and ed. Edward A. Shils and Henry A. Finch (Glencoe, IL: Free Press, 1949), conveniently reprinted and accessible in Maurice Natanson, ed., *Philosophy of the Social Sciences: A Reader* (New York: Random House, 1963). Natanson's reader was published the same year as Sellars's *Science, Perception and Reality*. Natanson happens to include as well (in part 3) papers by Ernest Nagel and Carl Hempel, two of the principal champions of versions of the unity-of-science conception, who were completely baffled (as their papers confirm) by Weber's proposal regarding "ideal-types." But, of course, here, Weber counts as a figure straddling empirical sociology and sociologically centered philosophy of science—under the circumstance that the relationship between human and natural sciences remains *disputed*. Could either Sellars or Brandom concede substantially different methodologies to the human and natural sciences?

45. In his 1903 "Lectures on Pragmatism," Peirce says, very neatly, that "the question of pragmatism . . . is nothing else than the question of the logic of abduction" (5.195), where logic, characterized as the second of three "normative sciences" (including phenomenology and metaphysics), is defined thus: "if, as pragmatism teaches us, what we think is to be interpreted in terms of what we are prepared to do, then surely *logic*, or the doctrine of what we ought to think, must be an application of the doctrine of what we deliberately choose to do, which is Ethics" (5.35). The entire set of seven lectures, delivered at Harvard University, comprise book 1, vol. 5 of *Collected Papers of Charles Sanders Peirce*, eds. Charles Hartshorne and Paul Weiss (Cambridge, MA: Harvard University Press, 1934/1962). I take the entire set, but especially lectures 1 and 7, to provide the strongest evidence of the deep convergence between Peirce and Dewey and, indeed, of Dewey's reliance on Peirce's account of pragmatism and the normative nature of logic.

46. McDowell, *Mind and World*, 108–09; see, also, p. 70, for a remark on Weber.

47. See McDowell, *Mind and World*, 73.

48. McDowell, *Mind and World*, 3.

49. See Margolis, *Moral Philosophy after 9/11*.

50. Cited in McDowell's first Woodbridge Lecture, "Sellars on Perceptual Experience," in *Having the World in View*, 6.

51. McDowell, "The Constitutive Ideal of Rationality: Davidson and Sellars," in *Having the World in View*, 218.

52. McDowell, "Towards a Reading of Hegel on Action in the 'Reason' Chapter of the Phenomenology," in *Having the World in View*, 166, 184.

53. Quoted in Eduardo Mendieta, *The Adventures of Transcendental Philosophy: Karl-Otto Apel's Semiotics and Discourse Ethics* (Lanham, MD: Rowman & Littlefield, 2002), 122; the passage is from Karl-Otto Apel, "Normatively Grounding 'Critical Theory' through Recourse to the Life World? A Transcendental-Pragmatic Attempt to Think with Habermas against Habermas," in *Philosophical Interventions in the Unfinished Project of the Enlightenment*, ed. Axel Honneth et al., trans. Willian Rehg (Cambridge, MA: MIT Press, 1992), 125–70.

54. On Apel's assessment of Peirce's "failed Kantianism," see Margolis, "Charles Peirce's Abductive Turn." Apel's well-meant "coaxing" of Peirce's semiotics in at least an equivocal transcendental direction (chiefly supported by appeal to Peirce's early papers) appears, most explicitly, in Apel, *Toward a Transformation of Philosophy*, chaps. 3–5. In effect, Peirce's papers are made to yield the essential clue on which *Apel* reads Peirce as having superseded Kant's "ontological" reading of transcendentalism, the first or lowest phase of transcendentalism (according to Apel), but also (then) the second phase of First Philosophy (by way of Kant's "transcendental theory of consciousness").

According to his own account, Apel thereupon formulates the third (now supposedly adequate) confirmation of a "transcendental semiotics" based on Peirce's unified theory of signs. The trouble is, Apel takes it for granted that Peirce *had* indeed found the adequate transcendental-semiotic premise on which Apel's own proposal depends: I find no confirmatory argument in Apel. Peirce, I concede, was divided in his assessment of Kant in his early work. In fact, the fallibilism of the "infinite long run" *is* the most important expression of that equivocation. My own conjecture (in "Charles Peirce's Abductive Turn") is that Peirce worries about the contrived (quasi-mathematized, cognitively paradoxical) nature of the formula and, in the last decades of his life—in some measure as a result of Josiah Royce's direct challenge and (very probably) a dawning appreciation of Dewey's having exorcised idealism rather successfully—Peirce begins to see the advantage of (what I've tagged) his abductive turn, which promises to outflank his idealist ontology and his own quasi-mathematical fiddling and to manifest a greater respect for the paradoxes of epistemology (as First Philosophy), *post*-Kant. I find the "infinite long run" argument loosely equated with the abductive turn and abduction itself explicitly designated as the logic of pragmatism in the Harvard Lectures on pragmatism, delivered in 1903.

For a sense of what may be Apel's most compendious account of his own transcendental semiotics, see Karl-Otto Apel, "Transcendental Semiotics and the Paradigms of First Philosophy," in *From a Transcendental-Semiotic Point of View*, ed. Marianna Papastephanou (Manchester: Manchester University Press, 1998), 43–63. As for my impression that Apel goes much too far in counting on Peirce as a Kantian, see Peirce's "A Survey of Pragmaticism," in *Collected Papers of Charles Sanders Peirce*, vol. 5, bk. 3, chap. 1 (pp. 317–45). I think a straightforward reading of no more than the paper's first two paragraphs (5.464–5.465) should provide the antidote to Apel's handsome (but ultimately futile) gesture.

55. Karl-Otto Apel, "The A Priori of the Communication Community and the Foundations of Ethics: The Problem of a Rational Foundation of Ethics and the Scientific Age," in *Towards a Transformation of Philosophy*, trans. Glyn Adey and David Frisby (London: Routledge / Kegan Paul, 1980), 277; see, also, the closing pages of Apel's piece, pp. 278–85. See, further, regarding Apel's transcendentalism, "Transcendental Semiotics and the Paradigms of First Philosophy" and "Normatively Grounding 'Critical Theory' through Recourse to the Life World?" See, also, Jürgen Habermas, "Discourse Ethics: Notes on a Program of Phenomenological Justification," in *Moral Consciousness and Communicative Action*, trans. Christian Lenhardt and Shierry Weber Nicholsen (Cambridge, MA: MIT Press, 1990), 43–115.

56. See Brandom, *Making It Explicit*, chaps. 1, 3. See, also, Sellars, "Language, Rules and Behavior," *Pure Pragmatics and Possible Worlds*. As already remarked, Sellars explicitly says there, "The mode of existence of a rule [a rule of material inference] is as a generalization written in flesh and blood, or nerve and sinew, rather than in pen and ink" (123), and, in "Inference and Meaning" (in the same volume), Sellars says, "There is nothing to a conceptual apparatus that isn't determined by its rules, and there is no such thing as choosing these rules to conform with antecedently apprehended universals and connexions, for the 'apprehension of universals and connexions' is already the use of a conceptual frame, and as such presupposes the rules in question" (237). Nevertheless, he adds, almost immediately, "We recognize that there are an indefinite number of possible conceptual structures (languages) or systems of formal and material rules, each one of which can be regarded as a candidate for adoption by the animal which recognizes rules, and no one of which has an intuitable hallmark of royalty. They must compete in the market place of practice for employment by language users, and be content to be adopted haltingly and schematically" (237). But how "compete"? And how determinately can we specify "haltingly" and "schematically" in context? All of this is, of course, very close to Brandom's sketch of Sellars's views (*Making It Explicit*, 102–07).

Brandom adds, in part citing Sellars and in part glossing Sellars's strenuous account, "Subjunctive conditionals . . . are the expression of material rules of inference, but . . . the authority of these rules is not derivative from formal rules," and "even though material subjunctive conditionals may be dispensable . . . it may nevertheless be the case that the function performed in natural languages by material subjunctive conditions is indispensable" (*Making It Explicit*, 103). Brandom explicitly says, "these [material inferences] are not logically valid inferences" (103). I find it hard to picture, as contributions to a unified account of "material inference" (which, in Sellars's view, *cannot be discerned semantically*, though it can be interpreted propositionally), such loosely linked ingredients as Sellars's strong reading of rules, the disjunction between logically and materially valid inferences, the indefinite plurality of competing inferential interpretations, the tendency to offer as exemplars of pertinent subjunctive conditionals those that implicate covering laws—without a workable sketch of how the interpretive results are to be tested and Sellars's justificatory procedures fleshed out. But Sellars is notably sanguine about his program. Brandom is as convinced as Sellars, but he adds very little to the argument needed—for instance, regarding how, precisely, to match a propositionalized inference to a rule "written in flesh and blood." The difficulties collected are serious enough to threaten the primacy of inferentialism itself. (Inferentialism appears to be inherently subaltern.)

57. Brandom, *Making It Explicit*, 5. Compare Brandom, *Between Saying and Doing*.

58. See Stephen P. Turner, *Explaining the Normative* (Cambridge: Polity), 60–63, for a sense of the deflection. For materials on Winch, Mauss, Weber, and Kelsen, see Turner, chaps. 2–4.

59. It's worth mentioning that Sellars's use of the "space of reasons" is clearly linked to his intuition (almost a gloss on the opening pages of Wittgenstein's *Investigations*) regarding the similarity between a child's first learning to respond to a word and a dog's learning to do something similar—hence, of course, bearing on Kant's account of the "spontaneity" of the understanding's transcendental resources, which McDowell makes so much of in the Woodbridge Lectures. Compare, in this regard, Sellars's remarks about animal intelligence in "Language, Rules and Behavior," which McDowell does not address, but which (per Wittgenstein, whose views McDowell very much admires) might have elicited a more engaged response.

60. Turner, *Explaining the Normative*, 148.

61. See, particularly, Turner, *Explaining the Normative*, pp. 113–14 and chap. 5, especially p. 129. See, also, Robert B. Brandom, "Freedom and Constraint by Norms," *American Philosophical Quarterly* 16 (1979): 187–96 (particularly p. 192); Wilfrid Sellars, "Imperatives, Intentions, and the Logic of 'Ought,'" in *Morality and the Language of Conduct*, ed. Hector-Neri Castañeda and George Nakhnikian (Detroit: Wayne State University Press, 1956), 203; and McDowell, *Mind and World*, 34–36. Turner cites all three passages. What, as I read him, Turner effectively shows is that the abiding transcendental dualism of Kant's first *Critique*, the dualism of causality (nature) and autonomy or freedom (normativity), which Cassirer does not disavow among his own neo-Kantian revisions, is an essential feature of the meaning

of "the space of reasons" that the Pittsburghers invoke. I find in this a devastatingly compelling objection to McDowell's quietism, since this quietism keeps McDowell from actually addressing the normativity issue in any explicit way.

62. McDowell, *Mind and World*, 35–36. Here, McDowell explicitly invokes the relevance of Gadamer's "fusion of horizons." It's remarkable that Kelsen's theory of the *Grundnorm* of positive law should have hit on an analogue of the Sellarsian thesis. But then both figures are engaged in recovering the nerve of Kant's account of normativity. For a sense of Kelsen's treatment of the relationship between "positive" and "constitutional" law, intended to be read in just this spirit, see the passage cited from Kelsen, *General Theory of Norms* ([1979] 1991), in Turner, *Explaining the Normative*, 75.

63. See Wittgenstein, *Philosophical Investigations*, pt. 1, §621.

Notes to Chapter Thirteen

1. Sen has mounted a very strong critique of Rawls's theory of justice, and of liberal economic theory in general, in a larger discussion of economic inequality and interpersonal comparisons of utility and value. He demonstrates how formal comparisons fail to come to grips with the actual differences in the lives of would-be consumers of commodities. The argument centers on the paradoxes of the measurement of economic inequality. But the corrections needed would require a thorough knowledge of the actual circumstances in which consumers are in a position *to use* their apparent entitlements in ways that actually fulfill them. I find a pertinent analogy here, admittedly lax on formal grounds but entirely apt in terms of political "capacitation," between interpersonal comparisons of utility and international comparisons of justice in world politics. I mention this only as a suggestion for reflecting on the implications of 9/11. See Amartya Sen, *On Economic Inequality*, exp. ed. (Oxford: Clarendon Press, 1997), especially the annexe to the expanded edition, "*On Economic Inequality* after a Quarter Century," by James Foster and Amartya Sen. See also John Rawls, *A Theory of Justice* (Cambridge, MA: Harvard University Press, 1971). Sen's emphasis is always on the practical functioning of human beings in the circumstances of their actual lives, bypassing all contextless or merely mathematized measures of interpersonal comparisons. But, of course, his purpose is to correct methodological abuses in a humane way.

2. I take constructivism to be distinct from idealism, although Kant, as opposed to Hegel, is both a constructivist and an idealist. I use the term primarily to signify that a viable realism with respect to scientific knowledge must escape the paradoxes of pre-Kantian philosophy or epistemology, which it accomplishes by affirming that, relative to objective knowledge, there can be no principled disjunction between cognizer and cognized. Pre-Kantian realism, often called Cartesianism, assumes the opposite. Idealists (Kant, for instance, as a transcendental idealist)

believe one way or another that we literally construct the world we know from the representational materials of the mind—that is, from the formative powers of understanding. Hegel, for instance, as a new kind of empiricist, holds that what we construct is a picture or conception of the world-presented-in-experience, not the world itself—and certainly not in any of Kant's paradoxical senses. Kant is a unique figure in this regard. He holds, for transcendental reasons, that knowledge entails a grasp of the necessary conceptual and perceptual structures of the world we know—and (in a sense) construct or constitute. Hegel, however, construes the conceptual and perceptual structures we impute to the world as the result of the contingent and evolving work of our reflexive account of the world-as-we-experience-it. (These distinctions are very laxly formulated here.) The advantage of the Hegelian account is that it helps to show the sense in which the objectivity of science and morality is seen to depend essentially on the same subjective conditions—in a way that yields maximal flexibility, without paradox, wherever needed. In particular, Hegel's account shows by its own example (apart from Hegel's personal convictions) how objectivity in science and morality can be coherently construed in constructivist terms, can be historicized, and can even adjust the notions of objective validity and legitimation in relativistic ways, without yielding to Kantian idealism. The account I offer *is* Hegelian, but only in the broadest and most generous sense. I take Hegel's *Phenomenology* more as a heuristic guide than an accurate model of how to construct an objective science and morality. The validity of the account I offer does not rely at all on Hegel's specific arguments. I venture to say that a viable philosophy in our time, whether with regard to science or morality, cannot fail to be Hegelian in the heuristic sense I favor. But I don't deny that a good account of science or morality may well favor some later, sparer Hegelian strategy—perhaps a version of pragmatism, for instance, or perhaps an account like the one I offer here. See G. W. F. Hegel, *The Phenomenology of Spirit*, trans. A. V. Miller (Oxford: Clarendon Press, 1957).

3. Here I begin to fill out my general philosophical orientation and my use of Hegelian themes. I give fair warning that I favor a heterodox reading of Hegel. I emphasize, however, certain philosophical issues that may not seem particularly pertinent at first glance—and the contributions spanning Kant and Hegel in particular—in assessing the reasonableness of the moral theory I am advancing. Frankly, I don't believe it is possible to assess the validity of any moral theory entirely apart from the fortunes of certain large philosophical visions. If Aristotle's or Descartes's or Kant's theories of knowledge and reality were true, then moral philosophy would (in my opinion) have to be very different from what I suggest counts as a reasonable theory now!

4. Effectively, I mean to favor by this epithet whatever may be defensibly yielded by confirming my account within the terms of a second-best morality—that is, either by rejecting any moral realism that draws objective moral norms from our cognition of independent nature or the independent world (or from revealed

sources, for that matter) *or* by affirming a constructivist realism based on the initial data of our *Sitten*. In my view, that would preclude realisms of both the natural-law sort and the Darwinian sort. See, for example, Edward O. Wilson, *On Human Nature* (Cambridge, MA: Harvard University Press, 1978); and Daniel C. Dennett, *Darwin's Dangerous Idea: Evolution and the Meanings of Life* (New York: Simon and Schuster, 1995).

    5. In a sense, my entire labor has been centered on the analysis of what it is to be a self or person. In a curious way, that is also the phantom issue that hovers over the work of both Kant and Hume. I'm persuaded that Hegel thought Kant lacked a coherent account of what a specifically human person is (as opposed to Kant's transcendental subject); Thomas Reid found Hume's *Treatise of Human Nature* to be a scandal for the same reason English-language analytic philosophy has proved to be notoriously shy about airing the cultural complexities of human nature. And in continental philosophy—even in the work of figures like Husserl, Heidegger, Althusser, Lacan, Levinas, and Foucault—specific discussions of the self are notoriously unclear and deficient. For a more ramified sense of the principal themes of my own account, I suggest Margolis, *Historied Thought, Constructed World: A Conceptual Primer for the Turn of the Millennium* (Berkeley: University of California Press, 1995). My intuition here is that it is impossible to give an account of either science or morality without a careful analysis of the self (whatever one's objections to treating the self as an entity may be). The essential considerations are these: that the analysis of the nature of the human self and the possibility of an objective morality (or science) are not independent inquiries, that philosophical accounts of the self are wildly diverse, and that these facts are largely ignored.

    6. I take the Aristotelian and Kantian traditions to be the most influential in Western moral philosophy. Both, I think, are seriously defective. Here, I single out Rawls and Habermas as the most important contemporary Kantians on moral/political questions and return, very lightly, a number of times, to their particular views. Both, I would say, exhibit the characteristic abstractness and relative indifference to context that mark Kant's own critical emphasis. Rawls, for instance, requires—in *A Theory of Justice*—the posit of an "initial position" that blocks or disallows an agent's knowledge of their own personal history, knowledge that Rawls insists cannot be called on if we are to construct a "rational" account of justice. (He's got things topsy-turvy, I'm afraid.) Habermas insists on strict universality in formulating the "rational" principles of morality. But then, he finds it impossible to decide whether he himself is an adherent of the Critical Kant or of a Hegelianized Kant, or of a pragmatized or Marxified or Frankfurt-Critical Kant, which affects the logic of universality itself. I regard both Rawls's and Habermas's notions as completely unworkable. See Jürgen Habermas, "Discourse Ethics: Notes on a Program of Philosophical Justification," in *Moral Consciousness and Communicative Action*, trans. Christian Lenhardt and Shierry Weber Nicholsen (Cambridge, MA: MIT Press, 1990), 43–115.

7. I touch here on an extraordinarily important but difficult metaphysical matter, the full implications of which I only partly understand. But I must venture a clue at least. In holding that selves are hybrid artifacts, that selves have Intentional natures as culturally emergent entities, or in suggesting that selves have (or are) histories rather than that they have natures (as *Homo sapiens* does), I mean to contrast physically formed phenomena and culturally emergent phenomena. I hold that the cultural is indissolubly incarnate, or embodied, in the physical (or material) world. But, in the sense in which physical things are said to possess determinate properties (size and shape and mass, for instance), cultural phenomena are, qua Intentional (that is, culturally significant—interpretable and subject to historical transformation), determinable only. Though the formal distinction is still too crude, I mean by this that the conceptual relationship between the determinate and the determinable is systematically different in the analysis of the physical and the cultural. The contrast is particularly helpful in analyzing the description, interpretation, and appraisal of moral deeds, history, artworks, speech, and the like, which I collect as what human selves utter (make, say, do, create). I regard it as astonishing that these themes first take their familiar form, in the West at least, only after the French Revolution—in Hegel, of course, in their most masterful early form. There's a great deal that needs to be clarified here, without which, I would say, moral theory cannot fail to be unacceptably primitive. The best explorations of these themes that I have been able to pursue are centered in the analysis of the fine arts. For a promising sample, but hardly more, see Margolis, *Interpretation Radical but Not Unruly: The New Puzzle of the Arts and History* (Berkeley: University of California Press, 1995).

Index

Abrams, Meyer, 243
abduction, 4–7, 10, 389–90, 410–13, 417, 430–31, 442, 450, 539, 543–45
abortion, 355, 365, 458, 468, 470–71
Adorno, Theodor, 195
Aeschylus, 102, 310
aesthetics: analytic, xiii; 295–300, 321–47 *passim*; theories of, 258–59, 267, 271, 301–5, 478
American Civil War, 2, 254, 466
American Constitution, 254
American foreign policy, 452, 469
analytic-synthetic, 3–4, 12–20, 104, 112, 126, 142, 176, 324–27, 408, 445
anarchism, 33, 49, 55, 60, 61, 353, 384, 480
anthropocentrism, 133
anthropology: and ethics, 113, 272, 395, 459; philosophical, xiii, 404–5, 433, 443
anthropomorphism, 129, 155, 177–79, 197–203, 211, 225–27, 231, 238, 259
Apel, Karl-Otto, 103, 142, 195, 351, 354, 356, 359, 361, 381, 383, 405, 410, 438–40, 446–47, 482n32, 544–45n54

a priori: and *a posteriori*, 12–17, 118–22, 130–35, 142, 324–27, 439, 541; and necessity, 3, 44, 69, 74–81, 120–26, 382–83, 405–11, 365–66, 408, 445
Anscombe, Elizabeth, 91–92, 487n61
Aquinas, Thomas, 98, 105, 282, 365–66, 369, 371, 373
Aristotle, xv, 13, 24–25, 27–28, 45, 81, 98, 101–2, 104–5, 107–8, 110–15, 118, 125, 140, 147–51, 165, 168, 170–71, 173, 181, 184–85, 195–96, 205, 221, 263–69, 282, 286–87, 293–97, 299, 306, 351–54, 360–61, 367–72, 374–81, 383, 419, 446, 455, 463, 482n31, 491n21, 492n30, 499n17, 507n8, 529–30n2, 540n34, 548n3
art: and beauty, 100, 271; as intentional, 24, 234–42, 294–98, 307–14, 319, 323–46; defining art, 289–300, 304–12 *passim*, 321–47 *passim*; theories of, 258–59, 267, 271, 301–5, 478
art interpretation, 24–28, 42, 53, 224–25, 232–33, 239, 292–95, 307–19, 337–46
Auden, Wystan Hugh, 257
Austin, John Langshaw, 123

Ayala, Francisco, 101

Balzac, Honoré de, 30, 253, 303–4
Barthes, Roland, 30, 38, 45, 243, 253, 302–4, 313, 316, 329, 513n28, 526n19
Bauman, Zygmunt, 358
Beardsley, Monroe, xii, xv, 28, 31, 39, 41, 246, 257, 294–302, 304–6, 311, 315–16, 321–22, 326, 328–30, 339, 344, 523n12, 526n19
behaviorism, 207, 325, 342, 508
Berlin, Isaiah, 357
Bernstein, Richard, 52–56, 58–59, 480–81n4, 482n27
Bhaskar, Roy, 94
Bildung. See culture
biologism, 98, 105, 108, 114
biology, 11, 13, 18, 100, 103–9, 113, 118, 191–94, 207, 286–87, 407
Bloom, Harold, 38, 316, 329
Bourdieu, Pierre, 204, 232–33
brain, 179, 228–29, 292, 342, 489
Brand, Myles, 487n63
Brandom, Robert, xii, 4, 19, 119, 403, 417, 420–22, 425, 427–31, 440–42, 445, 447, 538n19, 541–42n41, 542–43n42, 545–46n56
Braudel, Fernand, 226, 514n33
Brentano, Franz, 36, 153–54, 165, 195, 213, 311, 326
Bruner, Jerome, 197, 201, 504–5n1
Bunge, Mario, 187, 499n16
Burke, Edmund, 9

Campbell, James, 531n6
Carnap, Rudolf, 2, 4, 7, 9, 19, 68–69, 101–2, 108, 112, 125, 195, 488n1
Cartwright, Nancy, 5, 77, 80, 161, 390, 397, 484–85n23, 511n24, 537n15, 539n22, 540n28

Cassirer, Ernst, 2–3, 15, 118–20, 128, 141–42, 153, 274, 390, 409–11, 413–14, 422, 492n29, 537n12, 538n22, 546n61
Castoriadis, Cornelius, 226
categorical imperative, 356, 390–404, 413, 422, 436, 438, 536–37
categories: of language, 10, 234–36, 275–77, 437; of knowledge, 13–14, 17, 50, 107, 118–25, 133–34, 140, 153, 313
causality, 77–82; in agency, 88–94, 398–401, 413, 432, 537; in fate, 72–74; in science, 17, 66–75, 83–86, 114, 175; in society, 221
causation, 80, 114, 537
certainty: and apriori, 12, 62, 121, 129, 285; and subjectivity, 52, 127, 448
Cezanne, Paul, 336
Chomsky, Noam, 83, 87–88, 156, 178, 193, 196–97, 199–201, 213, 275–76, 425, 489n5, 496n6, 496n7, 504n1, 505n3, 506n5, 508n11, 510n21
Christianity, 369; and the Bible, 254, 296
Churchland, Paul, 9, 81, 162, 172, 217, 498n13, 500n23, 504n38, 511–12n25
common sense, 232, 413, 423
consciousness, 131–34, 139, 197, 265, 379, 425
continental philosophy, xiii–xiv, 1, 101, 107, 110, 128, 186–87, 323, 327–28, 341, 549
Culler, Jonathan, 243
culture: and enculturation, xi–xvii, 11, 23–39, 108–9, 136, 141, 192, 233–40, 266–70, 280–84, 297, 462–65; and nature, 19, 97–103,

111–15, 159–60, 181–83, 286–88, 315–18, 344–45, 461; and mind, 137–39, 151–57, 168–71, 191–230 *passim*

Damasio, Antonio, 230
Danto, Arthur, xii, xv–xvi, 36–37, 40–41, 181, 244, 315, 321, 326, 336–39, 344, 497n8, 502n32, 523n16, 524n35
Darwin, Charles, 11, 13, 100–1, 103–5, 107–8, 113, 118–19, 121, 136, 193, 395, 405, 437, 489n5
da Vinci, Leonardo, 223, 309, 513n31
Davidson, Donald, 53, 63–64, 80–81, 89–92, 119, 128, 157–61, 169, 184, 195, 224, 327, 363–64, 385, 393, 437, 482n32, 497n9, 503n34, 507n7, 509n15, 514n32
Davies, Stephen, 478n5, 522n3
Dawkins, Richard, 101, 283, 489n5, 502n31
deconstruction, 67–75 *passim*, 83–84, 236, 332–33, 340–41, 358
democracy, 470
Democritus, 147, 499n21
Dennett, Daniel, 10, 81, 93, 223, 499n19, 501n23, 513n30
determinism, 69–70, 148, 158, 162, 388, 398
Dewey, John, xii, 1, 4–6, 95, 103–4, 119, 121–23, 195, 278, 345, 353, 403, 422, 429, 431, 442, 460, 495n4, 531n6, 542–43n42, 543n45, 544n54
Derrida, Jacques, xii, 95, 236, 340, 343, 358, 526n19
Descartes, René, 8–9, 12, 18, 54, 103–5, 118–19, 123, 169, 173, 191–96, 200, 231, 340, 458, 461–62, 506n7, 548n3

Descombes, Vincent, 9
Dickie, George, 336
Dilthey, Wilhelm, 42, 105, 119, 153, 195, 278, 300, 328, 360
discourse ethics, 356–57, 362, 438
Dretske, Fred, 179, 502n28
dualism, 116, 140, 283, 286, 413, 445, 500–501; of mind-body, 8–9, 20, 114, 169–74, 177–78, 200
Duhem, Pierre, 512n26
Dürer, Albrecht, 186, 291, 309, 314
Dworkin, Ronald, 351, 535n73

economics, 394, 465, 547
education, 465
Elisabeth, Princess of Bohemia, 9
emergence: and physicalism, 69, 175–77, 184, 227–28, 343–44, 425, 499; of art, xvii, 290–92; of culture, 100, 105–9, 112–14, 117, 159, 163, 175–77, 180, 185–88, 202, 208, 215, 220, 227, 238–41, 280, 462, 503; of mind, 138, 154–56, 172, 197, 227, 238; of selves, xvi, 119, 136–37, 175, 227, 260, 281–84, 359, 392–93, 403, 463–64
emotion, 129, 139, 230, 239, 379, 380, 516
empiricism, 52, 78, 103–5, 265, 321, 325, 330, 337, 392, 415, 421, 509; logical, xii, 2, 247; and positivism, xii, 1–2, 73, 98, 161, 187, 221, 269, 322, 499, 511
enculturation, xi–xvii, 11, 23–39, 108–10, 136, 141, 192, 233–40, 266–70, 280–84, 297, 462–65; as *Bildung*, xvi, 8–18, 104, 110–18, 136, 141, 265, 399, 401, 414, 437, 536
environment, 196–97, 489, 504
environmentalism, 472

epiphenomenalism, 114
epistemology, 11–12, 20, 54, 61–62, 120–21, 324, 331, 342, 359, 506, 509; naturalizing it, 181, 212, 216, 221, 284, 326–28
equality, 465, 547
essentialism, xv, 26, 49, 52, 58–62, 81–82, 104, 290, 293, 336, 352, 360, 367–71, 460
ethics, 268, 352, 356–57, 369–79, 434, 438, 446, 452–56
ethics, 127, 268, 352, 356–57, 369, 375–79, 434, 438–46, 452–56
Evans, Gareth, 437
evil, 401, 452–55
evolution: cosmic, 125; cultural, 15, 18, 94, 101, 136, 238, 407; Darwinian, 11, 13, 18, 100, 103–9, 113, 118, 191–94, 207, 286–87, 407
experiment, 5, 76–80, 88, 250, 312

fallibility, 4–7, 126, 438, 544
Faraday, Michael, 5
Feigl, Herbert, 158, 247, 497n10
Feyerabend, Paul, 60, 63, 161, 363, 479–80n20, 480n2, 498n12, 511–12n25, 539n22
Fichte, Johann Gottlieb, 152, 285, 495n4
firstness, 125, 205
Fish, Stanley, 302–3, 316, 329
flux. *See* process philosophy
Fodor, Jerry, 193, 196, 502n30, 505n3, 518n33
Foucault, Michel, 25, 34–35, 41–42, 95, 105, 123–24, 152–53, 168, 195, 199, 204, 221, 223, 226, 232, 272, 302, 304, 328, 340, 342, 354, 358, 371, 460–61, 513n28, 549n5
foundationalism, xv, 11, 49, 52–54, 58, 62, 110, 321, 346, 390, 509

Fraassen, Bas van, 69, 161, 389–90, 397, 415, 511n24
Frankfurt School, 2, 105, 396, 414, 417, 438, 442–46
freedom: and culture, 99, 265, 285, 313, 436–37, 537; and indeterminism, 148, 382, 398–402, 432
Frege, Gottlob, 2, 4, 18, 119, 195, 277, 403, 405, 431, 441
French, Steven, 17
Freud, Sigmund, 73–74, 85–86, 89, 93, 213, 223, 232, 510n21, 513n31

Gadamer, Hans-Georg, 42, 53, 58–59, 70–73, 113, 123–24, 168, 187, 195, 198–99, 202, 204–5, 226, 232, 253, 300–302, 328, 340, 351, 353, 355, 360–63, 368, 371–72, 480–81n4, 506n6, 508n13, 512–13n27, 547n62
Galison, Peter, 250–51
Garver, Newton, 278
Galileo, 15, 107
Geach, Peter, 253, 429
generals: constructed, 379; ontological, 167, 376–78
gesture, 243, 307, 429
Gewirth, Alan, 351, 354
Gibson, James J., 179, 419, 437
Giere, Ronald, 397
Goethe, Johann Wolfgang von, 98, 232
Goldman, Alvin, 216, 514n32
Goodman, Nelson, xv, 62, 195, 239, 241–42, 244, 247, 292, 315, 321, 330–36, 339, 341, 344, 485n35, 507n9
Gracia, Jorge, 240–42, 244, 246–47
Greenblatt, Stephen, 258, 316
Greimas, Algirdas Julien, 155
Grene, Marjorie, 287, 490n8

Grünbaum, Adolf, 70–75, 81, 85–87, 93, 486n44

Habermas, Jürgen, 4, 53, 70–75, 103, 142, 153, 195, 351, 353–54, 356–64, 371, 374, 376–77, 381, 383, 405, 410, 438–40, 446–47, 464–65, 532n20, 549n6
Hacking, Ian, 5, 64, 79–80
Hampshire, Stuart, 370–71
Hawking, Stephen, 9, 98
Hegel, Georg Wilhelm Friedrich, xiii, xvi, 2, 41–43, 72–73, 95, 98–100, 104–36 *passim*, 142, 152–53, 168, 195, 204, 226, 237, 265, 267–68, 270–80, 283–85, 306, 328, 345, 353–57, 362, 400, 411, 436, 457–64, 488n2, 492n30, 531n6, 532n20, 547–48n2, 548n3, 549n5, 550n7
Heidegger, Martin, 2, 42, 84, 95, 99, 102–5, 107, 119, 123–24, 126, 128–29, 131, 134, 139–42, 195, 269, 278, 281–82, 328, 340, 360, 460, 506n6, 536n9
Hempel, Carl, 4, 19, 68–70, 92, 160, 390, 543n44
Heraclitus, 147, 264
Herder, Johann Gottfried, 98, 108, 123, 268, 422
hermeneutic circle, 219–23, 235–40, 298, 300, 303, 325, 495–96
hermeneutics, 2, 40, 46, 57–59, 73, 105, 186, 198, 246–48, 253, 259, 296, 333–35, 340–41, 360–62, 445
Hesse, Mary, 53
Hirsch, Eric Donald, 28, 31, 39–41, 246, 296–302, 304–6, 311, 315–16, 329, 512n27
historicism, xv–xvii, 50–51, 58–59, 107–12, 150–73, 171–89 *passim*, 248, 252–53, 278–86, 301–5, 341–47, 353–59, 366–73, 376, 384

historicity: of humanity, 11, 14–19, 117–22, 143–44, 168–88 *passim*, 195–210, 230–37, 258–63, 273–74, 294; of knowledge, 32, 37, 44–45, 54, 62, 70–72, 95, 223, 251–53, 361–66, 450–53
historiography, 325
history, 14, 20, 67, 73, 138–39, 147–72, 180–86, 196–99, 221–24, 236–38, 252–53, 271–74, 280–83, 300–7, 316–19, 360–63, 371–74, 447–52; and enculturation, xi–xvii, 11, 23–39, 108–9, 117–18, 152–62, 192, 225–40, 259–70 *passim*, 280–84, 297, 301–14, 372–89, 409, 432, 462–65
Hobbes, Thomas, 378, 458, 467
Horkheimer, Max, 42
human sciences, 65, 77, 90–95, 161, 188, 297–99, 392; and natural sciences, 70–77, 207, 217, 268, 284, 393, 461, 513
humanism, xii, xv
human nature, 41, 66, 108, 111, 203, 264–66, 368–71, 431, 454–57, 465, 473, 530, 549
Humboldt, Wilhelm von, 98, 422
Hume, David, xv–xvi, 76, 90–91, 105, 108, 115, 123, 135–36, 138, 143, 191–94, 196, 252, 351, 374, 378, 506n7, 509n17, 511n22, 529–30n2, 549n5
Husserl, Edmund, xvii, 2–3, 7, 12–16, 18, 36, 52, 67, 101–7, 110, 118, 121–36 *passim*, 140–43, 153–54, 165, 193, 195, 207, 266, 269, 272, 282, 299, 301–3, 311, 340, 342, 423, 493n38, 505n2, 549n5

idealism, 4, 66, 99, 134, 153, 231, 236, 269, 323, 335; and realism, 120, 135, 182, 343, 381

imagination, 271, 296–97, 335, 339, 380
indeterminacy, 29, 40, 60, 84, 210–12, 224, 294–96, 324–25, 375
individualism, 368
individuality, 70, 206
induction, 93, 331, 430, 485
Ingarden, Roman, 299–301, 525n45
intentionality, 65, 86–9, 109, 235–36; and art, 24, 234–42, 294–98, 307–14, 319, 323–46; and culture, xvii, 35–42, 115, 150–51, 172–81, 184–99, 203–16, 248–60, 304, 314–19, 420–26; and mind, 13, 43–46, 137–39, 152–69, 188–98, 202–11, 217–28, 239–46, 393, 401, 404, 495–96, 501–2; and personhood, 36, 155, 192, 200, 205–8, 224, 233–35, 420–26
interpretation, xv, 37, 107, 121, 163, 169, 180, 208–9, 219–20, 430; of art, 24–28, 42, 53, 224–25, 232–33, 239, 292–95, 307–19, 337–46; of texts, xvii, 30, 36–38, 41, 45, 157–59, 163–66, 222–27, 236–60 *passim*, 295–306, 328–30, 384–85, 428
invariance: as lawful, 69–76, 79–81, 94–95, 406; as metaphysical, 25, 28, 147–52, 265, 270, 273, 297, 316, 367, 376; as modal, 26, 293, 306, 351–54, 363, 367, 378–86 *passim*
Iser, Wolfgang, 299–306, 311, 315–16, 329
Islam, 224, 452, 456, 469–70

James, Henry, 268, 369, 375, 378–81
James, William, xii, 123
justice, 194, 549

Kant, Immanuel, xiii, xv–xvi, 2–5, 7–8, 12–18, 52, 67, 98–99, 103–8, 110–11, 113, 115–31 *passim*, 135–36, 141–43, 152–54, 191–96, 209–10, 231, 265–69, 271, 273–74, 276–78, 282–85, 340, 351–56, 360–62, 388–91, 394, 396–427 *passim*, 431–32, 437–40, 442, 445, 447–48, 455, 459–61, 463–65, 511n22, 537n12, 537n15, 540n34, 544n54, 547–48n2, 548n3, 549n5
Kelsen, Hans, 443–49, 547n62
Kiefer, Anselm, 43
Kierkegaard, Soren, 119, 123
Kim, Jaegwon, xvi, 101–2, 114, 116–17, 247, 491n22
Klee, Paul, 23–24
Korsgaard, Christine, 391, 397–401, 405, 410, 447, 536n7, 537n12, 537n15
knowledge, 10–11, 23, 141–42, 149, 211–16, 248, 327, 345, 411, 415–16, 461; and categories, 13–14, 17, 50, 107, 118–25, 133–34, 140, 153, 313; as historical, 32, 37, 44–45, 54, 62, 70–72, 95, 223, 251–53, 361–66, 450–53; and perception, 413–26, 432; and truth, 10, 121–22, 220, 234–35, 266, 285–57, 306, 406–8, 459
Kuhn, Thomas, 25, 34–35, 39, 41, 53–55, 60–61, 63–64, 105, 112, 121, 161, 182, 223, 250, 284, 306, 363

Lakatos, Imre, 53
language: categories in, 10, 234–36, 275–77, 437; personhood in, 16–20, 155–57, 192–93, 200–3, 392–94, 412, 447–48
Laplace, Pierre-Simon, 382
Leibniz, Gottfried Wilhelm, 141, 249, 345
Levinas, Emmanuel, 140, 269, 282, 358

Levinson, Jerrold, 515–16n7
Levi-Strauss, Claude, 62, 232–33, 496n7
Lewis, Clarence Irving, 2, 4, 7, 121–22, 128, 141–42
liberalism, 341, 368, 439
literature, 297, 313–14, 333, 380
literary criticism, 295–300, 312–19
Locke, John, 110, 192–94, 214, 226, 511n22
logic, 27, 61–62, 68, 164, 218, 346, 383–85; and bivalence, 27–44 *passim*, 48, 218, 248, 293–99, 307, 332, 383–86, 474–75
Lovibond, Sabina 351, 353–55, 371–72
Lyotard, Jean-Francois, 352, 358

Macbeth, Danielle, 4
MacIntyre, Alasdair, 53, 351, 353, 355, 361, 364–74, 376–77, 383, 443, 455
Mackie, John Leslie, 352–53, 375
MacKinnon, Catharine, 351, 358
Marx, Karl, 42, 94–95, 105, 119, 121, 123, 195, 204–5, 226, 232, 278, 328, 354–55, 451, 460, 508n13
mathematics, 3–7, 17, 20, 97
Mauss, Marcel, 443
McDowell, John, 18–19, 104, 108–22 *passim*, 125, 395, 403–4, 410–27 *passim*, 431–32, 435–38, 442–47, 492n30, 540n34
Mead, George Herbert, 103, 117, 123, 136
Meinong, Alexius, 167
memory, 9, 13, 210, 212, 235, 251, 305, 471–72
Merleau-Ponty, Maurice, 103, 123–24, 521n31
metaphysics, 110, 115, 127, 147, 168, 169–80, 189, 266, 340, 426
Michelangelo, 157, 239, 308
Milton, John, 44, 303

mind: and body, 8–9, 20, 114, 169–74, 177–78, 200; and culture, 137–39, 151–57, 168–71, 191–230 *passim*; emergence of, 138, 154–56, 172, 197, 227, 238; and intentionality, 13, 43–46, 137–39, 152–69, 188–98, 202–11, 217–28, 239–46, 393, 401, 404, 495–96, 501–2
Moore, George Edward, 153, 159, 195, 214, 497n9
morality, 365, 368, 475; as historicized, 370–74, 462; as intuitive, 351, 362, 400; as objective, 386; as *sittlich*, 41–45, 270–73, 279, 352–55, 461–75; historicity of, 459–64, 473–75; truth of, 454, 460, 470
Murdoch, Iris, 202
Murphey, Murray, 121

Nagel, Thomas, 505–6n5
naturalism, 70–77, 207, 217, 268, 284, 393, 461, 513
nature: and persons, 83, 115–16, 176, 203, 282, 408–9, 419–26, 500–501; and culture, 19, 97–103, 111–15, 159–60, 181–83, 286–88, 315–18, 344–45, 461; and science, 69, 175–77, 184, 227–28, 343–44, 425, 499
Nazism, 1, 43, 180, 296, 370, 400, 472
necessity, 3, 44, 69, 74–81, 95, 98, 117, 120–26, 142, 156–63, 245, 254, 408–11; modal, 26, 293, 306, 351–54, 363, 367, 378–86 *passim*; as nomological, 75, 78, 85, 388
Neurath, Otto, 5, 397
Newton, Isaac, 233, 389–90, 396, 408
Nietzsche, Friedrich, 42, 123, 168, 195, 202, 204, 226, 278, 328, 354, 396, 460

Nicholas of Cusa, 6
nominalism, 42, 82, 246, 321,
  331–34, 341, 377, 485
normativity, 112, 127, 178, 390–98,
  401–28, of *sittlich*, 204, 270–73,
  374–77, 404–47, 417, 422, 433,
  436, 445–59 *passim*
Nussbaum, Martha, 268, 369, 374–76,
  378–81, 383

Oakeshoot, Michael, 271
objectivity, 3, 27, 33–35, 42, 207,
  218, 456, 464
objectivism, 32, 35, 37, 44, 47–64
  passim, 66, 237, 250, 300, 304,
  329, 333, 341–43
observation, 5, 76, 78, 84, 88, 127
Oppenheim, Paul, 69
O'Shea, James, 4, 541n36

Parfit, Derek, 172, 500–501n23
Parmenides, 20, 25, 263–66, 268,
  270, 274, 277, 282, 284
peace, 12
Peirce, Charles Sanders, xii, 2, 4–7,
  10–11, 103–4, 114, 119–29 *passim*,
  153, 163, 169, 205, 224, 243, 388–
  89, 405, 408, 410, 413, 422, 426,
  429–31, 439–40, 442, 450, 498
perception, 13, 76, 86, 129, 143,
  208–9, 219–20, 248; as knowledge,
  180, 210–14, 411–26, 432
personhood: as artefact, xv–xvii, 40,
  78–80, 105–6, 169–70, 287, 311,
  359, 390, 402–6, 414, 432–33,
  473; as cultural, 78, 94, 105–6,
  148, 174–75, 206–20, 225–27,
  256, 339, 359, 390–95, 445–47,
  461–63, 473–74; as intentional,
  36, 155, 192, 200, 205–8, 224,
  233–35, 420–26; as linguistic,
  16–20, 155–57, 192–93, 200–3,
  392–94, 412, 447–48; as natural,
  83, 115–16, 176, 203, 282, 408–9,
  419–26, 500–501
Pettersson, Torsten, 31
phenomenology, 16, 67, 76–77, 84, 99,
  103–7, 121–42, 152–54, 165, 266,
  276, 436; of art, 301–3, 333–43
philosophy of art, xv, 289–319 *passim*,
  329–40
physicalism, 69, 175–77, 184, 227–28,
  343–44, 425, 499
physics, 14–15, 17, 20, 70–72, 81,
  250, 315, 387–89, 410
Piaget, Jean, 196–97, 200, 504n1
Picasso, Pablo 46, 240, 312–13
Pihlström, Sami, 4
Plantinga, Alvin, 103, 490n7
Plato, 23–25, 28, 140, 147, 149,
  194, 196, 199, 263–67, 269–76
  passim, 278, 280, 282, 284–85, 291,
  306, 370–72, 396, 414, 451, 454,
  456–57, 460, 507n8
Platonism, 42–43, 193, 249–52, 269,
  275, 492
Plessner, Helmuth, 287, 395, 490n8
pluralism, xvii, 50, 53, 343, 383–85,
  535
poetry, 31, 53, 149, 287, 290
Polanyi, Michael, 10, 488
politics, 41, 221, 246; and ethics, 270,
  275, 285–86, 352, 375, 452–59,
  463–76 *passim*
Popper, Karl, 53, 61–62, 81–82, 160,
  181, 486n36, 498n11
positivism, xii, 1–2, 73, 98, 161, 187,
  221, 269, 322, 499, 511
postmodernism, 32, 38, 212, 336,
  340–41, 352, 358
pragmatism: history of, xii–xiii, 1–5,
  103–5, 120–22, 413, 430; theses
  of, 10–13, 142–43, 327, 343–45,
  468–69

process philosophy, 3, 19, 25, 58–59, 80, 104, 109, 114, 131, 148–45, 167–69, 252–54, 264, 282–87, 305–13, 353, 367
Prokofiev, Sergei, 43
Protagoras, xv, 25, 28, 31, 35, 39, 45, 264–65, 276, 293, 388, 541n36
Protestantism, 458
psychology, 155, 231, 323
Putnam, Hilary, xi–xiii, xvi, 2, 53, 62, 69, 121–22, 133, 153, 165, 216, 359, 380, 385, 410, 508n11, 511n23

Quine, Willard Van Orman, xii, 2, 34–35, 60, 79, 84, 102, 119, 128, 154, 159–60, 162, 166, 176, 181, 189, 192, 195, 198, 211, 223, 249, 284, 324–27, 329–30, 342, 345, 359, 385, 507n7, 512n26

Ramsey, Frank, 63–64
rationalism, 3–7, 11, 17–20, 389, 394, 409; and irrationalism, 55, 59, 61, 353
Rawls, John, 195, 351, 354, 357, 361, 363–64, 368, 373–74, 377, 381, 383, 410, 439, 444, 451, 455, 464–65, 470, 547n1, 549n6
realism; 120–23, 249, 285, 377, 385; as abductive, 6, 413; and irrealism, 331–33; as logical, 30, 120; as scientific, 62, 66, 77–81, 161, 231, 412, 423–24
reason: normativity of, 374–77, 404–7, 417, 422, 433, 436, 445–59 *passim*; space of, 116, 396, 403, 417–26, 429–48 *passim*
reductionism, 69, 77, 81, 101, 109, 114–17, 158–63, 176, 192, 283, 297, 393, 491
Reichenbach, Hans, 17, 68, 160, 162, 175

Reid, Thomas, 549
relativism, xv, 25–30, 37–38, 264, 355, 384–85, 476; of culture, 30–37, 40–46, 51, 314–18, 332–33, 343–46, 355; of morality, 355, 365, 476–77; of truth, 27–28, 31–37, 44–45, 47–64 *passim*, 121–22, 248, 252, 293, 384–85
religion: and gods, 23, 114, 152, 193, 202, 236, 388; and magic, 56
representationalism, 119, 459
Ricouer, Paul, 53, 335, 502–3, 527
rights, 362, 455, 474, 511
Rorty, Richard, xi–xiii, 2, 54, 59, 119, 128, 160, 198, 324–28, 340–42, 345, 352, 377, 385, 403, 417, 421, 430, 503n34, 509n15, 517n18
Rousseau, Jean-Jacques, 232, 362, 404, 436, 449
Royce, Josiah, 2, 4, 117, 121, 544n54
Russell, Bertrand, 2, 4, 195, 214, 277, 500n22

Salmon, Wesley, 69, 71, 74, 382–83
Sandel, Michael, 351, 353, 355
Sartre, Jean-Paul, 123, 131, 142, 272, 337, 496n7
Saussure, Ferdinand de, 155–56
Schapiro, Meyer, 513n31
Schelling, Friedrich Wilhelm Joseph, 282
Schleiermacher, Friedrich, 259, 300, 512n27
science, 70–77, 207, 217, 268, 284, 393, 461, 513
scientific knowledge, 5, 77, 121–22, 383, 392
scientific realism, 62, 66, 77–81, 161, 231, 412, 423–24
Searle, John, 228, 495n5, 505n2
self: emergence of xvi, 119, 136–37, 175, 227, 260, 281–84, 359, 392–93, 403, 463–64

Sellars, Wilfrid, 2, 4, 10, 19, 81, 101–2, 115–17, 119, 125, 162, 325, 327, 342, 396, 402–5, 411–37 *passim*, 440–42, 444–45, 447–48, 538n19, 540n28, 540n34, 541n36, 542n41, 542–43n42, 545–46n56, 546n59
semiotics, 35, 41, 109, 164, 208, 236, 307, 311, 333, 439
Sen, Amartya, 451–52, 547n1
September 11, 2001, 451, 453–54, 463–64
Shakespeare, William, 254, 256–58, 291, 303, 308, 507n9
skepticism, 24, 33, 49, 53–56, 60–64, 206, 352, 375, 450
slavery, 355, 466
Smart, J. J. C., 69, 71, 387
social sciences, 93, 186–88, 268–76. *See also* human sciences
sociology, 233, 235, 246, 370, 417, 427, 430, 438, 443–44
Socrates, 28, 35, 39, 44, 270, 273, 278, 284–85, 287, 306, 371, 454, 456, 469, 476, 507
Sontag, Susan, 337–38
Sophocles, 102, 273, 454, 507n9
Spinoza, Baruch, 7–8, 18
Stecker, Robert, 478–79n5, 522n11, 524–25n45
Stich, Stephen, 81
stoicism, 118, 472
Strawson, Peter, 7, 174–75, 501n23
suicide, 355, 383, 470–73
supervenience, 114, 158–63, 247, 491
Suppes, Patrick, 4

Taylor, Charles, 53, 56–59, 226, 351, 353, 481–82, 501, 536–37
technology, 26, 65–71, 78–88, 250, 465

teleology, 98, 104, 114, 153, 178–79, 395, 402, 498
temporal, 149–51, 167, 184, 194, 233
terrorism, 451, 468
texts, xvii, 30, 36–38, 41, 45, 157–59, 163–66, 222–27, 236–60 *passim*, 295–306, 328–30, 384–85, 428
thirdness, 224
Thomson, George, 253, 310
Thucydides, 148–49
Tinbergen, Nikolaas, 86–87, 89
transcendental ego, 13, 52, 106, 124–26, 132–6, 197, 266–67, 394
transcendentalism: Kantian, 3, 99, 103–8, 117–23, 141–43, 152–54, 267–68, 277–78, 345, 404–8, 412–27, 440–44; as invariance, 11–20, 118–21, 189, 206–10, 363, 388–89, 438–41, 460–63
translation, 60, 63–64, 84, 324–25, 363–64
truth, 7, 10, 12–13, 28–29, 48–50, 60–63, 152, 212–13, 253–54, 344–46, 384–85; and knowledge, 10, 121–22, 220, 234–35, 266, 285–87, 306, 406–8, 459; and relativism, 33–35, 47–64 *passim*; as bivalent, 27–44 passim, 48, 218, 248, 293–99, 307, 332, 383–86, 474–75; as fallible, 4–7, 126, 438, 544; as necessary, 3, 14–20, 121, 130–35, 142, 324–27, 439; as objective, 3, 27, 33–35, 42, 207, 218
Turner, Stephen, 443–45, 447

universals, 42, 85–89, 94, 160, 235–39, 290–91, 375–79

Vaihinger, Hans, 3
Vietnam War, 471

Velazquez, Diego, 27, 254
Vendler, Helen, 254–59, 303
Vermeer, Johannes, 24
Vico, Giambattista, 108, 286, 516n9

war, 451–58, 468; and peace, 12
Weber, Max, 395, 418, 426–27, 430, 432–33, 435, 438, 440, 443–45, 447, 536n8, 543n44
West, Nathanael, 38
Winch, Peter, 53, 56–57, 443, 480, 487, 546
Winograd, Terry, 88

Wittgenstein, Ludwig, 2, 5, 10, 13, 41, 62, 105, 119, 123, 133, 153, 156, 199, 204, 213–14, 236, 244, 251, 275–80, 285–86, 306, 345, 353, 376–77, 411, 426, 436, 441, 443–44, 447–48, 496n5, 507n8, 508n13, 510n19, 512n26
Wollheim, Richard, 244, 315, 515, 522
Wolterstorff, Nicholas, 291
Worrall, John, 17
Wright, Crispin, 541n40

Zahavi, Dan, 126, 131–33, 494n48

www.ingramcontent.com/pod-product-compliance
Lightning Source LLC
Chambersburg PA
CBHW051842300426
44117CB00006B/236